P9-CNI-353

VENONA

VENONA

Decoding Soviet Espionage in America

John Earl Haynes and Harvey Klehr

NEW HANOVER COUNTY
PUBLIC LIBRARY
201 CHESTNUT STREET
WILMINGTON, N. C. 28401

Yale University Press
New Haven and London

To *my wife, Marcia Steinberg*

—HARVEY KLEHR

To *my wife, Janette*

—JOHN EARL HAYNES

Copyright © 1999 by Yale University.
All rights reserved.
This book may not be reproduced, in whole or in part, including illustrations, in any form (beyond that copying permitted by Sections 107 and 108 of the U.S. Copyright Law and except by reviewers for the public press), without written permission from the publishers.

Designed by James J. Johnson and set in Sabon Roman type by Rainsford Type, Danbury, Connecticut.
Printed in the United States of America.

Library of Congress Cataloging-in-Publication Data

Haynes, John Earl.
  Venona: Decoding Soviet espionage in America / John Earl Haynes and Harvey Klehr.
    p. cm.
  Includes index.
  ISBN 0-300-07771-8

  1. Communist Party of the United States of America—History—Sources. 2. Espionage, Soviet—United States—History—Sources. 3. Communism—United States—History—Sources. 4. Spies—Soviet Union—History—Sources. 5. Spies—United States—History—Sources. 6. Cryptography—United States—History—Sources. I. Klehr, Harvey. II. Title.
JK2391.C5H39 1999
327.1247'073'0904—dc21   98-51464

A catalogue record for this book is available from the British Library.

The paper in this book meets the guidelines for permanence and durability of the Committee on Production Guidelines for Book Longevity of the Council on Library Resources.

10 9 8 7 6 5 4 3 2 1

Contents

Acknowledgments

Everyone who studies Soviet espionage owes a debt of gratitude to Sen. Daniel Patrick Moynihan, who was instrumental in persuading the American intelligence community to expedite the release of the Venona material. We are also grateful for the work of Michael Lostumbo, a member of Senator Moynihan's staff, and Eric Biel, the director of the Commission on the Protection and Reduction of Government Secrecy. We are particularly appreciative of the help and encouragement we have received from Robert Louis Benson and the late Cecil Phillips of the National Security Agency. They not only patiently answered our sometimes naive queries about cryptology; they also read the manuscript and saved us from many errors. A number of scholars, writers, journalists, retired FBI agents and intelligence officers, and independent researchers helped us in a variety of ways. We are in their debt. They include Joseph Albright, Alan Cullison, Michael Dobbs, Fridrikh Igorevich Firsov, Robert Harris, David Horowitz, Gary Kern, Marcia Kunstel, Robert Lamphere, David McKnight, Harry Mahoney, Eduard Mark, Daniel Menaker, Hayden Peake, Richard Powers, Ronald Radosh, Rosalee Reynolds, Herbert Romerstein, Stephen Schwartz, Sam Tanenhaus, John Walsh, and Michael Warner. None of these people, however, is responsible for any of our interpretations, and our errors and mistakes are ours alone.

We remain indebted to our friends and colleagues at Yale University Press who have once again forced us to work much harder than we anticipated. Richard Miller's excellent editing sharpened our prose and organization. Jonathan Brent is a model of what a sponsoring editor should be. And we thank Susan Abel. Our families—particularly Amanda and Bill Haynes and Benjamin, Gabriel, and Joshua Klehr and Aaron Hodes—deserve lots of credit for tolerating six years of obsession with Moscow archives, decrypted cables, one-time pads, Communists, and Soviet spies.

A Note about Transcription of the Documents

American and Soviet intelligence agencies had the practice in written documents and messages of printing proper names, including cover names, completely in capital letters. This was done to signal that when one read "on Monday PILOT reported," the source of the report was not a real pilot. Persons not used to reading intelligence material, however, frequently mistake the purpose of such capitalization for emphasis. To avoid distraction, the practice will not be followed in this book; only the initial letter of a cover name will be capitalized.

The documents decrypted in the Venona Project were translated from Russian over the period 1946–1981. During that time National Security Agency practices on transliterating Russian words and names from the Cyrillic to the Latin alphabet changed several times. Furthermore, a portion of work was done by British linguists, who rendered the translations in British English rather than American English. To avoid distracting readers who will wonder, understandably, if the "Anatolii" of one document is the same person as the "Anatoly" of another, all such words will be rendered under a single standard of anglicization.

Every deciphered cable of the Venona Project is given a unique citation that identifies the message by the sending and receiving station, the date of transmission, the agency of transmission, and an "external" message number given to the cable by the National Security Agency.

(The NSA derived the external number from a sequential number actually placed in the outgoing cable by Soviet code clerks.) A citation of "Venona 722 KGB New York to Moscow, 21 May 1942" refers to a ciphered cable message sent by the KGB station in New York to the KGB headquarters in Moscow on May 21, 1942, and given the external number 722 by the Venona Project. Complete sets of the Venona messages are available at the Manuscript Division of the Library of Congress, at the NSA's National Cryptologic Museum, Fort Meade, Maryland, and, as of 1998, on the NSA's World Wide Web page (www.nsa.gov).

Glossary

Organizations and acronyms are identified when they are first used in the text. This glossary lists organizations mentioned in more than one chapter in order to minimize the need to search back for the original identification. See the appendixes for names of individuals.

Arlington Hall: informal name for the predecessors to the National Security Agency.

BEW: see Board of Economic Warfare.

Board of Economic Warfare (BEW): wartime U.S. agency that gathered information on and coordinated strategic international economic affairs.

Comintern: see Communist International.

Comparty: Comintern abbreviation for Communist party.

Coordinator of Information (Office of the Coordinator of Information): Set up by President Roosevelt in 1941, in 1942 this agency was split into two parts, the Office of Strategic Services and the Office of War Information.

Communist International (Comintern): founded by Lenin in 1919 as the international headquarters of all Communist parties.

CPSU: Communist Party of the Soviet Union.

CPUSA: Communist Party of the United States of America.

Daily Worker: flagship newspaper of the CPUSA.

Dies committee: Special Committee on Un-American Activities, a committee of the U.S. House of Representatives headed from 1938 to 1944 by Rep. Martin Dies (Democrat, Texas).

FBI: Federal Bureau of Investigation, chief American internal security agency.

FEA: see Foreign Economic Administration.

FOIA: Freedom of Information Act.

Foreign Economic Administration (FEA): wartime U.S. agency for foreign aid and successor to the Board of Economic Warfare. Coordinated strategic international economic affairs.

Great Terror: the most intense period of the Stalin-era purges of Soviet society, lasting roughly from 1936 to 1939.

GRU: Glavnoe razvedyvatelnoe upravlenie (Chief intelligence directorate of the Soviet general staff), the Soviet military intelligence agency, not part of the KGB.

House Committee on Un-American Activities: U.S. House of Representatives standing committee, created in 1945, that investigated subversion, sedition, espionage and terrorism.

HUAC: common acronym (from the informal name House Un-American Activities Committee) for the House Committee on Un-American Activities.

International Brigades: Comintern army of about thirty thousand foreign volunteers that fought in the Spanish Civil War of 1936–1939.

International Lenin School: Comintern school for mid- and upper-level foreign Communists and for Soviet Communists who worked with foreign Communists.

KGB: Komitet gosudarstvennoi bezopasnosti (Committee for state security), chief security service of the USSR. The KGB had a complex organizational history and in some periods the foreign intelligence apparatus was organizationally separated from the much larger internal security apparatus.

National Security Agency (NSA): chief American intelligence agency for signals and ciphers.

Naval GRU: Soviet naval intelligence agency (separate from the KGB).

NSA: see National Security Agency.

Office of Emergency Management: wartime economic mobilization agency, predecessor to the War Production Board.

Office of Price Administration (OPA): wartime agency to control prices and ration goods.

Office of Strategic Services (OSS): chief American intelligence and covert action agency in World War II. Officially disbanded in 1945; the remnants of its officers and functions were transferred either to the State Department or to the military Joint Chiefs of Staff and in 1947 transferred back to the newly organized Central Intelligence Agency.

Office of the Coordinator of Inter-American Affairs: wartime U.S. agency headed by Nelson Rockefeller that coordinated American diplomacy, information gathering, and propaganda in South and Central America.

Office of War Information (OWI): chief American propaganda agency in World War II, directed at both foreign and domestic audiences.

OPA: see Office of Price Administration.

OSS: see Office of Strategic Services.

OWI: see Office of War Information.

Popular Front: term used to describe the Communist political stance from 1935 to 1939 when Communists sought to create and lead a broad liberal-left alliance based on antifascism and reformist policies. Also used to describe similar stances in the 1942–1950 period.

Profintern: Krasnyi internatsional professional'nykh soiuzov (Red international of labor unions). The Profintern was the Comintern's trade union arm.

RTsKhIDNI: Rossiskii tsentr khraneniia i izucheniia dokumentov noveishei istorii (Russian center for the preservation and study of documents of recent history), archive holding records of the Comintern (1919–1943), the CPUSA up to 1944, and the CPSU up to 1953.

Senate Internal Security Subcommittee (SISS): informal name for the U.S. Senate Committee on the Judiciary's Subcommittee to Investigate the Administration of the Internal Security Act and Other Internal Security Laws.

SISS: see Senate Internal Security Subcommittee.

Trotskyists (Trotskyites): followers of Leon Trotsky, a Bolshevik leader defeated by Stalin in the struggle to succeed Lenin; accused of left-wing ultrarevolutionary ideological deviation.

United Nations Relief and Rehabilitation Administration (UNRRA): wartime U.S. agency that coordinated U.S. foreign economic aid and relief.

UNRRA: see United Nations Relief and Rehabilitation Administration.

War Production Board (WPB): U.S. wartime agency that controlled and coordinated military industrial production.

WPB: see War Production Board.

YCL: see Young Communist League.

Young Communist League (YCL): youth arm of the CPUSA.

INTRODUCTION: THE ROAD TO VENONA

For more than forty years, nearly three thousand telegraphic cables between Soviet spies in the United States and their superiors in Moscow remained one of the United States government's most sensitive secrets. Hidden away in guarded archives at Fort Meade in Maryland, these messages, decrypted shortly after World War II in an operation known as Venona, may change the way we think about twentieth-century American history.

Fort Meade is only a half-hour's drive from Washington, but our route to the Venona decryptions began with a nine-thousand-mile journey to a forbidding gray stone building that fills one block of Puskinskaia Street in central Moscow. This building houses archives of the Communist Party of the Soviet Union (CPSU) and the enormous records of the Communist International. The Comintern, as it is known, supervised Communist parties the world over from 1919 until Joseph Stalin dissolved it in 1943.

The CPSU kept tight control over which researchers would be allowed into its archive and what materials they would be allowed to see. As American scholars, neither of us ever expected to receive such permission. But in December 1991, the Soviet Union collapsed and the new Russian government of Boris Yeltsin seized the property of the Communist party. The archive, renamed the Russian Center for the Preservation and Study of Documents of Recent History (RTsKhIDNI, pronounced "ritz-kidney"), soon opened for the first time for research by Western scholars. In six visits to RTsKhIDNI, we spent many weeks requesting files, reading records, taking notes, and copying documents about the history of communism in America.

At first, the staff at RTsKhIDNI were hospitable and eager to accommodate our research needs. On later visits, however, one official in particular seemed bent on slowing our work by interpreting archival rules in the most restrictive ways possible. We came to call her a "remnant of the era of stagnation," using the Russian phrase for the stifling bureaucracy of the Brezhnev era. When we asked another RTsKhIDNI official why this change from warmth to frost, he replied that she had assumed we were American Communists at the time of our first visits but now realized that we were not. While most RTsKhIDNI staff members clearly welcomed the openness of the new Russia and were very helpful to our research, the "remnant" was not the only one who missed the old days. A larger-than-life statue of Lenin stared out over the spacious foyer of the RTsKhIDNI building, and some devotee of the old order kept putting fresh flowers at his feet every day. This Lenin, however, gazed down with his stony eyes on the office cubicles of that quintessential capitalist enterprise, a private bank, to which the archive had rented out half the foyer.

After our first visit to study the Comintern archives, RTsKhIDNI officials asked whether we might also be interested in the archive of the American Communist party, the CPUSA. That those records existed was a stunning revelation to us. No such collection exists in the United States, and although historians had joked that the CPUSA's records were hidden in Moscow, no one knew that to be true. The CPUSA archive, RTsKhIDNI staff explained, was stored at a remote warehouse because in the Soviet period it had rarely been consulted. Did the archive really have the files of the American Communist party's headquarters? Or was this just a small collection of CPUSA reports and yellowing copies of the *Daily Worker?* When the records arrived from the warehouse, an archivist wheeled in a cart with the first batch of what turned out to be more than forty-three hundred files. We blew the thick dust off the folders, untied the ribbons that bound them, and looked inside. There, just as the Russians had said, were the original records of the CPUSA, shipped secretly to Moscow many years ago.

Our research in that archive has produced two books, *The Secret*

World of American Communism (1995) and *The Soviet World of American Communism* (1998), which examine the relationship of the CPUSA to the Comintern and clarify contested parts of American Communist history. Early in our RTsKhIDNI research, we came across a series of queries about specific American Communists which had been sent in 1943 and 1944 to Georgi Dimitrov, then head of the Comintern. The queries ordered the Comintern to provide any background information it had on those Americans and were signed simply "Fitin." We were intrigued because we recognized the named individuals as Americans who had been accused of being Soviet spies in the late 1940s. The queries had been made by Pavel Mikhailovich Fitin, the Soviet Union's spymaster and head of the foreign intelligence section of the KGB from 1940 to 1946. The meaning of the messages to Dimitrov became clear: they were vetting inquiries. The KGB was in the process of recruiting American Communists as spies and was conducting background checks with the Communist International.

The subject of one of Fitin's inquiries, Judith Coplon, brought an obscure American code-breaking project into our research. Coplon, an analyst working in the Foreign Agents Registration section of the U.S. Justice Department, had access to FBI counterespionage files. The FBI had arrested her in 1949 in the act of handing over some of those files to Valentin Gubitchev, a KGB officer who nominally worked as an official of the United Nations. In his 1986 memoir, the retired FBI agent Robert Lamphere related that the FBI had been alerted that Coplon was a Soviet spy when the National Security Agency (the NSA) deciphered a 1944 KGB message regarding her recruitment. Lamphere also said that similar deciphered messages had led the FBI to identify Klaus Fuchs, a British physicist working on the atomic bomb project, as a spy, a discovery that ultimately brought about the arrests of Julius and Ethel Rosenberg on charges of espionage for passing atomic secrets to the Soviet Union. The deciphered messages that set all this in train, said Lamphere, were from the NSA code-breaking project. But he provided few details about the operation. David Martin, in his 1981 history of espionage, had also discussed a highly secret American code-breaking project that had provided key evidence against the Rosenbergs and other Soviet spies, a finding affirmed by the historians Ronald Radosh and Joyce Milton in their 1983 history of the Rosenberg case. Other histories of espionage gave the NSA project a name: Venona.[1]

Another message from Fitin to Dimitrov concerned the willingness of a French political leader, Pierre Cot, then in wartime exile in the United States, to assist the Soviet cause. Peter Wright, a retired officer for the British counterintelligence agency, MI5, reported in his 1987 memoir that deciphered messages of the Venona Project had led British and American security officials to identify Cot as a Soviet agent.[2]

We realized that the Fitin queries that we found in the RTsKhiDNI archives pointed to Venona. But what exactly was the Venona Project? Had the NSA deciphered only a few Soviet messages or many hundreds? Were other spies besides Cot, Coplon, and Fuchs identified? What did the messages say?

The NSA was notoriously closemouthed about its activities and by reputation far more secretive than either the Central Intelligence Agency or the FBI. During the height of the Cold War, Washington insiders joked that the initials "N.S.A." really stood for "No Such Agency." When we asked various government officials about Venona, we ran up against a stone wall. One official told us that yes, there had been a code-breaking project called Venona; yes, it had produced much valuable information that had never been made public; and yes, the project was old, with all its deciphered messages from the World War II era; but no, neither we nor anyone else would have access to Venona's records for many decades to come. Such cryptographic intelligence, we were told, was too sensitive to allow the public to examine.

In *The Secret World of American Communism* we presented RTsKhiDNI documents confirming that the CPUSA maintained an underground arm, a fact long denied by the party and by many historians. Other documents reproduced in the book showed that on several occasions the American Communist underground and high CPUSA officials had cooperated with Soviet intelligence agencies in espionage against the United States. That volume reproduces the full text of the Fitin messages about Judith Coplon and Pierre Cot and discusses the apparent tie between those Moscow documents and what little was known about Venona.

Soon after the book was published, we received a telephone call from Sen. Daniel Patrick Moynihan of New York. Senator Moynihan had read the book, wanted to discuss a few points, and also had a request. He noted that he chaired the newly established Commission on Protecting and Reducing Government Secrecy, consisting of eight persons selected by Congress and four appointed by President Bill Clinton. Moynihan thought that the end of the Cold War required a drastic revision of the regime of secrecy and security classification set up during the forty-five-year confrontation with the Soviet Union. He explained that in order to get across why the end of the Cold War should bring about a rethinking of secrecy policies, he wanted the commission to gain a better understanding of why those policies were established in the first place. To that end, he asked us to testify before the commission.

When the commission met in May 1995, we described the findings of our book. With reference to the documents tied to Venona, we observed that it seemed improper and ironic that American scholars could find messages linked to the Moscow end of the Soviet cable traffic in an *open* Russian archive but that the messages themselves were still locked up in *closed* American archives. With the Cold War ended and the messages more than forty years old, the rationale for continued secrecy, we asserted, seemed weak. Senator Moynihan then turned to his right and spoke to John Deutch, a presidential appointee to the commission, who was head of the Central Intelligence Agency (CIA) and hence the coordinator of all U.S. intelligence activities. Moynihan asked that Deutch discuss with the NSA what the status of Venona was and whether its secrecy might no longer be necessary. Deutch indicated that he would, but he made no promises regarding the outcome.

In view of the adamant refusals to consider declassifying Venona that we had met with earlier, we were not optimistic that even Senator Moynihan's influence and persuasiveness could pry Venona open. We were not aware that behind the outward wall of silence, figures inside the U.S. intelligence community had already been advocating opening Venona. The NSA, it turned out, had long ago decided that the project had ceased to have any operational value to American intelligence and had shut it down in 1980. It was, literally, history. James Angleton, the former head of CIA counterintelligence, had told colleagues before his death in 1987 that the deciphered Venona messages should be made public. Open the messages up, he had argued, and historians and journalists with perspectives different from those of professional security officers would probably be able to attach real names to the cover names of Soviet sources that the combined efforts of the FBI, the CIA, and the NSA had been unable to identify. His insight would prove to be correct.

Robert Louis Benson, an NSA officer who had an interest in the history of American counterintelligence, argued within the agency that the time was ripe for Venona to become public and for the record to be set straight about Soviet espionage. Cecil Phillips, a retired NSA officer who had been one of the earliest cryptanalysts (code-breakers) working on the project, spoke for many Venona veterans who hoped that their astounding success in breaking what the Soviets had believed to be an unbreakable cipher would become public before they all passed from the scene. Nor could it have been lost on senior security officials that Senator Moynihan hoped to persuade the Congress to support a bill mandating a drastic reduction in government secrecy. If executive-branch officials refused to voluntarily lift the secrecy on a project involving Soviet cables that were more than forty years old, they would appear intransigent and unreasonable and would risk having Congress mandate a more sweeping reduction in secrecy. Making Venona public would show that officials could act reasonably under the current system without statutory directives. Further, Venona had been a great success for American counterintelligence; opening it up would allow intelligence professionals to take a few bows in public—something they rarely had a chance to do.

None of this internal debate, however, was public knowledge. So it was a complete surprise when just two months after the secrecy commission hearing, we received calls inviting us to CIA headquarters in Langley, Virginia, on July 11, 1995, for the official disclosure of the Venona Project. At the public ceremony the heads of the CIA, FBI, and NSA, along with Senator Moynihan, jointly announced that Venona was being opened and gave the surviving members of the Venona code-breaking team, almost all of whom had retired from government service years earlier, some well-deserved public pats on the back. They also brought the first batch of Venona messages to the light of day. These forty-nine messages detailed Soviet atomic espionage and unmistakably showed that Julius Rosenberg was a Soviet agent, an assertion that some historians and much of the American public had rejected as unsupported by documentary evidence. Here, at last, was the evidence.

Over the next two years, the National Security Agency released the remaining messages, more than twenty-nine hundred, amounting to more than five thousand pages of text. Reading—and, more to the point, comprehending—these thousands of messages, all written in an abbreviated telegraphic style and strewn with cover names, many only partially deciphered, was difficult. But the effort was worthwhile, for the Venona decryptions fill in many gaps in the historical record and corroborate testimony from FBI files and congressional hearings. We also found that the new evidence required us to modify earlier judgments.

In 1992, before RTsKhIDNI was open and long before the Venona decryptions were made public, we published a one-volume history of the CPUSA, entitled *The American Communist Movement: Storming Heaven Itself.* In it we put forward convincing evidence that some American Communists had assisted Soviet espionage against the United States. But the limitations of the evidence then available made us cautious in our broader judgment of the American Communist party: "Ideologically, American Communists owed their first loyalty to the motherland of communism rather than to the United States," we wrote, "but in practice few American Communists were spies. The Soviet Union recruited spies from the Communist movement, but espionage was not a regular activity of the American C.P. The party promoted communism and the interests of the Soviet Union through political means; espionage was the business of the Soviet Union's intelligence services. To see the American Communist party chiefly as an instrument of espionage or a sort of fifth column misjudges its main purpose."[3]

As our computers correlated the evidence we found, first at RTsKhIDNI in Moscow and then in the Venona decryptions; as they printed out the names, not of "few," but of hundreds of American Communists who abetted Soviet espionage in the United States; as we read the deciphered messages showing that regional CPUSA officials, members of the party's most powerful body, the Politburo, and the party chief himself knowingly and purposely assisted Soviet spies, it became clear that espionage was a regular activity of the American Communist party. To say that the CPUSA was nothing but a Soviet fifth column in the Cold War would be an exaggeration; it still remains true that the CPUSA's chief task was the promotion of communism and the interests of the Soviet Union through political means. But it is equally true that the CPUSA was indeed a fifth column working inside and against the United States in the Cold War.

CHAPTER 1

VENONA
AND THE
COLD WAR

The Venona Project began because Carter Clarke did not trust Joseph Stalin. Colonel Clarke was chief of the U.S. Army's Special Branch, part of the War Department's Military Intelligence Division, and in 1943 its officers heard vague rumors of secret German-Soviet peace negotiations.[1] With the vivid example of the August 1939 Nazi-Soviet Pact in mind, Clarke feared that a separate peace between Moscow and Berlin would allow Nazi Germany to concentrate its formidable war machine against the United States and Great Britain. Clarke thought he had a way to find out whether such negotiations were under way.[2]

Clarke's Special Branch supervised the Signal Intelligence Service, the Army's elite group of code-breakers and the predecessor of the National Security Agency. In February 1943 Clarke ordered the service to establish a small program to examine ciphered Soviet diplomatic cablegrams. Since the beginning of World War II in 1939, the federal government had collected copies of international cables leaving and entering the United States. If the cipher used in the Soviet cables could be broken, Clarke believed, the private exchanges between Soviet diplomats in the United States and their superiors in Moscow would show whether Stalin was seriously pursuing a separate peace.

The coded Soviet cables, however, proved to be far more difficult to read than Clarke had expected. American code-breakers discovered that the Soviet Union was using a complex two-part ciphering system involving a "one-time pad" code that in theory was unbreakable. The Venona code-breakers, however, combined acute intellectual analysis with painstaking examination of thousands of coded telegraphic cables to spot a Soviet procedural error that opened the cipher to attack. But by the time they had rendered the first messages into readable text in 1946, the war was over and Clarke's initial goal was moot. Nor did the messages show evidence of a Soviet quest for a separate peace. What they did demonstrate, however, stunned American officials. Messages thought to be between Soviet diplomats at the Soviet consulate in New York and the People's Commissariat of Foreign Affairs in Moscow turned out to be cables between professional intelligence field officers and Gen. Pavel Fitin, head of the foreign intelligence directorate of the KGB in Moscow.[3] Espionage, not diplomacy, was the subject of these cables. One of the first cables rendered into coherent text was a 1944 message from KGB officers in New York showing that the Soviet Union had infiltrated America's most secret enterprise, the atomic bomb project.[4]

By 1948 the accumulating evidence from other decoded Venona cables showed that the Soviets had recruited spies in virtually every major American government agency of military or diplomatic importance. American authorities learned that since 1942 the United States had been the target of a Soviet espionage onslaught involving dozens of professional Soviet intelligence officers and hundreds of Americans, many of whom were members of the American Communist party (CPUSA). The deciphered cables of the Venona Project identify 349 citizens, immigrants, and permanent residents of the United States who had had a covert relationship with Soviet intelligence agencies (see appendix A). Further, American cryptanalysts in the Venona Project deciphered only a fraction of the Soviet intelligence traffic, so it was only logical to conclude that many additional agents were discussed in the thousands of unread messages. Some were identified from other sources, such as defectors' testimony and the confessions of Soviet spies (see appendix B).

The deciphered Venona messages also showed that a disturbing number of high-ranking U.S. government officials consciously maintained a clandestine relationship with Soviet intelligence agencies and had passed extraordinarily sensitive information to the Soviet Union that had seriously damaged American interests. Harry White—the second most powerful official in the U.S. Treasury Department, one of the most influential officials in the government, and part of the American delegation at the founding of the United Nations—had advised the KGB about how American diplomatic strategy could be frustrated. A trusted personal assistant to President Franklin Roosevelt, Lauchlin Currie, warned the KGB that the FBI had started an investigation of one of the Soviets' key American agents, Gregory Silvermaster. This warning allowed Silvermaster, who headed a highly productive espionage ring, to escape detection and continue spying. Maurice Halperin, the head of a research section of the Office of Strategic Services (OSS), then America's chief intelligence arm, turned over hundreds of pages of secret American diplomatic cables to the KGB. William Perl, a brilliant young government aeronautical scientist, provided the Soviets with the results of the highly secret tests and design experiments for American jet engines and jet aircraft. His betrayal assisted the Soviet Union in quickly overcoming the American technological lead in the development of jets. In the Korean War, U.S. military leaders expected the Air Force to dominate the skies, on the assumption that the Soviet aircraft used by North Korea and Communist China would be no match for American aircraft. They were shocked when Soviet MiG-15 jet fighters not only flew rings around U.S. propeller-driven aircraft but were conspicuously superior to the first generation of American jets as well. Only the hurried deployment of America's newest jet fighter, the F-86 Saber, allowed the United States to match the technological capabilities of the MiG-15. The Air Force prevailed, owing more to the skill of American pilots than to the design of American aircraft.

And then there were the atomic spies. From within the Manhattan Project two physicists, Klaus Fuchs and Theodore Hall, and one technician, David Greenglass, transmitted the complex formula for extracting bomb-grade uranium from ordinary uranium, the technical plans for production facilities, and the engineering principles for the "implosion" technique. The latter process made possible an atomic bomb using plutonium, a substance much easier to manufacture than bomb-grade uranium.

The betrayal of American atomic secrets to the Soviets allowed the Soviet Union to develop atomic weapons several years sooner and at a substantially lower cost than it otherwise would have. Joseph Stalin's knowledge that espionage assured the Soviet Union of quickly breaking the American atomic monopoly emboldened his diplomatic strategy in his early Cold War clashes with the United States. It is doubtful that Stalin, rarely a risk-taker, would have supplied the military wherewithal and authorized North Korea to invade South Korea in 1950 had the Soviet Union not exploded an atomic bomb in 1949. Otherwise Stalin might have feared that President Harry Truman would stanch any North Korean invasion by threatening to use atomic weapons. After all, as soon as the atomic bomb had been developed, Truman had not hesitated to use it twice to end the war with Japan. But in 1950, with Stalin in possession of the atomic bomb, Truman was deterred from using atomic weapons in Korea, even in the late summer when initially unprepared American forces were driven back into the tip of Korea and in danger of being pushed into the sea, and then again in the winter when Communist Chinese forces entered the war in massive numbers. The killing and maiming of hundreds of thousands of soldiers and civilians on both sides of the war in Korea might have been averted had the Soviets not been able to parry the American atomic threat.

Early Soviet possession of the atomic bomb had an important psychological consequence. When the Soviet Union exploded a nuclear device in 1949, ordinary Americans as well as the nation's leaders realized that a cruel despot, Joseph Stalin, had just gained the power to destroy cities at will. This perception colored the early Cold War with the hues of apocalypse. Though the Cold War never lost the potential of becoming a civilization-destroying conflict, Stalin's death in March 1953 noticeably relaxed Soviet-American tensions. With less successful espionage, the Soviet Union might not have developed the bomb until after Stalin's death, and the early Cold War might have proceeded on a far less frightening path.

Venona decryptions identified most of the Soviet spies uncovered by American counterintelligence between 1948 and the mid-1950s. The skill and perseverance of the Venona code-breakers led the U.S. Federal Bureau of Investigation (FBI) and British counterintelligence (MI5) to the atomic spy Klaus Fuchs. Venona documents unmistakably identified Julius Rosenberg as the head of a Soviet spy ring and David Greenglass, his brother-in-law, as a Soviet source at the secret atomic bomb facility at Los Alamos, New Mexico. Leads from decrypted telegrams exposed the senior British diplomat Donald Maclean as a major spy in the British embassy in Washington and precipitated his flight to the Soviet Union, along with his fellow diplomat and spy Guy Burgess. The arrest and prosecution of such spies as Judith Coplon, Robert Soblen, and Jack

Soble was possible because American intelligence was able to read Soviet reports about their activities. The charges by the former Soviet spy Elizabeth Bentley that several dozen mid-level government officials, mostly secret Communists, had assisted Soviet intelligence were corroborated in Venona documents and assured American authorities of her veracity.

With the advent of the Cold War, however, the spies clearly identified in the Venona decryptions were the least of the problem. Coplon, Rosenberg, Greenglass, Fuchs, Soble, and Soblen were prosecuted, and the rest were eased out of the government or otherwise neutralized as threats to national security. But that still left a security nightmare. Of the 349 Americans the deciphered Venona cables revealed as having covert ties to Soviet intelligence agencies, less than half could be identified by their real names and nearly two hundred remained hidden behind cover names. American officials assumed that some of the latter surely were still working in sensitive positions. Had they been promoted and moved into policy-making jobs? Had Muse, the unidentified female agent in the OSS, succeeded in transferring to the State Department or the Central Intelligence Agency (CIA), the successor to the OSS? What of Source No. 19, who had been senior enough to meet privately with Churchill and Roosevelt at the Trident Conference? Was the unidentified KGB source Bibi working for one of America's foreign assistance agencies? Was Donald, the unidentified Navy captain who was a GRU (Soviet military intelligence) source, still in uniform, perhaps by this time holding the rank of admiral? And what of the two unidentified atomic spies Quantum and Pers? They had given Stalin the secrets of the uranium and plutonium bomb: were they now passing on the secrets of the even more destructive hydrogen bomb? And how about Dodger, Godmother, and Fakir? Deciphered Venona messages showed that all three had provided the KGB with information on American diplomats who specialized in Soviet matters. Fakir was himself being considered for an assignment representing the United States in Moscow. Which of the American foreign service officers who were also Soviet specialists were traitors? How could Americans successfully negotiate with the Soviet Union when the American negotiating team included someone working for the other side? Western Europe, clearly, would be the chief battleground of the Cold War. To lose there was to lose all: the task of rebuilding stable democracies in postwar Europe and forging the NATO military alliance was America's chief diplomatic challenge. Yet

Venona showed that the KGB had Mole, the appropriate cover name of a Soviet source inside the Washington establishment who had passed on to Moscow high-level American diplomatic policy guidance on Europe. When American officials met to discuss sensitive matters dealing with France, Britain, Italy, or Germany, was Mole present and working to frustrate American goals? Stalin's espionage offensive had not only uncovered American secrets, it had also undermined the mutual trust that American officials had for each other.[5]

The Truman administration had expected the end of World War II to allow the dismantling of the massive military machine created to defeat Nazi Germany and Imperial Japan. The government slashed military budgets, turned weapons factories over to civilian production, ended conscription, and returned millions of soldiers to civilian life. So, too, the wartime intelligence and security apparatus was demobilized. Anticipating only limited need for foreign intelligence and stating that he wanted no American Gestapo, President Truman abolished America's chief intelligence agency, the Office of Strategic Services. With the coming of peace, emergency wartime rules for security vetting of many government employees lapsed or were ignored.

In late 1945 and in 1946, the White House had reacted with a mixture of indifference and skepticism to FBI reports indicating significant Soviet espionage activity in the United States. Truman administration officials even whitewashed evidence pointing to the theft of American classified documents in the 1945 *Amerasia* case (see chapter 6) because they did not wish to put at risk the continuation of the wartime Soviet-American alliance and wanted to avoid the political embarrassment of a security scandal. By early 1947, however, this indifference ended. The accumulation of information from defectors such as Elizabeth Bentley and Igor Gouzenko, along with the Venona decryptions, made senior Truman administration officials realize that reports of Soviet spying constituted more than FBI paranoia. No government could operate successfully if it ignored the challenge to its integrity that Stalin's espionage offensive represented. In addition, the White House sensed that there was sufficient substance to the emerging picture of a massive Soviet espionage campaign, one assisted by American Communists, that the Truman administration was vulnerable to Republican charges of having ignored a serious threat to American security. President Truman reversed course and in March 1947 issued a sweeping executive order establishing a comprehensive security vetting program for U.S. government employees. He also created the Central Intelligence Agency, a stronger and larger version of the OSS, which he had abolished just two years earlier. In 1948 the Truman administration followed up these acts by indicting the leaders of the CPUSA under the sedition sections of the 1940 Smith Act. While the Venona Project and the decrypted messages themselves remained secret, the substance of the messages with the names of scores of Americans who had assisted Soviet espionage circulated among American military and civilian security officials. From the security officials the information went to senior executive-branch political appointees and members of Congress. They, in turn, passed it on to journalists and commentators, who conveyed the alarming news to the general public.

Americans' Understanding of Soviet and Communist Espionage

During the early Cold War, in the late 1940s and early 1950s, every few months newspaper headlines trumpeted the exposure of yet another network of Communists who had infiltrated an American laboratory, labor union, or government agency. Americans worried that a Communist fifth column, more loyal to the Soviet Union than to the United States, had moved into their institutions. By the mid-1950s, following the trials and convictions for espionage-related crimes of Alger Hiss, a senior diplomat, and Julius and Ethel Rosenberg for atomic spying, there was a widespread public consensus on three points: that Soviet espionage was serious, that American Communists assisted the Soviets, and that several senior government officials had betrayed the United States. The deciphered Venona messages provide a solid factual basis for this consensus. But the government did not release the Venona decryptions to the public, and it successfully disguised the source of its information about Soviet espionage. This decision denied the public the incontestable evidence afforded by the messages of the Soviet Union's own spies. Since the information about Soviet espionage and American Communist participation derived largely from the testimony of defectors and a mass of circumstantial evidence, the public's belief in those reports rested on faith in the integrity of government security officials. These sources are inherently more ambiguous than the hard evidence of the Venona messages, and this ambiguity had unfortunate consequences for American politics and Americans' understanding of their own history.

The decision to keep Venona secret from the public, and to restrict knowledge of it even within the government, was made essentially by senior Army officers in consultation with the FBI and the CIA. Aside from the Venona code-breakers, only a limited number of military intelligence officers, FBI agents, and CIA officials knew of the project. The CIA in fact was not made an active partner in Venona until 1952 and did not receive copies of the deciphered messages until 1953. The evidence is not entirely clear, but it appears that Army Chief of Staff Omar Bradley, mindful of the White House's tendency to leak politically sensitive information, decided to deny President Truman direct knowledge of the Venona Project.[6] The president was informed about the substance of the Venona messages as it came to him through FBI and Justice Department memorandums on espionage investigations and CIA reports on intelligence matters. He was not told that much of this information derived from reading Soviet cable traffic. This omission is important because Truman was mistrustful of J. Edgar Hoover, the head of the FBI, and suspected that the reports of Soviet espionage were exaggerated for political purposes. Had he been aware of Venona, and known that Soviet cables confirmed the testimony of Elizabeth Bentley and Whittaker Chambers, it is unlikely that his aides would have considered undertaking a campaign to discredit Bentley and indict Chambers for perjury, or would have allowed themselves to be taken in by the disinformation being spread by the American Communist party and Alger Hiss's partisans that Chambers had at one time been committed to an insane asylum.[7]

There were sensible reasons (discussed in chapter 2) for the decision to keep Venona a highly compartmentalized secret within the government. In retrospect, however, the negative consequences of this policy are glaring. Had Venona been made public, it is unlikely there would have been a forty-year campaign to prove that the Rosenbergs were innocent. The Venona messages clearly display Julius Rosenberg's role as the leader of a productive ring of Soviet spies.[8] Nor would there have been any basis for doubting his involvement in atomic espionage, because the deciphered messages document his recruitment of his brother-in-law, David Greenglass, as a spy. It is also unlikely, had the messages been made public or even circulated more widely within the government than they did, that Ethel Rosenberg would have been executed. The Venona messages do not throw her guilt in doubt; indeed, they confirm that she was a participant in her husband's espionage and in the recruitment of her brother for atomic espionage. But they suggest that she was essentially an accessory to her husband's activity, having knowledge of it and assisting him but not acting as a principal. Had they been introduced at the Rosenberg trial, the Venona messages would have confirmed Ethel's guilt but also reduced the importance of her role.

Further, the Venona messages, if made public, would have made Julius Rosenberg's execution less likely. When Julius Rosenberg faced trial, only two Soviet atomic spies were known: David Greenglass, whom Rosenberg had recruited and run as a source, and Klaus Fuchs. Fuchs, however, was in England, so Greenglass was the only Soviet atomic spy in the media spotlight in the United States. Greenglass's confession left Julius Rosenberg as the target of public outrage at atomic espionage. That prosecutors would ask for and get the death penalty under those circumstances is not surprising.

In addition to Fuchs and Greenglass, however, the Venona messages identify three other Soviet sources within the Manhattan Project. The messages show that Theodore Hall, a young physicist at Los Alamos, was a far more valuable source than Greenglass, a machinist. Hall withstood FBI interrogation, and the government had no direct evidence of his crimes except the Venona messages, which because of their secrecy could not be used in court; he therefore escaped prosecution. The real identities of the sources Fogel and Quantum are not known, but the information they turned over to the Soviets suggests that Quantum was a scientist of some standing and that Fogel was either a scientist or an engineer. Both were probably more valuable sources than David Greenglass. Had Venona been made public, Greenglass would have shared the stage with three other atomic spies and not just with Fuchs, and all three would have appeared to have done more damage to American security than he. With Greenglass's role diminished, that of his recruiter, Julius Rosenberg, would have been reduced as well. Rosenberg would assuredly have been convicted, but his penalty might well have been life in prison rather than execution.[9]

There were broader consequences, as well, of the decision to keep Venona secret. The overlapping issues of Communists in government, Soviet espionage, and the loyalty of American Communists quickly became a partisan battleground. Led by Republican senator Joseph Mc-Carthy of Wisconsin, some conservatives and partisan Republicans launched a comprehensive attack on the loyalties of the Roosevelt and Truman administrations. Some painted the entire New Deal as a disguised Communist plot and depicted Dean Acheson, Truman's secretary of state, and George C. Marshall, the Army chief of staff under Roosevelt and secretary of state and secretary of defense under Truman, as participants, in Senator McCarthy's words, in "a conspiracy on a scale so immense as to dwarf any previous such venture in the history of man. A conspiracy of infamy so black that, when it is finally exposed, its principals shall be forever deserving of the maledictions of all honest men."[10] There is no basis in Venona for implicating Acheson or Marshall in a Communist conspiracy, but because the deciphered Venona messages were classified and unknown to the public, demagogues such as McCarthy had the opportunity to mix together accurate information about betrayal by men such as Harry White and Alger Hiss with falsehoods about Acheson and Marshall that served partisan political goals.[11]

A number of liberals and radicals pointed to the excesses of McCarthy's charges as justification for rejecting the allegations altogether. Anticommunism further lost credibility in the late 1960s when critics of U.S. involvement in the Vietnam War blamed it for America's ill-fated participation. By the 1980s many commentators, and perhaps most academic historians, had concluded that Soviet espionage had been minor, that few American Communists had assisted the Soviets, and that no high officials had betrayed the United States. Many history texts depicted America in the late 1940s and 1950s as a "nightmare in red" during which Americans were "sweat-drenched in fear" of a figment of their own paranoid imaginations.[12] As for American Communists, they were widely portrayed as having no connection with espionage. One influential book asserted emphatically, "There is no documentation in the public record of a direct connection between the American Communist Party and espionage during the entire postwar period."[13]

Consequently, Communists were depicted as innocent victims of an irrational and oppressive American government. In this sinister but widely accepted portrait of America in the 1940s and 1950s, an idealistic New Dealer (Alger Hiss) was thrown into prison on the perjured testimony of a mentally sick anti-Communist fanatic (Whittaker Chambers), innocent progressives (the Rosenbergs) were sent to the electric chair on trumped-up charges of espionage laced with anti-Semitism, and dozens of blameless civil servants had their careers ruined by the smears of a professional anti-Communist (Elizabeth Bentley). According to this version of events, one government official (Harry White) was killed by a heart attack brought on by Bentley's lies, and another (Laurence Duggan, a senior diplomat) was driven to suicide by more of Chambers's malignant falsehoods. Similarly, in many textbooks President Truman's executive order denying government employment to those who posed security risks, and other laws aimed at espionage and Communist subversion, were and still are described not as having been motivated by a real concern for American security (since the existence of any serious espionage or subversion was denied) but instead as consciously antidemocratic attacks on basic freedoms. As one commentator wrote, "The statute books groaned under several seasons of legislation designed to outlaw dissent."[14]

Despite its central role in the history of American counterintelligence, the Venona Project remained among the most tightly held government secrets. By the time the project shut down, it had decrypted nearly three thousand messages sent between the Soviet Union and its embassies and consulates around the world. Remarkably, although rumors and a few snippets of information about the project had become public in the 1980s, the actual texts and the enormous import of the messages remained secret until 1995. The U.S. government often has been successful in keeping secrets in the short term, but over a longer period secrets, particularly newsworthy ones, have proven to be very difficult for the government to keep. It is all the more amazing, then, how little got out about the Venona Project in the fifty-three years before it was made public.

Unfortunately, the success of government secrecy in this case has seriously distorted our understanding of post–World War II history. Hundreds of books and thousands of essays on McCarthyism, the federal loyalty security program, Soviet espionage, American communism, and the early Cold War have perpetuated many myths that have given Americans a warped view of the nation's history in the 1930s, 1940s, and 1950s. The information that these messages reveal substantially revises the basis for understanding the early history of the Cold War and of America's concern with Soviet espionage and Communist subversion.

In the late 1970s the FBI began releasing material from its hitherto secret files as a consequence of the passage of the Freedom of Information Act (FOIA). Although this act opened some files to public scrutiny, it has not as yet provided access to the full range of FBI investigative records. The enormous backlog of FOIA requests has led to lengthy delays in releasing documents; it is not uncommon to wait more than five years to receive material. Capricious and zealous enforcement of regulations exempting some material from release frequently has elicited useless documents consisting of occasional phrases interspersed with long sections of redacted (blacked-out) text. And, of course, even the unexpurgated FBI files show only what the FBI learned about Soviet espionage and are only part of the story. Even given these hindrances, however, each year more files are opened, and the growing body of FBI documentation has significantly enhanced the opportunity for a reconstruction of what actually happened.

The collapse of the Union of Soviet Socialist Republics in 1991 led to the opening of Soviet archives that had never been examined by independent scholars. The historically rich documentation first made available in Moscow's archives in 1992 has resulted in an outpouring of new historical writing, as these records allow a far more complete and accurate understanding of central events of the twentieth century. But many archives in Russia are open only in part, and some are still closed. In particular, the archives of the foreign intelligence operations of Soviet military intelligence and those of the foreign intelligence arm of the KGB are not open to researchers. Given the institutional continuity between the former Soviet intelligence agencies and their current Russian successors, the opening of these archives is not anticipated anytime soon. However, Soviet intelligence agencies had cooperated with other Soviet institutions, whose newly opened archives therefore hold some intelligence-related material and provide a back door into the still-closed intelligence archives.

But the most significant source of fresh insight into Soviet espionage in the United States comes from the decoded messages produced by the Venona Project. These documents, after all, constitute a portion of the materials that are still locked up in Russian intelligence archives. Not only do the Venona files supply information in their own right, but because of their inherent reliability they also provide a touchstone for judging the credibility of other sources, such as defectors' testimony and FBI investigative files.

Stalin's Espionage Assault on the United States

Through most of the twentieth century, governments of powerful nations have conducted intelligence operations of some sort during both peace and war. None, however, used espionage as an instrument of state policy as extensively as did the Soviet Union under Joseph Stalin. In the late 1920s and 1930s, Stalin directed most of the resources of Soviet intelligence at nearby targets in Europe and Asia. America was still distant from Stalin's immediate concerns, the threat to Soviet goals posed by Nazi Germany and Imperial Japan. This perception changed, however, after the United States entered the world war in December 1941. Stalin realized that once Germany and Japan were defeated, the world would be left with only three powers able to project their influence across the globe: the Soviet Union, Great Britain, and the United States. And of these, the strongest would be the United States. With that in mind, Stalin's intelligence agencies shifted their focus toward America.

The Soviet Union, Great Britain, and the United States formed a military alliance in early 1942 to defeat Nazi Germany and its allies.[15] The Soviet Union quickly became a major recipient of American military (Lend-Lease) aid, second only to Great Britain; it eventually received more than nine billion dollars. As part of the aid arrangements, the United States invited the Soviets to greatly expand their diplomatic staffs and to establish special offices to facilitate aid arrangements. Thousands of Soviet military officers, engineers, and technicians entered the United States to review what aid was available and choose which machinery, weapons, vehicles (nearly 400,000 American trucks went to the Soviet Union), aircraft, and other matériel would most assist the Soviet war effort. Soviet personnel had to be trained to maintain the American equipment, manuals had to be translated into Russian, shipments to the Soviet Union had to be inspected to ensure that what was ordered had been delivered, properly loaded, and dispatched on the right ships. Entire Soviet naval crews arrived for training to take over American combat and cargo ships to be handed over to the Soviet Union.

Scores of Soviet intelligence officers of the KGB (the chief Soviet foreign intelligence and security agency), the GRU (the Soviet military intelligence agency), and the Naval GRU (the Soviet naval intelligence agency) were among the Soviet personnel arriving in America.[16] These intelligence officers pursued two missions. One, security, was only indirectly connected with the United States. The internal security arm of the KGB employed several hundred thousand full-time personnel, assisted by several million part-time informants, to ensure the political loyalty of Soviet citizens. When the Soviets sent thousands of their citizens to the United States to assist with the Lend-Lease arrangement, they sent this internal security apparatus as well. A significant portion of the Venona messages deciphered by American code-breakers reported on this task. The messages show that every Soviet cargo ship that arrived at an American port to pick up Lend-Lease supplies had in its crew at least one, often two, and sometimes three informants who reported either to the KGB or to the Naval GRU. Their task was not to spy on Americans but to watch the Soviet merchant seamen for signs of political dissidence and potential defection. Some of the messages show Soviet security officers tracking down merchant seamen who had jumped ship, kidnapping them, and spiriting them back aboard Soviet ships in disregard of American law. Similarly, other messages discuss informants, recruited or planted by the KGB in every Soviet office in the United States, whose task was to report signs of ideological deviation or potential defection among Soviet personnel.

A second mission of these Soviet intelligence officers, however, was espionage against the United States, the size and scope of which is the principal subject of this book. The deciphered Venona cables do more than reveal the remarkable success that the Soviet Union had in recruiting spies and gaining access to many important U.S. government agencies and laboratories dealing with secret information. They expose beyond cavil the American Communist party as an auxiliary of the intelligence agencies of the Soviet Union. While not every Soviet spy was a Communist, most were. And while not every American Communist was a spy, hundreds were. The CPUSA itself worked closely with Soviet intelligence agencies to facilitate their espionage. Party leaders were not only aware of the liaison; they actively worked to assist the relationship.

Information from the Venona decryptions underlay the policies of U.S. government officials in their approach to the issue of domestic communism. The investigations and prosecutions of American Communists undertaken by the federal government in the late 1940s and early 1950s were premised on an assumption that the CPUSA had assisted Soviet espionage. This view contributed to the Truman administration's executive order in 1947, reinforced in the early 1950s under the Eisenhower administration, that U.S. government employees be subjected to loyalty and security investigations. The understanding also lay behind the 1948 decision by Truman's attorney general to prosecute the leaders of the CPUSA under the sedition sections of the Smith Act. It was an explicit assumption behind congressional investigations of domestic communism in the late 1940s and 1950s, and it permeated public attitudes toward domestic communism.

The Soviet Union's unrestrained espionage against the United States from 1942 to 1945 was of the type that a nation directs at an enemy state. By the late 1940s the evidence provided by Venona of the massive size and intense hostility of Soviet intelligence operations caused both American counterintelligence professionals and high-level policy-makers to conclude that Stalin had already launched a covert attack on the United States. In their minds, the Soviet espionage offensive indicated that the Cold War had begun not after World War II but many years earlier.

This book describes Soviet espionage in the United States in the 1930s and 1940s. It concentrates on operations during World War II, the most aggressive and effective phase of Soviet activity. It also shows how the success of the wartime espionage offensive rested on the extensive base prepared in the 1930s by the Communist International and the American Communist party. Separate chapters deal with the role of American Communists in Soviet espionage, Elizabeth Bentley's extensive spy rings, the lesser but still significant American activities of Soviet military intelligence (GRU and Naval GRU) compared with that of the larger KGB, the broad scope of Soviet industrial and scientific espionage, and the Soviet Union's waging of a secret war on American soil against its ideological enemies: Trotskyists, Zionists, defectors, and Russian exiles of various types. The Venona decryptions are central to documenting this activity, and the next chapter details the history of that highly successful and long-secret project.

CHAPTER 2

BREAKING THE CODE

Soviet agencies in the United States during World War II used three channels to communicate with Moscow. Most material went by diplomatic pouch and courier. But in wartime the pouch, though secure, was quite slow, often taking many weeks and sometimes months to reach its destination. For time-sensitive material the Soviets had a choice of in-house short-wave radio, commercial radiograms, or international commercial telegraphic cables. None of these, however, was totally secure. Radio messages could be intercepted by anyone with the proper equipment and sufficient listening personnel, while messages sent by telegraphic cable could be copied easily by authorities in any nation through which the cable passed. And during the war, the United States and other nations routinely kept copies of international cables as a military precaution.[1]

The solution to the lack of security of radio and cable was encryption. If messages were sent in a code that other parties could not read, then it was largely a matter of indifference to the Soviets if they were intercepted. For communications with their offices in the United States, the Soviets usually chose commercial cable and radiogram rather than in-house radio transmission. The Venona messages discussed in this book were sent largely by commercial telegraphic cable, although some went as commercial radiograms. For simplicity, all will be referred to as cables.

The technology of the early 1940s did not allow for reliable short-wave radio links between Moscow and North America unless one was using a large and powerful transmitting station, which the Soviets could not build within the confines of their diplomatic compounds. Further, such transmitters were illegal in the United States. The Soviets equipped their American diplomatic posts with short-wave stations but rarely used them. The transmitters appear to have been established chiefly as backup for emergencies such as breakdowns in commercial telegraphic traffic.

One Soviet agency, the Communist International (Comintern), had made heavy use of short-wave radio in the 1930s for communications with the foreign Communist parties that it supervised. But most of this radio traffic was with Central and Western European parties, radio links far more reliable than those with more distant North America. None-theless, the Comintern maintained a clandestine radio link with the American Communist party (CPUSA) in the 1930s. The records of the Comintern in the RTsKhIDNI archive in Moscow contain hundreds of decoded radio messages that passed between the CPUSA and the Communist International.

Throughout much of the 1930s, the Comintern's radio link to the United States ran through a resident agent operating under a false identity. His real name was Solomon Vladimirovich Mikhelson-Manuilov. Numerous decoded cables between Moscow and Mikhelson-Manuilov show him supervising the distribution of Comintern funds to the United States, overseeing the arrival from and departure to Moscow of CPUSA and Comintern couriers, passing along Moscow's orders to the CPUSA leadership, and answering requests from Moscow for information about CPUSA activities. The CPUSA and the Comintern maintained two covert short-wave sending-and-receiving stations in the United States, one primary (in New York City) and one backup (on Long Island), both unlicensed and illegal. Mikhelson-Manuilov supervised their operation, but the stations were usually manned by trusted American Communists. One man, Arnold Reid, submitted to the Comintern's International Brigades an autobiography that proudly noted, as a sign of the CPUSA's confidence in him, his assignment to set up and run the covert radio station on Long Island in 1935.[2]

The Comintern's radio links to foreign parties, however, also illustrate the vulnerability of that medium. In late 1997 the Government Communications Headquarters (GCHQ), the British equivalent of the American National Security Agency, released for public access thousands of these messages. GCHQ's 1930s predecessor had intercepted the broadcasts from 1934 to 1937 and broken the Comintern's code in a project given the name Mask.[3]

The Comintern was hardly the only agency to have its messages intercepted and its code broken. Several of the greatest successes of the Allied powers in World War II had their origins in code breaking. The American breaking of one of the Japanese navy's chief radio codes helped U.S. Navy forces to maximize their limited resources and reverse the tide of war in the Pacific at the Battle of Midway. Similarly, British success in breaking a key German machine-generated cipher called Enigma allowed the Royal Air Force to concentrate its resources to best advantage and turn back the numerically superior Luftwaffe in the Battle of Britain.

Soviet diplomatic offices and the intelligence officers who operated out of them were well aware of the vulnerability of coded messages to being broken and read. Nonetheless, they sent thousands of coded cables, many containing highly sensitive information, even about Soviet espionage against other nations. They did so because they were using a coding system that was far more difficult to break than that used by the Germans and the Japanese (or the Comintern radio code)—an encryption system that, if employed correctly, was unbreakable.

The Soviet Code and Cipher System

The following description of probable Soviet encryption procedures is constructed from comments by National Security Agency cryptanalysts who worked on the Venona Project, from information supplied by defecting Soviet code clerks, and from the knowledge of functions necessary in encoding and decoding texts and then further enciphering them with a one-time pad.[4]

The Soviet intelligence officer first writes out his message in Russian in as concise a form as possible, to reduce the cipher clerk's work and the expense of transmitting the cable. (The exact texts of the outgoing messages were prepared in the code clerk's office, and incoming texts were kept in that office, with the intelligence officer only permitted to bring in or take out notes or extracts of texts.) Proper names of people and places were replaced with cover names by the intelligence officer—both to conceal their identity from intermediaries who might see the text and, perhaps, to make the identity more specific to the receiving intelligence officer.

Using a code book, the code clerk converts the message text into four-digit numerical codes. The code book is a sort of dictionary that contains numerical groups for letters, syllables, words, entire phrases—even for punctuation and for numbers. If a word or phrase is not present in the code book, it is spelled out using letter or syllable equivalents. If the word is a name spelled with Latin letters, it is spelled out using a separate "spell table."[5]

Let's say the KGB receives a report from one of its spies, in this case William Ullmann, who provided information on U.S. Army Air Force experiments on a new rocket. (Ullmann was an Army Air Force officer assigned to the Pentagon.) The KGB sends Ullmann's detailed report about the rocket experiment to Moscow by diplomatic pouch. But it notifies Moscow by cable that Ullmann's report is on the way. The KGB officer might originally write (in Russian), "Ullmann delivered report about rockets." He then (or at the time of writing) substitutes Ullmann's cover name (Pilot) and hands the cipher clerk a message saying, "Pilot delivered report about rockets." The cipher clerk then consults his code book and converts the message to four-digit numbers:

Pilot	delivered	report	about	rockets
7934	2157	1139	3872	2166

The clerk then converts these four-digit groups into five-digit groups by shifting a digit from the second group to the first, and so on: 79342 15711 39387 22166.

Next the cipher clerk turns to the one-time pad. Each page of the pad contains 60 five-digit numerical groups, called the additive or the key. The clerk takes the first group in the upper lefthand corner of the page (26473 in this illustration) and writes it down as the first group of the message before he enciphers any text. This serves to tell the deciphering clerk on the receiving end (who has the same pad) which page to use or, more precisely, to confirm that the message he has just received was enciphered on the next page of the one-time pad.[6]

Starting with the second five-digit group on the key page, the code clerk places the numbers from the pad beneath the numbers from the code book. He then adds the numbers together; if the sum is greater than 9, nothing is carried (8 plus 6 yields 4, not 14, because the 1 is not carried). This produces a new set of enciphered five-digit numbers, which are placed after the first group from the key page, which serves as an indicator.

From the code book:		79342	15711	39387	22166
From the one-time pad:	26473	56328	29731	35682	23798
The enciphered message:	26473	25660	34442	64969	45854

Finally, the five-digit groups are converted to five-letter groups by the code clerk using the following substitution to Latin letters: o=O, 1=I, 2=U, 3=Z, 4=T, 5=R, 6=E, 7=W, 8=A, 9=P.[7] This produces:

UETWZ UREEO ZTTTU ETPEP TRART . . . TEERP 23412

At the end of the message text he enters the next five-digit group from the one-time pad after the last one actually used for encipherment (46659 in the letter form of TEERP) and also enters *as digits* a five-digit group (23412 in this illustration), of which the first three digits are a serial number for all of the messages on that circuit and the last two digits are the date of encipherment.[8]

In Moscow the cable is determined to be KGB by an initial receiving point and then routed to the KGB cipher office and converted back to:

(26473) 25660 34442 64969 45854 . . . (46659)

The deciphering clerk then goes to his copy of the one-time pad. If no messages have been reordered in transmission, the group 26473 should confirm that he has the proper page for decipherment. Further, if the group 46659 appears at a point that corresponds exactly to the number of cipher groups received, it confirms that all cipher groups have been received. The clerk then subtracts the five-digit numbers given by the one-time pad. When the number to be subtracted is larger than the number being subtracted from, ten is added without borrowing (4 minus 6 yields 8). If the clerk does his arithmetic correctly, he now has the original five-digit groups: 79342 15711 39387 22166. After rebreaking this string of numbers into four-digit groups—essentially reversing the encryption procedure—he consults the code book and uncovers the message:

7934	2157	1139	3872	2166
Pilot	delivered	report	about	rockets

The message is then passed to the appropriate KGB officer at head-quarters. The officer consults his own records and converts the cover name to the real name, Ullmann.[9]

Compromise of the Soviet Cipher System

Cecil Phillips, one of the American cryptanalysts who eventually broke the Soviet cipher, described the Soviet system: "The messages broken by the Venona program were both coded and enciphered. When a code is enciphered with a one-time pad, the cryptographer who designed the system expects the encipherment to provide absolute security—even if an adversary somehow obtains an underlying codebook or de-briefs a defecting code clerk. . . . The security of such an encipherment-decipherment system depends on both the randomness (that is, unpredictability) of the "key" on the one-time pad pages and the uniqueness of the one-time pad sets held by the sender and the receiver."[10] If con-structed correctly, each message in the Soviet one-time pad system was in a unique cipher. There was no repetition of the random cipher in any other message, which meant there was no way for the code-breaker (cryptanalyst) to decipher the message.

But this total security had a price. Because each coded message was further enciphered by a unique additive key (the one-time pad page) and there were hundreds of thousands of messages produced in war-time, the code-makers (cryptographers) had to manufacture hundreds of thousands of unique, nonrepeating key pages.[11] To be unbreakable, the key pages truly had to be used just one time. In an era before high-speed digital computers, this put a tremendous strain on code-makers to produce one-time pads.

German and Japanese cryptographers were as aware of the unbreak-ability of the one-time pads as were the Soviets. But in view of the daunting requirements for skilled personnel to produce huge quantities of one-time pads, each page containing a unique random-number ci-pher, they chose another route. They developed ciphers that, while the-oretically less secure than one-time pads, could be much more easily manufactured and used. The German "Enigma" machine cipher, for example, was produced by a primitive electromechanical computer. Both the Germans and the Japanese believed that these ciphers, while in theory vulnerable to cryptanalysis, were as a practical matter un-breakable. Their error, based on an underestimation of the capabilities of British and American code-breakers, contributed to their defeat in the war.

The Soviets, who had a well-deserved reputation for obsession with secrecy, chose to do things the hard way, using one-time pads and paying the price of employing a small army of code-makers. For a while, though, Soviet cryptographers were unable to produce new key pages fast enough to meet demand. In June 1941 Adolf Hitler broke his alliance with Joseph Stalin and invaded the USSR. Overnight the production of ciphered messages by Soviet diplomatic and intelligence offices skyrocketed. It is not known for certain, but it appears that the existing stock of one-time pads began to melt away, and the Soviet cryptographic office in Moscow faced an emergency. Individuals who failed to meet military production quotas faced severe, sometimes mortal consequences, so the crisis was not only national but also personal. The solution, in early 1942, was to produce duplicate key pages. Whether this expedient was introduced intentionally by a panicky senior official or a desperately overworked staff of cryptographers is not known. In any case, tens of thousands of duplicate key pages were bound in one-time pads during 1942.[12]

Thus, for a period Soviet cryptographers doubled their output by duplicating cipher pages, almost certainly by the simple expedient of using extra carbon sheets in the machines that typed out the key pages. This, of course, turned their one-time key pages into two-time key pages. Perhaps they thought the risk minimal. Many professional cryptographers believed that a single duplication, while voiding the theoretical unbreakability of the cipher, in practice only marginally degraded the security of the system. Further, for a duplication to be of any use to cryptanalysts, both messages using the duplicated key page had to be copied, and some strategy had to be developed to establish that both messages had used the same key. To minimize this risk, the Soviets did not duplicate entire pads. Rather, they duplicated individual pages, then shuffled them into different pads, often with different page numbers, and distributed them to Soviet offices across the globe. Only a code-breaking agency with extensive sources throughout the world would be in a position to gather enough of the duplicated messages even to attempt to attack the Soviet cipher. And the attack itself would require resources to deploy a team of cryptanalysts of the highest order for many years.

The National Security Agency of the United States (NSA), however, had those resources. The NSA originated as the Army's Signal Intelligence Service. Before World War II, the Army had only a limited cryptographic capacity. In September 1939, when Germany invaded Poland, the entire staff of the Signal Intelligence Service numbered merely nineteen. By the time of the Japanese attack on Pearl Harbor, more than two years later, the staff had grown to nearly four hundred; yet this included not just code-makers and code-breakers but also large radio interception staffs in Washington and in various field locations, support personnel, and the headquarters section. With America in the war, however, the Army quickly added thousands of staff members to its communications intelligence and code-breaking effort, and the service's personnel grew to more than ten thousand by 1945. To accommodate its greatly enlarged staff, the Signal Intelligence Service took over Arlington Hall, the campus of a private girls' preparatory school in northern Virginia, across the Potomac River from Washington, D.C. For many years the agency was informally known within the government as Arlington Hall, if for no other reason than that its formal title kept changing. In 1949, when signals and cryptographic intelligence units from the Navy and Air Force were added, Arlington Hall was transformed into the Armed Forces Security Agency, removed from Army control, and placed under the Joint Chiefs of Staff. In 1952 the agency was given its current name, the National Security Agency, and came under the supervision of the secretary of defense. It also moved to a new site, at Fort George Meade, Maryland, outside Washington. For simplicity, the name National Security Agency will be used throughout this book.

The prewar Army's few professional cryptographers were vastly outnumbered by the new staff mobilized for World War II. These new code-breakers came from a variety of backgrounds: philologists and linguists with a range of foreign language skills, mathematicians to whom numerical ciphers were a technical challenge, engineers and technicians who worked on radio interception and construction of cipher machines, and English majors with a love for puzzles. Arlington Hall veterans note that card games emphasizing mathematical skills, such as bridge, as well as the maddeningly difficult crossword puzzles of the *London Times* and the *New York Times*, were a common form of relaxation among staff. Much of the new staff was female because the uniformed services took so many males for other military duties. Almost all the new personnel had to be taught, or in many cases had to teach themselves, the skills and principles of cryptography. Very quickly, though, Arlington Hall scored valuable successes against both German and Japanese ciphers. By the end of World War II this little-known agency, built almost from the ground up by wartime amateurs, rivaled the British Government Communications Headquarters as the most skilled code-breaking agency in the world.

The NSA's predecessors began to collect enciphered Soviet and other telegrams in 1939. But for several years little was done with the Soviet messages because German and Japanese codes had a higher priority and because American cryptanalysts had made very little headway against Soviet ciphers in the past. In 1942, however, NSA success against the Japanese military attaché code stimulated a second look at Soviet messages. The NSA deciphered cables between the Japanese army's general staff and its military attachés in Berlin and Helsinki regarding the work of Finnish cryptanalysts on Soviet ciphers. The Finns had an excellent cryptographic staff that concentrated almost entirely on the Soviet Union, the chief threat to Finland. The Finns had not broken any of the Soviet diplomatic ciphers, but they had developed a partial understanding of their external characteristics and were able to sort most diplomatic messages into a series of identifiable variants. They relayed the information to the Japanese, who shared the Finns' antipathy toward the Soviets.[13]

This Finnish-Japanese information allowed American cryptanalysts to separate messages into homogeneous sets—a prerequisite to starting any cryptanalytic attack. It also suggested—incorrectly—that the Russians employed reusable key tables rather than one-time pads. This may have encouraged American cryptanalysts to believe that the Soviet cipher might yield rapidly to their analysis. It was at this time, in 1943, that Carter Clarke of the Army's Special Branch authorized the examination of the Soviet cables. Initially the project had no special name and was referred to by such phrases as the "Russian diplomatic problem." The deciphered messages themselves later received a formal code name—first Jade, then Bride, then Drug, and finally, in 1961, Venona. Eventually the entire code-breaking effort became known as the Venona Project.

NSA analysts soon identified five variants of the Soviet one-time pad cipher. One was called Trade, because it carried the traffic of Amtorg, the Soviet trading agency, and the Soviet Government Purchasing Commission, which oversaw Soviet receipt of American Lend-Lease aid. A second variant was used by diplomats in the Soviet foreign ministry.

The other three variants, however, were used by officers of the three Soviet intelligence agencies: the KGB, the GRU, and the Naval GRU. These intelligence officers were operating out of the Soviet embassy and consulates as well as Amtorg and purchasing commission offices in Washington, New York, and San Francisco.

A breakthrough came in autumn 1943, when Lt. Richard Hallock, analyzing Trade messages, demonstrated that the Soviets were making extensive use of duplicate key pages assembled in separate one-time pad books. The work of Hallock and his colleagues opened the first crack in the walls of the Soviet code and yielded methods for discovering duplicate pages.[14] Over time, and after a prodigious amount of analytic work, American cryptanalysts showed that even a single duplication of a one-time pad cipher rendered the messages vulnerable to decryption.

As World War II was drawing to a close, the staff working on Venona increased as cryptanalysts who had been assigned to Japanese and German ciphers sought new projects. One of these newcomers was a brilliant and innovative cryptanalyst named Samuel Chew. Working on Trade traffic, he discovered some highly predictable patterns in the shipping messages. Many of the Trade messages were time-sensitive but otherwise routine notifications to Moscow that certain ships were leaving American ports with specified cargoes of Lend-Lease supplies.

Chew's work had a dramatic impact on the efforts of those who were recovering cipher keys. They were now able to solve or remove the one-time pad cipher for stretches of Trade code text and thereby to reveal significant strings of KGB code. These strings, though still in digital code-group form for which the Russian meanings were unknown, accumulated rapidly in the latter half of 1945 as the work effort was sharply increased thanks to staff coming off the Japanese code and cipher problems.

While breaking the one-time pad cipher was a key to the success of Venona, it was not the end of the code-breaking project, because the Soviets used a two-stage system. The Soviet code clerk first encoded the message from a code book and then further complicated the code by use of the one-time pad cipher. The duplicated cipher pages allowed the NSA to break the second part, but not the first. To solve the first part and make the message readable, cryptolinguists had to re-create the Soviet code book.[15]

Although Chew developed a fair amount of Russian language skill, solving the underlying coded text called for a full-time linguist "book-breaker." In the parlance of cryptography, a book-breaker seeks to establish the textual meanings of numerical ciphers by "breaking" into the code book used by the opponent. It was at this time, early in 1946, that Meredith Gardner transferred to the Venona Project and became the principal book-breaker for all the codes of the Soviet cable project. A tall, gangling, soft-spoken Southerner, Gardner read German, Sanskrit, Lithuanian, Spanish, and French and had taught languages at universities in Texas and Wisconsin. Shortly after Pearl Harbor, the Army had recruited him to work on German and Japanese codes, and he had taught himself Japanese in the process. In 1946 he began a new language, Russian. His linguistic work was helped by the now expanding body of plain code groups (what was left when the overlying one-time pad cipher was removed) being extracted from Trade and KGB messages that had used the duplicate key pages. By about mid-summer 1946, Gardner had recovered enough code groups and text to be sure that the messages involved Soviet espionage. By the end of 1946, he had broken out the text of a message that revealed Soviet atomic spying.

Eventually it would become clear that Gardner had reconstructed the code book used by the KGB from November 1943 into early 1946. This work allowed the reading of hundreds of KGB messages from that period and provided some of the most complete text that the Venona Project produced. It also became clear, however, that the KGB had used a different code book for 1942 and most of 1943. NSA analysts made little progress on those messages for several years. Then in late 1953 Samuel Chew was able to solve a set of code clerk "key-saving" cases that Cecil Phillips had identified earlier.[16] This breakthrough afforded significant progress on earlier messages.

Shortly after Chew's analysis, the NSA also determined that a copy of a badly burned Soviet code book in American hands contained some of the code used in these earlier KGB messages. Finnish troops had captured the code book when they overran the Soviet consulate at Petsamo, Finland, in June 1941.[17] The Germans then obtained the book from the Finns. In May 1945 a U.S. Army intelligence team headed by Lt. Col. Paul Neff found a copy at a German signals intelligence archive located in a castle in Saxony, Germany. The archive was in territory assigned to the Soviet zone of occupation, and Neff's team removed the copy only a day before the Soviets pushed into the area.[18] Although badly damaged, the book assisted Meredith Gardner in reconstructing part of the KGB code book for the earlier years. The reconstruction, however, was not as complete as that achieved for the KGB code book for November 1943–1946, and the decryptions for that earlier period are less complete.

This burned code book is not the same as the code and cipher materials that were obtained from Finnish officers by another American intelligence agency, the Office of Strategic Services, in late 1944. In that case, the State Department learned of the matter and, in a remarkably naive act, successfully urged President Roosevelt to order the OSS to hand the material over to the KGB as a gesture of goodwill. So far as is known, the OSS did not even keep a copy.[19]

The third of the five main Soviet systems to be breached successfully was that used by the diplomats of the Soviet foreign ministry. A small amount of progress in finding duplicate key pages among messages was made in late 1946, but these instances were essentially unexploitable. Real success in deciphering foreign ministry messages was achieved by the mathematician Richard Leibler in 1950. Leibler's work led to finding a large number of duplicate key pages among foreign ministry messages, and between foreign ministry messages and other systems, and ultimately pointed the way to the success in decrypting some GRU and Naval GRU messages.

The nature of the key page indicator (used to identify messages ciphered from duplicate key pages) and the underlying code made both the GRU and Naval GRU systems more resistant to NSA analysis than the KGB system was. It was not until 1952 that computer assaults, devised by the mathematician Hugh Gingerich on the basis of Leibler's earlier work, allowed duplicate key pages to be found among a limited number of GRU messages. The attack was grounded in observations of code practices made by the cryptolinguist Charles Condray and others. It was even later, in 1957, that Naval GRU messages gave way, in the face of an analytic offensive by British cryptanalysts who were working with the Venona Project.

Although from the late 1940s through the 1970s many hundreds of messages were entirely or almost entirely read, a significant number were only partially decrypted. Analysis yielded a paragraph or two, or several sentences and partial phrases split up by the cryptanalyst's bracketed comment "[37 unrecovered code groups]," "[two unrecovered code groups]," or some other total of numerical code groups that the NSA was never able to render into readable prose. In the Venona Project more than twenty-nine hundred messages amounting to more than five thousand pages of text were decrypted and read. But as impressive as that feat was, the messages represented only a fraction of the total Soviet cable traffic. Venona uncovered, in whole or in part, roughly half (49 percent) of the messages sent in 1944 between the KGB New York office and its Moscow headquarters, but only 15 percent of the messages from 1943 and a mere 1.8 percent of the messages from 1942 (only twenty-three out of nearly thirteen hundred). Only 1.5 percent of the 1945 traffic between the KGB Washington office and Moscow was deciphered. Venona cryptanalysts read half of the Naval GRU's Washington traffic in 1943 but not a single Naval GRU message for any other year.

The National Security Agency also established relations with Britain's highly regarded cryptographic service (GCHQ), and several of their linguists and analysts joined the Venona Project in 1948. (The British contribution can be observed in a number of messages that are rendered into British English rather than into American idiom.) Initially, of course, the NSA had copies of ciphered Soviet cables sent to and from Soviet diplomatic offices in the United States. Through a variety of means the NSA garnered ciphered Soviet cables from other nations as well, eventually including Soviet offices in Canada, Great Britain, France, the Netherlands, Sweden, Germany, Czechoslovakia, Bulgaria, Turkey, Iran, Japan, Manchuria, Ethiopia, South Africa, Australia, Chile, Uruguay, Colombia, Mexico, and Cuba. The Venona Project continued until October 1, 1980, although on a reduced scale in the 1970s. But even in the last year new messages, thirty-nine in all, were broken. By that point, the NSA deemed the material so old that it no longer had operational value to American intelligence, and the project ended. Its product, however, remained secret until 1995.

Until late 1947 the NSA worked virtually alone on Venona and shared it with only a few officials in Army intelligence. But at that point Carter Clarke, now a general and the Army's deputy G-2 (military intelligence), concluded that the information required wider dissemination if it were to be properly understood and used. In particular, while some of the identities of cover names in the Venona traffic were obvious, others were not. For example, by mid-1947 Gardner had broken messages that discussed a Soviet agent who at first had the cover name Antenna and later was called Liberal. Gardner did not know his identity, but one of the decrypted messages from the New York KGB office to Moscow reported that Liberal's wife of five years was named Ethel and was twenty-nine years old.[20] These investigative leads required further work. The NSA, however, was a cryptologic agency: it did not have street investigators who could check on candidates for Antenna/Liberal and see which one had a wife named Ethel.

General Clarke spoke with S. Wesley Reynolds, the FBI liaison with Army G-2. Initial cooperation was tentative, but in October 1948 Reynolds brought Special Agent Robert Lamphere to the Venona Project as its full-time FBI liaison. The result was a fruitful partnership that allowed rapid progress in identifying cover names in Venona. Gardner handed over deciphered Venona messages showing cover-named Soviet agents at certain places on certain days, holding certain jobs, with certain family circumstances and individual characteristics. In turn, the FBI looked at its own investigative files and undertook new checks to identify persons who fit the information provided by the deciphered Venona messages. Over the next years hundreds of cover names were identified. In 1950 this cooperation allowed the NSA and the FBI to identify Antenna/Liberal as Julius Rosenberg, who in the right year had married Ethel Greenglass, who was the right age.

Cover names played a security role in obscuring the identity of a person. But they also were used because they lessened the work of code clerks and promoted clarity. Proper names and other words not found in the code book had to be laboriously spelled out letter by letter from a table that had two-digit code groups for each letter. This was further complicated by having to convert English names from the Latin alphabet to the Cyrillic. It was easier to establish a cover name that was in the code book, or at least to use a short cover name, than to spell out a lengthy name. Use of cover names also minimized the risk of confusion that might result from spelling out similar names, particularly non-Russian ones.

The Soviets believed that the real security of their cables lay in their use of the unbreakable one-time pad cipher, not in the lesser security device of cover names. Consequently, although cover names predominate in the Venona messages, the real names of agents on occasion also appear in clear text. Often, when the KGB in the United States established a relationship with a new source, it would send a message to Moscow giving the agent's real name and then stating a new cover name that would be used in the future.[21] Cover names frequently hinted at a person's profession or character—a serious error if security is a primary consideration. George Silverman, a Soviet source in the U.S. Army

Air Force, had the cover name Aileron. Harold Glasser, a Soviet agent in the U.S. Treasury, received the cover name Ruble, the name of the Soviet currency. One writer has waggishly referred to the "semiotics of Venona," referring to the way Soviet intelligence officers indulged in insider humor and, consciously or unconsciously, expressed their attitudes by their choices of cover names.[22] The KGB gave Trotskyists and Zionists, both hated enemies, the cover names Polecats and Rats, respectively. Expressing their view that American intelligence and counterintelligence agencies were unsophisticated compared with themselves, the KGB assigned to the OSS the name Izba, the Russian word for log cabin, while the FBI received the similarly belittling designation Khata, or the Hut. KGB cables used the cover name Babylon for San Francisco, an obvious reference to the city's cultural reputation, while Washington, as the capital of the United States, received the name Carthage—and we know what happened to Carthage.

In a later era, when the Cold War led to heightened sensitivity about communications security, both Soviet and American security practices required that cover names be purely random. Several American agencies even had computers generate a random cover name when needed to ensure that a human choice might not unconsciously produce a cover name that would give an enemy clues to what or who was being camouflaged. Certainly the assistance provided to American counterintelligence by the Soviets' frequent disregard for security in choosing Venona cover names was an object lesson in why such practices were later adopted.

Venona provided the FBI with information that allowed it to neutralize several major Soviet espionage networks and scores of individual agents. (In most cases the Soviet agents were not prosecuted, for reasons that we discuss later.) But Venona did more than that. It identified, on a smaller scale, Soviet agents operating in Britain, Canada, Australia, and other nations. American authorities shared information with appropriate national counterintelligence agencies, and these agents, too, were largely neutralized. Australia was a striking example of the power of Venona's deciphered messages to convince otherwise skeptical politicians to take action. Rather like the Truman administration in the United States, Australia's left-of-center Labour government in 1946 abolished its wartime internal security apparatus, not wishing a rerun of the 1920s and 1930s, when Australia's conservative governments had used the internal security agencies to harass left-wing groups. Internal security became simply a secondary task of the Commonwealth Investigation Branch, the police section of the attorney general's office charged with a broad array of criminal investigative tasks. The same Labour government, however, reversed direction in 1949 when the United States and Great Britain handed over to the Australian government deciphered KGB messages (Venona decryptions) from the Soviet embassy in Canberra that pointed to well-placed Soviet sources inside the Australian government. Both countries also informed the Australians that unless the leaks were dealt with, Australia could not expect a significant role in British and American atomic research or other high-level security matters. In response the Labour government created the Australian Security Intelligence Organization, with responsibility for counterespionage and internal security and a specific mandate to track down the real identities of the spies in the KGB's Canberra traffic.[23]

Venona provided the FBI and the CIA with crucial information about the professional practices and habits of Soviet intelligence agencies—"tradecraft" in espionage jargon. It also revealed details about scores of professional Soviet intelligence officers who would be the West's opponents in the espionage arena of the Cold War. Young intelligence officers who show up often in Venona continued to serve with the KGB into the 1980s.

Most of all, American intelligence agencies used Venona as a standard against which to judge information from less reliable sources. One of the major sources of intelligence and counterintelligence information was the testimony of defectors: former Soviet intelligence officers, former Soviet spies, and former Soviet officials of various sorts. But defectors were driven by a variety of motives: ideological conversion, personal spite, fear, or greed. Most were voluntary, but some were coerced or blackmailed into defection. Many were truthful, but some otherwise truthful defectors had limited understanding of what they were reporting and inadvertently misled American intelligence officers. Others told the truth about some matters but also exaggerated their own importance or inflated the value of what they knew or lied about other things if it served their interests. And, of course, there were fake defectors, Soviet agents who pretended to defect in order to subvert American intelligence with false and misleading information.

Often defectors in the early decades of the Cold War gave information about topics or persons who were the subject of Venona messages, in particular the assignments and careers of Soviet intelligence officers in the 1940s. In those cases, American intelligence could compare what the defector said with what was known from Venona. If the defector's story matched the Venona information, it showed that on those matters he was telling the truth and gave a basis for confidence in his story on other matters. If, on the other hand, the defector's information was contradicted by Venona, his credibility plummeted. As an NSA-CIA history of Venona stated, "Venona thus became a touchstone of American counter-intelligence—a kind of super-secret central reference point for FBI and CIA leaders to use in judging the accuracy of subsequent information."[24]

Venona and Historical Documentation

Some of those who do not wish to believe the evidence of Venona have denied that the messages are authentic. They have maintained that the Venona messages are forgeries wholly or partially concocted by the American government.[25] A number of points, however, substantiate the authenticity of Venona.

First, the accusation of forgery, while easily made, is most unlikely in regard to the Venona decryptions. There are cases where U.S. government agencies prepared and distributed forged documents in deception operations during World War II and the Cold War. In wartime, forged documents may be successfully foisted on an enemy when that party must make a quick decision, lacks the opportunity to seek corroborative evidence, and is denied the clarity of hindsight.

Successfully forged *historical* documents, however, are much more difficult to prepare. The likelihood of the forger's making a mistake that will lead to exposure is high. Errors in formatting, in language and nomenclature, in references to individuals and events, and in printing, handwriting, and typefaces are common. Moreover, scholars examining historical documents are not under time pressure, have the opportunity to seek corroborative evidence, and will judge the document in the light of how it fits with independently derived historical knowledge. There are, to be sure, cases of forgery of historical documents, but they tend to center on a very small number of documents—often a single one. In the case of Venona, there are more than five thousand pages of messages. A successful forgery of historical documents in this quantity that could not be easily exposed is not only unprecedented, it is as a practical matter impossible.

Forgers of historical documents attempt to disguise the documents' origins in order to deflect critical attention from the true source. In the case of Venona, however, the origins are openly proclaimed and the identity of the chief cryptanalysts, linguists, and investigators in the project are known. Though some are dead, others are still alive and have made themselves available to scholars investigating the Venona messages. Venona could only be a forgery if it had been supported by a massive conspiracy involving hundreds of people. Further, over the more than three decades of its operation, the Venona Project employed many who later left government service and hence are under no legally enforceable restraint to remain silent about what would be a criminal enterprise under cover of government authority.

Second, in this book Venona is not treated in isolation. The documentation of Venona is integrated with a broad range of other corroborative evidence, including testimony, both written and oral, by a wide variety of persons over many decades. It includes voluntary statements from defectors from Soviet intelligence, reluctant testimony from persons under legal compulsion, and candid discourse gathered by listening devices, as well as information available in published works. The corroborative documentation also includes written primary material from a range of public and private archives as well as contextual historical material from the work of earlier scholars. As we shall see, the documentation of Venona fits, and fits very well, with this other evidence.

Ultimately the authenticity of Venona will be confirmed when Soviet-era intelligence archives are opened. Although unrestricted access seems unlikely in the near future, some documents have been released. The Russian Foreign Intelligence Service, successor to the KGB, has provided selected documents to current and retired Russian intelligence officers to publish narratives of certain aspects of KGB history. The largest opening from the KGB archive came in early 1999 with the publication of *The Haunted Wood: Soviet Espionage in America—The Stalin Era* by the American historian Allen Weinstein and the retired KGB officer Alexander Vassiliev.[26] These documents confirm the participation in Soviet espionage of fifty-eight persons identified in Venona.[27] They also establish the real identity of nine persons who were hidden behind cover names in the Venona messages, as well as uncovering other Soviet spies who are entirely absent from Venona.

There is also a back door into the Soviet intelligence archives, and we have already located documentary corroboration for Venona in those Moscow archives that are open, documents that would not exist if the claims that Venona is a forgery had any basis in reality.

Corroboration for Venona: Moscow Documents

From 1919 until 1943, the Communist International (Comintern), headquartered in Moscow, supervised the activities of Communist parties throughout the world. After the Comintern dissolved in 1943, its records were stored in an archive that in late 1991 became RTsKhIDNI, the Russian Center for the Preservation and Study of Documents of Recent History. This archive holds the bulk of the records of the central bodies of the Communist Party of the Soviet Union (CPSU) from the early 1920s to Stalin's death in 1953.

The records of the Comintern deal chiefly with its main task, the promotion of communism and world revolution by political means. The Comintern, although not itself an arm of Soviet intelligence, nonetheless cooperated with Soviet intelligence agencies. After Venona was made public, it was discovered that the Comintern's records contained communications with the KGB and GRU that corroborated a number of Venona documents.[28]

The case of Anwar Muhammed illustrates how Comintern records verify the authenticity of Venona. One deciphered Venona cable, from the New York KGB station to the KGB Moscow headquarters in July 1943, reports that the station has been unable to gather any information about Muhammed.[29] It also notes that Jacob Golos, the CPUSA's chief liaison with the KGB, reported that he knew nothing of Muhammed. The footnotes to this message by NSA and FBI analysts show that they were never able to identify Muhammed and had no idea why the New York KGB was interested in him.

A document found in 1993 in the RTsKhIDNI archive, however, explains the matter. In January 1943 the Comintern received an inquiry about Muhammed from a Soviet official named Sharia.[30] Sharia is unknown, and the agency on whose behalf he was writing is not clearly identified, although it was likely the KGB. Sharia stated that his agency's office in Kabul, Afghanistan, reported that Anwar Muhammed, director of a Kabul teachers' school, wanted to visit Moscow. Before this visit was approved, Sharia wanted to confirm Muhammed's claim that he was a Communist of some years' standing. Muhammed had told Soviet officials in Kabul that he held a doctorate in biochemistry from the Johns Hopkins University in Baltimore and that while a student at Johns Hopkins he had been recruited into the CPUSA through Albert Blumberg, head of the Maryland Communist party and a Johns Hopkins faculty member. Muhammed also said that his wife was an American and a fellow Communist. Sharia asked if the Comintern had any records that might verify Muhammed's claims.

The RTsKhIDNI document clarifies the meaning of the deciphered Venona message and verifies its authenticity. The Moscow KGB had asked its New York office, just as it had asked the Comintern, to corroborate Muhammed's story. In its July 1943 message the New York KGB reported that neither it nor the CPUSA was able to provide the requested confirmation.

Another objection to the Venona evidence is that in order to impress their Moscow superiors, KGB officers in the United States might exaggerate and falsely claim to have recruited as sources entirely innocent people they had casually met. This is very unlikely. Soviet intelligence officers could not simply report that they had recruited John Smith as a source. The KGB had elaborate procedures governing source recruitment.

A field officer who had spotted a candidate for recruitment had first to review the case with the head of the KGB station and receive permission to proceed. The next step was the "processing" of the candidate, to use Soviet tradecraft jargon. The intelligence officer gathered background information from various sources to verify the individual's biography and assess his or her fitness for espionage work. The CPUSA's liaisons with the KGB, Jacob Golos and Bernard Schuster on the East Coast and Isaac Folkoff on the West Coast, were often called upon to provide background material on prospective recruits. Sometimes the reports were not satisfactory and a candidate was dropped. If they were positive, the head of the KGB station would endorse the field officer's recommendation and ask the KGB Moscow headquarters for "sanction" to proceed with "signing-on," as the KGB called the formal recruitment of a source.

Moscow's sanction for a recruitment was not automatic or routine. Often the KGB headquarters asked its American station for additional documentation of a candidate's fitness. The KGB headquarters also did its own independent checking, sending queries to the Communist International to see if its extensive records on the American Communist movement contained relevant information. One case involved Marion

Davis, a candidate then working for the Office of the Coordinator of Inter-American Affairs in Washington, whom the New York KGB wanted to recruit. The field officer's report noted that she had earlier worked at the U.S. embassy in Mexico City and had had contact with Soviet diplomats. Not only did General Fitin of the KGB request Comintern records on Davis, but he refused to sanction her recruitment until he received a report from the head of the KGB station in Mexico City.

Once Moscow sanctioned a recruitment, the actual signing-on usually consisted of a meeting between the candidate and a professional KGB officer or, more rarely, one of the KGB's full-time American agents. The officer who conducted the signing-on then filed a report with Moscow confirming that recruitment had been completed. The Moscow KGB expected its field officers to provide regular reports on a source's productivity. The head of the KGB station in the United States also periodically shifted responsibility among his field officers for contact with sources. Under these circumstances, a faked or exaggerated source would show up quickly and might entail severe consequences for the offending officer. In most cases Moscow expected the delivery of actual or filmed documents or reports written personally by the source. Those were delivered to Moscow by diplomatic pouch; and when a source failed to deliver material, Moscow demanded an explanation. The KGB station in the United States sometimes transmitted only reports of verbal briefings by a source. Under special circumstances, this was acceptable to Moscow, but usually it was not. In 1945, for example, General Fitin became irritated that KGB field officers dealt with one of their most highly placed sources, the White House aide Lauchlin Currie, only through intermediaries provided by the Silvermaster network of American Communists. Further, Currie usually gave only verbal briefings. KGB officers were reluctant to press Currie because he was not under CPUSA discipline and cooperated with the KGB cautiously and on his own terms. Fitin demanded direct KGB contact with Currie, and his order was carried out. These KGB tradecraft practices greatly reduce the possibility that the Venona messages are replete with field officer braggadocio.

Finally, the Venona decryptions, while they contain extraordinary information, are otherwise an ordinary set of archival documents with all of the strengths and weaknesses of such records. They ought to be treated and judged in the same way that similar historical records are dealt with. Historical scholarship must be based on documentary records. One or another document may occasionally mislead or be mis-interpreted, but in time other documents from other archives or reex-amination by other scholars will bring about correction of errors. That is the normal course of historical scholarship, and is as true in this case as it is in others.

The Zubilin Affair

On August 7, 1943, the director of the FBI received an anonymous letter written in Russian.[31] It purported to name leading KGB officers oper-ating under diplomatic cover in Soviet offices in the United States, Can-ada, and Mexico and charged that they were engaged in espionage on a broad scale. The letter stated that the chief KGB officer in the United States was Vasily Zubilin, that Zubilin's real name was Zarubin, and that his wife, Elizabeth, was also a KGB field officer running her own network of American sources.[32] Other KGB officers named in the letter were Pavel Klarin and Semyon Semenov, officials at the Soviet consulate in New York; Vasily Dolgov and Vasily Mironov, officials at the Soviet embassy in Washington; Grigory Kheifets, Soviet vice-consul in San Francisco; Leonid Kvasnikov, an engineer with Amtorg; Andrey Shev-chenko and Sergey Lukianov, officials with the Soviet Government Pur-chasing Commission; Vladimir Pavlov, second secretary of the Soviet embassy in Canada; and Lev Tarasov, a diplomat at the Soviet embassy in Mexico.[33]

The FBI was, not surprisingly, perplexed by the letter and suspicious that it was a fraud. But an investigation of the activities of the Soviet diplomatic personnel named in the letter quickly convinced the bureau that they probably were indeed Soviet intelligence officers. Years later, the deciphered Venona messages further confirmed the accuracy of the identifications provided in the letter.

The motive behind the letter was clear: the anonymous author hated Vasily Zubilin and accused him of a variety of sins, including partici-pating in the murder of thousands of Polish prisoners of war in the Katyn forest. This last accusation caught the attention of American au-thorities because at that time they were not sure what had happened at Katyn, and out of nowhere came a letter asserting inside knowledge about one of the participants in the Katyn action. Only a few months earlier, the German government had announced that it had uncovered a mass grave containing the bodies of thousands of executed Polish military officers in the Katyn forest near Smolensk, on Soviet territory overrun by Nazi forces. According to the Nazis, the Soviet Union had captured these Poles in 1939 when it conquered eastern Poland under the terms of the Nazi-Soviet Pact. The USSR blamed the mass murder on the Nazis, saying that the Germans had captured the Poles alive when they overran Soviet prisoner-of-war camps and had subsequently murdered them. In fact, the Soviets had murdered the Poles: on March 5, 1940, Stalin ordered the KGB to shoot 14,700 Polish prisoners of war.[34]

The anonymous letter also correctly asserted that Zubilin had some role in the KGB's Katyn operation. The FBI had no way to verify it at the time, but eventually the Venona Project deciphered a KGB cable in which Zubilin himself confirmed having played a role. On July 1, 1943, he reported to Moscow that he thought he had noticed surveillance of his activities by a hostile intelligence agency and speculated that it had found out about his 1940 service at one of the camps at which the Poles had been murdered.[35]

But while the claim that Zubilin had taken part in the Katyn massacre was accurate, the letter also contained the outlandish claim that he had betrayed the Soviet Union and was spying on the United States in the service of Japan. It urged American authorities to reveal Zubilin's treachery to Soviet authorities and asserted that when his betrayal was revealed, one of the other KGB officers, Vasily Mironov, would surely execute Zubilin on the spot. Mironov, nominally a Soviet diplomat, was described as a patriotic KGB colonel who hated Zubilin.

The FBI suspected that the author of the anonymous letter was a disgruntled KGB officer, but it was never sure of his identity. A passage in the 1994 memoir of a retired KGB general, Pavel Sudoplatov, suggests that Mironov wrote the letter. Sudoplatov, who held a headquarters role in KGB foreign intelligence operations during World War II, states that Mironov, a KGB lieutenant colonel, had sent a letter to Stalin denouncing Zarubin (the anonymous letter was correct about Zubilin's real name) as a double agent. Sudoplatov explains that "Mironov's letter caused Zarubin's recall to Moscow. The investigation against him and Elizabeth lasted six months and established that all his contacts were legitimate and valuable, and that he was not working with the FBI. Mironov was recalled from Washington and arrested on charges of slander, but when he was put on trial, it was discovered that he was schizophrenic. He was hospitalized and discharged from the service."[36]

Although Mironov had denounced Zubilin both to the FBI and to Joseph Stalin for imaginary crimes, virtually everything else in the letter has been independently documented as accurate.

Not only did the anonymous letter arrive in 1943, but that same year the FBI also opened, probably not coincidentally, an investigation labeled the Comintern Apparatus, which grew into a file containing thousands of pages of reports and memorandums. In December 1944 it completed a massive internal study entitled "Comintern Apparatus Summary Report."[37] More than six hundred pages, this report reviewed what the FBI knew at that point about Soviet espionage and about its overlap with the American Communist party.

The FBI understood that the Soviet Union, in alliance with the American Communist party, was mounting a major espionage attack on the United States. But although the bureau grasped the broad outlines of the espionage offensive, its knowledge of specific operations was spotty and its understanding of Soviet intelligence practices limited. Though convinced that espionage was taking place, in most cases the FBI did not feel it had sufficient evidence to bring successful criminal prosecutions. A tone of frustrated resignation pervaded the report; leading policy-makers in the government would not want trials and public revelations of Soviet espionage to threaten the wartime political alliance with the USSR.[38] In 1944 the FBI still regarded the Soviet Union as a secondary threat to American security; there was little sense of urgency about Soviet espionage.

The FBI also had difficulty sorting out the activities of American Communists and Soviet spies. Some of the CPUSA activities highlighted in the report as involving espionage certainly did not. This clarity, however, exists only in retrospect. And other CPUSA activities that the report mentions clearly did involve spying on the U.S. government. Espionage, of course, is not a mass movement, and most individuals who joined the CPUSA did not directly participate in espionage. Even many party leaders and officials never directly assisted Soviet intelligence. But there was no fire wall between the CPUSA's work in politics, in the trade union movement, or in other arenas, on the one hand, and its assistance to Soviet espionage, on the other. Rather, the transition between these activities was seamless. Scores of CPUSA members and officials were engaged both in political or labor organizing and in assistance to the intelligence services of a foreign power. Nor was this latter assistance provided by individual Communists. The American Communist party as an organization covertly cooperated with Soviet espionage. The CPUSA made party members available to Soviet intelligence when they were needed. For the FBI, and for all later observers, the overlap between the activities of the CPUSA and Soviet intelligence presented a difficult analytic problem. With no clear line of separation, it was easy to overstate or understate the extent to which the two intermeshed.

When Did the Soviets Learn of Venona?

Soviet cryptographic officials had great confidence in the unbreakability of their one-time pad system and appear to have done little about early reports of attacks upon it. In late 1941 a Soviet agent in Berlin informed Moscow that the Germans had obtained a copy of the Petsamo code book from the Finns. Confident that the overlying one-time pad cipher would protect the system, the Soviets did not get around to replacing the code book until 1943. They appear to have learned of the existence of the NSA's Venona Project within a year and a half of its origin. Elizabeth Bentley told the FBI that in the spring of 1944 Lauchlin Currie, one of the sources in her KGB-CPUSA network, reported that the United States was on the verge of breaking the Soviet code. Currie, one of President Roosevelt's assistants, may well have heard an overly optimistic report sent to the White House about the early Venona effort.[39]

There is evidence of what may have been a Soviet reaction to Currie's report. But the change was superficial, the sort made to placate nervous higher-ups by professionals who think their superiors' worries are unjustified. In late April 1944 the KGB issued a circular to all stations to use a new message starting-point or key page indicator in ciphered cables. This minor change was easily made, allowing KGB cryptographic officers to report to superiors that they had altered their system. Whatever the reason for the alteration in procedure, it backfired disastrously for the Soviets. Cecil Phillips, then a nineteen-year-old cryptanalyst newly assigned to the Venona Project, noticed the change in message formatting and after a few months identified the first five-digit cipher group as the key-page indicator. Consequently, when any two messages were found to have the same initial five-digit cipher group, the two were identified as having been enciphered using the duplicated one-time pages. Phillips's insight enabled American cryptanalysts to examine their collection of intercepted Soviet cables and rapidly find duplication of key pages between KGB messages and Trade messages, a fundamental step in breaking into the KGB traffic.[40]

There is also evidence, although it is not conclusive, that Currie attempted to kill the Venona Project before it revealed the contents of Soviet cable traffic. Col. Harold Hayes and Lt. Col. Frank Rowlett, senior officers at Arlington Hall, reported that in 1944 Colonel Clarke, their Army Special Branch supervisor, told them that he had received instructions from the White House to cease work on Soviet ciphers. Clarke, however, advised the two not to take the instruction seriously and to continue the Venona Project. Independently, veterans of the OSS counterintelligence branch also reported that in 1944 they received instructions from the White House to stop collecting information on Soviet intelligence operations. The OSS appears to have taken the order more seriously than the Army's Special Branch. It did not protest, and it obeyed the White House and State Department order to give Soviet officials cipher material on Soviet codes that the OSS had obtained from Finland. Nor did the OSS counterintelligence branch establish a Russian desk.[41]

No written record exists of these instructions to halt work on Soviet ciphers, and the memory of OSS and Arlington Hall veterans attributed them to the White House and not to anyone in particular. But in view of Bentley's testimony about Currie's knowledge of the attack on the Soviet codes, and Currie's intervention to frustrate counterintelligence investigations of KGB spy Gregory Silvermaster (chapter 5), Lauchlin Currie would be the most likely White House initiator.[42]

Shortly after the close of World War II, Soviet intelligence received two more warnings about their wartime cipher that surely must have seized their attention. One was from William Weisband. Born in Egypt to Russian parents, Weisband came to the United States in the 1920s and gained American citizenship in 1938. He joined the Army in 1942, and his considerable linguistic skills and an Officer Candidate School commission earned him an assignment to the Signals Security Agency, one of the NSA's earlier incarnations. His wartime duties took him to North Africa and Italy. In late 1944, however, he returned to the United States, and in 1945 he received an assignment as a "roving" language consultant assisting various NSA projects, including Venona. Meredith Gardner, the chief code-breaker on the Venona Project, remembered consulting Weisband on obscure points of Russian grammar and recalled that Weisband was present in late 1946 when he read a 1944

KGB espionage message about scientists working on the atomic bomb project. Although Weisband was never directly involved in the Venona Project, his position gave him some knowledge of its activities. Cecil Phillips, one of Venona's leading cryptanalysts, commented that Weisband "managed to roam around with great ease. He cultivated people who had access to sensitive information. He used to sit near the boss's secretary, who typed everything we did of any importance."[43]

Venona, however, also led indirectly to the unmasking of Weisband's treachery. Weisband himself is not clearly identified in Venona, although he is a candidate for the unidentified cover name Link.[44] Link occurs in three Venona messages, but two are very fragmented and give few clues to Link's identity. In the third, dated June 23, 1943, the New York KGB reported that Link had completed a language course in Italian in Arlington, Virginia, and was expected to be sent overseas shortly. It then gave recognition signals for the London KGB to contact Link when he passed through there. These details fit Weisband, who was at an Army language school in Arlington in June 1943 and then shipped out to Britain in July. From there he later went to North Africa and Italy. This message, however, was not fully broken until 1979 and played no role in Weisband's identification as a Soviet agent.[45]

What put the FBI on to Weisband was not the Link messages but the deciphering of fourteen Venona messages discussing a KGB agent with the cover name Nick. These messages provided enough information for the FBI to identify Nick as Amadeo Sabatini. The FBI also found that years earlier, during routine surveillance of Soviet diplomats, its agents had observed that Sabatini "exchanged envelopes and packages on the streets of Los Angeles with Kheifets."[46] Grigory Kheifets was a KGB officer who operated out of the Soviet consulate in San Francisco under diplomatic cover. At that time, however, the bureau had lacked sufficient evidence regarding Sabatini to proceed further.

Sabatini had joined the CPUSA in 1930 and soon earned selection to the governing board ("district buro") of the party's Pennsylvania district. By 1935 he had shifted from open political work for the CPUSA to covert work as an international courier for the Comintern. He joined the International Brigades in 1937 and fought in the Spanish Civil War. Records in Moscow show that among his assignments was membership in the CPUSA "Control Commission," which exercised political discipline over American Communists serving with the International Brigades. After his return from Spain he undertook assignments for the

KGB, including serving on a team that shadowed Walter Krivitsky, a high-ranking GRU defector who publicly exposed several Soviet intelligence operations. Krivitsky died in 1940, probably a suicide, although there were some puzzling aspects to his death that suggested murder.[47]

Venona shows that in the early 1940s Sabatini became a highly active courier linking the KGB to its American sources. He lived in Los Angeles and worked for the Bohn Aluminum and Brass Company, which made parts for aircraft plants. Sabatini used that position to develop and service Soviet industrial and technical espionage contacts in the aviation industry. The KGB reimbursed him for travel and living expenses and paid a monthly stipend to his wife. The FBI confronted Sabatini in 1949. Under questioning he denied much, but the FBI had enough on him that he conceded some matters and pointed the FBI toward a second Soviet agent, an aircraft engineer named Jones York. York was also identified in four deciphered Venona messages under the cover name Needle.[48]

The FBI tracked down York, and under questioning he provided considerable information about his role in Soviet espionage. He stated that in 1935, when working for Douglas Aircraft's El Segundo Division, he met a group of visiting Soviet engineers. One in particular, Stanislau Shumovsky, befriended him and convinced him to turn over Douglas Aircraft technical information in return for payment. Shumovsky was a KGB officer operating under cover of the Soviet Government Purchasing Commission. He specialized in industrial espionage, and York was but one of his recruits. York admitted that he continued to sell technical intelligence to the Soviets until late 1943, when he lost touch with them. During eight years of spying he went through a number of Soviet contacts, most known to him only by pseudonyms: Brooks, Werner, Bill, and a woman whose name York had forgotten.

York, however, provided a number of details about Bill. Bill bought him an expensive camera for photographing documents and paid him about fifteen hundred dollars over the year they were in contact. York said he had given Bill a number of rolls of film of technical documents he had photographed. The only particulars he could remember concerned technical documents about the P-61, an advanced night-fighter developed by Northrop Aircraft. (One Venona message, from 1943, shows York handing over to the Soviets, through Sabatini, five rolls of film, including several on the design and motors for the experimental

XP-58 aircraft.) York stated that he had met with Bill about ten times, three or four of them at York's residence, and that they had developed a friendly and relaxed relationship. He remembered that Bill had admired a poem York had written about the Soviet resistance to the Nazi invasion and had taken a copy to show his Soviet superiors. York also recalled that during their chats Bill had mentioned his family name, which York thought was something like Villesbend.[49]

In 1950 the FBI had York observe an individual walking along a street. York identified him as the man he had known as Bill. It was William Weisband. Weisband was repeatedly interviewed by the FBI. In 1950 he denied any participation in espionage but refused to sign a statement to that effect. He also refused to obey a grand jury subpoena. He was sentenced to a year in prison for contempt of court and lost his job with the NSA. Reinterviewed in 1953, he admitted to knowing York but refused to explain the circumstances. This time he declined to either affirm or deny involvement in espionage.[50] Considering his position inside America's chief cryptologic agency, there is every reason to assume that he did significant damage to American security. Weisband certainly was in a position to tell the KGB a good deal about the NSA's success against the KGB system used for most of 1944 and 1945. He was exposed, however, before any breakthroughs on earlier KGB traffic or on GRU and Naval GRU cables, and the Soviets may have thought those still immune.

The second major breach of Venona's secrecy came through H. R. "Kim" Philby, a senior British intelligence officer and also a longtime Soviet agent. In 1949 the British Secret Intelligence Service sent Philby to Washington for a tour as its liaison with American intelligence agencies. British cryptanalysts of GCHQ were partners in the Venona Project and shared in its product, and GCHQ's liaison with the NSA gave summaries to Philby. Philby also visited the NSA's Arlington Hall facility for discussions with its officials. He quickly informed the KGB that American code-breakers were beginning to read wartime KGB cables between New York and Moscow. A London KGB report from February 1950 laid out the dire situation:

Stanley [Kim Philby] asked to communicate that the Americans and the British had constructed a deciphering machine which in one day does "the work of a thousand people in a thousand years." Work on deciphering is facilitated by three factors: (1) A one-time pad used twice;

(2) Our cipher resembles the cipher of our trade organization in the USA; (3) A half-burnt codebook has been found in Finland and passed to the British and used to decrypt our communications. They will succeed within the next twelve months. The Charles [Klaus Fuchs] case has shown the counter-intelligence service the importance of knowing the past of civil servants. . . . Stanley, Paul [Guy Burgess], and Yan [Anthony Blunt] consider that the situation is serious.[51]

It was particularly serious because some of those early Venona successes of which Philby received summaries struck very close to Philby himself. Philby, Donald Maclean, Guy Burgess, John Cairncross, and Anthony Blunt are known in KGB lore as "the Magnificent Five," among the most productive moles ever developed within the governing establishment of a major Western nation. The first four had all been students at Cambridge University in the early 1930s; Blunt, a Cambridge don and art expert, recruited prospective spies from among the students. Philby became a high-ranking professional British intelligence officer, Maclean joined the foreign office and became a senior diplomat, Burgess transferred back and forth between British intelligence and the foreign office, and Cairncross worked for British intelligence and on military and intelligence matters for the British Treasury. In addition to his work as talent-spotter and recruiter, Blunt also did wartime service for British counterintelligence (MI5), thus greatly enhancing his value to Moscow as a spy. After the war Blunt became chief art adviser to the British monarch and acted as intermediary between Burgess and the KGB.[52]

As soon as Philby arrived in Washington, in the fall of 1949, the FBI discussed with him Venona decryptions about a KGB agent with the cover name Homer who appeared to be connected with the British embassy in 1945–1946. The initial decryptions about Homer provided few details, and there were hundreds of candidates for Homer among the many British subjects who had served at the United Kingdom's diplomatic office in Washington in that period. Philby, however, immediately recognized Homer as his friend and fellow spy Maclean and warned Moscow.

The son of a prominent British Liberal party politician, Donald Maclean had become a Communist by 1933 and was quickly convinced to forego political activity and serve the cause by becoming one of Stalin's agents inside the British government. In 1935 he placed highly in the British foreign service exam and coolly told his questioners, who had heard of his student radicalism, that he had been working to shake off his Communist views but had not yet entirely succeeded. They bought his deception, and he joined the diplomatic corps in late 1935. In 1944 he was posted to the British embassy in Washington; for much of his four-year stay he held the senior position of first secretary. In that capacity he had access to virtually everything passing through the embassy.

Maclean and his wife arrived in the United States on May 6, 1944. By the end of June he was in touch with Vladimir Pravdin, a KGB officer operating under the cover of a journalist for the TASS news agency. The New York KGB station cabled Moscow on June 28 that Pravdin had met with Homer/Maclean three days previously and would see him again on the thirtieth in New York, where his wife was living with her mother. Although Maclean lived and worked at the Washington embassy, his wife, who was American and pregnant, lived in New York to enable Maclean to have a plausible excuse to travel there to meet his Soviet controller. After the birth of their son, Maclean and his wife moved to Washington.

Nearly a dozen Venona messages over the next year and a half detail the rich haul of intelligence that Maclean provided to the KGB. He offered details of secret telegrams between Prime Minister Winston Churchill and President Roosevelt, discussions of military plans, and synopses of issues they discussed at their Quebec meeting in September. Maclean also provided details of British plans for dealing with Greece, which had been under German occupation until late 1944. Chaos reigned in the wake of the German retreat, as pro- and anti-Communist Greek resistance forces and the Greek government-in-exile battled for control. British forces were entering the country to stabilize the situation and had no intention of allowing Communists to seize power. The New York KGB station told Moscow that in regard to the latter, "Homer hopes that we will take advantage of these circumstances to disrupt the plans of the British."[53]

One long, only partially decrypted New York KGB cable from August 1944 illustrates the wide range of sensitive material to which Maclean had access and which he passed on to the KGB. The cable reported that British and American officials were establishing a high-level joint commission to decide on political and economic policies for those areas of Western Europe then being liberated by advancing American and British troops. The cable reported that in regard to the commission almost all the work is done by H. [Homer/Maclean] who is present at all the sessions. In connection with this work H. obtains secret documents . . . including the personal telegraphic correspondence of Boar [Churchill] with Captain [Roosevelt]. . . . H. was entrusted with the decipherment of a confidential telegram from Boar to Captain which said that [British general Henry] Wilson and other generals of the Island [Great Britain] were insisting strongly on a change in the plan to invade the South of France, suggesting instead an invasion through the Adriatic Sea, Trieste and then north-eastwards. Boar supported this plan. From the contents of the telegram it is clear that Boar did not succeed in overcoming the strong objection of Captain and the Country's [America's] generals. Yesterday H. learnt of a change in the plans . . . and Anvil [Anglo-American invasion of southern France] will be put into effect possibly in the middle of August.[54]

Among his other duties Maclean represented Great Britain as diplomatic liaison between the American atomic bomb program, the Manhattan Project, and its British counterpart in 1944 and 1945. In 1946 he continued this role as the British liaison with the U.S. Atomic Energy Commission (AEC), the successor to the Manhattan Project. He made at least twenty visits to the AEC in 1947 and 1948, including one conference to discuss what atomic bomb data should not be declassified. Maclean continued to provide the Soviet Union with reports about the British and American discussions of early Cold War policy until his reassignment and departure in September 1948.

Although the initial deciphered message about Homer in 1949 provided few clues to his identity, as more messages were broken the list of possibilities began to narrow. With MI5 and the FBI cooperating, the hundreds of possibilities of 1949 declined to thirty-five by the end of 1950 and to fewer than a dozen by the spring of 1951. As Philby well knew, Maclean was on the rapidly shrinking list. In April 1951 a newly decrypted Venona message noted that in June 1944 Homer was traveling back and forth between New York and Washington to see his pregnant wife, who was living with her mother. That settled it. There was only one name on the list that fit: Donald Maclean. Philby, as British intelligence liaison, immediately learned that his comrade was in danger. But MI5 had to gather evidence to support an arrest, a delay that Philby used to his advantage. Guy Burgess, who was then working at the British embassy in Washington and lodging with the Philbys, was returning to London in disgrace after a drunken escapade. Philby briefed Burgess and told him to leave at once and contact their KGB controller in London to arrange Maclean's escape. He did, and on May 25 Maclean and Burgess took a channel ferry to St.-Malo, picked up false papers from a waiting KGB contact, and traveled on to Moscow.

After Maclean and Burgess fled, both American and British counterintelligence wondered who had warned them. Suspicion quickly fell on Philby because of his close relationship with the two, particularly Burgess. The evidence against Philby was largely circumstantial. The CIA, however, demanded that the British find a new liaison officer, and Philby was withdrawn from Washington. MI5 thought him guilty but also concluded that it had insufficient evidence for a criminal charge. The Secret Intelligence Service ordered Philby into retirement in December 1951. Philby then worked as a journalist, but he remained under suspicion and as time went on, evidence accumulated pointing to his treachery. In 1963 he too fled to Moscow. Philby's access to Venona information ended in the summer of 1951. Like Weisband's information, Philby's probably indicated to the KGB that the NSA's success to that point was confined to messages from 1944 on and did not reach back to earlier KGB cables or to GRU and Naval GRU messages.[55]

Weisband's and Philby's information about Venona did not appear to trigger any sudden changes in Soviet diplomatic cryptographic habits. Nor should it have. After all, the vulnerability of the Soviet code was limited to the duplicate one-time pad pages produced in 1942. By 1946 most of these had already been used, although a few would turn up in outlying Soviet stations as late as 1948. But the warnings of the three about the NSA breakthrough did allow the KGB to alert agents who were at risk of exposure to prepare for FBI scrutiny and, if they were still active, to cease any espionage activity that could be uncovered and used against them in a criminal trial. Philby, for example, warned Moscow that British and American counterintelligence had identified one of the atomic spies in the Venona traffic as the British scientist Klaus Fuchs. This information allowed Moscow to withdraw at least one and perhaps several of its officers operating covertly in the West who might be compromised when Fuchs was arrested.[56] The KGB also warned a number of its American agents who were linked directly or indirectly to Fuchs. Several of them fled to the Soviet Union (Morris and Lona Cohen, Joel Barr, and Alfred Sarant), others were arrested while in flight (Morton Sobell was caught and returned after fleeing to Mexico) or when preparing to leave the United States (Julius and Ethel Rosenberg), and several attempted to ride out the investigation (David and Ruth Greenglass and William Perl).

Even after it sank in at the NSA, sometime in the 1950s, that Venona had been exposed by Weisband and Philby, the agency still had reasons for keeping the project highly secret. It did not want Moscow to learn of its subsequent success with GRU, Naval GRU, and the earlier KGB traffic. Nor did it want Moscow to know the extent of the NSA's success: it did not want Soviet intelligence to find out which messages had been read and which remained opaque. American interests, at least in the short run, were served by Moscow's uncertainty over how much the United States had really learned. That uncertainty enhanced the ability of American intelligence and counterintelligence agencies to use Venona as a standard for evaluating other sources of intelligence information.

CHAPTER 3

THE AMERICAN COMMUNIST PARTY UNDERGROUND

The size and success of the Soviet espionage offensive in World War II rested on the preparatory work of the CPUSA in the 1930s. The American Communist party was born as the organizational center of a revolutionary movement. The manifesto of the movement's 1919 founding convention declared that "Communism does not propose to 'capture' the bourgeoisie parliamentary state, but to conquer and destroy it. . . . It is necessary that the proletariat organize its own state *for the coercion and suppression of the bourgeoisie.*"[1]

Initially, American communism operated legally. American Communists proclaimed their revolutionary goals at an open convention. Official harassment was limited to the ripping down by irritated Chicago police of the convention's red rose floral arrangements and pictures of Marx, Trotsky, and Lenin. Spurred on, however, by a series of left-wing terrorist bombings a few months later, the federal government began arresting radical noncitizens and deporting them. Since the overwhelming majority of the new American Communist movement consisted of immigrants without U.S. citizenship, this response posed a direct threat, and the movement went underground. Members of the nascent American Communist party, in any case, needed little encouragement to operate clandestinely. With the model of the conspiratorial

Bolshevik party in Tsarist Russia in mind, most regarded underground activity as the natural mode for a revolutionary Marxist movement.[2]

By 1921 the postwar fear that Bolshevism was about to sweep the world had subsided, and the federal government ceased taking much of an interest in the Communist party. American Communists, enthralled by the Bolshevik model, nevertheless insisted on staying underground. In fact, the Communist International, the Soviet agency that supervised all foreign Communist parties and ensured their fealty to Moscow, had to order the American party to surface, as it did in 1922.[3] In the 1920s a few state and city governments undertook sporadic harassment of Communists, but in most places the Communist movement was free to operate openly and legally. It did so even while continuing to proclaim revolution and the abolition of constitutional liberties as its mission. In 1928 William Z. Foster, then the CPUSA's presidential candidate and one of the top party leaders until his death in 1961, told cheering American Communists, "When a Communist heads a government in the United States—and that day will come just as surely as the sun rises [Applause]—that government will not be a capitalistic government but a Soviet government and behind the government will stand the Red Army to enforce the Dictatorship of the Proletariat."[4] The CPUSA would later downplay and even deny its commitment to revolution and one-party rule, but it was an open aim as late as the early 1930s. In 1932 Foster, again running for president on the CPUSA ticket, foretold a Communist future for Americans:

> One day, despite the disbelief of the capitalists . . . the American work-
> ers will demonstrate that they, like the Russians, have the intelligence,
> courage and organization to carry through the revolution. . . .
>
> By the term "abolition" of capitalism we mean its overthrow in
> open struggle by the toiling masses, led by the proletariat. . . . To put
> an end to the capitalist system will require a consciously revolutionary
> act by the great toiling masses, led by the Communist party; that is, the
> conquest of the State power, the destruction of the State machine cre-
> ated by the ruling class, and the organization of the proletarian dicta-
> torship. . . .
>
> Under the dictatorship all the capitalist parties—Republican, Dem-
> ocratic, Progressive, Socialist, etc.—will be liquidated, the Communist
> party functioning alone as the Party of the toiling masses. Likewise will
> be dissolved all other organizations that are political props of the bour-
> geois rule, including chambers of commerce, employers' associations,
> rotary clubs, American Legion, Y.M.C.A., and such fraternal orders as
> the Masons, Odd Fellows, Elks, Knights of Columbus, etc. . . .

The press, the motion picture, the radio, the theatre, will be taken over by the government.[5]

Even though the U.S. government treated Foster's revolutionary threats with indifference, the party always feared that authorities might decide that tolerating an antidemocratic and anticonstitutional movement was dangerous. Consequently, the CPUSA always kept the need for illegal operations in mind. The movement's commitment to maintaining an underground arm was reinforced by the instructions of the Communist International. Under Comintern orders American Communists created "illegal departments" charged with protecting the party's internal security, preserving its ability to function in the event of government repression, infiltrating non-Communist organizations for political purposes, and otherwise using clandestine means to serve the interests of the world revolution. These Communist party underground organizations were not primarily espionage or intelligence agencies. But, as we shall see, it was relatively easy for such underground apparatuses to move from assisting the world revolution politically to helping the homeland of the world revolution through espionage.

The Communist International itself was not primarily an intelligence organization, but it too was linked to Soviet intelligence. Within the Comintern the OMS (International Liaison Department) oversaw the covert financing of foreign parties and the activities of Comintern emissaries. Numerous American Communists worked for this agency, which served as the Comintern's own covert apparatus. In the course of its mission to secretly transfer Comintern agents and money around the world, it produced false passports, developed mail drops, procured safe-houses, and established systems of coded telegraphic and radio communications. The OMS was supervised by the "Illegal Commission," made up of senior Comintern officials but usually including an official of the foreign intelligence arm of the KGB as well. In 1923, for example, the Illegal Commission consisted of two senior Cominternists along with Mikhail Trilisser, the KGB's foreign intelligence chief in the 1920s. In May of that year it met to consider whether the American Communist party was maintaining the proper balance between legal and illegal work. After a discussion with Israel Amter, the CPUSA's representative to the Comintern, it issued a number of directives designed to enhance the CPUSA's capacity for "secret work."[6]

In 1929 the CPUSA's flagship newspaper, the *Daily Worker,* announced that the party had undertaken to "make all necessary preparations for illegal functioning of the leading organs of the Party." It was, however, a symptom of the indifference of the American authorities toward the CPUSA at the time and the sense of security of CPUSA officials that its newspaper openly published a resolution about its intent to form a secret organization. In 1930 the Comintern again reminded American Communists that "legal forms of activity must be combined with systematic illegal work." The Comintern reinforced the point with another memo to the CPUSA noting that "all legal Parties are now under the greater responsibility in respect to the creation and strengthening of an illegal apparatus. All of them must immediately undertake measures to have within the legally existing Party committees an illegal directing core." The next year, 1931, Solomon Lozovsky, head of the Profintern, urged Communist trade unionists to disregard the "mystic secrecy" of governmental institutions and expose the secrets of capitalist nations by operating "in the holy of holies of capitalist society, in the armed forces and diplomatic service," and another Comintern official, Boris Vasiliev, reminded Communists that "it is obvious that any secret treaties, government proposals and military orders which by one means or another fall into the hands of Communist Party organizations must be published without delay."[7]

During the 1920s the American party had an underground, but, distracted as it was by its vicious internal factional battles, its covert apparatus was not carefully maintained. This debilitating factionalism, however, ended in 1929 after the systematic expulsion of Trotskyists, Lovestoneites, and other dissidents had produced a thoroughly Stalinized party. The person chosen to revitalize the CPUSA's secret apparatus for the 1930s was Josef Peters.[8]

J. Peters and the Secret Apparatus

J. Peters, as he was known in Communist ranks, was an example of the professional revolutionaries of European origin who populated the Communist underground and intelligence world of the 1930s and 1940s. During his life he used a variety of names—Alexander Goldfarb, Isador Boorstein, and Alexander Stevens. Born in Cop, then part of the Austro-Hungarian empire, into a working-class Jewish family, he dropped out of college because of lack of funds and went to work in an office. Peters served in the Austro-Hungarian army during World War I and was made an officer because he was a high school graduate.

When the Austro-Hungarian empire collapsed in 1918, the newly formed Communist party briefly seized power in newly independent Hungary. Peters, on furlough at the time and caught up in the revolutionary fervor, joined the Communists, organized railroad workers, and fought the White (anti-Communist) armies. He continued his party work after the defeat of the Hungarian Communists and held several minor positions in the regional party organization. In 1924 he moved to the United States and worked in a New York factory for eight months before becoming an organizer for the Hungarian-language federation of the CPUSA.[9]

By the end of the decade, Peters was the leading functionary in the Hungarian federation and had been a delegate to the Sixth Congress of the Comintern in Moscow. The CPUSA was convulsed by factional warfare in 1929, and dozens of leading party functionaries loyal to the party leader, Jay Lovestone, were expelled. Peters, who had been a Lovestoneite, made his peace with the new leadership and was appointed head of the CPUSA's National Minorities Department at the end of 1929. Shifted to mainline party work in 1930, he became organizational secretary of the New York Communist party, the CPUSA's largest regional unit. In that capacity he was responsible for building an illegal apparatus for the New York organization.

In 1931 Peters was sent to Moscow for training with the Communist International. He worked at the Comintern's Anglo-American Secretariat as a senior intern and late in 1932 returned to the United States, where the Central Committee, in the words of a Comintern document, "assigned him to work in the secret apparatus. He was at this post until June of 1938."[10] Peters's headquarters was in the CPUSA main office at Union Square in New York City.

The secret apparatus under Peters's leadership carried out a variety of tasks. Some of these concerned party security: to detect surveillance by hostile police, expose infiltrators, and protect special party assets, such as sensitive records, from seizure. The secret apparatus was also responsible for preparing the party to function underground. Peters purchased printing presses that were secretly stored around the country to be used for printing Communist material in an emergency. One, for example, was located at the back of the Intimate Bookshop in Chapel Hill, North Carolina. This press had been bought by Alton Lawrence, ostensibly a member of the Socialist party but actually a secret Communist, with funds provided by Peters.[11] In an offensive mode the secret apparatus carried out the surveillance, infiltration, and disruption of rival groups such as the Socialist party and the Socialist Workers party (Trotskyist).

The Washington Communist Underground

Another of Peters's duties was maintaining contact with sensitive groups of secret party members in Washington. In the 1930s the CPUSA recruited several hundred persons among the many thousands of new employees hired by the federal government under the impact of the New Deal's rapid expansion of governmental programs. While the CPUSA operated legally in the 1930s, federal regulations forbade partisan political activity by federal employees, and open membership in the Communist party brought discharge. The CPUSA evaded the law by organizing caucuses of government employees that met in secret, studied party literature, paid dues, and listened to visiting party officials explain party policies.

The existence of a significant Washington Communist underground in the 1930s became a matter of public debate in 1948 when Whittaker Chambers described his role in it. Chambers related how in the spring of 1934 Peters introduced him to Harold (Hal) Ware in New York and soon afterward the three of them met again in Washington to coordinate the activities of what came to be known as the Ware group. Ware was the CPUSA's point man for farm issues, and the Ware group initially consisted of young lawyers and economists hired by the Agricultural Adjustment Administration (AAA), a New Deal agency that reported to the secretary of agriculture but was independent of the long-established Department of Agriculture bureaucracy. In origin the Ware group was a secret Communist political club. Espionage on behalf of the USSR was not part of its agenda, although from the beginning its members gave inside government information to the CPUSA.

By the time Chambers became involved, the Ware group had grown to about seventy-five persons and was in the process of being broken up into smaller, more manageable units. It leading figures were Alger Hiss, Lee Pressman, John Abt, Charles Kramer, and Nathan Witt, who all originally worked for the AAA, as well as Henry Collins of the National Recovery Administration (the NRA was the leading New Deal agency for reorganizing industry), George Silverman, an economist with the Railroad Retirement Board, Marion Bachrach (John Abt's sister), Donald Hiss (Alger's brother and also a government attorney), and Victor Perlo, a statistician for the NRA. After Harold Ware's death in an automobile accident in 1935, Peters took over direct supervision of Ware's Washington underground organization. Although based in New York, Peters served on the CPUSA's Baltimore district committee, making frequent trips to the Washington area to meet with members of the growing group of government employees that Ware had put together.

When Chambers first discussed the Washington Communist underground in 1948, those he named as members either flatly denied that it existed or refused to say anything at all. While some people believed Chambers, others thought the idea of a CPUSA underground nothing but a paranoid fantasy. But over the years the accumulated evidence has become overwhelming. In 1950 Lee Pressman testified that he had been a formal, albeit secret member of the CPUSA in 1934 and 1935 and, although no longer officially a party member, a firm ideological Communist from 1936 to 1950. He agreed that there had been a group in the AAA which had met with Peters. Although he depicted the group as an innocuous study club of government employees who got together to discuss political theory, he admitted that several of its leading figures (he, Nathan Witt, John Abt, and Charles Kramer) were Communists. Later, he privately admitted to Jerome Frank, a leading AAA official, that the group had been a Communist party enterprise. Also in 1950, Nathaniel Weyl, a former AAA economist, stated that he had been an original member of the Ware group, and that it was a Communist caucus that met to discuss how CPUSA policies could be applied to the agricultural issues with which they dealt.[12]

Another of the original members of the Ware Group was John Abt, a lawyer for the AAA. In his posthumously published autobiography, Abt, who admitted to party membership only when he was eighty years old, acknowledged that Hal Ware invited him to join the CPUSA in 1934 and he had accepted. He also said that Ware had recruited his sister, Marion Bachrach, as well. According to Abt, the party decided to keep his membership a closely held secret in order to protect his usefulness during his government service and, later, as a leading labor lawyer. After Hal Ware's death, Abt wrote, J. Peters would come to the capital once a month to meet the group members. Although Abt denied that he and his comrades had engaged in espionage, he admitted that they provided Communist party leaders with information about government policies.[13]

Another member of the Ware group was John Herrmann, the husband of the radical writer Josephine Herbst. Herbst's biographer wrote of Herrmann: "From early 1934 until the summer of 1935 he was a paid courier for the Communist Party whose job was to deliver to New York material emanating from the secret cells of sympathetic government employees being cultivated by Harold Ware. . . . John's superior in the network was Whittaker Chambers. . . . According to his widow, whom I met in 1974, John Herrmann was the man who introduced Chambers to Alger Hiss."[14]

The most intimate look at the CPUSA Washington underground and the Ware group in the 1930s comes from Hope Hale Davis in her *Great Day Coming: A Memoir of the 1930s.* She and her husband, Hermann Brunck, both worked for the National Recovery Administration, and both were recruited into the CPUSA and its underground organization. Davis wrote that her unit, led by Charles Kramer, was a subgroup of what had been the Ware group. From her initial group meeting she retained a vivid memory of Victor Perlo lecturing earnestly about Mao Tse-tung's Long March in China. Her husband was soon passing sensitive, confidential documents from the National Labor Relations Board (NLRB), then part of the NRA, and from the NRA's shipping industry regulatory board to the CPUSA to assist its union organizing efforts. She noted that Peters appeared from time to time at her group meetings, not as an education lecturer, as Pressman and Abt claimed, but as the authoritative head of the party underground.

By the late thirties, Davis explained, the original Ware group had evolved into a large number of small secret Communist clubs operating in a great variety of federal agencies, including congressional committee staffs. These clubs were linked to each other and to the CPUSA through a hierarchy of intermediary leaders. Victor Perlo had several of these small caucuses reporting to him. For example, Herbert Fuchs headed one of the CPUSA's secret caucuses at the National Labor Relations Board from 1937 to 1942, a period in which his unit grew from four members to seventeen. He said that his NLRB unit's link to the larger apparatus was initially through Perlo. Davis and her husband eventually became heads of their own subgroups, and her residence was used to store documents kept by a mysterious Latvian immigrant whom she understood to be connected with some sort of anti-Trotsky operation.[15]

These secret Washington Communist caucuses were not formed for espionage. Instead, they were engaged in politics, albeit secret politics, and political subversion, inasmuch as they attempted to secretly manipulate government decisions, to serve Communist party interests.[16] However, such covert organizations were adaptable to espionage operations. Whittaker Chambers's account of his role in Soviet espionage in the mid-1930s is one example of such adaptation.

Peters's secret apparatus was the CPUSA's covert arm, and Peters reported to Earl Browder, head of the CPUSA. On Browder's direction Peters also cooperated with Soviet intelligence. In the 1930s the chief Soviet intelligence agency operating in the United States was the GRU, Soviet military intelligence. Chambers explained that Peters recognized that the network of secret Communists in government agencies offered espionage potential and that he had selected a few people who held sensitive positions as possible intelligence sources. Among other goals, he hoped that the Soviets would pay for services rendered and thereby assist in meeting the high costs of the party's underground operations. In early 1936 Peters had Chambers obtain documents from two secret Communist sources, Julian Wadleigh in the State Department and Ward Pigman at the National Bureau of Standards. Peters then offered these documents to his chief GRU contact, known to Chambers only by the pseudonym Bill, who was unenthusiastic about Peters's plans but agreed to send the documents to Moscow for review.

Two examples of documents stolen by secret Communists in the U.S. State Department in this era were found in the CPUSA's own records, which were surreptitiously shipped to Moscow decades ago and only opened to research after the collapse of the USSR. One is a copy of an October 19, 1936, letter from William Dodd, the U.S. ambassador to Germany, to President Roosevelt. Dodd reports on conversations he had with Hjalmar Schacht, president of the Reichsbank and Hitler's chief economic adviser, Hans Heinrich Dieckhoff, shortly to become the German ambassador to the United States, and Baron Konstantin von Neurath, then German foreign minister. The other document, from an unidentified source in the State Department, is entitled "Excerpt of a letter enclosed to Judge Moore of the State Department and written by Ambassador Bullitt, written confidentially." It quotes from a letter from

William Bullitt, the U.S. envoy to France, to Assistant Secretary of State R. Walton Moore regarding how economic conditions in Europe might affect growing international tensions. The document then quotes from Moore's written comment on Bullitt's observations and notes that Moore's comment was also confidential. The thief who stole the document also offered his own judgment that the quoted remarks are "interesting and important because they show attitudes of men in key positions. . . . Moore has great influence on President Roosevelt. And Bullitt is not undangerous in Paris." Both documents are from the fall of 1936 and are date-stamped as reaching the CPUSA on January 5, 1937—swift work by the CPUSA source.[17]

In late 1936 Bill was replaced by a new GRU officer, Col. Boris Bykov, who endorsed the espionage project (possibly Moscow had found the sample documents of interest). Chambers soon found himself the link between Bykov and a network of sources in various U.S. government agencies drawn from the CPUSA underground but essentially transferred to a GRU-supervised espionage apparatus.[18]

By late 1937 Chambers had lost much of his once fervent ideological loyalty to communism and was increasingly disturbed by rumors that Soviet intelligence officers and agents were being recalled to Moscow and vanishing. The rumors were well founded. Stalin used his Great Terror not only to purge the Soviet Communist party and the Soviet state of all possible opposition to his rule but to clean out his own security agencies as well. Hundreds of officers of the KGB's internal security apparatus found themselves facing the same fate to which they had sent hundreds of thousands: the labor camps of the Gulag or a bullet in the back of the head. Nor were the foreign intelligence arms of the KGB and the GRU exempt, and their senior officials and scores of their field officers also fell victim to the Terror.

Chambers, however, did not publicly renounce the Communist party, nor did he contact U.S. authorities. Given American politics at the time, he thought little would result from either course and did not wish to risk imprisonment for espionage if he were to turn himself in and confess. Instead, in April 1938 he simply dropped out of Soviet espionage and the CPUSA in a way he hoped would protect himself and his family and allow him to reenter normal life. Fearing immediate retaliation, he initially fled to Florida with his family and remained in seclusion for several months. Through intermediaries he got word back to his former colleagues that if they left him alone he would not go to the authorities. He also warned that he had hidden material that would embarrass them if any move were made against him. By the end of the year he felt that it was safe to gradually reenter society and moved his family to a farm in Maryland. Reviving old journalistic contacts from the 1920s, he sought and found a position with *Time* magazine.

Chambers's defection caused considerable turbulence in the organization of Soviet espionage and the CPUSA underground. Potentially he could compromise a number of Soviet officers and American sources. Someone had to take the blame, and one victim was J. Peters. In June, two months after Chambers disappeared and a frantic search by underground Communists failed to locate him, Peters was removed as head of the secret apparatus and replaced by Rudy Baker. After Chambers's story became public in 1948, Peters, then using the name Alexander Stevens, was subpoenaed by a congressional investigating committee. He refused to answer any questions. He had never gained American citizenship and was deported to Communist Hungary.

Rudy Baker and the Secret Apparatus

Although he served as head of the secret apparatus from 1938 through the end of World War II, Rudy Baker always remained in the Communist shadows. Baker was never called before a congressional committee, never drew the attention of the media, and was never deported from the United States. Instead he quietly slipped out of the country in the late 1940s: not even the year he left is certain. But he later turned up in Communist Yugoslavia as a translator for a state publishing house and a government research institute.

Rudy Baker's anonymity was well planned. In a 1939 report to the Comintern, he identified one of the weaknesses of the secret apparatus: "The problem with this work was that it became generally known that this work was being directed by Peters." He noted that in choosing him as the new head of the underground, Earl Browder "was above all concerned that this work be passed on to me in such a way that my participation in the work of the special apparatus not become generally known, as had been the case with Com. Peters." To hide his "special work," Baker was also given other party assignments, which, while taking up time and energy, achieved the aim that his "special work goes unnoticed and unknown."[19] The plan succeeded. Not only did Baker's role remain secret within the CPUSA, but the FBI took a very long time to identify him. The Comintern Apparatus file shows that from 1943 on, the FBI was trying to identify "Al," the cover name for the head of the apparatus. Later it identified Al as Ralph Bowman, but this too was a pseudonym. Not until several years later did it identify Al/Ralph Bowman as Rudy Baker.

Like the man he replaced, Rudy Baker was an immigrant from Eastern Europe and a veteran of Communist organizing in the United States. Baker was born in 1898 in Vukovar, Croatia, probably under the name of Rudolph Blum. He arrived in the United States with his family in 1909. He had little formal education, having finished four years of primary school and briefly attended an evening technical school. He became a radical militant at an early age and was arrested during a Westinghouse strike in Pittsburgh. Convicted of inciting to riot, he was jailed for a year and a half. Released from prison in May 1918, he was arrested in August for further radical agitation, held as an enemy alien (his native Croatia was part of the Austro-Hungarian empire, with which the United States was at war), but released after two months. Baker joined the Communist party when it was founded in 1919. He worked as a machinist until 1926, when he became the party's district organizer in Detroit. From 1927 to 1930 he studied at the Comintern's prestigious International Lenin School in Moscow, where he became a member of the Soviet Communist party.[20]

A biography found in the Comintern's archives shows that after returning from the International Lenin School in 1930, Baker directed the CPUSA's organizational department for a period and carried out unspecified "illegal work" in Korea, Canada, and England. For much of the 1930s Baker directed the clandestine work of the San Francisco bureau of the Pan-Pacific Trade Union Secretariat, a covert agency of the Profintern (the Comintern's trade union arm) which sought to promote Communist unionism in those Asian countries where Communist organizing was illegal or restricted. With its heavy shipping traffic with China, Japan, and other Asian ports, San Francisco was one of the secretariat's key regional offices. In 1938 Baker told the Comintern that this work had kept him out of CPUSA activities since 1932, and this low profile would assist in keeping his role as head of the CPUSA's covert arm a secret.[21]

Baker became head of the CPUSA underground in late 1938 and lived in Peekskill, New York, as a gentleman farmer with his wife, Lilly (the former wife of J. Peters). He had a desk at the New York City offices of the CPUSA's literary-intellectual magazine, *New Masses,* and publicly carried out several minor Communist party tasks while at the same time directing a large clandestine organization. Because it was a "secret apparatus" that was largely successful in maintaining its secrecy, many details of Baker's organization remain unknown. There is now enough evidence, however, from recently declassified FBI files, recently unearthed Comintern files, and the recently released Venona decryptions to provide an outline of the apparatus, identify some of its personnel, and describe some of its methods.

Baker visited Moscow in January 1939 to confer with Comintern officials regarding his new post as head of the underground. Shortly after returning to the United States, he began to communicate via coded radio and telegraphic cables with Georgi Dimitrov, head of the Communist International. Copies of some of these messages were located in Comintern archives. During World War II he also sent reports to the Comintern by diplomatic pouch via the KGB. There are two mentions of Baker in deciphered Venona cables. In one the New York KGB station reports receiving a letter from him that it was forwarding to Moscow. In the other the New York KGB notes that it had received a cable for Baker from Moscow and requested instructions on whether its agents should deliver the message or whether Soviet diplomats could be used for the chore.[22]

Moscow absorbed a significant share of the cost of the CPUSA's secret apparatus. In November 1939 Baker and Browder sent Dimitrov a message requesting that he "send several 1000 bill every 2 or 3 weeks" hidden inside the cover of a book and addressed to a mail drop in the Bronx; another message from Baker repeated the plea for money and gave a different address. In early 1942 Baker alerted Dimitrov that he had received "85" during 1941. From the context, it seems likely that this meant Baker had gotten $85,000. Baker reported that of this total $35,000 had gone to Alexander Trachtenberg, head of International Publishers, while Baker had retained $10,000. Baker was forwarding the remainder to sites abroad, mostly stations in Latin America. Early in 1943 Baker wrote a report, transmitted to the Comintern, on his apparatus's activities during the preceding year, indicating expenditures of $11,311 in 1942 with $18,834 remaining for 1943 operations. The total 1942–1943 sum in Baker's report, $30,145, would be more than $200,000 in 1998 dollars.[23]

These coded messages were sometimes addressed to Browder and

Baker separately and sometimes jointly. Similarly, the messages to the Comintern were signed by them separately and jointly. In his 1943 report to Dimitrov, Baker explained that although for security reasons "our apparatus is kept strictly isolated from party . . . periodically all questions are discussed and considered by son [Baker] and father [Browder]."[24] And in the report itself Baker discussed several matters about the secret apparatus's work that he had referred to Browder for an authoritative decision.

One of Baker's tasks as head of the secret apparatus was to ensure communications with the Soviet Union. Immediately after the Nazi-Soviet Pact, on September 2, 1939, Dimitrov had informed him and Browder, "According to the new situation I propose that the automobile man start to work with us from the tenth this month"—"automobile" being a Comintern cover term for clandestine short-wave radio operations. Two weeks later Dimitrov sent a second message to Baker and Browder, repeating his earlier admonition: "The new situation demands also from us new methods of connections. It is of great importance to organize with the necessary reserves the automobile connections."[25] The Comintern also used Baker and the CPUSA secret apparatus to maintain clandestine short-wave radio links to Communist parties in Latin America and Canada. One section of Baker's 1942 end-of-year report to the Comintern was devoted to one of his short-wave radio operators with the cover name Louis. Baker told Dimitrov:

> *Louis:* Your suggestion of more than year ago that he set up auto [short-wave radio] in Argentina had been conveyed to him and 5,000 sent to him as per your suggestion. We also invited him to come to Gilla [unknown location] but he informed us that if he left he could not return. Now your present suggestion that he organize auto in Gilla is very much along same lines. Insofar as his trip to Gilla will mean that he loses his connection in South American countries and cannot return[,] Father [Browder] is firmly opposed to his leaving. More than one years [*sic*] ago son [Baker] reported to you that our comrades in Gilla investigated problem of auto and reported that it would cost about $4000 which is over five times its cost here. . . . We will send person to Gilla to work on this problems [*sic*] from here again.[26]

In addition to radio links, Baker also established other communication ties to Moscow. In the 1930s only a few countries subjected international mail to close scrutiny. American authorities rarely looked at international mail unless the sender or the recipient was on a special watch list. Consequently, the CPUSA used mail drops, generally inactive rank-and-file Communist party members who had never attracted official attention, to receive letters from the Comintern. Once World War II began, however, government authorities everywhere began to examine international mail more closely. In early 1940 Baker informed the Comintern that he would be using microdots for sending "largess [*sic*] possible quantity mail," and a later message read, "Please acknowledge receipt invisible micro under stamps. Letters in future examine all envelopes, some of them will have micro under flaps or postage stamps."[27]

In addition to radio and microdots, Baker also used sailors as couriers to carry messages and material to Moscow. The Comintern was used to seaman couriers, and in September 1939 Dimitrov, while urging more work on the short-wave radio link, had told Browder and Baker that "it is good to utilize the sailors."[28] The Comintern archives also turned up this 1942 Dimitrov message to Baker: "We think that now is just [the] time to organize a courier connection between you and us using some comrades among ship crew on U.S. cargo steamers that come every week from American ports to South Persia ports with munitions for Russia. We hope that you find trustworthy boys among crews who could deliver us your mail and take back. We shall secure transit connections through Persia with our man who will meet your mailmen in Persian Ports. Please inform us can you organize this business."[29] In April 1943 Baker told Moscow that the system was in place. "After long delay," he wrote, "am now able to ship material through Persia," and he named a crew member of a U.S. ship then bound for Persia carrying material for transmission to Moscow.[30]

The Comintern and the CPUSA had, in fact, employed Communist seamen to transport political literature, messages, and information for years. In 1932 George Mink, former head of the CPUSA's Marine Workers Industrial Union, was in Moscow preparing for a tour as a maritime organizer for the Profintern, which had long encouraged the establishment of clandestine seaman courier networks. Mink assured them that as head of the Marine Workers Industrial Union he had been "in charge of maintaining contact through the seamen, with India and Cuba, Mexico" and that he had "secured many passports for our work."[31]

The FBI's 1944 "Comintern Apparatus Summary Report" (chapter 2) devoted one section to the Communist seaman courier network. It identified the chief overseers of the system as Frederick "Blackie" Myers (vice-president of the National Maritime Union), Joseph Kenegsberg (or Koenigsberg, a long-time official of the San Pedro Club of the Los Angeles Communist party), Rudy Lambert (head of the California Communist party labor commission), and Albert Lannon (a key Communist maritime organizer on the East Coast).[32] The FBI could not, however, differentiate between sailors who were carrying batches of Communist and maritime union agitational literature to foreign ports (of little interest to the FBI) and those who were carrying clandestine party communications to other Communist parties and the Comintern. But it knew that Communist sailors returning from foreign ports who were seen delivering letters to CPUSA officials or Soviet consulate staff were not carrying routine political literature.

J. Peters had met directly and frequently with Soviet intelligence officers while he was supervising the CPUSA secret apparatus. This is one reason that Chambers's defection initially panicked both the Soviets and the CPUSA underground. Chambers not only could compromise the agents and the Soviet controllers of his own particular network but, owing to his association with Peters, he also threatened the entire CPUSA underground and other Soviet intelligence officers and operations to which Peters was directly linked. Rudy Baker was far more circumspect. It appears that after he took over the CPUSA secret apparatus, direct liaison with Soviet intelligence on the East Coast was assigned to another senior CPUSA official, Jacob Golos, so that the link between the head of the CPUSA underground and Soviet intelligence became less direct.

Connections between the CPUSA's secret apparatus and Soviet intelligence ran through the most senior Soviet intelligence officers in the United States. In the Comintern archive is a copy of an October 1941 message, in poor English, that Dimitrov sent to Baker: "One of our friends name cooper who works in your county and whom [we] trust is authorized to establish [contact] wi[th] your . . . . We gave him the address. . . . His slogan by meeting you: 'I have something for your from brother, some greetings.' After you established direct connections with him continue this connections not directly but through one of your secret comrades. Acknowledge."[33]

Cooper and Baker did establish contact. In Baker's end-of-year report on 1942 activities he told Dimitrov that because the war had made use of the regular international mail too insecure, "this year we began sending mail through Cooper." Later in the report Baker stated that "we are also cooperating very closely with Cooper which accounts also for his helpful aid in communication with you." As an example of the cooperation, Baker cited his agent George, whom he described as having been "loaned . . . to Cooper for auto building work"—short-wave radio operations.[34]

Was Cooper another Comintern representative sent to promote communism as a political movement? In April 1943 Steve Nelson, the West Coast head of the CPUSA secret apparatus, received a visitor named Cooper. The FBI, which had bugged Nelson's house, recognized Cooper as Vasily Zubilin, nominally a Soviet diplomat. It assumed that Zubilin was a Soviet intelligence officer, but only years later would it become clear that he was the chief of KGB operations in the United States.

Nelson and Cooper/Zubilin, using guarded language, discussed espionage and how Nelson's West Coast underground, which they referred to as the apparat, could assist Soviet intelligence. They referred to Rudy Baker ("Al") and to Earl Browder's support for cooperation between Soviet intelligence and the CPUSA underground. Nelson told Zubilin that between thirty and forty-five seamen were available for courier activities for the Communist party between West Coast ports and the Pacific rim and assured Zubilin of their availability for Soviet use. Nelson, however, also complained to Cooper/Zubilin that there were too many cases of Soviet intelligence officers co-opting West Coast CPUSA members to assist their operations without coordinating with Nelson. Zubilin handed over a sum of cash, although the amount is not known. Whether Zubilin was transmitting funds from the Comintern or providing a KGB subsidy is unclear. By this time the Comintern was preparing for its dissolution and the KGB was taking over selected parts of the Comintern's covert operations.[35] In any case, the links between Rudy Baker and Steve Nelson of the CPUSA and Zubilin illustrate the tie between Soviet intelligence and the American Communist party.

American Communists on Intelligence Missions Abroad

In the 1930s the CPUSA supplied several recruits for Soviet intelligence operations abroad. Two of them, Robert Switz and Arvid Jacobson, landed in European jails. And one, sent to Asia, paid with his life.

Born in Japan in 1903, Yotoku Miyagi immigrated to the United States in 1919. An aspiring painter, he graduated from the San Diego

Public Art School in 1925. Already by that time he had developed chronic tuberculosis. He settled in Los Angeles and in the late 1920s he joined the Proletarian Art Society, a CPUSA affiliate. He formally joined the CPUSA in 1931 and was quickly spotted by Tsutomu Yano, who had arrived in California in the early 1930s to help revive the CPUSA's languishing Japanese section. But Yano's duties also included recruiting agents to assist Soviet intelligence. Yano recruited Miyagi in 1931 and in 1933 sent him back to Japan, where he became part of a Soviet spy ring headed by Richard Sorge. Sorge, a German Communist operating under the cover of being a pro-Nazi German journalist stationed in Japan, became an unofficial adviser to Germany's ambassador. Sorge's access to the German embassy and that of his subagents to the Japanese government allowed him to provide the Soviets with highly valuable intelligence on both Japan and Germany.

Miyagi was one of Sorge's chief assistants, but his CPUSA past was the undoing of the Sorge ring. Japanese security police in 1940 began to look for Communists among expatriates who had returned to Japan. The investigation turned up a returnee who had joined the CPUSA in Los Angeles at the same time as Miyagi and knew him as a fellow Communist. On the basis of that information Japanese police put Miyagi under surveillance and arrested him in October 1941. He attempted suicide by leaping head-first from an upper-storey window of the police station, but shrubbery broke his fall. Under torture he confessed, and the security police rolled up the rest of the Sorge network, including Sorge himself. Miyagi, in poor health even before his arrest, died in prison in 1943.[36]

During World War II the CPUSA secret apparatus supplied personnel for clandestine Soviet operations in Europe. In September 1940 Dimitrov, by ciphered message, told Earl Browder, "It is of great importance to have some of your peoples not known as members of Party in the organization that have to be organized in your country for various relief to people of Europe." Dimitrov explained that those picked "have to be very carefully chosen from the well developed, absolutely sure" in order "to penetrate committees we propose to utilize for the international connection work." By "international connection work" Dimitrov meant that these persons, serving as relief officials, would use their freedom of movement among the warring nations of Europe (America was not yet a belligerent) to act as covert couriers for the Soviets.[37]

One month after Dimitrov's message to Browder, Noel Field, a secret American Communist who worked on disarmament issues for the League of Nations, resigned his post. He then went to work for an international relief organization, the Unitarian Service Committee, and began work in early 1941 directing their refugee services in Europe from offices in Marseilles. Field used that position to serve as a courier for the underground German Communist party and to convey messages to and from representatives of the Hungarian, Polish, Bulgarian, and Yugoslav parties as he traveled around Europe on refugee business.

Field was not new to Soviet and Communist clandestine work. A mid-level State Department official in the 1930s, he had been the object of a tug of war between two separate Soviet espionage networks. Hede Massing, who worked then for the KGB, later wrote that she had attempted to recruit Field but he had told her he preferred to work with his old friend Alger Hiss, who was part of a GRU network. (Field left the State Department to work for the League of Nations in 1936.)[38]

After the Hiss case became public in 1948, Field, fearing he would be called to testify against his old comrade, fled to Eastern Europe with several members of his family. His timing, however, was poor. Joseph Stalin was then purging the leadership of the Communist regimes in Hungary and Czechoslovakia. Field, in his clandestine role for the Comintern, had also been in touch with underground Communists, including many targeted for liquidation in the late 1940s. During World War II Field had provided information on conditions in Nazi-occupied Europe to Allan Dulles, the American OSS station chief in Switzerland. At the time, this activity was compatible with his Communist loyalties. Those conducting Stalin's purges, however, found Field a convenient way to link their targets to American intelligence. Although he was in fact a Soviet spy, Field, his wife, his brother, and a foster daughter were all arrested and imprisoned by Hungary's Communist regime as American spies, and Field's activities were cited in the indictments of Hungarian and Czechoslovak officials imprisoned or executed in the purges. After Stalin's death in 1953, Field was released and rehabilitated. Despite his imprisonment Field remained a loyal Communist. He never returned to the United States. He died in Hungary in 1970.[39]

Field was only one of the reliable comrades Dimitrov had asked Browder to find for infiltration of international relief agencies. A memorandum sent from the foreign intelligence directorate of the KGB to the Comintern in 1942 suggests that Browder may have found at least one more. General Fitin informed Dimitrov that someone on the staff of the Unitarian Service Committee, identified only as "Doctor Joe," had successfully delivered letters from the CPUSA to the Communist Party of Great Britain.[40] Nothing else, however, is known of Doctor Joe.

On September 13, 1939, Dimitrov also ordered the CPUSA "to select two comrades with good bourgeois references as salesmen or journalists of a solid bourgeois newspaper who will be able to live in Europe and to move from one country to the other. They have to go to Stockholm and wait there for our instructions." Dimitrov supplied the passwords and meeting places they were to use.[41]

Shortly after this cable was sent, the CPUSA handed over a young Communist journalist working for the *Brooklyn Eagle,* Winston Burdett, to the Comintern for clandestine work. Burdett had secretly joined the CPUSA in 1937. Early in 1940 a fellow reporter, Nathan Einhorn, who was then serving as executive secretary of the New York local of the American Newspaper Guild and was also a secret Communist, asked Burdett to meet with Joseph North, a prominent Communist and editor of *New Masses.* North informed Burdett that "we" had a mission for him and introduced him to a man whose name Burdett was not told. Burdett later identified a photograph of Jacob Golos as the man he had met. Golos, a shadowy figure in the CPUSA's leadership, was also the liaison between the CPUSA and the KGB. Golos instructed the young reporter that he should persuade the *Eagle* to give him credentials as a foreign correspondent, with Burdett financing his own way (Golos promised to furnish the funds) and the *Eagle* paying only for those stories it used. Golos told Burdett to suggest as his first assignment going to Finland to cover the war that had just broken out between the Finns and the Soviets. Golos also had Burdett turn in his CPUSA membership card, hand over photographs of himself (for use by Soviet agents to identify him), and write out an autobiography, the latter a standard Soviet intelligence practice for new agents.[42]

The *Eagle* was delighted to obtain a war correspondent on the cheap, and Golos provided Burdett with funds and instructions for a covert meeting with a Soviet contact in Stockholm. Burdett left the United States in February 1940. When he reached Stockholm he cabled confirmation of his arrival to a name he recalled only as that of a woman and sounding Anglo-Saxon, with an address in New York City. He met his Soviet contact in Stockholm and was instructed to use his position as a reporter to find out about the morale of the Finnish population and its psychological willingness to continue fighting. (Finland was vastly overmatched by the USSR, and the Soviets had been shocked when the Finns not only failed to collapse after the Soviet invasion but halted the initial Soviet assault.) His Stockholm contact also handed over more funds to supplement those Golos had provided to him.

After the Finnish-Soviet war ended in March 1940, Burdett made a final report to his Stockholm contact and received an additional payment. He then undertook other journalistic assignments for American newspapers, reporting from Norway, Romania, Yugoslavia, and Turkey, all the while meeting with Soviet intelligence contacts as well. Burdett gradually grew dissatisfied with his clandestine work, and his ideological loyalty to Communism weakened. He quietly dropped his ties to Soviet intelligence in 1942 when he went to work for CBS Radio News, where he eventually became a prominent correspondent.

When Elizabeth Bentley, the Soviet spy and former associate of Jacob Golos, defected in late 1945, she told the FBI that in 1940 she had received a cable from Burdett which was a signal to Golos that he had reached Stockholm. The FBI interviewed Burdett in 1951. He initially admitted being close to the CPUSA in the 1930s but denied any knowledge of Bentley, Golos, or Soviet intelligence. Upon being reinterviewed, however, he admitted that in the early 1940s he had furnished the Soviets with information while overseas. In 1955 he testified to a congressional committee about his recruitment through Einhorn and North and his work for the Soviets.

In his testimony Burdett mentioned in passing that while in Stockholm in early 1940 he had run into another American reporter, Peter Rhodes, who then worked for the United Press wire service. Burdett said he knew nothing about Rhodes except that from talking to him it was obvious that he was pro-Communist. Burdett did not know it, but Rhodes, like himself, was a clandestine contact of the Soviets via the CPUSA and Golos. The Comintern archive contains a February 1940 coded cable to Dimitrov in which Rudy Baker reports that Peter Rhodes had not gone to Bucharest as planned earlier and his scheduled contact there with Soviet agents had to be rescheduled. A year later, while conducting a surveillance of Jacob Golos, the FBI observed him meeting with Peter Rhodes and his wife, Ione.[43]

Rhodes's attachment to communism was of some years' standing. After attending Oxford University from 1934 to 1936, he joined the

United Press. He wrote extensively about the Americans fighting with the International Brigades in Spain and became an ardent partisan of their cause, to the point of serving as an American delegate to the International Coordinating Committee for Aid to Republican Spain. A German Communist who had been with the International Brigades even entered the United States illegally using Rhodes's passport. In 1939 and 1940 Rhodes signed nominating petitions to put Communist party candidates on the New York State ballot. After America entered the war Rhodes first worked for the Foreign Broadcasting Monitoring Service of the Federal Communications Commission and then transferred to the Office of War Information; by 1944 he was the chief of its Atlantic News Section.

In August 1944 Ione Rhodes met with Bernard Schuster, then the CPUSA liaison with the KGB (replacing Golos). A deciphered Venona message of the New York KGB reported that Mrs. Rhodes had told Schuster that her husband had lost contact with Soviet intelligence.[44] Schuster recommended that the KGB reestablish contact and reminded the KGB that earlier Rhodes had been in liaison with them through Jacob Golos.

Ione Rhodes's reference to her husband's having lost contact most likely points to Golos's death in 1943. When Elizabeth Bentley defected in 1945, she told the FBI that Golos had described Peter Rhodes as one of his covert contacts and had met with him on a number of occasions in 1941 and 1942. Bentley also said that though she had met Ione Rhodes, she had had no personal contact with her husband and did not know what sort of information he provided. She said that from her contact with Ione and from what Golos had said, she knew that the Rhodeses were secret Communists, that he had been born in the Philippines and she in Belgium. Bentley also understood that Rhodes was a journalist who later became a government official involved in broadcasting, and that there had been a family tragedy: Rhodes's mother had killed his father. The FBI checked Bentley's knowledge about the Rhodeses' background and found it accurate.[45]

Bentley's statement to the FBI also demonstrated that the KGB attempted, although without any immediate success, to follow up on Schuster's recommendation of reestablishing contact with Rhodes. Bentley reported that in early 1945 one of her KGB contacts, Joseph Katz, directed her to reapproach Ione Rhodes. Bentley said she tried to do so but that Ione was wary and refused to meet. A few months later, Anatoly Gromov, who had replaced Katz as her KGB liaison, again asked her to contact Ione. Bentley, who was only a few months from her own defection, declined, citing Ione's suspicious attitude.[46]

The FBI interviewed Peter Rhodes in June 1947. He flatly denied ever having met Jacob Golos and claimed not to recognize his photograph. The FBI had observed Golos meeting with the Rhodeses in 1941, so it knew this statement to be false. Much of the rest of Rhodes's statement also lacked credibility. He denied knowing that his friends from the International Brigades were Communists and dismissed the matter of the fraudulent use of his passport as something that he did not need to explain. He also left his interviewers flabbergasted by delivering a strident defense of the Nazi-Soviet Pact.[47]

The CPUSA Secret Apparatus and False Passports

In the early and mid-1930s, the CPUSA's secret apparatus under J. Peters engaged in the wholesale procurement of false American passports for use by American Communists traveling abroad and by Soviet intelligence for espionage purposes. This task was largely dropped when Baker took over in mid-1938, for reasons that will become obvious.

American passports were greatly prized in the intelligence world because of their international acceptability to most border authorities. Moreover, because of the polyglot population of the United States, agents from a variety of ethnic and racial backgrounds and speaking English with all kinds of accents could plausibly claim to hold valid American passports.

The lack of a system of national identification in the United States made obtaining false passports relatively easy. In 1938, shortly after his defection, Whittaker Chambers wrote an essay about this aspect of Soviet espionage and gave it to an old friend and journalist colleague, Herbert Solow. Signed by "Karl," Chambers's pseudonym in the underground, it was entitled "The Faking of Americans." Chambers claimed that in 1932 a Latvian agent of the KGB, known as Ewald, arrived in New York to assume responsibility for the production of false passports. Chambers never knew Ewald's real name, but documents that have surfaced in Russian archives identify him as Arnold Ikal. Chambers wrote that Ewald's chief contact was a man Chambers called Sandor, "the organizer of most of the illegal activities of the Communist Party of America."[48] From this and other descriptive phrases Chambers provided, it is clear that Sandor was Chambers's pseudonym for J. Peters.

In his 1938 essay Chambers asserted that producing fake passports was a source of money for the secret apparatus: "The greatest handicap to Sandor's expensive work is lack of funds and here was a sizable slice of the secret service budget at his disposal." Peters and Ewald/Ikal struck a deal: "The Party supplied the secret service with naturalization papers, birth certificates, business and social fronts, cover addresses and reliable contacts of various kinds. And the Soviet Government pumped life-blood into the underground Communist Party in the form of money payment for such services."[49]

Members of Peters's secret apparatus looked in the genealogical division of the New York Public Library for the names of dead children. The researcher would obtain a copy of the child's birth certificate, which would then be used to apply for a false passport. The CPUSA underground also provided witnesses who would falsely swear to the identity of the applicant before a passport official. By the time Ikal was arrested in Moscow in 1937, he had received hundreds of fraudulent American passports from the CPUSA underground.[50]

The productivity of the CPUSA-Soviet passport fraud ring is illustrated by the arrest in 1935 in Denmark of George Mink, Leon Josephson, and Nicholas Sherman. Mink, born in Russia in 1899, came to the United States in 1912. He was a leading CPUSA maritime union organizer in the 1920s and for a time headed its Marine Workers Industrial Union. In the early 1930s he became an operative for the Profintern, coordinating Communist trade union activities in the maritime field around the world.

When he was arrested in Denmark, Mink had in his possession four American passports, one in his name, one fraudulent passport with his photograph but in the name of Al Gottlieb, one for Harry H. Kaplan, and one for Abraham Wexler. The Kaplan passport was authentic; when American authorities asked Harry Kaplan how his passport had gotten into Mink's hands, Kaplan stated that it had been stolen from him by Barney Josephson, Leon Josephson's brother. The Wexler passport was also authentic; Wexler claimed it had been stolen but could not say when, where, or by whom. Wexler was a member of the small Marine Workers Industrial Union, of which Mink was the first national chairman, and Kaplan was an associate of the Josephson brothers and Mink. The obvious inference was that both had turned their passports over to Mink for later alteration by insertion of new photographs.[51] A Danish court convicted Mink of espionage, and he served eighteen months in prison. He was then deported to the USSR. His history after that time is unclear.[52]

Leon Josephson, who had been arrested with Mink, spent four months in jail. At that point a Danish court decided that the evidence was insufficient to proceed, and Josephson returned to America. State Department handwriting experts later determined that the application for the fraudulent Gottlieb passport carried by George Mink was in Josephson's hand. Nor was this Josephson's only venture into the illegal passport business. An analysis of the application for a fraudulent American passport in the name of Samuel Liptzen carried by Gerhart Eisler, the Comintern's illegal representative in the United States in the mid-1930s, was in Josephson's hand, as was the statement of a witness falsely vouching for Liptzen's identity.[53]

Josephson had joined the CPUSA in 1926. He was a lawyer and in the late 1920s represented Amtorg and the party's interests in a variety of legal proceedings. In 1930 he was one of a group of Communist lawyers helping several unionists convicted of killing a local sheriff during a textile strike in Gastonia, North Carolina. Those convicted jumped bail and fled to the Soviet Union. One of them, Fred Beal, later returned to the United States, announced his disillusionment with communism, and served his prison sentence. He stated that Josephson had arranged for the false passports that he and the others had used to flee.[54]

The third person arrested with Mink and Josephson claimed to be Nicholas Sherman. He carried a U.S. passport in that name but also had in his possession a Canadian passport in the name of Abraham Goldman and a German passport in the name of Wilhelm Brettschneider. The Sherman passport was fraudulent, obtained by using the naturalization papers of a man who had died in 1926 and a false witness supplied by Peters's secret apparatus. When arrested, Sherman had on him correspondence from a business firm operated by Harry Kaplan, the same Kaplan whose passport was in Mink's possession. The Danish court convicted Sherman of espionage; he served eighteen months in prison and was deported to the USSR.

Who was the fake Nicholas Sherman? Robert Switz, an American who worked for Soviet military intelligence in the 1930s, later identified a photograph of Sherman as that of a senior GRU officer operating illegally in the United States whose name was Aleksandr Petrovich Ulanovsky. Whittaker Chambers, who worked for Ulanovsky's GRU espionage apparatus in the early 1930s, discussed him in detail in his memoir, *Witness*.[55]

The arrest of Mink, Josephson, and Sherman/Ulanovsky demonstrates not only the productivity of the CPUSA-Soviet fraudulent passport operations. Traveling together and arrested together were a CPUSA unionist and Profintern operative (Mink), a CPUSA lawyer and associate of its clandestine arm (Josephson), and a GRU officer and professional spy (Ulanovsky). Communist trade unionism, the CPUSA (aboveground and below), and Soviet espionage were intermingled. To use the jargon of Cold War espionage, there was no "compartmentalization." In the 1930s and early 1940s the organizational blending of these different aspects of the Communist movement allowed the Soviet Union to maximize its return on the assets it possessed. But after World War II, when American authorities belatedly started to pay attention and the FBI began an aggressive investigation, the vulnerability of this arrangement also became clear. An organization as large as the CPUSA had too many areas of weakness. Many party-linked espionage operations were exposed and neutralized by American counterintelligence in the late 1940s and 1950s. And of course the CPUSA itself became tainted with disloyalty. That, however, was for the future. In 1935 the State Department noticed the Danish arrests and began to look into the matter of false passports, but follow-up was slow, the Justice Department had little interest in prosecuting Soviet espionage, and the popular press paid scant attention.

Nor was much notice taken in 1936 when two Comintern agents, Arthur Ewert and his wife, Elsie, turned up in Brazil with fake American passports. Ewert, a German Communist leader in the early and mid-1920s, became a covert Comintern agent in the late 1920s. In the mid-1930s he and his wife arrived by separate routes in Brazil. Arthur Ewert's American passport gave his name as Harry Berger, while his wife's American passport was in the name of Machla Lencsyski. The real Berger had died as an infant; the CPUSA passport ring had again simply used the infant's birth certificate and provided witnesses who falsely swore that Ewert was Berger. Elsie Ewert's passport had been gained by using the naturalization papers of Machla Lencsyski. When the passport fraud came to light, the real Lencsyski claimed that her naturalization papers had been lost and she had no idea how they had come to be used to obtain a fake passport. Her brother, however, was one of the perjuring witnesses to the fake Berger passport and part of the CPUSA fake passport apparatus.

The Ewerts were in Brazil to assist a Communist-backed insurrection against the authoritarian Vargas regime. The insurrection failed when it was uncovered by Brazilian police, and the Ewerts were arrested. The U.S. embassy initially took an interest in their fate when it was thought that they were American citizens. Once it became clear the two were using fraudulent passports and were not Americans, U.S. diplomats withdrew from the matter.[56]

The passport issue gained more attention in 1937 with the arrest of Arnold Ikal, the GRU's contact with Peters's passport operation. Ikal was not, however, arrested in the United States for his role in the wholesale faking of American passports. Diplomats at the U.S. embassy in Moscow got word that an American woman, Mrs. Donald L. Robinson, needed assistance at the nearby Hotel National. They visited the distraught woman, who said that her husband, also an American, had disappeared. The officials returned to the embassy to check their records, then went back to the hotel, only to find the room occupied by a new person and the hotel staff claiming that Mrs. Robinson had departed without leaving a forwarding address. The American chargé d'affaires, Loy Henderson, refused to accept that story, went to Soviet authorities, and insisted that Mrs. Robinson be located and that embassy officials be allowed to speak to her. After lengthy delays, Henderson was allowed to visit Mrs. Robinson, in a Moscow prison. She told Henderson that she neither needed nor wanted American diplomatic assistance.

Meanwhile, a search of State Department passport records showed that the Robinsons also possessed a second set of passports, as Mr. and Mrs. Adolph A. Rubens. The wife of a former U.S. diplomat at the American consulate in Latvia also recognized the photograph of Donald Robinson as that of a Latvian believed to have been a Soviet intelligence agent. It turned out that the real Donald Robinson was born in Queens in 1905 and had died in 1909. Mrs. Robinson, meanwhile, had used the birth certificate of Ruth Norma Birkland, who was born in 1909 and died in 1915, for her passport. At this point Henderson concluded that the two were not innocent Americans but Soviet agents of some sort caught up in the nightmarish purges then sweeping the Soviet Union and saw little reason for the U.S. embassy to pursue the case.

The Moscow incident, however, generated considerable press coverage and interest in how the Rubenses got two sets of false American passports. Chambers's friend, Herbert Solow, used the Rubens case and the information Chambers provided as the basis of an article, "Stalin's American Passport Mill," in the popular *American Mercury,* which outlined the sizable joint CPUSA-Soviet passport forgery operation.[57]

Ikal was merely one of many hundreds of KGB, GRU, and Comintern agents who in the late 1930s fell victim to Stalin's Terror. When recalled to Moscow in 1937, he was arrested by his colleagues and charged with being part of a Trotskyist-fascist plot to destroy the Soviet Union. Like many of those arrested during the Terror, Ikal signed a false confession, admitting to having made contacts with the American followers of Leon Trotsky on behalf of Latvian fascists, at whose head stood Gen. Yan Berzin, head of the GRU. Ikal's confession also claimed that through Philip Rosenblit, a New York dentist and participant in the CPUSA underground, he had funneled money to James Cannon, head of the American Trotskyist movement (Cannon and Rosenblit were married to sisters). Rosenblit, who in the 1920s had played a key role in the clandestine transfer of Comintern subsidies to the CPUSA and had been part of the CPUSA underground that had assisted the GRU in the early 1930s, had unwisely emigrated to the USSR in the mid-1930s. He disappeared in 1937, the same year as Ikal's faked confession, having been either executed or sent to the Gulag.

As for Ikal, after signing the confession he went to the Gulag. In 1939, no longer under immediate threat of execution, he repudiated his 1937 confession, strenuously denied any ideological deviation, and asked for reconsideration of his sentence. He remained in prison, however, and died in the camps. His wife, although holding two false American passports, really was an American. Her true name was Ruth Buerger, and she was a Communist. After she cooperated with Soviet authorities by declining American diplomatic assistance, she was released from Soviet prison but not allowed to leave the USSR. Her family in the United States received a visit from an intermediary for the Soviets who warned that they should make no public outcry about their daughter's fate. They did not, and she was allowed to live out her natural life in the Soviet Union.[58]

Although fake American passports had surfaced by this time in the hands of Comintern and Soviet intelligence agents in Denmark, Brazil, and Moscow, the U.S. government still did little about the matter until war broke out in Europe in September 1939. Authorities then launched an investigation that included the seizure of the records of World Tourists, a travel agency headed by Jacob Golos. These documents showed that World Tourists had provided travel services for at least sixteen persons who possessed false American passports, and that the passage tickets and other charges for these persons were assigned to two special accounts, one labeled George Primoff and the other A. Blake. Charges to these accounts, it turned out, were actually paid by the American Communist party.[59]

On the basis of the passport investigation in 1939, the Justice Department launched several prosecutions. Most prominently, it indicted Earl Browder, head of the CPUSA, for use of fraudulent passports. He was arrested in October 1939, tried, convicted, and, after his appeals failed, imprisoned in 1941. Although he was sentenced to four years in prison, after Browder had served fourteen months President Roosevelt commuted his sentence as a gesture of goodwill toward the Soviet Union, by that time an ally of the United States against Nazi Germany. William Weiner, the CPUSA's national treasurer, was also convicted, but the court suspended his sentence when he claimed to have a life-threatening heart condition. The government indicted the party official Harry Gannes for passport fraud, but his case was repeatedly delayed, and he died in 1941 before trial. Virtually all the other Communists identified in the investigation as having obtained fraudulent passports, as well as the many witnesses who falsely vouched for them, escaped prosecution.

Jacob Golos and World Tourists were also indicted, but they got away remarkably lightly. Under a plea bargain, on March 14, 1940, Golos pled guilty to failing to register as the agent of a foreign power, namely, the USSR. He was fined five hundred dollars and given a suspended jail sentence.

American Counterespionage: Other Priorities

With the exception of jailing Earl Browder, the government's response to the CPUSA-Soviet passport fraud operation was anemic, and it was symptomatic of the disarray in American counterintelligence. In the 1930s the U.S. government had a hodgepodge of internal security laws, no clear executive order on what constituted government secrets, no clear policy on the security fitness of government personnel with access to sensitive information, and divided and unclear authority as to which government agencies were responsible for internal security enforcement.

This disarray had historical precedents. America had entered World War I in 1917 with a governmental structure ill-prepared for a major international conflict. Nor had the nation's history given it any serious experience with the espionage, sabotage, or political subversion linked to a foreign power. Yet these became legitimate concerns, if in retrospect exaggerated, when the United States entered the war against Imperial Germany. In 1917 and 1918 the government under emergency wartime conditions created a large security system based on the Justice Department's Bureau of Investigation (predecessor to the FBI) and the counterintelligence sections of Army military intelligence and the Office of Naval Intelligence. Unable to expand its own agencies rapidly enough, the federal government also sponsored the creation a series of state and local authorities (for example, the New York City Committee on Aliens) as auxiliaries of the national government. The federal government also sanctioned an array of quasi-private organizations manned by eager volunteers (the American Protective League and the American Defense Society were among the largest) that watched for sabotage, espionage, or other acts of resistance to the war effort.[60]

This hastily created arrangement worked. German government financial support for American antiwar activities, significant before the United States entered the war, was stopped and its recipients were largely silenced. German intelligence made a number of efforts to penetrate the United States, but most were blocked or thwarted. Domestic resistance to conscription was also suppressed. The cost, however, had been high. The hastily thrown-together arrangements were inefficient, inconsistent, and prone to abuse. Several of the state-level security agencies became tools of partisan politics. The Minnesota Commission of Public Safety, for example, used its extensive official power to suppress the political ambitions of Minnesota's Non-Partisan League, a populist farm organization that threatened the position of the dominant Republican party. Several of the private organizations that received federal government support also ventured into vigilante justice and engaged in egregious violations of basic legal norms.

After the war ended in November 1918, some parts of the wartime security apparatus continued to operate, turning their attention to Bolshevism, which seemed on the threshold of sweeping Europe. But the panic over the new Red threat receded by 1921, and the Harding administration completed the dismantling of the wartime security apparatus. The Bureau of Investigation withdrew almost entirely from the internal security field.[61] The military's intelligence agencies shrank drastically in size. Both the Army's and the Navy's counterintelligence branches continued to monitor domestic radicalism, but neither service had any jurisdiction to prosecute espionage or subversion that did not directly involve military personnel. Their reports went largely unread by military commanders and usually were not shared with civilian agencies that might actually have had jurisdiction.

In the mid-1930s President Roosevelt, concerned about the pro-Nazi German-American Bund and domestic fascist groups such as the Silver Shirts and the Black Legion, ordered the Federal Bureau of Investigation to reenter the domestic security field. Bureau head J. Edgar Hoover did so eagerly and included American Communists among those under observation. The FBI of the 1930s, however, was very small, with barely three hundred agents in 1933 and fewer than nine hundred even by the end of the decade. While the agency had become skilled in criminal investigation, it took some years for its agents to develop knowledge and procedures geared to counterintelligence activities.

Internal security concerns grew in the late 1930s when it appeared that fascists had created a new strategy of combining internal subversion with external military aggression. During the Spanish Civil War the Nationalist forces of Gen. Francisco Franco, backed by Nazi Germany and Fascist Italy, advanced in four columns on Madrid, the besieged capital of the Spanish Republicans. The Nationalist general directing the offensive, Emilio Mola, boasted that he had a secret "fifth column" of fascists inside the city sowing disaffection and defeatism which would assail the Republicans from within as his troops assaulted the city's defenses from without. Thus was born the image of the "fifth column" as a clandestine underground that spread subversion, engaged in sabotage and espionage, and prepared the way for military conquest. Fifth-column imagery grew stronger as Hitler used covertly organized Nazi sympathizers, first in Austria and then in Czechoslovakia, to pave the way for German conquest.

As a consequence, the FBI devoted more of its resources to internal security. Both the Army and the Navy also expanded their efforts, although all three agencies were still on Depression-era austerity budgets with limited personnel until mobilization began in earnest in 1941. The

State Department took an interest in the area, and the Treasury Department, which oversaw the Secret Service, thought it might have a role as well. Even the Post Office claimed a role with its jurisdiction over the mail, and the Commerce Department, concerned about foreign trade manipulation, asserted an interest. It became clear to Attorney General Frank Murphy that the overlapping and uncoordinated efforts in this field were wasting what limited resources the government had. In 1939 he asked President Roosevelt to issue an order clarifying the situation. The president did so in a June 26, 1939, confidential memorandum to the secretaries of state, treasury, war, navy, and commerce and to the attorney general and postmaster general: "It is my desire that the investigation of all espionage, counterespionage, and sabotage matters be controlled and handled by the Federal Bureau of Investigation of the Department of Justice, the Military Intelligence Division of the War Department, and the office of Naval Intelligence of the Navy Department. . . . [Y]ou will instruct the heads of all other investigative agencies other than the three named, to refer immediately to the nearest office of the Federal Bureau of Investigation any data, information, or material that may come to their notice bearing directly or indirectly on espionage, counterespionage, or sabotage."[62]

Roosevelt's order imposed some system on the threatening chaos of American counterintelligence operations. As it worked out, the Navy and the Army would take care of internal security for their own personnel, bases, and facilities. The FBI would cover everything else. There was overlap in regard to war plants and civilian workers as American military mobilization got under way, and the military agencies kept a finger in civilian counterintelligence, but the main jurisdictional lines were clear. Interagency cooperation, however, continued to be poor.[63]

The system worked fairly well on its chief targets. After the invasion of Poland in 1939, German intelligence made repeated efforts to establish espionage and sabotage networks in the United States, with little success. In a 1940 report Hoover boasted, with justifiable pride, that the FBI had so infiltrated German intelligence networks that a German clandestine short-wave radio was run by FBI penetration agents. He noted that "all material furnished by German Agents through their complicated channels of communication to this station for transmittal to Europe is cleared by State, War and Navy Department officials prior to the time that it is actually transmitted to Germany."[64] Once the United States entered the war in December 1941, German and Japanese intelligence networks were easily rolled up, and new penetrations were few. Dozens of Americans who had covertly accepted German and Japanese money between 1939 and 1941 to finance pro-Nazi propaganda, anti-intervention literature, or antisemitic publications were prosecuted or silenced. The German-American Bund collapsed and its chief figures were imprisoned. Pro-Mussolini Italian-American networks were dispersed. Key leaders of other domestic fascist organizations were also imprisoned, or they faced such strict official attention that their ability to impede the war effort was reduced to nil. With the glaring exception of the internment of West Coast Japanese-Americans, an act that Hoover and the FBI advised against, the internal security regime in World War II also worked with much greater sensitivity to individual rights and democratic liberties than did the security regime in World War I. Because of the abuses that had occurred, the World War I experience of delegating internal security authority to semi-autonomous state and local governmental entities or semi-private volunteer organizations was not repeated.

It would be poor history to use the clarity of hindsight to fault officials for not giving Soviet espionage priority consideration in this era. German, Italian, and Japanese espionage was the overriding concern of security officials in the late 1930s and during World War II, and rightly so. But even though Soviet intelligence operations in the United States were a secondary or even a tertiary concern, the American response to Soviet espionage was noticeably weak, and the limited follow-through on the uncovering of the massive CPUSA-Soviet passport operation was but one example.

The Missed Opportunity: Whittaker Chambers in 1939

During most of 1939 Whittaker Chambers continued his effort to reenter normal life. He solidified his position at *Time* magazine and managed to avoid both public and official notice. The Nazi-Soviet Pact in August 1939, however, caused Chambers to change his stance. He realized that the pact made war inevitable and that the Soviet Union had become a de facto nonbelligerent ally of Nazi Germany. He anticipated, correctly, that the pact would put Soviet supporters in the United States in conflict with American national policy. Isaac Don Levine, a journalist who wrote extensively on communism and had a rough idea of what Chambers had been involved in, convinced him that he had to alert

American authorities. Chambers agreed, with the proviso that he wanted immunity from prosecution. Levine approached Marvin McIntyre, the White House appointments secretary, summarized Chambers's story, and asked for a meeting with President Roosevelt himself. McIntyre declined a meeting with FDR but arranged for Levine to take Chambers to see Assistant Secretary of State Adolf Berle.

Levine and Chambers met with Berle on the evening of September 2. A day earlier Nazi armored columns had smashed into Poland. Soviet Red Army forces would wait two weeks and then, with the Poles fully engaged in the west, would strike from the east and annex half of Poland. Chambers told Berle a large part, although not all, of the story of the CPUSA-GRU network of which he had been a part. Concerned about his own vulnerability to imprisonment, he held back how deeply he himself had been involved in spying. There was no doubt, however, that Berle understood that he was being told of espionage. Berle kept written notes of the meeting, headed "Underground Espionage Agent." They show that Chambers gave him the names and provided short descriptions of a number of mid-level government officials whom he described as secret Communists and members of covert CPUSA caucuses operating within the U.S. government. He also provided the names of persons outside the government who supported the operations of the CPUSA underground. In several cases, according to Berle's notes, Chambers implied that the person in question might be engaged in espionage against the United States as well as in covert Communist activity.

The Venona decryptions confirm that eight of those whom Chambers named in September 1939 later cooperated with Soviet espionage against the United States.[65] They were Alger Hiss, then a mid-level State Department official; Laurence Duggan, then head of the State Department's Division of the American Republics, which supervised diplomatic relations with Central and South America; Frank Coe, a Treasury Department official who worked in international economics; Charles Kramer, on the staff of the National Labor Relations Board; John Abt, a prominent labor lawyer with wide contacts in the Congress of Industrial Organizations; Isaac Folkoff, a senior leader of the California Communist party; Lauchlin Currie, recently brought into the White House as a senior aide to President Roosevelt; and Harry Dexter White, assistant to the secretary of the Treasury. (Isaac Don Levine also kept notes on the meeting, and his notes contain White's name. Berle's notes do not. Chambers, in his memoir, names White as an espionage contact but thought he had not mentioned him to Berle.)

In addition to these eight, five others named by Chambers and listed in Berle's notes are confirmed to have participated in Soviet espionage by evidence other than that of Venona.[66] These were Julian Wadleigh, a State Department official who confessed to his role in Soviet espionage in 1949; Vincent Reno, a civilian official at the Army's Aberdeen Proving Grounds who also confessed in 1949 to his role in spying for the Soviets; Noel Field, who had been a State Department official in the mid-1930s; Solomon Adler, a senior Treasury Department official whom Elizabeth Bentley would later name as one of the sources for her CPUSA-KGB network; and Philip Rosenblit. Unknown to Chambers, by this time Rosenblit had fallen victim to Stalin's terror and was no longer a threat to the United States.

In accordance with Roosevelt's 1939 order, the president's appointments secretary should have sent Levine and Chambers to the FBI. Similarly, Assistant Secretary of State Berle, once he understood that Chambers was raising an issue of possible espionage, had a responsibility under Roosevelt's order, as well as by common sense, to notify the FBI. He did not. Exactly why he did not is not clear, but it certainly had nothing to do with any sympathy for the Soviet cause. Berle was, and was known to be, a firm anti-Communist, which is why Levine and Chambers felt comfortable discussing these issues with him. In his diary for that night Berle recorded that he had met with Levine and Chambers regarding what he described as "Russian espionage" and that "it becomes necessary to take a few simple measures."[67]

The measures he took were simple, but they were also ineffective. He did not file a report on the interview with the FBI, either military counterintelligence agency, or even the State Department's own personnel security office, although Chambers's information dealt with several State Department employees. In March 1941, more than a year after the interview, Berle checked on Chambers's veracity by asking the FBI if it was investigating Chambers or had information on him. The bureau told Berle that it was not investigating Chambers and only had him on a list that noted past participation in radical activities. Berle did not pass on Chambers's warnings or explain why he wanted to know about Chambers. His diary also shows that he discussed the matter with Marvin McIntyre, but not until 1942, and Berle did not know if McIntyre ever told President Roosevelt.[68]

As the years passed, several sources told FBI agents that Whittaker Chambers, by then a senior *Time* journalist, had information worth hearing. In May 1942 the FBI interviewed Chambers, who told them that he had already given all the information he had to Berle in 1939. The FBI contacted Berle and, a year later, in June 1943, his notes finally reached the FBI.[69] Even then the matter had a low priority, and nothing was done for many months—only after other evidence, the Katherine Perlo letter (chapter 5) and the FBI's own Comintern Apparatus investigation of 1944 (chapter 2) produced a body of corroborative documentation. And still the FBI accorded little urgency to the matter until Elizabeth Bentley turned herself in to the FBI in the fall of 1945.

Chambers had given the assistant secretary of state a list that included no fewer than thirteen persons, eight of them serving officials, several of them senior officials of the U.S. government who had had compromising relationships with Soviet intelligence. But the government did not act, in part because the information did not reach the proper agency for more than three and a half years, and even then the follow-up was slow. Had the government acted on Chambers's information in 1939, significant damage to U.S. national interests would have been avoided and a great deal of the basis for the bitter postwar domestic controversy about communism and subversion would have been removed.

CHAPTER 4

THE GOLOS-BENTLEY NETWORK

The American Communist party's secret apparatus under Josef Peters and Rudy Baker performed a multitude of tasks. It protected the CPUSA from infiltrators, hunted down internal ideological deviators, infiltrated and disrupted left-wing rivals and right-wing enemies, and maintained contact with secret party caucuses of members who were government employees. Not the least of its duties, however, was assisting the Comintern in its international operations and helping Soviet intelligence with its espionage activities.

After war broke out in 1939, and particularly after Nazi Germany invaded the Soviet Union in June 1941, sections of the CPUSA's underground shifted from being party networks to being primarily Soviet espionage networks. The most extensive of these ran through Jacob Golos and his assistant and successor, Elizabeth Bentley. It was not, in fact, a single apparatus, but several networks and a number of singleton agents, all of whom at some point were linked to Soviet intelligence through Golos and Bentley.

Jacob Golos

The story of the Golos-Bentley networks begins with Jacob N. Golos. A good deal about Golos's life remains unknown or unclear. He was born

Jacob Raisen in 1890 in what today is Ukraine. He later told Elizabeth Bentley that he had been involved in radical agitation against the Russian government at an early age, and was imprisoned and sent into Siberian exile. After several years he escaped via Japan and came to the United States to join his parents, who in the meantime had emigrated. The details and dates are unclear, but he or his parents arrived in the United States about 1908, and one source states that he became a naturalized citizen in 1915. In any event, around that time Golos became active in the Russian-language federation of the Socialist party, the core of its growing left-wing faction from which the American Communist movement developed. When the left wing was ejected from the Socialist party in 1919, it formed two rival organizations, the Communist Labor party and the Communist Party of America. Raisen went with the latter. (The two parties merged in 1921.) Raisen, then, had the status of a founding member of the American Communist party. Like many Communists of that era, he also adopted a new name, Golos, the Russian word for "voice." (In an obvious play on his name, the KGB in the Venona cables gave him the cover name Zvuk, or "sound" in Russian.)[1]

Golos's activities in the early 1920s are murky. He told Bentley that he returned to his native Russia in 1919 to work for several years for the Bolshevik regime, serving for a time as a foreman in a Siberian coal mine but also joining the Cheka, the powerful political police of the Soviet state and predecessor of the KGB. If Golos had been a "Chekist," it would have prepared him for his later role as a liaison between the CPUSA and the KGB.

The records of the Comintern in Moscow contain an autobiographical questionnaire that Golos filled out. It is undated, but the information on it indicates that he wrote it at some point after 1927. Unfortunately, the questionnaire was an American party form, and its questions related to American matters. Golos's answers refer to his birth in Russia and, in response to a question about his arrest record, states that he had been jailed for three years in Russia, probably a reference to his internal exile under the Tsarist regime. Otherwise the questionnaire is silent on whether Golos was in the Soviet Union in the early 1920s. It does state that he became a "full time functionary" (employee) of the CPUSA in 1923, so if he had gone to Russia in 1919, he was back four years later.[2]

After 1923 Golos worked for *Novy Mir*, one of the CPUSA's Russian-language journals, served as a party organizer in Detroit and

Chicago, and rose to the position of secretary (chief administrator) of the Society for Technical Aid to Soviet Russia, an organization that recruited technicians and specialists for work in Russia and shipped machinery, tools, and other needed goods to the new Soviet state.

His work for the Communist movement took a new direction in 1927. That June, Golos was one of the incorporators of World Tourists, a travel agency, and became its chief official, serving in that position until his death from a heart attack in 1943. All of World Tourists' officers and key staff were members of the CPUSA, and its capital was covertly provided by the party as well. On paper Golos was the principal owner of its stock.

World Tourists had a contractual relationship with Intourist, the official Soviet travel agency, and its chief business was the selling of Intourist services on commission. These included travel tickets, customs services, and documentation for transport to and from the USSR as well as lodging, travel, and tourist services inside the Soviet Union. It also arranged the shipment of parcels to the USSR, a major source of business because of the large number of immigrants who had family in the Soviet Union. Like any travel agency, it sold travel arrangements for other destinations as well. World Tourists' arrangement with Intourist guaranteed the agency a steady flow of business because Intourist was the only agency allowed to provide commercial tourist services inside the USSR. Further, Amtorg, the Soviet Union's trading arm, encouraged American businessmen seeking to do business with the Soviet state to make their travel arrangements through World Tourists. World Tourists, then, provided a method for the Soviet Union to indirectly subsidize the American Communist movement because the agency's covert owner was the CPUSA itself.

World Tourists also served the CPUSA in other ways. American Communists on party business, seeking to avoid notice by both American officials and those of foreign nations, often traveled abroad carrying false passports and deceptive travel documents. World Tourists not only never raised questions about the authenticity of the documents offered to it by CPUSA personnel; it also assisted in the subterfuge. It provided this service not only for the American party but even for foreign Communists on missions for the Communist International or Soviet intelligence agencies who were using false American travel documents.

At this point the story of Jacob Golos and World Tourists overlaps with that of the American Communist party's underground. The services Golos and World Tourists provided for the CPUSA secret apparatus and for Soviet intelligence resulted in World Tourists' indictment and plea bargain in 1940 as an unregistered agent of a foreign power.

Although the government's prosecution of World Tourists amounted to little more than a slap on the wrist, it signaled that authorities were not entirely blind to Golos's activities. So Golos changed his mode of operations in several ways. First, with World Tourists tainted as an agent of a foreign power, he and the CPUSA created a new cover business: U.S. Service and Shipping Corporation. Second, fearing himself under surveillance, he made Elizabeth Bentley, then unknown to the FBI, his courier and assistant for his covert operations.

U.S. Service and Shipping Corporation

To function as a new cover, U.S. Service and Shipping Corporation also needed a respectable head. Earl Browder arranged for a socially prominent and wealthy party sympathizer, John Hazard Reynolds, to become the president of the new company. To finance it the CPUSA put up fifteen thousand dollars as initial capital, delivered in cash to Reynolds, who laundered the funds through his own accounts. Although Reynolds put in only five thousand dollars of his own money, he initially held all of the company's stock. As a front man, he was far better than Golos, who was a Russian immigrant, an open although little-known CPUSA official, and a convicted criminal. Reynolds, by contrast, was from a wealthy Long Island family, his father was a New York judge, and his wife, Grace Fleischman, was an heiress to the Fleischman Yeast fortune. In the 1920s Reynolds, a member of the New York Stock Exchange, had by good luck or good judgment cashed in most of his holdings before the 1929 crash; he had also inherited a healthy share of the family's wealth in 1930. He had served as an Army officer in World War I and, taking a commission in the finance corps, became a lieutenant colonel in the Army in World War II.

Despite his elite background, Reynolds had been a Soviet sympathizer since the early 1920s. Although he never joined the CPUSA, he lent his name and some of his wealth to party-linked causes. One was the journal *Soviet Russia Today,* which promoted Stalin's USSR as a place where the idealistic goals of socialism had actually been realized. Theodore Bayer, president of the CPUSA-aligned Russky Golos Publishing Company, managed this journal, got to know Reynolds, and recommended him to Browder.[3] Lemuel Harris, a long-time CPUSA agricultural specialist who shared Reynolds's elite social background, served as the chief link between the party and Reynolds.

In 1947, when the FBI questioned Reynolds about U.S. Service and Shipping, he confirmed much of what Bentley had earlier told them but put it in a benign light. Reynolds explained that Bayer, whom he described as a friend, had introduced him to Browder and Golos, who had suggested the venture that became U.S. Service and Shipping. But, he assured the FBI, it had been purely a business enterprise. He denied that there were any party funds involved in the company and explained that the fifteen thousand dollars he had accepted from Lemuel Harris was a personal loan, not a CPUSA investment. Although insisting that all of this was strictly business, Reynolds also admitted that Harris's loan had not been accompanied by a written loan agreement, promissory note, or other documentation. The FBI did not believe him.[4]

When U.S. Service and Shipping was organized in 1941, Elizabeth Bentley was named vice-president. De facto she was the manager of the company, because Reynolds took little interest in its day-to-day affairs and, after he resumed Army duty in late 1942, was absent in any case. Bentley was Golos's proxy within U.S. Service and Shipping and the link to World Tourists, which Golos continued to head and which did much of the work for U.S. Service and Shipping on what amounted to a subcontractor basis.

The importance of U.S. Service and Shipping to Soviet intelligence as a cover is illustrated by two decrypted KGB messages from late 1944. Several persons connected with Russian War Relief, a major supplier of donated goods to the USSR, asked Amtorg to authorize other firms to offer the same services as did the U.S. Service and Shipping/World Tourists combination. The New York KGB urged its Moscow headquarters to derail this proposal because it "directly threatens the existence of Myrna's cover" and from the KGB's view it was "essential to continue the contract with Myrna's firm."[5] Myrna was the cover name used by the KGB at that time for Elizabeth Bentley.

Elizabeth Bentley

Elizabeth Bentley, born in 1908 in Connecticut, came from a socially respectable but not wealthy family. She graduated from Vassar, went to Italy on a student exchange program, and earned a master's degree from Columbia University. While at Columbia she joined the American League Against War and Fascism. This organization was covertly controlled by the CPUSA, and Bentley was drawn to the Communists within the league, all of whom kept their party membership secret. After she had proved her worth, they sponsored her for membership in the party in 1935.[6]

Over the next several years Bentley gradually moved into the CPUSA's underground. The CPUSA initially used Bentley for its basic covert work, infiltrating and reporting on organizations of interest to it. In 1938 Bentley got a job at the Italian Library of Information, a pro-Mussolini institution. Her reports on the pro-fascist propaganda put out by the library, however, did not seem to arouse much interest in the CPUSA. One of the party officials she reported to, however, took an interest in *her*. It was Jacob Golos. Golos had a wife and son, but both had emigrated to the Soviet Union in the mid-1930s. By the time Bentley met him Golos was lonely, and the two formed a romantic attachment. They would remain together until Golos's death in 1943.

Golos also began to use Bentley as an assistant in his covert work, although initially her tasks were minor. In 1939 she acted as a mail drop for Golos, receiving letters from Sam Carr and Tim Buck of the Canadian Communist party. (The Canadian government later imprisoned Carr, the national organizing secretary of the Communist Party of Canada, for espionage.) She also acted as a go-between for another Golos mail drop, Rose Arenal, who received mail for Golos from her brother-in-law, Leopolo Arenal, a Mexican Communist. Arenal helped to organize and participated in an armed assault in 1940 on the Mexican home of Leon Trotsky, the exiled Soviet leader. Trotsky escaped assassination then, but the assailants murdered one of Trotsky's guards, a young American.[7]

In late 1939 Golos also infiltrated Bentley into the office of the McClure newspaper syndicate to check on rumors that its chief was a Nazi agent. Bentley, who had taken a secretarial job, found no indication that he was, and she left the job early in 1940. Meanwhile, the government's legal attack on World Tourists had begun, and Golos started to suspect that he was under FBI surveillance. He responded by creating U.S. Service and Shipping and by increasingly relying on Bentley to meet with his sources and contacts.

Early in 1941 Golos, fearing that his trips outside New York would be watched, made Bentley his courier to his sources who were now located in Washington. One was Mary Price, secretary until mid-1943 to one of America's most respected press commentators, Walter Lippmann. Lippmann had wide access to the nation's decision makers, and Price furnished Golos with items that Lippmann chose not to write about or the names of Lippmann's sources, often not carried in Lippmann's stories but useful to the Soviets for weighing Lippmann's comments on American foreign policy.

Mary Price: The Spy as Secretary

Price shows up in the Venona traffic in mid-1943.[8] The two versions of what happened at that time, one from Bentley and the other from the KGB cables, do not contradict each other as concerns the facts. The two differ, however, with regard to the motives Bentley attributes to the KGB and those the KGB attributes to Bentley. Bentley told the FBI that Price had recurrent bouts of ill health exacerbated by the nervous strain of her espionage work. She left Lippmann's employ and went for an extended visit to Mexico to recover her health. Bentley's view was that the burden of the covert world was getting to be too much for Price and she should be withdrawn. Bentley claimed, though, that in early 1944 the KGB officer known to her as Bill pressed her to turn over Price to direct KGB control. From her description of Bill and Bill's wife, the FBI later concluded that Bill was Iskhak Abdulovich Akhmerov, a senior KGB officer. This identification is confirmed by deciphered Venona messages.[9] Bentley told the FBI that for some months in 1944 she and Bill/Akhmerov argued about Price's next mission, and she suspected him of reserving Price for "honey-trap" assignments, using sex as a means of recruiting sources. In the meantime Price was used as an intermediary with members of Bentley's network.

The Venona cables cast the same story in a different light. In June 1943, when Price was preparing for her extended vacation in Mexico, the New York KGB made a preliminary move to take her under its direct control and out of the Golos-Bentley network, reporting that it planned to have her courier material to its agent Nora (unidentified) in Mexico. In two decrypted KGB cables in April and May of 1944, Akhmerov reported to Moscow that he had met with Price and been at her New York apartment. (After returning from Mexico, Price had moved from Washington to New York.) Then in a July Venona message Akhmerov reported on his feud with Bentley about Price. He said that Browder and Bentley, citing Price's health and strained nerves, were insisting that she be withdrawn from intelligence work and given CPUSA political assignments. Akhmerov agreed to try to persuade Browder to turn Price over to the KGB, explaining he did not want to lose someone who "has been working for a long time and has acquired considerable experience."[10] He said that even if Price's health was delicate, her apartment could be used as a safe-house and she could function as an intermediary. Akhmerov made no comments that would support Bentley's suspicions that he meant for Price to do honey-trap work. Although Bentley attributed her stance to concern for Price, Akhmerov told Moscow that he thought Bentley had taken a personal dislike to Price and wanted her out of intelligence work for that reason.

In Bentley's account, she finally persuaded Earl Browder to her way of thinking. The decrypted Venona messages in fact confirm that in mid-1944 Browder told the KGB he was withdrawing Price from the underground and assigning her to political work, and the KGB finally acquiesced. Price became director of the Legislative and Educational Department of the Communist-dominated United Office and Professional Workers of America, a small CIO union, in 1945. In 1946 she moved to North Carolina to serve as secretary-treasurer of the North Carolina Committee of the Southern Conference for Human Welfare and ran for governor on the Progressive party ticket in 1948. Both of those organizations had numerous hidden Communists in their top leadership.

Although the Soviets found the information from Lippmann's files of interest, scavenging was not Price's most important work for them. Price acted as liaison with Maurice Halperin, one of the most productive agents in the Golos-Bentley networks, and assisted in recruiting one of their most highly placed sources, Duncan Lee.

Maurice Halperin: The Scholar Spy

Like almost everyone in the Golos-Bentley apparatus, Halperin came to Soviet espionage through the CPUSA. In the 1930s he was a Latin American specialist at the University of Oklahoma and at some point secretly joined the Communist party. Nathaniel Weyl and his wife knew him as a party member in 1936–1937 when Sylvia Weyl became organizational secretary of the Texas-Oklahoma district of the CPUSA.[11]

Although he kept his party membership secret, Halperin was a highly visible champion of far-left political causes. In 1940, with Communists subject to public opprobrium over the Nazi-Soviet Pact, this activism got him into trouble at the University of Oklahoma. Although he vigorously (and falsely) denied CPUSA membership, the Oklahoma legislature pushed for his dismissal. The university's president, however, believed Halperin and arranged a soft landing for him: a fully paid sabbatical, followed by Halperin's resigning rather than being fired. Almost immediately, in the late summer of 1941, a new federal agency, the Office of the Coordinator of Information, offered Halperin a position in its research section. This agency, renamed the Office of Strategic Services, became the U.S. government's chief intelligence arm in World War II, and Maurice Halperin became head of the Latin American division of its research and analysis section.

Halperin's party membership was secret, and he now worked for a sensitive government agency, so he did not approach the open CPUSA organization in Washington. According to Bentley, he made contact with the party through Bruce Minton, an editor of the party's literary intellectual journal, *New Masses*. Minton, recognizing his potential, notified Jacob Golos. Golos arranged for Bentley to contact Halperin at the Washington residence of his friend and fellow Latin American specialist, Willard Park, who worked for another federal agency, the Office of the Co-ordinator of Inter-American Affairs. Park, although not a CPUSA member, was a sympathizer. Initially, Bentley presented herself as a covert party contact (rather than an espionage link) and, using Mary Price's apartment as a meeting place, collected dues from Halperin and donations from Park. But she soon pressed them to deliver documents and information. She said that Park's material was of low quality, and eventually he ceased providing information. Halperin, however, was a fountain of material. Initially he delivered information to Mary Price, who passed it on to Bentley, although on occasion he handed his material directly to Bentley. Deciphered KGB messages confirm Bentley's account of Halperin's productivity as a spy: Halperin "reports," Halperin "has handed over material," "according to the information of" Halperin, Halperin "handed over . . . telegrams," Halperin "handed over a copy of an 'Izba' [OSS] document," "according to information sent to the 'Bank' [U.S. State Department] . . . and received by us from" Halperin, and so on.[12]

Halperin was particularly assiduous in getting copies of sensitive

U.S. diplomatic dispatches that were furnished to the OSS. Bentley rarely read them, and later she could tell the FBI only that there were a lot of them. The twenty-two Venona messages about Halperin's espionage alerted Moscow to the subjects dealt with in the stolen documents that the CPUSA was sending by diplomatic pouch. Halperin handed to the Soviets U.S. diplomatic cables regarding Turkey's policies toward Romania, State Department instructions to the U.S. ambassador in Spain, U.S. embassy reports about Morocco, reports from Ambassador John Winant in London about the internal stance of the Polish government-in-exile toward negotiations with Stalin, reports on the U.S. government relationship with the many competing French groups and personalities in exile, reports of peace feelers from dissident Germans being passed on by the Vatican, U.S. perceptions of Tito's activities in Yugoslavia, and discussions between the Greek government and the United States regarding Soviet ambitions in the Balkans.[13]

Nor did Halperin confine his work on behalf of the Soviets to collecting information. A number of the OSS reports written under his supervision were distorted to reflect Communist views. One Halperin OSS report depicted the Movimiento Nacionalista Revolucionario, which took power in Bolivia in 1943, as dangerous and pro-Nazi. Another described exiled Trotskyists and European anti-Stalinist Socialists in Mexico as pro-Hitler and linked the Socialist Workers party, the chief Trotskyist organization in the United States, to the Gestapo. In pursuit of a claim that a Roman Catholic political movement in Mexico was pro-Nazi, Halperin had OSS agents intercept and read mail between Mexican Catholic clergy and leading bishops and cardinals in the United States in hopes of finding evidence that the American church was aiding a pro-Nazi movement. All of these claims were false but fully in accord with CPUSA and Soviet stances.[14]

Halperin stayed with the OSS until it dissolved in 1945, but he was able to transfer to the State Department and continue to work on Latin American questions. By 1946, however, as American-Soviet tensions rose, and probably warned by the KGB of Bentley's defection to the FBI, he concluded that his days were numbered, and resigned. When the FBI interviewed Halperin in 1947, he emphatically denied that he was a Communist, that he had ever met Elizabeth Bentley, and that he had had any contact with Soviet intelligence. Many years later Halperin contradicted his FBI statement, telling a biographer that on the recommendation of an unnamed relative of Bruce Minton, he had met with

Bentley on several occasions, including at his residence. But, he insisted, she was simply a research assistant to Earl Browder who was interested in Latin America, and their conversations were innocent.[15]

Bentley's statements about Halperin became public in 1948, but press attention centered on others, and in the elite academic world in which Halperin moved, Bentley was widely dismissed as a fantasist. By 1953 Halperin was head of the Latin American regional studies program at Boston University. In that year the Senate Internal Security Subcommittee called him to testify. He promptly refused, citing his Fifth Amendment rights. When called to appear before a Boston University committee he once again refused to answer questions. The academic leadership at the university, however, did not want to press the matter and worked out a compromise whereby Halperin told the committee he was not a member of the CPUSA and the committee mildly criticized him for not being more forthcoming, but he kept his job and his position as head of the Latin American studies program.

The issue received more attention when Attorney General Herbert Brownell made public a 1945 FBI report specifically naming Halperin as a Soviet spy. University authorities privately told Halperin that its committee would like to discuss the matter with him once more. Halperin did not wait; he and his family left abruptly for Mexico. Once there, he refused a university offer to pay his way back to Boston to talk over his status. He was then discharged, not for taking the Fifth but for abandoning his job. He remained in Mexico until 1958 and then, fearing he might be deported to the United States, moved to Moscow. There the Soviets gave him a position with their leading scholarly institution, the Academy of Sciences. By 1962, disillusioned with Soviet communism, he moved to Cuba in hopes that the Castro variety might come closer to his ideals. He worked for the government Central Planning Commission and taught at the University of Havana.

By 1967, soured on Castroist communism as well, he moved yet again, to Canada to teach at Simon Fraser University in British Columbia. In his later years he wrote critically of both Soviet and Castroist communism. Don Kirschner, a colleague of Halperin's at Simon Fraser, described him as having become a "New Deal liberal" who was "immovably hostile to any variant of socialism." Halperin continued, however, to deny that he had ever cooperated with Soviet intelligence. After his death Kirschner published *Cold War Exile: The Unclosed Case of Maurice Halperin,* which appeared before the Venona decryptions became available. Kirschner wrote that his study had been "a distressing exercise" because, as he marshaled the evidence about Bentley's statements and Halperin's life, he had concluded, "In the essentials of the story, I believe the lady."[16] Venona shows that his judgment was correct.

Duncan Lee: The Ivy League WASP Spy

Duncan Chaplin Lee was descended from the Lees of Virginia. His father was an Episcopal priest and rector for many years at Chatham Hall, an elite girls' school in Virginia. Duncan attended the equally prestigious St. Alban's preparatory school in Washington, went to Yale, played football, and was graduated first in his class in 1935. He then went to Oxford as a Rhodes scholar, returned to Yale to get a law degree, and in 1939 joined the prominent Wall Street law firm Donovan, Leisure, Newton and Lumbard. In 1942 he accepted a commission in the Office of Strategic Services, an agency whose upper echelons included many Yale alumni who shared Lee's high-establishment background, a fact that inspired a witticism from the regular military that OSS stood for "Oh So Social."

Initially Lee served as an aide and adviser to Gen. William Donovan, head of the OSS and the senior partner of Lee's law firm. Later Lee took an OSS field assignment in China. (Lee's parents had served many years in China as missionaries, and he had lived there until he was twelve.) Most OSS officials held Army rank, and by the time the war ended he had become a lieutenant colonel.

Lee, however, was a secret Communist. It is not known when he became one, although mostly likely it was at Oxford. There he met and married Ishbel Gibb, whose hard-left sympathies were unconcealed. Oxford possessed a highly active Communist student group in the mid-1930s, and it may or may not be a coincidence that no fewer than four young Americans who attended Oxford in the mid-1930s (a time when Americans at Oxford were rare) had compromising relationships with Soviet intelligence: Duncan Lee, Peter Rhodes, Donald Wheeler, and Carl Marzani.

In 1940, just as Lee was completing his final year at Yale Law School, a neighbor notified the FBI that the Lees were Communists, citing the accumulation of party literature in their residence and their political statements. At the time, anxious citizens were deluging the FBI with reports on suspected Nazi and Communist fifth columnists, and the New Haven FBI office simply filed a brief report with the New York office, which in turn filed the statement away: the politics of a newly minted lawyer were not of interest to the FBI. Once established in New York, Duncan Lee worked during the day for various Wall Street clients. On his own time, however, he volunteered his services to CPUSA causes. By the end of 1941 he was the legal adviser to Russian War Relief, and early in 1942 he was on the executive board of the China Aid Council. The council, which directed assistance to Chinese organizations aligned with the Chinese Communist party, was headed by Mildred Price, Mary Price's sister and an ardent secret Communist.[17]

Bentley explained that Mary Price had met Lee through his association with her sister and, having learned that General Donovan had asked him to join the OSS, brought this to Golos's attention. Golos directed Price to develop Lee as a source. She did so, but according to Bentley the information Price passed on from Lee was limited in both quality and quantity. Hoping for more, Golos had Bentley meet Lee in Washington. Lee, she discovered, was willing to help but very cautious. She told the FBI, "After my initial meeting with Lee, he began to supply me with O.S.S. information of a varied nature. These data were always given by him orally, and he would never furnish any thing in writing, nor would he allow me to make notes of the information he gave me." All the time she dealt with him he remained "extremely apprehensive about the possibility of being under FBI surveillance."[18]

Bentley recalled that Lee furnished much information about OSS operations in Europe that might adversely affect Soviet interests and identified OSS sources in foreign countries. In her November 1945 FBI deposition she gave as an example Lee's "mentioning O.S.S. agents being parachuted into Hungary and Yugoslavia and peace maneuvering going on between the satellite Axis nations through the medium of O.S.S. representatives."[19] The FBI attached no special significance to this remark, and neither did Bentley. What neither Bentley nor the FBI knew was that she had referred to a highly secret OSS project, the Sparrow mission, designed to persuade the Hungarian government to surrender to the Allies in the fall of 1944 and collapse the entire Nazi position in the Balkans.[20]

When Bentley's statements became public in 1948, many OSS veterans refused to believe that one of their leading officers, one who so embodied the OSS's Ivy League WASP image, could have betrayed them. Similarly, much of the press treated Bentley's charges about Duncan Lee as preposterous on the face of it. Lee did not resort to the Fifth Amendment when called to testify and firmly denied the charges. He was not pressed, however, about his background or the circumstances of his relationship with Bentley. This omission helped to maintain the facade of his innocence because the story he had told the FBI when it interviewed him was not one that inspired belief. Lee admitted meeting with Bentley on a number of occasions over a period of two years, both in Washington and during trips to New York. But, he insisted, he had known Bentley only as "Helen." As for Golos, Lee admitted he had met Helen's friend "John," and the description matched that of Jacob Golos. He said he never knew Helen's last name and knew nothing of her activities. Helen, said Lee, was simply a social acquaintance he had met through his friend Mary Price. That a highly placed OSS officer engaged in intelligence work in wartime would over two years meet privately with someone and never learn that person's full name or occupation strains credibility. Lee also claimed that he was a New Deal liberal. He did not disclose, and the FBI at the time did not know, that when the Lees married in the 1930s they honeymooned in Moscow.[21] As the public controversy over domestic communism and Soviet espionage grew in the early 1950s, Duncan Lee left the United States. Although he returned for periods, he largely lived abroad for the rest of his life.[22]

Decoded KGB cables show Lee reporting to the Soviets about British and American diplomatic strategy for negotiating with Stalin over the fate of postwar Poland, American diplomatic activities in Turkey and Romania, and OSS operations in China and France. Venona confirms Bentley's comment about Lee's caution. In May 1943 the New York KGB office informed Moscow that "we discussed with Koch [Lee] the question of his removing documents for photographing. Koch said that in some cases he agrees to do this, but as a rule he considers it inexpedient."[23] In discussing Lee's espionage, Bentley wrote:

> When we discovered he had access to the [OSS] security files, we had asked him to bring us information that might be of value. Thereupon, he had given me a slip of paper on which he had written down the names of people that the O.S.S. considered dangerous risks, divided into three categories—"known Soviet agents," "known Communists," and "Communist sympathizers." In the first group were three names—none of whom I knew; in the second was an active member of the Perlo

group, and in the third, Maurice Halperin. We had quite promptly alerted Maurice and told him to be careful; the other since he was more reckless, we had "put on ice" and told to abstain from any activities for a six-month period.[24]

Three Venona messages confirm the essential elements of this passage unambiguously. A September 15, 1944, New York KGB message states:

> According to Koch's [Lee's] advice, a list of "reds" has been compiled by the Security Division of Izba [OSS]. The list contains 4 surnames of persons who are supplying information to the Russians. . . .
>   The list is divided into two categories: 1. Open Fellowcountrymen [Communists] (among them "Izra" [Donald Wheeler]) and 2. Sympathizers, left-wing liberals etc. (among them "Hare" [Halperin]). Koch is trying to get the list.[25]

Lee did get the list, and it constituted the text of a follow-up message of September 22.[26]

These messages confirm Bentley's statement that Lee supplied an OSS security list containing three elements: names of persons OSS security had identified as Soviet sources, names of Communists serving in the OSS, and names of Soviet sympathizers. The only difference from Bentley's FBI statement, made several years after the event in question, is that the Venona messages show the names of four suspected Soviet sources on the list, whereas she had remembered it as containing only three, and that she characterized the list as having three categories, whereas the messages refer to two categories and a third element, the designation of four persons as Soviet sources.

Bentley also wrote that the list had named Maurice Halperin. Venona confirms this. Bentley said the list contained the name of a source who was part of the Perlo group (discussed in chapter 5). Venona confirms that too, as Donald Wheeler was part of that network. A third Venona message, from the KGB headquarters in Moscow, further corroborates Bentley's account. This message of September 20, in reply to the New York message of September 15 about Lee's list, advises the New York KGB to "tell 'Myrna' [Bentley] to cease liaison with 'Izra' [Wheeler] and 'Hare' [Halperin]. In future liaison may be re-established only with our permission."[27] Bentley's version largely conforms to this one, stating that Wheeler was placed on inactive status for six months but that Halperin was simply warned to be careful.

In late 1944 the OSS sent Lee to China to supervise an attempt to penetrate Japan via Japanese-occupied China and Korea. A decoded Venona message shows that Bentley made arrangements with Lee so that Soviet agents in China could approach him and he could continue his service to the Soviet cause.

Julius Joseph: From Political Subversion to Espionage

Julius Joseph was yet another of Bentley's sources within the OSS. In 1938 he received a master's degree in economics and public administration from the University of Michigan, and in 1940 he got a job with the government's National Resources Planning Board. From there he went in 1941 to the Federal Security Agency (a welfare agency) and the Social Security Board, in 1942 to the Office of Emergency Management (war industries mobilization), and in 1943 to the Labor War Manpower Commission, where he became a senior administrative officer. He was also a not-too-secret Communist, writing for the *Daily Worker* in 1936, signing New York electoral petitions for the CPUSA in 1940, and speaking at a forum of the Communist-aligned *Science and Society* in 1942.[28]

In 1942 Joseph contacted the CPUSA with government information he thought of value. Bentley picked up material from him during the next two years, chiefly information on labor-related matters of interest to the CPUSA's labor cadre inside the CIO but not to Soviet intelligence. In May 1943, however, Joseph was drafted. At Golos's urging he applied for and got a position with the Office of Strategic Services, as did his wife, Bella: he in the Far Eastern section, she in the motion picture and publicity divisions. By 1945 Joseph was deputy chief of his section, working chiefly on Japanese intelligence. Bentley said that he supplied useful OSS information, not only on the work of the Far Eastern section but also on the Russian section of the OSS, on the basis of his discussions with colleagues in that division. Joseph shows up in two Venona cables, once in a June 1943 report on Soviet agents the New York KGB office maintained in the OSS, and once in a 1944 cable reporting information on the OSS Russian section that Joseph had learned from a pro-Soviet OSS staff member.[29]

After the OSS dissolved, Joseph went to work for the United Nations Relief and Rehabilitation Administration and then directed the New York Committee for the Arts, Sciences, and Professions, a Popular Front political advocacy group. He was later called to testify about his wartime activities by the Senate Internal Security Subcommittee, in 1953. He declined to answer key questions, taking the Fifth.[30]

Joseph's sister, Emma, was also a Communist and also worked for the OSS. Although Bentley never mentioned it to the FBI, deciphered Venona messages show that in 1944 Bentley informed the KGB that Emma Joseph was well suited for KGB work and Bentley would give her recognition procedures so that she could be contacted by the KGB when she reached Ceylon on her next OSS assignment.[31]

Cedric Belfrage: Betrayer of Two Nations

One of the more unusual sources of the Golos-Bentley network was a British intelligence officer. Cedric Belfrage was born and grew up in Great Britain, first came to America in the mid-1920s, and returned on frequent visits while pursuing a career as a writer and journalist. He secretly joined the CPUSA in 1937 and filed an intent to become an American citizen with U.S. immigration authorities, but he never completed his naturalization. After the Nazi attack on the USSR, he went to work for the British Security Coordination Office, an arm of British intelligence under the direction of William Stephenson. Stephenson's agency acted as British intelligence liaison with the American OSS and FBI.

Elizabeth Bentley told the FBI that starting in late 1942 or early 1943 Belfrage met on a number of occasions with Jacob Golos. She remembered that either Earl Browder or V. J. Jerome (a senior CPUSA official) brought Belfrage to Golos. Bentley recalled Belfrage's turning over to Golos a variety of items that came to him at the British Security Coordination Office, both material on British concerns and American material that had been given to the British. She also said that after Golos died, the KGB in 1944 asked her to establish contact with Belfrage. Bentley, however, had replied that she had not dealt with him directly, being aware of his activities only through Golos, and that Belfrage would be wary of her. At the direction of the KGB, she contacted Browder because Belfrage had come to Golos through the CPUSA and his material was shared with Browder himself. But Browder refused to put Bentley in touch with Belfrage, stating that Belfrage should be kept out of further espionage. Later, at KGB insistence, she found out where Belfrage was living but did not make contact with him and did not know if the KGB reestablished contact.[32]

When the war ended Belfrage took a position with the Allied occupation government in Germany. He returned to the United States as a founder of the *National Guardian,* which first appeared in 1948 and for a number of years was the most influential journal on the Popular Front left.

In 1947 the FBI asked Belfrage about Bentley's statements. Belfrage told the bureau that in 1942 he had met with Earl Browder and a man whose name he did not know but who, he admitted, looked a great deal like the FBI's photograph of Jacob Golos. He also said that in 1943 he had met with V. J. Jerome eight or nine times. As to the purposes of these meetings, Belfrage explained that he met with Jerome "with a view to finding out what I could about Communist and Russian politics." Belfrage reported that in order to induce Jerome to provide him with information, he answered Jerome's questions about British policy toward the Soviet Union while the latter took notes and "I supplied him with information about Scotland Yard surveillances and also with some documents relative to the Vichy Government in France, which were of a highly confidential nature with respect to their origin but which contained information of no value whatever." Belfrage did not know it, but his statement about giving Jerome material on Scotland Yard surveillance matched closely with a Bentley statement that among the documents Belfrage had handed over was a British security service manual on procedures and techniques for the proper running of agents. He also insisted that he was not and never had been a Communist.[33]

The FBI did not find Belfrage's statement very credible. Belfrage did not provide any explanation about why he would be attempting to learn about Russian politics from Jerome, whose longtime area of responsibility in the CPUSA was supervising American intellectuals allied with the party, and Belfrage did not relate anything of interest that he learned from Jerome. He also admitted that his contact with Jerome and his turning over of British Security Coordination documents was not authorized by his superiors, that he never told his superiors what he had done, and that he might be subject to prosecution under British law.

The decrypted Venona cables show that the bureau's skepticism was well founded.[34] Belfrage lied. The cables show Belfrage giving the KGB an OSS report that British intelligence had received on the anti-Communist Yugoslav resistance forces of Gen. Draza Mihailovic, then in competition with the Communist resistance led by Josip Tito; reporting on the contacts and activities of British Security Coordination's own Yugoslav specialist; telling the Soviets what his superior, William Stephenson, had said about British policy on a second front after a meeting with Prime Minister Churchill; describing the sometimes tense relationship between British Security Coordination and the FBI over the former's U.S. activities; offering to establish covert contact with the Soviets if he were assigned to permanent duty in Britain; and delivering to Golos documents he had obtained during a visit to London. The subject matter of the London documents was not described, but the New York KGB reported that it was sending them to Moscow by diplomatic pouch. The Venona cables also corroborate Bentley's story that Golos shared Belfrage's information with Browder. One Venona message noted Golos's irritation over Belfrage's insistence on a personal meeting with Browder.

The FBI informed U.S. immigration authorities of its view that Belfrage had had a compromising relationship with Soviet intelligence. The Immigration and Naturalization Service then moved to deport Belfrage to Great Britain. He fought the action in court and in public, proclaiming his innocence and depicting the deportation order as political persecution. In 1955, however, he accepted voluntary deportation and returned to England. He later published two books, *The Frightened Giant: My Unfinished Affair with America* and *The American Inquisition, 1945–1960,* describing American concern about Soviet espionage as baseless paranoia.[35]

Bentley's Other Singleton Agents

Bentley told the FBI of several other individual espionage contacts who reported to her. These included Helen Tenney of the OSS and Michael Greenberg, a China specialist who worked for the Board of Economic Warfare and its successor agency, the Foreign Economic Administration, as well as Joseph Gregg and Robert T. Miller, both of the Office of the Coordinator of Inter-American Affairs.[36] This latter body was one of the hybrid wartime agencies created by the White House. Headed by Nelson Rockefeller, it supervised economic warfare, propaganda, and intelligence operations in Central and South America. In addition to a research staff in Washington, it had representatives working out of various American embassies.

In 1942 Grace Granich, a CPUSA and Comintern veteran, called Golos's attention to Helen Tenney, a secret Communist who worked for Short Wave Research, a firm on contract for the Office of War Information to recruit people with foreign language skills. Golos recruited Tenney as a source, but Short Wave Research soon disbanded. Golos then encouraged her to seek a job with OSS headquarters in Washington. Tenney had excellent Spanish language skills and in late 1942 got a job in the Spanish section of the OSS. Bentley arranged for Tenney to sublet the Washington apartment of Mary Price, who was then returning to New York. Wartime Washington suffered from an acute housing shortage, and this arrangement made it easier for Tenney to take a Washington job with the OSS—and kept the apartment available for use as an espionage safe-house by the Golos-Bentley network. (When interviewed by the FBI, Price denied that Bentley had any role in Tenney's getting her apartment, claiming that Tenney had simply been the first person to answer a newspaper ad.) In Venona, Tenney appears under the cover name Muse. A 1943 OSS report on Spain, marked secret, found in the Moscow archives of the Communist International may be among the fruits of Tenney's espionage. The report was an appraisal of the strength of the Communist party in Catalonia.[37]

After the FBI became convinced of Bentley's bona fides and began to follow up on the various Soviet sources she had named, the bureau found Tenney ensconced in the State Department. After the OSS disbanded, Tenney was able to move with one of its surviving offices to a newly created State Department research section assigned to analyze American intelligence on the Soviet Union. The FBI quietly had her fired, and the State Department revoked her passport. Tenney realized that she was under suspicion and suffered a partial nervous collapse. Friends had her hospitalized briefly in January 1947 when she started babbling about Soviet spies and being under FBI surveillance. This was not paranoia, as her worried friends thought: she really was under FBI surveillance and she really was a Soviet spy.[38]

The FBI thought that perhaps she would break if Bentley, then cooperating with the bureau, approached her. Bentley did so in early February 1947. Tenney, clearly unaware that Bentley had defected, said that she had been out of touch with the Soviets for some time. The isolation from her Soviet contact, along with her sense that the FBI was closing in, had produced a sense of abandonment, and she hoped that Bentley was reestablishing Soviet contact. Tenney, however, did not indicate any disaffection with the Soviet cause, and the FBI dropped hopes of turning her. Later, when the bureau formally interviewed her,

Tenney denied having done any work for the Soviets. Apparently unaware that their meeting just a few months earlier had been observed by FBI agents, she admitted knowing Bentley, but under another name and only during 1942 and 1943.[39]

Tenney's loss of her KGB liaison in 1946 is evidence that the Soviets, realizing that Bentley's networks had been compromised, had cut off contact with her sources. In most cases Soviet intelligence appeared to have succeeded in warning its sources of what was happening, but for some reason the KGB was unable to brief Tenney.

Michael Greenberg had become a secret Communist while a student at Cambridge University in the 1930s. Born in Britain, he immigrated to the United States in 1939 and became editor of *Pacific Affairs,* a prestigious journal published by the Institute of Pacific Relations. His tenure, however, caused one trustee of the institute to complain that Greenberg had imposed a pro-Communist slant on the journal's articles. In 1942 he became a China specialist for the Board of Economic Warfare and an assistant to that agency's de facto head, Lauchlin Currie. (Currie's links to Soviet intelligence are discussed in chapter 5.) Bentley stated that she never met directly with Greenberg but received his information via Mary and Mildred Price.[40]

Civil Service Commission security officials learned something of Greenberg's Communist background and wanted him discharged as a security risk. He appealed, and naive superiors overruled the security officials. In 1945 he won a transfer to the State Department. He resigned in 1946, however, probably after being warned that Bentley's network had been compromised. When questioned by the FBI in 1947, Greenberg agreed that he knew the Price sisters and had met with them on a number of occasions but denied passing them any information. He had no explanation for how Elizabeth Bentley had come to know of his relationship with the Price sisters. Although he had become a U.S. citizen in 1944, shortly after the FBI interview he moved back to Britain.[41]

Robert T. Miller III had visited the Soviet Union in 1934 and liked it well enough to stay in Moscow, supporting himself by becoming a part-time correspondent for an American newspaper. He also met his wife there, Jenny Levy, who worked for the English-language *Moscow News,* a pro-Soviet paper. He left Moscow in 1937 to become press agent for the Spanish Republican government. After the Spanish Civil War ended, Miller teamed up with an American veteran of the International Brigades, Jack Fahy, to found Hemispheric News Service, which concentrated on Latin American affairs. Miller served as president, Fahy as vice-president, and Jenny Levy Miller as secretary. In 1941 the firm moved to Washington and Joseph Gregg joined as its manager. Gregg had also served in the Comintern's International Brigades during the Spanish Civil War. Under the name of Export Information Bureau, their agency first became a contract research arm of the Office of the Coordinator of Inter-American Affairs and then was entirely absorbed by it. Fahy, meanwhile, was recruited by the Naval GRU as one of its spies.

Bentley said that Gregg and Miller were recruited by Golos via the CPUSA and handled as separate agents, and that neither knew that the other was in touch with the KGB.[42] Gregg, she said, was the more active, turning over to the Soviets U.S. naval intelligence, military intelligence, and FBI reports on Soviet and Communist activities in Central and South America. Gregg transferred to the State Department in late 1944, concealing on his employment form his service with the International Brigades.[43]

Miller also transferred to the State Department in 1944, obtained a position working on Soviet-American diplomatic matters, and rose to the position of assistant chief of the Division of Research and Publication. Probably warned that Bentley's defection had compromised him, he resigned in December 1946. When questioned by the FBI, Miller admitted knowing Bentley under the name Helen, acknowledged that both he and his wife met her on several occasions in New York and Washington, and allowed that he may have casually discussed confidential information with her. Miller also took the same bizarre position that Duncan Lee had, insisting that although he had met Helen/Bentley repeatedly and perhaps even discussed confidential information with her, he had never known her family name.[44]

Greenberg, Gregg, and Miller are not identified in those KGB cables that were deciphered in the Venona Project. Given, however, the high degree of corroboration of Elizabeth Bentley's testimony, her statements about these persons must be regarded as having great credibility. There are, moreover, numerous unidentified cover names in Venona that one or more of these persons might hide behind, such as Charlie (provided the KGB with government reports on China), Dodger (provided diplomatic information), Eagle, Fakir (provided diplomatic information), Harold, Hedgehog, Horus, Levi, Mirage (provided diplomatic information), Reed, Robert, Vick, Vita, and Whitefish. The information supplied in the cables was sufficient to identify these cover names as Americans who passed information to the KGB but was insufficient to identify who precisely was spying for the Soviet Union.

CHAPTER 5

FRIENDS IN HIGH PLACES

Elizabeth Bentley ran two networks of American Communist party members employed in the federal government. The Perlo group developed Soviet sources on the War Production Board, on a key Senate committee, and in the Treasury Department. The Silvermaster group established contacts not only in Treasury and the Army Air Force but in the White House itself. These were small groups of Communists who had known each other for years, socialized together, met secretly to discuss party policy and pay their party dues, helped each other get jobs and promotions in the government, and dreamed together of the day when America would attain the perfection already achieved by Russia under Stalin.

The Perlo Group

Victor Perlo was one of the original members of the Ware group of young Communist professionals that Whittaker Chambers met when he arrived in Washington in 1934. Perlo's parents were immigrants from Russia, and he attended Columbia University, gaining bachelor's and master's degrees in mathematics. After leaving Columbia he became a statistician for the National Recovery Administration and transferred to the Federal Home Loan Bank Board in 1935. In 1937 Perlo-went to the Brookings Institution for two years to hone his credentials as an economist. He reentered government employment in 1939 at the Commerce Department. In 1940 he moved to an agency that eventually became the wartime Office of Price Administration, and three years later he became a senior economist at the War Production Board. In 1945, with the wartime agencies disbanding, he transferred to the Division of Monetary Research at the Treasury Department, then headed by Frank Coe, a fellow secret Communist.

The accounts of Hope Davis and Herbert Fuchs depict Perlo as a senior member of the Communist underground in Washington in the late 1930s. Perlo is mentioned in numerous deciphered KGB cables of the Venona Project and was a central figure in Elizabeth Bentley's account of Soviet espionage in the 1940s.[1]

Bentley said that in November 1943 Earl Browder put Golos in touch with a group of Washington Communists that she later came to designate as the Perlo group. Golos met once in New York with the leading figures of the group to discuss their cooperation with his espionage apparatus. He died the same month, however, before a second meeting. Bentley at that point had not met any of its members and knew little about them.

Since Bentley had been acting as Golos's assistant and courier to many of his sources, both the KGB and Earl Browder initially welcomed her taking over much of Golos's role. Early in 1944 Browder urged her to renew Golos's attempt to approach the Perlo group and arranged a meeting, which most likely took place on Sunday, March 5.[2]

Bentley met the group at the New York apartment of John Abt, who had been the intermediary between Browder and this Washington-based group. Abt, however, was an increasingly visible labor lawyer, and both he and Browder thought it wise to withdraw him from covert activity. Bentley explained that Abt had introduced her to the group and from that point on had no contact with her espionage apparatus. In addition to Abt, she recalled that Perlo (War Production Board), Charles Kramer (Senate Subcommittee on War Mobilization), Edward Fitzgerald (War Production Board), and Harry Magdoff (War Production Board) had all traveled to New York from Washington for the meeting.

Bentley learned at this meeting that other members of the group included Donald Wheeler (Office of Strategic Services) and Allan Rosenberg (Foreign Economic Administration). Later she was told that the group included among its contacts Harold Glasser (Treasury), Sol Leshinsky (United Nations Relief and Rehabilitation Administration), and George Perazich (United Nations Relief and Rehabilitation Administration).

Three deciphered KGB cables corroborate Bentley's account. In these Venona cables of April 27, May 13, and May 30, 1944, the KGB officer Iskhak Akhmerov reported on the reorganization of the KGB system of collecting intelligence from the American Communist party after Golos's death. Golos had worked with Soviet intelligence for a very long time, at least since the mid-1930s and probably earlier, had been born and raised in Russia, and was an "Old Bolshevik" who had been part of the movement before the 1917 revolution and, if the story he told Bentley is true, even a veteran Chekist (Soviet secret policeman). His death disrupted long-established relationships and required shifting arrangements regarding who reported to whom.

These three cables are Akhmerov's initial report on the Perlo group.[3] Akhmerov stated that after Golos's death, Bentley, acting on Browder's instructions, had taken over liaison with two covert Communist groups in Washington that had reported information to the CPUSA. The messages are not completely deciphered and contain several garbled passages. But in regard to the Perlo group the messages show that Bentley established contact through John Abt. The readable sections of the April 27 KGB cable name as part of the group Charles Kramer, Victor Perlo, Charles Flato, Harold Glasser, and Edward Fitzgerald and state that several other, unnamed persons belonged as well. Flato, an official in the Board of Economic Warfare, is unusual in that he was not named by Bentley in her deposition to the FBI or in her memoir *Out of Bondage*. Bentley either forgot about him or chose for some reason not to disclose his name. The May 13 message adds this judgment: "They are reliable Fellowcountrymen [Communists], politically highly mature; they want to help with information." It also names Harry Magdoff as a participant.

That Abt's name does not occur in any readable Venona messages after those of April 27 and May 13 conforms to Bentley's account that he handed over the Perlo group and then left clandestine work. Of the ten persons she named as members of the Perlo group (Abt, Perlo, Kramer, Fitzgerald, Magdoff, Wheeler, Glasser, Rosenberg, Leshinsky, and Perazich), the first seven come up in the three deciphered Venona messages discussed here as well as in numerous others.[4]

An eighth, Allan Rosenberg, appears in a partly deciphered December 1944 KGB message noting the acquisition of a State Department report and promising that a full translation would be forwarded to Moscow by courier. Rosenberg is named in clear text, apparently as the source of the report. Rosenberg's close relationship with others in the Perlo group went back to the early days of the Communist underground in Washington. When John Abt became chief attorney for the Civil Liberties Subcommittee of the Senate Education and Labor Committee in 1935, he saw to it that his staff included several of his fellow secret Communists—Rosenberg, Kramer, and Flato. Rosenberg later joined the legal staff of the National Labor Relations Board, where Herbert Fuchs knew him as one of the members of his secret Communist caucus. When a congressional committee questioned Rosenberg about these matters, he refused to answer.[5]

The April Venona message on the Perlo group also stated that aside from those specifically named, two or three other persons were part of the group. Bentley's two remaining names, Leshinsky and Perazich, were probably among them. The first Akhmerov report (April 27) on the Perlo group has all of the names in clear text because, obviously, cover names had not yet been assigned, except in the case of Glasser, who had been designated Ruble during earlier work with Soviet intelligence. By Akhmerov's second and third reports, cover names had been assigned to most and were easily identified: Kramer was Plumb; Fitzgerald was Ted; Magdoff was Kant; Perlo was Raider; and Wheeler was Izra.

But in Akhmerov's reports of May 13 and 30, one unidentified cover name, Storm, is connected to the Perlo group in an unspecified fashion. Storm is unlikely to have been Rosenberg, whose name occurred in later Venona messages in the clear, or Abt, because his name occurs in the clear in the May 13 message also mentioning Storm. Possibly Storm was Flato, but the cable of May 30 includes a partially decrypted sentence with a partially deciphered name, beginning "Char . . ." The text at that point describes Char . . . as a very close friend of another Soviet agent, Jane Foster, who in her autobiography calls Charles Flato one of her closest friends of that period.[6] If "Char . . ." was Charles Flato, then Storm was not Flato. Leshinsky and Perazich are obvious candidates for Storm, but there are other possibilities as well. The deciphered Venona messages show that Bentley did not remember all the Soviet sources with whom she had had contact.

Another possibility for Storm is Josef Peters. When Peters headed the CPUSA's underground in the mid-1930s, he cooperated with both the GRU and the KGB and knew the KGB officer Iskhak Akhmerov. Akhmerov's cables to the KGB in 1938 used Storm as Peters's cover name.[7] Usually cover names for active sources were changed from time to time, but the cover names of KGB officers changed only at great intervals. Peters was not a source but a CPUSA staff officer, and it is therefore possible that his cover name was not changed. Akhmerov is also the author of both of the 1944 messages that used the cover name Storm.

Peters was removed as head of the CPUSA secret apparatus after Chambers's defection in 1938, but he continued to work on the CPUSA's Central Committee staff on what a 1947 Soviet Communist party personnel report guardedly called "special assignments" and may have continued to act as a liaison with some of the party underground groups in Washington not then connected with Soviet intelligence.[8] An examination of the Comintern's records turned up two 1943 messages from the GRU (Soviet military intelligence) referring to a GRU officer in Washington as having come across "a group of workers singled out by the American Comparty CC [Central Committee] for informational work and headed by the CC worker 'Peter.' " Though usually called "Peters" in the United States, in Comintern records Peters's name is often rendered as "Peter."[9] "Informational work" was GRU jargon for clandestine intelligence activity. The GRU asked the Comintern whether its officer had stumbled on a Comintern apparatus. The messages have the look of the GRU's appraising a covert CPUSA group for possible takeover into its own espionage work.

Another of the GRU messages reported that "certain workers in that group are unhappy with 'Peter,' since he pays almost no attention to informational work and takes no interest in the information received."[10] This complaint sounds remarkably close to that reported by Akhmerov in April 1944 about the Perlo group. He told Moscow that Bentley reported that during her first meeting with the Perlo group "they told her that this group was neglected and that nobody was interested in them."[11] Mention of Storm appears in deciphered KGB cables about the Perlo group only in Akhmerov's two May 1944 reports on the group's background as the KGB prepared to take it over. Storm never occurs later as a source. The passages in which Storm is named are sufficiently garbled that a firm judgment cannot be made; but it is possible that Storm was Peters and the references to Storm are references to his earlier relationship with the group before its absorption by Bentley's KGB-connected apparatus.[12]

Akhmerov said something else in his April 27 report to the KGB in Moscow in regard to the group: "For more than a year Maksim [Zubilin] and I tried to get in touch with Perlo and Flato. For some reason Helmsman [Browder] did not come to the meeting and has just decided to put Clever Girl [Bentley] in touch with the whole group. If we work with this group, it will be necessary to remove her."[13] And remove her they did. Bentley first met with the Perlo group in March 1944. By the end of the year, on Soviet orders, she had cut all ties to it. Bentley reported constant pressure by her Soviet contacts during 1944, particularly by Akhmerov, to gain direct control not only of the Perlo group but of all of the sources that Golos had built up and she had taken over.

Bentley essentially functioned as a transitional figure. She took a group that had reported to the CPUSA directly and to Soviet intelligence only through intermediaries (Browder and Golos) and transformed it into one that reported directly to Soviet intelligence, initially through her. The KGB clearly intended to remove her as intermediary as soon as it was practical to do so. On orders from her KGB contacts Bentley prepared biographies of those sources she knew best, a preliminary step for reducing the need to keep her involved. Also as part of the KGB vetting process, in September 1944 General Fitin of the KGB asked Dimitrov of the Comintern to "provide any information at your disposal on the following members of the Compary of America. 1. Charles . . . Flato, in 1943 worked at the US Office of Economic Warfare. 2. Donald Wheeler . . . , works in the Office of Strategic Services. 3. Kramer, works in a government institution in ˌWashington. 4. Edward Fitzgerald, works on the WPB. 5. Magdoff, works on the WPB. 6. Harold Glas[s]er, currently on assignment abroad. 7. P[e]rlo, works on the WPB."[14]

The KGB was satisfied with the checking of the Perlo network, and it proceeded to phase Bentley out. In December 1944 she met covertly with Anatoly Gromov, the chief of the KGB Washington office and Zubilin's successor as head of KGB operations in the United States. In her memoir Bentley reconstructed the conversation: "[Gromov:] We have at last decided what to do about all the contacts that Golos handled. You cannot, obviously, continue to handle them; the set-up is too full of holes and therefore too dangerous. I'm afraid our friend Golos was not too cautious a man, and there is the risk that you, because of your connection with him, may endanger the apparatus. You will therefore turn them over to us; we will look into their backgrounds thoroughly and decide which ones we will keep."[15] He ordered Bentley to inform her sources of the pending change and to confine her activity to the U.S. Service and Shipping Corporation. Gromov also suggested that later she would be removed from that task as well and placed on inactive status for a period.

Bentley's memory of the KGB's concern that Golos's practices did not meet its increasingly professional security standards is corroborated by Venona. In October 1944 a deciphered KGB message reports that Gregory Silvermaster, head of another and larger network managed by Golos and Bentley, was resisting KGB advice that the group be broken into smaller units and that the KGB establish direct liaison with key agents. Akhmerov complained to Moscow that Silvermaster's reluctance unfortunately showed that Golos's "education is making itself felt."[16]

The logic of the KGB's position was clear. Bentley simply was not attuned to the rules of espionage tradecraft it was implementing. Golos, Bentley, and their agents moved back and forth between CPUSA political activities and Soviet espionage, readily socialized with one another, and only barely disguised their political attitudes. In the 1930s and early 1940s, with government policy-makers largely oblivious to Soviet espionage and the FBI's then-limited resources focused elsewhere, these amateurish practices had had few serious consequences. But the KGB feared that this era was ending and a higher professional standard of tradecraft was needed.

The KGB, however, did not handle Bentley well in this transition. Bentley had been in love with Jacob Golos and had sustained a great loss when he died in late 1943. She had then thrown herself into continuing his work. But by the end of 1944 the KGB had taken that away. In 1945 it further urged her to give up the U.S. Service and Shipping Corporation, the only thing she had left of her life with Golos. Her morale hit rock bottom. By the late summer of 1945 she was convinced that the FBI was closing in. It was not, but her fear of arrest and her disillusionment led her to defect. The KGB had pushed Bentley out because it wanted a more secure system. What it got by doing so was the exposure and neutralization of the very networks it was trying to protect.

The Perlo Group's Espionage

The extent of the espionage performed by the spies of the Perlo group is not clear. Bentley collected documents and reports from her sources but usually did not read them, and kept no notes or copies; she provided to the FBI only general descriptions and a few specifics that stuck in her memory. She told the FBI that she had met with Perlo and other members of his group at Mary Price's apartment, where they handed over documents. She remembered memoranda on aircraft production (from Perlo), OSS intelligence summaries and OSS copies of State Department cables (from Wheeler), and plans for the occupation of Germany (from Rosenberg). She reported that Leshinsky, although a member of the group, never handed over documents during her tenure. She said that, through Perlo, Perazich supplied some information on Yugoslavia and that she thought the KGB had made arrangements to contact him when he traveled to that country for the United Nations Relief and Rehabilitation Administration.

The decrypted Venona cables provide more definite information, but they are only brief summaries of much more voluminous information sent by courier. In any case, the Venona Project decrypted only a portion of all KGB traffic from the United States to Moscow. The readable Venona messages on the Perlo group corroborate Bentley's recollection of the types of information that Perlo group sources provided. Wheeler of the OSS, for example, passed information to the Soviets regarding the organization and policies of the British intelligence services, with which the OSS had a close relationship and which the Soviets regarded at that time as a more serious opponent than American intelligence. Perlo, an economist with the aircraft production division of the War Production Board, supplied data on aircraft production and U.S. shipments to various fronts and reports about development difficulties for a jet engine for America's first and very secret jet fighter, as well as information on clashes between U.S. military and civilian policy-makers over allocation of economic resources.

Charles Kramer: The Spy as Congressional Aide

A number of members of the CPUSA underground in the 1930s worked at one time or another for a congressional committee. Marion Bachrach, one of the original Ware group members (and John Abt's sister), was the chief aide to one member of Congress, Rep. John Bernard, a Farmer-Labor party member elected from Minnesota in 1936 for a single term. Bernard was unusual in that he himself was secretly a Communist.[17] Charles Kramer, however, was more than an underground Communist. He was a Soviet spy. He also worked for four congressional committees in his career, the Senate Civil Liberties Subcommittee in the 1930s, the Senate Subcommittee on War Mobilization and the Senate Subcommittee on Wartime Health and Education during the war, and the Senate Labor and Public Welfare committee after the war. His congressional employment was interspersed with work in the executive branch, including the Agricultural Adjustment Administration, the National Labor Relations Board, and the Office of Price Administration (OPA).

Fellow members of the CPUSA underground assisted him in obtaining all his jobs. Abt hired Kramer for the Civil Liberties Subcommittee, Nathan Witt (another Ware group veteran) helped him get the job with the NLRB, and at the OPA Victor Perlo signed his job performance rating and was listed as an employment reference. During this period Kramer publicly posed as a committed liberal Democratic political activist, and he took time off in 1944 to work for the Democratic National Committee and in 1946 to assist the reelection campaign of California Democratic representative Ellis Patterson.[18] After Kramer's exposure by Bentley, he abandoned the Democratic party to work for the Progressive party and was far more open about his radical loyalties, although he never admitted CPUSA membership.

Venona cables show Kramer, from his position as a professional staff member of the Senate Subcommittee on War Mobilization, providing information about the dispute among American policy-makers concerning what the U.S. attitude should be toward Charles de Gaulle's Free French movement and an internal U.S. government investigation of German corporate links to American companies. After Roosevelt's death, the cables show that Kramer passed on to the KGB insider political information from the Democratic National Committee about

President Truman's likely changes in State Department leadership and appraisals of Truman by U.S. senators with whom Kramer had contact.

Harold Glasser: The Discreet Stalinist

Although not in the top tier of American government, Harold Glasser was nonetheless a very important bureaucrat. He had joined the Treasury Department in 1936 as an economist and had risen to the position of assistant director of the Division of Monetary Research by late 1938. The Treasury and the State Department sent Glasser to Ecuador in 1940 to act as the chief American economic adviser to its government. He served there until 1942. After that he held increasingly high-level wartime positions: vice-chairman of the War Production Board, economic adviser to American forces in North Africa, U.S. Treasury representative to the United Nations Relief and Rehabilitation Administration, and Treasury representative to the Allied High Commission in Italy. Immediately after the war he became economic adviser to the American delegation at the Council of Foreign Ministers meeting in Moscow in 1947 and economic adviser to the Treasury secretary at the board of governors meeting of the World Bank. When he resigned in December 1947 Glasser was serving as assistant director of Treasury's Office of International Finance.

When Glasser left government service, Treasury secretary John Snyder wrote a glowing letter of recommendation, assuring Glasser's prospective employers that he "has no hidden facets to his personal qualities."[19] Snyder could not have been more mistaken. Throughout Glasser's distinguished career with the U.S. government he was an underground Communist and a Soviet source.

A decrypted 1944 Venona message from the New York KGB station stated that "Harold Glasser is an old fellow countryman," the latter the standard KGB term for a Communist party member.[20] But exactly how old a Communist is not clear. When questioned by the FBI in 1947, Glasser would admit only to having had a casual curiosity about communism in the early 1930s. When asked later about these matters under oath, he declined to answer.[21]

Glasser shows up as a trusted member of the CPUSA underground in 1937. In that year Whittaker Chambers's CPUSA-GRU network had as one of its sources Harry Dexter White, then assistant director of the

Division of Monetary Research in the Treasury Department. Chambers, however, thought that White was providing less material than he expected both in quality and in quantity. Chambers recalled that his GRU controller, Boris Bykov, "fumed" that White should supply more. But White was not a CPUSA member, only a sympathizer. Though he was willing to cooperate with Soviet espionage, he did so on his own terms and did not respond to orders as committed CPUSA members did. Chambers discussed the problem with Josef Peters, and Peters transferred to Chambers's network Harold Glasser, who was a member of the party's covert organization but had not been linked to Soviet intelligence. Chambers had Glasser, then in his second year as an economist at Treasury, check on the sort of material to which White had access. Glasser reported that, as far as he could ascertain, White was providing everything of importance. This task done, Chambers cut off his contact with Glasser and after 1937 knew nothing more of his activities.[22]

That Glasser continued to work for Soviet intelligence is clear from a Moscow document obtained by the historian Allen Weinstein: an April 1945 memo from Pavel Fitin, head of KGB foreign intelligence, to Vsevolod Merkulov, then head of the overall KGB organization. Fitin asked for equitable treatment in terms of awards for a longtime KGB agent, Ruble. The Venona decryptions indicate that Ruble was Harold Glasser. Fitin informed Merkulov that Ruble/Glasser had worked for Soviet intelligence since May 1937, usually for the KGB but also at times for the GRU. The 1937 dating coincided, of course, with Chambers's account.

Fitin went on to explain that one of those tours with the GRU had led to his agent Ruble/Glasser's being slighted in regard to Soviet awards. (For ideologically motivated agents, Soviet decorations had great psychological value.) Fitin stated that "the group of agents of the 'military' neighbors [GRU] whose part Ruble was earlier, recently was decorated with orders of the USSR. Ruble learned about this fact from his friend Ales [Alger Hiss], who is the head of the mentioned group." Fitin asked, in view of Glasser's valuable work for the KGB and because only "as a result of transfer to our station [KGB], Ruble [Glasser] was not decorated together with other members of the Ales group," that the KGB put him in for the Order of the Red Star.[23]

Glasser appears in two KGB Venona cables in July 1943.[24] At the time of these messages he was the U.S. Treasury representative to American military forces in North Africa. The cables are only deciphered in part but appear to say that Glasser had been asked to give an opinion on Eugene Dennis or about something in which Dennis was involved, or possibly that Dennis had asked that Glasser be told of something. Dennis was one of the leading figures in the CPUSA and became its head (general secretary) in 1946. He was also involved in the party's covert activities during World War II and maintained contact with secret Communists in the Office of Strategic Services and the Office of War Information.

Glasser came to Elizabeth Bentley's attention in mid-1944, after he returned from a wartime Treasury mission to Italy. Bentley told the FBI that Victor Perlo had informed her that Glasser had reestablished contact. Perlo explained that Glasser had been part of the group earlier, before Bentley had been involved with it. He had been transferred to assist another Soviet network, but that task had ended, and he wished to work once more with the Perlo group. Bentley mentioned that Perlo did not know who headed the network to which Glasser had been temporarily transferred, but Charles Kramer told her that it was Alger Hiss in the State Department. This story is corroborated by the Fitin-Merkulov document just discussed.[25]

Glasser came back into the Perlo group but then went abroad on another Treasury assignment, and by the time he returned, the KGB had taken direct control of the Perlo group and had restricted Bentley's work to the U.S. Service and Shipping Corporation. Consequently, she had no direct knowledge of what sort of espionage tasks Glasser performed in this period. Several decrypted Venona cables, however, allude to his work.

One cable from March 28, 1945, shows Glasser working as a talent-spotter. Glasser reported that in April the Treasury Department was sending a young lawyer, Josiah DuBois, to Moscow to serve as its representative on the American delegation to the Allied Reparations Commission meeting. Glasser explained that he had established "most friendly relations" with DuBois and judged him to be ideologically a Communist, although he was not a CPUSA member. Glasser stated that he had counseled DuBois to be more "discreet" in expressing his left-wing views and noted that his personal relationship with DuBois was such that he could "normally obtain by asking" anything he wanted.[26]

Three June 1945 KGB cables report Glasser's handing over a State Department analysis of Soviet war losses, a State Department report on a Finnish company that was believed to be hiding Nazi financial assets, and an OSS report on the movement of Nazi gold through Swiss banks. In a fourth June cable Glasser reported that he had won a seat on the Treasury committee advising Supreme Court justice Robert Jackson, the U.S. member of the Allied War Crimes tribunal.

Although Glasser was an able economist, his rise in the Treasury Department was assisted by the network of fellow underground Communists inside Treasury. At various times in his Treasury career, his promotions and job ratings were determined by fellow Communists Frank Coe and William Ullmann. His promotions and job ratings were also reviewed and backed by Harry Dexter White, director of the Division of Monetary Research and later assistant secretary of the Treasury. Coe, Ullmann, and White, like Glasser, cooperated with the KGB.[27] This hidden network also helped Glasser when security officers first ran across evidence of his Communist background. In December 1941 the Secret Service, the Treasury Department's investigative arm, forwarded a report indicating that it had evidence of Glasser's involvement in Communist activities. Had the report been acted on, Glasser's subsequent work for Stalin's intelligence agencies might never have taken place. The report, however, went to Harry White, and nothing happened.[28]

Neutralization of the Perlo Group

By 1947 the FBI was convinced that the Perlo group's members had spied during World War II, but the authorities also judged that without additional evidence successful prosecution was unlikely. The bureau decided the only practical step it could take was to remove the opportunity for the members of the Perlo group to damage the United States further. In the case of those still working for the U.S. government, the FBI alerted appropriate officials to its findings. It was all done quietly; those involved were allowed to resign, or their posts were abolished, rather than being publicly fired for cause. Perlo lost his job with the Division of Monetary Research, Magdoff and Fitzgerald resigned from the Commerce Department, Kramer left the staff of the Senate Labor and Public Welfare Committee, and Glasser was forced out of his high-ranking Treasury post. For many years Perlo refused to admit that he was a Communist, declining to answer questions about CPUSA membership when asked by congressional committees and stating that he had only been "helping in my humble way to carry out the great New Deal program under the leadership of Franklin D. Roosevelt." In 1981, however, he discarded his pretense of having been just another New Deal liberal; he emerged openly as a member of the national leadership of the CPUSA. When the American Communist party split between hard-line Marxist-Leninists and supporters of Gorbachev's attempt to democratize Soviet communism in 1991, Perlo, a member of the CPUSA's National Board, sided with the hard-liners and denounced Gorbachev's reforms as "treachery" and "betrayal."[29]

None of the Perlo group members were ever prosecuted for espionage; some of the key evidence against them could not be used in court, and what could was not sufficient to gain their conviction. But material from Moscow's archives, and particularly the evidence of Venona, make their culpability very clear.

The Silvermaster Group

While the Perlo group provided the Soviets with useful information, it was easily outdone by another network, the Silvermaster group, that reported to the Soviets first through Jacob Golos and then through Elizabeth Bentley.

Bentley told the FBI that in the late summer of 1941 Golos had sent her to establish contact with a network that had been reporting to the CPUSA but which, in view of the recent Nazi invasion of the Soviet Union, was being made available for espionage. Gregory Silvermaster, assisted by his wife, Helen, and William Ullmann, a close family friend who lived with them, led the group. Bentley herself dealt chiefly with the Silvermasters and Ullmann, who passed on material from a diverse group of sources, most of whom Bentley rarely met and some of whom she never met face to face. These other sources included Solomon Adler, William Taylor, George Silverman, Frank Coe, William Gold, Sonia Gold, Irving Kaplan, Norman Bursler, Lauchlin Currie, Anatole Volkov, and Harry Dexter White.

Bentley said she traveled frequently to Washington, sometimes every month, sometimes twice a month, to pick up material from this group until it was fully turned over to direct Soviet control in 1944. The volume of material grew so great that Ullmann obtained a high-quality camera and set up a darkroom in the Silvermaster residence so that documents could be photographed rather than laboriously copied by hand. Bentley explained that initially she had picked up material and delivered it to Golos, who turned it over to the Soviets. Later, she herself met with a KGB contact and delivered the material. She also reported that after Golos's death the KGB repeatedly pressed her and Browder to transfer the group to its direct control. She said that they were reluctant to do so, but in mid-1944 Browder agreed, and the transfer was made over a period of months.

Eighty-five deciphered KGB cables, dating from 1942 to 1945, mention one or more of the persons Bentley named as members of the Silvermaster group. Eleven of the fourteen persons she named feature in Venona messages: both Silvermasters, Ullmann, Silverman, Coe, both Golds, Bursler, Currie, Adler, and White.[30] Not identified in any deciphered Venona messages are three members of the group: Kaplan, Taylor, and Volkov.

An unidentified cover name, El, is associated with the Silvermaster group in several Venona messages, but it is difficult to tell whether El is a source or someone assisting Iskhak Akhmerov, the KGB officer, in managing the group. It is possible that El was merely a shortened form of Elsa, the cover name for Akhmerov's wife and espionage assistant, Helen Lowry. Finally, the unidentified cover name Tur appears in a message alongside those of Gregory Silvermaster and Ullmann, but it is not clear whether Tur is a fellow member of the Silvermaster network or an independent source supplying the KGB with the same information—in this case, news of a delay in the Anglo-American invasion of southern France.

Various deciphered KGB cables corroborate details of Bentley's story about her relationship with the Silvermaster group. Several cables noting members of the Silvermaster group as the source of information refer to Golos as the intermediary. The first reference to Bentley in a Venona message occurs in December 1943, after Golos's death. The message, though only partly deciphered, indicates that Bentley had met Earl Browder and would "continue work"—presumably Golos's work.[31] In February 1944 the New York KGB reported to Moscow that the information coming from the Silvermaster network flowed through Bentley and then to Akhmerov. Several messages also report Akhmerov's irritation that Bentley was dragging her feet about implementing his plan to take direct control over the Silvermaster apparatus, and note her unhappiness when in mid-1944 Browder agreed to KGB absorption of the group.

One New York message notes that the KGB was sending by diplomatic pouch fifty-six "films"—probably rolls of film—delivered by the Silvermaster network.[32] Bentley said that she rarely picked up fewer than two or three rolls on her visit to the Silvermasters and remembers being given forty rolls on one visit. The KGB cable said that these films included photographic copies of seventeen different stolen American reports, including Board of Economic Warfare reports on Germany and the Far East, a memo from President Roosevelt regarding Lend-Lease policy toward France, a related Lend-Lease Administration report on its plans for France as well as one on Italy, a report by the U.S. embassy in Spain on German assets located there, an analysis of German industrial organization, an analysis of American military industrial capacity, and American plans for the dissolution of the Nazi party. Later, when the Silvermasters advertised their Washington home for sale, the real estate ad noted the extra amenity of a superbly equipped darkroom.[33]

Gregory Silvermaster: The Spy with Friends in High Places

Nathan Gregory Silvermaster was born in Russia in 1898 and came to the United States in 1914. He attended the University of Washington, where he established a record as a exceptional student and earned a bachelor's degree in philosophy in 1920. He also secretly joined the Communist party. The poet Kenneth Rexroth, in *An Autobiographical Novel,* described his experiences in Seattle's heady radical milieu during that era and noted that the theoretician of the nascent Communist movement there was a brilliant philosophy student at the University of Washington. Rexroth did not name him, but the details of the description clearly point to Silvermaster.[34] He became a U.S. citizen in 1926 and went on to graduate study in economics, receiving a doctorate at the University of California, Berkeley, in 1932; his dissertation was entitled "Lenin's Economic Thought Prior to the October Revolution." In 1935 he received an appointment as an economist with the Resettlement Administration, a New Deal agency attached to the Department of Agriculture. In 1938 he moved on to the U.S. Maritime Labor Board, and in 1940 to the Farm Security Administration (formerly the Resettlement Administration), where he stayed until 1944. Late that year he transferred to the War Assets Division of the Treasury Department. Silvermaster was transferred, along with the rest of the division, in mid-1945, first to the Commerce Department and later to the Reconstruction Finance Corporation, where it became the War Assets Corporation.

Though nominally remaining on the employment rolls of the Farm Security Administration, in 1942 Silvermaster arranged through contacts of his espionage apparatus to be detailed to the Board of Economic Warfare. The transfer, however, triggered objections from the Office of Naval Intelligence and from War Department counterintelligence. Neither agency had evidence that Silvermaster was engaged in espionage, but both believed that he was a hidden Communist and regarded him as a security risk at an agency with access to U.S. intelligence information.

Silvermaster flatly denied any Communist beliefs, past or present, and appealed to Under Secretary of War Robert Patterson to overrule the security agencies.[35] Silvermaster also called upon hidden Communists and Soviet sources within the government to bring pressure on Patterson. Harry White, then assistant to the secretary of the Treasury, got in touch with Patterson and told him that the suspicions about Silvermaster were baseless. White was a secret admirer of Stalin's regime and cooperated with the Soviets through Silvermaster's network. Lauchlin Currie, a presidential aide who also cooperated with Soviet intelligence, personally phoned Patterson and urged a reconsideration of Silvermaster's case. Calvin B. Baldwin, head of the Farm Security Administration and Silvermaster's superior, also vouched for him. Baldwin, while no spy, was a secret Communist. Patterson chose to trust and accommodate these highly placed persons and overruled military counterintelligence.[36] His naive decision facilitated the work of a man who headed one of the largest and most productive spy rings that Stalin's espionage agencies maintained inside the U.S. government. It would also provide substance to the postwar Republican charge that high officials in the Roosevelt and Truman administrations aided Soviet espionage against the United States.

The Silvermaster group's success in manipulating the under secretary of war illustrated as well the continued gaps in U.S. internal security procedures. The evidence that military counterintelligence possessed about Silvermaster was incomplete. Neither Naval nor Army intelligence knew that Silvermaster had come to the attention of the FBI as a contact of Gaik Ovakimian, a KGB officer who directed Soviet espionage from 1933 to 1941 under cover of being an Amtorg official.[37] Nor did Patterson, when weighing Currie's and White's support for Silvermaster, have knowledge that in 1939 Whittaker Chambers had informed Assistant Secretary of State Adolf Berle that both of them had cooperated with the CPUSA's Washington underground in the 1930s.

Silvermaster's security problems did not, however, end in 1942. Although detailed to the Board of Economic Warfare, he was still officially on the employment rolls of the Department of Agriculture. Its personnel office and the Civil Service Commission were not under Patterson's jurisdiction, and they opened an inquiry on Silvermaster in 1943 and called in the FBI. Once more, Silvermaster's high-placed friends swung into action. Lauchlin Currie assured the FBI that there was no basis for the suspicions that Silvermaster was a Communist. And the FBI had yet to get Berle's notes with their indication that Whittaker Chambers had identified Currie as an ally of the Communist underground in 1939. The FBI also appears to have been unaware of the details of the earlier Naval and Army counterintelligence investigations of Silvermaster. The FBI investigation produced nothing concrete, and the matter was dropped. In 1944 Silvermaster's tenure at the Board of Economic Warfare (by then merged into the Foreign Economic Administration) was ending, and he sought a new post. Although no adverse action had been taken in the Agriculture Department security probe, a security cloud surrounded him. White and Currie again intervened, and Under Secretary of Agriculture Paul Appleby sent a memo to his subordinates:

> The other day when Harry White, of the Treasury Department, was in to see me on other business, he lingered to ask whether or not I could do anything about placing Gregory Silvermaster, who has been in Farm Security Administration for some years. . . . Silvermaster has been under some attack by the Dies committee, I believe, principally or exclusively because he happens to have been born in Russia and has been engaged most of his life as an economist and more particularly a labor economist. He is a highly intelligent person and is very close both to Harry White and to Lauch Currie. There is no reason to question his loyalty and good citizenship.[38]

Appleby's statement was inaccurate. The Dies committee (House Special Committee on Un-American Activities) had raised questions about Silvermaster's having concealed Communist loyalties, not about his birth or occupation. It is unlikely, however, that Appleby was lying. He was neither a Communist nor even a fellow traveler but merely gullible. He was easily manipulated by men as unscrupulous as Currie and White, and his memo reflected his naive trust in their honesty.

Silvermaster briefly returned to the Department of Agriculture, but White soon found him a better post in the War Assets Division of his own Treasury Department.

In 1943 Lauchlin Currie reported to the Silvermaster network that the FBI had interviewed him about Silvermaster's Communist sympathies. The network passed this report on to the New York KGB, which informed Moscow. From the nature of the FBI inquiries to Currie and its questions to Silvermaster himself, the KGB deduced correctly that American authorities were suspicious of his Communist convictions but had not as yet picked up evidence of espionage. Consequently, the KGB decided that although increased caution was needed, Silvermaster could continue his work.

In her November 1945 statement to the FBI Bentley had said that Akhmerov had sought to convince Silvermaster of the need for direct KGB contact with the network's chief sources, but that Silvermaster had long resisted the move. The deciphered Venona cables confirm Bentley's recollection. Several Venona messages show Akhmerov urging Silvermaster to split his large network into smaller groups and to allow the KGB to take several members under its direct supervision. The New York KGB, however, told Moscow that Akhmerov described Silvermaster as "jealous about encroachments" on his apparatus and that "an attempt to 'remove members of the group, however, circumspectly, will be received . . . unfavorably by Robert [Silvermaster].' "[39]

Although seeking to convince him of the advisability of a change, Akhmerov was aware that Silvermaster had created and managed an espionage network of impressive size. He informed Moscow that "it is doubtful whether we [the KGB] could get same results as Robert [Silvermaster]." He gave the example of two Treasury Department employees, William and Sonia Gold, who were Silvermaster network "probationers," the KGB term for agents who were not professional KGB officers. Akhmerov described them as devoted to the Communist cause but difficult to manage because of unspecified "caprices." He told Moscow that "it costs Robert great pains to keep the couple and other Probationers in line. Robert being their leader in the CPUSA line helps him give them orders." Akhmerov stressed that Silvermaster's position as an underground CPUSA leader added to his ability to direct such ideologically motivated agents, noting "that our workers [KGB officers] would not manage to work with the same success under the CPUSA flag." Akhmerov further reported that he was at pains to convince Silvermaster that the breaking up of the network into smaller groups was a security measure, not a reflection on Silvermaster's leadership, and that Silvermaster would "retain general direction."[40]

Elizabeth Bentley wrote that Helen Witte Silvermaster was an active partner in her husband's work, did much of the copying, met sources to pick up material, and passed on material to Bentley herself. Helen Silvermaster was Russian-born, like her husband. She had immigrated to the United States in 1923 and become a U.S. citizen in 1930. Her marriage that year to Gregory Silvermaster was her second, and she had a son from her first marriage, Anatole Volkov. Bentley reported that Volkov, born in 1924, had occasionally performed courier duties for the Silvermaster network but dropped out of the picture when he was drafted into military service. Under the cover name Dora, Helen Silvermaster shows up in the deciphered KGB cables as a fully knowledgeable assistant in her husband's work. When she was interviewed by the FBI in 1947, she denied any belief, past or present, in communism, complaining that "anyone with liberal views seemed to be called a Communist now-a-days." She agreed that she had known Elizabeth Bentley and that Bentley had often met with her and stayed overnight at the Silvermaster residence, but claimed that she had believed Bentley to be an OSS speech writer collecting material for speeches for U.S. government officials.[41]

The deciphered Venona cables show that, in recognition of their hard work, the KGB provided Silvermaster with a regular stipend and in late 1944 paid him a bonus of three thousand dollars. This KGB cable is partially garbled, but it appears that the KGB also gave Silvermaster a Soviet medal for his service to the USSR. Akhmerov reported that "Robert [Silvermaster] is sincerely overjoyed and profoundly satisfied with the reward given him in accordance with your instructions. As he says his work for us is the one good thing he has done in his life. He emphasized that he did not take this only as a personal honor, but also as an honor to his group. He wants to see the reward and the book."[42]

It is impossible to differentiate between what information Silvermaster provided in his own right and what he delivered from the various members of his group. Deciphered Venona messages mentioning Silvermaster, sixty-one in total, report his handing over huge quantities of War Production Board data on weapons, aircraft, tank, artillery, and shipping production; Board of Economic Warfare documents on

German industry and on American reserves of manpower, foodstuffs, and raw materials; summaries and copies of U.S. diplomatic cables, particularly those dealing with American negotiations with the USSR; OSS reports on a wide variety of subjects; analyses of rivalries inside the U.S. government and of the increasingly tense relations between Secretary of State Cordell Hull and President Roosevelt; American reports about British intentions in the Balkans after Hitler's defeat; and postwar U.S. military planning documents. Silvermaster also accepted KGB requests for specific items of information. One KGB cable, for example, reported that he delivered requested technical and operating manuals for various models of American bombers and attack aircraft. Probably these were supplied by William Ullmann, then an officer with the Army Air Force headquarters at the Pentagon.[43]

William Ullmann: The Spy as Family Friend

William Ullmann was born to a prosperous Missouri family in 1908. He graduated from Harvard Business School in 1932 and arrived in Washington in 1935 to take a job with the National Recovery Administration. At that time he also met the Silvermasters. In 1938 they jointly bought a house that they shared until Ullmann and Gregory Silvermaster were forced out of the government in 1947. All three then moved to Harvey Cedars, New Jersey, where they were partners in a building construction firm.

Ullmann transferred to the Resettlement Administration (which later became the Farm Security Administration) in 1937. In 1939 Harry White, director of Treasury's Division of Monetary Research, hired him. Ullmann received a strong recommendation for the position from C. B. Baldwin, then assistant administrator of the Farm Security Administration. His immediate supervisor at Treasury was Frank Coe. White later told the FBI that he hired Ullmann on the recommendation of his close friend George Silverman. As noted earlier, Baldwin was a secret Communist, and White, Coe, and Silverman were all part of Silvermaster's espionage network. Ullmann worked in White's office until 1942, when he was drafted. He then obtained a commission in the Army Air Force. Bentley told the FBI that Silverman, then a civilian official in the Army Air Force, had arranged for Ullmann to be assigned to work in his division at the Pentagon, an assignment that allowed him to resume living in the Silvermaster/Ullmann residence and carrying on his espionage activities. When interviewed by the FBI in 1947, Ullmann confirmed that Silverman had arranged his assignment to the Pentagon.

Ullmann is mentioned in twenty-four deciphered Venona messages under the cover names Pilot and Donald and was clearly both a major source in his own right and Silvermaster's partner in managing the rest of the network.[44] After his military duty he returned to the Treasury Department, where he worked under Harold Glasser, yet another Soviet agent, until he was quietly forced to resign in 1947.[45]

George Silverman: The Link to Highly Placed Sources

Abraham George Silverman's roots in the CPUSA underground of the 1930s were deep. When Hope Hale Davis and her husband joined in the mid-1930s, he was already a leading member. In early 1935 her husband, Hermann Brunck, had written an economic study concluding that the New Deal's reforms were beginning to work. Such a position was a serious ideological error before the CPUSA's shift to a Popular Front position (late 1935) in support of Roosevelt, and Silverman ferociously attacked Brunck's findings at a meeting of their underground Communist group.[46]

Whittaker Chambers knew Silverman as a secret Communist and as a contact of the espionage network that he had supervised in the mid-1930s. Chambers noted that Silverman, along with Alger Hiss, Harry White, and Julian Wadleigh, had been a recipient of expensive Bokhara rugs, which he distributed to leading figures of his network in January 1937. (The giving of New Year's presents, a sort of Christmas bonus, to agents was common Soviet intelligence practice in the 1930s and early 1940s. Bentley in her testimony reported the same custom.) Chambers explained that the rugs were shipped to Silverman's residence, from which they were then distributed. Chambers said that Silverman was a close friend of White, and his chief task for the network was keeping White in a cooperative mood. It was Silverman, according to Chambers, who actually delivered the rug to White.

Silverman later admitted knowing Chambers in the 1930s but described him as only a casual social acquaintance. Silverman also admitted having received two rugs from him, but he said they were repayment for a seventy-five-dollar loan he had made to Chambers. In Silverman's version he paid Chambers three hundred dollars for the rugs in addition to canceling the debt. He could not, however, produce any receipts for the loan to Chambers or his payment to Chambers for the rugs.[47]

Silverman worked as an economist and statistician for a variety of government agencies in the 1930s: the National Recovery Administration, the Tariff Commission, and the Railroad Retirement Board. While he had been active in the CPUSA underground and assisted Chambers's GRU-linked network, none of these positions offered significant access to information of intelligence interest. This changed, however, in 1942, when Silverman became civilian chief of analysis and plans in the office of the assistant chief of the Army Air Force Air Staff for Material and Service. He brought William Ullmann into this division. In the Venona cables, where he has the cover name Aileron, Silverman furnished the KGB with reports on American aircraft production and allocation and on training and provisioning of air crews.[48]

Although this information was of intelligence value to the Soviets, Silverman's close association with two highly placed government officials, Harry White and Lauchlin Currie, remained his most critical work for Soviet intelligence. Bentley told the FBI that Silverman was the network's chief link to both, although Gregory Silvermaster himself developed a close relationship with the two men as well.

Harry Dexter White: A Most Highly Placed Spy

Among all the covert sources that Stalin possessed in the American government, none held a higher position than Harry Dexter White, assistant secretary of the Treasury. He joined the Treasury Department in 1934, and his brilliance as an economist and his ability to explain and propose solutions to complex monetary issues to nontechnically trained policy-makers soon made him one of the department's most influential officials. Secretary of the Treasury Henry Morgenthau's extensive and detailed diary shows that no individual had greater influence on Morgenthau's own thinking in the late 1930s and during World War II than White.

Rising steadily, White became director of monetary research in 1938 and assistant to the secretary of the Treasury in 1941. He and John Maynard Keynes were the chief architects of the historic Bretton Woods monetary agreement in 1944 that structured international monetary policy for decades to come, and he became assistant secretary of the Treasury, the second-ranking position in the department, in 1945. The next year President Truman appointed him the American director of the International Monetary Fund, one of the chief institutional pillars of the postwar international economic order. He came close to rising even higher. Henry Wallace, vice-president from 1941 to 1945 and a candidate for president in 1948, told the press that White was his first choice for secretary of the Treasury. Had Roosevelt died a year earlier or not decided to replace Wallace on the ticket in the 1944 election, Wallace would have become president.[49]

Whittaker Chambers stated that in the mid-1930s White was valued because of his talent and potential, but that he was not a very productive source for Chambers's GRU-CPUSA network. He was then only establishing his influence at Treasury and, in any case, at that time the Treasury Department was not involved in issues of much intelligence interest to the Soviets. Chambers also noted that White was not a CPUSA member; he cooperated with the Communist underground on his own terms and could not be ordered to do anything in particular.

Although White was not one of Chambers's most productive sources in the mid-1930s, he was nonetheless a source. After Alger Hiss sued Chambers for slander in 1948, Chambers responded by producing a collection of documents and microfilm that he had hidden in 1938. Most of the material had come from Hiss, but it also included a long memo in Harry White's own handwriting.

Chambers later wrote that when he stopped spying for the Soviets he met briefly with his chief sources and urged them to cease as well, hoping that they would either rethink their loyalties or at least break contact out of fear of exposure. Elizabeth Bentley heard that White did draw back after Chambers's defection. She said that Silvermaster told her that White "had been giving information to the Russians during the thirties but ceased abruptly when his contact . . . turned 'sour' in 1938."[50] But, Silvermaster explained to Bentley, in 1940 White had renewed his ties with the CPUSA underground in Washington.

White facilitated Soviet espionage by sponsoring government employment of a number of Soviet sources. Working for the Treasury Department during his tenure as one of its most powerful officials were at least eleven Soviet sources: Frank Coe, Harold Glasser, Ludwig Ullmann, Victor Perlo, Sonia Gold, Gregory Silvermaster, George Silverman, Irving Kaplan, William Taylor, and Solomon Adler. He also used his position to protect Silvermaster and Glasser when they came under security scrutiny.

In addition, in 1941 White successfully urged the Chinese Nationalist government's Ministry of Finance to employ in a senior position Chi Ch'ao-ting, a Chinese national trained as an economist in the United States. Chi Ch'ao-ting was educated at Tsinghua College in Peking and then attended the University of Chicago and Columbia University. He also secretly joined the American Communist party in 1926 and was part of its Chinese bureau until 1941. He worked as an interpreter for the Communist International in Moscow in the late 1920s and was a member of the Chinese Communist party's delegation to the Sixth Congress of the Comintern in 1928. In the United States in the 1930s he wrote for the *Daily Worker, Amerasia,* and other publications under the pseudonyms of Hansu Chan, R. Doonping, Huang Lowe, and Futien Wang. Chi's Communist activities, however, were secret.

In 1940 Chi traveled to Chungking, the capital of China after the capture of Beijing by the Japanese. Comintern records show that in August Mao Tse-tung informed Georgi Dimitrov that Chi had met with Chou En-lai, Mao's chief lieutenant and representative in Chungking. Mao asked Dimitrov to inform Earl Browder that Chi would be returning to the United States to recruit Japanese-American Communists for espionage against the Japanese forces in China, oversee a courier system using American Communist seamen to link the Chinese Communist party via Hong Kong with Japan, the Philippines, and the United States, and supervise a program by the CPUSA's Chinese Bureau to collect funds from Chinese immigrants that would go to the Chinese Communists. Chi's return to the United States was brief, however. With U.S. government support, arranged through White, Chi returned to Chungking in 1941 to become an official of the Chinese government's finance ministry. There he supplied the Chinese Communists with information and disrupted Chiang Kai-shek's regime from within. When Chiang and his Nationalist government retreated to Taiwan in 1949, Chi stayed on the mainland, openly announcing his status as a veteran Chinese Communist party operative, and became a senior official of Mao Tse-tung's government.[51]

There are fifteen deciphered KGB messages during 1944 and 1945 in which White was discussed or which reported information he was providing to Soviet intelligence officers.[52] The KGB mentioned that White offered advice concerning how far the Soviets could push the United States on abandoning the Polish government-in-exile (which was hostile to Stalin) and assured the Soviets that U.S. policy-makers, despite their public opposition, would acquiesce to the USSR's annexation of Latvia, Estonia, and Lithuania. White was also a senior adviser to the U.S. delegation at the founding conference of the United Nations in San Francisco in May 1945. During the negotiations on the UN charter he met covertly with Soviet intelligence officers and provided them with information on the American negotiating strategy. He assured the Soviets that "Truman and Stettinius want to achieve the success of the conference at any price" and advised that if Soviet diplomats held firm to their demand that the Soviet Union get a veto of UN actions, that the United States "will agree."[53] He offered other tactical advice on how the Soviets might defeat or water down positions being advanced by his own government and that of Great Britain. The KGB officer meeting with White even carried with him a questionnaire on a variety of issues about which Soviet diplomats wanted to know the American negotiating strategy; White answered in detail.

In November 1944 the KGB told Moscow that Silvermaster had spoken with Terry Ann White, Harry's wife. She told him that her husband was considering a position in private business in order to finance college education for one of their daughters. Silvermaster, according to a Venona decryption, responded that the KGB "would willingly have helped them and that in view of all the circumstances would not allow them to leave Carthage [Washington]. Robert [Silvermaster] thinks that Richard [Harry White] would have refused a regular payment but might accept gifts as a mark of our gratitude for [unrecovered code groups] daughter's expenses which may come to up to two thousand a year. Albert [Akhmerov] said to Robert that in his opinion we would agree to provide for Richard's daughter's education."[54] The New York KGB endorsed Akhmerov's offer to finance the college education of White's daughter and asked for Moscow's sanction. (Moscow's reaction, however, is not among the Venona messages decrypted.)

The Venona messages show that Silvermaster had protested the KGB's bypassing him and meeting directly with White, an objection that was overridden. White did not meet just with Americans who were part of Soviet intelligence, but also directly with Soviet intelligence officers. An August 1944 deciphered cable reported on a July meeting between Kolstov, the cover name of an unidentified KGB officer, and Jurist, White's cover name at the time:[55]

As regards the technique of further work with us Jurist said that his wife was ready for any self-sacrifice; he himself did not think about his personal security, but a compromise would lead to a political scandal and the discredit of all supporters of the new course, therefore he would have to be very cautious. He asked whether he should [unrecovered code groups] his work with us. I replied that he should refrain. Jurist has no suitable apartment for a permanent meeting place; all his friends are family people. Meetings could be held at their houses in such a way that one meeting devolved on each every 4–5 months. He proposes infrequent conversations lasting up to half a hour while driving in his automobile.[56]

In addition to these particular examples of White's espionage, he also attempted—sometimes successfully, sometimes not—to influence American policy to serve Communist interests. One case of White's acting as an agent of influence is the matter of a Soviet loan for postwar reconstruction. On January 3, 1945, the USSR asked the United States to give it a loan of six billion dollars repayable under generous terms: over thirty years at a rate of 2¼ percent. A week later White, then assistant secretary of the Treasury, persuaded Secretary Morgenthau to urge President Roosevelt to offer Stalin an even larger loan on even more generous terms: ten billion dollars repayable over thirty-five years at a rate of 2 percent. Internal U.S. government discussions about a Soviet loan were highly sensitive and were kept secret, or so government officials thought. White, however, was a central participant in these conversations, and several KGB cables in January 1945 relay information from White on these discussions, including his and Morgenthau's loan proposal. The State Department, however, opposed any postwar loan as ill-advised at that time, as did President Roosevelt, and the idea was dropped. If the loan proposal had moved to the point of serious negotiations, the Soviets would have been in the enviable position of having covert communications with a leading member of the American negotiating team who was their secret partisan.

Another case in point is the Chinese gold loan. In 1942 the U.S. Congress authorized a $500 million loan to Nationalist China. In 1943 the Chinese government asked for a $200 million delivery of gold to be charged against this loan. China's currency was inflating rapidly under wartime conditions, with great damage to that country's economy. A supply of gold to back the currency would assist in slowing inflation, which was rising to ruinous levels. Roosevelt approved the gold loan, and in July 1943 Secretary Morgenthau signed a letter to the Chinese government pledging transfer of the gold.

White, with the assistance of Frank Coe (director of the Division of Monetary Research) and Solomon Adler (Treasury representative in China), opposed carrying out the transfer and repeatedly won Morgenthau's support for delaying delivery, arguing that pervasive corruption in the Nationalist government and its failure to adopt financial reforms would result in the gold's doing little good. By July 1945, two years later, only $29 million in gold had been sent to China. Meanwhile, the hyperinflation of this period, more than a thousand percent a year, did immense damage to the Chinese economy and severely weakened the standing of the Nationalist government when civil war with the Chinese Communists resumed at the end of 1945.

White, Coe, and Adler were right about the corruption of the Nationalist regime, but their position that China needed to institute a monetary reform in the midst of World War II, with the Japanese occupying China's most productive regions, was an excuse rather than a reason. They effectively delayed the transfer while only going through the motions of offering alternatives. By mid-1945 Morgenthau, who had supported delaying the transfer, realized that he had been misled on key points. He told Coe, White, and the others that they had put him "in an absolutely dishonorable position, and I think it's inexcusable."[57] Morgenthau, however, thought his aides had merely mishandled the gold transfer but were well motivated, and he never suspected that they had an entirely separate agenda from his.[58]

Frank Coe was one of the persons Whittaker Chambers had identified as a covert Communist to Assistant Secretary of State Berle in 1939. Frank Coe had the cover name Peak, which appears in four deciphered Venona cables.[59] Only one conveys much of the substance of Coe's work, a New York KGB message in December 1944 informing Moscow that five reels of filmed documents provided by Peak/Coe were on the way. The cable briefly described the documents as reports and memoranda about American Lend-Lease plans and negotiations with the British.

After White became the American director of the International Monetary Fund in 1946, he found a post for Coe there. In 1947 the FBI interviewed Coe, and he denied any participation in Soviet espionage, any sympathy for communism, or any association with Communists. In

1948 he testified to the House Committee on Un-American Activities and denied Elizabeth Bentley's statements about his activities. When American authorities decided to force those identified as Soviet agents from public employment in 1947, Coe's position at the International Monetary Fund put him beyond immediate firing. But by 1950 American pressure forced Coe out. In 1952 he was called before a congressional investigating committee. Considerable evidence had accumulated since he had testified in 1948, and this time he chose not to take a chance that a perjury charge might be brought. He refused to answer most questions, citing the right not to provide evidence against himself. In 1956 he was once more called to testify. He denied having engaged in espionage but again refused to answer questions on most specifics, including his relationship with the CPUSA. He then moved permanently to Communist China in 1958 to work for Mao Tse-tung's government. By 1959 he was writing articles justifying the "rectification campaign," a massive Maoist purge of Chinese society instituted the previous year, and claiming that the resulting Marxist-Leninist ideological purification had led to prodigious increases in economic production.[60]

Solomon Adler is identified under the cover name of Sachs as a member of the Silvermaster network in a deciphered Venona message regarding delivery of information about China. Elizabeth Bentley remembered Adler as a source who had been in China during part of the war but little else about him. She did not even recall meeting him. When interviewed by the FBI in late 1947, Adler stated that he had met Bentley, introduced to her by Ludwig Ullmann at a social occasion also attended by Helen Silvermaster. Adler denied any sympathy or association with Communists. The FBI wanted him fired from his senior Treasury post, but its evidence was not as strong as for other members of the Silvermaster group, and he kept his job until 1950. By then the evidence accumulated by the FBI convinced Treasury Department authorities, and he quietly resigned under pressure. At that time he also obtained a passport and left the United States, traveling initially to Britain. (Adler had been born in Britain and had become a U.S. citizen in 1936, the same year he became a U.S. government employee.) He remained abroad for more than three years and allowed his American passport to expire. This subjected him to denaturalization and he lost his American citizenship.[61]

At some point in the 1950s Adler also emigrated to the People's Republic of China. Sidney Rittenberg, another American Communist who emigrated to China, wrote in a memoir that in 1960 Adler, Coe, and he were working together on translating Mao's writings into English. In 1983 a Chinese Communist journal identified Adler as having worked for twenty years for the Chinese Communist party's Central External Liaison Department, an agency that included among its duties foreign espionage. He also appeared in a photograph in a memoir published in China as a colleague of Henshen Chen, a senior official in Mao's government who had worked as an intelligence operative in the United States from the late 1930s until the Communist victory in China in 1949. In his memoir Chen described how during that period he, Chen, had worked as an agent for the Chinese Communist party and its liaison with the CPUSA, while using as cover the position of editor at *Pacific Affairs* and researcher for the Institute of Pacific Relations.[62]

In the late 1940s and 1950s some Republicans charged that a cabal of secret Communists in the Roosevelt and Truman administrations had "lost China" to the Communists.[63] The duplicitous role that White, Coe, and Adler played in the matter of the Chinese gold loan figured among the particulars of the charge. This was exaggeration for partisan purposes. The chief reasons for China's fall to Mao's forces lay in China. The obstruction of the gold loan made a minor, not a major, contribution to Mao's victory. White, Coe, and Adler were minor actors, but actors they were, and China's Communist government showed its gratitude by hiring the latter two as advisers. Both spent the rest of their lives in Communist China, Coe dying there in 1980, Adler in 1994.

Lauchlin Currie: White House Aide as Soviet Spy

Harry White and Alger Hiss were the two most highly placed Soviet sources in the American government. Lauchlin Currie, however, was a close third. Born in Nova Scotia and educated at the London School of Economics, he went to Harvard to pursue a doctorate in economics and became an American citizen in 1934. He became a U.S. government employee the same year, working with Harry White in Treasury's Division of Research and Statistics before moving to the Federal Reserve Board.

These technical positions ended in 1939 when he joined the White House staff as a senior administrative assistant to the president. The growth in the White House staff was just getting under way; presidential aides were few and exercised significant authority. Roosevelt sent Currie to China in 1942 for several months as his personal representative and head of the American economic mission to the Nationalist government. In 1943 the Board of Economic Warfare, part of the Lend-Lease Administration, and several other war agencies merged to form the Foreign Economic Administration. Currie was detailed from the White House to serve as deputy administrator and day-to-day head of the agency. Currie was, then, a powerful figure in wartime Washington, both as a presidential aide and as an administrator of an agency.

His ties to the Washington Communist underground went back to the mid-1930s. Chambers described him in his memoir as working with the underground as a fellow traveler rather than a party member, in the same manner as Harry White. Adolf Berle's 1939 notes on his conversation with Chambers describe Currie as someone who cooperated with the underground but who "never went the whole way."[64] Bentley also described his relationship with the Silvermaster group as cautious and calibrated by Currie himself. She remembered Currie as providing only verbal briefings, through George Silverman and Gregory Silvermaster, and refraining from handing over documents. She also said that Akhmerov had urged Silvermaster to arrange for direct KGB contact with Currie, but that Silvermaster had resisted. She recalled Currie's warning that American cryptanalysts were on the verge of breaking the Soviet diplomatic code, an apparent reference to the origins of the Venona Project. Otherwise the only specifics Bentley remembered were Currie's intervention to assist Silvermaster with his security probes and his helping various Soviet intelligence contacts get jobs in the government.

There are nine deciphered Venona messages that discuss Currie, who had the cover name Page.[65] They show that Currie gave assistance to Soviet intelligence cautiously and on a limited basis, just as Bentley said. The KGB cables also demonstrate that, although Bentley did not know or did not remember, on occasion he did turn over documents to the KGB. An August 1943 New York KGB cable reports to Moscow that Currie had given Silverman a memorandum on a political subject, otherwise unspecified, that was either from or for the State Department. In June 1944 the New York KGB reported receipt of two items from Currie. One was information on President Roosevelt's reasons for keeping Charles de Gaulle at arm's length. The other, however, was of greater importance to Stalin. Currie told the Soviets that Roosevelt was willing to accept Stalin's demand that the USSR keep the half of Poland that it had received under the Nazi-Soviet Pact of 1939 and that FDR would put pressure on the Polish government-in-exile to make concessions to the Soviets. In public the United States was supporting the Polish government-in-exile, and President Roosevelt had personally assured Polish-Americans, prior to the 1944 election, of his support for the Polish cause. Currie's private information let Stalin know that he could disregard these public stands and need not make serious concessions to the Poles.

The Venona cables also confirm Bentley's statement that the Soviets sought direct contact with Currie. In February 1945 the Moscow KGB headquarters reminded its officers in the United States to find out from Akhmerov and Silvermaster "whether it would be possible for us to approach Page [Currie] direct."[66] The cables also show that by this point Moscow had begun to grow impatient. General Fitin, head of KGB foreign intelligence, told its New York office in March that it wanted more out of Currie. Fitin acknowledged that "Page trusts Robert [Silvermaster], informs him not only orally, but also by handing over documents"—further confirmation that Currie delivered documents to Soviet intelligence. But, said Fitin, "up to now Page's relations with Robert were expressed, from our point of view, only in common feelings and personal sympathies. [unrecovered code groups] question of more profound relations and an understanding by Page of Robert's role. If Robert does not get Page's transfer to our worker, then he [unrecovered code groups] raising with Page the question of Page's closer complicity with Robert."[67]

Fitin was being unduly harsh on his New York station, since earlier messages show Currie doing much more than merely expressing personal sympathies. But it served to make the point about Moscow's expectation that Currie could do much more. This March 1945 message was the last concerning Currie that the National Security Agency deciphered, so Venona does not show the New York KGB's response. There is, however, other evidence that Moscow's instruction to establish direct contact between Currie and its officers, bypassing Silverman and Silvermaster, was carried out. After Bentley defected in late 1945, the FBI opened an investigation of her Soviet supervisor at the time, Anatoly Gromov, a KGB officer operating out of the Soviet embassy in Washington under the guise of being a Soviet diplomat. A report on the investigation in February 1946 cited several meetings between Gromov and Currie. In 1947 the FBI interviewed Currie, who stated that he had met twice with Gromov in early 1945, once at Gromov's residence and once at his, and that they had had at least two other meetings after his leaving government service in June 1945. He described them as innocent discussions of cultural matters and denied any knowledge that Gromov was a KGB officer. Many years later it was discovered that Currie had also met with Vasily Zubilin, Gromov's predecessor as KGB station chief, in 1943. White House records show that Currie gave an innocuous reason for his meeting with Zubilin, who was nominally a Soviet diplomat. But the date, August 1943, coincides with that of the "anonymous Russian letter" (chapter 2) in which a Soviet KGB officer stated that Zubilin "has some high level agent in the office of the White House."[68]

The FBI also asked whether Currie had ever discussed with George Silverman the possibility that American code-breakers were close to breaking Soviet codes, one of the few specifics of his espionage that Bentley had remembered. Currie's answer was peculiar; he stated that while he did not specifically remember discussing breaking Soviet codes with Silverman, he might have done so casually because Silverman was a trusted friend. He further admitted that he might have been indiscreet on various other matters, all of which suggests that he was setting up a claim of carelessness as his defense against an espionage charge.

Indeed, the more the FBI learned of Currie's activities over the years, the more that "indiscreet" seemed a mild term for his behavior. In early 1941, for example, the Washington Committee for Aid to China planned to raise funds for victims of the Japanese war. It announced that Paul Robeson would sing at a fund-raising concert under the sponsorship of Cornelia Pinchot, the social-activist wife of Gifford Pinchot, the respected conservationist and former Republican governor of Pennsylvania, and Eleanor Roosevelt, the First Lady.[69] What neither Mrs. Pinchot nor Mrs. Roosevelt knew was that the CPUSA controlled the Washington Committee for Aid to China. They also did not know until a few days before the concert that only half the funds were to go to the Chinese relief; the rest would go to the National Negro Congress. Communists covertly led the latter organization, and in accordance with the requirements of the Nazi-Soviet Pact it had spent the last year and a half denouncing President Roosevelt in harsh terms.[70]

When Mrs. Pinchot and Mrs. Roosevelt discovered that they had been misled and manipulated, they demanded that either the concert go forward as they had originally been told (all funds to China) or that they not be named as sponsors. At that point Lauchlin Currie, who was a member of the Washington Committee for Aid to China, intervened and urged the two to avoid controversy and allow half the funds to go to an avowedly anti-Roosevelt organization. They refused, and issued a public statement withdrawing their sponsorship. That a Roosevelt aide should act in such a manner seems bizarre, unless his secret ties to the CPUSA are understood.[71]

The FBI lacked sufficient direct evidence to sustain a criminal prosecution against Currie. Bentley had dealt with him only through Silverman and Silvermaster and could not personally testify about his actions. Even if she had, it still came down to her word against his, not nearly enough to win a conviction. Venona would later provide more direct evidence, but Venona was a secret and could not be cited in court.

In 1948 Currie testified before the House Committee on Un-American Activities. Perhaps realizing that the FBI had only Bentley's indirect evidence, he shifted from his defensive stance in the 1947 interview with the FBI to a more aggressive posture. He rejected any possibility of indiscretion on his part and stated that he had no reason to suspect that Silvermaster, Silverman, Ullmann, Coe, and Glasser, whom he readily acknowledged as close friends and associates, had any Communist sympathies. Currie claimed that he had intervened with Under Secretary of War Patterson at the request of an official whose name he could not remember. He said that in his call to Patterson he had not urged a favorable consideration, and he also insisted that it was "customary procedure" in Roosevelt's White House for presidential aides to get in touch with officials at Patterson's level about individual personnel security investigations. This was false: it was unusual for one of the president's half-dozen administrative assistants to intervene in such a matter, but only one member of the committee, Richard Nixon, taxed Currie with the weaknesses of his explanation.[72]

Indeed, one of the committee's most vocal and reactionary members, Democratic representative John Rankin of Mississippi, rushed to Currie's defense. Rankin was an ardent racist who believed that slavery had been a blessing for African Americans. The chief object of his hatred, however, was Jews. He identified the New Deal, liberalism, racial equality, and communism as a Jewish conspiracy. Communism in itself was not really of interest to Rankin unless he could connect it with Jews; he even occasionally had kind words for Stalin, in whom he recognized a fellow anti-Semite. When Bentley testified that Currie had provided information to her espionage network through Silverman and Silvermaster, Rankin lashed out at her for "smearing Currie by remote control through two Communists." Rankin readily believed that Silverman and Silvermaster were Communists because they were Jews. But he could not believe Bentley about Currie because, as Rankin twice said, Currie was a "Scotchman" and therefore ethnically immune to communism.[73]

By 1950, however, Currie felt more vulnerable. The FBI had accumulated more evidence and the then-secret Venona Project had confirmed much of Bentley's story. Exactly what precipitated his decision is unclear, but in late summer of that year he emigrated to Colombia and a few years later renounced his American citizenship.[74]

Bentley's Defection

Although Elizabeth Bentley thought the FBI was closing in, it actually knew nothing about her when she suddenly appeared at an FBI office in August 1945. Was she a defector or a lunatic confessing to imaginary crimes? After several extensive interviews with Bentley and some quick checking on parts of her story, by the late fall of 1945 the FBI became convinced that she was genuine and had been deeply involved in espionage.

One item the FBI discovered was that it already had in hand a letter from Katherine Perlo that had made accusations about some of the same people that Bentley named. Katherine had married Victor Perlo in 1933, but in 1943 he divorced her. Distraught and bitter, in April 1944 Mrs. Perlo sent an unsigned letter to President Roosevelt denouncing her former husband and others as participants in clandestine Communist activities in Washington in the 1930s. The FBI traced the letter back to her, and she confirmed when interviewed that she had written it. In addition to her husband, she named George Silverman, John Abt, Charles Kramer, Harold Glasser, Harry White, Hermann Brunck, Hope Brunck (Hope Hale Davis), and Henry Collins.[75]

Bentley did not defect until more than six months after the KGB had taken over her networks, severed her contact with her agents, and changed her status to inactive. Once she had been replaced as their liaison, her former sources would have regarded any contact by her as a sign that something was amiss and would have been put on their guard. The FBI did, of course, begin extensive surveillance of those she named, in hopes of observing contact with Soviet agents and evidence of criminal activity. But by late 1945, when the FBI began surveillance of those Bentley named, the Soviets appeared to have suspected that their networks had been compromised and warned their sources to cease activity.

Indeed, one contact between a Bentley source and a Soviet intermediary that the FBI did observe appears to have been the actual delivery of a KGB warning that the network was in danger and that contact was being cut. One of the earliest Bentley contacts put under surveillance was Gregory Silvermaster. On December 1, 1945, bureau agents noted a man meeting with Gregory and Helen Silvermaster for several hours. The man was followed, and FBI suspicions were heightened when on his journey back to New York he "executed a number of diversionary maneuvers which appeared to the surveilling Agents to be calculated to ascertain the presence of a surveillance." The FBI identified the man as Alexander Koral, a Communist and maintenance engineer working for the New York City school system.[76]

The FBI had come across Koral several years earlier when it placed Gaik Ovakimian under surveillance. Ovakimian, an Amtorg official, had worked in the United States from 1933 to 1941. After the Nazi-Soviet Pact and the start of World War II, the U.S. government, which had paid little attention to Soviet espionage, belatedly looked into the matter briefly and spotted Ovakimian as an intelligence officer. He was arrested in May 1941 as an unregistered foreign agent. The FBI wanted him prosecuted, but the State Department negotiated an agreement that allowed him to leave the United States in return for the release of six Americans or spouses of Americans whom Soviet authorities had refused to allow out of the USSR. Although the FBI did not know it at the time, Ovakimian was the head of KGB operations in the United States. During its surveillance the FBI noted that Ovakimian met on a number of occasions with Koral and, although nothing could be proved, it was assumed that a Soviet intelligence officer and a school district maintenance man were not meeting for benign purposes.[77]

Confronted by the FBI in 1947, Koral admitted that from 1939 to 1945 he had worked as a clandestine courier. He explained that he had been paid two thousand dollars by someone known to him only as Frank to travel to different cities in order to pick up and deliver small packages and envelopes to different persons, including the Silvermasters. Koral stated that at his last meeting with Gregory Silvermaster, the one observed by the FBI in December 1945, he had also delivered a verbal message from his employer that "no more visits would be made to him." This was probably the KGB's message breaking contact with those compromised by Bentley's defection.[78]

Koral identified a photograph of Semyon Semenov, a KGB officer in New York working under Amtorg cover, as one of the persons to whom he delivered material. Koral's admissions, however, were a strategic retreat, acknowledging what he feared the FBI had observed. He then attempted to put his admissions in a context that would protect him from criminal prosecution. He hid his ties to the CPUSA, apparently unaware that the FBI already knew of his Communist background. He denied all knowledge of the content of the packages and messages he couriered. He presented himself simply as someone doing an odd job on the side for extra money and suggested that those he dealt with were involved in some sort of shady business deals over government war contracts.

The deciphered Venona cables show that Alexander Koral was part of a husband-and-wife KGB courier team. He, under the cover name Berg, and she, under the names Miranda and Art, show up in eleven KGB cables during 1944 and 1945.[79] These cables show that the KGB paid each a regular stipend of a hundred dollars a month in 1945. The cables also show Helen Koral (or more likely the Korals jointly) as one of three KGB courier links assigned to pick up material from the Silvermasters and as a link between Olga Valentinovna Khlopkova, a KGB officer working under diplomatic cover, and the KGB's illegal officer Iskhak Akhmerov. In the latter case, the arrangement usually was for Olga Khlopkova to meet with Helen Koral, who would also meet with Helen Lowry, Akhmerov's wife and assistant. The KGB assumed that these meetings would appear to be normal female socializing and would be less likely to attract FBI attention than contact between male links.

Alexander Koral's work for the KGB as a liaison agent also showed up in statements made to the FBI by Michael Straight. The son of wealthy American liberals who had founded the magazine the *New Republic*, Straight attended Cambridge University in England in 1934 and joined the Communist Party of Great Britain in 1935. He also developed a friendship with Anthony Blunt, the art expert, Cambridge don, and KGB recruiter. Soviet documents made public in 1998 include a 1943 autobiographical report that Blunt made to the KGB in which he discussed his "trying to combine the difficult task of not being thought left-wing and at the same time being in the closest contact with all left-wing students in order to spot likely recruits for us. As you already know the actual recruits whom I took were Michael Straight and . . ."[80] Straight gave his version of what happened in his memoir *After Long Silence*. He said that early in 1937 Blunt ordered him to drop his open Communist connections, return to the United States, and use his family connections to establish a career as a Wall Street banker while secretly working for the Communist cause. Straight protested that he had little interest in business and planned to stay in England and become a British subject. He recorded this conversation with Blunt:

> "Our friends have given a great deal of thought to it. . . . They have instructed me to tell you that that is what you must do."
> "What *I* must do? . . . What friends have instructed you to tell me—"
> "Our friends in the International. The Communist International."[81]

According to Straight, Blunt promised that his objections would be considered. A week later Straight met with Blunt again and learned the party's decision. "If I refused to become a banker that would be accepted. But my appeal was nonetheless rejected. I was to go back to America, and I was to go underground. . . . That was the bargain that was offered to me. I accepted it."[82] Straight publicly distanced himself from his student Communist connections, and shortly before he left Great Britain Blunt introduced him to a "stocky, dark-haired Russian," who gave him a brief introduction to conspiratorial technique.[83]

Through his family connections Straight met with both President Roosevelt and Mrs. Roosevelt to discuss his employment prospects and was hired as an unpaid assistant at the State Department in the fall of 1937. In late 1938 he accepted a paid job as a presidential speechwriter while nominally an employee of the Interior Department. There in 1939 he worked closely with Roosevelt's chief speechwriters and political advisers, James Rowe, Tom Corcoran, and Ben Cohen. In 1940 he returned to the State Department, this time as a regular employee of its European division. In 1941, however, he left State to take a post with the *New Republic* and remained there until he entered the military in 1942.

Meanwhile, early in 1938 Straight was contacted by a Soviet agent who identified himself as Michael Green. For the next four years, Straight says, he met occasionally with Green. At several of these meetings, he gave Green memoranda and reports that he had written at the

State Department and at Interior, none of which were important, he says. Michael Green was an alias, one of the several used by Iskhak Akhmerov, the KGB's leading illegal officer in the United States.

In espionage parlance, a "legal" intelligence officer is one who operates under diplomatic cover. Officers of the KGB working at the Soviet embassy or other recognized agencies of the Soviet government, such as Amtorg, were "legal" officers. Although they pretended to be diplomats or trade officials and often went by false names, they were openly Soviet officials, and their presence in the United States was part of a recognized Soviet activity. Vasily Zubilin, nominally a Soviet diplomat with the Soviet embassy, was a "legal" officer. "Illegals" such as Akhmerov are the classic spies of espionage novels, who have no diplomatic status, no official connection with the Soviet government, and a wholly false identity, often including a false nationality as well.

According to a biography prepared by the Russian Foreign Intelligence Service, Iskhak Abdulovich Akhmerov, born in 1901, was of Tartar background and joined the Communist party in 1919, shortly after the Bolshevik revolution. Recognizing his talent, in 1921 the party sent him to the Communist University of Toilers of the East, a school that principally served the USSR's Asian nationalities, and later to the elite Moscow State University, where he specialized in international relations. He joined the KGB immediately after graduating and served initially in its internal security arm aiding in the suppression of anti-Soviet movements in the USSR's Central Asian republics. He transferred to foreign intelligence in 1932 and served as a legal intelligence officer in Turkey under diplomatic cover. In 1934 he became an illegal officer and, using false identity papers, entered China, where he enrolled at an American-run college in order to improve his English and prepare for his next assignment. He entered the United States in 1935 with false identity documents and remained there for ten years, serving as the chief of the KGB's illegal station from 1942 to 1945. The admiring biography from the Russian Foreign Intelligence Service credits him with having "recruited a number of agents in the State Department, the Treasury Department, and the intelligence services" from whom "important political, scientific-technical, and military information" was obtained. He returned to the USSR in 1945 and became deputy chief of the illegals branch of the KGB's foreign intelligence arm, receiving the rank of full colonel and numerous medals, including the Badge of Honor, two Orders of the Red Banner, and the title of Honored Chekist.[84]

Those Americans who had contact with Akhmerov report that his English, while good, was accented and clearly not native, so most likely he pretended to be an immigrant. Some of the aliases he used are known, but what sort of false identity documents he kept and what profession he claimed are not, although American counterintelligence officers found indications that he maintained a business front as a clothier. He lived on the East Coast, probably in New York, and there are reports that he moved to Baltimore in 1945 shortly before he was withdrawn from the United States. His secret move to the USSR at that time was probably a reaction to concern that Bentley's defection would eventually lead the FBI to him, although there are also some indications that he was in poor health.[85]

Michael Straight records that he once had dinner with Green/Akhmerov and his wife, whom he described as a native-born American with a Midwestern accent. Mrs. Akhmerov, certainly, was a major contributor to Akhmerov's success as an illegal. She was a full partner in his espionage work and acted as his liaison with many of the sources he developed. As a native-born American and a woman, she attracted far less attention than he. She is known to have used the name Helen Lowry. According to several Soviet and American sources, she was also the niece of the CPUSA leader Earl Browder, although through which of his siblings the relation went is unclear. The Browder family was from Kansas (Earl himself never lost his Kansas accent), and Straight's description of Mrs. Akhmerov's accent and origins is compatible with the claim that she was Browder's niece. Bentley also knew the Akhmerovs, as Bill and Catherine. Like Straight, she knew that Bill was Russian and his wife American. Both Iskhak Akhmerov and Helen Lowry show up in scores of Venona messages.[86]

In his memoir Straight, making light of his connections with Soviet intelligence, insists that his contacts with Akhmerov were intermittent and largely inconsequential and that he never committed espionage. Although the KGB archive is not open for research, it has released selected documents, some of which deal with Michael Straight. In 1938 Straight was fresh out of college and working at the State Department job that the White House had arranged for him. In May Akhmerov sent a cable to Moscow informing his KGB superiors that Nigel (Straight's cover name at the time) had recommended one of the State Department rising stars, Alger Hiss, as someone with "progressive" (i.e., pro-Communist) views. Akhmerov, who knew that Hiss was already working for Soviet intelligence through the GRU, appeared to fear that Straight's youthful enthusiasm might compromise an already productive Soviet agent. Akhmerov reported to Moscow that he faced a dilemma because if he told Straight to stay away from Hiss, "he might guess that Hiss belongs to our family." He also worried that from the other side the GRU might order Hiss to recruit Straight and "in this case 'Nigel' would find out Hiss's nature." The message implied that Akhmerov expected the Moscow KGB to make contact with the GRU and make sure that their respective networks did not start tripping over each other. It also suggested that Akhmerov thought it unwise for Straight, a young and undeveloped contact, to know too much about Hiss, a Soviet source of proven reliability and great promise.[87]

Straight claimed that he was appalled by the Nazi-Soviet Pact. By late 1939 he felt himself increasingly estranged from communism and identifying himself inwardly as well as outwardly as a New Deal liberal. He had left government service, he wrote, to extricate himself from his link to Soviet intelligence, but he continued to meet Akhmerov until 1942, when he entered the U.S. armed forces. Unbeknownst to Straight, the KGB had dispatched Arnold Deutsch, a KGB illegal officer who had operated in England from 1934 to 1937, to the United States to renew contact with him and several other sources. Deutsch, however, died when the Soviet ship on which he was traveling was sunk in the Atlantic by a German U-boat in 1942.[88]

After World War II, Straight visited Britain and met his old friend and KGB recruiter, Anthony Blunt. KGB documents show that Blunt informed Moscow that Straight "in principle remains our man," but that he was increasingly disenchanted with the CPUSA.[89] Straight still had a sufficiently Popular Front orientation to align himself with Henry Wallace. When Straight was publisher of the *New Republic* he gave Wallace an editorial position that served as a platform for launching his Progressive party campaign for the presidency in 1948. But Straight was repelled by the CPUSA's secret leading role in the Progressive party, distanced his journal from it, and subsequently moved toward mainstream liberalism. In 1960 he supported John Kennedy, an exemplar of anti-Communist liberalism. In 1963 President Kennedy asked him to chair the Advisory Council on the Arts. Faced with an FBI security check, Straight informed Arthur Schlesinger, Jr., then working in the Kennedy White House, of his past and soon told his story to the FBI. The bureau arranged for him to tell British counterintelligence, MI5, about his contact with Anthony Blunt. Although MI5 had long suspected Blunt of espionage, it had had no firm evidence. With Straight's information in hand, British authorities confronted Blunt, and he confessed his guilt, although he provided few details. The confession and Blunt's spying were kept secret but were exposed by British journalists in 1979, at which time Straight's role also became public.[90]

Straight added to the picture of Alexander Koral as a KGB liaison agent, a go-between linking KGB officers to their sources. Straight told the FBI that because their face-to-face meetings were infrequent, Akhmerov also provided him with a telephone contact: Alexander Koral. The New York School Board later fired Koral when he refused to testify to a congressional investigating committee. The dismissal led one writer in the 1970s to present Koral as a victim of McCarthyism. He was, in fact, a spy, and his loss of public employment was a remarkably light penalty given the seriousness of his offense.[91]

In addition to Koral's meeting with the Silvermasters, the FBI in 1946 may have gotten a second indication that Bentley's various sources had been warned. FBI agents watching Charles Kramer, identified by Bentley as a member of the Perlo network, observed him leaving his residence carrying packages. He then proceeded to an isolated bus stop some distance from his residence and disposed of the material in a streetside trash can. The agents were understandably curious about what he had disposed of in so surreptitious a manner. They checked the can and found an accumulation of CPUSA literature. The obvious conclusion was that he was preparing for a possible search of his home.[92]

It is not known how the KGB learned about Bentley's defection and proceeded to warn her former sources of the need to break contact and cease activity.[93] Shortly after Bentley made contact with the FBI, it arranged for her to schedule a meeting with her KGB supervisor, Anatoly Gromov, head of the KGB office operating out of the Soviet embassy. The FBI observed the meeting on November 21, 1945. It is possible that KGB countersurveillance detected the FBI's surveillance or that Gromov surmised from his discussion with Bentley that she had turned. A still stronger possibility is that a Soviet agent within the Justice Department warned the KGB. Among the earliest Venona messages deciphered (late 1946 or early 1947) was one referring to a Soviet source hired by the Justice Department in 1944 who had access to counterintelligence information. Not surprisingly, that message initiated a crash FBI program to find the rotten apple in its own barrel, and in December 1948 it identified Judith Coplon, an analyst who had been working since early 1945 in the Foreign Agents Registration section of the Justice Department.

Fourteen deciphered KGB Venona messages, a KGB document regarding Coplon found in a Moscow archive, and the Justice Department's prosecution of her provide a fairly complete picture of Coplon's betrayal of the United States.[94] She attended Barnard College and was graduated in 1943. As an undergraduate she participated in the Communist student group at the school. Coplon got her first job in 1944, working for the New York office of the Economic Warfare Section of the Justice Department. A routine personnel security check at the time of her hiring noted her undergraduate Communist activities, but most personnel security offices were on the lookout for Nazi sympathizers, and Coplon's Communist links neither disqualified her nor even earned a flag on her file for future reference. Among Coplon's friends was another young Communist, Flora Wovschin, who already worked for the KGB. Coplon's new job had obvious intelligence interest, and Wovschin sounded her out and reported to the KGB that she was an excellent prospect. The New York office of the KGB agreed, and in July 1944 it requested Moscow's permission to recruit her as an agent.

The New York KGB temporarily suspended further action on her case when a change in personnel forced a reassignment of responsibilities for contact with various covert agents. The KGB headquarters did not get around to Coplon's case for several months. It was not until October that General Fitin sent an inquiry to the Comintern asking if it had any background information on Coplon.[95] Wovschin reported in November that Coplon was impatient for direct contact, and in December the New York KGB office, having received Moscow's approval, announced that it was proceeding and that Coplon's espionage potential had greatly increased since she had obtained a transfer to the Foreign Agents Registration section of the Justice Department.

Vladimir Pravdin, a KGB officer who worked under the cover of a journalist for the TASS news agency, met with Coplon in January 1945 and reported to Moscow that she was a "serious person who is politically well developed and there is no doubt of her sincere desire to help us. She had no doubts about whom she is working for."[96] Pravdin went on to say that he expected that Coplon would provide the KGB with highly valuable information on FBI operations. The remaining deciphered Venona messages regarding Coplon, all from the first half of 1945, report that she was working well, but the KGB had advised her initially to refrain from stealing documents until she was confident that she had consolidated her position at Justice.

In one Venona cable the New York KGB reported that Coplon was studying Russian to assist in getting assigned to work on Soviet-related matters. This gambit succeeded, and she gained access to files on FBI operations directed at possible Soviet agents. There is every reason to believe that Coplon gave the KGB early warning of many FBI counter-intelligence operations from 1945 until she was identified in late 1948. Her alerts allowed the KGB to warn its sources to cease activity and break contact. Consequently, as in the Bentley case, by the time a case got to the point of the FBI's instituting surveillance in order to produce enough evidence to bring a criminal charge, the sources were fore-warned and surveillance produced little.

The FBI arrested Coplon in 1949 in the act of handing over Justice Department counterintelligence files to Valentin Gubitchev, a KGB of-ficer working under cover of being an official of the United Nations. Gubitchev claimed diplomatic immunity and was allowed to return to Moscow. Coplon, though, was tried and convicted of espionage.[97]

Coplon's trial, however, illustrated the difficulties of successfully prosecuting an espionage case under peacetime conditions. Coplon's de-fense attorneys, by insisting that the government add to the public rec-ord the counterintelligence files that Coplon had been transferring to Gubitchev when they were arrested, gave the Soviets in open court the confidential information that their arrested source had stolen. One doc-ument, for example, may have surprised key members of the CPUSA's underground arm. It was an FBI report that in 1944 its agents had surreptitiously entered the residence of Philip Levy, a member of the Communist underground apparatus. Among other things, the agents reported discovering that Levy was storing files belonging to Leon Jo-sephson, a figure in the party underground (chapter 3). Josephson's files contained material that had been stolen in 1938 from the residence of Jay Lovestone, a leading opponent of the CPUSA. Thus, a Soviet agent's theft of government files produced a report of an FBI burglary of a Communist's residence that had turned up the booty of an earlier CPUSA theft of the files of one of its critics.[98]

Once they paid the price of revealing some of the secrets they wanted to protect, government prosecutors had little difficulty winning a conviction. Coplon, after all, had been arrested while actually passing documents to a Soviet official. But though the evidence was clear, its admissibility under the complex standards of U.S. criminal justice was not. The government had no intention of revealing that the FBI had initiated surveillance and wiretaps of Coplon in response to its having broken the cipher to KGB cables that the Soviets believed unbreakable. Authorities feared that if the Soviets learned of the success of American code-breakers, they would end contact with their sources and close down operations revealed in the cables. Such an outcome would prevent the FBI from doing what it had done with Coplon: using Venona to identify a Soviet agent, institute surveillance, and catch the spy in the act. But because the government did not produce Venona as the basis for its actions, an appeals court held that the reasons the government did give lacked probable cause for the surveillance and arrest, and ordered a new trial.

The government reformulated its evidence to avoid the legal technicality that had voided the first trial, but still it did not reveal Venona. For a second time the government tried and convicted Coplon of espionage. But for a second time an appeals court found key evidence inadmissible, owing to lack of probable cause, and returned the case to the trial court. Utterly frustrated, prosecutors had to allow a Soviet agent to walk away free. The only punishments they could inflict were that Coplon lost her job working for the Justice Department and her indictment remained alive, keeping the door open for a third trial. In fact, however, she was never retried. The case also left the public in a sour mood because most people were enraged that an obviously guilty spy had escaped punishment.

As the Coplon case showed, the requirements for a successful criminal prosecution under the American legal system were high—too high for the evidence that the government could produce in court against most of those Elizabeth Bentley had named. And in most instances the government had less direct proof than it did against Coplon: only the testimony of a single witness, Bentley, an admitted ex-spy, whose credibility was vulnerable to attack by a defense attorney. There was a great deal of supporting evidence, but it was largely circumstantial and concerned actions several years in the past. There were no stolen documents or other direct physical evidence of spying. As one FBI official bitterly commented about the Bentley investigation in early 1947, "The subjects in this case are extraordinarily intelligent, at least they are unusually well educated, and include some very prominent people, including Harry Dexter White. It can be expected that some of the finest legal talent in the country would be retained for their defense in the event of prosecution. With the evidence presently available, the case is nothing more than the word of Gregory [Bentley's FBI cover name] against that of the several conspirators. The likely result would be an acquittal under very embarrassing circumstances."[99]

The FBI concluded that its only chance for conviction would be to interview the suspects and hope that "one of the subjects of this case, probably the weakest sister," would break and give them a second witness to join Bentley, or that those interviewed would make provably false statements that would allow a prosecution for perjury.[100] It did not, however, expect this to happen, and with one exception it did not.

When interviewed, most of those whom Bentley had named gave evasive answers or refused to say anything at all, and most refused to sign statements. Later, they would be called before grand juries and congressional committees. There, under oath and conscious that a false answer might result in a perjury charge, most refused to testify, relying on their right under the Fifth Amendment not to incriminate themselves. Four of those Bentley named did testify, denied her charges, but then put themselves beyond prosecution for perjury by leaving the United States: Maurice Halperin, Duncan Lee, Frank Coe, and Lauchlin Currie. Two others, Michael Greenberg and Solomon Adler, left the United States, never to return, before they could be called to testify.

The prudence of these actions is illustrated by the fate of one of those Bentley named who failed to take the Fifth or to leave the United States. Bentley stated that one of her less important sources was William Remington, an employee of the War Production Board when she had contact with him. She explained that one of the CPUSA talent-spotters, Joseph North, an editor of *New Masses,* had introduced Remington to Jacob Golos. Golos completed his recruitment, and Bentley later testified that Remington had furnished information on airplane production, high-octane gasoline, and synthetic rubber and paid her his CPUSA dues money. Bentley described Remington as very nervous about his covert work and as not a major source, and she explained that contact had ceased when he entered the Navy in 1944.[101]

As a result of Bentley's information, the FBI interviewed Remington in 1947. He confirmed that he had known North and that North had introduced him to Golos and Bentley, known to him only as John and

Helen. He even agreed that he had met with Helen/Bentley and given her information. He insisted, however, that none of this was espionage, that he had thought Bentley was a journalist and that he had only handed over publicly available information. He agreed that he had paid Bentley money, but said it was not CPUSA dues but payment for copies of newspapers she had given him. As for North and Golos, he described his meetings with them as innocuous and claimed that only much later did he realize that Joseph North might be a Communist. To prove his loyalty, Remington offered to work as an FBI informant, meet with North, and trap him into making compromising statements. Remington denied that he had ever been a Communist and insisted that although he had been a member of the Communist party's antiwar front group, the American Peace Mobilization, during the period of the Nazi-Soviet Pact, he had actually opposed the group's positions.

Remington's motive for his not very credible statements is unclear. When the FBI interviewed him in 1947, Remington was in the process of applying for a job with the Atomic Energy Commission. He may have tried to account for Bentley's evidence because he hoped that it might still be possible to pursue a government career if he convinced the FBI of his innocence. What he did not know was that the FBI had become convinced of his guilt even before the interview and had already torpedoed a previous attempt of his to get an important government job. After his wartime naval duty, Remington had gotten a position with the Office of War Mobilization and Reconversion. In December of 1946 the FBI learned that Remington was about to be transferred to a professional position in the White House as an aide to one of President Truman's special assistants. An FBI warning that Remington was a suspected Soviet agent put an end to that promotion. The FBI was equally unenthusiastic about the prospect that a Soviet intelligence contact would get a job at the Atomic Energy Commission, and that bid also came to nothing.[102]

Called before a grand jury, Remington did not invoke the right against self-incrimination when asked about his Communist background. In the course of his testimony he made statements that the government was able to prove to have been false. Among other points, Remington denied having taken part in Communist activities, a fact the government easily refuted with, among other evidence, the testimony of his former wife. He was convicted of perjury and imprisoned. Espionage, however, played only a background role in his perjury trial.[103]

Another person named by Bentley was imprisoned under special circumstances. In 1954 Congress passed the Compulsory Testimony Act, which granted authorities the option of offering immunity from prosecution in exchange for testimony. Immunity, of course, removed grounds for taking the Fifth. Edward Fitzgerald, one of those whom Bentley had named as a Soviet source, was given immunity. Fitzgerald still refused to testify and went to jail.

Aside from these two, however, none of the several dozen persons whom Bentley named as spies was tried, much less convicted and imprisoned. Because there were no trials, the FBI's collaborative evidence, impressive in its totality, remained confidential, kept secret in the FBI's files for more than three decades. Congressional investigative committees, chiefly the House Committee on Un-American Activities and the Senate Internal Security Subcommittee, called many of those whom Bentley had named to testify, but again most invoked the Fifth Amendment to avoid testifying. The committees put on the record some of the evidence corroborating Bentley's story, but it was incomplete, only part of what the FBI had accumulated. Further, the congressional investigative committees became enmeshed in partisan politics; a large segment of the public and many commentators dismissed anything brought out in the hearings as suspect. In light of these factors, the doubt that many people came to feel about Bentley's story produced, as one scholar wrote, the consensus that Bentley's charges were the "imaginings of a neurotic spinster."[104] The consensus, however, was wrong. The deciphered Venona cables show that Elizabeth Bentley had told the truth.

CHAPTER 6

MILITARY ESPIONAGE

Most examinations of Soviet espionage focus on Soviet spies linked to the foreign intelligence arm of the KGB. But the KGB's predominance was of recent origin, dating from the early years of World War II.[1] In the 1920s and 1930s the intelligence branch of the Soviet army, the GRU (Glavnoe razvedyvatelnoe upravlenie, or chief intelligence directorate of the Soviet general staff), had more extensive foreign intelligence operations than the KGB.[2] In the late 1920s the GRU had set up the first organized Soviet espionage operation in the United States. Alfred Tilton, a Latvian, and Lydia Stahl, a Russia-born American citizen, put together a courier service and photographic facilities and sought out military information. Tilton also recruited Nicholas Dozenberg, the first American GRU agent about whom much is known.

Nicholas Dozenberg

Born in Latvia in 1882, Nicholas Dozenberg immigrated to the United States in 1904. He joined the radical Lettish Workingmen's Society, the Latvian-language affiliate of the Socialist party, which split from that party in 1919 to form the new American Communist movement. By 1923 Dozenberg held the position of literature director of the Workers party, as the CPUSA then termed itself. He dropped out of open party work in 1927 to become an agent of the GRU under Alfred Tilton.[3]

Over the next decade Dozenberg carried out a variety of tasks for Soviet intelligence. Several involved use of American territory as the staging grounds for Soviet espionage operations aimed at foreign nations, particularly France and Romania. (In that era those nations as well as others were of higher priority to Soviet intelligence than was the United States.) He also assisted a Soviet GRU officer in obtaining American identity documents and a U.S. passport as Frank Kleges (the real Kleges was dead). The fake Kleges then proceeded to France to carry out GRU operations there under cover of his American identity. While working for the GRU, Dozenberg also established cover offices in China, representing an American radio manufacturer, and in the Philippines, marketing Bell and Howell motion picture equipment.

The ease with which Dozenberg was able to gain a Bell and Howell franchise for a cover business illustrates another aspect of Soviet intelligence operations in the United States in the 1930s. Dozenberg received authorization to represent Bell and Howell with the assistance of William Kruse, head of the company's film division.[4] Like Dozenberg, Kruse had been a mid-level CPUSA leader in the 1920s and had also served with the Comintern in Moscow for a time. In 1929 Jay Lovestone and several hundred of his adherents, including Kruse, were expelled for ideological deviation. For several years Lovestone and his followers termed themselves the "Communist Party (Opposition)" and continued to proclaim their loyalty to the Soviet Union, which several covertly demonstrated by assisting Soviet espionage.[5] Dozenberg had entered GRU service before Lovestone was expelled from the CPUSA, but he had been aligned with Lovestone and made full use of the continued willingness of some of Lovestone's followers to undertake Soviet intelligence tasks.

In the late 1930s Stalin unleashed a purge of the Soviet intelligence services in which hundreds of GRU and KGB officers were executed. Numerous Soviet intelligence officers serving abroad were recalled and arrested. Fearing for their lives, some dropped out of Soviet service. Whittaker Chambers, who worked for a GRU network in the United States, attributed his defection in part to fear of being called to Moscow. Nicholas Dozenberg also dropped out in the late 1930s. He attempted to live quietly in Oregon, but a more vocal GRU defector, Walter Krivitsky, exposed him as a GRU agent in an article published in the *Saturday Evening Post*. Arrested in December 1939, Dozenberg confessed, in exchange for being allowed to plead guilty to a single charge of using a false passport, and was sentenced to a year in prison in 1940. Dozenberg's statement confirmed, among other points, that Philip Rosenblit, a Communist dentist in New York, was part of the courier system for delivering Soviet money to Soviet intelligence networks in the United States as well as funds to subsidize the CPUSA itself. Dozenberg also stated that he had recruited Philip Aronberg, a veteran American Communist, for GRU assignments.[6]

Other American Agents of the GRU in the 1930s

A surprising fallout from Dozenberg's confession, however, was that what had earlier been regarded as an ordinary case of currency counterfeiting turned out to be part of a Soviet intelligence operation. In 1933 the U.S. Secret Service, which had jurisdiction over counterfeiting, traced some counterfeit money through an intermediary to Dr. Valentine Burtan, who refused to reveal to authorities the source of nearly $100,000 in counterfeit bills. He received a sentence of fifteen years. After Dozenberg's arrest in 1940 and his confession to having been a GRU agent, Burtan talked. He told the FBI that Dozenberg had been his source and that the money was to be used to finance Soviet covert operations. In addition to his role in the failed counterfeiting scheme, Burtan had been Dozenberg's partner in the American Rumanian Film Corporation, one of the business covers that Dozenberg had established to assist Soviet intelligence infiltration of Romania. Burtan had been a member of the CPUSA in the 1920s and had been expelled with Lovestone in 1929.[7]

Burtan's work for the GRU earned him reentry into the Communist movement. While in federal prison in 1935 he received a visit from a jeweler named Julius Heiman. In the early 1920s some of the Soviet subsidies provided to the American Communist movement had been in the form of jewelry rather than cash, and Heiman, a secret party member, was one of the outlets the CPUSA had used to convert the jewelry into currency. Max Bedacht, a senior CPUSA official, raised funds to assist Burtan's wife and family while he was in prison. William Edward Crane, who worked for the GRU in the 1930s—he was one of Whittaker Chambers's photographers—told the FBI that he remembered taking money, at the request of either Chambers or Boris Bykov, his GRU controller, to a woman in upper Manhattan who he thought was the wife of someone in jail for counterfeiting money. It was probably Mrs. Burtan. After Burtan left prison (he was paroled after ten years), he reestablished ties with the CPUSA.[8]

In the early 1930s the GRU replaced Tilton as head of its U.S. operations with Mark Zilbert, also known as Moishe Stern and later, in the Spanish Civil War, as General Kleber. One of his major operations was foiled when a source he had recruited to steal military secrets went to the Office of Naval Intelligence and for months turned over faked material to the Russians. One of Zilbert's successors was Aleksandr Ulanovsky, who supervised Whittaker Chambers's early espionage endeavors. Another of Ulanovsky's contacts was Robert Gordon Switz, son of wealthy American parents, who obtained military plans pertaining to the Panama Canal through a network of American Communists. One of Switz's sources, U.S. Army corporal Robert Osman, was convicted of taking defense information but won reversal of the verdict on appeal. The Army, however, discharged him. Switz, arrested in 1933 while on a mission to France by French counterintelligence, made a full confession.[9] Another GRU agent, the Finnish-American Communist Arvid Jacobson, was also arrested, when he went on a GRU mission to Finland in 1933.

Some of the GRU's known activities in the United States during World War II are not mentioned in the decrypted Venona cables. Undoubtedly, these are among the thousands of cables that were never deciphered. But enough was decrypted to give a picture that looks remarkably like the outlines of the activities of the KGB, but on a smaller scale. In particular, like the KGB, the GRU habitually used ideologically motivated American Communists (Dozenberg and Chambers, for example) and veterans of the International Brigades as sources and agents.

Alger Hiss

A prime example of ideologically driven espionage was the activity of the most infamous Soviet spy linked to the GRU, Alger Hiss. Hiss was one of the original members of the Ware group of young American Communists in the Agricultural Adjustment Administration in the early 1930s, and he became a valued member of the CPUSA-GRU network managed by Whittaker Chambers. Hiss was only a mid-level State Department official at the time of Chambers's defection in 1938, but he was already marked as a rising star. And rise he did. By the end of World War II he was a senior assistant to the secretary of state and part of the American diplomatic delegation that accompanied President Roosevelt to Yalta in 1945 to negotiate the final stages of the war with Joseph Stalin and Winston Churchill. He headed the State Department's Office of Special Political Affairs, which oversaw United Nations diplomacy, and he presided at the founding conference of the UN in San Francisco in 1945. He left the State Department in 1946 to lead the prestigious Carnegie Endowment for International Peace.

Hiss was a highly respected member of the Washington establishment. Unbeknownst to the public and the press, however, Hiss had been very quietly eased out of the government by Truman administration officials who feared that he was a security risk and might become an embarrassment because of accumulating indications that he was in covert contact with Soviet intelligence. In 1945 Igor Gouzenko, a GRU cipher clerk who had defected in Ottawa, handed over to Canadian authorities more than a hundred Soviet military intelligence documents and his personal knowledge of GRU operations. Shocked Canadian authorities learned that the Soviets had used their wartime alliance with Canada as an opportunity to launch extensive espionage operations on Canadian soil. Gouzenko's documents and information allowed Canadian authorities to break up several GRU spy networks, discharge a number of government employees who had surreptitiously assisted the Soviets, and send five Soviet spies to prison. Those imprisoned included Allan Nunn May (a British scientist working in Canada on part of the British-American atomic bomb project), Fred Rose (a Communist member of the Canadian parliament), and Sam Carr (the national organizing secretary of the Communist Party of Canada). Canadian prime minister Mackenzie King contacted President Truman, and the Royal Canadian Mounted Police shared with American officials those parts of the Gouzenko investigation that bore on American matters. One of these was that Gouzenko had heard other GRU officers bragging that the agency had a source who was an assistant to the American secretary of state.[10] In the same year, and independently of Gouzenko, Elizabeth Bentley told the FBI that one member of the Perlo group had earlier been part of a separate Soviet network headed by Alger Hiss. And, of course, by this time the FBI had begun to pay attention to Chambers's 1939 information, given to Assistant Secretary of State Berle, that Hiss had been part of a covert Communist group.

Chambers told the House Committee on Un-American Activities in 1948 that Hiss had been a member of the Ware group in the early 1930s. Initially he did not accuse Hiss of espionage, only of having been a Communist. Hiss demanded and got an opportunity to reply. He flatly denied any Communist links and denied even knowing Chambers. Hiss's rebuttal carried the day with the press, but the committee persisted, and Hiss's story began to crumble. Chambers provided details of a close relationship with the Hiss family during the 1930s, and Hiss began to backtrack, stating that he had known Chambers, but under a different name and only casually. He continued to deny any Communist connections.

Hiss increasingly found himself on the defensive. Chambers said, for example, that Hiss had given the Communist party an old car he no longer needed for use by a party organizer. Hiss testified that he had sold the car to Chambers as part of a deal in which Chambers rented an apartment from Hiss. Congressional investigators, however, produced motor vehicle records bearing Hiss's signature to show that ownership of the auto had been signed over to an official of the Communist party. Press coverage began to shift from overwhelmingly pro-Hiss to a more neutral stance. Chambers was protected from a slander suit when testifying before a congressional committee, and Hiss then attempted to regain the offensive with a challenge to Chambers to repeat his claims outside of a congressional hearing. It was an ill-advised ploy. Chambers repeated his charges on the television program *Meet the Press*. After a three-week delay that caused consternation among his supporters, Hiss sued.

In preparation for the slander trial, Hiss's lawyers demanded that Chambers produce any documents relevant to his charge that Hiss had been a Communist. Chambers, to the lawyers' surprise, did have documents, ones he had not discussed with the House Committee on Un-American Activities. They included four sheets of paper in Hiss's handwriting with summaries of State Department information, sixty-five typewritten pages copied from confidential State Department material that had passed through Hiss's office in 1938 (and many pages that experts identified as having been typed on Hiss's typewriter kept at his residence), and two microfilm reels of State Department documents from 1938 with Hiss's initials on them. Although the documents did not prove that Hiss had been a Communist, they were powerful evidence that he been a spy. A grand jury looked into the matter and indicted Hiss for perjury. The statute of limitations had expired for an espionage charge, but the charge of having lied under oath to the grand jury when he made statements to the effect that he had never passed documents to Chambers was a way of getting at the same offense. After one hung jury, Hiss was convicted in 1950 and imprisoned for three and a half years.

The evidence at the trial and that which has appeared subsequently from Russian archives firmly establishes Hiss's espionage on behalf of the Soviet Union in the 1930s.[11] But what was until recently left open was whether Hiss's betrayal of the United States continued beyond the 1930s. Chambers's personal knowledge and the documents he produced were all from that decade. A number of persons who spied for the Soviet Union in those years later deserted the Communist cause. Some, like Chambers, later publicly acknowledged their role. Others quietly dropped out of espionage.

Some commentators have thought Hiss belonged to the latter group and speculated that when the Nazi-Soviet Pact was concluded in 1939, someone of Hiss's idealism would have seen that his faith in the Soviet cause was misplaced. In 1990, however, a onetime KGB officer, Oleg Gordievsky, stated that Hiss had continued to work for the Soviets in the 1940s.[12] The Venona decryptions support his claim. Hiss is named openly in one message, a 1943 GRU cable noting that a KGB report about the State Department mentioned Hiss. The remainder of the message was undeciphered and the significance of the cable unknown.[13] The Venona Project also deciphered a KGB message about a meeting between a KGB officer and a GRU source with the cover name Ales. And Ales, the evidence indicates, was Alger Hiss. While the KGB, GRU, and Naval GRU tended to keep their networks independent of each other, cross-agency contacts were far from rare. Further, the KGB had the authority to poach on the territory of the GRU and Naval GRU, appropriating their sources if it wished. In the history of Soviet espionage, the most notable example of this is atomic spying. The GRU penetrated Britain's early atomic bomb program and developed one of the Soviets' most important sources, Klaus Fuchs. But when Stalin made atomic espionage a priority, the KGB took over much of the GRU's atomic espionage operation, and when Fuchs came to work on the American atomic bomb program, he was already firmly under KGB jurisdiction.[14]

Before dealing with the Venona message on Ales, however, we should take note of a KGB document located by the historian Allen Weinstein. This cable, dated March 5, 1945, from the KGB office in Washington to Moscow, states that the Washington office had asked one of its agents, Ruble, to report on Ales. Ruble was the cover name in the Venona traffic for Harold Glasser, a Treasury Department official who spied for the Soviets. According to the cable, " 'Ruble' gives to 'Ales' an exceptionally good political reference as to a member of the Communist Party. 'Ruble' informs [me] that 'Ales' is a strong, determined man with a firm and resolute character."[15] Glasser, who, like Hiss, had been an active member of the Washington Communist underground in the 1930s, would have been qualified to give this evaluation of Hiss.

The March 5 cable is then followed by a deciphered March 30 Venona message about Ales. The NSA/FBI footnote to the Ales message identifies Ales as "probably Alger Hiss." It was not a difficult identification to make. The description of Ales in the KGB message fits Hiss, and it is difficult to imagine its fitting anyone but Hiss.[16]

"As a result of A.'s chat with Ales," the report notes, "the following has been ascertained: 1. Ales has been working with the Neighbors continuously since 1935." The Neighbors was KGB jargon for the GRU. Chambers had Hiss entering the CPUSA underground in 1934 and beginning to steal documents in 1935, and contended that Hiss was part of a group that came under GRU supervision. A. is unidentified, but the context of other KGB Venona messages suggests that it was the initial of Albert, the cover name of the illegal officer Iskhak Akhmerov. (The defector Gordievsky had linked Akhmerov to Hiss.)

"2. For some years past he has been the leader of a small group of the Neighbors' probationers, for the most part consisting of his relations." "Probationers" was standard KGB jargon for agents. Hiss's closest associates in his espionage work were his wife, Priscilla, who typed many of the documents he stole from the State Department, and his brother Donald, who also worked for the State Department for a time.

"3. The group and Ales himself work on obtaining military information only. Materials on the Bank allegedly interest the Neighbors very little and he does not produce them regularly. 4. All the last few years Ales has been working with Pol [unidentified] who also meets other members of the group occasionally. 5. Recently Ales and his whole group were awarded Soviet decorations." This passage indicates that Ales worked for the State Department (Bank), as Hiss did. It also says that the Neighbors/GRU were pressing Ales to produce military rather than the diplomatic information more readily available to him. In the 1920s and early 1930s, when the GRU dominated Soviet foreign intelligence operations, its networks sought political and strategic information as well as more narrowly defined military intelligence. But as the KGB established its supremacy in foreign intelligence, the GRU's jurisdiction was steadily narrowed. It had to get its agents to produce more strictly military information or risk losing them to the KGB. The GRU's stress on military intelligence may explain the extraordinary proposal Hiss made in September 1945, that the State Department create a new post, that of "special assistant for military affairs" linked to his Office of Special Political Affairs. The GRU's need for military intelligence also explains why when security officers belatedly began to look closely at Hiss in 1946 they discovered that he had obtained top secret reports "on atomic energy . . . and other matters relating to military intelligence" that were outside the scope of his Office of Special Political Affairs, which dealt largely with United Nations diplomacy.[17]

"6. After the Yalta Conference, when he had gone on to Moscow, a Soviet personage in a very responsible position (Ales gave to understand that it was Comrade Vishinski [the deputy Soviet foreign minister]) allegedly got in touch with Ales and at the behest of the Military Neighbors passed on to him their gratitude and so on." This passage indicates that Ales had been at the Yalta conference and had returned to the United States through Moscow. After the Yalta conference, most of the American delegation returned directly to the United States via Iran. Those Americans attending from the U.S. embassy in Moscow returned to Moscow but did not, as Ales did, then proceed quickly to the United States. (This message came only a month after the Yalta conference ended.) There was, however, a small party of four State Department officials who flew to Moscow to wrap up some details with the Soviets and then proceeded after a brief layover to Washington. There has never been any allegation or evidence that three of them— Secretary of State Edward Stettinius, Director of the Office of European Affairs H. Freeman Matthews, and Wilder Foote, Stettinius's press aide—were Soviet agents. The fourth official was Alger Hiss.[18]

Another illustration of the overlap and mutual corroboration of the testimony of Whittaker Chambers, various Venona messages (that on Ales/Hiss discussed in this chapter and those on Glasser, Victor Perlo, and Charles Kramer discussed in chapter 5), and the KGB documents cited by Weinstein is a passage from Elizabeth Bentley's FBI deposition in 1945:

> Referring again to Harold Glasser, I recall that after his return from his assignment in Europe, probably in Italy, for the United States Treasury Department, Victor Perlo told me that Glasser had asked him if he would be able to get back in with the Perlo group. I asked Perlo how Glasser happened to leave the group and he explained that Glasser and one or two others had been taken sometime before by some American in some governmental agency in Washington, and that this unidentified American turned Glasser and the others over to some Russian. Perlo declared he did not know the identity of this American, and said that Charley Kramer, so far as he knew, was the only person who had this information. Sometime later I was talking with Kramer in New York City, and brought up this matter to him. At this time Kramer told me that the person who had originally taken Glasser away from Perlo's group was named Hiss and that he was in the U.S. State Department.[19]

Between Bentley's testimony, the Ales Venona cable, and the new KGB documents Weinstein located in Moscow, there is little doubt that Hiss's service to Soviet intelligence continued beyond the 1930s and at least until 1945.

Arthur Adams

Arthur Adams was a long-term Soviet agent whose American ties went back to the earliest years of a Soviet presence in the United States. The connections he developed immediately after the formation of the Soviet Union enabled him to build an agent network that paid dividends in the 1940s. While the FBI apparently was able to neutralize his efforts at atomic espionage far more successfully than it countered the KGB's, many of the details of his network of agents and their activities remain obscure. Adams himself was not identified in the Venona messages, nor were several of his close collaborators. Either they are among the cover names that have never been identified or else the messages dealing with them were never decrypted.

Adams was an Old Bolshevik. Born either in one of the Scandinavian countries or the Baltic regions of the Russian empire, he knew Lenin from pre-revolutionary days in Russia. He entered the United States in 1910 as an immigrant and first came into public view as the head of the "technical department" of the Soviet Russian Information Bureau during 1919–1921. The United States did not officially recognize Lenin's new Soviet regime, and the Information Bureau was the Soviet government's unofficial embassy. The head of the Information Bureau, Ludwig Martens, said that Adams had been born in Russia but had acquired British citizenship and was a graduate of the School of Science in Kronstadt, Russia, and the University of Toronto. The U.S. government expelled Martens and Adams in 1921 and ordered the Information Bureau closed.[20]

Adams returned to the United States in the 1920s and 1930s, ostensibly on missions for Amtorg but actually in his role as a GRU officer. In the 1920s he also divorced his first wife (who had arrived in the United States in 1914) and married Dorothea Keen, the American-born daughter of a Russian immigrant, who had also been on the staff of the Soviet Russian Information Bureau. Adams entered the United States through Canada with a false passport in 1938. Soon afterward he set up a business called Technological Laboratories with a New Jersey man named Philip Levy. On the surface Levy, born in Russia in 1893, was a respectable businessman, the president of Federated Trading Corporation in New York, a textile firm engaged in import-export. In 1935, however, an associate of his, Leon Josephson, was arrested in Copenhagen and charged with espionage on behalf of the Soviet Union. Josephson claimed he was on a business trip in connection with Levy's firm. One of the men arrested with Josephson was traveling under a false American passport made out to Nicholas Sherman. Sherman was Aleksandr Ulanovsky, the GRU officer who directed Soviet espionage in the United States in the early 1930s. Levy did more than merely provide a business cover for Josephson's covert activities. Josephson's files and those of other members of the CPUSA's underground arm were hidden in Levy's residence, where they were found in a secret FBI search in 1944. Levy, however, told a congressional committee that he was not aware of Josephson's activities, and he also denied knowing anything about Technological Laboratories, the firm headed by Adams, although Levy was one of the company's officers.[21]

Adams had other associates who were part of the CPUSA underground. Just like Akhmerov, the KGB's leading illegal officer, the GRU's Adams treated the CPUSA as a recruiting pool for the GRU and the party's underground as an auxiliary to his espionage activities. When the FBI undertook surveillance of Adams during World War II, its agents observed that Adams visited Victoria Stone, owner of the Victoria Stone Jewelry Corporation, almost daily either at her home or at her store on Madison Avenue. In 1935 Stone had approached an attorney to get legal help for Dr. Valentine Burtan, the Lovestoneite who had been convicted of involvement in a counterfeiting scheme run by the GRU agent Nicholas Dozenberg. Julius Heiman, who visited Burtan in prison, was the secretary-treasurer of Stone's jewelry company. Heiman, as noted above, had arranged to convert jewels sent by the Comintern in the early 1920s into cash for the CPUSA. Still another business associate of Adams in the late 1930s was M. G. Kahn, who had been arrested in 1919 for smuggling jewels into the United States from Russia.[22]

The FBI became interested in Adams in 1943 when he was observed attempting to recruit as sources several scientists working at the Manhattan Project's Chicago laboratories. After observing these meetings, FBI and Manhattan Project security men surreptitiously entered Adams's apartment in New York. They discovered very sophisticated camera equipment, materials for constructing microdots, and notes on aspects of experiments being conducted at the atomic bomb laboratories at Oak Ridge, Tennessee.[23]

As cover for his espionage activities, Adams was employed by two companies headed by Communists. The Electronics Corporation of America, led by Sam Novick, held Navy contracts for the manufacture of radar. Novick, who had signed Adams's immigration papers when he entered the United States illegally from Canada in 1938, had falsely stated that Adams had been employed by him for ten years. The Keynote Recording Company, headed by Eric Bernay, a former editor of *New Masses,* paid Adams a salary. Early in 1945 Bernay helped Adams escape FBI surveillance and leave New York. Adams left Victoria Stone's apartment and walked a dog up a one-way street, then hailed a taxicab and fled before FBI agents could follow. He then boarded a train with Bernay. The FBI picked them up in Chicago, trailed Adams to Portland, and prevented him from boarding a Soviet ship. The State Department, fearful of offending the Soviets, ordered the FBI not to arrest him but also not to let him leave the country. Adams, however, later evaded FBI surveillance, disappeared, and presumably returned to the USSR.[24]

Joseph Bernstein and *Amerasia*

Although Adams's activities are not visible in the few GRU messages deciphered by the Venona Project, other GRU agents were identified. One agent whose activities were exposed was Joseph Bernstein, whose cover name in Venona is Marquis. Bernstein was a suspect in the first major post–World War II espionage case, the *Amerasia* affair, but was never indicted. Venona documents Bernstein's other activities on behalf of Soviet intelligence, while throwing some light on *Amerasia* itself.

Security officers from the Office of Strategic Services, investigating how portions of a secret report had come to be printed in the journal *Amerasia,* which was published by the wealthy, pro-Soviet greeting-card entrepreneur Philip Jaffe, secretly entered the magazine's offices in the spring of 1945 and discovered hundreds of classified government documents. When the case was turned over to the FBI, it wiretapped and bugged several of the editors and their contacts in Washington. One such bug, in a Washington hotel room occupied by Jaffe on May 7, 1945, picked up a conversation with Andrew Roth, a lieutenant in the Office of Naval Intelligence assigned as a liaison officer to the State Department. Jaffe mentioned to Roth that Joseph Bernstein, a former *Amerasia* employee, had told him that for many years he had worked for Soviet intelligence. According to Jaffe, Bernstein had said, "I would like to ask you whether you are willing to give me the dope you get on Chungking out of the Far Eastern Division of the State Department."[25]

Jaffe was willing to help Bernstein, but he insisted on checking his bona fides as a Soviet agent. The day after Bernstein's request, Jaffe visited first John Stuart, a writer for *New Masses,* and then Earl Browder at his home in Yonkers. Although the FBI observed Jaffe's meetings with Bernstein, Stuart, and Browder, it was not able to overhear the conversations. But Jaffe recounted them to Roth and to the hidden FBI microphones. Browder had advised Jaffe to insist on meeting Bernstein's Soviet contact. If he was genuine, "he'll find a way to prove it. If he can't find a way, don't deal with him. It may be that he [Bernstein] is . . . on his own, and he just wants to put a feather in his own cap, if he can get a little something. And if it's just personal, nothing doing. Don't touch it."[26]

Although Jaffe and Bernstein held several more meetings, monitored by the FBI, and may even have exchanged some information, Bernstein apparently had not yet been able to arrange a meeting between Jaffe and his Soviet superiors when Jaffe, Roth, and several associates were arrested on June 6 on charges of conspiracy to commit espionage. Although the FBI believed that Bernstein was a Soviet agent, it never arrested him, in part because the stenographer who transcribed the bugged conversation rendered his name as Bursley and perhaps because the evidence gained by bugging was inadmissible in court.[27]

Confirmation that Bernstein was a GRU agent comes from the Venona decryptions. They make clear that he provided the GRU with information he received from several sources. And they shed light on the activities of two other spies, Philip and Mary Jane Keeney, who worked for both the KGB and the GRU.

There are five decrypted messages mentioning Marquis/Bernstein, all from 1943.[28] In one, Pavel Mikhailov, the GRU chief in New York, noted that Marquis had reported that he had become friends with T. A. Bisson, who was named in plain text and then given the cover name Arthur. Bisson had just left the Board of Economic Warfare and was with the Institute of Pacific Relations and "in the editorial office of Marquis's periodical."[29] Bernstein was then working for *Amerasia,* and Bisson was a close collaborator of Jaffe's. Bisson, who had been a staunch supporter of the Chinese Communists for many years, had been a founding editorial board member of both *China Today* and *Amerasia.* He was also a leading promoter of the view that the Chinese Communists under Mao Tse-tung were not real Marxist-Leninists. He wrote that the correct terminology for "so-called Communist China" was "democratic China," and that the system in place in Mao's areas was "in fact, the essence of *bourgeois* democracy."[30] When he testified before the Special Committee on Un-American Activities in 1943, Bisson denied Communist sympathies. All of his activities, he swore, had been devoted to promoting greater understanding of the USSR and China in the United States. Presumably in the interest of promoting greater understanding, Bisson turned over confidential Board of Economic Warfare reports to Bernstein in 1943, and the GRU dispatched them by diplomatic pouch, meanwhile notifying Moscow by cable that the reports included a valuable joint British-American evaluation of the military situation on the Russian-German front as well as reports on American troops shipped to China, a report by the Chinese embassy in Washington about trade between Chinese industrialists and the Japanese in China, and a report by the American consul on conditions in Vladivostok.[31]

In another message, Bernstein reported on the views of William Phillips, FDR's special envoy to India, and provided information about material *Amerasia* had received from a journalist who had interviewed the Chinese minister of war. A third Venona message contained more information from Bisson about Chiang Kai-shek's efforts to combat the Chinese Communists and discussions within the U.S. government about making direct contact with the Chinese Communists to arrange the establishment of air bases on territory they controlled.[32]

The Librarian Spies: Philip and Mary Jane Keeney

Bernstein also supervised another pair of agents with interesting radical credentials—Philip and Mary Jane Keeney. The Keeneys were librarians who first came to prominence in 1937 when Philip's firing by the president of the University of Montana for radical activity elicited widespread protests. While awaiting resolution of their court challenge to the dismissal, the Keeneys lived in Berkeley, California, and were in frequent contact with Communists; indeed, Mary Jane's diaries indicate that they were members of the Marin County CPUSA club. In 1940 Philip was hired at the Library of Congress and soon transferred to the Office of Strategic Services, where he served as a librarian. Mary Jane worked for the Board of Economic Warfare during World War II. Both were active in CPUSA fronts in Washington and friendly with many of those later accused of espionage, including the Silvermasters, William Ullmann, and Maurice Halperin. On November 1, 1945, Mary Jane left for Europe, where she worked for the Allied Staff on Reparations. Philip, meanwhile, left for Tokyo, where he worked on General MacArthur's staff, helping rebuild the Japanese library system. Mary Jane Keeney returned to the United States on March 9, 1946, to be met by the GRU agent Joseph Bernstein. Philip came home in the fall before returning to Japan in January 1947.[33]

The Keeneys are mentioned in three deciphered Venona messages.[34] The first is a KGB message from General Fitin in Moscow to Vasily Zubilin in New York in May 1942. The message has been only partially deciphered, but it appears to contain either suggestions by the Moscow KGB headquarters on persons who might be used to penetrate the OSS or comments by Moscow on suggestions made earlier by Zubilin. At that time a large section of the OSS staff was housed at the Library of Congress, and the cable mentions that Jacob Golos met Philip Keeney there. In response, on May 22 Zubilin noted that Keeney "is being entrusted to our agentura," a statement that his recruitment would be undertaken.[35] Keeney, however, was not recruited by the KGB in 1942. The reason may be that he was already working for the GRU. Sergey Kurnakov, a Russian immigrant and one of the KGB's most industrious agents, noted in a report in 1944 that "Keeney and his wife were signed on apparently by the Neighbors [GRU] for work in 1940."[36]

In 1944, however, the KGB decided that it was time to push the GRU out of the picture. Through "a highly confidential source," an FBI euphemism for a break-in, the bureau obtained a copy of Mary Jane Keeney's diaries from 1938 to 1945. It also intercepted and read correspondence between Mary Jane and Philip. This material chronicles Kurnakov's takeover of the two for the KGB. One month before Kurnakov's report about their GRU affiliation, the Keeneys had dinner with someone identified in the diaries as Colonel Thomas. Thomas "takes us to dinner and then discovers he came on a wild goose chase," in Mary Jane's words.[37] Thomas was, the FBI determined, Mary Jane's cover name for Kurnakov. One factor identifying Kurnakov as Thomas was that the diary records Colonel Thomas's leaving the United States to return to his homeland at the same time as Kurnakov returned to the Soviet Union. Several letters refer to Thomas's impending departure. On December 20 Philip noted in regard to Thomas, "It is wonderful for him that he is returning. It makes me green with envy." A handwritten note from Thomas was found indicating that around January 10, 1946, he would be going home. Kurnakov left the United States in January 1946. The "wild goose chase" was, of course, Thomas's discovery that the Keeneys were already working for Soviet intelligence.

Kurnakov, however, was not deterred by the GRU connection, and sometime between August 1944 and November 1945 the Keeneys went to work for the KGB. In November Philip was in New York, preparing to leave for Japan. He wrote Mary Jane several letters that make his intentions and loyalties clear. On November 22 he noted that "our friends, including Thomas, have made it clear there is a job to do and it falls to my lot to do it." On November 24 he indicated that while in New York he intended to see Colonel Thomas and Joe Bernstein. On November 29 he proudly wrote that he had spent several hours "with Col. Thomas which is a pass word to use in the higher circles." On December 1: "Last night I had a long session with Col. Thomas and I left with a terrible sense of responsibility."[38]

Philip Keeney had been recruited by the KGB but had not yet provided intelligence information when he went to Japan. Several letters to his wife suggested that his work for Soviet military intelligence under Joseph Bernstein had not been very productive. On February 2, 1946, he wrote to Mary Jane from Tokyo that "I presume word from Col. Thomas will be reaching us both in due course. I am certain we will be reached when something turns up for us to do. I have the feeling, at any rate, that we are both on call now which is more that I have felt for months past." And, two months later, he reflected that "probably, I might not have come to Japan, had it not been for my serious confabs with Col. Thomas. Now that I am here it seems as if I were repeating the long dry spell that twice occurred when we were part of Joe B's plans. I should have followed Greg's advice and relaxed."[39]

The Keeneys' equanimity was disturbed by the escalating investigations into Soviet espionage in 1946, prompted by Elizabeth Bentley's defection and that of Igor Gouzenko in Canada. In March 1946 Mary Jane sent a letter to Philip in Japan via a friend, warning him to be careful of what he wrote to such old acquaintances as the Silvermasters. Their friends were afraid they were being wiretapped and their mail examined. She concluded that "Joe told me to be on the lookout as well as several others in New York. There is no reason for alarm on your part or mine only it is well to remember that it's better to be safe than sorry." Two months later she wrote that their old GRU contact was temporarily on ice: "Joe B. [Bernstein] doesn't expect to be back in the swim for a long long time. He says that the Canadian affair will have a very lingering effect."[40] The "Canadian affair" was a reference to Gouzenko's defection in Ottawa.

The Keeneys both lost their government jobs but never were prosecuted for their espionage. Mary Jane secured a job at the United Nations, from which she was also fired under pressure from the American government. They were called to testify to a congressional investigating committee, were uncooperative and convicted of contempt of Congress. The convictions, however, were reversed on appeal. The two then opened an art film club. Joseph Bernstein, their original GRU handler, also escaped prosecution and worked as a translator and writer.

The GRU and the Lincoln Battalion

Several GRU agents identified in Venona were veterans of the Abraham Lincoln battalion. There is only one Venona message about Daniel Abraham Zaret, named in plain text in a message from New York to Moscow. Zaret, who served as aide-de-camp to the commander of the International Brigades' Fifteenth Division in Spain, returned to the United States in November 1938. Until August 1943 he worked in various explosives factories, at the last one as assistant director in Williamsport, Pennsylvania. He was slated to become production safety inspector in the Explosives Division of the War Department in Chicago when the New York GRU office informed Moscow that Zaret had already passed on to his GRU contact some data on material being used for shells, bombs, and torpedoes.[41]

Other information came to the GRU from Thomas Babin, a Communist organizer and Spanish Civil War veteran. Babin, born in 1901 in Croatia, was deported from the United States for Communist activities in 1925 but reentered by 1928 and remained illegally, serving as a leader of the Croatian Communists in America and one of the CPUSA leaders on the New York waterfront. He served in Spain from 1937 to 1939, first in a Balkan unit and then in the Abraham Lincoln battalion. During World War II Babin worked as a longshoreman in Hoboken, New Jersey, and briefly served in the OSS.[42]

Under the cover name Brem in Venona, Babin kept the GRU closely informed about his OSS activities.[43] Babin was apparently being trained, along with a group of other Yugoslavs, to be sent first to Cairo and then to Yugoslavia itself as liaison with anti-Nazi partisans. Babin vouched for several of his fellow trainees as potential GRU contacts, but an illness or injury prevented him from accompanying them when they left the United States. In one message, in July 1943, the New York GRU station queried Moscow: "Since they were recommended to the school by Brem [Babin] at our request, he asks what is to be done if they go without him."[44] Apart from his activities with the OSS, Babin provided a steady stream of information to the GRU about American shipping in New York harbor. The data on cargoes, types of ships, and destinations probably came to Babin from a network of Communist sailors and longshoremen.

Leonard Mins: The Spy Who Was Hard to Miss

The most blatant GRU agent was Leonard Mins. That he could ever have been in a position to provide classified information to the Soviet Union testifies to the ease with which the American government could be infiltrated. Mins worked for the OSS for a little over a year, from 1942 to late 1943, spending most of his time on a survey of strategic minerals and oil reserves in Asia and the USSR. He was called before the Dies Committee in 1943. He flatly denied being a member of the CPUSA or a Communist of any kind, but Mins conceded that he had taught at the Communist-controlled Workers School, served on the editorial board of *Partisan Review* when it was under party control, been a member of the CPUSA's John Reed Clubs, written for the CPUSA's *New Masses,* and been a member of the CPUSA-aligned League of American Writers. He admitted living in Moscow from 1934 to 1936 but insisted that he had done nothing more than undertake translations for the Soviet Academy of Sciences.[45]

His testimony was difficult to believe, and within a few months the OSS fired Mins. His record was more incredible than even the Dies Committee had thought. Although he had testified that he had been working for the Soviet Academy of Sciences during his time in Moscow, actually he was working for the Communist International. In 1935 the American representative to the Comintern asked the CPUSA to corroborate information that Mins had provided to the Comintern in Moscow. Mins had told the Comintern that he had joined the CPUSA in 1919, worked for the Communist movement in Germany in 1920 and 1921, worked for the Executive Committee of the Comintern as a translator in 1924 and 1925, worked for the Communist movement in Germany from 1925 to 1927, done party work in the United States from 1927 to 1932, and had transferred his party membership to the Communist Party of the Soviet Union in 1934.[46] Mins was in France in 1938 working with exiled anti-Nazi German writers, one of whom was the father of the later notorious East German spymaster and Stasi (secret political police) officer Markus Wolf. In his memoirs Wolf recalled his old friend Leonhard [Leonard] Mins, "a Communist exile who had been my parents' close friend" in Russia. "He had been the channel through which my father was able to communicate with us during his internment in France."[47]

Elizabeth Bentley later wrote that one member of her network had run into Mins at OSS headquarters and was afraid to be seen in his company, as he was such a well-known Communist. Bentley complained to Golos, who agreed that it was folly to use Mins as a spy: he was so obviously a Communist "that he might just as well go around

Washington with the hammer and sickle painted on his chest and waving a red flag."[48]

Nonetheless, Mins, who had the cover name Smith in the GRU Venona messages, worked in the Russian section of the OSS.[49] The messages show him reporting to the GRU on the training of American military intelligence officers to break Soviet codes, and trying to obtain a highly secret OSS report on discussions between President Roosevelt and Prime Minister Churchill concerning the USSR.

Mins also worked as a talent-spotter for other potential Soviet sources. He told the GRU that one of his friends, Isador Steinberg, had been hired "in the War Department as a member of the publications bureau and expert on military publications matters." Steinberg, Mins reported, "is a Corporant [GRU term for CPUSA members] and owner of the firm Production Illustration in New York." Mins, who had known Steinberg for fifteen years, strongly recommended him for recruitment. The New York GRU station commented, "We consider that the latter [Steinberg] will be useful to us both as a source for secret publications of the War Department and for general military and political information."[50] Another message reported the potential recruitment of an unidentified government employee given the cover name Clarke, and observed that Clarke was not a Communist and that Mins was approaching him cautiously. A further GRU message reported that Mins had met with a U.S. Army lieutenant colonel and had suggested an economics professor in Nashville as a possible recruit. Because of the OSS investigation of Mins, the New York GRU noted that he had "been instructed to refrain for the moment from private meetings" with these potential sources.[51]

An August 1943 GRU message demonstrated Mins's attitudes toward loyalty and betrayal. After General Donovan fired Mins from the OSS, Mins appealed for reinstatement to the Civil Service Commission. In this message Mins proudly reported to Soviet intelligence that six of his OSS colleagues, including Arthur Robinson, chief of the OSS Russian Section, testified that Mins was loyal and could be trusted.

The GRU Mole

The GRU also planted in the United States at least one long-term penetration agent, the classic "mole" of espionage fiction. Although he posed as an immigrant, he was actually a professional GRU officer. He appeared in Los Angeles in 1938 claiming to be a Canadian immigrant of Polish birth and carrying a Canadian passport identifying him as Ignacy Witczak. He enrolled in the University of Southern California, earned bachelor's and master's degrees in political science, and was admitted to a doctoral program. He had a wife and young child. He was exposed in 1945 when Igor Gouzenko, a GRU code clerk, defected from the Soviet embassy in Canada. Gouzenko was familiar with Witczak because of an error the GRU had made in creating his fake identify.

The GRU's Witczak (his real name is unknown) had taken the passport of a real person of Polish birth who had immigrated to Canada in 1930 and become a Canadian citizen in 1936. The real Ignacy Witczak had also fought in Spain with the International Brigades, which had collected the passports of many of its American and Canadian volunteers and turned them over to Soviet intelligence for their use. The GRU had thought that Witczak had died in Spain and so appropriated his identity for one of their agents. The real Witczak, however, had survived and returned to Canada. This produced a problem in 1945 when the fake Witczak's Canadian passport expired. Renewal of the passport could trigger a discovery that there were two Witczaks. GRU officers directed Sam Carr, head of the Canadian Communist party and a Soviet agent, to pay a bribe of three thousand dollars to a Canadian official to take care of the problem. Less than a week after this successful transaction, Gouzenko defected and alerted Canadian authorities to the scheme.

Informed of the Witczak matter by the Canadians, the FBI put him under surveillance. The bureau discovered that although his only known employment since 1938 was as a part-time instructor at the University of Southern California with an annual salary of $1,700, he had banked $16,000. Witczak traveled from Los Angeles to New York and Washington in 1946, all the while under FBI surveillance. He was observed passing material to an attorney, Leonard Cohen, who worked for the Interior Department and whom he appeared to have met by prearrangement at the Library of Congress. In New York FBI agents surreptitiously searched his hotel room and turned up a notebook with names and addresses, one of which was that of the family residence of Winston Burdett (chapter 3). Probably alerted about Gouzenko's defection, Witczak appeared to have detected the surveillance and vanished in late 1945 and is presumed to have returned to the Soviet Union.

Gouzenko had the impression that Witczak was establishing a deep-cover reserve espionage apparatus to be activated if a break in American-Soviet diplomatic relations or some other trauma disrupted the networks run by GRU officers operating under diplomatic cover. According to the retired FBI agent Robert Lamphere, the bureau had located several persons in California whom Witczak had recruited and obtained confessions from some of them, although none was ever prosecuted. Dr. Arnold Krieger, a former Communist, later testified that Witczak had attempted to recruit him for secret missions in Asia and Latin America. Although not identified by NSA/FBI analysts, Witczak is almost surely the Soviet illegal officer identified in the Venona traffic only by the initial "R." The San Francisco KGB reported to Moscow in January 1946 that R.'s family had surreptitiously boarded the Soviet ship *Sakhalin* and left the United States. Inasmuch as FBI surveillance of Witczak's wife, Bunia, who also had a false Canadian passport, and their American-born son indicated that they had slipped aboard the *Sakhalin* at that time, it is very likely that R. was Witczak.[52]

One Canadian GRU agent mentioned in the decrypted Venona documents was Fred Rose, a leader of the Canadian Communist party. Born in Poland, Rose had become a Canadian citizen in 1926. Early in the 1940s he was in secret communication with Jacob Golos. Elizabeth Bentley reported that Sam Carr and Rose turned over several Canadians to Golos for liaison with the KGB. One was Hazen Sise, a veteran of the Spanish Civil War who worked in the Canadian Film Bureau Office in Washington.[53] Rose was elected to the House of Commons in 1943 as a candidate of the Labor-Progressive party, the political arm of the Canadian Communists at the time. In a message dated August 12, 1943, Pavel Mikhailov, the GRU station chief in New York, proudly cabled Moscow that "Fred, our man in Lesovia ["Forestland," i.e., Canada] has been elected to the Lesovian parliament."[54] Rose was arrested after Gouzenko's disclosures and sentenced to six years in prison. After his release in 1951 he left for Communist Poland, where he died in 1983.

Other American Agents of the GRU in the 1940s

Another ring of GRU agents was connected with Charles Irving Velson, a member of the Communist party's secret apparatus. Velson had a distinguished Communist pedigree. His mother, Clara Lemlich Shavelson, was a rank-and-file garment worker, whose impassioned speech in

1909 was credited with sparking an industry-wide walkout led by the International Ladies Garment Workers' Union. She went on to a long career as a Communist. Charles Velson (he changed his name in 1939 or 1940) was a machinist who worked at the Brooklyn Navy Yard from 1931 to 1938. Congressional investigators believed that while there he was a mail drop for J. Peters, who headed the secret apparatus, and that Velson was also involved in Cpl. Robert Osman's espionage activities on behalf of the GRU in the Panama Canal Zone. The latter suspicion is supported by Robert Gladnick, a former CPUSA functionary and Lincoln Brigade veteran who knew Velson. He wrote that in the early 1930s Velson assisted Bernard Chester, then director of the CPUSA's antimilitarist work, in a program to develop secret Communist groups among American military personnel. In the mid-1930s, Gladnick said, Velson replaced Chester as head of the antimilitarist effort. (Chester was the party name of Bernard Schuster, who in the early 1940s became the liaison between the CPUSA and the KGB.) When a congressional committee asked him about his relationship with Peters, Velson refused to answer.[55]

The deciphered Venona messages show Velson performing a number of tasks for the GRU.[56] In one he is assigned to approach a prospective Soviet source. In another he reports that he has heard about some experiments dealing with the testing of a seventy-five-millimeter cannon but has thus far been unable to get the data. One message notes that Velson has endorsed the request of another GRU agent, Milton Schwartz, for a GRU loan of $1,200 to pay off debts incurred in taking care of his sick father.

The Naval GRU

Soviet naval intelligence, known as the Naval GRU, was the smallest of the three Soviet spy agencies, much smaller than the Soviet army's intelligence arm, the GRU, and only a fraction of the size of the KGB. Nonetheless, it maintained a station in the United States and developed a number of valuable sources. One was Jack Fahy, who came into the Soviet orbit through service with the Comintern's International Brigades in the Spanish Civil War. Born in Washington, D.C., in 1908, he grew up in New York, where his father was senior partner of Walter J. Fahy and Co., a stock exchange firm. After working for Sen. George Moses and campaigning for Herbert Hoover's election to the presidency in

1928, Fahy joined the family firm. The stock market crash of 1929 jolted him out of Republicanism, and he joined the Socialist party. Fahy was both adventurous and peripatetic; at various times he attended New York University, the Institute of International Affairs in Geneva, San Marcus University in Peru, Black Mountain College in North Carolina, and Montana State University, where he took courses in animal husbandry. He established several small companies, including a food business in Peru in 1933. In 1937 he went to Spain to fight in the International Brigades but did so under the auspices of the Socialist party, not the Communist party.[57]

Fahy served as a truck driver in Spain, was wounded in 1938, and returned to the United States. He quickly quarreled with Norman Thomas, head of the Socialist party, over policy toward the Spanish Civil War and publicly resigned from the Socialist party in a letter published in the Communist *Daily Worker*. In the summer of 1939 Fahy met Robert Miller, a onetime Moscow correspondent, who had worked for the Spanish republic as a propagandist. Miller and Fahy set up the Hemisphere News Service to provide American newspapers with information from Latin America, with much of the money coming from Miller's family inheritance. They hired Joseph Gregg, who had served as a truck driver with Fahy in Spain, to handle the business side of Hemisphere. The company limped along until 1941, when it gained a contract from and was later absorbed by the Office of the Coordinator of Inter-American Affairs, a wartime agency that coordinated diplomacy, propaganda, and economic warfare in Central and South America.[58]

Fahy soon left the Office of the Co-ordinator of Inter-American Affairs and moved on to the Board of Economic Warfare, where he held a position as "Principal Intelligence Officer." In 1943, just as he was about to move to the Department of the Interior to become chairman of the Territorial Affairs Bureau, Rep. Martin Dies included him on a list of government employees suspected of communism. Fahy testified before the Kerr Commission set up to investigate the charges. He claimed that his letter of resignation from the Socialist party was "silly and foolish" and described his past association with Communists as a youthful misadventure. The commission agreed, concluding that after 1938 he "returned to his affairs, has joined no organizations, written no articles and made no speeches" and noted that many persons had testified to his good character. It praised his "loyal service" and concluded that he "has not been guilty of any subversive activity."⁵⁹ Deciphered Venona cables show that the Kerr Commission could not have been more mistaken.⁶⁰ Almost precisely when he was denying before a congressional committee any Communist involvement and proclaiming his divorce from political activity, Fahy was transmitting material to Georgy Stepanovich Pasko, secretary to the Soviet Naval attaché in Washington and a Naval GRU officer. In January 1943 the Naval GRU in Moscow approved a special payment to Maxwell, Fahy's cover name, as recognition of his service. In February two messages emphasized the importance of Fahy's information; the Naval GRU commander in Moscow directed the Naval GRU station in Washington to "communicate each item of information from Maxwell [Fahy] on political questions to the Master [Soviet ambassador] and telegraph it to me with the postscript 'reported to the Master.' "⁶¹

Eugene Franklin Coleman never held an important government position, was never hauled before a congressional committee, and was never pulled from obscurity into the limelight by charges by an ex-Communist or anti-Communist. But Venona documents indicate that he was an important Soviet agent. In August 1942 the Naval GRU sent a query to the Comintern asking for any information it had about Coleman; it described him as an employee for a telephone company and a Communist.⁶² Coleman, an electrical engineer, is the subject of six Venona messages. They show that the Naval GRU was still considering in early 1943 whether to recruit him and made a final decision to go ahead in July. By this point he was working for an RCA laboratory in New Jersey on devices to assist in radio navigation for high-altitude aerial bombardment. Indeed, according to one cable, he was engaged in writing the manual for the equipment. In addition, Coleman furnished the Naval GRU with the names and backgrounds of four other Communist engineers who were working at various defense establishments, as possible intelligence sources. Given its limited staff, Naval GRU asked the KGB in Washington to check up on these potential sources.⁶³

The Naval GRU also had to ask for assistance with another project, an effort to smuggle an illegal officer into the United States. Called the Australian Woman or Sally in the deciphered Venona messages, her real name was Francia Yakilnilna Mitynen, and once in the United States she assumed a false identity, that of Edna Margaret Patterson. A Soviet citizen born in Australia, Sally/Mitynen was the subject of nineteen decrypted messages. In December 1942 the Washington Naval attaché sent a lengthy cable to Moscow detailing what was necessary for the "dispatch and legalization of the Australian Woman." He included information about such documents as birth certificates and driver's licenses, problems associated with smuggling her off a Soviet ship (he pointed out, among other problems, that Soviet women sailors stood out from Americans "because of their stockings, their berets . . . their handbags and their untidiness. They do not take any trouble over their hair or their make-up"), the advantages and disadvantages of using San Francisco or Portland, and the options for traveling across country to New York.[64]

Over the next several months the details were ironed out. San Francisco was chosen as the port of arrival, arrangements were made for contacts in San Francisco and New York, code words and recognition signals were set up, appropriate American clothes were purchased, and a detailed "legend" was constructed for the illegal agent. But the Naval GRU had to seek assistance. On June 10, 1943, Moscow angrily complained, "You have had eight months to prepare for Sally's reception at the port of disembarkation, and when, moreover, you have so many people of your own, you should be ashamed to turn to the Neighbors [KGB or GRU] for help." It demanded final details, for Sally was leaving the USSR that day. Sally arrived in August 1943 and was successfully inserted into American society under her false identity; the FBI later learned that she left the United States in 1956. Her mission here remains unknown.[65]

There were other GRU sources in the United States. Two more were identified either by name in cables or through counterintelligence work: Theodore Bayer, editor of *Russky Golos* and a senior Communist party official, and "L. Gordon," a female Communist functionary being considered to head a group of GRU sources in New York. Although L. Gordon is not identified in the Venona decryptions, she is probably Lottie Gordon. In the 1930s she served in Ohio as organizational secretary of the Young Communist League. Her husband, David, was a veteran of the Abraham Lincoln Brigade.[66]

Twenty-five other GRU sources were never identified by the FBI or the NSA. They ranged from Cerberus, a Treasury Department employee who lost touch with the GRU and in 1945 was trying to reestablish contact via the CPUSA, to Jack, who provided information on American testing of guided bombs.[67] Others served in the War Production Board, the U.S. Navy, the Board of Economic Warfare, and the Bureau of Shipping or worked as journalists. The GRU might not have run as many spies as the KGB, but nonetheless it procured a steady stream of important information from the United States.

CHAPTER 7

SPIES IN THE U.S. GOVERNMENT

The Soviet intelligence community enjoyed the cooperation of key persons in high positions in the U.S. government—among them, Harry White (assistant secretary of treasury), Alger Hiss (assistant to the secretary of state), and Lauchlin Currie (administrative assistant to the president). But just as impressive is the number of lower-ranking officials in virtually all major U.S. government agencies, civilian and military, who passed information to Soviet intelligence. This chapter will survey, agency by agency, Soviet penetration of the federal government for purposes of espionage.

Office of Strategic Services

At the start of the war in Europe, American leaders recognized that the United States possessed limited foreign intelligence capability. The intelligence branches of the Army and the Navy were oriented toward military applications, chiefly combat and signals intelligence, and had only limited capability to carry out political, diplomatic, and economic intelligence. The State Department had an interest in diplomatic and strategic intelligence but did not regard covert and clandestine information gathering as part of its mission. Nor did any of these established agencies have much capacity for behind-the-lines commando and guerrilla operations or propaganda and psychological warfare. Consequently, in mid-1941, before the attack on Pearl Harbor, President Roosevelt authorized Gen. William Donovan to establish the Office of the Coordinator of Information to deal with these matters. In 1942 Donovan's agency, which had grown enormously since the United States entered the war, was split; its propaganda operations aimed at domestic and Allied audiences were broken off to form the Office of War Information and some analysis and propaganda operations aimed at Central and South America assigned to the Office of the Coordinator of Inter-American Affairs, headed by Nelson Rockefeller. The FBI also had responsibility for intelligence gathering in Central and South America. The core of foreign intelligence gathering and analysis, covert action and commando operations, and propaganda aimed at enemy nations remained under General Donovan and was named the Office of Strategic Services (OSS).

Donovan's OSS developed the nation's first capacity for analytic strategic intelligence by bringing in hundreds of academic specialists (economists, political scientists, historians, psychologists, anthropologists, and sociologists) and supplying them with information from both covert and overt sources. The resulting intelligence estimates then supported the strategic decision making of the president, the military Joint Chiefs of Staff, and the State Department. The OSS also established a network of field officers who recruited and ran clandestine agents in Europe and Asia, trained and supplied anti-Nazi partisans in occupied Europe and anti-Japanese guerrillas in Asia, parachuted sabotage teams into occupied Europe, and beamed radio propaganda and dropped into enemy areas leaflets designed to dishearten enemy forces and arouse the resistance of those under German or Japanese occupation. The Office of Strategic Services became the chief American foreign intelligence agency in World War II and the predecessor to the contemporary Central Intelligence Agency.

In March 1945 a congressional committee, concerned by rumors of Communists in the OSS, asked Donovan about four OSS officers. Milton Wolff, Vincent Lossowski, Irving Fajans, and Irving Goff were International Brigade veterans then serving with the OSS in Italy. General Donovan testified that he had investigated all four and "did not find that they were Communists. I found that they were not." He was also asked whether any of the four had been in the Young Communist League; he said no.[1] In fact, all were Communists and three of the four,

Fajans, Wolff, and Lossowski, had been Young Communist League members in the 1930s.[2]

Donovan assured the Committee on Military Affairs that everyone in the OSS had been vetted: "I try to determine whether a man is or is not a Fascist or a Communist—I have never taken a man of whom I had any doubt." One congressman asked whether, perhaps because of the highly special qualifications needed for some types of intelligence work, Donovan had recruited someone even though "he had been a member of the Communist Party . . . or a contributor to . . . some Communistic magazine." Donovan, offered wiggle room, rejected it: "I should say right here no such case has ever happened."[3]

Donovan lied to the Congress. From the origins of his agency in mid-1941 he recruited dozens of persons he knew to be Communists. Through Milton Wolff, Donovan recruited veterans of the Comintern-led International Brigades for OSS commando operations in occupied Europe. Most were Communists, but they had attributes Donovan needed for OSS personnel working with various resistance and guerrilla forces: foreign language skills, experience working with foreign soldiers, and combat experience. In some cases the resistance groups with which the OSS wanted to establish contact were Communist-led, and having some OSS officers who shared that loyalty offered advantages.

After World War II some former senior OSS officers kept up Donovan's deception that the OSS had never recruited Communists and that only a handful had ever succeeded in joining the organization. Others were more candid and did not deny that they recruited Communists, explaining that they used Communists when the individuals in question had the appropriate skills, did not conceal their Communist background, and were willing to subordinate themselves to OSS policies. Indeed, it is known that Donovan discharged several OSS employees for concealing Communist membership or for allowing Communist loyalties to interfere with OSS goals. Among these was Stephen Dedijer, a Serbian recruited for OSS work in occupied Yugoslavia. The OSS released Dedijer when it concluded that he was a Comintern agent sent to the United States to edit a Serb-language Communist newspaper and that his brother was an aide to the Yugoslav Communist leader Tito. OSS officials decided that Dedijer's Communist partisanship was so blatant that he could not work successfully with non-Communist Yugoslavs.[4] Another example, discussed in chapter 6, was Donovan's firing of Leonard Mins for lying about his Communist connections.

With more honesty than when testifying to the Congress, Donovan once remarked to an aide, "I'd put Stalin on the OSS payroll if I thought it would help us defeat Hitler."[5] Between those who were known to be Communists when Donovan recruited them and those whose Communist affiliation was unknown when they were hired, it could be said that Donovan did put Stalin on the payroll: researchers have identified Communists in the Russian, Spanish, Balkan, Hungarian, and Latin American sections of the OSS's Research and Analysis Division and its operational Japanese, Korean, Italian, Spanish, Hungarian, Indonesian, and German divisions.[6] There is no exact count of the number of Communists who worked for the OSS, but the total was easily more than fifty and probably closer to a hundred or even more.

In the midst of World War II, when Hitler was the main enemy, General Donovan's attitude was a justifiable one, but it was also fraught with risk. Although the arrangement allowed the OSS to make use of Communists, the price of using their talents was high because it also facilitated KGB and GRU recruitment of sources within America's chief intelligence agency. Donovan's decision to employ Communists was defensible, but his egregious dishonesty when testifying to the people's elected representatives was not. Nor was his policy in accord with official government rules. Early in the war, in 1942, a Roosevelt administration task force authorized immediate discharge of Communists from government service. Later, in 1944, a directive specified that Communists could serve in the military but were to be excluded from duty in posts dealing with highly secret military technologies, cryptography, and intelligence.[7]

Other chapters in this book identify twelve Soviet agents within the OSS.[8] The deciphered Venona cables also have the cover names of four other Soviet intelligence contacts within the OSS, one whose real identity has not been established, and three whose real names are known.[9] The unidentified KGB source in the OSS had a cover name whose numeric cipher was never broken to yield a legible word. Referred to by the NSA as "unbroken cover name No. 6," this person was a member of an OSS team in Algeria in 1943. The KGB cable reporting on No. 6 suggests that this person was one of the veterans of the International Brigades serving with an OSS field unit in Algeria. These units chiefly worked with resistance forces in Italy and the Balkans.

The three additional identified sources are Franz Neumann, Linn Farish, and John Scott. Neumann, cover name Ruff, fled Germany in the early 1930s, reached the United States in 1936, and became a naturalized American citizen. An economist, he joined the OSS in 1942 as a member of its German section. Farish, cover name Attila, was an OSS officer who served as OSS liaison with Tito's Partisan forces in Yugoslavia. He died in a aircraft crash in the Balkans in September 1944. As for Scott, in a report discussing the Russian section of the OSS sent in May 1942, Vasily Zubilin noted that "our source Ivanov" was an OSS analyst on Soviet industry.[10] The son of radical writer Scott Nearing, he never publicly admitted CPUSA membership but was an organizer for the CPUSA's Trade Union Unity League in the late 1920s and early 1930s. He migrated to the USSR in 1932 and worked for much of the decade in Magnitogorsk, created under Stalin's five-year plans to be the Soviet Union's premier steel-making city. He returned with a Russian wife and in 1942 published *Behind the Urals: An American Worker in Russia's City of Steel,* recording his personal observations on the building of Magnitogorsk and presenting it as an awe-inspiring triumph of collective labor. Scott's book, however, was not a pure propaganda piece. He also described the painful human price of industrial accidents, overwork, and the inefficiency of the hyperindustrialization program, the wretched condition of peasants driven from the land in the collectivization program and coerced into becoming industrial workers, and the harshness of the ideological purges. These experiences, however, did not disillusion him with Soviet communism. He stated that the Soviet people believed (and Scott indicated he shared this belief) that "it was worthwhile to shed blood, sweat, and tears" to lay "the foundations for a new society farther along the road of human progress than anything in the West; a society which would guarantee its people not only personal freedom but absolute economic security."[11]

In addition, Venona has several unidentified cover names of Soviet sources who may have worked for the OSS or who may have been employed by another wartime agency with access to OSS material. A single 1945 message, for example, reported the delivery of an OSS document by a KGB source identified only by the initial "I." A 1943 KGB message noting KGB assets in the Office of Strategic Services and the Office of War Information included one unidentified cover name. This "unbroken cover name no. 19" (the numeric code was never converted to a readable name) was in one of the agencies, but which one is not clear.[12] Horus also reported what may have been OSS information to the New York KGB. Khazar was a naturalized American citizen, probably of Yugoslav origin, who gave the KGB information on OSS personnel inserted into occupied Yugoslavia. One message reported that the OSS discussed with Khazar his participation in such an operation. It is not clear, however, whether he became an OSS operative. Finally, Okho (possibly Ojo, Spanish "eye"), an asset of the New York KGB, furnished information on the OSS in 1944, but whether Okho was actually in the OSS is unclear.

How many Soviet agents operated inside the OSS? Because of the possibility of duplication between some unidentified cover names in Venona and persons otherwise established as Soviet sources, the exact number cannot be stated. There were at least fifteen Soviet agents inside the OSS, with the actual number probably being about twenty. These numbers may also be on the low side, because most GRU and many KGB messages were never deciphered. Since the total number of Communists in the OSS was at least fifty and perhaps as high as a hundred, at least one in seven and perhaps as many as one in three Communists in the OSS were spies.[13]

The Office of War Information

The Office of War Information (OWI) was America's chief propaganda agency in World War II. Originally part of Donovan's Office of the Coordinator of Information in 1941, it was broken off in June 1942 and placed under the direction of Elmer Davis, a prominent radio commentator and ardent Roosevelt supporter. The OWI's duties included providing supportive and motivational war information by print, radio, film, and all other media to domestic audiences and to audiences in Allied and neutral nations abroad. The task of preparing propaganda aimed at enemy nations remained largely with Donovan's OSS. While the OWI lacked formal censorship powers over domestic media, it monitored the domestic press and informally pressured U.S. newspapers and magazines that failed to conform to its guidelines. In the case of nonconforming radio broadcasts, its pressure included threats to urge the Federal Communications Commission, which regulated radio broadcasting, to lift a station's broadcasting license.

Like the OSS, the OWI hired Communists. Eugene Dennis sent a message to the Soviets informing them that the party was maintaining contacts with staff members in the propaganda sections of the OWI and the OSS. Both during and after World War II several congressmen and others complained that the OWI had allowed Communists on its staff to shape its policies on several matters in a way that served Soviet interests. In 1943 Rep. John Lesinski, a Michigan Democrat with a Polish-American constituency, warned OWI head Elmer Davis in a speech on the House floor that several members of the OWI's Polish-language section were pro-Soviet. Davis received a similar but private warning from Ambassador Jan Ciechanowski of the Polish government-in-exile. Infuriated by the criticism, Davis blasted Lesinski's speech for containing "more lies than were ever comprised in any other speech made about the Office of War Information" and rebuked Ambassador Ciechanowski for interfering with internal American matters. But after the war several members of the OWI's Polish-language section emerged as defenders of the Communist takeover of Poland and as close relatives of officials in the new Polish Communist regime; one section official, Arthur Salman, became chief editor of *Robotnik* (Worker), a leading Communist newspaper in Warsaw. In addition, the head of the OWI's Czechoslovak desk in New York emerged as a high-ranking Czechoslovak Communist and became the ambassador to France of the Czechoslovak Communist regime.[14]

Vanni Montana, an official of the International Ladies Garment Workers' Union and a former Communist, visited liberated Italy in 1944 and reported finding a number of American Communists on the staff of Radio Italy, a propaganda station operated by the Office of War Information. Montana complained that Radio Italy's programs, beamed toward Nazi-occupied northern Italy, supported the political ambitions of Italian Communists in postwar Italy.[15]

After World War II Elmer Davis testified to Congress that he had fired about a dozen OWI employees, including the head of the OWI's labor news desk and its Greek desk in New York, when evidence surfaced that they were actively involved in Communist party activities while working for the OWI. But he refused to concede anything about the Polish issue and, dismissing evidence about OWI employees who were Communists as unimportant, he flatly denied that any could have influenced OWI activities. The congressional committee specifically asked Davis about OWI treatment of the matter of the Soviet murder of some fifteen thousand captured Polish officers at Katyn and other prisoner-of-war camps. The OWI had endorsed the Soviet story that the Nazis had executed the Poles, and it pressured several domestic radio stations to stop carrying commentaries suggesting that the Soviets were responsible for the Katyn massacre. Davis explained that he had believed the Soviet explanation, and he denied that Communists in the OWI influenced acceptance of the Soviet cover story.

Venona contains the unidentified cover names of several Soviet espionage contacts in the Office of War Information. These include Philosopher (OWI French section), Fred, and Leona.[16] The KGB stated that Philosopher was being used for "processing"—that is, providing background information and character appraisals—of OWI personnel. Fred was an employee of a U.S. government agency and supplied information about Austria. The OWI is most likely the agency for which he worked, but there are other possibilities as well. The KGB described Leona as the wife of a New York radio journalist and said that she was attempting to get an OWI job. It is not clear that Leona got the post.

The most active Soviet agent in the OWI revealed in Venona was Flora Wovschin. Twenty KGB cables deciphered by the Venona Project detail her service to Soviet intelligence.[17] Both her mother, Maria Wicher, and her stepfather, Enos Regnet Wicher, were active members of the CPUSA. The Wichers, in addition to being Communists, appear in deciphered Venona messages as KGB contacts.[18] Maria Wicher had the cover name Dasha in the Venona traffic and was aware of both her husband's and her daughter's work. Enos Wicher received the cover name Keen. His liaison with the KGB ran through the KGB agent Sergey Kurnakov. Enos Wicher was a source for information on American military electronics. At that time he worked for the Wave Propagation Group of Columbia University's Division of War Research. In July 1945 Wicher reported to his KGB controller that his supervisor had shown him a letter from Army counterintelligence indicating that he was suspected of having concealed Communist ties. Enos told the KGB that the letter even listed the pseudonym he had used many years earlier when he worked as a CPUSA organizer in Wisconsin.

Flora Wovschin was a far more active spy than the Wichers. She got a job with the Office of War Information in September 1943 and worked there until February 1945. The Venona messages show her performing a variety of tasks for Soviet intelligence. In 1943 the KGB was considering recruiting a young radio engineer who worked in the design office of Hazeltine Electronics Corporation. It assigned Wovschin the task of checking on his background. She also spotted and carried out the recruitment of at least two other Soviet agents: Marion Davis and the invaluable Judith Coplon, both of whom had been fellow students of hers at Barnard College.

While not as valuable a source as Coplon, Marion Davis was a useful addition to Soviet espionage. The earliest record of the KGB's interest in Davis was found in the archives of the Communist International and dates from September 1944. The KGB's General Fitin asked the Comintern if it had any information about *"Marion Davis,* an employee of the American embassy in Mexico."[19] Davis at that time worked on the staff of the Office of Naval Intelligence at the U.S. embassy in Mexico. Fitin's message was one of a series of requests for background checks on Americans whom the KGB was considering for recruitment. Given later Venona messages describing Wovschin as the KGB's initial link to Davis, it seems likely that she suggested Davis as a prospect.[20]

Three deciphered Venona messages discuss Davis's recruitment. She was back in the United States at the end of 1944 and in touch with Flora Wovschin. A New York KGB message on December 5 states that Wovschin was "drawing [Davis] into active work" and told Moscow that the KGB planned "to entrust to Zora [Wovschin] after Lou [Davis] gets work of interest to us (Zora all the time is aiming Lou at this) the gradual preparation of Lou's signing on."[21] "Signing on" referred to formal recruitment as an active KGB agent. These messages also indicate that the KGB office in Mexico City had earlier entered into preliminary contacts with Davis. In response to its New York office's plans to go forward with her formal signing on, the KGB headquarters in Moscow on December 8 ordered Lev Tarasov, head of the Mexico City office, to send an appraisal of Davis based on his meetings with her. In January 1945 the New York KGB told Moscow that Davis was reporting for a new assignment with the Office of the Coordinator of Inter-American Affairs in Washington. It asked sanction for Wovschin to complete Davis's recruitment, stating that "since Lou [Davis] is beginning to work it is extremely important to direct her efforts from the very beginning along a line which we need and for this direct contact and leadership are necessary."[22]

As for Wovschin, her KGB controllers were pleased with her dedication. One KGB officer who met with her praised her for being "extremely serious, well-developed and understand[ing] her tasks."[23] Her KGB controllers were also impressed by the volume of her production.

An August 1944 New York KGB cable reported that it had shipped to Moscow a batch of OWI material that Wovschin had gathered. Then in November, in slightly amazed tones, the New York KGB reported that already "in her apartment are lying a lot of materials that she is supposed to turn over to us but up to now has not had an opportunity."[24] In December 1944 it reported that it had taken possession of Wovschin's new collection of OWI documents. It noted, however, that the material she had turned over was not of high value because her OWI job "is poor in opportunities for our line." Consequently, the New York KGB urged Wovschin to find a position that would better serve Soviet interests and reported that the ever-responsive young woman was "in search of work that would suit us."[25] She succeeded and in February 1945 transferred from the OWI to the U.S. State Department, a far more profitable intelligence target.

Wovschin's productivity was indeed impressive. Venona messages refer to the New York KGB office's forwarding to Moscow four reports she wrote in January and February 1945 alone. Nor did the reports go unread. The Moscow KGB headquarters ordered its New York office to follow up on a report about Ralph Bowen, a State Department economics official. Wovschin, it noted, had known Bowen and his wife in the Young Communist League.

By the end of March, however, someone in the Moscow KGB headquarters concluded that her energy had crossed over into impetuousness and that the New York KGB, impressed with her productivity, had let security slip. Appalled officials at KGB headquarters told their field officers that Wovschin's reports, written by her and not by her KGB controllers, used standard KGB cover names for various American agencies: Bank for the U.S. State Department, Cabaret for the Office of the Coordinator of Inter-American Affairs, and others. Only KGB officers, not their American agents, were supposed to know these cover names. Other items in her reports indicating that she was pressing various persons for information and initiating risky contacts were also cited.

Warning that it could lead to "serious political complications" between the USSR and the United States if her promiscuous espionage became public, Moscow ordered the New York KGB to see that steps were "taken to curtail Zora's [Wovschin's] dangerous activities." It further ordered the New York KGB to admonish the KGB officer who supervised Wovschin about his mistakes, "forbid Zora [Wovschin] to recruit all her acquaintances one after the other," and "as an ultimatum warn Zora that if she does not carry out our instructions and if she undertakes steps without our consent, we shall immediately terminate all relations with her."[26]

This message from March 1945 was the last KGB cable regarding Wovschin deciphered in the Venona Project, so the New York response is not documented. Wovschin continued to work for the State Department until September 1945. Only a few points about her subsequent life are known. When the Venona Project deciphered the KGB messages about Wovschin in the late 1940s, the FBI tried to find her but could not. In 1949 the FBI forwarded a memo to the National Security Agency stating that its information indicated that at some point, probably 1946 or 1947, she fled to the Soviet Union and renounced her American citizenship, and that she later married a Russian. The timing of her flight suggests that in reaction to Elizabeth Bentley's defection, the subsequent increase in FBI counterintelligence activity, and possibly knowledge that the Venona Project was under way, the KGB withdrew Wovschin from the United States because it expected her to be uncovered. In 1954 a postscript added to the 1949 FBI memo stated that information had been received that Wovschin had later gone to Communist North Korea to work as a nurse and had died there.[27]

The State Department and Wartime Diplomatic Agencies

While the U.S. Department of State was America's chief diplomatic agency, during World War II President Roosevelt created a number of temporary specialized wartime agencies that conducted war-related diplomatic and foreign affairs tasks. These included the Board of Economic Warfare (BEW), which later became part of the Foreign Economic Administration (FEA), the Office of the Coordinator of Inter-American Affairs, and the United Nations Relief and Rehabilitation Administration (UNRRA). At the end of World War II most of these agencies were dissolved and their remnants merged into the State Department.

In addition to Flora Wovschin (State) and Marion Davis (Inter-American Affairs), eighteen other sources within these foreign relations agencies are discussed elsewhere in this book.[28] The deciphered Venona cables identify three other Soviet sources in the diplomatic community. The most important was Laurence Duggan, a respected member of the Washington establishment. He had joined the U.S. State Department in 1930 and was chief of the Division of American Republics from 1935 until 1944. After leaving the State Department he served as a diplomatic adviser to the United Nations Relief and Rehabilitation Administration and then as president of the Institute for International Education. He was a close adviser on foreign policy to former vice president Henry Wallace.

The FBI interviewed Duggan in late 1948 about whether he had had contact with Soviet intelligence in the 1930s. Duggan admitted that during his tenure as a State Department official he twice had been the object of recruitment by Soviet intelligence, once by Henry Collins and once by Frederick Field, but he could not offer a satisfactory explanation for why he never reported either approach to the State Department, as had been his duty.[29] He denied participation in espionage but cut short the interview. Ten days later he fell to his death from a window of his sixteenth-floor office.

Sumner Welles, FDR's former under secretary of state, Eleanor Roosevelt, the poet and former Librarian of Congress Archibald MacLeish, and the influential journalists Drew Pearson and Edward R. Murrow all defended Duggan's reputation and denounced suspicions of his involvement in espionage as baseless. Even Attorney General Tom Clark, who should have known why Duggan was under suspicion, announced that Duggan was "a loyal employee of the United States Government."[30] His death closed access to investigatory files for several decades, and in many historical accounts Duggan has been presented as a loyal and innocent public servant driven to suicide by unfounded accusations. In fact he was a KGB agent.

Duggan's role in the CPUSA's underground and in Soviet espionage was first brought to the attention of Assistant Secretary of State Adolf Berle by Whittaker Chambers in September 1939. Chambers explained that in the mid-1930s his GRU-CPUSA network had tabbed Duggan as a Communist sympathizer. Henry Collins, a member of the CPUSA underground and one of Chambers's contacts, had been a friend of Duggan's at Harvard and knew his views. Collins approached Duggan about assisting the underground, but he seemed uninterested. Boris Bykov, the GRU officer who supervised Chambers's network, thought Duggan too good a prospect to ignore and ordered a second try. This time Frederick Field, a socially prominent figure in diplomatic circles and a secret Communist, pressed Duggan and found out that he was already working for the Soviets, having been recruited by Hede Massing for a KGB-linked network. In 1947 the FBI interviewed Massing, who had quietly defected in 1938, and she confirmed Chambers's story. In 1997 KGB documents from Moscow appeared that further confirm Massing's account.[31]

Deciphered Venona cables provide ample evidence that Duggan continued his cooperation with Soviet espionage into the 1940s. Nine cables from 1943 and 1944 show Duggan reporting to Soviet intelligence officers about Anglo-American plans for the invasion of Italy, consideration of an invasion of Nazi-occupied Norway (a plan later canceled), U.S. diplomatic approaches to Argentina's military government, and secret discussions regarding a common Anglo-American policy toward Middle Eastern oil resources.[32]

Duggan resigned from the State Department in mid-1944. He had been a protégé of Under Secretary of State Sumner Welles, and most likely his resignation was a result of the feud between Welles and Secretary of State Cordell Hull, which led Welles to resign earlier, at the end of 1943. In a July 22 Venona cable the New York KGB office reported the resignation of their source "Frank" (Duggan's cover name at the time) from the State Department. (Duggan officially resigned on July 18.) The cable glossed over the loss of this asset with an assurance to Moscow that "prospects for the future are being looked into." An August 4 message then reported that Frank/Duggan had gotten a new post with the United Nations Relief and Rehabilitation Administration. (Duggan officially received his appointment to UNRRA in late July 1944.) The New York KGB also reported that before his resignation from the State Department, Duggan had warned his Soviet controller, the illegal KGB officer Akhmerov, that his position was precarious. The text of the August 4 message was partially garbled owing to some unbroken code groups, but it appears to indicate that Akhmerov had told Duggan to hold on at State as long as possible.

In a November 18 cable Soviet officers reported their expectation that President Roosevelt would shortly remove Secretary of State Hull and speculated that Duggan might then be able to reenter the State Department in "a leading post." The hope was based on the rumor, reported in the same cable, that Roosevelt might name Henry Wallace secretary of state as recompense for having dropped him as vice president in the 1944 election. Even if Wallace did not get the State Department appointment, the cable went on to say, Duggan could still aid the Soviets by "using his friendship" with Wallace for "extracting ... interesting information" that would inevitably come to someone of

Wallace's political standing. Roosevelt did in fact replace Hull after the 1944 election but installed Edward Stettinius as secretary of state. Wallace received the lesser position of secretary of commerce.

The earliest Venona cable mentioning Duggan is dated June 30, 1943. Only parts of the long message have been deciphered and are readable, but the cable appears to give what the message itself describes as Duggan's resume. It refers to someone as "by profession an author-ess," which would be a reference to Duggan's mother, who was an established writer. The presence of the resume may indicate a routine re-vetting, or it may mean that Duggan had been a source who had been kept on the shelf for a period and had just been revived. It is very likely that after Chambers's defection in 1938, the GRU and the KGB put those who had been in contact with Chambers into "cold storage," to use Soviet intelligence jargon, until it was learned whether he had gone to authorities. Possibly Duggan was among them.

The second diplomatic source identified in Venona is Helen Keenan, a free-lance journalist active in the CPUSA in the 1930s, who went to work for the Coordinator of Inter-American Affairs as a writer and editor in January 1945.[33] By mid-1945 it was clear that this office would be dissolved at the war's end, and Keenan found a position with the Office of U.S. Chief of Counsel for Prosecution of Axis War Criminals. The Washington KGB office told Moscow that it approved the change because "there is certainly no doubt that while working for this com-mission El [Keenan] will have access to material of interest to us and with skillful guidance will be able to be [unrecovered code groups] of us."[34] The Washington KGB provided Moscow with recognition signs so that KGB agents could make contact with her when she reached Europe.

The third diplomatic source identified in Venona was Samuel Rod-man, a UNRRA employee. In late 1944 the New York KGB reported that its CPUSA liaison, Bernard Schuster, had been in contact with Rod-man, a CPUSA member, and arranged for him to gather information during a trip that Rodman was making on behalf of UNRRA to Yu-goslavia.[35]

In addition to identified Soviet sources, Venona contains a number of cover names of sources within American diplomatic agencies whose identities were never established by American analysts.[36] In several cases it is difficult to tell whether the cover-named person is an original source within an American government agency or an intermediary passing on information from a source. These cover names include, for the KGB, Dodger (who provided information on American diplomats specializing in Soviet matters), Fakir (who passed along State Department documents and was considered for an assignment in Moscow by his agency), Flora (who supplied information on UNRRA), Godmother (who provided diplomatic information on American policy toward the USSR), and Mirage (who reported on U.S. diplomatic activities in Latin America).[37]

The Venona cables also describe cover names of two GRU sources among these diplomatic agencies.[38] These were "Source No. 12" (the GRU on occasion used numeric cover names), whose information and documents suggest he was with the Board of Economic Warfare. The second GRU source is described in a 1945 KGB cable under the KGB cover name Robert. Robert had appeared on a list of targets for recruitment at the U.S. State Department, but the Moscow KGB told its New York office that it had learned he was already a GRU source.

An intriguing but unidentified and ambiguous cover name in Venona related to diplomacy is "Source No. 19." This name occurs in a single KGB message in May 1943. The KGB only rarely used numeric cover names, and it is possible that here the New York KGB was reporting about a GRU contact. Source No. 19 reported on a private conversation he had had with President Roosevelt and Prime Minister Churchill during the just-ended "Trident" conference of the two Allied powers in Washington. The message, from the New York KGB office to Moscow, is signed by the KGB illegal officer Iskhak Akhmerov. It states that "19 reports that Kapitan [Roosevelt] and Kaban [Churchill], during conversations in the Country [USA], invited 19 to join them and Zamestitel." Unfortunately, much of the subsequent text is only partially deciphered. It is clear, however, that Source No. 19 reported Churchill's views that an Anglo-American invasion of continental Europe in 1943 was inadvisable. The message also reported that Zamestitel supported a second front and that it appeared that Roosevelt had been keeping Zamestitel in the dark about "important military decisions."[39]

There is too little material for a firm judgment on the identity of Source No. 19. It appears that this source was at the Trident conference or one of its ancillary events and was very highly placed, since he was asked to join a private conversation with Roosevelt and Churchill. Beyond that, however, it is difficult to get much of a clue about No. 19's identity. It is not even clear that Source No. 19 was American: possibly he was part of the British delegation that accompanied Churchill, and a few Trident events were attended by senior officials of other Allied powers and several governments-in-exile. Unfortunately, the deciphered parts of the message do not give the exact date of Source No. 19's conversation with Roosevelt and Churchill.

Nor is it known who Zamestitel was. The word *zamestitel* means "deputy" in Russian, and originally analysts thought it referred to Vice President Henry Wallace. In five later Venona messages, however, Wallace was clearly designated by the cover name Lotsman.[40] While the KGB had a practice of changing the cover names of its covert sources for security reasons, it rarely changed the cover names used in its cable traffic for institutions or individuals who were written of frequently but were not covert sources. The KGB, for example, used the cover names Captain (Kapitan) and Boar (Kaban) for Roosevelt and Churchill throughout the span of Venona traffic. Having second thoughts about the Zamestitel identification, analysts later added an annotation to the message from Source No. 19 suggesting that Zamestitel might be Harry Hopkins, Roosevelt's chief aide, rather than Wallace. But Hopkins's name appears in the clear in several later Venona messages, whereas Zamestitel never again occurs.[41] Although KGB cipher clerks did not always use a cover name when one had been set, the fact that they generally did suggests that Zamestitel was not Hopkins.

One is left, then, with the knowledge that at the Trident conference the Soviets had a very high level contact, Source No. 19, who reported on a sensitive political and diplomatic conversation between Roosevelt, Churchill, and a third high American official, possibly Wallace or Hopkins.[42]

Military and War Production Agencies

The KGB and the GRU maintained a plethora of sources in the American military and war industrial production agencies. Twenty-six of these are discussed elsewhere in this book.[43] Elizabeth Bentley identified two additional minor sources in military-related agencies: Vladimir Kazakevich, an instructor at a wartime U.S. Army school, and Bernice Levin, a clerical employee of the Office of Emergency Management and the Office of Production Management.[44]

Venona also has a number of unidentified cover names for Soviet sources within various American military and war economic agencies.

The unidentified KGB sources were Iceberg (who provided information about the movement of American aircraft in Asia), Liza (a secretary in the War Department), Nelly (who reported on the Lend-Lease Administration), Staff-Man (someone in the U.S. Army who was valuable enough for the KGB to assign him a cipher), and Tur (who reported on U.S. plans for the invasion of France). The GRU cover names that were not identified were Donald (a U.S. Navy captain), Farley (who delivered information from the War Production Board and the War Department), and an unidentified clerk in the Strategic Directorate of the Allied Joint Staff.[45]

Treasury and Other Agencies

Eight Soviet sources in the U.S. Treasury are discussed in the chapters dealing with the Perlo and Silvermaster groups.[46] In addition, one 1945 KGB message mentioned Cerberus, an employee of the U.S. Treasury Department who was a GRU asset. He had, however, lost touch with his GRU contact and was attempting to reestablish a connection through the Communist party. The KGB heard of this through its CPUSA contacts and reported it to Moscow.[47]

Other Government Agencies

Soviet sources were also scattered thoughout other sections of the U.S. government. The KGB maintained two sources, William Gold and Charles Kramer, on the staff of the Senate Subcommittee on War Mobilization, a rich source of military information. Both are discussed in earlier chapters on the Perlo and Silvermaster groups. Also discussed elsewhere are Norman Bursler (anti-trust section of the Justice Department), Judith Coplon (Foreign Agent Registration section of the Justice Department), James Walter Miller (postal censorship) Ward Pigman (National Bureau of Standards), and Jack Fahy (Interior Department). Two other unidentified Soviet sources inside the government were noted in Venona. An October 27, 1944, New York KGB message refers to a Soviet source in the FBI. It is unclear, however, whether this was a reference to Judith Coplon or to another Soviet source.[48] A 1943 GRU message also notes information from an unidentified source in the Bureau of Shipping.[49]

FELLOW-COUNTRYMEN

CHAPTER 8

Earl Browder: Helmsman

The KGB in its coded cables gave Earl Browder, who headed the CPUSA from 1930 to 1945, the cover name Helmsman. It was, of course, a reference to his leadership of the party. But it was also appropriate in that Browder's own involvement with Soviet intelligence set the example for other Communists.

Margaret Browder, Earl's sister, was herself a Soviet intelligence operative. In January 1938 Earl Browder sent a memorandum to Georgi Dimitrov, head of the Comintern:

> For about 7 years my younger sister, Marguerite Browder, has been working for the foreign department of the NKVD [KGB], in various European countries. I am informed that her work has been valuable and satisfactory, and she has expressed no desire to be released. But it seems to me, in view of my increasing involvement in national political affairs and growing connections in Washington political circles, it might become dangerous to this political work if hostile circles in America should by any means obtain knowledge of my sister's work in Europe and make use of this knowledge in America. I raise this question, so ... steps can be taken by you to secure my sister's release from her present work.[1]

Dimitrov agreed and wrote to Nikolai Yezhov, then head of the KGB: "I am forwarding you [this] note from Comrade Browder. . . . I, for my part, consider it politically expedient to relieve his sister of her duties in the foreign department of the NKVD."[2]

Browder's concern that his sister's work as a Soviet agent might become public and embarrass him may have been prompted by the late 1937 defection of Walter Krivitsky, a senior Soviet military intelligence officer. Margaret had for a time been part of an operation supervised by Krivitsky. If this was the cause of Browder's fear, it was well founded. In 1939 Krivitsky publicly revealed that Margaret Browder, using a fraudulent American passport identifying her as Jean Montgomery, had worked as a Soviet espionage agent in Europe.[3]

The House Special Committee on Un-American Activities questioned Browder and his brother William about their sister in 1939, but their responses were carefully phrased. Asked whether she was employed by either the Comintern or the Soviet government, Earl answered, "I think not. . . . To the best of my knowledge, she is not now and has not in the past been officially connected with any government institution." William Browder testified that "to the best of my knowledge and belief," his sister did not work for the Soviet government.[4] When examining the CPUSA's fraudulent passport operations, government investigators determined that the photograph for an American passport issued to "Jean Montgomery" was that of Margaret Browder and that the signature on her passport application that purported to be that of Jean Montgomery's brother was in the handwriting of William Browder.[5]

The Browders were also in contact with Vasily and Elizabeth Zubilin, both senior KGB officers, over a lengthy period. Margaret later admitted knowing Vasily Zubilin in Germany under the name Herbert. She also identified a picture of Zubilin and his wife and told the FBI that she had met them both at the home of William and Rose Browder sometime in the late 1930s. She claimed that Zubilin was merely a talent scout for a movie studio and that she knew them in the United States as Poppy and Mommy. Although Margaret Browder denied meeting with the Zubilins in 1942, Lucy Booker, a former Soviet agent who later cooperated with the FBI, told the bureau that in 1942 she and Margaret had spent a weekend with the Zubilins at an estate on Long Island. A Venona message confirms meetings in 1943 and 1944 between Zubilin and William Browder.[6]

Twenty-six deciphered Venona messages mention Earl Browder.[7] Some of the references are trivial, others show the KGB acting as the communications link between the CPUSA and the Comintern over political matters, but a number document Browder's personal involvement in Soviet espionage against the United States.

In some deciphered cables Browder passes on to the KGB diplomatic and political information he had gained through the CPUSA's own contacts. In May 1943, for example, he delivered a report on what Under Secretary of State Sumner Welles had told an influential writer about turmoil inside the Italian government. Occasionally, the cables show intelligence information going *to* Browder rather than coming from him. In January 1945 the KGB illegal officer Iskhak Akhmerov reported that Solomon Adler, a source of the Silvermaster group, demanded that certain information on Chinese matters he had obtained be shared with Browder.[8] This attitude was one left over from the CPUSA's Washington underground of 1930s, when many of the KGB's sources got their introduction to the secret world. As John Abt, one of the leaders of the Washington underground, later admitted in his autobiography, the secret CPUSA caucuses inside government agencies provided "the national Party leadership" with "commentary and analyses" of government plans and programs.[9] The intent, of course, was to assist the CPUSA's political activities. Even after these networks were shifted to Soviet espionage control in the 1940s, some of their members had difficulty understanding why the results of their espionage should not be made available to the CPUSA as well; in their eyes, it was all part of the same struggle.

Akhmerov cabled Moscow about Adler's demand because such sharing was, as he stated, "an exception" to KGB tradecraft. The KGB's policy, however, was of recent origin. Elizabeth Bentley related that when Jacob Golos had been the chief link between the KGB and several CPUSA espionage networks, he regularly met with Browder to discuss the information being obtained and provided him with summaries or copies of material of interest to the American Communist party.[10] But Golos was of the old school of Soviet espionage. He was an open CPUSA official and had spent his entire adult life working for the party. He mixed open Communist activity, underground party work, and Soviet espionage in a way that the increasingly professional KGB of the 1940s thought risky.

In her FBI deposition Bentley stated that the day after Golos's death

Arlington Hall, headquarters of the Army's code-breaking operations and the Venona Project, in 1944.

Courtesy National Security Agency

Reissue (T1362)

From: NEW YORK
To: MOSCOW
No: 1340

21 September 1944

To VIKTOR[i].

Lately the development of new people [D% has been in progress]. LIBERAL[ii] recommended the wife of his wife's brother, Ruth GREENGLASS, with a safe flat in view. She is 21 years old, a TOWNSWOMAN [GOROShANKA][iii], a GYMNAST [FIZKUL'TURNITsA][iv] since 1942. She lives on STANTON [STANTAUN] Street. LIBERAL and his wife recommend her as an intelligent and clever girl.

[15 groups unrecoverable]

[C% Ruth] learned that her husband[v] was called up by the army but he was not sent to the front. He is a mechanical engineer and is now working at the ENORMOUS [ENORMOZ][vi] plant in SANTA FE, New Mexico.

[45 groups unrecoverable]

detain VOLOK[vii] who is working in a plant on ENORMOUS. He is a FELLOWCOUNTRYMAN [ZEMLYaK][viii]. Yesterday he learned that they had dismissed him from his work. His active work in progressive organizations in the past was the cause of his dismissal.

In the FELLOWCOUNTRYMAN line LIBERAL is in touch with CHESTER[ix]. They meet once a month for the payment of dues. CHESTER is interested in whether we are satisfied with the collaboration and whether there are not any misunderstandings. He does not inquire about specific items of work [KONKRETNAYa RABOTA]. In as much as CHESTER knows about the role of LIBERAL's group we beg consent to ask C. through LIBERAL about leads from among people who are working on ENORMOUS and in other technical fields.

Your no. 4256[a]. On making further enquiries and checking on LARIN[x] we received from the FELLOWCOUNTRYMEN through EKhO[xi] a character sketch which says that they do not entirely vouch for him. They base this statement on the fact that in the Federation LARIN does not carry out all the orders received from the leadership. He is stubborn and self-willed. On the strength of this we have decided to refrain from approaching LARIN and intend to find another candidate in FAECT [FAKhIT][xii].

No 751
20 September

MAJ[xiii]

VENONA

A deciphered Venona message. The New York KGB station reports to Moscow headquarters that Liberal (Julius Rosenberg) and his wife (Ethel) recommend recruiting Ruth Greenglass, Ethel's sister-in-law, as a Soviet agent. The local KGB stations in the United States had to request formal permission from Moscow for recruitments. Venona 1340 KGB New York to Moscow, 21 September 1944.

Courtesy National Security Agency

Cecil Phillips in Paris in 1946. Phillips came to Arlington Hall at age eighteen. In 1944 he made the breakthrough in cracking the Soviet code by identifying Soviet cables that were vulnerable to cryptanalysis.

Courtesy National Security Agency

Army cryptanalysts at work at Arlington Hall in 1944. The man at the far left is Meredith Gardner, who in 1946 became the chief book-breaker (a cryptolinguist who breaks codes) on the Venona Project. The vast majority of code-breakers were young women.

Courtesy National Security Agency

Carter Clarke, chief of the Special Branch of the Army Military Intelligence Division. Clarke initiated the Venona Project in 1943.

Courtesy National Security Agency

William Weisband, the Arlington Hall linguist who in the late 1940s alerted the Soviets that the Venona Project had succeeded in deciphering messages about Soviet espionage in the United States. After Weisband was identified as a KGB agent, he was fired from his job at the National Security Agency and imprisoned for refusing to obey a grand jury subpoena.

Courtesy National Security Agency

Vasily Zubilin (Zarubin), chief of KGB espionage operations in the United States from late 1941 to early 1944.

Courtesy National Security Agency

Duncan Lee being asked to identify a photo of Jacob Golos in 1948 for the House Committee on Un-American Activities. Lee insisted that his relationship with Bentley was purely social.

UPI/Corbis-Bettmann

Elizabeth Bentley in 1948, around the time of her testimony before the House Committee on Un-American Activities. An American Communist and a KGB agent, Bentley turned herself in to the FBI in 1945 and identified scores of Soviet sources.

Courtesy Library of Congress

Judith Coplon reading accounts of her conviction for espionage in 1949. Coplon was convicted twice, but both verdicts were overturned on technicalities.

UPI/Corbis-Bettmann

Victor Perlo appearing before the House Committee on Un-American Activities in 1948. In response to questions from committee members, Perlo, the leader of a large espionage cell, invoked the Fifth Amendment protection against self-incrimination.

UPI/Corbis-Bettmann

Gregory Silvermaster appearing before the House Committee on Un-American Activities in 1948. He was called to respond to Elizabeth Bentley's charges that he supervised an extensive ring of U.S. government employees who spied for the Soviet Union. Silvermaster refused to testify, invoking the Fifth Amendment protection against self-incrimination.

UPI/Corbis-Bettmann

Laurence Duggan testifying before a Senate committee in 1946. Duggan had first begun turning information over to Soviet agents in the mid-1930s. In 1948 he fell to his death, an apparent suicide, after having been questioned by the FBI.

UPI/Corbis-Bettmann

Lauchlin Currie in 1945. An administrative assistant to President Franklin Roosevelt, Currie was also a secret Soviet sympathizer and a source for the KGB. After denying any involvement in Soviet espionage, he left the United States in the early 1950s and renounced his American citizenship.

Courtesy Library of Congress

Harry White in 1946. Assistant secretary of the Treasury in the Roosevelt administration, White was the KGB's highest-ranking source in the U.S. government. He passed information to Soviet intelligence and used his position to promote more than a dozen KGB sources within the federal government. He died of a heart attack in 1948, shortly after denying that he had participated in espionage.

Courtesy Library of Congress

Alfred and Martha Dodd Stern, socially prominent millionaires and secret Communists who assisted Soviet intelligence operations in the United States. They fled, first to Mexico and then to Czechoslovakia, to avoid indictments for espionage.

UPI/Corbis-Bettmann

David Greenglass preparing to testify in 1951 that his sister and brother-in-law, Ethel and Julius Rosenberg, recruited him to pass along atomic secrets from Los Alamos.

UPI/Corbis-Bettmann

Ruth Greenglass testifying that she assisted her husband in atomic espionage at the request of the Rosenbergs.

UPI/Corbis- Bettmann

in November 1943 she met with Browder at his office, and he urged her not to turn over Golos's sources directly to the Russians. Bentley continued to meet Browder about every two weeks at his office. Three imperfectly decrypted cables dealing with Golos went from the KGB in New York to Moscow in the weeks after his death. Zubilin reported to General Fitin that Bentley had twice seen Earl Browder to consult with him about Golos's networks.[11] But Bentley lacked Golos's standing in both the party and the intelligence world to negotiate successfully with the Soviets or to serve as the party's liaison with the KGB. While the KGB kept Bentley in the role of liaison with Golos's networks, from the start it intended her role to be a transitional one as it took direct control.

Browder also acted as a talent-spotter for the KGB. In the fall of 1940 he delivered a report regarding Pierre Cot, a member of the Radical party in France who had served in more than half a dozen of the short-lived French cabinets of the 1930s. A passionate supporter of a Franco-Soviet alliance against Germany, Cot was accused of handing over to the Soviet Union secret information he had obtained in his capacity as aviation minister during the Spanish Civil War. When Walter Krivitsky defected in 1937, he named Cot as a Soviet source within the French government. After the fall of France in 1940 Cot fled to London but was rebuffed in his efforts to join General de Gaulle's Free French movement, which regarded him as an embarrassment.[12]

In September 1940 Cot arrived in the United States, where he quickly established contact with Earl Browder. Browder's report on the meeting originally went via KGB cable from General Fitin, head of the KGB's foreign intelligence directorate, to Lavrenty Beria, chief of the KGB, who briefed both Stalin and Molotov about its contents and forwarded it to the Comintern, in whose archive it was eventually found. Browder reported that Cot had asked him to notify the USSR that he continued to work "for a full alliance between France and the Soviet Union," a coalition that could "be achieved only through the French Comparty [Communist party]." He also passed on that Cot "wants the leaders of the Soviet Union to know of his willingness to perform whatever mission we might choose, for which purpose he is even prepared to break faith with his own position"[13]—a reference to the politics of the Nazi-Soviet Pact. After the pact was concluded in August 1939, the French Communist party had dropped its bellicose anti-Hitler stance and adopted a defeatist attitude toward France's decision to go to war with Nazi Germany. After France's surrender in mid-1940, French Communists did not actively support the pro-Nazi Vichy regime, but neither did they oppose it. Moreover, French Communists were hostile to de Gaulle and his supporters, who refused to recognize the surrender and continued the fight against Hitler. Cot, too, had refused to accept the surrender or the Vichy regime and fled into exile. Through Browder, however, he offered to give up this position if that was the Soviets' wish. (After the Nazi attack on the Soviet Union in June 1941, the French Communist party reversed its stance: it opposed the Vichy regime, sought an alliance with de Gaulle's Free French, and became a major element in the anti-Nazi resistance in the German-occupied areas of France.)

The KGB followed up on Browder's report. Vladimir Pravdin, a KGB officer with a cover as a Soviet journalist, took advantage of a speech Cot gave in June 1942 to meet him. A decrypted Venona message indicates that Cot welcomed the overture. In response to this message, on July 1, 1942, Moscow cabled "about the signing on of Pierre Cot (henceforth 'Daedalus')."[14] For at least the next year, KGB contact with Cot was under the direct supervision of Vasily Zubilin. A number of deciphered KGB messages show that Cot turned over reports on his activities and analyses of events throughout 1943.[15] In addition to cooperating with the KGB, he worked closely with the Comintern and the French Communist party; one KGB cable from San Francisco refers to a message for Cot from the French Communist leader and Comintern official André Marty. In one imperfectly decoded message, dated July 1, 1943, Zubilin relayed a report in which Cot offered to go to Algiers to assist on some problem; Zubilin noted that Cot "will obey unquestionably." Cot also sent analyses of exiled French politicians with whom he had contact in French North Africa and in the United States. After World War II he successfully reentered French politics and briefly served once again as aviation minister. He continued to champion French-Soviet friendship and in 1953 received the Stalin Peace Prize. By the time the Venona documents revealing his cooperation with Soviet intelligence were decrypted, his political career was over, and French authorities chose to keep secret his relationship with the KGB.[16]

Although Browder performed many valuable services for Soviet intelligence, he also inadvertently provided it with misinformation about President Roosevelt. In July 1943 both the KGB and the GRU in the United States informed their superiors in Moscow that a friend of Browder's who was a secret member of the CPUSA was surreptitiously meeting with Franklin Roosevelt, who was using her as a back channel to communicate with Browder.

In a message to Moscow on July 18, a senior KGB officer in New York, Pavel Klarin, stated that Jacob Golos had told the New York KGB that Roosevelt had informed Browder that the invasion of Sicily was a prelude to a large-scale invasion of Europe during the summer, but that Churchill was objecting. In addition, according to Golos, the president was pleased with the positions of the CPUSA in New Jersey politics.[17] The very next Venona message, sent the same day, begins by stating that Browder had asked the KGB to get a message to Dimitrov. Most of the remainder of the lengthy cable, nearly two hundred code groups, was not deciphered, except that the name Carnero appears.[18]

Located in the archive of the Comintern in Moscow are two related documents, a covering note from General Fitin and a Browder report for the Comintern sent through the New York KGB station, both dated July 23, 1943, five days after the two Venona cables. The report discussed, among other points, American plans for following up on the invasion of Sicily, Churchill's reluctance to launch a continental assault, and Roosevelt's praise for the CPUSA's position in New Jersey. A section about Mexico notes the role of Carnero, a leading Mexican Communist, in party factionalism.[19] These documents in the Comintern's archive obviously derive from the two earlier cables that were later partially deciphered in the Venona Project. The report Fitin forwarded to Dimitrov was an in-clear version of the second, and largely undeciphered, Venona cable of July 18. The striking point about the version in the Comintern archive is its statement that President Roosevelt had conveyed the comments on the Sicilian invasion and on New Jersey politics to Browder "verbally."

Just one day after the KGB in New York sent along its information on FDR, Soviet military intelligence in New York also cabled Moscow. Although only fragments of the message were decoded by American cryptanalysts, it too appears to be about some Communist source with access to President Roosevelt. Two weeks later, obviously in response to queries from Moscow, Pavel Mikhailov, the GRU chief in New York, cabled Moscow that his source for the story was Theodore Bayer, cover name Simon. A Communist who headed the Russky Golos Publishing Company, Bayer described the CPUSA source near Roosevelt as a woman "from an aristocratic family, [who] has known the President and his wife for a long time, evidently a secret member of the Corporation [CPUSA]." Mikhailov passed along from Bayer gossipy tidbits from the woman's alleged conversations with Roosevelt, including praise of Stalin's leadership and the claim that Mrs. Chiang Kai-shek was "a narcotics addict," but he said that Bayer had not provided her name. Mikhailov warned that the information was thirdhand but speculated that FDR might be trying to improve his political standing "with the masses before the 1944 election" by lauding the CPUSA (a sign of how little the GRU officer understood American politics). In mid-August Mikhailov cabled that he had gotten the name of the woman: Josephine Treslow.[20]

Who was Josephine Treslow? The GRU in Moscow did not know. On August 21 it sent this memo to Dimitrov: "According to information we have received, an American citizen, Josephine Treslow, on instructions from Browder is meeting systematically with the president of the U.S. Roosevelt. Please advise whether this is in fact the case, and whether you have any information on this issue."[21]

The memo's Josephine Treslow was Josephine Truslow Adams, born in Brooklyn in 1897. From 1934 to 1941 she taught art at Swarthmore College and, without openly acknowledging her Communist loyalties, joined numerous Communist-led organizations. Adams's contact with the Roosevelt family began when she was commissioned to paint a picture for Eleanor Roosevelt. When Mrs. Roosevelt visited Swarthmore in 1941, they met. Adams then sent Mrs. Roosevelt another painting and began bombarding her with long letters.[22] Among the subjects Adams stressed was the advisability of freeing Earl Browder from federal prison, where he was serving a sentence for use of fraudulent passports; Adams was a mainstay of the Citizens' Committee to Free Earl Browder. President Roosevelt released Browder in May 1942, as a goodwill gesture to the Soviet Union at the time of Molotov's arrival in Washington and as a reward to Communists for their recent support for his war policies. There is no evidence that Josephine Truslow Adams's lobbying had any effect on the president's decision. Earl Browder, however, thought otherwise. He met with her at a Communist gala in July 1942 and believed her story that she had met with President and Mrs. Roosevelt on many occasions, had become an intimate family friend, and had successfully lobbied for his release.

Adams misled Browder not least because she suffered from delusions. By 1956 she was in and out of hospitals for psychiatric treatment.

In 1943, however, her mental delusions were not so manifest, and Browder believed he had a private pipeline to the White House. Browder gave Adams material on various political matters to discuss with President Roosevelt during their (as he thought) frequent chats. Actually, Browder's political information became the texts of the letters Adams continued to send Mrs. Roosevelt, who recognized the political interest of some of Adams's letters and forwarded them to her husband—noting on one, however, "I know nothing of her reliability." Mrs. Roosevelt sent polite responses to Adams, the most encouraging being a note that "your letters go directly to the president. What then happens I do not know."[23] That, however, is not what Josephine Adams told Earl Browder. She represented that she met in person with FDR, and she gave Browder substantive messages that she said were the president's responses to Browder. Adams in fact simply made up FDR's responses, basing them on the analysis offered by political commentators and on what Browder wanted to hear.[24]

Convinced that he had Roosevelt's blessing for his effort to build closer ties between American Communists and the Democratic party, and encouraged by the dissolution of the Comintern and by the Teheran meetings of Roosevelt, Churchill, and Stalin in 1943 that promised postwar cooperation among the Allies, Browder put American communism on a new course in 1944. He converted the American Communist party into the Communist Political Association and set out to make it the left wing of the Democratic party. Browder's influence also appeared in the CPUSA's decision to oppose New Jersey reformers' attempt to create a third party, the decision of Communists who secretly controlled Minnesota's Farmer-Labor party to merge it with the Democratic party in 1944, and the decision in early 1945 of the secret Communists who controlled the Washington (State) Commonwealth Federation to end its separate existence and attempt to integrate it into the Washington Democratic party.[25]

The Soviets, however, did not approve of Browder's new tack. Dimitrov warned Browder that he was veering away from Moscow's guidance, but Browder pushed ahead anyway. It is not known whether the KGB ever learned that Browder had been systematically misled by Adams. Did the Soviets worry that Browder had become too close to FDR? Or did they conclude that he had been played for a fool? In any case, sometime in the fall of 1944 someone in Moscow drafted what became known as the Duclos article, which harshly criticized Browder's policies.

After it was published in the spring of 1945, American Communists realized that their leader no longer had Moscow's approval. The Communist Political Association called an emergency convention, transformed itself back into the CPUSA, removed Earl Browder from its leadership, and later expelled him altogether.[26]

Adams not only encouraged Browder to travel down a path that proved disastrous for him but also contributed to the souring of postwar American politics. Browder would often hint at his relationship with Roosevelt. Rumors of his back channel to the White House circulated in the upper levels of the CPUSA. From there the story seeped out to Popular Front liberal allies of the party, who were thus reassured that there was nothing improper in their own relationship with the CPUSA. The rumors also reached anti-Communists; in some cases Communists who had become disillusioned and quit the party carried with them what they thought was inside knowledge of a Browder-Roosevelt relationship.[27] Many anti-Communists discounted the rumors, but some conservative anti-Communists who intensely disliked both FDR and the CPUSA found a Roosevelt-Browder connection believable. They were wrong, but their belief was based on credible sources from within the Communist party itself. Thus, Josephine Adams's fantasies and Browder's credulity misled some liberals into believing that association with the CPUSA had Roosevelt's backing and promoted the belief among some conservatives that Roosevelt had a conspiratorial relationship with the CPUSA. This perception in turn contributed to partisan divisiveness about the nature of the domestic Communist problem in the postwar period.

As for Adams, after Earl Browder was expelled from the CPUSA, she also drifted away from the party. The FBI interviewed her several times and examined her papers but concluded that she was unreliable. While in a New York mental hospital in late 1956, she got through to the staff of the Senate Internal Security Subcommittee and said she wanted to reveal her role as the secret link between President Roosevelt and the Communist party. She also asserted that "Communist doctors" were giving her shock treatments, drugs, and lobotomies to convince her she was mentally ill. That should have been a clue to her reliability, but nonetheless she was invited to Washington and testified in executive session in January 1957. Excerpts of her testimony were released in February and provided a sensation for those who believed that the New Deal was essentially a Communist conspiracy. In the excerpts Adams claimed to have had nearly forty personal meetings with the president at Hyde Park or the White House.[28]

The sensation, however, was brief. Following her testimony, Adams signed a book contract and hired Isaac Don Levine, the veteran anti-Communist journalist, as her ghostwriter. When Adams sent a file of what she said were letters between herself and President Roosevelt to Levine, however, he became suspicious. Included in Adams's material were more than a score of letters from FDR to Adams, displaying the irreverence and flightiness that characterized Adams's style, not FDR's. Further, of the twenty-one dates on which FDR supposedly wrote from Washington, Levine discovered that the president was not there on ten. Levine confronted Adams, who eventually admitted that the letters were forgeries. The planned book, tentatively entitled *I Was Roosevelt's Secret Emissary,* was dropped. Adams drifted deeper into her delusional world and in 1958 was committed to Norristown sanitarium in Pennsylvania, where she remained until her death in 1969.

Eugene Dennis and Infiltration of the OSS and OWI

Next to Earl Browder, Eugene Dennis was the most important figure in the CPUSA during World War II. Born Francis Waldron in 1905 in Seattle, he had become a full-time organizer shortly after joining the party in 1926. He fled to Moscow in 1930 after being indicted for criminal syndicalism in California in connection with Communist union organizing, changed his name to Tim Ryan, and undertook a series of covert tasks for the Comintern in China, South Africa, and the Philippines. Using the name Gene Dennis and leaving his American-born son behind in Moscow to be raised in Comintern boarding schools as a Russian, he arrived in Wisconsin in 1935 to serve as district organizer. Two years later he was back in the USSR as the CPUSA's representative to the Communist International for one year. On his return to the United States, he became a member of the national party leadership; he was ordered underground in 1940 in anticipation of a move to illegality if the U.S. government suppressed the party because of its support for the Nazi-Soviet Pact. The following year he once again visited Moscow to consult with Comintern leaders. When Browder was ousted from the party leadership in 1945, Dennis was selected to succeed him; he remained general secretary until 1959, when, in poor health, he was replaced by Gus Hall.

Louis Budenz, a former CPUSA leader turned anti-Communist, charged in 1948 that during World War II Dennis had directed a ring of Communist agents in the Office of Strategic Services (OSS) that included Carl Marzani.[29] In the 1920s Budenz had been a labor activist, an early official of the American Civil Liberties Union, and a supporter of the Socialist party. In the 1930s he moved to the left, first joining the American Workers party, led by the independent radical A. J. Muste; but Muste's radicalism was insufficient for Budenz, and he moved to the CPUSA. Budenz rose rapidly to membership on the Communist party's New York state committee, then on the national central committee. In 1941 he became managing editor of the *Daily Worker* and was on the fringe of the CPUSA's top leadership, even irregularly attending meetings of the party's ruling Political Bureau. In 1945, however, Budenz underwent a spiritual crisis, left the CPUSA, and was received into the Roman Catholic Church. He then joined the faculties of Notre Dame and Fordham universities and wrote, lectured, and testified widely about communism as a subversive threat.[30] Many scholars scoffed at Budenz's assertions, but documents found in Russian archives and deciphered material from Venona demonstrate that Budenz was correct about Dennis: he oversaw a CPUSA operation that placed Communists in the OSS during World War II.

In November 1941 Col. William Donovan, head of the OSS, approached Milton Wolff, the last commander of the Abraham Lincoln battalion in Spain. Wolff had been a member of the Young Communist League in the United States and the Communist Party of Spain.[31] When he returned to the United States he became the commander of the Veterans of the Abraham Lincoln Brigade, which encompassed all Americans who had served in the International Brigades as well as veterans of the Abraham Lincoln battalion. As its commander he steered it firmly in line with the policies of the Communist party. During the period of the Nazi-Soviet Pact, this meant that the Veterans of the Abraham Lincoln Brigade opposed any U.S. assistance to Britain in its war with Germany. Once Germany attacked the USSR in June 1941, however, the organization became an enthusiastic supporter of such aid. Donovan wanted Wolff to recruit Spanish Civil War veterans to serve with British commando units being prepared for operations in occupied Europe. (America was officially neutral at that time, but President Roosevelt was offering Britain all possible aid short of U.S. entry into the war.) Wolff agreed to Donovan's plan. After Pearl Harbor and America's declaration of war in December, Donovan redirected Wolff's recruits to his own agency, where several dozen International Brigades veterans served in the OSS units that worked with resistance forces in enemy-occupied areas.

On April 3, 1942, Dimitrov sent a coded cable to the CPUSA leadership that "we have information that Wolff, repeat Wolff, from Abraham Lincoln Brigade is recruiting comrades from this brigade for special work" in the name of the Communist party. "Special work" was a euphemism for intelligence work. Dimitrov instructed CPUSA leaders to "examine carefully this question and inform us urgently."[32] A week later Gene Dennis responded with a brief coded cable, assuring Dimitrov that "Wolff has our approval working for government."[33] Some weeks later Dennis met with a KGB officer in New York and delivered a more detailed report for forwarding to Moscow. In this report, found in the Comintern's archive, Dennis described Donovan's approach to Wolff the previous November and explained that Donovan had "proposed selecting dependable veterans and putting them at the disposal of the British for deployment in the interior of the Axis countries for diversionary work. Wolff conveyed this proposal by the intelligence service to the Comparty [CPUSA] and was given a sanction for it. . . . By the time the US entered the war, Wolff had provided the British with 12 Yugoslavs, 3 Czechs, and 1 Italian. . . . Wolff has provided American intelligence with 10 Americans, 1 Greek, and 3 Yugoslavs, who are considered on active duty in the army and undergoing training in special ('commando') groups." All were Communists, Dennis reported, but in addition Wolff had also handed over from among the veterans of the International Brigades "6 nonparty Hungarians and 4 Czechs to American intelligence." The report went on to explain that in December 1941 the CPUSA had appointed Dennis to negotiate with Donovan about the party's cooperation with the OSS. It noted that Dennis had provided the OSS with a "selection of Italian and German immigrants for the compilation of propagandistic materials and radio broadcasting."[34]

On May 13 General Fitin, head of KGB foreign intelligence, sent a sobering memo to Dimitrov. He noted that the KGB "regard[s] this entire matter as a political mistake by the leadership of the US Comparty, thanks to which the American and British intelligence services have been given the opportunity to infiltrate not only American Comparty channels but also the Comparty organizations of other countries."[35] (Fitin's fears were misplaced: as a matter of policy the OSS made no attempt to penetrate the CPUSA or Soviet intelligence.)[36] Dimitrov was not one to disagree with the KGB, and the same day he responded by telling Fitin that he agreed that "allowing Wolff to recruit people for English and American intelligence [was] a mistaken policy" and suggested "curtailing that recruitment and all connection with the indicated intelligence services." A handwritten note by Dimitrov on Fitin's memo said, "A directive has been given to New York for the discontinuation of this work."[37] Dennis, too, toed the line: on June 1 he sent a message to Dimitrov through the KGB: "We fully agree with your proposals regarding the activities of Wolff and we have taken all necessary measures for their discontinuation."[38] Wolff promptly closed down his recruiting operation.

Still, that left a body of Communists who had already been recruited. Via the KGB, Dennis explained to Dimitrov: "We are in contact with the department of foreign propaganda and with the information coordinator of the US. That department is one of three departments in the so-called *Donovan* Committee and is directly controlled by the White House. We also have several persons working in the Czech and Italian radio-broadcast sections of that department and influencing certain broadcasts in Germany [in German], although not in the overall program. We consider it expedient to prolong that contact and keep these persons in the radio-broadcast section, if, of course, you are in agreement. We have a similar contact with the inter-American Committee."[39]

In the last message Dennis was telling Dimitrov and the KGB that the CPUSA planned to retain contact with party members in the U.S. Office of Strategic Services, the Office of War Information, and the Office of the Coordinator of Inter-American Affairs. One Venona message from 1943 lists six Soviet agents working in the OSS and the OWI. The message was only partially decrypted, but five of the Soviet sources can be identified: Maurice Halperin, Duncan Lee, Franz Neumann, Bella Joseph, and Julius Joseph, all of whom worked with Elizabeth Bentley. One possibility for the unidentified source is the man Budenz named: Carl Marzani, who was hired by the Presentation Division of the OSS in 1942.[40]

Born in Italy, Marzani emigrated to the United States in 1924. After graduating from Williams College in 1935, he won a scholarship to attend Oxford in England. A member of the English Communist party, he went to Spain to fight but, oddly enough, enlisted in an anarchist rather than a Communist battalion. Back in the United States, Marzani joined the CPUSA on the day the Nazi-Soviet Pact was signed. Under the name of Tony Whales, he worked fervently for the party on the Lower East Side of New York. He insisted in his autobiography that he quit the party in 1941 and that when he joined the OSS he told people that he was an ex-Communist. After World War II he became a State Department official but was later convicted of making false statements in denying that he was a Communist when he joined the OSS. After his jail term he headed Marzani and Munsell, a left-wing publishing house. A retired KGB officer in 1994 identified Marzani as a contact and a recipient of KGB subsidies for his publishing house in the 1960s.[41]

Dennis is mentioned in only two Venona messages, and in neither one was enough of the message deciphered to make much sense of what it concerned. In both messages he is linked to Harold Glasser, a member of the Silvermaster espionage network.[42]

KGB Liaison with the CPUSA

In June 1943 Vasily Zubilin cabled Moscow regarding a realignment of liaison for several of the New York KGB's major contacts. He specified that his wife would supervise contact with Jacob Golos but would use an intermediary for communication. He would retain as his own liaisons three major contacts: Pierre Cot, Iskhak Akhmerov, and Earl Browder.[43] Very shortly thereafter, however, Moscow ordered a general reorganization of KGB contact with Communist parties around the world. In September General Fitin sent a circular order to KGB stations in Australia, Canada, and the United States warning that by continuing to meet with Communist party leaders, regional KGB offices risked giving Russia's allies the impression that the Comintern's recent dissolution had been a sham. He ordered his officers to stop meeting with prominent Communist party officials and no longer to routinely accept Communist party material for forwarding to Moscow. Henceforth all meetings had to take place "only with special reliable undercover contacts of the Fellowcountryman [Communist party] organizations" and were to be "exclusively about specific aspects of our intelligence work, acquiring [unbroken code group] contacts, leads, rechecking of those who are being cultivated, etc."[44]

The subsequent reorganization of liaisons was further complicated by the death of Jacob Golos in November 1943. By early 1944 there was a new liaison between the CPUSA and the KGB, Bernard Schuster or, as he was known in the CPUSA, Bernard Chester. A soft-spoken man of average height and build, Schuster was, according to FBI agents who watched him in 1945, "suspicious, nervous, tail conscious."[45] He had good reason to be. Venona cables clearly demonstrate that in the next two years he became deeply enmeshed in KGB operations, including atomic bomb espionage.

Schuster was born October 14, 1904, in Warsaw and came to the United States in 1921 with his father. He graduated from New York University in 1925, but mediocre grades discouraged his plans for medical school. Instead, he became an accountant. He may have worked for Amtorg in 1930. In the early 1930s he directed the CPUSA's anti-militarist work, a program to develop secret Communist groups among American military personnel. By 1935 he was treasurer of the Wholesale Book Corporation, which distributed Communist literature. In the next few years Schuster became a director, along with William Browder, of the Commonwealth Minupress Company, which printed party literature. He also formed the Bernador Sales Company and became co-owner of National Mercantile Trading Company, an import-export firm serving clients in Mexico, Uruguay, and Argentina, and a limited partner in Screenmakers, Inc., manufacturers of radio equipment.

Schuster's business interests were probably all fronts for the Communist party, which he served in a variety of second-rank positions. In 1938, as Bernard Chester, he was New York state membership director of the Communist party; the following year he was president of the Fifth Assembly District Club of the Communist party in the Bronx. By 1943 he was treasurer of the New York state Communist party and was often dispatched to do special audits by Charles Krumbein, the party's national treasurer. Several ex-Communists briefly mentioned Schuster in their memoirs. Louis Budenz identified "Comrade Chester" as the "man in charge of secret work in the New York district" in the late 1930s. Elizabeth Bentley recalled "Berny Schuster" as an old friend of Jacob Golos's who had "turned contacts for espionage over to us." Bella Dodd, a New York Communist activist turned anti-Communist, wrote about "Chester," whom she knew as the head of the party's intelligence service. Chester, according to Dodd, received reports from secret Communist agents in other left-wing organizations and government agencies and collected money from various businesses with ties to the CPUSA.[46]

The Venona decryptions confirm Bernard Schuster's critical role in Soviet espionage in America. He is mentioned in more than three dozen messages from 1944 and 1945.[47] In line with Fitin's directive of September 1943, the New York KGB used Schuster as its intermediary with Earl Browder rather than meeting with him directly, as had been done earlier, and often checked with Moscow first when it needed to approach Browder through Schuster. Browder also went through Schuster when he passed on to the Soviets his assessment of political conditions in the United States. And Schuster passed along Browder's request that the Soviets approve the new theoretical positions he was developing about postwar détente between the USA and the USSR.[48]

A number of Venona messages dealt with KGB requests that Schuster check on potential recruits. In one cable, Soviet intelligence asked what the CPUSA knew about Marion Schultz, a Russian-born American working as a mechanic in the Philadelphia shipyards and active in Russian War Relief and Slavic organizations.[49] When Mary Ann Grohl, an American Communist once employed by the Joint Anti-Fascist Refugee Committee, moved to Mexico to live with a KGB agent who was being prepared for an assignment, Schuster told the KGB that she had been fired for incompetence.[50] Schuster arranged for Samuel Rodman, an employee of the United Nations Relief and Rehabilitation Administration leaving for Yugoslavia, to provide information to the KGB.[51] Schuster assured the KGB that Joseph Rappoport, a long-time party member active in Russian War Relief, was "a reliable and responsible comrade."[52] Sometimes he reported that a potential recruit was not known to the party.[53] The Soviets refused to maintain contact with an agent code-named Phloke and her husband until it received a report about them from Schuster, and it was through Schuster that Earl Browder warned the KGB about potentially unreliable or untrustworthy sources.[54]

Schuster's liaison role brought him into the KGB's efforts to steal scientific information and American atomic bomb secrets. (See chapter 10.) He met regularly with Julius Rosenberg to receive his CPUSA dues. The New York KGB office told Moscow that Schuster wanted to know whether the KGB was satisfied with the work of the Rosenberg apparatus. A number of Communist party members were working as scientists and engineers on projects relating to the atomic bomb, and the Communist-dominated Federation of Architects, Engineers, Chemists and Technicians (FAECT), to which Rosenberg belonged, was a natural recruiting ground for the KGB. When Schuster investigated a possible candidate for recruitment and reported that the individual was a disruptive force in the FAECT, the KGB decided not to approach him and instead to "find another candidate" from the union. Schuster had been so helpful that the New York office requested permission from Moscow to ask Schuster "through Liberal [Julius Rosenberg] about leads from among people who are working on Enormous [the Manhattan Project] and in other technical fields."[55] When Saville Sax and Theodore Alvin Hall—both young Communists—approached the KGB with the news that Hall, a physicist, was being dispatched to Los Alamos to work on the atomic bomb, Schuster was entrusted with the task of checking up on their backgrounds.[56]

Schuster also located safe-houses where KGB officers could meet in secrecy with their sources, and provided them with the names of two long-time CPUSA members, Louis Horvitz and Paul Burns. New York sent this information to Moscow on August 16, 1944; three days later General Fitin of the KGB directed a memo to Dimitrov asking for information on Horvitz, identified as working in a judicial office, and Paul Burns, a social worker and Lincoln battalion veteran.[57] Leonid Kvasnikov, a KGB officer, used the apartment of a CPUSA member for his first meeting with one source at the end of 1944, although it is not clear whether the apartment was Horvitz's or Burns's.[58]

Toward the end of 1944 Schuster began to balk at the demands placed on him by the KGB. His reasons are not clear. The CPUSA had recently been dissolved and replaced by the Communist Political Association. Possibly Earl Browder may have developed doubts that continued extensive American Communist involvement in Soviet espionage was compatible with moving communism into the mainstream of American politics. In any case, in October 1944 the New York KGB complained to Moscow that Schuster had begun to refuse to carry out assignments. During a meeting with the KGB agent Joseph Katz, Schuster declined several assignments, stating that his position within the Communist Political Association did not give him the authority to obtain safe-houses, find candidates to infiltrate the FBI, or perform other tasks. Schuster suggested that the KGB ask Browder "for a responsible worker to be assigned to us, one who is capable of carrying out the necessary measures without asking permission from the authorities each time."[59] In another message the KGB passed along Schuster's complaint that he could work effectively only within the New York area and that for anything else he had to go to Browder and get specific approval.[60] Both messages noted Schuster's claim that getting Communist party members to carry out espionage tasks for the KGB had become more difficult since Browder's reforms. (This latter observation did not, of course, recommend Browder's new course to Moscow and may have contributed to its decision to reverse the reforms.)

Moscow's response clearly demonstrated that the KGB had little use for any show of independence by an American Communist. The Communist party's secret apparatus was beholden not to the party leader, Earl Browder, but to the KGB. General Fitin angrily ordered the New York KGB to tell Schuster that "henceforth he must carry out our tasks without resorting to the help of Helmsman [Browder]."[61] Following this order Schuster took a holiday in Mexico from November 1944 to January 1945. While he was gone, the KGB planned his future assignments; the New York office reported that he would be asked to obtain information about the structure of the OSS. When he returned, Schuster desisted from complaining and once again began carrying out the tasks allotted to the Communist party by the KGB.[62] And, of course, via the Duclos article, by mid-1945 Moscow had disposed of Browder and his reforms, and the Communist Political Association had once more become the Communist Party of the USA.

Schuster's foot-dragging also coincided with a disagreement within the KGB about how crucial CPUSA cooperation was to intelligence operations in America. In 1944 Stepan Apresyan headed the KGB's New York station, but he did not have the broad authority over all KGB operations that his predecessor had had. Vasily Zubilin's move from New York to Washington in 1943 indicated that the senior KGB officer in the United States would henceforth be in the capital. Zubilin was hastily recalled from the United States in 1944, however, after his subordinate, Vasily Mironov, accused him of treason (chapter 2). Until the arrival of Anatoly Gromov several months later as Zubilin's replacement, this gap temporarily left uncertain who was the chief of KGB activity, and Vladimir Pravdin, the head of TASS in the United States and a senior KGB officer, asserted authority independently from Apresyan. Each sent a cable to Moscow accusing the other of poor performance. Apresyan denounced Pravdin for believing that "without the help of the Fellowcountrymen [American Communists] we are completely powerless." Apresyan disagreed: although "we shall have to have recourse to the Fellow Countrymen [American Communists] . . .

they ought not to be the one and only base especially if you take into account the fact that in the event of Kulak's [Thomas Dewey's] being elected [U.S. president] this source may dry up."[63]

Apresyan's irritation at the CPUSA and Browder was undoubtedly related to the KGB's effort to take direct control of the sources previously supervised by Jacob Golos, particularly the large Silvermaster group. Some of the group's activities, set up and run by enthusiastic but amateur spies, appalled the professional KGB officers. Its members socialized with each other, mixed Communist party activity with intelligence work, violated elementary rules of security, kept documents in the Silvermaster home, and even planned to buy a farm together. Akhmerov tried to professionalize the group's operations but ran into resistance from Gregory Silvermaster, who explained "that he did not believe in our orthodox methods."[64] One KGB initiative resisted by members of the Silvermaster group was the attempt to stop the sharing of espionage with the CPUSA leadership. As already noted, Akhmerov had to ask Moscow to make an exception to its rule and allow him to transmit some information to Browder. Otherwise, the frustrated Akhmerov stated, the "Fellow Countrymen [American Communists] may try to realize transmission passing us by," which would be even more insecure than if Akhmerov did it.[65]

The West Coast

There was a separate California branch of the CPUSA's secret apparatus, dating from the early 1930s. Its head in those years was a longtime Communist, Isaac Folkoff, often called Pop Folkoff. Born January 10, 1881, in Lutzin (Latvia), Folkoff came to the United States in 1904 and became a citizen in 1912. A charter member of the CPUSA, Folkoff kept a low profile until 1932, although the FBI believed that he had visited the Soviet Union in the early 1920s. Folkoff was a partner in the Model Embroidery and Pleating Company in San Francisco. For much of the 1930s he was the chairman of the Finance Committee of the California Communist party. While head of the West Coast party underground, Folkoff worked with Whittaker Chambers, and, like J. Peters, he was removed from his position after Chambers's defection in 1938 put him at risk of exposure. Indeed, Chambers identified him to Under Secretary of State Berle in 1939.[66]

Another West Coast figure was William Crane, a newspaper reporter who had worked for the *Wall Street Journal* in San Francisco and joined the Communist party in 1932. Crane, a native of Minnesota, had graduated from Stanford. His stay in the aboveground party was brief, however. He told the FBI years later that Pop Folkoff introduced him to John Loomis Sherman (just as Max Bedacht introduced Chambers to Sherman), who asked him to drop out of the CPUSA "in order to engage in special work." For the next several years Crane assisted Sherman in several operations that benefited both the party and Soviet intelligence. His first assignment was a survey of the Japanese and Chinese populations on the West Coast. Next, he taught English to a Japanese Communist whom he knew only as Joe. The FBI suspected that it was Joe Koide, an immigrant who worked for the Profintern's Pan-Pacific Trade Union Secretariat in the 1930s. Crane and Sherman also published a small Japanese newspaper in Los Angeles. In 1934 Crane, who was receiving $125 a month for his underground work, went to New York and met Whittaker Chambers, as well as the Soviet officer who headed the GRU apparatus in the United States.[67]

When he returned to San Francisco, Crane became more involved in Soviet intelligence operations. He served as the contact for Morris Asimow, who was originally used as a mail drop but who began to supply industrial formulas he obtained from his work at U.S. Steel in 1936. Asimow later acknowledged to American authorities that he had supplied Crane information about an industrial steel alloy. Crane also picked up materials from Vladimir De Sveshnikov, a ballistics expert employed by the U.S. government. In 1949 De Sveshnikov confirmed to the FBI that he had been recruited by the Soviets in the mid-1920s and regularly received a hundred dollars a month in return for patent information and American military journals dealing with artillery and engineering. He handed over material regularly throughout the 1930s. Crane also received from Lester Marx Huettig, who worked for Remington Arms in Bridgeport, Connecticut, the blueprints for automatic shell loaders, which Crane turned over to Boris Bykov of the GRU.[68]

Chambers was dispatched to San Francisco in 1935 with a money belt containing approximately twenty thousand dollars. He contacted Crane, whom he knew by the pseudonym Keith. Crane, in turn, introduced Chambers to Pop Folkoff, who took the money belt. Chambers assumed that the money was for the Pan-Pacific Trade Union Secretariat courier system to Japan; for some reason it was not used, and in 1935 Crane returned it to him in New York. Crane began working as a photographer for Chambers's Washington, D.C., espionage ring in 1937. He left the apparatus at the end of 1937 and returned to California; under the name Will Morgan he resumed activity in the above-ground CPUSA, writing for its West Coast newspaper, *People's World*. Not until 1947 did he break with the party. When the FBI found him in 1948, he confirmed Whittaker Chambers's story of espionage, although they differed on small details.[69]

After the KGB began operating out of the Soviet consulate in San Francisco in the early 1940s, Folkoff began to appear in Venona messages—more than a dozen from 1943 to 1946. He is portrayed as doing many of the same things as Bernard Schuster did on the East Coast. He arranged meetings for KGB officers with West Coast Communists they wanted to contact, such as Nat, described in the deciphered message as a leading Communist in the San Francisco area.[70] Folkoff, under the cover name Uncle, also passed along to the KGB the names of likely candidates for recruitment. In February 1944, for example, Uncle/Folkoff suggested as a likely source an engineer named Darcy Henwood, who worked for Standard Oil. The KGB message mentioning Henwood also indicated that Folkoff was being paid five hundred dollars. Another 1944 message suggests that Folkoff was helping the Soviets recruit Bay Area longshoremen, among whom the CPUSA had many supporters.[71]

One of Folkoff's most valuable agents was James Walter Miller, a Russian-language translator with the financial and trade section of the U.S. government wartime mail censorship office. With its legal access to mail and to U.S. security agencies' watch list of mail to be given special scrutiny, this office was of considerable interest to Soviet intelligence.[72] A Russian native, Miller had been a member of the Communist party in Los Angeles under the name of Victor Milo. He had worked for the party's *Russky Golos* and the American-Russian Institute and done translating for the *People's World*. Several times in 1943 Folkoff gave the KGB material he had received from Miller. In November San Francisco requested permission from Moscow "to sign on Vague [Miller]" but warned that because he was "talkative" it wanted to have Folkoff arrange for him to pass his material through Communist party contacts, so that he "will have no inkling that the information is coming to us." Because Miller was so eager to help, the KGB worried that he might be a double agent, but Grigory Kheifets, the KGB's San Francisco chief, reported that "the Fellowcountrymen [CPUSA] categorically rule out such an assumption."[73]

Miller was soon passing information to the KGB through an old friend at the *People's World,* Harrison George, himself a veteran of the Comintern's Pan-Pacific Trade Union Secretariat. One message indicated that Miller had enabled some KGB operation in Mexico to proceed with assurances that its communications had not been compromised. Late in 1943 Miller was able to warn his contacts that the Mail Censor's office had found secret writing upon opening a letter that a Naval GRU officer had sent to Moscow. The KGB warned Moscow to make sure the Naval GRU was alerted. Miller, however, came into the sights of the FBI in 1944 during its "Comintern Apparatus" investigation. His CPUSA membership was barely concealed. The bureau also observed Miller meeting the KGB officer Kheifets at least six times in the early months of 1944. The two would often walk along deserted streets, Miller talking and Kheifets taking notes. Under prompting from the FBI, Miller's superiors subjected his activities to extra scrutiny. When they found that he had copied a letter without authority to do so, they forced him to resign.[74]

Another important West Coast CPUSA official linked to Soviet espionage was Steve Nelson, who had years of experience in clandestine work. A native of Croatia, he joined the Young Communist League in 1923 in Philadelphia. After working in Pittsburgh, Nelson was encouraged to move to Detroit by Rudy Baker, a fellow Yugoslav with whom he shared an apartment before Baker went off to the International Lenin School in Moscow. By 1929 Nelson had become a full-time functionary (Communist party professional). The CPUSA sent him to the Lenin School in 1931 at Baker's suggestion. During his two-year stay there, Nelson was sent on clandestine missions to Germany, Switzerland, France, India, and China, while his wife also served in the Comintern's courier service. After another sojourn organizing within the United States, Nelson went to Spain to serve as political commissar of the Abraham Lincoln battalion. Nelson had traveled under false passports to the Soviet Union and to Spain.[75]

Nelson proved to be an effective political commissar, and upon his return to the United States the CPUSA, having marked him as an up-and-coming leader, sent him to southern California as a party functionary. He headed a covert special commission that both ferreted out infiltrators of the CPUSA and stole the files of hostile organizations. In 1939 the Civil Liberties Subcommittee of the U.S. Senate Education and Labor Committee, headed by Wisconsin Progressive senator Robert

La Follette, held hearings on labor relations in California. As part of its investigation the La Follette subcommittee subpoenaed the records of the Associated Farmers, a leading employer group in California that was hostile to the Communist role in the California CIO.

Committee investigators seized the records to ascertain the Associated Farmers' role in the use of labor spies and physical assaults on farm unionists in California. As part of its anti-Communist campaign the Associated Farmers had gathered extensive documentation on Communist activities. Eager to learn what the Associated Farmers knew (and to learn the identity of its informants), Nelson's apparatus secretly stole, photographed, and returned the subpoenaed records.[76] He also worked with Japanese-American Communists to produce propaganda and arranged with longshoremen and sailors to smuggle it onto ships bound for Japan. Transferred to San Francisco in the fall of 1939, Nelson went underground early the next year, preparing to function illegally in case the CPUSA was outlawed.

During World War II Nelson served as head of the local Communist party organizations in San Francisco and Oakland. Early in 1943 Rudy Baker informed Dimitrov that "we have assigned one responsible person in California (Mack) to be responsible for all our work from there." Although there is no direct evidence that Nelson was Mack, a bugged conversation between Nelson and Vasily Zubilin in April 1943 indicated that Nelson had been appointed to head the West Coast apparatus late in 1942. And although Nelson's name does not appear among the decrypted agent names in Venona, he is a candidate for Butcher, a KGB source on the West Coast, who identified possible recruits in the aviation and oil industries in California.[77] One part of Nelson's task was to gather information on the atomic bomb project. He was seen and overheard meeting with young Communist scientists working at the radiation laboratory at Berkeley. Information gleaned from FBI bugging and wiretaps indicated that several had discussed the atomic bomb project with him. Nelson made notes of what the scientists told him regarding their work, and he was subsequently observed passing materials, which the FBI assumed were his notes, to a Soviet intelligence officer operating under diplomatic cover at the USSR's San Francisco consulate.

The FBI's listening devices overheard Nelson meeting with Zubilin, the KGB's senior officer in the United States, on April 10, 1943. The conversation opened with Zubilin counting out a roll of bills and passing it to Nelson, who responded, "Jesus, you count money like a

banker." Zubilin answered, "Vell, you know I used to do it in Mos-
kva." Nelson and Zubilin discussed the role of Al, the head of the
CPUSA's secret apparatus in the United States, whom the FBI later identified as Rudy Baker. Nelson indicated that Earl Browder knew about
his activities and the work of the apparatus on behalf of the Soviet
Union. Nelson also went into considerable detail about his underground
party work on the West Coast. Although most of the members of the
secret apparatus were referred to by code names, Nelson openly identified Dr. Frank Bissell and his wife, Nina. Both were active Communists
who had served in medical units in the Spanish Civil War.[78]

Nelson had a number of complaints about the operations of his own
apparatus and the way it was being used by Soviet intelligence. He was
dissatisfied with courier operations to the South Pacific and contacts
with Japanese Communists in the relocation camps. Two members of
the underground apparatus, George and Rapp, came in for particularly
strong condemnation. Nelson felt that George (later identified as Getzel
"Joe" Hochberg) and Rapp (Mordecai "Morris" Rappaport) were inefficient. Hochberg was an intermediary with Earl Browder on secret
apparatus matters. Rappaport supervised the West Coast seamen couriers. Soon after this conversation, Hochberg, who had previously been
employed by the Jewish Communist newspaper *Die Freiheit* and had
traveled as a bodyguard for Earl Browder, was transferred from New
York to Detroit and stripped of his party responsibilities.[79]

Morris Rappaport was a far more prominent party figure, but Nelson's complaint ended his leadership role. A longtime party functionary,
he had directed Communist activities in the Pacific Northwest for much
of the 1930s. Born November 1, 1893, in Ekaterinoslav, Russia, Rappaport came to the United States by way of Vancouver in 1922. The
government had unsuccessfully attempted to deport him in 1930, when
he left no doubt about his beliefs. Questioned whether he believed in
the overthrow of the government by force and violence, he replied that
"in the interest of the working class of the government, I think it would
be historically necessary to overthrow it by revolution." Rappaport was
arrested for deportation again in 1941 and let out on bail. He then
vanished to assume a leading role in the party underground. After Nelson's complaint, he was transferred from San Francisco to Los Angeles,
where FBI agents located him in 1944 living under the name of John
Fox and running a retail cigar and candy store. He was still in touch
with Communists known to have ties to the underground, including

Leo Baroway and Rudy Lambert, and the head of the California Communist party, William Schneiderman. Rappaport never resumed a public leadership role in the CPUSA, although he remained active in the party in Petaluma, California, where he owned a chicken farm. He died in 1982.[80]

Nelson's most significant complaint to Zubilin reflected just how aggressive Soviet intelligence had become. Soviet intelligence agents were directly approaching Communist party members in California and asking for their help on specific assignments. Nelson was upset, not that Communists were being asked to work for the KGB, but that the KGB was bypassing the CPUSA organization when making the requests. According to an FBI summary of the conversation, "Nelson suggested to Zubilin that in each important city or State, the Soviets have but one contact who was trustworthy, and [that they] let that man handle the contact with party members who were to be given special assignments by the Soviets."[81]

One of the close contacts of Grigory Kheifets, the KGB San Francisco chief, was a wealthy San Francisco Communist, Louise Bransten—so close that she was frequently referred to as Kheifets's mistress. Born in San Francisco in 1908, the only child of a wealthy Jewish merchant who founded a produce company, Louise Rosenberg inherited more than a million dollars from her parents. Married to and then divorced from Richard Bransten, a prominent Communist journalist, she was active in the American-Russian Institute in San Francisco. The FBI, which closely monitored her activities during World War II, described her as "the hub of a wheel, the spokes thereof representing the many facets of her pro-Soviet activities, running from mere membership in the Communist Party . . . to military and industrial espionage and political and propaganda activities."[82]

The FBI observed her making contact with a remarkable number of Soviet agents. In addition to her relationship with Kheifets, Bransten was a longtime friend of Gregory Silvermaster and visited him in Washington. She met frequently with Pop Folkoff. Willard Park and Mary Price, both named by Bentley as sources, were friends. Martin Kamen, an atomic scientist who had been observed by the FBI meeting with the KGB officer Kheifets and who admitted providing information to him, met with Bransten. So did Haakon Chevalier, who approached Robert Oppenheimer to pass on atomic bomb data. Two of her friends at the

American-Russian Institute were Dolly Eltenton and Rose Isaak. The former's husband, a chemist at Shell Development Laboratories, had asked Chevalier to approach Oppenheimer about providing information to the Soviets. Rose Isaak advised the KGB in 1945 that she intended to resign from her job at the American-Russian Institute and "henceforth not to communicate with us."[83]

Still another contact of Bransten's was Vladimir Pozner, a Russian émigré.[84] Pozner's family had fled the Bolshevik Revolution, but Pozner became a Communist sympathizer while living in Europe. Pozner was chief engineer of the European branch of Metro-Goldwyn-Mayer in Paris in 1938. He fought in the French army until its defeat and then fled to the United States with his French wife and son in 1941. In 1943 he headed the Russian section of the film department of the U.S. War Department. A Venona message that year noted that "we are planning to use Vladimir Aleksandrovich Pozner (henceforth Platon)," discussed his background, and lauded his extensive connections. The same message noted that one of his secretaries was being "redeveloped by us for use in connection with Platon" and asked Moscow to "check Platon and sanction his use as a probationer [agent] and a source of leads."[85]

Although Bransten's name was not among those identified in Venona, she is a candidate for an unidentified agent with the cover name Map. The subject of half a dozen messages from the San Francisco KGB, Map served as a liaison between the KGB and several intelligence sources.[86]

Senior CPUSA Figures and Soviet Espionage

A substantial number of senior American Communists had compromising relationships with Soviet intelligence. These include Rudy Baker (Central Control Commission), Theodore Bayer (president of the Russky Golos Publishing Company), Max Bedacht (head of International Workers Order), Earl Browder (general secretary), William Browder (assistant to Earl Browder), Morris Childs (Illinois Communist party leader), Eugene Dennis (Political Bureau), Nicholas Dozenberg (National Literature Director), Isaac Folkoff (California Communist party treasurer), Jacob Golos (Central Control Commission), Bruce Minton (an editor of *New Masses*), Steve Nelson (Bay Area Communist party head), Joseph North (an editor of *New Masses*), Josef Peters (head of the Organizational Department), and Bernard Schuster (New York Communist party treasurer).[87]

In addition, deciphered Venona cables show that Boleslaw (Bill) Gebert, a CPUSA district organizer for many years, actively assisted the KGB. Gebert had immigrated from Poland in 1918 and gone to work as a miner. A charter member of the CPUSA, he had headed the Polish-language bureau of the party in the late 1920s before moving into a leadership role as district organizer in Chicago and Pittsburgh in the 1930s. When the CIO was formed, Gebert used his position as head of the Communist fraternal society Polonia to mobilize ethnic steelworkers to join the organization. After World War II Gebert returned to Communist Poland, where he assumed a leading position in the state-controlled labor unions. He came back to the United States in 1950 as UN representative of the Communist-dominated World Federation of Trade Unions and later served as a Polish ambassador. Louis Budenz claimed that Gebert engaged in espionage. He charged that during World War II Gebert, the district organizer in Detroit, frequently visited Chicago to meet covert contacts in the Slavic community. According to Budenz, there was conflict between Gebert and Morris Childs (district organizer for Illinois) over Gebert's intrusion into Chicago and, in particular, over a "Czech comrade who was doing vital underground work for Gebert."[88]

Budenz was right about Gebert; he appears in nine Venona messages written between May and October 1944.[89] In one, the KGB in New York gave Gebert's real name and cover name—Ataman—in plain text, noting that his father was a peasant of German background and his mother was Polish. Several of the messages dealt with political developments within the Polish-American community; others involved Gebert's transfer to another control agent. In one message it is reported that the New York KGB had promised Gebert a subsidy of one thousand dollars to publish a Polish-language book but had paid only five hundred dollars and Gebert was now demanding the rest. The most interesting cables dealt with Gebert's cultivation of Oskar Lange, a prominent Polish-American intellectual and economist. They also bear on the contentious issue of the postwar Polish government and the "betrayal" of Poland to Stalin.

Well known as a left-wing socialist critical of Stalinism, Oskar Lange, who was born in Poland in 1904, had achieved renown as an economist before moving to the United States in 1937. He taught at the University of Chicago and became an American citizen in 1943, when he began to involve himself in Polish émigré and diaspora politics. Most American Poles were vehemently anti-Communist and supported the London-based exile government of Prime Minister Stanislaw Mikolaj-czyk. In March 1944 an array of Polish-American groups formed the Polish American Congress to support Poland's independence from Soviet domination. Two smaller groups supported the Soviet Union and endorsed its demands to annex large portions of eastern Poland and provide eastern Prussia as compensation to Poland: the Kosciuszko League, based in Detroit and led by Father Stanislaw Orlemanski, and the American Slav Congress, led by the pro-Communist labor leader Leo Krzycki. As the Red Army moved into Poland in 1943, Lange emerged from political obscurity and attached himself to the pro-Soviet forces. By 1944 Joseph Stalin was suggesting to a slightly shocked American ambassador Averell Harriman that Lange, Krzycki, and Orlemanski, all American citizens, become members of an entirely new Polish government. Although the Roosevelt administration was unenthusiastic, it did expedite a trip by Orlemanski and Lange to Moscow in April and May of 1944.[90]

While in Moscow, Lange met with Molotov and Stalin. The same day as the meeting with Stalin, the KGB in New York sent a cable with information that Bill Gebert felt was essential for Lange to have during his Moscow visit about internal émigré politics in the United States. At the end of May, Gebert provided information to the KGB about Lange. Although the beginning of the cable was poorly deciphered, it suggests that Lange's change of heart toward the USSR had come in 1943. At that point Lange had no cover name.[91] Lange returned to the United States at the end of May, met with Polish prime minister Mikolajczyk, who was in Washington, to stress how reasonable Stalin was prepared to be, and with a State Department official to urge that the United States put pressure on the exiled Poles (particularly Mikolajczyk) to cooperate with the Soviet Union. The Venona documents suggest that Oskar Lange had reached a tacit agreement with the Soviets, via the KGB, even before he went to Moscow in 1944. At that time the KGB also gave Lange a cover name—Friend—and told Moscow that he would "undoubtedly play a political role in Poland in the future."[92] In 1945 Oskar Lange renounced his American citizenship and returned to Poland. He was not out of the United States long, though. He came back to Washington as the first ambassador of Communist Poland to the United States.

The CPUSA, Journalists, and Espionage

As the CPUSA grew in the 1930s, it acquired adherents from all walks of life, including journalism. Journalists were of interest to Soviet intelligence as sources of information; reporters were, after all, in the business of finding out what was happening. Journalism also provided a convenient cover profession for espionage. Two of Jacob Golos's agents, Winston Burdett and Peter Rhodes, were journalists recruited through the CPUSA. Joseph Bernstein of the GRU was also a reporter by trade.

The *Daily Worker*'s Moscow correspondent, Janet Weaver Ross, illustrates one kind of assistance that Communist journalists provided to the USSR. Janet Ross accompanied her husband, Nat, to Moscow in 1939. In the early 1940s Nat Ross was the highest-ranking CPUSA member stationed in Moscow. Janet attended press briefings at the American embassy, was accorded interviews with American diplomats, and was given invitations to "Americans only" social events. But she did not just file her stories with the *Daily Worker;* she used her access to the American embassy to prepare secret reports for the Comintern about what she had heard. Georgi Dimitrov then forwarded her reports to Molotov, the Soviet foreign minister. A number of such reports, dated from August 1942 to June 1943, when the Rosses left the USSR to return to the United States, were located in the files of the Comintern. While Ross did not commit espionage—she conveyed no secret information and stole no embassy files—she functioned as an informer for the Soviet Union. As Dimitrov noted to Molotov when he sent one of Ross's reports, she was "*our* American correspondent comrade Janet Ross."[93]

Other Communist journalists also assisted the KGB's activities, either by providing information or by working to discredit anti-Communists. During Whittaker Chambers's years at *Time* magazine, he became a fierce anti-Communist. For a period in 1944 and 1945, Chambers was in charge of the foreign news department, where his editing of stories to bring out matters that depicted the USSR in a poor light enraged several correspondents, who demanded that publisher Henry Luce remove him. Two of the most hostile were John Scott and Richard Lauterbach. Lauterbach, described by one scholar as "the correspondent Chambers trusted least," had been *Time*'s correspondent in Moscow.[94] Two Venona cables refer to Lauterbach. The KGB agent Jack Soble reported in December 1944 that Lauterbach was a secret member of the CPUSA, had just returned from the USSR, and had passed on to Soble the information that *Time* (Chambers, most likely) had pressured him to write an anti-Soviet series but that he had refused and threatened to resign. Impressed by Lauterbach's defense of the USSR, Soble "recommends drawing him in" to the KGB apparatus. Vladimir Pravdin had started to study him, and the cable asked Moscow to check on his activities while he had been in the Soviet Union. It assigned him the cover name Pa. A few weeks later, another cable asked Moscow to "please expedite checking and telegraph your instructions about Pa," because he might soon be leaving on another foreign assignment. Moscow's response was not decrypted.[95]

As discussed above, John Scott, another of Chambers's enemies on *Time,* had been an active KGB source when he worked for the OSS. Whether Scott continued to provide assistance to the KGB after he joined *Time* is not clear.[96]

Another influential figure at *Time* was Stephen Laird, who for a period supervised *Time* foreign correspondents. Half a dozen deciphered Venona cables show that he, too, was a KGB agent.[97] In August 1944 the New York KGB station handed liaison with Laird over to a new case officer, Konstantin Shabenov. He cabled Moscow his assessment of his new charge:

Yun [Laird] gives the impression of a politically well-developed person who wishes to help us. However, he considers his potentialities to be limited, for he deals only with technical work on the magazine. He can pass on correspondents' telegrams but we receive them from other sources. Using his connections among journalists and studying the magazine's materials he could draw up political reports for us but he lacks perseverance for that. Besides, [unrecovered code group] breakup with his wife. Yun declares that he is used to reporters' work and would like to go abroad again, but the owner of the magazine will not send him because he disapproves of his radical views. The other day the film company RKO took him on as a film producer, which he succeeded in getting thanks to social connections in actor and producer circles. According to Yun's words, Vardo [Elizabeth Zubilin] in her time did not object to such a maneuver and afterwards it may give him an opportunity to make trips to Europe and do work useful to us. In the middle of September Yun is moving to Hollywood. We consider it expedient to continue liaison with him in Hollywood. Telegraph whether a new password should be agreed upon.[98]

Subsequent cables show that the KGB gave Laird verbal recognition signals for use when the KGB made contact after his move to Hollywood. (He was to meet his KGB contact at the Beverly Hills Hotel.) Before he left for Hollywood, Laird turned over to the Soviets material obtained by a *Time* correspondent on diplomatic negotiations between the United States and Portugal over American use of the Azores as a military base.

While pursuing a Hollywood career, Laird also continued to work as a journalist and to promote Soviet causes. When the 1947 election in Poland was held, almost all American correspondents described it as a fraud preceded by a campaign of terror, intimidation, and coercion. Laird, however, did not see it that way. In the *New Republic* he insisted that the election was free, saw no reason to doubt the Communist regime's claim of having won 85 percent of the vote, and favorably compared the extent of political democracy in Communist Poland with that in the United States.[99] (One amusing note is that in 1945 Stepan Apresyan, then the San Francisco KGB chief, used the difficulty of meeting Laird in automobile-oriented Los Angeles as an argument for an adjustment in his budget so that he could have a car. He told Moscow, "In a town like Caen [Los Angeles] I should be simply walked off my feet.")[100]

Another Communist journalist mentioned in Venona was Walter Sol Bernstein, better known today as a screenwriter with such credits as *Fail Safe, The Front, The Molly Maguires,* and *Semi-Tough.* Bernstein's Communist loyalties led to his blacklisting by Hollywood studios in 1950. For the next decade he was forced to use "fronts" to survive professionally. In his 1996 memoirs Bernstein wrote that he had joined the Young Communist League while a student at Dartmouth in 1937. A writer for the *New Yorker* for several years, during World War II he was a correspondent for *Yank* in Europe and the Middle East. His greatest coup came in 1944, when with help from Communist contacts he became the first Western correspondent to obtain an interview with Josip Tito, the leader of the Yugoslav Communist Partisans.

In his memoirs Bernstein noted that after he returned to New York in 1944, his aunt, who worked in Communist party headquarters, asked if he would meet with some party leaders who wanted information on Tito. Gene Dennis and Avrom Landy, who supervised the party's work with ethnic minorities, came to his apartment. "I told them what I knew," Bernstein recalled, "which was no more that what I had already written. They asked intelligent questions, refused a drink and left with thanks." And Bernstein admitted, "I had myself been approached at a party by an affable secretary from the Soviet Embassy. I was still in uniform and what he wanted to know was trivial; what I thought about the morale of American troops. He knew me as a friend of the Soviet Union and if I would just write a few words on the subject. . . . I declined as politely as I could, feeling vaguely guilty afterward. Was I betraying the cause? The Russians were allies; where was the harm? I had gone against American policy in Yugoslavia, acting subversively in a time of war. What was the difference now? Should I have told my superior officer? (I didn't.)"[101]

Bernstein's story about his own brush with Soviet officialdom is given a different twist in one Venona message. In October 1944 the New York KGB reported to Moscow that a certain Khan had met with Bernstein, whose name is given in plain text. Bernstein "welcomed the re-establishment of liaison with him and promised to write a report on his trip by the first of November."[102]

Even though NSA and FBI analysts were never able to identify Khan, he is probably Avrom Landy. The other mentions of Khan—or Selim Khan, as he was later called in Venona—show him to be a liaison between the KGB and agents with connections in the CPUSA's ethnic societies. Khan handled liaison with Bill Gebert, Albert Kahn, and Mikhail Tkach, all of whom Landy would have met naturally in the course of his duties in the CPUSA. Moreover, Elizabeth Bentley reported that Landy had been recruited by Jacob Golos as a "look-out" for likely espionage recruits.[103]

Landy, born in 1902 to poor Russian immigrants, attended Ohio State University and the University of Wisconsin, earning election to Phi Beta Kappa. He was an editor on the *Daily Worker* in the early 1930s and educational director of the CPUSA before World War II. After his stint in charge of minority work for the party, Landy became co-publisher of International Publishers. He quietly dropped out of the CPUSA sometime in the late 1940s or early 1950s and died in 1992.

The October 1944 KGB cable is not necessarily in conflict with the story Bernstein told in his memoirs. The message noted that Bernstein welcomed the "re-establishment" of contact with the KGB. It is, of course, possible that Bernstein believed that he was merely resuming contact with the CPUSA. But it is also clear that Khan, the KGB contact, regarded the incident as a reestablishment with his agency.

Johannes Steele, a radio commentator and columnist known for his pro-Communist views, was the subject of several Venona cables.[104] One, from July 1944, shows Steele serving as a talent scout for the KGB. Vladimir Pravdin of the New York KGB told Moscow that for some time he had been deflecting the efforts of Roman Moszulski, director of the Polish Telegraphic Agency (a Polish-language wire service, aligned with the Polish government-in-exile) in the United States, to meet him. Then Steele, code-named Dicky, told Pravdin that Moszulski was secretly pro-Soviet and wanted to make contact with the KGB. Steele said he had known him for several years—that he was critical of "Polish fascists" and wanted to quit his job.

Steele had suggested to Moszulski that he remain where he was, to counteract the efforts of Polish reactionary propaganda. Steele set up a meeting with Pravdin at which Moszulski explained that he realized the future of Poland rested on its having good relations with the USSR and, "having thought over the full seriousness and the possible consequences of his step, he was putting himself at our disposal and was ready to give the Communists all the information he had and to consult with us on questions concerning his activities." Moszulski explained to Pravdin that he realized he could win the KGB's confidence only by deeds and that he would have to prove himself, given that Steele's endorsement of his bona fides was insufficient. "In reply he was told that we welcomed people well-disposed towards us and that naturally the proof of his sincerity would depend on himself."[105] Moszulski, attempting to provide the proof, delivered to the KGB the next month a list of Polish exiles and Polish-Americans, including an evaluation of how they stood on Polish-Soviet relations.[106]

Journalists who covered foreign news were useful to Soviet intelligence as couriers and intermediaries between KGB stations in the United States and elsewhere. Ricardo Setaro, deputy chief of the Latin American department of CBS Radio, functioned in those roles.[107] A deciphered 1943 Venona message identifies him as a way station for KGB funds for use in its Central and South American operations. In response to an inquiry from Moscow, an August 1944 message from the New York KGB station summarized his work: "Gonets [Setaro] is working as deputy chief of the Provincial [Latin American] department of the 'Columbia Broadcasting System.' He was used by us earlier for the most part on liaison with Arthur, as a meeting point for couriers. At the same time we used him on the processing of Provincial [seventeen unrecoverable code groups] as a Fellowcountryman [Communist]. We are using him here on the processing of the CBS and of the diplomatic representation of the Country [United States] in the Provinces [Latin America]."[108] By "processing," the KGB meant providing background information. Arthur, the person with whom Setaro was a liaison for the KGB, was not identified by NSA and FBI analysts. He occurs in dozens of Venona messages and appears to have been the principal courier between KGB stations in the United States and its stations in various Latin American capitals.

Newsmen are obvious targets for espionage recruitment. A reporter legitimately searching for legally available information has excellent cover for spying out secrets. Even when Soviet intelligence recognized that particular journalists were impossible targets for recruitment as spies under discipline, it cultivated them to obtain inside information or insights into political affairs. Walter Lippmann, for example, had no sympathy for communism. Golos's CPUSA-KGB network, however, placed Mary Price in his office as a secretary in order to find out what sources and additional information lay behind the prominent journalist's columns.

Another example of the KGB's cultivation of journalists as "legal" sources occurs in a fall 1944 deciphered Venona message. At that time the New York KGB station sent a message to Moscow about the activities of Vladimir Pravdin, a TASS correspondent and a senior KGB officer. The cable reported that several of his journalist "acquaintances are persons of great interest from a legal point of view. They are well informed and although they do not say all they know, nevertheless they provide useful comments on the foreign policy" of the United States. The message specifically named Joseph Barnes, an official in the OWI and later foreign editor of the *New York Herald Tribune*. Barnes was often accused of being a Soviet agent; he denied it under oath, and this Venona cable supports that denial. The message stated that "the signing up of Barnes is obviously not only inadvisable but unrealizable; however, it is desirable to use him without signing him up."[109]

Even without being agents, journalists had access to a great deal of information, their stock in trade. They knew many more things than they could print. In 1945, when Philip Jaffe, the editor of *Amerasia,* was trying to persuade his friend, Navy lieutenant Andrew Roth, to cooperate in spying for the USSR, Roth raised several objections. He was, naturally, worried whether Jaffe's contact with Soviet intelligence (Joseph Bernstein) was sincere or whether he was an American counterintelligence plant. But, he also suggested to Jaffe that it would be less risky to simply publish classified information in *Amerasia* and other media outlets as a way of informing the Soviets: "This country is so wide open and obvious, and [it is] so easy for dozens of newspapermen to get the information, and they proceed to state it very openly in dozens of forms, that I don't see why I shouldn't." After some additional argument, however, Roth gave in, reasoning that since TASS no doubt forwarded summaries of the contents of *Amerasia* to Soviet leaders anyway, Jaffe might as well go ahead and deal directly with Bernstein. He agreed that "if the situation warrants it, whenever anything comes up that you feel is significant, you can tell Joe [Bernstein]."[110]

Another Communist journalist who played a key role in the KGB's efforts to find journalistic informants and agents was Samuel Krafsur, an American who worked for TASS. Not much detail is available about his background and life. He was born in Boston around 1911 and attended Northeastern University for one year. Krafsur was a member of the CPUSA and fought with the International Brigades in Spain, where he was wounded in 1937. Krafsur went to work for TASS in 1941, first in New York and then in Washington, where he was assistant head of the local bureau. After leaving TASS in 1949 he worked in a toy factory. Krafsur was subpoenaed by the House Committee on Un-American Activities but was uncooperative.

Venona makes clear that Krafsur was an important Soviet agent, first recruited by the TASS correspondent and KGB officer Vladimir Pravdin.[111] Krafsur was particularly valued for the extensive contacts he had developed as a newsman. In May 1944, the New York KGB cabled Moscow to report that after months of study it proposed to use Krafsur, who was given the cover name of Ide, "for cultivating newspapermen's circles in Washington." Krafsur was described as a Communist, a Lincoln battalion veteran, and "absolutely devoted to the USSR, [someone who] always zealously carries out minor tasks" given by Pravdin to obtain information. Work with his wide circle of friends "will give opportunities for obtaining valuable information and also of studying individual subjects for signing on."[112] After checking with the Comintern about Krafsur's background, the KGB headquarters in Moscow approved his recruitment.[113]

The Venona cables show that Krafsur provided at least twenty leads for the KGB. One was Joseph Berger, a personal aide to the chairman of the Democratic National Committee. There is no evidence that Soviet intelligence succeeded in recruiting Berger, but the KGB clearly targeted him. A message one year later noted that Berger had left for Moscow as an American delegate to the Reparations Commission and discussed his background.

Joseph Berger was born in 1903 in Denver, Colorado. He graduated from the University of Missouri School of Journalism in 1924 and took a job as a reporter on the *Kansas City Star*. In 1934 he came to Provincetown, Massachusetts, with his wife and young daughter and worked as a free-lance writer. The Bergers lived in extreme poverty for a year, begging food from local residents. His fortunes changed when he got a job with the Federal Writers' Project under the Works Progress Administration, writing for the American Guide Series. Berger's *Cape Cod Pilot,* published in the series under the by-line Jeremiah Digges, won great praise, enabling Berger to obtain a Guggenheim Fellowship and launching his writing career. One of his many children's books detailed the adventures of a mythical figure, Bowleg Bill, an eight-foot bronco buster from Wyoming.[114]

In 1941 Berger moved to the Democratic National Committee (DNC), where he worked as a speechwriter for Pres. Franklin Delano Roosevelt, Sen. Harry Truman, Rep. Lyndon Johnson, and other national Democratic figures. In 1945 he served as a member of the Reparations Commission and traveled to Moscow. According to one KGB message, Robert Hannegan, the DNC chairman who had been appointed postmaster general, had hired Berger at ten thousand dollars a year to serve as his special assistant when he returned from Moscow. After leaving the government, Berger wrote scripts for daytime television shows. In 1950 he became a speech writer for the March of Dimes but continued to write short stories and articles until his death in 1971.[115]

In his 1945 message to Moscow about Berger, who had just left for the Soviet Union with the Reparations Commission, Pravdin reported that Krafsur had known Berger for five years and described him as a progressive and as well disposed toward the Soviet Union. According to Krafsur, Berger had expressed a desire to live in the USSR and maintained contact with the CPUSA. The message noted that given his connections and future job, "he could be a valuable probationer [agent]. I would recommend using B.'s trip to Smyrna [Moscow] for working on him and possibly signing him on." Pravdin also noted that Berger had met with Krafsur just before leaving and "insistently inquired" about what friends he should meet in Moscow.[116]

There are no further decrypted messages indicating whether Berger was actually recruited by the KGB. And the fact that he left government service and political work in 1946 suggests that in any case he might not have had access to sensitive information. Indeed, it is possible that Berger's decision to leave government work was linked to a desire not to have anything to do with Soviet espionage.

The cable requesting permission to sign up Krafsur noted that one of his leads, in addition to Joseph Berger, was "[deleted]- brother of the well-known journalist [deleted]. Ide [Krafsur] is very friendly with them both." In its notes to the cable, the NSA blacked out both names of the brother journalists, but noted that the well-known one was born in 1897 and his brother in 1899. Very likely these references are to Drew Pearson, born in 1897, and his younger brother, Leon, also a journalist. Leon worked for Drew until they had a falling-out and he pursued an independent career in journalism. He accompanied Secretary of State James Byrnes to Moscow in 1945 and later headed the International News Service's Paris Bureau and did newscasts for NBC Radio.

There is no evidence that Leon Pearson responded to a KGB approach, if one was ever made. Drew Pearson wrote in his diaries that in 1951 the FBI approached several persons and asked if Leon knew an unnamed Russian and "a newspaperman named Barger." Lou Nichols, a high-ranking FBI official, told Drew Pearson that "questions were asked about Leon's friends because they are trying to track down a Russian agent in this country who knew Leon. However, Leon is in no way involved." Quite likely the cable referring to the KGB's interest in Leon Pearson had been partially decrypted by 1951, and the FBI was trying to learn about his connections with Joseph Berger, Samuel Krafsur, and Vladimir Pravdin.[117]

Krafsur also pointed the KGB toward an associate of Drew Pearson. In a badly broken message from June 1944 Pravdin told Moscow about "information received by Ide [Krafsur] from the journalist David

Karr."[118] David Karr was at that time the chief aide to Pearson, one of America's most widely read columnists. His incredible career, which included important positions in American industry and friendships with some of America's most distinguished politicians, was dogged by accusations that he was a Soviet agent. The one Venona document in which his name is mentioned is not clear enough to determine whether in passing information to Krafsur he was innocently sharing material with a fellow journalist or knowingly supplying reports to a Soviet agent. Karr's life, however, suggests the latter.

David Karr was born in Brooklyn in 1918 into a middle-class family. As a young man he wrote articles and book reviews for the *Daily Worker,* attended CPUSA meetings, and befriended Communists. In later years, he always denied joining the CPUSA and maintained that his ties to the Communists were a consequence of his fervent antifascism.

In 1943 Karr, then working for the Office of War Information, was among a group of government employees attacked by Rep. Martin Dies, chairman of the House Special Committee on Un-American Activities, for their Communist ties. He appeared before the committee, insisted that his associations were entirely innocent, and falsely claimed to have been an FBI informant. A special congressional investigation exonerated him at the same time as the Civil Service Commission was concluding that he was both untruthful and unreliable.[119] Karr resigned from the OWI and went to work for Drew Pearson. An indefatigable investigator, Karr earned a reputation as an unscrupulous and unrelenting reporter, who eavesdropped on conversations, read documents upside down on people's desks, and misrepresented himself to sources. He was active politically as well, providing advice and help in Henry Wallace's effort to remain on the presidential ticket in 1944.

The FBI investigated Karr twice during the war, once for obtaining a confidential report on Stalin written by Oskar Lange for President Roosevelt by claiming to be on Vice President Wallace's staff and once because he was the recipient of leaked material from several of those charged in the *Amerasia* spy case. In 1950 Sen. Joseph McCarthy launched a bitter attack on Pearson, in the course of which he denounced Karr as the columnist's "KGB controller" and accused him of orchestrating the character assassination of a string of prominent anti-Communists. Conservative columnists like Westbrook Pegler hammered at Karr as a Communist for the next decade.[120]

During the 1950s Karr became involved in corporate intrigue and wrote a book about the use of public relations in business takeovers. He soon moved from theory to practice. In 1959, following a corporate raid, Karr became chief executive officer of the Fairbanks-Whitney Corporation, a large defense contractor whose divisions included Colt Firearms. After three rancorous years, a stockholders' revolt pushed him out. Karr dabbled in the movie and hotel businesses before becoming associated with Armand Hammer in 1972. Through Hammer, who had long-standing ties to the USSR (he had laundered Soviet money for the CPUSA in the 1920s and assisted Soviet intelligence agencies for years), Karr made valuable connections in the Soviet Union. Within a few years, he was brokering deals for Western firms in the USSR, most notably the construction of the $175 million dollar Kosmos Hotel in Moscow.[121]

The approach of the 1980 Moscow Olympics provided numerous opportunities for profit to Western businessmen with good connections to influential Soviet figures. Karr, a close friend of Dzherman Gvishiani, a son-in-law of Soviet president Aleksei Kosygin, obtained North and South American rights to Misha the Bear, the mascot of the games. Along with Hammer, he formed a joint venture to make and sell Olympic commemorative coins, an enterprise estimated to be worth some $200 million.

David Karr's connections in the Soviet Union were matched by his entrée to prominent American politicians. He boasted of his close ties and substantial campaign contributions to prominent U.S. senators and presidential candidates. He also claimed to have carried messages and information back and forth between the Soviet and American governments on such issues as détente, trade, strategic-arms negotiations, and emigration of Soviet Jews.

In 1979, shortly after returning to his Paris home from Moscow, Karr suddenly died. Amid charges that Karr had been murdered, his widow halted the burial so that an autopsy could be performed. One claim was that Karr had been swindling his Russian partners. Shortly before his death, in secret testimony before the Securities and Exchange Commission, he had implicated Hammer in the bribery of Soviet officials. Rumors circulated linking his friend Gvishiani to bribery scandals. Israeli intelligence officials spread rumors that Karr had been involved in secret Russian arms sales to Libya and Uganda. After the collapse of the Soviet Union a Russian journalist, citing a KGB file as her source, published an article in *Izvestia* charging that Karr was "a competent KGB source" who "submitted information to the KGB on the technical capabilities of the United States and other capitalist countries."[122]

Another Krafsur candidate for recruitment was I. F. "Izzy" Stone. Charges and countercharges about whether Stone had been a KGB agent roiled intellectual circles in the 1990s. By that time Stone, who had died in 1989, was a cultural hero. That a journalist celebrated for his fierce independence and iconoclastic writings about American government officials could have collaborated with the Soviet government was regarded by many on the American left as impossible, and they dismissed the charge as a McCarthyite smear.

Born Isidor Feinstein in Philadelphia in 1907 to Jewish immigrants from Russia, Stone dropped out of the University of Pennsylvania to become a journalist. He wrote for the *New York Post,* the *Nation,* and *PM,* before beginning *I. F. Stone's Weekly,* a highly regarded muck-raking newspaper, in 1953. Stone was briefly a member of the Socialist party in the 1930s and was long sympathetic to the Soviet Union. In *The Hidden History of the Korean War* Stone spread the falsehood that it was South Korea that had sparked the war by invading the North with American backing. Although he was occasionally critical of aspects of Soviet policy, it was not until the mid-1950s that he lost his illusions about the Soviet regime, but he remained extremely critical of the United States and its policies throughout his life. In retirement Stone learned classical Greek and wrote a book on Socrates and Athens, part of his lifelong concern with issues of free speech and dissent.[123]

The question of Stone's relationship with the KGB heated up in 1992 when Oleg Kalugin, a retired KGB general, told a British journalist that "we had an agent—a well-known American journalist—with a good reputation, who severed his ties with us after 1956. I myself convinced him to resume them. But in 1968, after the invasion of Czechoslovakia . . . he said he would never again take any money from us." Herbert Romerstein, a former staff member of the House Committee on Un-American Activities, identified the journalist in question as Stone. The British journalist then reinterviewed Kalugin, who admitted that he had been referring to Stone but denied that Stone was a spy. Later, in his autobiography, Kalugin characterized Stone as a fellow traveler "who had made no secret of his admiration for the Soviet system" before the mid-1950s. He wrote that when he was asked to reestablish contact with Stone, KGB headquarters in Moscow "never said that he had been an agent of our Intelligence service, but rather that he was a man with whom we had regular contact."[124]

When Kalugin was stationed in the United States in the 1960s, he regularly met with journalists to glean their insights into the political scene. Since he was the official press attaché at the Soviet embassy, Kalugin had valid reasons to meet with American journalists, Stone's defenders noted. Even if Stone knew that Kalugin was a KGB officer, there was no evidence that Stone had done anything more than talk to him. Because Stone was not privy to government secrets, there was no illegality in his actions. Kalugin wrote that after the Soviet invasion of Czechoslovakia, Stone denounced the USSR, refused to meet with him again, and would not allow him to pick up the restaurant check, which Kalugin had customarily done.

The Venona decryptions provide a more complex background to this controversy. The KGB, it appears, had marked Stone as a promising source for recruitment. In September 1944 the New York KGB reported to Moscow that Stone "occupies a very prominent position in the journalistic world and has vast connections." In order to figure out "precisely his relations to us we will commission Echo to make a check." Echo was Bernard Schuster, the CPUSA's liaison to Soviet intelligence. Both Krafsur and Pravdin made several attempts to contact Stone, but to the former he was "coy" and to the latter he pleaded the press of business.[125]

Finally, in October 1944, Pravdin met with Stone, to whom the KGB gave the cover name Bliny, or Pancake. Stone knew he was not dealing with an ordinary journalist and told Pravdin "that he had noticed our attempts to contact him, particularly the attempts of Ide [Krafsur] and of people of the Trust [Soviet embassy] but he had reacted negatively fearing the consequences. At the same time he implied that the attempts at rapprochement had been made with insufficient caution and by people who were insufficiently responsible. To Sergey's [Pravdin's] reply that naturally we did not want to subject him to unpleasant complications, Pancake gave him to understand that he was not refusing his aid but one should consider that he had three children and did not want to attract the attention of the FBI."[126]

The tenor of this message suggests that Stone was flirting with the KGB. Had he thought he was simply dealing with TASS employees, he would hardly have been so cautious or frightened. No left-wing or even mainstream journalist in America would have been afraid to meet a

TASS correspondent or think that meeting with one in 1944 would incur the wrath of the FBI. Stone was perfectly willing to meet with Kalugin regularly during the 1960s, when the climate for Soviet government officials was far less hospitable. There is no evidence in Venona that Stone ever was recruited by the KGB, but Kalugin's comments in the 1990s that he "reestablished" contact leave open the possibility that Stone may have met with KGB agents on some basis after the meeting documented in Venona.

CHAPTER 9

HUNTING STALIN'S ENEMIES ON AMERICAN SOIL

In the 1930s and 1940s the Soviet Union carried out a maniacal campaign against Stalin's arch-rival, Leon Trotsky, and others abroad who posed ideological threats to Soviet communism. The foreign intelligence arm of the KGB spied on, infiltrated, and on occasion assassinated those Soviet dissidents who had been able to go into exile, as well as their foreign comrades and political allies.

The Venona decryptions, together with newly released FBI files, document the extensive involvement of the CPUSA and its secret apparatus in Trotsky's 1940 murder, as well as efforts to free his assassin and to spy on Stalin's ideological enemies. A dedicated revolutionary and brilliant Marxist theoretician who organized the Red Army and engineered its victory over the Whites in the civil war of 1918–1920, Leon Trotsky had appeared to many to be Lenin's obvious successor. He could not, however, match Stalin in the ruthless bureaucratic struggle inside the Soviet Communist party that followed Lenin's death in 1924. He and his supporters were subjected to a furious political attack both within the party and before the Soviet public. There was no free press in the USSR, and Trotsky was denied the right to reply. His ideas became thought crimes, and he was expelled from the Communist party and sent into internal exile. By the end of the 1920s very little remained of the once sizable Trotskyist faction.

For reasons that are not clear, Stalin allowed Trotsky to go into foreign exile in 1929. But thereafter Stalin's fury seemed to grow. By the mid-1930s it had reached nightmarish proportions, and Stalin set out to obliterate Trotsky and Trotskyism in both an ideological and a physical sense. Trotsky, to be sure, hoped to see Stalin overthrown and then to return to the Soviet Union in triumph as its new leader. He attempted to maintain contacts with supporters within the USSR, but in time few escaped imprisonment or execution. For example, when Trotsky initially went into exile in Turkey, the KGB learned that one of its senior officers there, Jacob Blumkin, was quietly communicating with Trotsky. Blumkin was recalled to the Soviet Union and shot. (There is also a minor American aspect of this affair. Blumkin was betrayed by his lover, Lisa Gorskaya. She was herself a KGB officer and later married Vasily Zubilin. As Elizabeth Zubilin she would serve with him in the United States as an effective espionage operative.)

Soviet pressure soon led the Turks to ask Trotsky to move on. As he wandered across Europe looking for a refuge, the campaign to destroy him escalated. Soviet intelligence operatives infiltrated his entourage, reported on his activities, stole his archives, and murdered a number of his associates. The campaign culminated in Mexico in 1940, when a KGB assassin smashed Trotsky's skull with an axe. Even Trotsky's murder, however, did not end Stalin's obsession with his movement and his small band of followers. Soviet intelligence continued to spy on Trotsky's widow and his associates and mounted a major clandestine campaign to free his assassin from a Mexican prison.

Infiltrating the Trotskyists

A long-standing Soviet counterintelligence tactic was to infiltrate and disrupt dissident organizations. As Trotsky struggled to establish a network of supporters from his exile in Prinkipo, Turkey, he was already encircled by KGB agents. Two of the earliest were a pair of Lithuanian Communist brothers, known in America as Jack Soble and Robert Soblen, recruited by the KGB to infiltrate the nascent European Trotskyist movement in the late 1920s. They were born in Lithuania to a wealthy Jewish family with the name Sobolevicius, which they anglicized slightly differently when they came to the United States. Their path through Europe and America spanned more than two decades of service to the Soviet Union.

Jack was born in 1903 and went to Leipzig in 1921 to attend college. There he joined the German Communist party at the age of eighteen. Graduating in 1927, he traveled to the USSR, where he married. Returning to Germany, he studied at the University of Berlin, becoming a Trotskyist and being expelled from the Communist party in 1929. When he testified at his brother's espionage trial in 1961, he claimed that he was recruited by the KGB in 1931 after his wife returned to the USSR to see her sick mother; he maintained he was summoned to the Soviet embassy and coerced into espionage with threats against his wife. The truth of this claim, however, is unclear, and there is evidence he was in Stalin's service by 1927, before he nominally became a Trotskyist.

Known as Abraham Senin in the European Trotskyist movement, Jack Soble visited Trotsky in Prinkipo in 1931 and in Copenhagen in 1932. Both he and his brother, known as Roman Weil to the Trotskyists, were important figures among German Trotskyists until 1932, when Trotsky grew suspicious of their maneuverings and ousted them. Robert Soblen/Roman Weil then openly emerged as a Stalinist and joined the German Communist party in 1933. Jack Soble returned to the USSR in 1933 and worked for a Profintern publication. He was apparently considered a possible witness in one of the Soviet purge trials but was spared.[1]

Lavrenty Beria, head of the KGB, personally allowed the entire Soble family to leave Russia in 1940. Three generations were sent across Siberia to Vladivostok, then on to Japan and into Canada. Soon afterward, Jack and Robert entered the United States to resume their espionage careers. Robert Soblen practiced medicine (he was a graduate of the University of Bern medical school) and assisted his brother in espionage. Jack Soble supervised a major KGB intelligence network that specialized in infiltration of the Trotskyists and other Russian exiles in America. In the deciphered KGB messages they are referred to by names derived from the false identities they had used while operating inside the European Trotskyist movement—Jack was called Abram (from Abraham Senin) and Robert was Roman (from Roman Weil).

The ouster of Jack Soble and Robert Soblen in 1932 did not leave the KGB without highly placed operatives among the Trotskyists. In 1956 Mark Zborowski, a prominent American anthropologist, confessed that he had worked as a KGB spy within the European Trotskyist movement in the 1930s.

Mark Grigorievich Zborowski was born in Uman, Russia, on January 21, 1908. He moved to Poland in 1921 and then went to France in 1928. The KGB's own file on Zborowski indicates that he had joined the Communist party in 1926 in Lodz, Poland, had been arrested in 1930, and had fled to Germany and then France after being sentenced to prison. Having been assigned to infiltrate the Trotskyist movement, he began working for the KGB in France in 1932. Zborowski, known in the movement as Etienne, worked for several years as a volunteer inside its Paris headquarters and became a close friend and confidant of Leon Sedov, Trotsky's son. He, Sedov, and Lilia Estrine Dallin were joint editors of the *Bulletin of the Opposition,* the authoritative voice of the Trotskyist movement. When the Fourth International (Trotsky's pale answer to the Communist International) was founded in 1938, he was its designated reporter on Russian issues, which were its chief concern at the time.[2] Zborowski, obviously, was in a position to report to the KGB on many of the details of the Trotskyist movement. To cite one example, his information is credited with enabling Soviet intelligence to steal a portion of Trotsky's archives.[3]

After Sedov took the lead in exposing Stalin's mass terror in Russia in 1937, the KGB targeted him for elimination. In 1938 he entered a French clinic suffering from abdominal pains, and after a routine appendectomy he died. Zborowski had alerted the KGB to the location of the clinic, owned by a French Stalinist, and later investigations established that Stalinist agents had been in and out of the clinic after Sedov was admitted. It may, of course, have been a natural death, but the KGB's activity surrounding the matter also raises the possibility that Sedov may have been medically murdered.

Following his secret defection in 1938, Aleksandr Orlov, a senior KGB officer, wrote an anonymous letter to Trotsky warning him about a KGB agent named Mark who had been close to his son. Convinced that the warning was an KGB provocation, Trotsky ignored it, but other Trotskyists became increasingly mistrustful of Mark Zborowski. He drifted away from the movement and finished his degree in anthropology at the Sorbonne. In 1941 he immigrated to the United States, where he was soon returned to work for the KGB.

Zborowski and Kravchenko

Nearly two dozen Venona messages discuss Zborowski's work in the United States under the code names Tulip and Kant.[4] Although the Ven-

ona traffic shows that originally the KGB directed Zborowski to spy on
the Trotskyists, he then by chance became the lead agent in the KGB's
effort to deal with Victor Kravchenko, a defector who deeply embarrassed the Soviets. A Soviet engineer and mid-level bureaucrat, Kravchenko arrived in Washington in 1943 as a member of the Soviet Government Purchasing Commission. Already secretly hostile to Stalin, he
carefully prepared to defect. On April 3, 1944, he held a news conference, denounced the USSR's oppressive government and placed his life
"under the protection of American public opinion."[5] Kravchenko was
an embarrassment not only to the Soviets but to those in the U.S. government who did not want the image of a major American military ally
sullied. He came very close to being handed back to the Soviets. But
his public defection and the ties he developed with sympathetic journalists kept him safe from deportation.

He was, however, subject to a ferocious attack by the Soviet government and the CPUSA. Over the next several years, Kravchenko was
harassed and threatened. Undaunted, he wrote *I Chose Freedom* (1946),
a searing indictment of the Soviet Union as a terrorized and repressed
society. Kravchenko's book became a best-seller, and the Soviet assault
on his credibility intensified. In 1949 the French Communist journal
Les Lettres Françaises published an article by Siam Thomas, identified
as an American journalist, asserting that Kravchenko's book was a
fraud manufactured by American intelligence agencies. Kravchenko,
however, sued in a French court, established that Siam Thomas did not
exist, and turned the trial into an indictment of Stalinism by calling as
witnesses Russian refugees who testified to the accuracy of his assertions
about the brutal collectivization campaigns, purges, and concentration
camps of the 1930s. Numerous Communists and fellow travelers, on
the other hand, testified in defense of the honor of Stalin's USSR. Kravchenko won his court case.[6]

One American witness against Kravchenko in Paris was Albert
Kahn, a left-wing journalist and secret CPUSA member. Elizabeth Bentley told the FBI that in 1942 Jacob Golos had taken her to Kahn's home
in New York and that he had provided them with information he had
gathered on exiled anti-Soviet Ukrainian nationalists. According to
Bentley, her contacts with Kahn ended in 1943. Kahn is a likely match
for an unidentified KGB asset with the cover name Fighter, whom the
Venona cables show to have been recruited in 1942. Fighter provided

the KGB with information on émigré Ukrainian groups and the political leanings of American journalists. He was put "in cold storage" in 1944.[7]

Although he did not know what he had stumbled on, in 1944 Zborowski actually gave the KGB advance warning of Kravchenko's defection. Zborowski lived in the same apartment building as David and Lilia Estrine Dallin. One day in March, Zborowski spoke to a Russian who was looking for the Dallin residence. Later, the Dallins told Zborowski about a potential Soviet defector whom they had met, but they did not reveal his name. Lilia Dallin had never believed the rumors that Zborowski had KGB links. When General Orlov had written Trotsky warning about Mark, she had believed that the letter was a provocation. She also had sponsored the Zborowski family's entry into the United States in 1941. Her husband, David, was friendly with many exiled Russian Mensheviks (Social Democrats) and wrote voluminously on Soviet repression. Given the Dallins' standing as proven anti-Stalinists, their friendship protected Zborowski from suspicion. Zborowski repaid them by reporting on their activities to the head of his KGB network, Jack Soble. Soble passed Zborowski's news of a potential defector along, prompting a panicky Vasily Zubilin to visit Soble, demanding information about the threatened defection.[8] Kravchenko, however, defected before his identity was uncovered.

When Kravchenko defected in early April 1944, the KGB assigned Zborowski to befriend him. (In a not unusual display of KGB attitudes, in their cables the KGB gave Kravchenko the cover name Gnat.) A few weeks later, despite his best efforts, Zborowski had still not been able to meet Kravchenko, and he was afraid to push the Dallins too hard for information lest they become suspicious.[9] The KGB also received information about Kravchenko's defection from a source, identified as Green, who furnished the KGB with the unwelcome news that Kravchenko had been meeting with Eugene Lyons and Joseph Shaplen, two prominent anti-Stalinist journalists.[10] Lyons, a former Associated Press correspondent in Moscow, later translated Kravchenko's book into English and assisted in editing it. Shaplen, also an AP reporter, advised Kravchenko on how best to present himself to the American press so as to promote widespread news coverage.

The KGB also received information from one of its agents in the U.S. Office of War Information, Christina Krotkova. Like Zborowski, Krotkova had cultivated Lilia Dallin as a way to gain information on anti-Stalinist Russian refugees. Krotkova got one Russian immigrant, a U.S. Marine sergeant who had played a role in Kravchenko's defection, drunk in order to get information about Kravchenko's intentions. She also met with Shaplen and, the KGB office in New York reported, "has been given the task of cautiously endeavoring to enter into closer relations" with him to get more information.[11] Another Soviet agent, Vasily Sukhomlin, a staff member of the Czechoslovak government-in-exile, reported to the KGB that Kravchenko was living in Connecticut in a cottage owned by Aleksandr Kerensky, the exiled leader of the Russian Provisional Government overthrown by Lenin in 1917.[12]

Zborowski, meanwhile, was also reporting what he heard from the Dallins. He had learned that Kravchenko had been an adherent of the views of Nikolai Bukharin, who, like Trotsky, had been a contender to succeed Lenin and had lost out to Stalin. (Stalin executed Bukharin in 1938.) Zborowski, confirming Green's information, reported that Kravchenko was dictating a manuscript to Lilia Dallin, writing an exposé of Soviet misuse of Lend-Lease aid, and seeing Isaac Don Levine, the energetic anti-Stalinist journalist. More ominously, Zborowski reported that Kravchenko was "well informed about the Krivitsky case."[13] Walter Krivitsky, a defector who had been a high-ranking Soviet military intelligence officer, had been found dead in a Washington hotel room in 1941, an apparent suicide, but suspicions that he had been murdered were widespread.

The suggestion that Kravchenko knew anything about Krivitsky must have alarmed both the KGB and Zborowski. Shortly after Krivitsky defected in France in 1937, he sought help from Leon Sedov and the Trotskyists. Sedov appointed Zborowski as Krivitsky's bodyguard, and he undoubtedly fed information about him to the KGB. Just before Krivitsky defected, his boyhood friend and fellow Soviet intelligence agent, Ignace Reiss, also broke with Stalin's regime. Reiss, a KGB officer, sent a defiant letter to the Central Committee of the Soviet Communist party in 1937 denouncing Stalin for betraying the ideals of the Bolshevik Revolution. The KGB caught up with him in Switzerland a few months later and murdered him. Else Bernaut, Reiss's widow, later charged in her autobiography that Zborowski had had a role in delivering her husband to the KGB murder squad.[14]

Finally, in late June 1944 Zborowski reported to the KGB that he had succeeded in meeting Kravchenko in the Dallins' apartment; their conversation began at nine in the evening and ended at four in the morning in Zborowski's nearby flat. One of Zborowski's tasks was to discover who had assisted Kravchenko in his defection. He was able to tell his KGB superiors that Kravchenko had told him the story of a Russian friend he identified only as Konstantin Mikhailovich, a winner of a Stalin Prize in metallurgy, who had been arrested in 1936 by the KGB. Set free in 1938, he had met Kravchenko in Moscow and encouraged him to work against the Soviet Union. In *I Chose Freedom,* Kravchenko identified his friend as Konstantin Mikhailovich Kolpovsky but made no mention of Kolpovsky's anti-Soviet views. With Zborowski's information in hand, the KGB presumably did not have to wait for the book to appear before dealing with Kolpovsky.[15]

Both Zborowski and Christina Krotkova continued to supply information about Kravchenko into 1945. Krotkova even became Kravchenko's typist and one of his translators in 1945. Zborowski reported gossip about Kravchenko's relationship with Isaac Don Levine, as well as his panic in early 1945 over reports that the U.S. government might hand him back to the Soviets and his well-founded fear that he was being shadowed by the KGB. The KGB concluded that Zborowski "is carrying out the task very diligently."[16]

Mark Zborowski continued to monitor the activities of other Soviet exiles and Trotskyists for the KGB. In late 1944 he reported on a conversation with Else Bernaut, the widow of the KGB defector murdered in Switzerland, and in 1945 he was accumulating information on the proposed trip to France of a Trotskyist leader. Zborowski never held any government jobs, nor did he steal government documents or industrial secrets: his espionage career was limited to betraying his friends and personal associates who were critics of Stalin. As a reward for his dedicated services, the KGB arranged with the CPUSA to enroll Zborowski as a member of the American Communist party. Bernard Schuster, the CPUSA's liaison with the KGB, reported that he would have to fill out an application and questionnaire, but if the KGB vouched for him, his membership would be approved and his real identify known only to Schuster and one other person.[17]

Jack Soble later testified that after 1945 Zborowski became a less productive agent and his regular KGB stipend was reduced. His growing prominence in American academic circles, however, easily compensated. After his arrival in America, he had worked at a screw factory in Brooklyn, but by 1944 Zborowski found employment compiling a Russian-American dictionary. In 1946 he went to work at the Yivo Scientific

Institute as a librarian. After meeting the well-known anthropologist Ruth Benedict, Zborowski became a consultant at Columbia University's Institute on Contemporary Culture and obtained a government grant, which led to the publication in 1952 of *Life Is with People,* a groundbreaking study of the Jewish shtetls of Eastern Europe. He then became study director of the American Jewish Committee. A series of grants enabled Zborowski to undertake projects on how people responded to pain. When published, the studies were well received and further enhanced his scholarly reputation.

Zborowski was exposed after Aleksandr Orlov went public in 1954. Orlov had remained in hiding in the United States ever since his defection in 1938. Following Stalin's death, he published an account of the dictator's crimes and offered a highly sanitized version of his own past.[18] Orlov met the Dallins and discovered that Mark, the KGB agent about whom he had warned Trotsky, was Mark Zborowski and lived in the United States. He told the FBI. Zborowski was interviewed and two years later testified before a Senate committee. Although he admitted spying on Trotskyists in Europe, he denied working for the KGB in the United States. He claimed that when the KGB had made contact with him in New York in 1941, he had refused to deal with them: "At this time, I became almost—I was almost hysterical and I remember well, I hit my fist on the table and said, 'I will not do anything with you any more.' And I walked out. Since then, I have not seen anyone."[19] Zborowski admitted that he was asked to spy on Kravchenko but claimed that he refused to do so. The deciphered Venona messages demonstrate that this statement, and much of the rest of his testimony, was false.

Convicted and sentenced to five years in jail for perjury, Zborowski successfully appealed on procedural grounds that his defense had not had access to certain information held by the prosecution. Retried in 1962 after having been given access to the contested information, he was again convicted and sentenced to three years and eleven months in prison. After serving his sentence, he moved to San Francisco, where he worked as a medical anthropologist at Mount Zion Medical Center.[20]

Spying on Other Enemies

Even when the KGB was not plotting the murder of Stalin's enemies, Soviet intelligence wanted to know what they were doing and with whom they were in contact. In some cases, infiltration of exile communities was designed to identify individuals as possible recruits for intelligence work. In others, there were efforts to discredit or disrupt their activities. One KGB circular order shows the broad sweep of Soviet interest; sent to KGB stations in New York, Mexico City, and Paris in 1945, it ordered forwarding of material on "old and new Russian and nationalist émigrés, the Russian, Armenian and Mohammedan clergy, Trotskyites and Zionists."[21]

Within the United States, the KGB had agents reporting on many of these groups. One unidentified agent, Alexandrov, reported on Russian émigrés, received a subsidy, and was promised Soviet citizenship. Another, Eugénie Olkhine, reestablished contact with the KGB in 1945 after a long break and supplied information about the Russian Orthodox Patriarch in the United States. She, too, was promised Soviet citizenship. Arrow (unidentified) worked among Carpatho-Russians, as did Eufrosina Dvoichenko-Markov, who also reported on Romanians and on several State Department employees with whom she had contact. Her son, Demetrius, was a U.S. Army sergeant on duty in Alaska. He was assigned to military counterintelligence duties and obtained some sort of manual that he turned over to the KGB. The KGB thought Demetrius had prospects, and it had a plan to fund his college education after the war.[22]

One of the most important Soviet agents working among émigrés was Sergey Kurnakov, a former tsarist cavalry officer who had immigrated to the United States and later became an ardent but undeclared Communist.[23] In addition to providing information about his fellow immigrant Russians, Kurnakov was a highly active KGB liaison agent. As a reward for his services, the KGB arranged for Kurnakov and his son to return to the USSR. The KGB also had sources who trolled for information about Bessarabians and Ukrainians. Mikhail Tkach edited a pro-Communist Ukrainian-language newspaper and supervised a small network of subagents. Tkach's daughter, Ann Sidorovich, and her husband, Michael, were part of Julius Rosenberg's espionage network.[24]

Several agents were assigned to infiltrate Jewish organizations. If the cover name Polecats, which the KGB used for Trotskyists, reflected Stalin's disdain for his ideological arch-enemy, the cover name for the Zionists in the KGB cables, Rats, was likewise a reflection of the Stalinist opinion of Jews. During World War II, for tactical reasons, the USSR encouraged the formation of Jewish groups in Russia that appealed to world Jewry for assistance. Always wary of Jewish nationalism, however, the KGB monitored all their activities. In 1943 Solomon Michoels and Itzhak Feffer, representatives of the USSR's Jewish Anti-Fascist Committee, toured the United States to great acclaim in Jewish communities. Feffer was himself a KGB agent. In 1947 Grigory Kheifets, who had run the KGB office in San Francisco for much of World War II, became Feffer's deputy. Kheifets's timing, however, was poor, as Soviet postwar purges took on an antisemitic air. Stalin had Michoels murdered in a fake accident, executed Feffer, and imprisoned Kheifets.[25]

The 1943 Michoels-Feffer tour of the United States was arranged by Ben-Zion Goldberg, son-in-law of the famed Yiddish writer Sholem Aleichem. Goldberg, born in Russia, returned there for a visit in 1945. During Stalin's purge of Soviet Jewish writers in the late 1940s, he was accused of being an American espionage agent, and several Soviet writers were executed because of their contacts with him. In fact, his situation resembles that of Noel Field (chapter 3). In *Out of the Red Shadows: Anti-Semitism in Stalin's Russia,* the Russian historian Gennady Kostyrchenko details how the KGB used contact with Goldberg by prominent Soviet Jews as evidence of complicity in American espionage, even though its own records stated that Goldberg had been a "foreign agent of the MGB [KGB] of the USSR abroad."[26]

The Venona messages confirm that the KGB maintained a number of informants in the Jewish community. Mark, a Jewish journalist (Menashe Unger is a likely candidate for Mark), reported not only on Jewish groups but also on exiled Social Democrats and Socialists. Mark was put on inactive status in 1944 because his information was of limited value. Hudson, the cover name of an unidentified American KGB agent, supervised a small group of subagents in various Jewish and Zionist organizations.[27] Esther Rand was one agent supervised by Hudson. A longtime Communist activist, Rand was born in Russia in 1907 and came to the United States as an infant. She moved to New York from Massachusetts in 1940. Rand had worked in 1944 for the United Jewish Appeal but in that capacity could report only on Zionist activity. The KGB encouraged her to obtain a position as administrative secretary to a group described as a "committee of Jewish writers and artists" where "she will be able to expand her opportunities for using Jewish organizations and prominent figures."[28] It is not clear that she got that position, inasmuch as she worked in Italy and Israel for the United

Jewish Appeal after World War II. Rand was named as an unindicted co-conspirator in the Soblen espionage case.[29]

Spying on the Socialist Workers Party

The KGB's infiltration of Jewish groups, however, was minor compared with that directed against American Trotskyists. James Cannon, one of the founders of the American Communist movement (and the party's chairman for a period in the early 1920s), had led about a hundred followers of Trotsky out of the CPUSA in 1928. Cannon's group went through a number of organizational permutations before becoming in the late 1930s the Socialist Workers party (SWP), the American affiliate of Trotsky's Fourth International. Without the prestige in radical circles of support by the USSR, and lacking the generous subsidies the Soviets provided the CPUSA, the American Trotskyist movement was never large, a few thousand members at its peak and barely more than a hundred militants. It never seriously challenged the many-times-larger and organizationally stronger Communist party for leadership of the revolutionary left in America. Nevertheless, the tiny Socialist Workers party was a prime target of the KGB.

In 1937 Louis Budenz was a rising CPUSA official on the fringe of the party's top leadership. Just before he went to Chicago to become editor of the *Midwest Daily Record,* a regional Communist newspaper, Budenz was asked by one of the CPUSA's Soviet intelligence contacts, Dr. Gregory Rabinowitz, to find someone there to infiltrate the Trotskyist headquarters in New York. The notion was that SWP activists would be likely to spot an infiltrator from New York's Communist community, but one from Chicago could more easily pass as a sincere Trotskyist. Jack Kling, head of the Young Communist League in Chicago, introduced Budenz to Sylvia Callen, a young Communist social worker who was eager to help. Her married name was Sylvia Franklin; her husband, Zalmond Franklin, already worked for the KGB. Budenz later testified that he had been told that Zalmond Franklin had done "secret work" in Spain and after his return had been sent on clandestine missions to Canada on behalf of Soviet intelligence. Budenz recalled that after Sylvia had successfully infiltrated the New York SWP headquarters, the KGB set up Zalmond in a separate apartment where the two could meet.[30]

A May 1944 Venona message documents essential points of Budenz's recollections of Zalmond Franklin. The message—a report from Bernard Schuster, the CPUSA's liaison with the KGB—described a complaint about Franklin from Nathan Einhorn, head of the American Newspaper Guild in New York and a secret Communist. After the Franklins divorced in 1943, Zalmond had married Rose Richter, whose sister, Frieda, was Einhorn's wife. Einhorn told Schuster that Zalmond was bragging to his new relations about his connection with the KGB. Einhorn thought this loose talk ill advised, although everyone in the family circle was a Communist. The KGB, too, thought it unwise. The New York KGB told Moscow that it was ordering Franklin to finish a report on his last assignment and then it would remove him from active work.[31] It also said that it would have Schuster keep an eye on Franklin in case of more insecure talk. An FBI inquiry into Zalmond Franklin's background also confirmed that he had served in the Spanish Civil War, working at least part of the time as a bacteriologist at a Spanish Loyalist hospital. He had worked in Alberta, Canada, in 1943. Michael Straight also told the FBI that during the period when he had been associated with the KGB, Franklin had been one of those with whom he was in contact.[32]

As for Sylvia Callen, she joined the Socialist Workers party in Chicago under the name of Sylvia Caldwell, according to instructions from the CPUSA. Following Rabinowitz's instructions, she moved to New York shortly afterward, assiduously undertook volunteer clerical tasks for the Trotskyist movement, and was rewarded by an appointment as secretary to the leader of the SWP, James Cannon. Callen later testified to a grand jury that she had provided information from the SWP offices to Rabinowitz, known to her as Jack. Jack, she stated, was later replaced by someone she knew as Sam, who was later identified as Jack Soble.[33] In confirmation, Callen turns up under the cover name Satyr in a number of deciphered Venona messages as a valuable KGB source in the Soble network that, as the KGB put it, "deals with the Polecats [Trotskyists]."[34] The Venona messages show her turning over to the KGB copies of the correspondence of SWP leaders, information on the household, health, and finances of Natalia Trotsky (Leon Trotsky's widow), and reports on the internal finances of Trotskyist groups.

Sylvia Callen dropped out of the SWP in 1947, a year before Louis Budenz, by then a Communist defector, exposed her as a Stalinist agent in the Trotskyist ranks. Her Trotskyist comrades, however, refused to believe Budenz's story. In 1954 Callen, then known as Sylvia Doxsee and living in Chicago, was called before a grand jury. Invoking the Fifth Amendment, she refused to answer questions about her membership in the SWP, her relationship to the KGB, Louis Budenz, or anything else bearing on her activities in New York. She was called back to another grand jury in 1958. This time she was more cooperative, confessing that she met regularly with Rabinowitz and Soble to pass on confidential Trotskyist material at an apartment rented by a woman named Lucy Booker. Callen was named as an unindicted co-conspirator when Robert Soblen was charged with espionage in 1960, but she never publicly testified.[35]

Lucy Booker, whose apartment had been used for meetings between Callen and Soble, was also named as an unindicted co-conspirator in the Soblen case. Booker had worked for Soviet intelligence in Germany in the 1930s along with Margaret Browder, sister of the head of the CPUSA. Booker returned to the United States in 1939 but lost touch with the KGB. In 1941 Jacob Golos told Elizabeth Bentley that he had been ordered to reestablish ties. Golos did so, and Booker worked at various times under the supervision of Golos, the longtime KGB liaison agent Joseph Katz, and the Soble-Soblen brothers. Jack Soble testified that Vasily and Elizabeth Zubilin had introduced him to Booker; he regularly paid her between $100 and $150 a month for her work. She cooperated with the FBI and was never called as a witness in a public forum.[36]

Still another Communist assigned to infiltrate the Socialist Workers party was Floyd Cleveland Miller, known in the SWP as Mike Cort. Miller confessed his activities to the FBI in 1954 and appeared as a witness in Robert Soblen's espionage trial in 1961. The story he told government investigators and the jury is confirmed by numerous decrypted Venona documents.[37]

Born in South Bend, Indiana, Miller went to school in Michigan and in 1934 moved to New York, where he found a job writing soap operas for radio station WMCA. He joined the CPUSA in 1936. Only a few months later, Gregory Rabinowitz recruited him to do "opposition work," as the CPUSA called covert action against rival political organizations. Miller's first assignment, which lasted a year, was to listen to a wiretap on James Cannon's home. Next he joined the SWP and became one of its activists, all the while writing up reports for the CPUSA and the KGB. The Trotskyists assigned him to the Sailors Union of the

Pacific in 1941, and he became editor of the union's journal, in addition to writing on military affairs for the *Fourth International,* a Trotskyist journal, during World War II. The Sailors Union of the Pacific, led by firm anti-Communists, challenged the Communist-led International Longshoremen's and Warehousemen's Union for leadership of maritime labor on the West Coast. Miller's position gave Communist unionists a spy in the upper ranks of a chief rival union. He later stated, "My job as a Stalinist was to keep track of the sailing of all Trotskyite seamen so a Stalinist agent would be at the port and have a surveillance on whatever Trotskyites entered the Soviet Union."[38]

Miller's primary KGB contacts were Joseph Katz, who himself had installed the listening device in Cannon's residence, and a woman he knew as Sylvia Getzoff. She has the cover name Adam in the deciphered Venona cables and is identified there as Rebecca Getzoff.[39] The Venona cables about Getzoff show that in addition to collaborating with Miller, she worked with Mark Zborowski, Joseph Katz, and Amadeo Sabatini (chapter 2). She was named as an unindicted co-conspirator in the Soblen indictment, but very little information about her was made public.

The Socialist Workers party decided to send Miller to Mexico in the spring of 1944 to meet with Natalia Trotsky and to show her a microfilm of the page proofs of her late husband's biography of Stalin. Before leaving, Miller met in New York with Jack Soble, and Soble copied the film for the KGB. Three Venona messages from that spring deal with the preparations for his trip and the methods by which he could best extract information of interest to the KGB about Trotskyist activity in Mexico. The New York KGB office asked Moscow's advice on whether Miller should arrange to spend time with Natalia Trotsky and collect information about the physical arrangements of her residence. One complication to his trip was that the FBI had Miller on a surveillance list because of his Trotskyist activities; KGB officials worried that he might be watched by American counterintelligence in Mexico, thus making more difficult its own contact with him.

These messages offer an example of KGB tradecraft of that era. The New York KGB reported Miller's departure for Mexico on June 11 and sent passwords and recognition codes to Moscow for transmittal to the Mexico City KGB. Miller would phone the Soviet embassy precisely at 9:30 A.M., ask for the ambassador's secretary, and identify himself as Mr. Leonard. This would mean he was setting up a meeting for seven o'clock that evening at the entrance to a specified movie house, where he would be holding a copy of *Life* magazine and wearing glasses, which he would periodically remove and wipe. His KGB contact should hold a copy of *Time* and ask in English, "Are you Mr. Toren?" to which Miller would reply, "No, my name is Charles Bruno."[40] Officials of the Mexico City KGB, however, were not impressed by the meeting place chosen by their New York colleagues. Mexico City complained to Moscow that the rendezvous New York had assigned to Miller was in full view of a café frequented by political émigrés who might spot the man meeting Miller as a Soviet embassy officer.[41]

Miller testified in 1961 that his 1944 Mexican assignment for the KGB had included investigating reports of a budding alliance between Trotskyists and anarchists and other radicals grouped around the exiled French writer Victor Serge. Miller admitted, and Venona cables confirm, that he had been given a contact at the Soviet embassy in Mexico City. He spent six weeks living in the Trotsky household and determined that no such alliance of radicals was brewing. Upon returning to New York, Miller delivered a written report on his mission to a KGB contact.[42] The New York KGB informed Moscow on August 10, 1944, that Miller had returned from Mexico and turned in a detailed report that not only described the relationship between the Trotskyists and Serge but also divulged the names and addresses of most of the active Trotskyists in Mexico. The cable also discussed future use of Miller. To avoid the military draft, he had taken a job as a seaman on a coastal steamer that would temporarily interrupt his spying on the Trotskyists. Nonetheless, "we will continue to put him forward for the staff [SWP headquarters] and strengthen his authority with the Polecats [Trotskyists]."[43]

Miller also testified that he was introduced to Lucy Booker, who served as a courier between him and Soble in 1945; his reports on the Trotskyists were typed in her apartment. In 1945 Soble informed Miller that he was being transferred to another controller and introduced him to his "cousin," who turned out to be Robert Soblen. A Venona message from May 1945 confirms that Jack Soble had handed over his agents in the Polecats and Rats to Robert Soblen. Miller insisted that he stopped working for Soviet intelligence in 1945, thereafter turning his energies to writing children's books.[44]

When he returned from Mexico, Floyd Miller expressed concern to the KGB that his true allegiance might be exposed to the Trotskyists. Another KGB agent pretending sympathy for the Trotskyist Fourth International, a friend of Miller's named Robert Owen Menaker, had returned to New York from Latin America. Menaker, Miller learned, had told some of his relatives that he was not a Trotskyist but associated with them on a Communist assignment. Miller, the KGB reported, "is afraid that this may get to the ears of the Polecats and they may become suspicious of Khe . . . [Miller] as he came to them through Bob [Menaker]."[45]

Robert Owen Menaker came from a radical family. His father, imprisoned for revolutionary activities in Russia, prospered in America as co-owner of a handkerchief factory. Determined not to exploit his workers, he abandoned manufacturing for farming. He named his sons after revolutionaries and radicals—Peter Kropotkin Menaker, William Morris Menaker, Robert Owen Menaker. One of Robert's brothers, Frederick Engels (Enge) Menaker, an openly Communist journalist, ran a League of American Writers home for anti-Nazi refugees in France. When the house was closed, he arranged shelter for some of the exiles in the home of the Arenal family in Mexico City, where he cooked for them. Years later, Enge's nephew and Robert's son, Daniel Menaker, wrote an affectionate portrait of his Communist uncle.[46]

In his account of his family Daniel Menaker noted that the Communist party had sent his father to Mexico "to keep an eye on Trotsky in exile."[47] He certainly did that, but more as well, although exactly what Menaker's assignment was is not clear from the sixteen Venona messages in which he is mentioned. As was noted in the Venona message just quoted, he assisted Floyd Miller's infiltration of the Socialist Workers party. Several of the messages relate to Menaker's employer, Michael Burd, owner of the Midland Export Corporation of New York. In 1944 and 1945 Menaker represented Midland in Chile, where he was associated with Christian Casanova Subercaseaux, a Chilean diplomat. Both Burd and Subercaseaux were KGB agents; Burd used his business to transfer large amounts of money to agents throughout Latin America and aided the KGB in a complicated effort to obtain American transit visas for Nicholas and Maria Fisher, the names used by two KGB illegal officers claiming Swiss citizenship who were to go to Mexico via the United States. Subercaseaux assisted in transferring funds and couriering messages and documents throughout Latin America.[48]

Menaker had difficulties as an agent. In 1944 he returned from a trip to Chile and tried to find permanent employment in the United States. Michael Burd complained to the New York KGB office that

Menaker had alienated several companies with whom he did business. The New York KGB station chief cabled Moscow that in working with Menaker "allowances should be made," since he had not been thoroughly trained or screened prior to being given his assignment.[49]

Later messages are only slightly clearer about Menaker's tasks. In one message the KGB speculated about the possibility that Laurence Duggan, one of its sources who had recently resigned from the State Department, might obtain a job in Chile to do some unspecified work with, or in place of, Menaker. A partially decrypted cable from October 1944 suggests that Menaker was distributing money to someone in Chile but also noted that "relations of Bob and X" (X was its veteran agent Joseph Katz) were "not quite normal." The cable asked for instructions about what should be done about Menaker's salary and noted that someone would be paying him thirty thousand dollars but that he might not receive it for a year.[50] Joseph Katz owned the Tempus Import Company in Manhattan in 1944; it is possible that Menaker was somehow connected with that firm.

Like his friend Floyd Miller, Robert Menaker apparently cooperated to some extent with the FBI in the 1950s. His name never surfaced in connection with investigations of Soviet espionage; he was never indicted or questioned by congressional committees. His son wrote of the frequent presence in the household in the 1950s of a friendly FBI agent, but his father never spoke about precisely what he did in Mexico or what he told the FBI.[51]

Katz, with whom Menaker was associated for a time, was one of the KGB's most active liaison agents. An immigrant to the United States (he was born in Lithuania in 1912), he is referred to in thirty-three deciphered Venona messages as the contact between Soviet KGB officers and numerous Soviets sources.[52] He went to work for Soviet intelligence in 1938 and at various times was the KGB go-between with such important contacts as Earl Browder, Elizabeth Bentley, Flora Wovschin, Harry Gold, Thomas Black, and Bernard Schuster. Deciphered Venona messages suggest that the KGB provided some of the capital for the business firms (Tempus Import Company and, earlier, Meriden Dental Laboratories) that afforded Katz cover for his work during World War II. Katz left the United States at some point after the war, probably in 1948, when the KGB decided that Bentley's defection or the Venona Project placed him in danger. He worked for Soviet intelligence in Europe but in 1950 had a falling out with his KGB superiors, dropped out of Soviet service, and emigrated to Israel.[53] He never talked to American authorities about his work for Soviet intelligence.

The Soble Apparatus

While one part of Jack Soble and Robert Soblen's apparatus concentrated on spying on Trotskyists and other political opponents, a second part ranged more widely. This group of agents infiltrated the OSS and created business covers for Soviet intelligence. In 1957 three of its principals—Jack and Myra Soble and Jacob Albam—pleaded guilty to espionage. Four years later, Robert Soblen was convicted of espionage. Several other members of the ring fled the United States and were never brought to trial. And one, Boris Morros, turned out to be a double agent working for the FBI.

Born in St. Petersburg in 1895, Boris Morros was a musical prodigy. He left Russia in 1922 and made his way to the United States. For sixteen years he was a producer and music director at Paramount Studios in Hollywood, responsible for such movies as *Flying Deuces,* which starred Stan Laurel and Oliver Hardy, and *Second Chorus* with Paulette Goddard and Fred Astaire. Morros aided the careers of stars such as Bing Crosby, Ginger Rogers, and Rudy Vallee. Morros later claimed that he agreed at first to help the KGB in order to ensure that the parcels of food he sent to his brothers and aged parents in the Soviet Union were delivered. A Russian he knew as Edward Herbert, claiming to be involved in anti-Nazi activities, used Morros in 1936 to obtain cover as a Paramount talent scout in Germany. Herbert once again approached Morros in 1942, identified himself as Vasily Zubilin, and obtained Morros's cooperation in return for allowing his father to immigrate to the United States.[54]

Morros later insisted that he resisted Zubilin's efforts to get him to hire and provide business cover for Soviet agents. But the anonymous Russian letter received by the FBI in 1943 (chapter 2), while asserting that a number of Americans cooperated with the KGB, specifically named only two—Earl Browder and Boris Morros. The letter identified Elizabeth Zubilin as the KGB officer who dealt with Morros. So it is likely that Morros was performing more important functions for the KGB than those he discussed in his exculpatory autobiography.

Morros's own story is that he attempted to discourage use of his company as cover for KGB operations by telling Zubilin that it was too small, but Zubilin had a solution. He informed Morros in the fall of 1943 that he had found a wealthy couple willing to invest in a sheet music company that would serve as cover for Soviet espionage. That December Zubilin drove Morros to Connecticut, where they met with Alfred and Martha Dodd Stern, who invested $130,000 in the Boris Morros Music Company.[55]

The Sterns were the epitome of Communist fellow-traveling chic. Alfred Stern, born in 1897, was educated at Phillips Exeter Academy and Harvard. In 1921 he married Marion Rosenwald, daughter of the head of Sears, Roebuck and Company, and directed the Rosenwald Foundation for a decade. After divorcing his wife in 1936 and receiving a million-dollar settlement, Stern met and married Martha Dodd, daughter of America's ambassador to Nazi Germany from 1933 to 1937.

Born in 1908, Martha Dodd was a femme fatale of the 1930s. Her long list of lovers included Carl Sandburg and Thomas Wolfe. She had shocked the diplomatic community in Germany with her torrid love affairs with Rudolf Dies, head of the Nazi Gestapo, and Boris Vinogradov, first secretary of the Soviet embassy. Vinogradov and Dodd asked the Soviet government for permission to marry in 1936, but they were turned down. Vinogradov returned to Moscow and their relationship came to an end. Decades later she learned from Soviet contacts that he had been executed in 1938. Although it is not certain, Vinogradov most likely was a KGB officer, and his execution was part of Stalin's late-1930s purge of his intelligence agencies. Jack Soble later testified that Martha Dodd had told him that she had worked as a Soviet source while at the U.S. embassy in Berlin and during her relationship with Vinogradov.[56]

After their marriage in 1938, Alfred and Martha Stern devoted themselves to promoting far-left causes, using both their wealth and their talents. In 1939 Martha Dodd published a best-selling book, *Through Embassy Eyes,* on her experiences in Berlin and the developing horror of the Nazi regime. She and her brother, William Dodd, Jr., published in 1941 an edited version of their deceased father's diaries of his time as ambassador. It, too, offered a revealing look at the nature of the Nazi regime and was a publishing success. The younger Dodd was himself a controversial figure. He had been an active participant in the late 1930s in such Communist front organizations as the American Friends of the Soviet Union and had worked for the American League for Peace and Democracy. He published an article in the March 1938 issue of *Champion,* the journal of the Young Communist League. He was a national sponsor of the League of American Writers annual conference in 1941, at a time when it was supporting the Nazi-Soviet Pact with such vehemence that most of its non-Communist members had long since departed. When a congressional investigating committee questioned him in 1943 about his activities, Dodd, then an assistant news editor for the U.S. government Foreign Broadcasting Monitoring Service, denied any Communist ties. He claimed not to know that *Champion* had connections with the Young Communist League and to be equally ignorant of any Communist role in the other organizations to which he belonged. His denials availed him little; Congress refused to appropriate money to pay his salary.[57]

William Dodd, Jr., is the subject of one Venona message. The KGB in New York asked Moscow in 1944 if it would allow Dodd, who had the cover name Sitsilla, to take a temporary job with TASS, the Soviet news agency. He had, it explained, worked for the Office of War Information, had supplied information in the past, and had most recently worked for Russian War Relief.[58]

Early in 1944 Jack Soble replaced the Zubilins as Morros's KGB contact. Several Venona messages detail the increasingly fractious business relationship between Morros and the Sterns, who were concerned that their KGB-inspired investment was being poorly managed. In four separate cables the New York KGB station informed Moscow that Alfred Stern, cover-named Louis, believed Morros had squandered large amounts of money and that he, Stern, refused to put any more cash into the business. In one message Stern linked the problems to the Zubilins' departure from the United States. He had been ordered not to make any contacts until the KGB got in touch with him, but the situation had become critical: "I want to reaffirm my desire to be helpful. My resources are sufficient for any solid constructive business but I don't intend to maintain silence when my resources, time and efforts are being spent for nothing." One of Stern's memos, given to Helen Lowry, Browder's niece and Akhmerov's wife, for transmittal to Elizabeth Zubilin, complained that the entire $130,000 initial investment had vanished: "In view of the poor business management and misguided artistic temperament unsuitable for conducting a very systematic business this sum is not enough. . . . My partner ignores my advice; my endeavors lead almost or completely to nothing and even evoke disdain."[59]

Jack Soble came to California in March 1945 to adjudicate the dispute between Stern and Morros. In April the partnership was dissolved and Morros repaid Stern $100,000 for his one-quarter interest in the company. The Sterns continued their socialite lives at their elegant Connecticut estate and New York apartment. A friendly journalist described the heady company: "Lillian Hellman, Marc Blitstein, Paul Robeson, Margaret Burke-White, Clifford Odets, and Isamu Noguchi were regular guests at the Sterns' parties, along with members of the Soviet and Eastern European diplomatic set. One evening a guest looked around the Stern's living room and, half in jest, dubbed the crowd 'La Très Haute Société Communiste.' "[60]

Morros, meanwhile, was brooding about his treatment and threats from Jack Soble that any lack of cooperation might result in trouble for his brothers back in the Soviet Union. He went to the FBI in 1947, confessed, and agreed to work as a double agent.[61] From then on he provided the U.S. government with information on the activities of Soble, while the FBI put the Soble network's members under periodic surveillance.

At the same time, the Sterns' work as highly visible advocates of Soviet causes attracted the attention of a congressional investigating committee. After they were subpoenaed by the House Committee on Un-American Activities in 1953, the Sterns fled to Mexico rather than testify. The government was finally ready to move against the Soble ring in 1957. Jack Soble and his wife, Myra, Jacob Albam (then Soble's assistant), and the Sterns were indicted for espionage.

Fearing extradition from Mexico, the Sterns fled to Communist Czechoslovakia. In the 1960s they moved for a time to Castro's Cuba but returned to Prague. Their indictments were dismissed in 1979, but they never returned home and died in Prague.

With the assistance provided by Morros, the government had ample evidence against Jack Soble, and he decided not to risk trial. He, his wife, and Jacob Albam pleaded guilty. Soble also made a detailed statement of his past activities. In addition to testifying about Mark Zborowski, he assisted the government in convicting his brother, Robert Soblen, of espionage in 1961. Sentenced to life in prison and suffering from leukemia, Soblen jumped bail and fled to Israel using a passport issued to a dead relative. The Israelis, however, refused to admit him and put him on a plane to the United States. During the flight he attempted suicide and the plane landed in London, where he underwent medical treatment and launched another battle for asylum. When he was ordered deported to the United States, Soblen took a large dose of barbiturates and died.

Two other members of the Soble network, Jane Foster and her husband, George Zlatowski, were also indicted in 1957. They were living in France at the time and refused to return home to face trial; the French government declined to extradite them, possibly because in return they provided information about Soviet espionage in France. Jane Foster was the daughter of a wealthy businessman. After graduating from Mills College in 1935, she toured Europe, married a Dutch government official in 1936, and moved with him to the Dutch East Indies (Indonesia). On a visit to her parents in California in 1938, she joined the American Communist party and soon afterward divorced her husband. Shortly after she moved to New York in 1941, friends introduced her to George Zlatowski. A Minnesotan, Zlatowski had joined the Young Communist League in 1937 and then went to Spain to fight with the International Brigades.[62] They married, but George was soon drafted.

Around the same time, Foster met Alfred and Martha Stern and became friends with them. She also met William Browder, the brother of the head of the CPUSA. She later wrote that both he and Martha told her "not to be so open in my Party work, as I could be more helpful to the Party if I were more discreet." Foster felt this was "a welcome suggestion." With George off on military duties, Jane moved in 1942 to Washington, where she rented a room from Henry Collins and his wife, Susan B. Anthony II, active members of the CPUSA Washington underground. In her autobiography Foster admitted that before she had left New York, William Browder had introduced her to a young woman (unnamed) who would visit her occasionally in Washington "so that I could still keep in touch with the Party."[63] With her Indonesian experience and Malay language skills Foster soon found work in the Netherlands Study Unit, a wartime agency set up to coordinate intelligence on the Dutch East Indies; the agency was later absorbed by the Board of Economic Warfare. She wrote that at the board her closest friend was the KGB agent Charles Flato. She transferred to the Office of Strategic Services in the fall of 1943, and early in 1944 she was sent to Ceylon.

According to Boris Morros, Jane Foster told him she had been recruited as a Soviet agent by Martha Dodd Stern in 1938. (Foster dated her acquaintance with the Sterns to the early 1940s.) In her autobiography Foster denied being a Soviet agent and offered a convoluted explanation of her relationships with Jack Soble and Boris Morros. In her telling, they were both unscrupulous businessmen who took advantage of her and her husband. She wrote that she had met Jack Soble in 1946, after returning to the United States, and had loaned him eighteen hundred dollars for a business venture in France, though she never later produced a receipt or an IOU. She also said that she had given him a copy of one of her OSS reports on Indonesia, labeled top secret, although she denied that it was really secret. Meanwhile her husband, George, had earned an officer's commission, and in 1946 he attended the U.S. Army Intelligence School. (The Army was then unaware of his Communist background.) George Zlatkowski became an interrogator with U.S. military intelligence in Austria. He was released from Army duty in 1948. In her account, what Morros had reported as Soble's espionage subsidies to the Zlatowskis was simply his belated repayment of her 1946 loan. She agreed that Soble had introduced her and her husband to Boris Morros, but said that the connection was entirely innocent and that they had even loaned Morros money.

Deciphered Venona messages show that Jane Foster lied in her autobiography. KGB cables prove that she was a spy, but that Morros was either mistaken or misinformed about when she was recruited. Zubilin notified Moscow in June 1942: "[Unrecovered code group] Liza [Martha Stern], we are cultivating the American Jane Foster with a view to signing her on. She is about 30 years old and works in Washington in the Dutch [two unrecovered code groups] translator of Malay languages. . . . She is a Fellowcountrywoman [CPUSA member]. She is described by the Fellowcountrymen [CPUSA] as a [unrecovered code group], dedicated person."[64] Under the cover name of Slang, she is mentioned in subsequent deciphered Venona messages from 1943 and 1944 as engaged in transmitting information and in other espionage tasks.[65]

The grand jury in the Soble case listed a number of other persons as coconspirators in the espionage network but did not indict them, because they either were foreigners no longer in the United States, were dead, had cooperated with the prosecution, or had spied on Trotskyists or Zionists but not the United States government. Spying on Trotskyists and Zionists on behalf of the USSR might be reprehensible, but it was not a criminal violation of federal law.

Three of those named were Germans: Johanna Koenen Beker (daughter of the prominent German Communist William Koenen), Hans Hirschfeld (a consultant for the OSS during World War II), and Horst Baerensprung (another OSS consultant). After the Nazi seizure of power in Germany, Johanna Beker, whose father had held high positions in the Comintern, moved to Moscow, where she worked as a translator for American businessmen. By her own testimony, she was recruited by the KGB in 1937 to spy on visiting Americans and then sent to the United States in 1939. Zubilin introduced her in 1942 to Robert Soblen, for whom she worked as a courier. Soblen paid her between thirty-five and forty dollars a month. Her regular job was as a file clerk in a New York law firm.[66]

Beker testified at the Soblen trial that Hirschfeld and Baerensprung had passed information to her for transmittal to Soblen. Baerensprung, she said, had supplied information on German émigré groups and biographical material from OSS files. After the war ended, Baerensprung returned to the Soviet occupation zone and became a police official in the new East German regime, but he died before the Soble case broke in the United States. Beker said that Hirschfeld also had given her material on other German émigrés, including their fields of interest and their political views, and had passed on information he had heard about the development of a new American weapon. After the war Hirschfeld moved to West Berlin, and in 1960 he became press chief for West Berlin mayor Willy Brandt. From West Berlin Hirschfeld denied Beker's charges but refused to return to the United States to testify unless he were granted complete immunity from prosecution. The U.S. government offered him only limited immunity: his testimony could not be used as evidence against him, but he would be liable to perjury charges if it could be shown that he had testified falsely. Faced with the possibility of an indictment for perjury if he denied Beker's testimony, he remained in Germany. In an interview with American intelligence agents, he admitted to "extended illegal activity and contacts with Communist agents in Europe prior to 1940" but again denied Beker's statements about his activities after that time. He resigned his position with Mayor Brandt.[67]

The Venona messages shed little light on this portion of Soble's ring. Johanna Beker probably appears in three Venona messages, under the cover names Clemence and Lee, although the identification is not certain.[68] Clemence/Lee is identified as an agent assigned to work among German immigrants and exiles and as the hostess of a safe-house. One Venona message, largely undecrypted except for a handful of names, refers to Robert Soblen's making a proposal to his brother Jack about Hans Hirschfeld and other German immigrants.[69]

Two mysterious figures listed in the Soble network indictment were Dr. Henry Spitz and his wife, Dr. Beatrice Spitz. Both physicians and naturalized citizens, in 1950 they lived in Albuquerque, New Mexico, where they allegedly took photographs of a military base where atomic weapons research was done and passed it to Dr. Soblen. That year they left for their native Austria; following Soblen's arrest they renounced their American citizenship.[70]

One other relative of Robert Soblen and Jack Soble also served as a member of their espionage ring. Ilya Wolston was the son of one of Robert and Jack's sisters. Boris Morros wrote in his autobiography that Jack Soble had told him that Ilya, whose cover name Morros remembered as Slava, had done work for the Russians in Alaska. Venona shows that Morros was correct.

Ilya Elliott Wolston entered the U.S. Army in World War II and became a military intelligence officer. He promptly began reporting to the KGB on the organization, curriculum, and personnel of the Army's intelligence school at Fort Ritchie, Maryland. In the Venona cables he describes the training that he and other American intelligence officers underwent as specialists in Soviet affairs. The deciphered KGB cable suggests that one of his missions was to spot other officers who might be susceptible to recruitment as Soviet agents. The KGB valued his position inside American military intelligence, and the New York KGB assured Moscow that "Slava was warned about appropriate secrecy and caution."[71]

After graduating, Wolston was posted to Alaska on an assignment to Army counterintelligence dealing with Soviet matters. At the time Soviet Lend-Lease traffic, both naval and air, through Alaska was heavy. Thus a Soviet spy was given what was from the point of view of the KGB a dream assignment, protecting the United States from Soviet spies. There are no Slava/Wolston Venona messages from his Alaska period. But cover names were changed from time to time, and he seems a likely candidate for Skrib, the cover name of an unidentified agent in a Venona cable who wrote to Frost (Boris Morros) from Alaska in December 1944 announcing that he was "ready to work if we want."[72]

After the war Wolston worked for the KGB network run by his uncle Jack. By the 1950s, however, he developed health problems and became a rural recluse. He ignored six subpoenas to testify before a federal grand jury. Tried for contempt, he pleaded guilty but claimed mental illness as a mitigating circumstance. He was given a one-year suspended sentence.

Most of the other unindicted co-conspirators in the Soblen case were people who had infiltrated the Trotskyists or Zionists: Floyd Miller, Sylvia Callen Franklin, Esther Rand, Sylvia Getzoff, and Lucy Booker. Infiltration of the Trotskyist movement, however, was not enough for Joseph Stalin. He wanted Trotsky dead. And the plan to murder Leon Trotsky and then to free his killer from prison had depended on the cooperation of members of the American Communist party's secret apparatus with the KGB.

Americans and Trotsky's Assassination

Pavel Sudoplatov, a senior KGB officer who had several successful KGB assassinations to his credit, was summoned to a meeting with Stalin and KGB head Lavrenty Beria in March 1939 and appointed deputy director of the KGB foreign department, with orders to eliminate Trotsky. Sudoplatov enlisted Leonid Eitingon, a veteran KGB officer, to run the operation. (Eitingon shows up in the Venona traffic under the cover name Tom.)[73] Another veteran Soviet intelligence officer, Lev Vasilevsky, who used the name Tarasov when in North America, helped coordinate the operation's communications and was posted to Mexico City, where Trotsky then lived in exile. Eitingon arrived in New York in October 1939 and set up an export-import company as a cover.[74]

Eitingon and Sudoplatov established several networks aimed at killing Trotsky. Eitingon had served in the Spanish Civil War under the name of General Kotov and supervised the training of special units of the International Brigades for commando and sabotage missions. He drew on those contacts for personnel for the anti-Trotsky operation. Caridad Mercader, a wealthy Spanish Communist, headed one of the networks, and Eitingon recruited her son, Ramón, to play the chief role in this network's mission. The Spanish painter David Siqueiros, who had moved to Mexico, headed a second apparatus. Eitingon may have had still another apparatus prepared to eliminate Trotsky if these efforts failed. Thomas Black, an American Communist, testified that Gaik Ovakimian, the KGB chief in New York, had recruited him for industrial espionage in the mid-1930s. Black said that the KGB ordered him to join the Trotskyists in 1937 and prepare to go to Mexico to join the Trotsky household. He later learned that he was to be part of an assassination attempt. For personal reasons, however, Black was unable to go to Mexico and took little part in the anti-Trotsky operation.[75]

The Siqueiros group struck first. Approximately twenty Spanish and Mexican Communists, many of them veterans of the Spanish Civil War, launched an armed raid on Trotsky's villa in May 1940; although one of Trotsky's American bodyguards, Robert Sheldon Harte, was killed, the operation failed to kill Trotsky.[76] Siqueiros, himself an International Brigades veteran, was arrested and insisted that the raiders, who had fired several hundred bullets, were merely trying to gather evidence of Trotsky's counterrevolutionary activities in Mexico. After being released on bail, he was spirited out of the country with the assistance of Pablo Neruda, a Communist and future Nobel Prize laureate in literature, then a Chilean diplomat in Mexico.[77]

Two of the gunmen named in the Mexican press as the murderers of Robert Harte were Leopolo and Luís Arenal, members of a wealthy Mexican family. (Harte was not killed in the gun battle at the Trotsky residence but was taken away by the raiders and murdered later.) In the spring of 1939 Jacob Golos had introduced Elizabeth Bentley to Leopolo Arenal. Leopolo's brother Luís was married to an American, Rose Biegel Arenal, who lived in New York. An Arenal sister, Angelica, was married to David Siqueiros. Golos had arranged for Bentley to pick up mail sent by Leopolo to Rose and deliver it to him. Rose Arenal later admitted to the FBI that she had received such letters, which she turned over to Bentley and Jacob Golos; although she never opened the letters, she assumed they might have had to do with the Trotsky assassination plot.[78]

Although Rose Arenal professed to be shocked by her possible involvement in murder, deciphered Venona cables show that she remained in touch with the KGB. She told a KGB officer in New York in July 1943 about Elena (identified by analysts as Elena Huerta Muzquiz), who needed financial help and who, evidently having some claim on the Soviets, was planning to appeal to Konstantin Umansky, Soviet ambassador to Mexico. Rose told the KGB that she had advised Elena against this course and asked the KGB to "report on the situation." She also alerted the KGB to an opportunity to recruit still another member of the Arenal family. She had received a letter from Mexico with news that her husband's cousin, Capt. Alberto Arenal, had been appointed a member of a Mexican military mission and would soon be leaving for New York. Alberto was "an honorable man and sympathetic to us," she told her KGB contact.[79]

The failure of the Siqueiros apparatus to kill Trotsky led Sudoplatov and Eitingon to put in motion an alternative plan using the Mercader group, whose elements had been carefully nurtured for several years. Louis Budenz later testified that one of the American Communists he had introduced to Gregory Rabinowitz in 1938 was Ruby Weil, a member of the CPUSA's secret apparatus. Weil had been cultivating a friendship with Sylvia Ageloff, an ardent Trotskyist who did not know that Weil was a secret Stalinist. On a trip to Paris in 1938 to attend an international Trotskyist meeting, Weil introduced Sylvia Ageloff to "Jacques Mornard," the alias being used by Ramón Mercader. Mornard pursued Ageloff, and they became lovers. After Ageloff returned to the United States, Mornard visited her in September 1939 in New York on his way to Mexico. A few months later, Sylvia Ageloff traveled to Mexico to do volunteer work for Trotsky and to join her boyfriend. (Much of Trotsky's household and office staff in Mexico consisted of young American Trotskyists who volunteered a few months' work. The murdered Harte was one such volunteer.) Mornard then used Ageloff's position in the Trotsky household to gain entrance to the residence and became acquainted with Trotsky's guards and aides. Presenting himself as interested in Trotsky's ideas but still working out his own views, he arranged a private meeting in August 1940 with Trotsky himself to discuss a philosophical manuscript he had prepared. Once alone with Trotsky, Mornard used a small ax to smash in Trotsky's skull.[80]

Mornard had planned to kill Trotsky silently and escape, but his victim had cried out, and he was seized by Trotsky's guards. Convicted of murder by a Mexican court, Mornard maintained that he was a disaffected Trotskyist, and initial efforts to ascertain his true identify were fruitless. He had entered Mexico using an altered Canadian passport belonging to a man who had served in the International Brigades. Despite widespread suspicion that he was a Soviet agent, there was no proof, nor even any firm evidence of his real nationality.

When he was captured, Soviet intelligence immediately set in motion plans to free him. Known in the Venona messages as the Rita Project, later as the Gnome Project—both names were used as cover names for Mercader—it involved Russian, Mexican, and American Communists. Just as the assassination of Trotsky depended on the cooperation of American Communists, the plot to free his killer revealed a large group of CPUSA members who worked for the KGB as agents, mail drops, and couriers. The extensive operation is the subject of dozens of cables from Moscow, New York, and Mexico City.

The KGB had used Rose Arenal as a mail drop in New York before the assassination. Afterward it employed a separate network of American Communists. Between November 1941 and November 1943 the FBI intercepted twenty-four messages in cipher or concealed writing that had been sent by mail and courier between the United States and Mexico. The FBI files released thus far do not indicate how the bureau first learned of the messages. The individuals who served as mail drops all lived in New York and Mexico City and were longtime members of the Communist party. The first mail drop discovered by the FBI was Lydia Altschuler, an immigrant from Germany and employee of Consumers Union. Before taking that job, Altschuler had worked for a distributor of Soviet films in the United States.[81]

Other mail drops included Pauline Baskind (wife of a New York attorney), Frances Silverman (member of the Communist-dominated New York Teachers Union), Louis Bloch (a New York motion picture operator employed by the Soviet government), Fanny McPeek (a clerk at Washington Irving High School), Barnett Shepard, and Ethel Vogel (her husband, Sidney, had served in the International Brigades as a medical doctor). Helen Levi Simon, a columnist at the *Daily Worker,* traveled to Mexico City in August 1943 to attend a Joint Anti-Fascist Refugee Conference and sent $3,700 to Mexico City in February 1944 for Mercader's use.[82]

The FBI followed Anna Colloms, whose address had been used as a mail drop, on a trip to Mexico in August 1943. She was carrying secret messages concealed in a box of blank stationery. United States Customs officials, having confiscated the box on August 15 when she left the United States, deciphered the messages and returned the box to her on her way home. The FBI laboratory discovered that all the messages dealt with efforts to free Mercader.[83]

A teacher at Washington Irving High School and a member of the CPUSA, Colloms continued her journey to Mexico City, where she made a half-hearted effort to get in touch with an American named Jacob Epstein, whom she had known previously. (Colloms must have suspected that she was under surveillance when Customs seized her stationery.) After picking up the seized material upon reentering the United States on September 16, 1943, she returned to New York and gave the stationery box to Ethel Vogel, her sister-in-law, who handed it over to Ruth Wilson Epstein, Jacob's wife. When asked in 1950 about her activities, Colloms took the Fifth.[84]

Several decrypted Venona messages reveal that both Lydia Altschuler and Anna Colloms had been used extensively as mail drops for KGB operations throughout Latin America, and that the KGB quickly learned that one of its mail drops had been compromised after her trip to Mexico. On December 6, 1942, a KGB agent in Buenos Aires cabled to New York that several of his letters sent to Lydia Altschuler had been intercepted by American mail censorship. He warned New York to "take measures with Lidia." The letters, which indeed had been seized by the government, had dealt with the movement of agents, the transfer of money, the setting up of clandestine radio contact and contacts for KGB agents in several South American countries.[85] On February 1, 1943, the New York KGB warned Buenos Aires to stop writing to one address and "for the time being use only Anna Collums' address." But on September 29, 1943, just two weeks after Colloms returned to New York, the New York KGB warned Buenos Aires, "Do not write any more to the address of Ana Colloms. Warn Alexander [unidentified] about this."[86] Colloms's trip was also the subject of a 1944 Venona message which reported that the KGB had spotted "surveillance of Non [Ruth Epstein] and the courier "A" [Anna Colloms] who came to the Countryside [Mexico] for liaison with Harry [Jacob Epstein] but achieved nothing." The message assured Moscow that appropriate measures were being taken to shake surveillance.[87]

Jacob and Ruth Wilson Epstein were Soviet agents whose activities are the subject of a number of Venona messages. Jacob Epstein, who was stationed in Mexico City, was born in Brooklyn to Russian parents on November 10, 1903. He attended public schools in New York and was graduated from Cornell University, where he met Anna Colloms, also a student, in 1924. He worked for several clothing companies in New York from 1924 to 1938, when he enlisted in the International Brigades. In the fighting Epstein was badly wounded. While recuperating, he met and married Ruth Beverly Wilson, who was serving as a nurse.[88]

While it is not clear whether Epstein was first recruited by the KGB in Spain or after his return to the United States, there is one intriguing bit of evidence that he was associated with the CPUSA's secret apparatus in 1941. When he applied for his passport for Mexico, one of his witnesses was Abraham Held, who was a business associate of J. Peters from 1939 to 1941. Jacob entered Mexico on a tourist visa in 1941. The following year he was granted resident status as representative of a business called Aldon Rug Mills, run by James Lewis Marcus, that served as a Soviet intelligence front. In 1943 he applied for and was granted student status, but later in the year his request to engage in the furniture business was denied by the Mexican government. Epstein's primary business in Mexico, however, was not tourism, schooling, or business. Epstein was in charge of the Gnome Project—the effort to free Mercader from his Mexican jail cell.[89]

Epstein reported to a series of senior Soviet intelligence officers. Lev Tarasov, nominally first secretary of the Soviet embassy but in reality a professional KGB officer, had been sent to Mexico to support Trotsky's assassination and was the KGB station chief in Mexico City. Pavel Klarin, another senior KGB officer, arrived from New York in November 1943 to supervise the jailbreak. And, from Moscow, Leonid Eitingon oversaw the entire operation. But despite the elaborate preparations, the escape attempt never took place.[90]

The first reference to Epstein's activities in the deciphered Venona documents came in a cable of May 28, 1943. Two days later, another message reported that Harry (Epstein) had placed two agents in the prison where Mercader was being held—one as a "consultant" and the other as a "patient." (The KGB adopted medical pseudonyms for this project. The Mexican prison, for example, was called the Hospital.) Arrangements were being made to transport Mercader out of Mexico once he was freed from jail, and other agents were being deployed. But Klarin admitted to Moscow from New York that planning was going "extremely slowly."[91]

The discovery by American counterintelligence of the couriers carrying secret messages between Klarin in New York and Epstein in Mexico persuaded Klarin that he had to travel to Mexico City to oversee the operation directly. He arrived on November 23, 1943, ostensibly as second secretary of the Soviet embassy. A December 23, 1943, cable from Tarasov in Mexico City to Beria in Moscow indicated that "the surgical operation is planned by the Doctors" to take place in four days and requested the immediate transfer of twenty thousand dollars to pay expenses.[92]

Less than a week later, however, Tarasov reported failure. The escape had been scheduled to occur when Mercader was being taken from prison to a courthouse. Epstein's team had bribed some of the guards to inform them of which of nine possible routes would be used to transport Mercader. KGB combat teams would then ambush the caravan, free Mercader, take him to a hiding place, and transport him out of Mexico. Several obstacles had derailed the operation. A key meeting between Klarin, Epstein, and Juan Godoy, a taxicab driver and the leader of a group of Mexican KGB agents providing much of the personnel, had not taken place. Other unspecified snags had arisen, and the operation had had to be scrapped.[93]

Epstein's usefulness to the KGB in Mexico also had come to an end. The KGB had discovered that he was being watched in Mexico and that his wife was under surveillance in New York. It decided that his continued presence in Mexico jeopardized the eventual success of the Gnome Project. Epstein left for the United States in May 1944. Nothing more is known of Epstein's activities at the time, but his wife remained in touch with Soviet intelligence into 1945.[94]

After the operation was aborted, on Eitingon's instructions, Klarin decided to disband the combat groups set up to carry out the original escape plan and inaugurated a long and fruitless search for alternatives. Tarasov identified two in a March 29, 1944, cable. The first possibility was to take advantage of relaxed security at the jail on Easter Sunday. An unidentified employee of the prison, with the cover name Kite, would enlist the help of a senior guard to free Mercader. The second option was to rely on a member of the Mexican Department of Justice cover-named Lord.[95]

Neither of these plans succeeded. Klarin departed from Mexico on May 24. In June, Tarasov sent a long message to Moscow describing a new plan using Invention, an agent in the prison who was close to the governor of the state of Hidalgo, Dr. Javier Rojo Gomez. Much of this message was not deciphered, but it appeared to involve a Communist doctor, Esther Chapa, who was then treating Mercader. The message contained a few cryptic references to getaway vehicles. This plan also failed.[96]

The KGB had still not given up hope of freeing Trotsky's assassin. Caridad Mercader surreptitiously entered Mexico in 1945 to look into her son's situation. Moscow ordered "a detailed study of Gnome's hospital [prison] routine and activities, what sort of watch is kept on him by the special agents of the Competitors [Mexican counterintelligence]," and warned that he was so well known that even genuine travel documents might not suffice to get him out of the country through legal checkpoints. Nothing availed; Mercader remained in a Mexican prison until he had finished serving his sentence and was released in 1960. He eventually retired to the Soviet Union on a KGB pension.[97]

Kitty Harris and the KGB in Mexico

Because the Mexican Communist party was small, the KGB found it convenient to seek links to other political forces in the country. The most significant was the powerful labor leader Vicente Lombardo Toledano, president of the Confederación General de Obreros y Campesinos de Mexico, Mexico's largest labor confederation. Toledano was the most prominent pro-Soviet figure in Mexican political life but remained aloof from the Mexican Communist party.

Toledano himself regularly provided political information and resources to the KGB and helped to obtain papers and visas for its agents. Toledano, whose Venona cover name was only partially decrypted (Sh . . .), worked very closely with one of the more fascinating Soviet KGB agents, an American woman named Kitty Harris, who worked for the Comintern and Soviet intelligence on several continents and through several decades. Thanks to the Venona decrypts another portion of her remarkable intelligence career has been uncovered, although some mysteries remain.

Kitty Harris was born in London around the turn of the century to Russian parents and came to the United States with her family by way of Canada. Kitty and several of her brothers and sisters became active Communists in the 1920s. One of Kitty's brothers and two of her brothers-in-law fought in the International Brigades in Spain. Another brother and a sister worked for Amtorg, while a second sister worked for TASS, the Soviet news agency.[98]

Kitty Harris joined the CPUSA in 1923. Soon afterward she became Earl Browder's lover and accompanied him to China in 1928. They lived together in Shanghai, and she assisted his work on behalf of the Pan-Pacific Trade Union Secretariat, a Comintern organization engaged in clandestine labor organizing. At that time she briefly irritated some of her fellow Comintern agents by failing to vacate her residence as quickly as she was ordered to after the Shanghai police got wind of Browder's activity and began hunting for him. Browder and Harris returned separately to the United States in 1929 and went their separate ways: he to the public leadership of the CPUSA, she deeper into the Communist underground. When she tried to renew her passport in 1932, American authorities turned her down; she was deported to Canada (she had never gained official U.S. citizenship) and dropped out of sight. In 1997 a nephew reported that family lore held that she had died while on a mission abroad for the Soviet Union in the 1930s.[99]

Whatever she was doing from 1932 to 1943, Kitty Harris was in Mexico in 1943, living under false papers and acting as a KGB contact with Vicente Toledano. What name she used and what position she occupied are unclear.[100]

Just as she had in China, Harris could display an independent streak in Mexico that exasperated her superiors. One of the projects on which Harris worked was a complicated effort by the KGB to obtain legal American transit documents for a couple, Nicholas and Maria Fisher, cover-named the Pair and the Reef. The mysterious Fishers, assumed to be KGB illegal officers, must have been important agents, because Moscow devoted much money and considerable effort to try to getting them through the United States with valid transit documentation and into Mexico. In Mexico, the KGB worked through Adolfo Orive de Alba, a Mexican politician. Alba was a member of the National Irrigation Commission; in December 1946 he was appointed minister of irrigation. In one message Moscow ordered Tarasov to "set Sh . . . [Toledano] the task through Ada [Harris] of organizing with Okh's [Alba's] help" in obtaining entry and transit visas for the Fishers.[101] Tarasov gave Alba money for his help, but Toledano "forbade him to take the money and explained to us" that it was well known that Alba lived on his salary alone and would not be able to account for a sudden windfall.[102] Michael Burd, the business partner of Robert Menaker, used his connections in Washington and appealed to David Niles, a presidential aide, for assistance in getting the transit visas, at first to no avail but at last successfully. (Burd claimed to have bribed political associates of Niles.) Even Niles's intervention, however, did not end the saga. As late as January 1945, the FBI was still holding up issuance of visas because of questions about how the Fishers had obtained their alleged Swiss citizenship in 1942. A KGB cable explained that the bureau paid careful attention to Mexico because it considered the country "one of the focal points for [KGB] intelligence organizations."[103]

Toledano's reluctance to allow his associate Alba to accept Soviet money was characteristic of his caution in his dealings with Soviet intelligence. Kitty Harris was apparently his only direct liaison with the KGB. When Toledano left for a visit to the United States in April 1944, Tarasov informed Moscow that Harris did not think it advisable, as had been suggested, to put him in touch with another agent. On another occasion, General Fitin instructed Tarasov not to risk meeting Toledano himself but to have him relay his information through Ambassador Umansky, who could meet Toledano in the regular course of his diplomatic duties.[104]

Several other messages indicate that Toledano set strict limits on what he would do for the KGB, limits that sometimes irritated Moscow. One of the major tasks of the Mexico City KGB residency was to "legalize" a number of agents, many of them Spanish refugees, who were being prepared for intelligence assignments in other countries. In one cable, Moscow, eager to obtain papers for someone code-named Patriot, ordered Mexico City to "approach Sh . . . [Toledano] through Ada [Harris]" for help in using Alba to obtain papers.[105] Harris, however, refused to approach Alba because "Sh . . . has forbidden her without his knowledge to approach" anyone. (Toledano was in the United States on a visit at the time.)[106] The implication that its agent deferred to Toledano angered Harris's superiors in Moscow. They quickly fired off a cable ordering Tarasov to tell Harris "that we require our orders to be carried out without any discussion. Explain to her that she receives instructions and tasks only from you and carries them out at your request." Harris was to be ordered once again to obtain the needed papers.[107]

Harris also engaged in incautious behavior that provoked Moscow. She was secretly communicating with members of her family in the United States. Harris underwent operations for appendicitis and removal of a tumor in December 1943. Early in 1944 Moscow learned that, perhaps because of her illness, she was in contact with one of her sisters. The security break was a source of concern to Moscow, which announced that "we absolutely forbid Ada [Harris]" to communicate with her family. Whether owing to her prior loyal work or to humanitarian concern, Moscow finally approved a method by which she could send and receive letters to this sister through secure KGB channels.[108]

It was not her communicating with her family, however, that brought an end to Harris's service for the KGB in Mexico. In June 1944 Tarasov warned Moscow that through carelessness on the part of Toledano and Vasily Zubilin, Alejandro Carrillo, editor of *La Popular* and a deputy in the Mexican Parliament, "has been put in the picture about the work of our illegal, Ada." In response, Moscow issued orders to "carefully work out a new cover-story for her."[109]

Later the KGB decided to end Harris's contact with Toledano. A message from Moscow in May 1945 has a partial sentence that warns "not to let Sh . . . feel a break in liaison"—a suggestion that Harris would no longer be his contact. A later message from Moscow requests ideas on "how she should be used in future and also state how you are thinking of completing or putting through her legalization." The last Venona message referring to Kitty Harris is dated April 28, 1946; Moscow inquired how preparations for her departure from Mexico were progressing. Her destination and fate are not known.[110]

CHAPTER 10

INDUSTRIAL AND ATOMIC ESPIONAGE

Theft of scientific and technical information constituted the earliest and perhaps the most widespread form of Soviet espionage in the United States. It ranged from stealing commercially valuable industrial secrets to penetrating America's most closely guarded military scientific secret, the atomic bomb.

As in other areas, the Soviets relied heavily on ideological sympathy as a lure for industrial spies. Recruitment was assisted by a shift in the demographic makeup of American Communists. In the 1920s the CPUSA's membership consisted largely of first-generation immigrants with limited formal education and little access to leading-edge technology. By the 1930s, however, its membership was mainly native-born, the level of education had increased markedly, and the CPUSA attracted scientifically and technically trained professionals. American Communists regarded the capitalist corporations they worked for as morally illegitimate institutions. Consequently, when Soviet intelligence officers approached and asked that the scientific secrets of these corporations be shared with the Soviet Union, referred to by Communists as "the Great Land of Socialism," few had any moral objections. The willingness of American Communists to turn over the technical secrets of their corporate and government employers further increased when the USSR faced possible defeat by Nazi Germany in World War II. When the homeland of communism was threatened, the "fellowcountrymen," as the KGB referred to American Communists, were eager to help in any way they could.

Harry Gold is an example of a Soviet agent whose espionage career was largely devoted to industrial spying. Arrested and convicted of espionage, he made a full confession of his activities. Gold's parents were Russian Jews. He was born in Switzerland in 1912 and brought to the United States before he was two. After graduation from high school, he worked as a laboratory assistant for Pennsylvania Sugar Company and entered the University of Pennsylvania in 1930. Money difficulties, however, forced him to drop his studies in 1932. Later that year he was also laid off from Pennsylvania Sugar. Entranced by the vision that the USSR had created a just society without unemployment or antisemitism, he considered emigrating to Birobidzhan, an area of the USSR that the Soviets had declared to be an autonomous Jewish region. But a friend and fellow chemist, Thomas Black, found him another job until Pennsylvania Sugar reinstated him.

Black also worked to recruit Gold into the CPUSA, but Gold had found party activities dull and declined formal membership. Black himself dropped out of the CPUSA in 1934 and ceased urging Gold to join. In 1935, however, Black approached Gold again. He explained that he had left the open party to take up secret work for Amtorg, the USSR's foreign trade agency. Black argued that while Gold may have found the CPUSA a dreary organization, as a sympathizer with Communist ideals he owed it to the Soviets to promote their economic success by handing over the scientific secrets of the capitalists to the world's only socialist state. Gold later remarked, "The chance to help strengthen the Soviet Union appeared as such a wonderful opportunity."[1]

Initially, Gold's espionage was confined to stealing the chemical processes developed at the laboratories of Pennsylvania Sugar, but later the Soviets expanded his work by making him their contact with a far-flung network of industrial spies. In his confession Gold described his life as a spy as one of continuous hard work:

> The planning of a meeting with a Soviet agent; the careful preparation for obtaining data from Penn Sugar, the writing of technical reports and the filching of blueprints for copying (and then returning them); the meetings with Paul Smith or Ruga or Fred or Semenov, in New York or Cincinnati . . . the cajoling of Brothman to do work and the outright blackmailing of Ben Smilg for the same purpose; and the many

lies I had to tell at home, and to my friends, to explain my whereabouts during these absences from home (Mom was certain that I was carrying on a series of clandestine love affairs and nothing could have been farther from the truth); the hours of waiting on street corners, waiting dubiously and fearfully in strange towns where I had no business to be, and the uneasy killing of time in cheap movies.[2]

Nonetheless, Gold kept at it, and his KGB controllers became his friends and confidants. When he had doubts about the cause, as he did over the Nazi-Soviet Pact, they assuaged his concerns and assured him that in the end Soviet communism would sweep all before it. By 1942 Gold worked under the direction of Semyon Semenov, a KGB technical and industrial intelligence specialist.[3] Semenov told Gold in 1943 that he, Gold, was being transferred to more important work and someone else would take over his existing sources. Gold was to be used once more as a go-between, but this time on a special project involving highly placed scientists. The chief one was Klaus Fuchs, a Soviet source within the American atomic bomb project.

What the deciphered Venona cables confirm about Gold's involvement in atomic espionage is discussed later in this chapter. Venona, however, also deals with Gold's industrial espionage.[4] One 1944 New York KGB message asked for Moscow's approval of a proposal that its industrial sources report to Gold (cover name Goose and later Arnold) and to Smart, the cover name of an agent who has never been identified. The message also noted that Gold was pressing for an explanation for the delayed delivery of his $100 monthly stipend. A December cable of the same year reported that Gold wanted to set up his own laboratory to work on thermal diffusion of gases and had asked the KGB for a $2,000 subsidy. The New York office, however, thought that Gold had underestimated the capital needed for the laboratory. The KGB declined to provide the subsidy, and Gold went to work for a firm headed by Abraham Brothman.

Gold identified Brothman as one of his chief associates in industrial espionage. He was a chemist who originally started spying for the Soviets when he worked for Republic Steel, supplying blueprints and documents on industrial processes. Among other points, Gold said that Brothman had helped to deliver industrial processes to the USSR for producing synthetic rubber and developing industrial aerosols. Venona has two 1944 KGB messages identifying Brothman, under the cover names Expert and Constructor, as one of Gold's sources. The messages report that Brothman was setting up a new engineering firm after leaving the company where he had been working on synthetic rubber and "the Aerosol problem (the work has partly been sent you)."[5] After Gold confessed in 1950, Brothman and an associate, Miriam Moskowitz, were convicted and jailed for obstruction of justice for lying to a grand jury about these activities.

Gold also identified Alfred Slack, a chemist, as one of his sources of technical espionage. Slack provided information from Eastman Kodak in Rochester, New York, on the recovery of silver from used film and on color photography as well as information on explosives developed at Holston Ordnance Works in Kingsport, Tennessee. After Gold identified him, Slack confessed and received a fifteen-year prison sentence.[6]

Another Soviet agent named by Gold was the man who recruited him into espionage, Thomas Lessing Black. When confronted by the FBI in 1950, Black confirmed Gold's account of his recruitment and admitted to industrial espionage, an activity whose legal status was unclear at that time and rarely prosecuted. He denied, however, any participation in espionage involving government secrets. Given his cooperation in corroborating Gold's testimony and the difficulty of establishing criminality in the case of industrial espionage, Black escaped prosecution.[7]

Black's own story was that he had joined the CPUSA in 1931 and in late 1933 or early 1934 approached Amtorg to inquire about employment opportunities in the USSR. He talked to Gaik Ovakimian, nominally an Amtorg official but actually a KGB officer.[8] Ovakimian told him that before he could be considered for employment in the Soviet Union, he had to prove his worth by supplying technical information. Once he began doing so, however, the KGB kept putting off discussion of his move, and he became caught up in his role as a full-time Soviet agent. On KGB instructions, he dropped out of the CPUSA and worked on industrial espionage.

Black also took on other assignments. The Soviets had him join the American Trotskyist movement around 1937. Black said that at one point his Soviet contact considered sending him to Mexico to attempt to infiltrate Trotsky's Mexican residence, but nothing came of the idea. (The KGB also briefly assigned Harry Gold to anti-Trotskyist work.) In 1940 Joseph Katz became his chief KGB contact. Black claimed that he actually met with Katz only a few times during World War II and that his last meeting was in 1946.[9]

Black is the subject of seven deciphered KGB messages.[10] They show that, probably seeking to avoid prosecution for espionage, he significantly understated his service to the Soviets during World War II. Chiefly, he appears to have worked as go-between for a network of Soviet sources. As far as can be discerned (several of the messages are incompletely deciphered), his sources appear to have engaged in the theft of industrial secrets. One message, however, states that Black had a source at the U.S. Bureau of Standards, which during World War II was deeply involved in high-technology military projects.

Harry Gold was not the only KGB agent who requested KGB funding to set up his own business. Another Soviet industrial source also asked for clandestine Soviet capital. William M. Malisoff was born in Russia and immigrated to the United States at an early age, obtaining citizenship through his father's naturalization. He held a doctorate from Columbia University and ran his own company, United Laboratories in New York. He was also a highly active Soviet source and the subject of nine Venona messages. In 1944 Leonid Kvasnikov, a KGB officer who specialized in scientific-technical espionage, reported to Moscow that he had met with Malisoff twenty times in the preceding year alone.[11]

In mid-1944 Malisoff asked the KGB for a large infusion of capital to add a manufacturing component to his firm. He was turned down, and the New York KGB cabled Moscow that "Anton [Kvasnikov] has informed Talent [Malisoff] of the impossibility of large-scale one-time aid. Just as we expected, Talent took this announcement exceptionally morbidly." The New York KGB noted that in addition to pleading with Kvasnikov, Malisoff had raised the subsidy issue with two of Kvasnikov's predecessors, Mikhail Shalyapin and Ovakimian. The New York KGB said that Malisoff complained "that the materials handed over by him on one question alone—oil, by his estimate had yielded the [Soviet] Union millions during past years and the aid requested by him was trifling." Offended that he had been turned down again, Malisoff threatened that in the future it would be "impossible to expect much help from him." Kvasnikov noted that "one cannot put him into cold storage in this condition, it will look like an attempt to get rid of him altogether." He recommended being patient and continuing contact until Malisoff had calmed down.[12]

While Gold and Malisoff were turned down for capital subsidies, others were not. The KGB set up at least two enterprises in New York using Soviet seed money. One, headed by an agent who had the cover name Odessan, was given a budget of two thousand dollars in KGB funds to purchase a camera, fans, printing press, cash register, studio fittings, shop window fittings, and stock. Another unidentified agent, with the cover name Second Hand Bookseller, was picked to head a second subsidized enterprise. The two enterprises were related in some fashion, and several messages suggest that they were engaged in producing false documents and photographing intelligence material.[13]

In addition to Gold, Brothman, and Black, the deciphered cables name numerous other sources of industrial and scientific intelligence. These included Aleksandr Belenky (a Russian immigrant working at a General Electric plant, who provided material to the KGB through another immigrant), Michael Leshing (superintendent of Twentieth Century Fox film laboratories, who in 1943 provided the Soviets with documents and a formula for color motion pictures and other film-processing technology), Frank Dziedzik (an employee of National Oil Products Company who supplied documents on medical compounds), Herman Jacobson (an employee of the Avery Manufacturing Company), Burton Perry (who gave the KGB the technical particulars of a radar-guided glide bomb), Kenneth Richardson (an employee of World Wide Electronics), Eugene Franklin Coleman (an electrical engineer who worked for Bell Telephone and RCA), Jones Orin York (an aircraft engineer who provided information on both civilian and military aviation design from 1935 to 1944), and Daniel Abraham Zaret (a safety inspector for the U.S. Army's Explosives Division).[14] Aside from sources identified in Venona, two other Soviet technical intelligence sources were Otto Alleman (a chemist who worked for Du Pont) and Arthur Gerald Steinberg (a zoologist who worked for the U.S. Office of Scientific Research and Development).[15]

Venona also provides the cover names of a number of Soviet technical sources whose identity has not been determined. These included Bolt (who provided documents on radio control technology in 1944), Brother (who engaged in aviation-related technical espionage), Oppen (a military industrial source of the New York GRU in 1943), Emulsion (who provided information on the military aircraft industry in 1944), Fisherman (a liaison with subagents involved in industrial espionage), I. (the initial of the name of a New York KGB asset working in industrial espionage, possibly with the oil industry), Serb (who was in contact with Leonid Kvasnikov), Jack (a GRU source who passed information on testing of guided bombs and was a liaison with the CPUSA), Johnny (a GRU source who delivered a 150-page technical report), Octane (active at least from 1943 to 1945 and perhaps as early as 1939), and Karl (who appears to have been engaged in technical espionage for the New York KGB; Karl may have been a member of a covert CPUSA apparatus, inasmuch as the New York KGB asked Moscow about the advisability of its picking up material that Karl had delivered to Earl Browder).[16]

One KGB industrial espionage effort that the FBI partly neutralized involved the military aviation industry in New York State. The United States provided the USSR with thousands of aircraft under the Lend-Lease program during World War II. One of the suppliers was Bell Aircraft, which produced the Bell Airacobra fighter (P-39) that saw extensive use on the eastern front. The Soviet Government Purchasing Commission, the conduit for American Lend-Lease aid, assigned an aviation inspector, Andrey Ivanovich Shevchenko, to the Bell Aircraft plants at Buffalo to approve aircraft before shipment to the USSR. He arrived in the United States in mid-1942 and remained until early 1946.

Trained as an aviation engineer, Shevchenko was a professional KGB officer charged with stealing secrets from the American aviation industry. He recruited and developed a number of sources in Bell Aircraft and in New York aviation plants. (Unlike many of the other Soviet sources, most of those recruited by Shevchenko do not appear to have had any links to the CPUSA.) It is not clear exactly when and how the FBI concluded that Shevchenko was a spy. It may well have been the anonymous August 1943 Russian letter (chapter 2) that caused the FBI to put him under surveillance. This letter named Shevchenko as a KGB officer and identified his place of work (Buffalo) and his cover (the Soviet Government Purchasing Commission). The FBI observed him meeting with Leona and Joseph Franey on July 26, 1944. Leona was chief librarian at Bell Aircraft, while Joseph worked in the rubber section of nearby Hooker Electro-Chemical. The bureau observed a second liaison on July 30, during which Shevchenko met the Franeys on the parkway near Niagara Falls and then took them to a leisurely dinner.

The FBI suspected that Shevchenko was cultivating the Franeys for possible recruitment. The bureau made contact with them in August 1944, and they agreed to assist the U.S. government. They reported that Shevchenko, whom Leona had met the previous November when he first began using the Bell Aircraft library, gave them theater tickets and small gifts, took them out to dinner, and related how social conditions in the USSR were superior to those in the United States. At the FBI's request, the Franeys allowed themselves to be recruited as spies, and in 1949 they testified to a congressional committee about their work as double agents. They stated that the KGB gave them cash bonuses and provided a camera to photograph the secret documents to which Leona had access in the secure section of Bell Aircraft's library. Shevchenko was particularly interested in material on Bell's development of one of the prototype American jet aircraft (the P-59), technical questions about jet engine design, and design problems with the innovative swept-back wing. Of course, the material the Franeys furnished was reviewed and sanitized by the FBI.[17]

The Venona Project eventually deciphered five KGB cables about Shevchenko and the Franeys.[18] The earliest, dated July 4, 1944, noted that Shevchenko had been cultivating Leona with small presents and wanted sanction to attempt recruitment. Both that cable and one on July 25 state that even prior to formal recruitment Leona had been persuaded to hand over one batch of secret material on jet aircraft development. This was before the FBI contacted the Franeys in August and puts a slightly different light on their subsequent role as double agents. It may indeed have been based on a patriotic desire to help the U.S. government, but their realization that they were already implicated in espionage may have encouraged cooperation.

The FBI also interviewed another potential Shevchenko recruit, Loren Haas, a Bell engineer who assisted in the technical training of Soviet personnel. Haas agreed to assist the FBI and allowed Shevchenko to recruit him. As with the Franeys, Shevchenko provided Haas with a camera to assist his espionage. One late 1944 Venona message notes that Haas had turned over to Shevchenko detailed drawings of a jet engine under development. Haas left Bell in 1945 to take a position with Westinghouse, soon to become a major producer of jet aircraft engines. Shevchenko renewed contact with Haas when he was at Westinghouse, and he continued to function as a double agent for the FBI.[19]

There is no indication in the twenty-nine deciphered Venona messages mentioning Shevchenko that the KGB ever suspected that he was under surveillance or that three of his sources were FBI counterintelligence contacts. The FBI wanted to arrest and either try or expel Shevchenko, but to its frustration the State Department objected that such action might upset Soviet-American relations. Shevchenko was allowed to continue his espionage, and the bureau had to content itself with neutralizing his activities to the extent it could.[20]

Aside from the Franeys and Haas (all working for American counterintelligence), Venona shows that Shevchenko's other sources included Aleksandr Petroff (an employee of Curtiss-Wright Aircraft Corporation who provided information on aircraft production methods), William Pinsly (also a employee of Curtiss-Wright), and William Plourde (an engineer with Bell Aircraft). In addition, Venona gives five cover names of unidentified Shevchenko sources: Spline, Splint, Bugle, Armor, and someone whose first initial was B.[21] Armor was clearly a source at Bell Aircraft. B. worked at Republic Aviation and provided information on research on the American equivalent of the German V-1, the first practical cruise missile. It is not clear which aircraft companies employed the other three sources.

Julius Rosenberg's Network of Communist Engineers

Julius Rosenberg is best known for his role in Soviet atomic espionage. But he was more important to the KGB as a source of nonatomic technical intelligence than for his role in stealing American atomic bomb secrets. Rosenberg had been an engineering student at the College of the City of New York (CCNY) in the late 1930s, one of the central figures of a close group of engineering students who were members of the Young Communist League. He later recruited many of them into Soviet espionage.[22]

Elizabeth Bentley told the FBI that in 1942 someone named Julius had contacted Jacob Golos to offer the services of a group of engineers to the Soviet cause. Golos handled them initially but in 1943 turned them over to the KGB. Bentley did not know Julius's family name, his address, or where he worked, and it would take the FBI five years to figure it out, but Bentley's physical description fit Julius Rosenberg precisely. How did Rosenberg know to contact Golos? One fellow Communist engineer later told the FBI that Rosenberg had simply kept approaching CPUSA officials until he found one who referred him to the right person.[23]

Twenty-one deciphered KGB cables, all from 1944 and 1945, discuss Julius Rosenberg. The first, from May 5, 1944, and the second, from May 22, 1944, show that the Rosenberg apparatus was already well in operation by that time. In the first, the New York KGB asked

Moscow to "carry out a check and sanction the recruitment of Alfred Sarant," provided a brief description of Sarant's background, and noted that he "is a lead of Antenna"—Rosenberg's cover name.[24] In the second, the New York KGB told Moscow that in view of the volume involved and in light of periodic FBI surveillance of official Soviet offices, it had concluded that its officers' practice of bringing stolen documents to the Soviet consulate for filming ought to be changed. The New York office reported that it was arranging for several officers to get cameras and to film at their own apartments the material that their sources brought. But in addition to decentralizing filming, "we consider it necessary to organize the filming of Antenna's Probationers' [agents'] materials by Antenna himself."[25] The two messages show that Julius Rosenberg's network was well established and produced enough material to justify its own filming operation. The KGB trusted Rosenberg sufficiently to assign the filming to him and to accept and pass on to Moscow his recommendation for a new agent.

A KGB message of July 26, 1944, deciphered by the Venona Project in 1950, allowed the identification of Julius Rosenberg as the man behind the cover name Antenna. In this message the New York KGB reported that Antenna had been to Washington to explore recruitment of a new source. The cable named the candidate for recruitment in plain text as Max Elitcher and described him as a old friend of Antenna's, an electrical engineering graduate of CCNY, and added that both Elitcher and his wife were Communists. It noted that Mrs. Elitcher worked for the War Department and that Elitcher himself headed a section of the U.S. Bureau of Standards working on a fire control system for heavy naval guns. Antenna said of Elitcher that "he has access to extremely valuable materials."[26]

When the NSA's cryptanalysts deciphered this message, neither the NSA nor the FBI knew who Antenna was. But Elitcher was a different matter. His name appeared in clear text. The government had already had its suspicions about his loyalty. The Office of Naval Intelligence had noted in 1941 that Elitcher and his friend Morton Sobell had attended a rally of the American Peace Mobilization, a CPUSA front. Naval intelligence investigated, but Elitcher denied any Communist links and the matter was dropped.

Elitcher, however, had been a party member and had participated in a secret caucus of Communists employed by the Navy Department and the Bureau of Standards. Armed with what it had learned from Venona, the FBI confronted Elitcher in 1950, and he broke. He admitted that he had been a Communist and said that in the summer of 1944 his old friend Julius Rosenberg had visited him in Washington and asked him to spy for the Soviet Union. Elitcher said that he had declined to make a decision at the time, and Rosenberg had repeated his recruitment appeal six or eight times between the years 1944 and 1948. He also said that Morton Sobell, another engineering colleague, was already a member of Rosenberg's network. Elitcher related how he had accompanied Sobell to a rendezvous in New York when Sobell furtively dropped off film to Julius Rosenberg. Sobell worked at the time for Reeves Electronic, which held U.S. government contracts for secret military research. It is another illustration of the laxness of American internal security practices in the 1940s that Sobell, whom Naval Intelligence had marked as a supporter of the American Peace Mobilization, who had worked as a counselor at a Communist youth camp, and whose admiration for Stalin was hardly camouflaged, received a security clearance to work on American defense contracts as late as 1949.

In 1997 Aleksandr Feklisov, one of the KGB officers who supervised Rosenberg's espionage apparatus, assessed Alfred Sarant and Joel Barr as among the most productive sources of the group.[27] Both were among Rosenberg's circle of young Communist engineers: Barr had been at CCNY with Rosenberg, while Sarant got his training at Cooper Union, also in New York City. The two electrical engineers were close friends and shared an apartment during part of their espionage career. During World War II, both also worked on military radar at the U.S. Army Signal Corps laboratories at Fort Monmouth, New Jersey. Barr lost his job at Fort Monmouth in 1942 when Army counterintelligence came across evidence of his Communist allegiance. But because concern about Communist espionage in that period was so uneven, Barr had no difficulty getting a job with Western Electric for a project developing the highly secret radar bombsight. Sarant also lost his position with the Signal Corps, but because of disruptive union activity rather than out of concern about his Communist leanings. He, too, then moved on to Western Electric to continue his work on radar.

There are seven deciphered KGB messages about Barr and four about Sarant. The KGB treated them as a team, and often both were discussed in the same cable. The first deciphered message about either is that of May 5, 1944, which discussed the recruitment of Sarant, who had not yet been assigned a cover name. The other messages, however, use their cover names. (Sarant was Hughes, and Barr had the cover name Scout, later changed to Meter.)[28]

The New York KGB reported to Moscow on November 14, 1944, that Julius Rosenberg "has safely carried through the contracting of Hughes [Sarant]," who, it noted, was a good friend of Meter [Barr]. "Contracting" was Sarant's formal recruitment as an active agent. The New York KGB proposed "to pair them off and get them to photograph their own materials having [been] given a camera for this purpose. Hughes [Sarant] is a good photographer, has a large darkroom and all the equipment but he does not have a Leica."[29] Later, when the FBI interviewed Sarant, he confirmed that he was an amateur photographer and had equipped one room in his apartment as a darkroom. He also said that Barr, his roommate, shared an enthusiasm for photography. He stated that Barr eventually obtained a Leica, but that he (Sarant) owned a less sophisticated camera.

The KGB cable went on to say that Rosenberg would pick up the film from the two and deliver it to the KGB. In addition, it pointed out that although Rosenberg was the chief link with Sarant and Barr, the two had also met with Harry Gold, another frequent intermediary between the KGB and its technical spies. Film of technical documents that the two stole was forwarded to Moscow for evaluation and use and was not usually commented on by the New York office. In one message, however, the New York KGB boasted that Hughes [Sarant] had just "handed over 17 authentic drawings relating to the APQ-7."[30] The APQ-7 was an advanced and secret airborne radar system jointly developed for the U.S. military by the Massachusetts Institute of Technology and Western Electric.

After World War II Sarant and Barr set up an engineering firm (Sarant Laboratories) that sought U.S. defense contracts, but it failed to prosper, and they went their separate ways. In 1946 Sarant moved to Ithaca, New York, where he worked in the physics laboratories at Cornell University and lived in a house next to Philip Morrison, a Cornell physicist and former Manhattan Project scientist who was a personal and political friend. (Morrison joined the Young Communist League in 1938 and the American Communist party in 1939 or 1940 while studying physics at the University of California, Berkeley.)[31] Barr worked on secret military radar systems for Sperry Gyroscope in late 1946, but lost his job a year later when the Air Force denied him a security clearance. He moved to Europe in 1948 to continued his graduate engineering studies.

The FBI arrested Harry Gold in late May 1950. The next month it arrested David Greenglass, Julius Rosenberg's brother-in-law. Joel Barr, living in Paris, disappeared around the same time. He told no one of plans to leave, and he abandoned his apartment without taking his clothes and other personal possessions. The FBI arrested Julius Rosenberg on July 17. Two days later, the bureau interviewed Alfred Sarant. Unsure of Sarant's role, the FBI did not arrest him but did warn him that he was the subject of an investigation and should notify the bureau of travel plans. Sarant told the FBI on July 25 that he was driving to Long Island for a week's vacation with relatives. Once there, however, he was joined by Carolyn Dayton, an Ithaca neighbor with whom he was romantically involved. With the help of his relatives Sarant evaded FBI surveillance, and the two took off on what he told his relatives was a cross-country vacation. In mid-August they entered Mexico (Sarant used the name of Carol's husband when crossing the border) and vanished. Both abandoned their spouses and children.

Nothing more was known of Sarant and Barr until 1983, when Mark Kuchment, a Russian émigré at Harvard University's Russian Research Center, read about Sarant and Barr in *The Rosenberg File* and linked them to two leading Soviet scientists who were native speakers of English. One, Joseph Berg, claimed to be a South African; the other, Philip Georgievich Staros, claimed to be of Canadian background. Later, another Russian immigrant scientist identified a photograph of Sarant as the man he had known in the USSR as Staros. (Staros/Sarant died of a heart attack in the the Soviet Union in 1979.)

Carolyn Dayton, who had had the name Anna Staros in the USSR, returned to the United States in 1991, and Barr came back in 1992. Only then did the rest of the story emerge. After reaching Mexico in 1950, Sarant and Dayton, fearing FBI surveillance, had avoided the Soviet embassy and reached the Soviets through the Polish embassy, had crossed over to Guatemala, and then had flown to Communist Poland. After six months in Warsaw, they traveled on to Moscow, where they caught up with Barr, who had arrived in the USSR via Czechoslovakia. Soviet intelligence gave them new identities as Joseph Berg and Philip Staros and set them up as electrical engineers in Communist Czechoslovakia. Sarant and Dayton, although never officially married, lived as the Staroses; Barr/Berg married a Czech woman.

In 1956 the Soviets transferred Sarant and Barr to Leningrad, put them at the head of a military electronics research institute, and provided them with the benefits of membership in the Soviet elite: government cars, large apartments, and substantial salaries. They were credited with founding the Soviet microelectronics industry, and Barr claimed that they created the first Soviet radar-guided anti-aircraft artillery and surface-to-air missiles, weapons that proved highly effective against American aircraft in the Vietnam War. Sarant was admitted to the Communist Party of the Soviet Union and in 1969 was awarded a state prize for his contributions to Soviet science.

After returning to the United States in 1992, Barr denied any participation in Soviet espionage, as did Dayton on Sarant's behalf. Both insisted that their covert flights to the USSR had been motivated by fear of American anticommunism. Despite these protestations of innocence, the deciphered Venona messages, along with other accumulated evidence, show that Barr and Sarant were among the KGB's most valuable technical spies.[32]

Morton Sobell also tried to disappear but did not succeed. At the same time Barr vanished in Paris, Sobell, who was working at Reeves Electronics, asked for leave, claiming a medical emergency. He hastily settled his private affairs and flew to Mexico with his family. Once there, he tried to make arrangements to reach the Soviet bloc but was hampered because he had not had time to obtain American passports. (Passports had not been needed to enter Mexico.) Before he could travel farther, Mexican police picked him up and delivered him to the U.S. border, where American authorities arrested him. Tried for espionage, he was convicted and sentenced to thirty years in prison.

Another member of the Rosenberg network, William Perl, was warned but, hoping to bluff it out, chose not to flee. He almost succeeded. Perl was a brilliant and highly placed aeronautical scientist who had taken part in a series of highly secret American military projects since the early 1940s. Another one of Rosenberg's engineer acquaintances, he had graduated from CCNY in 1940. His talent immediately earned him a position with the National Advisory Committee for Aeronautics, predecessor to the National Aeronautics and Space Administration. He worked first at Langley Field, Virginia, then at the Lewis Flight Propulsion Laboratory in Cleveland, Ohio. The National Advisory Committee for Aeronautics sent him to Columbia University in 1946 for doctoral work with Theodore von Karman, then chairman of the Air Force Scientific Advisory Board. In 1948 Perl was back at the Lewis Flight Propulsion Laboratory, where he supervised a fifteen-person group studying jet propulsion and supersonic flight. In 1950, when the FBI first began to understand the extent of Rosenberg's apparatus, Perl was under consideration for an appointment to a sensitive scientific post with the Atomic Energy Commission.

Perl did not get the appointment. Instead, on July 20, 1950, he got an interview with the FBI, who asked questions about his subletting of Sarant's New York City apartment several years earlier. At that point the FBI was interested only in what Perl might know about Sarant, Barr, and Julius Rosenberg. It did not suspect Perl of espionage, but Perl thought the FBI was toying with him. He approached the FBI on July 24 and told agents about a visit the previous day from Vivian Glassman, a visit he evidently thought the FBI had observed. (It had not; he was not even under surveillance.) He explained that he had known Glassman as Joel Barr's fiancée. He said she had acted strangely, chatted about trivial matters, mentioned Julius Rosenberg, and given him a sheet of paper. She had then urged him to leave the United States at once; the paper provided directions for fleeing to Mexico and offered two thousand dollars if he would go immediately. Perl told the FBI that he had no idea what any of this was about and had rejected all of Glassman's suggestions.

The FBI interviewed Vivian Glassman, and she presented herself as an innocent bystander. She said that a man whose identity she didn't know had persuaded her to go to Cleveland and offer Perl two thousand dollars to go to Mexico for an unknown purpose. After Perl had refused to take the money, she had traveled back to New York and returned the money to the unknown man, accepting no payment or reimbursement for her expenses. This was not very believable, but neither was it the sort of evidence that would convince a jury to send Glassman or Perl to prison. Perl, however, overstepped himself when called before a federal grand jury. Under oath he denied that he had ever known Julius Rosenberg or Morton Sobell. The government easily established that his statements were lies. Considering the government's unwillingness to expose Venona in court, had Perl admitted to knowing Rosenberg and Sobell, it is doubtful that charges would have been brought against him. His lies, however, resulted in a perjury indictment. Perl was convicted and sent to prison in 1953.

The Venona Project deciphered fourteen KGB cables that refer to William Perl.[33] They show that he was a productive and highly valuable source of secret technical information. Chronologically, the first, a New

York KGB report of May 10, 1944, referred to information Perl provided on a long-distance fighter under development by Vultee Aircraft and on a prototype American jet aircraft. Ten days later he provided information on the jet engine under development by Westinghouse. The New York KGB told Moscow in July 1944 that it had forwarded Perl's reports on the work of the National Advisory Committee for Aeronautics by diplomatic pouch. In September the New York KGB told Moscow that Perl thus far had received reimbursement only for the extra expenses incurred in his espionage work, but that it felt his productivity merited a bonus of five hundred dollars, similar to that granted other veteran sources of Rosenberg's network.

Moscow agreed to the bonus, and with good reason. In February the Moscow KGB told the New York KGB that evaluators had judged Perl's material to be "highly valuable."[34] In April some of his latest material was called "valuable" and the rest "highly valuable."[35] The FBI later determined that Perl had gained access to numerous files on advanced military aircraft research which did not appear to have relevance to his own research. On one special trip in 1948 from Cleveland to Columbia University, he removed classified files on the development of jet turbine–powered helicopters and the results of expensive wind-tunnel tests of prototype aircraft and airfoil designs.[36] Perl's position allowed him to deliver to the Soviets some of the most advanced aeronautical research undertaken by the United States, particularly in the development of high-performance military jet aircraft.

The New York KGB told Moscow in November 1944 that Perl's information was both valuable and ample enough to warrant sending a liaison team to Cleveland dedicated to handling Perl's intelligence information. Julius Rosenberg recommended Michael and Ann Sidorovich. The New York KGB concurred and told Moscow that Rosenberg had described Michael Sidorovich as follows: "Fellow Countryman [CPUSA member], was volunteer in Spain, lives in Western NY, no political work last three years, Liberal [Rosenberg] known him since childhood, including his political work, says he and wife are devoted. Wife is dressmaker who can open a shop in city for cover. . . . Liberal says Linza [Michael Sidorovich] ready to renew contact with us."[37]

The New York KGB also asked Moscow to arrange for the KGB station in Mexico to provide Leica film cassettes, in short supply in the

United States, both for the Rosenberg apparatus in New York City and for Sidorovich in Cleveland. It also reported in December that the Sidoroviches had sold their New York home and moved to Cleveland. They had received a $500 bonus for undertaking the liaison job, and Rosenberg was traveling to Cleveland to arrange an introductory meeting between Perl and the Sidoroviches. When the FBI later investigated the Rosenberg network, it found that the Sidoroviches owned a Leica and in 1945 had paid for an automobile in cash without having to withdraw any funds from their bank account.[38]

The Moscow KGB headquarters sanctioned a New York KGB plan in March 1945 to make more extensive use of Ann Sidorovich and pay her a monthly stipend of fifty dollars. Like her husband, she also had an background in the American Communist movement. She was the daughter of Mikhail Tkach, editor of the CPUSA's Ukrainian-language newspaper and himself a KGB asset, who reported on Ukrainian immigrants and functioned as an intermediary with several KGB sources.

The Rosenberg network was a large one. It included six sources: Barr, Perl, Sarant, Sobell, David Greenglass, and an unidentified source with the cover name Nile.[39] In addition to these sources, the network maintained two active liaison-couriers, Michael and Ann Sidorovich, and three others who carried out support work: Vivian Glassman, Ruth Greenglass, and Ethel Rosenberg.

In addition to running the network, Julius Rosenberg was also a source in his own right. For much of the war Rosenberg worked as a engineering inspector for the Army Signal Corps, checking on electronic equipment and projects under contract to the Signal Corps. This job gave him access to a wide array of secret American military technology. Army counterintelligence, however, came across evidence of his Communist loyalties in 1944 and forced him out. But as with Joel Barr, the hit-or-miss quality of American security procedures allowed Rosenberg to quickly find another job at Emerson Radio working on classified military projects. There he achieved a singular espionage coup, stealing a working sample of the proximity fuse, one of the most innovative advances of American military technology in World War II.[40] There is no doubting the value the Soviets saw in Rosenberg. Moscow ordered its New York office to award him a $1,000 bonus in March 1945 in recognition of his achievements and authorized smaller sums for his agents.[41]

Giving Stalin the Bomb

Even before the 1995 release of the Venona cables, several books reported rumors that deciphered Soviet cables had played a critical role in uncovering atomic spies.[42] Not only were the rumors true, but the decryptions exposed several theretofore-unknown Soviet agents responsible for the remarkable success of the USSR's atomic bomb program.

Klaus Fuchs and Harry Gold

The British began their atomic bomb program before the United States, and the Soviets quickly developed a key source within the project. One of the scientists enlisted to work on the British bomb project was a naturalized British subject and brilliant young physicist named Klaus Fuchs. A refugee from Nazi Germany, Fuchs had also been a member of the German Communist party. After he joined the British atomic project in 1941, Fuchs contacted a refugee German Communist leader, Jürgen Kuczynski, and offered to spy for the Soviets. Kuczynski put Fuchs in touch with a contact at the Soviet embassy, and Fuchs was soon reporting the secrets of the British bomb project to the GRU through Ursula Kuczynski (Jürgen's sister). After America entered the war, the British threw their resources into the U.S. bomb program, whose immense industrial capacities would be more likely to develop a practical atomic weapon swiftly.[43]

Fuchs arrived in the United States in late 1943, part of a contingent of fifteen British scientists augmenting the Manhattan Project. (By this point the KGB had also taken over control of Fuchs from the GRU.) Initially he worked with a Manhattan Project team at Columbia University, which was experimenting with uranium separation through gaseous diffusion.

Uranium in its natural state consists of two isotopes, U-235 and U-238. U-235 is highly radioactive and better suited for achieving an atomic explosion, but it accounts for less than 1 percent of natural uranium. The two isotopes are chemically identical, so their physical separation is difficult and constituted one of the major technical barriers to building an atomic bomb. The Manhattan Project developed several separation methods. One of them, gaseous diffusion, converted solid uranium into a gas and then pumped it through a porous screen through which the lighter U-235 isotope would diffuse faster than (and thus be separated from) the heavier U-238. The physics of the procedure was complex, and in that day many scientists thought the process impractical.

After his work on gaseous diffusion, Fuchs was transferred in August 1944 to Los Alamos, the top-secret heart of the U.S. atomic bomb project, to join its theoretical division. He continued working at Los Alamos until mid-1946, when he returned to England as one of the leaders of the once-again-independent British atomic bomb program. He also continued his work as a spy for the Soviet Union.

In late 1948 the FBI turned over to its British counterparts the Venona decryptions and the supporting evidence that Fuchs was a Soviet agent.[44] The British were convinced. In December officers of MI5 began to question Fuchs. Under interrogation, he collapsed quickly and began his confession on January 24, 1950, which led to his trial and conviction on charges of espionage. Released in 1959 after serving nine years of a fourteen-year sentence, Fuchs moved to Communist East Germany, where he became director of a nuclear research institute.

Because he did confess, the Venona cables serve primarily to confirm and enrich the story Fuchs told. They also corroborate the confession of Harry Gold, the American who was the chief link between Fuchs and the KGB. Gold first appears in the Venona cables in 1944 in connection with his work as the liaison with Fuchs. As noted earlier, Gould had been working as an industrial spy for the Soviets for nine years. On the basis of information from Fuchs's confession and on decrypted Venona cables, the FBI confronted Gold in 1950 and found ample evidence in his house of his long work as a Soviet agent. Like Fuchs, Gold easily broke and confessed. He received a thirty-year sentence for his crimes and served sixteen years before receiving a parole in 1966.

A February 1944 New York KGB message told Moscow that Fuchs, who had arrived in the United States in December 1943, and Gold had firmly established their relationship. Fuchs, the cable said, had turned over information about the organization of the U.S. atomic project and work on uranium separation, both gaseous diffusion and an alternative method, electromagnetic separation, developed at the University of California Radiation Laboratory at Berkeley. Other KGB messages report that Fuchs delivered information on the progress of the project and more technical details about gaseous diffusion. The New York KGB was so pleased by the quality of his information that it planned to give Fuchs a $500 bonus.

In August, however, the New York KGB reported that Fuchs had failed to show up for several meetings with Gold. Initially the KGB thought that Fuchs might have returned to Britain, but it sent Gold to see Fuchs's sister, who lived near Boston, and find out what had happened to him. Gold learned that Fuchs had been transferred to Los Alamos, where tight security had cut him off from his KGB links. Fuchs was able to phone his sister, however, while on a business trip to Chicago. Informed of Gold's inquiries, Fuchs told his sister to tell Gold that when he got leave from Los Alamos at Christmas he would reestablish contact. Once he did, Fuchs continued his espionage, this time from Los Alamos itself.[45]

Fuchs's transfer to Los Alamos increased the range of secrets he turned over to the Soviets. In addition to his long-standing work on uranium separation, he now gained access to work on the development of plutonium as an alternative to uranium U-235 as a bomb fuel and on the implosion mechanism as a way to detonate plutonium.

The Manhattan Project developed two different types of atomic bombs. The first, dropped on Hiroshima, was a pure uranium bomb with a "gun-type" detonator. The second, dropped on Nagasaki, was a plutonium bomb with an implosion detonator. In the first type, a small amount of U-235 is fired down a barrel at tremendous speed to hit another piece of uranium. The collision sets off a fission chain reaction that produces an atomic explosion. One of the difficulties with this type of atomic bomb is that it depends on the rare U-235 isotope, and the separation methods required the expenditure of tremendous industrial resources.

In the face of the daunting problem of obtaining enough U-235, the Manhattan Project developed an alternative. A team of Berkeley scientists in 1941 used a cyclotron to create (transmute) a new element that did not exist in nature: plutonium. Plutonium, they discovered, was more fissionable than U-235 and could be created in quantity in a nuclear reactor. This greatly reduced (although it did not eliminate) the need for laborious uranium separation.

A practical plutonium bomb, however, required a different method of detonation. Plutonium was so unstable that in a gun-type bomb system plutonium would began a premature chain reaction before the two pieces of plutonium were fully fused. A premature chain reaction would destroy the rest of the plutonium before it could be affected, thus producing a small nuclear explosion (a "fizzle") rather than a city-destroying blast. The solution worked out was implosion. An explosive sphere is shaped around a central core of plutonium. The sphere is then set off by a system of detonators that essentially allow all parts of the sphere to explode simultaneously. The result is that the core of plutonium is squeezed from all directions at the same time by a uniform force, and simultaneously all parts of the squeezed plutonium core undergo fission.

Fuchs's assignment to the theoretical division at Los Alamos gave him access to information on the plutonium bomb and use of implosion in a detonation device. Given Fuchs's position at Los Alamos, it is no surprise that messages from the Moscow KGB show intense interest in Fuchs and his work. Indeed, the messages from Moscow to the New York KGB attest not only that the KGB received the information but also that it quickly turned the information over to Soviet scientists working on an atomic bomb, because Moscow sent technical follow-up questions with instructions that the queries be passed to Fuchs and other Soviet sources inside the Manhattan Project.

Fuchs's confession in Britain led the FBI to Harry Gold in the United States. Gold's confession, in turn, uncovered other Soviet agents. The credibility of Gold's confession has been harshly attacked by those who refuse to believe that there was significant Soviet espionage in the United States. The Venona cables, however, offer independent confirmation of many points Gold made.

Greenglass and the Rosenbergs

Harry Gold's confession did more than corroborate Klaus Fuchs's story. Although most of his trips to New Mexico had been to get material from Fuchs, on one trip he picked up documents from another Soviet source at Los Alamos, whom he described, in the words of his FBI interrogators, as "a soldier, non-commissioned, married, no children (name not recalled.)"[46] Gold's description quickly led the FBI to Sgt. David Greenglass, a machinist working at one of Los Alamos's secret laboratories. Greenglass confessed to espionage and also implicated his wife, Ruth, and his brother-in-law, Julius Rosenberg. Ruth Greenglass also confessed, corroborating David's testimony that Julius Rosenberg had recruited David as a Soviet source. Under further interrogation, the Greenglasses implicated David's sister Ethel (Julius's wife) in espionage. Simultaneously the FBI was comparing the decrypted Venona cables containing their cover names with the confessions of Fuchs, Gold, and the Greenglasses and with the results of their investigative work. Fuchs, it had been determined earlier, had the cover names Rest and Charles, while Harry Gold was known as Goose and Arnold in the Venona traffic. By the latter half of June, the FBI and the NSA had identified the cover names Antenna and Liberal as Julius Rosenberg, Caliber as David Greenglass, and Osa as Ruth Greenglass.[47]

David and Ruth Greenglass were both fervent Communists who had joined the Young Communist League as teenagers. David had ambitions to become a scientist, but the need for a job forced him to drop out of Brooklyn Polytechnic Institute after only one semester. Just a few months after his marriage in late 1942 he was drafted. After he entered the Army, the young soldier's letters to his bride mixed declarations of love and longing with equally ardent profession of loyalty to Marxism-Leninism. One letter declared, "Victory shall be ours and the future is socialism's." Another looked to the end of the war when "we will be together to build—under socialism—our future." In yet another David wrote of his proselytizing for communism among his fellow soldiers: "Darling, we who understand can bring understanding to others because we are in love and have our Marxist outlook." And in a June 1944 letter he reconciled his Communist faith with the violence of the Soviet regime: "Darling, I have been reading a lot of books on the Soviet Union. Dear, I can see how farsighted and intelligent those leaders are. They are really geniuses, everyone of them. . . . I have come to a stronger and more resolute faith in and belief in the principles of Socialism and Communism. I believe that every time the Soviet Government used force they did so with pain in their hearts and the belief that what they were doing was to produce good for the greatest number. . . . More power to the Soviet Union and a fruitful and abundant life for their peoples."[48]

At the time David Greenglass wrote this last letter, he was a skilled machinist in an Army ordnance unit that was preparing to go overseas. But he was unexpectedly transferred to work on a secret project. By August he was in Los Alamos and assigned to work in a facility that made models of the high-technology bomb parts being tested by various scientific teams; specifically he worked on models of the implosion detonators being developed for the plutonium bomb.[49]

Through phone calls and letters David let Ruth know something about what he was working on. She, in turn, informed David's older sister, Ethel Rosenberg, and her husband, Julius. Although they did not know the details, both of the Greenglasses were aware that Julius was involved in secret work with concealed Communist engineers who worked in defense plants. Julius immediately understood the importance of the project on which David was working. He quickly reported this to the KGB. A September 1944 cable from the New York KGB states: "Liberal [Rosenberg] recommended the wife of his wife's brother, Ruth Greenglass, with a safe flat in view. She is 21 years old, a Townswoman [U.S. citizen], Gymnast [Young Communist]. Liberal and wife recommend her as an intelligent and clever girl. . . . Ruth learned that her husband was called up by the army but he was not sent to the front. He is a mechanical engineer and is now working at the Enormous [atomic bomb project] plant in Santa Fe, New Mexico."[50]

The Rosenbergs suggested to the Greenglasses that David should put the knowledge he was gaining in the service of the Soviet Union. David worked under secure conditions at Los Alamos, so in the initial approach guarded language was used in phone calls and letters. Nevertheless, in early November 1944 David wrote a letter to Ruth in which he said plainly that he would "most certainly will be glad to be part of the community project that Julius and his friends have in mind."[51]

Shortly afterward, David got five days of leave, and Ruth prepared to visit him in Santa Fe, the city nearest to the secret Los Alamos facility. She testified that she had dinner with the Rosenbergs just before she left. Julius and Ethel both pushed her to press David to take part in Julius's plan for espionage. According to those who believe the Rosenbergs to be innocent, Ruth's testimony was phony and there had been no such discussion. Among the Venona cables, however, there is a KGB message dated November 14, 1944, and devoted entirely to the work of Julius Rosenberg. Among other matters, it reported that Ruth Greenglass had agreed to assist in "drawing in" David, and that Julius would brief her before she left for New Mexico.[52]

As for Ethel's role, the same September KGB cable that first noted the contact with Ruth Greenglass stated that Ethel had recommended recruitment of her sister-in-law. Both Greenglasses later testified that Ethel was fully aware of Julius's espionage work and assisted him by typing some material. The only other deciphered reference to Ethel in the Venona cables came in November 1944, when the New York KGB responded to a Moscow headquarters inquiry about her: "Information on Liberal's wife. Surname that of her husband, first name Ethel, 29 years old. Married five years. Finished secondary school. A Fellow-countryman [CPUSA member] since 1938. Sufficiently well developed politically. Knows about her husband's work and the role of Meter [Joel Barr] and Nil [unidentified agent]. In view of delicate health does not work. Is characterized positively and as a devoted person."[53]

A December 13 KGB cable stated that the New York office had decided to designate Julius Rosenberg as the liaison with the Green-glasses rather than to shift them to another KGB link. A few days later, on December 16, a triumphant New York KGB reported that Ruth had returned from Sante Fe with the news that David had agreed to become a Soviet source and that he anticipated additional leave and would be visiting New York soon. The cable noted that Julius Rosenberg felt technically inadequate to ask the right scientific questions and wanted assistance in debriefing David during his visit. Finally, in a January 1945 Venona cable, the New York KGB reported that while David Green-glass had been on leave in New York, his recruitment had been completed and arrangements for delivery of material made. He had also given an initial report on his implosion detonator work. All this information matches the later testimony of both David and Ruth Greenglass.

The Venona cables greatly assisted the FBI's investigation by providing a documentary basis against which interrogators could check Fuchs's, Gold's, and Greenglass's confessions and the statements made by others. It provided leads for follow-up questions and the tracking down of additional witnesses. Because of the policy decision not to reveal the Venona secret, prosecutors could not use the cables as evidence in court. Nonetheless, they provided the FBI and other Justice Department officials with the sure knowledge that they were prosecuting the right people.

Initially, the FBI's investigation gave promise of being a classic case of "rolling up" a network link by link. First Fuchs was identified, and he confessed. His confession led to Gold, and Gold's confession led to David Greenglass. Greenglass then confessed, followed swiftly by his wife Ruth. But there it ended. The next link in the chain was Julius Rosenberg, and he refused to admit anything. So did Ethel.

The government charged Julius and Ethel Rosenberg with espionage. They were swiftly convicted, even without use of the deciphered Venona cables. The eyewitness testimony of David and Ruth Greenglass, the eyewitness testimony of Max Elitcher, the corroborative testimony of Harry Gold, and an impressive array of supporting evidence led to a quick conviction. David Greenglass was sentenced to fifteen years in prison. In view of her cooperation and that of her husband, Ruth Greenglass escaped prosecution. Morton Sobell was tried with the Rosenbergs and also refused to confess, but Elitcher's testimony and his flight to Mexico led to Sobell's conviction and to a term of thirty years.

The stonewalling by the Rosenbergs and Sobell took its toll, however, on the ability of the government to prosecute additional members of the Rosenberg network. William Perl was convicted, but only of perjury rather than of espionage. Barr and Sarant secretly fled to the USSR and avoided arrest. Others suffered nothing more than exclusion from employment by the government or by firms doing defense work.

The government asked for and got the death penalty for the Rosenbergs, and they were executed on June 19, 1953. It appears that government authorities, hoping to use the death sentences as leverage to obtain their confessions and roll up other parts of the Soviet espionage apparatus, did not expect to carry out the executions. But the Rosenbergs were Communist true believers and refused to confess.

The deciphered KGB messages of the Venona Project do more than confirm the participation of Fuchs, Greenglass, and Rosenberg in Soviet atomic espionage. They also show that the Soviet Union's intelligence services had at least three additional sources within the Manhattan Project.

Quantum: The Unidentified Atomic Spy of 1943

The New York KGB reported in a message of June 21, 1943, that a source, given the cover name Quantum, had met with Soviet officers in Washington a week earlier, on June 14.[54] The message is only partially decrypted, but several points are clear. The cable shows that Quantum met initially with a high-ranking Soviet diplomat. The New York KGB referred to the official as "Grandfather's deputy." Grandfather was the KGB cover name for the Soviet ambassador to the United States, Maksim Litvinov. Analysts at the NSA and the FBI concluded that the reference to his deputy was most likely to Andrey Gromyko, Litvinov's chief aide and his eventual successor. After a short discussion Gromyko turned Quantum over to Egor. Egor has never been identified, but another cable shows that it was the cover name for a KGB officer at the Soviet embassy. Egor heard out Quantum and then (this is unclear owing to the incomplete decryption) either brought in immediately or later consulted Semyon Semenov, a KGB officer who worked on scientific intelligence. Semenov also had long been involved in the Soviet program to penetrate Enormous, the KGB cover name for the U.S. atomic bomb project.

The KGB cable reported that Quantum was "convinced of the value of the materials and therefore expects from us a similar recompense for his labor—in the form of a financial reward." The reference to "materials" indicates that Quantum not only provided a verbal briefing but brought documents with him as well. Asking for money was unusual. While the cables show that the KGB habitually gave its productive sources annual gifts of some sort, rewarded many with cash bonuses, and provided regular stipends for those with heavy work loads or expenses, in this period money was not the usual inducement for betrayal of the United States. Ideological sympathy for communism—not greed—was the most common motivation for treachery. Monetary payment for specific deliveries was not the usual practice.

Because only a portion of all KGB cables has been decrypted, we cannot be sure when Quantum first made contact with the Soviets. The partial decryption of the June 21 message further hampers a firm conclusion. But the June 14 meeting appears to have been, if not the first, then a very early contact. Egor called on Semenov to evaluate the information; had Quantum been a developed source, his material would have been dealt with more routinely. Further, the nature of the contact suggests an early meeting, perhaps even a "walk-in." Though Soviet diplomats cooperated with the KGB, both they and the KGB avoided becoming directly involved in meeting with spies; diplomats regarded direct involvement in espionage as interfering with their main work, and the KGB did not care to deal with persons not under its direct control. Yet on June 14 Quantum met first with a senior Soviet diplomat. Possibly Quantum had no established contact with the KGB before that time, came to the Soviet embassy, and secured a meeting with a senior diplomat. Once he realized that espionage was on Quantum's mind, the diplomat turned him over to a KGB officer.

Semenov was impressed with Quantum's material and quickly paid him three hundred dollars. A lengthy second message, sent in three parts over the next two days, shows why Semenov was pleased.[55] Quantum had turned over a detailed scientific description of one variant of the difficult process of uranium separation through gaseous diffusion. Russian scientists working on a Soviet bomb in 1942 and early 1943 had thought the process of separation through gaseous diffusion to be not worth pursuing.[56] Espionage changed their minds. Not only did the Soviet intelligence agencies learn that in both Britain and America scientists had devised a practical method, but the KGB handed the process to their own scientists on a platter. Quantum was one of the sources.

Who was Quantum? The FBI never identified him. He probably was a scientist or engineer of some sort, for it seems unlikely that someone without a sophisticated technical background would have realized the importance of gaseous diffusion. Quantum's ability to win an audience with a senior Soviet diplomat and to persuade a KGB officer also suggests someone with scientific credentials and some professional standing. The cover name Quantum seems to point to a physicist. None of this is certain, however. The only thing that can be said with confidence is that Quantum had access to highly valuable scientific information on the U.S. atomic bomb project and handed it over to the Soviet Union at a meeting at the Soviet embassy on June 14, 1943.

What happened to Quantum? In August another cable mentioned in passing the report of mid-June. But Quantum does not appear again in the Venona cables. Possibly he is mentioned later under another cover name or in cables never deciphered. Possibly his handover of June 14 was a one-time act of perfidy for cash. Perhaps the KGB, as surely it would have tried to do, developed Quantum into a long-term asset. We cannot tell.

Fogel/Pers: The Unidentified Atomic Spy of 1944

A second unidentified Soviet source shows up in several 1944 New York KGB cables. This source initially had the cover name Fogel, changed in September 1944 to Pers, Russian for Persian.[57] The New York KGB sent Moscow a very lengthy report in February 1944 on the sort of atomic bomb information that was being turned in by Fogel. Unfortunately, only a few parts of the report were deciphered. There was enough to see that it was technical in nature, but the details are unknown. A June message from the New York KGB noted that it was forwarding to Moscow a layout of one of the Manhattan Project's manufacturing facilities that Fogel had provided. The facility was not specified, but what is known of the intelligence information turned over to Soviet scientists at this time suggests that the plans were of one of the plants at the Manhattan Project's Oak Ridge, Tennessee, facility.[58] Finally, a December message dealt with Fogel's work. The actual description was not decrypted, but it does associate Fogel with Camp-1, the KGB cover name for Oak Ridge. All that can be said about Fogel with certainty is that he had access to technical information about the atomic bomb project; very probably he was an engineer or scientist of some sort, but even that is a guess.

Youngster: The Treachery of Theodore Hall

The greatest surprise in the Venona traffic was that it revealed the identity of a major Soviet spy who, although long known to U.S. authorities, was unknown to the general public, had never been prosecuted, and was living in comfortable and respected retirement in England. In its initial release of the Venona cables in 1995 the NSA blacked out its footnote giving the identity of a Soviet agent with the cover name Youngster. The text of the messages, however, provided sufficient information about Youngster to enable a *Washington Post* reporter, Michael Dobbs, to break the story of the espionage carried out by Theodore Alvin Hall.[59] The NSA, which apparently had already made a decision to withdraw it redaction, did so, and the footnotes showed that the U.S. security officers had identified Hall as a Soviet spy long ago. In September 1997 a new book, *Bombshell,* appeared that focused on Theodore Hall's role as a Soviet source.[60] The authors, Joseph Albright and Marcia Kunstel, based the book on the Venona decryptions, hours of interviews with Hall himself, and other documentation and interviews.

Eight KGB cables deal with Theodore Hall, covering his initial recruitment in November 1944 through his work as a source at Los Alamos in July 1945.[61] An intellectual prodigy, Hall graduated from Harvard in 1944 at age eighteen. Not surprisingly, Manhattan Project talent hunters recruited this young star physicist to work on the program. Hall was dispatched to Los Alamos early in 1944 and assigned to a team attempting to master the physics of implosion, the key to the U.S. plutonium bomb.

Los Alamos was under tight security, and Hall could not communicate easily with anyone about what he was working on. But in October 1944 he returned home to New York on leave and spoke with his best friend and Harvard roommate, Saville Sax. One of the bonds between Hall and Sax was that both were fervent young Communists.

The two agreed that the Soviet Union ought to have the secrets with which Hall had been entrusted. (Like Fuchs, Hall was a volunteer: he made contact with the Soviets, not the other way around.) Sax then visited the CPUSA headquarters in New York City. At one point he tried to obtain an appointment with Earl Browder, head of the CPUSA, but the Harvard student, even if he was a young Communist, could not talk his way past Browder's secretary. Eventually, though, someone sent him to the right man. In this case it was Sergey Kurnakov, a journalist who wrote on military affairs for the CPUSA's *Daily Worker,* as well as for more mainstream publications. He was also a KGB agent.[62]

Kurnakov heard Sax out and then met with Hall. The New York KGB told Moscow that Kurnakov reported Hall to have "an exceptionally keen mind and a broad outlook," and to be "politically developed," meaning that Hall was a loyal Communist.[63] The historian Allen Weinstein gained access to the detailed written report that Kurnakov submitted to the KGB, which was sent to Moscow via diplomatic pouch. Quoting from Kurnakov's 1944 report, Weinstein wrote:

> Hall also "proposed organizing meetings, if needed, to inform [us] about the progress of . . . practical experiments on explosion [*sic*] and its control, the shell's construction, etc . . ."
>
> Kurnakov was fascinated but still cautious, possibly fearing that this off-the-street agent might have been planted by the FBI so he asked Hall: "Do you understand what you are doing? Why do you think it is necessary to disclose U.S. secrets for the sake of the Soviet Union?" Hall responded: "There is no country except for the Soviet Union which could be entrusted with such a terrible thing."[64]

At this first meeting Hall gave Kurnakov a report he had prepared on the Los Alamos facility, the progress of the research, and the roles of the chief scientists working on the bomb. Kurnakov had immediately reported to his KGB superiors, Anatoly Yatskov, a KGB officer who specialized in scientific intelligence, and the chief of the New York KGB office, Stepan Apresyan, both nominally Soviet diplomats. The New York KGB had to act quickly because Hall was about to return to Los Alamos. On Apresyan's instructions, Kurnakov met again with Hall, reached an initial understanding, and picked up a photograph to assist the KGB in future contacts. Because it had to act rapidly and without the usual background checks, the KGB decided to use Sax as its initial liaison with Hall rather than risk one of its regular agents. As the contact man, Sax traveled to New Mexico to pick up material from Hall.

Later Lona Cohen, an American Communist and career KGB agent, made at least one trip to New Mexico for Hall's material in the late spring of 1945.

Other deciphered messages show the KGB carrying out its background checks on Sax and Hall through its CPUSA liaison, Bernard Schuster. The KGB gave Hall the cover name Mlad, meaning Youngster in Russian (Hall was only nineteen at that point), while his friend Sax was named Star, or Oldster. Hall delivered reports on the implosion detonation system for the plutonium bomb and on the methods the Manhattan Project had developed to separate the needed uranium U-235 from the unneeded U-238. While not a senior scientist like Klaus Fuchs, Hall held a very sensitive position at Los Alamos, and his access to highly valuable secret material was broad. Moscow told the New York KGB office in March 1945 that Hall's material was of "great interest."[65] The basis for the KGB's opinion was an evaluation of Hall's material by Igor Kurchatov, the scientific head of the Soviet atomic bomb project.[66] Hall was also drafted into the Army while at Los Alamos, but given his scientific talent he was immediately offered a commission. He accepted and swore the oath of true faith and allegiance to the United States required of all officers. He then returned to Los Alamos and proceeded to break his oath.

After the war ended, Hall was released from the atomic bomb program. He attended the University of Chicago and received a doctorate in physics in 1950. His research interests also turned toward radiobiology and the medical uses of X rays, and he later worked at the Sloan-Kettering Institute for Cancer Research. In 1962 he moved to Great Britain to take a position as a biophysicist at the Cavendish Laboratories at Cambridge University, where he still lives in retirement. Hall's espionage continued beyond the period documented by Venona, into the early 1950s, and included his recruitment in the late 1940s of two other American atomic scientists to work for the KGB.

Theodore Hall and Saville Sax came to the attention of the FBI in 1949, when an early, partially decrypted Venona message produced both their names in clear text. (In this initial New York KGB report on the first contact with Hall and Sax, the two had not yet been given cover names.) The FBI interviewed Sax and Hall in 1951. Neither, however, broke under interrogation, and both denied any contact with Soviet intelligence. Hall also repeatedly accused the FBI of harassing him simply because of his progressive political beliefs. Given the decision not to reveal the Venona cables in court and the absence of alternative evidence of their crimes of five years earlier, prosecution was not practical. In addition, by this time Hall was no longer involved in military-related science, nor was there evidence that either Sax or Hall was then currently involved in espionage. The FBI dropped its interest in the two in 1952. Although later additional Venona decryptions would further document Hall's and Sax's guilt, the matter was not reopened. Indeed, FBI policies kept their treachery secret from the American people until the release of the Venona cables in 1995.[67]

Atomic Espionage and Morris and Lona Cohen

In the aftermath of the collapse of the Soviet Union, the Russian Foreign Intelligence Service, successor to the foreign intelligence section of the KGB, released selected documents to the Russian press. These documents and the stories that accompanied them by retired Soviet and active Russian intelligence officers highlighted past successful intelligence operations. One of the operations praised for its success was Soviet penetration of the American atomic bomb project during World War II.

Col. Vladimir Chikov, a press officer with the Russian intelligence service, wrote a lengthy article in 1991 about Soviet atomic espionage which singled out two Americans who worked for Soviet intelligence, Morris Cohen and his wife, Lona (Leontine).[68] The Russian Foreign Intelligence Service has been adamant in continuing to protect the identities of Soviet agents, whether living or dead, and within Russia uses legal sanctions to prevent disclosure of Soviet-era foreign agents. The only exceptions are agents who publicly identified themselves or who had been identified by the Soviet government for reasons of state. The Cohens, who cooperated with Chikov's research, fell into both categories. They secretly left the United States in 1950 and went to the Soviet Union. There they prepared for a new assignment and, holding fraudulent New Zealand passports, reappeared a few years later in London as antiquarian book dealers under the names of Peter and Helen Kroger. In 1961 British security officials arrested the two as part of a Soviet espionage network that had penetrated the British navy. The Cohen residence housed the ring's elaborate radio and microfilming equipment.[69]

The Cohens stuck to their cover and insisted that their name really was Kroger. But British security had been in touch with the FBI and identified them as the Cohens. The FBI had stumbled onto the Cohens when an informant in 1953 mentioned having known Morris Cohen as an ardent Communist. The FBI routinely checked on him and found that he and his wife had vanished in September 1950. Morris, a New York City school teacher, had abruptly resigned, and the couple also abandoned their furniture in the apartment they vacated. They had told their relatives that they were moving to the West, but correspondence from them had been brief, had not provided a new address, and had then ceased. The FBI thought this chain of events suspicious but had no reason to treat it as other than a routine matter until 1957, when the bureau arrested KGB colonel Rudolf Abel, a Soviet spy operating under a false identity in the United States. In his safe-deposit box the FBI discovered photographs of the Cohens, along with recognition phrases used to establish contact between agents who have not met previously. Not surprisingly, that discovery spurred a major FBI effort to find out more about the Cohens. The investigation generated information on their backgrounds but no real clues to what had happened to the couple after September 1950. There the matter had stood until 1961, when British security arrested the Krogers, whose photographs and fingerprints identified them as the long-missing Cohens.[70]

A British court convicted and imprisoned the Cohens for espionage. In an extraordinary act, the Soviet government in 1967 admitted that the two were Soviet agents and obtained their release by exchanging them for a British subject held by the Soviet Union. The Cohens then lived in Moscow on KGB pensions until their deaths—Lona in 1992 and Morris in 1995.

In writing about the Cohens, consequently, Chikov was not revealing previously unknown spies but praising acknowledged KGB agents who had spent a lifetime in the service of the Soviet Union. The Cohens, indeed, were treated as heroes by both the KGB and the successor Russian Foreign Intelligence Service. During the Soviet era both received the Order of the Red Banner and the Order of Friendship of Nations for their espionage work. After the collapse of the USSR they also were given the title of Heroes of the Russian Federation by the Yeltsin government.[71]

Chikov claimed key roles for the Cohens in Soviet penetration of the Manhattan Project. He stated that in 1942 Morris, who then had the cover name Louis, personally recruited a key scientist working on the U.S. atomic bomb project. Chikov published a 1942 message from a KGB officer in the United States that said, "The physicist . . . contacted our source 'Louis,' an acquaintance from the Spanish civil war. . . . We propose to recruit him through 'Louis.' 'Louis' has already carried out a similar task, and very successfully."[72] One of the cover names given this physicist, according to Chikov, was Perseus. Morris Cohen was drafted in mid-1942 and was unavailable for espionage until released from duty in 1945. Chikov credited Lona with acting as the courier to Perseus, including making trips to New Mexico to pick up Perseus's material from Los Alamos. Support for these claims also came from the retired KGB officer Anatoly Yatskov, a senior KGB officer in the United States during World War II.[73] Both Chikov and Yatskov refused to identify the physicist, Chikov saying only that Morris had originally met him in some connection during the Spanish Civil War.

In fact, it was in Spain that Cohen became a spy. Cohen had joined the American Communist party in 1935, at age twenty-five. Two years later he was among the more than two thousand young American Communists who traveled to Spain to fight with the Communist-led International Brigades. He served with the Mackenzie-Papineau battalion, a nominally Canadian but largely American unit. Always an ideological militant, he quickly became one of the battalion's Communist political officers. During fighting at Fuentes del Ebro in October 1937, Cohen was wounded and hospitalized. When he recovered, rather than being returned to the front, he was sent to a secret Soviet-run school in Spain for training in covert radio operations and recruited as a Soviet agent. After returning to the United States, Morris Cohen worked at the Soviet exhibit at the 1939 New York World's Fair and later for Amtorg. He also worked as a substitute teacher in the New York schools. These, however, were his "day" jobs. He also served KGB officer Semyon Semenov as a courier and talent-spotter for new sources. In 1941 he married Lona Petka, a fellow Communist, and she soon became a full partner in his espionage work.[74]

There are difficulties in relying on Chikov's account about the details of Perseus. His articles and his book were reviewed by the Russian Foreign Intelligence Service, and any material it found objectionable was removed or changed. Chikov's account appeared before the Venona cables, original documents not sanitized by the Russian Foreign Intelligence Service, became public. Their evidence is far more reliable than Chikov's censored and deliberately distorted secondary account. The cables reveal that Chikov provided a mixture of truth, half-truth, and deliberate deception. With regard to Perseus, Chikov states that this cover name was later changed to Youngster. But Youngster, as Venona shows, was actually the cover name of Theodore Alvin Hall. Hall/Youngster was not recruited until late 1944, and the Cohens had no role in his recruitment. When Chikov prepared his articles and book, Hall was still alive and had never been publicly identified as a Soviet agent. Chikov's claim that Perseus and Youngster were one and the same has the look of an attempt by the Russian Foreign Intelligence Service to muddy the historical waters and obscure the identity of as yet unexposed agents.

One is then left with the problem of deciding what can be trusted in Chikov's account. That the Cohens were valuable Soviet spies is surely true. The highly unusual Soviet decision to acknowledge their service and get the Cohens out of prison through a spy exchange is evidence of their value. That the Cohens had some role in Soviet atomic espionage is true as well. Albright and Kunstel in *Bombshell* detail the evidence that Lona Cohen acted as a courier in 1945 at least once and perhaps twice to Hall in New Mexico. But beyond that, the particulars provided by Chikov cannot be relied upon. The Perseus of Chikov's account may have been constructed out of the stories of two different agents, Fogel/Pers and Youngster, and perhaps of a third altogether unknown spy.

An intriguing part of Chikov's story is that he puts the recruitment of the unidentified physicist in the first half of 1942, at the earliest stages of the Manhattan Project. Given what is known of Soviet atomic espionage, it is very likely that the Soviets had penetrated the U.S. project in 1942, but the identify of the source is unknown. Klaus Fuchs did not arrive in the United States until the end of 1943. The unidentified Quantum appeared in mid-1943, and Fogel/Pers was present only in 1944. Hall and David Greenglass are figures from late 1944 and 1945. Gen. Pavel Sudoplatov, the retired KGB officer who for a time supervised atomic espionage, wrote in his memoirs that Semyon Semenov had a valued source inside the Manhattan Project in the latter half of 1942. Sudoplatov asserted that the source provided a full report on the achievement of the first controlled nuclear chain reaction at the project's University of Chicago facility. This and other stolen atomic material were among the information that Stalin's aide Vyacheslav Molotov turned over to the Soviet nuclear physicist Igor Kurchatov in February

1943. Molotov had just picked Kurchatov to head the Soviet atomic bomb program. Hence Chikov's claim of a 1942 recruitment of a source in the Manhattan Project is probably accurate, but Morris Cohen's role is uncertain, and the identify of the source remains a mystery.[75]

As for the Cohens, they make only the briefest appearances in the Venona cables, in part because Morris was drafted and unavailable for espionage during the period covered by most of the deciphered messages. Here Chikov's account does give some assistance. Chikov notes that Lona had the cover name Lesley for a period and that the apparatus set up by the Cohens was called the Volunteers. Albright and Kunstel in their research found that Morris himself had the cover name Volunteer and that Lona was Lesley. A 1945 Venona message relayed a report that Volunteer had been killed while on Army duty in Europe.[76] Chikov's account, which appeared before Venona was made public, provides corroboration, because he wrote that in 1945 Lona was briefly grief-stricken when a erroneous report came that Morris had been killed. Lona shows up in Venona cables of the New York KGB office both under the cover name Lesley and as "Volunteer's wife."[77]

None of these Venona messages, however, reveal anything of substance about the work of the Cohens. Both Albright and Kunstel and Chikov reported that Lona was running a network that included engineers and technicians at munitions and aviation plants in the New York area while Morris was on military duty. One of her sources even smuggled a working model of a new machine gun out of his plant. The FBI later learned that Lona had herself worked at two defense plans, the Public Metal Company in New York City in 1942 and the Aircraft Screw Products plant on Long Island in 1943. In a 1993 interview released by the Russian Foreign Intelligence Service, Morris Cohen alluded to contact with Hall in the late 1940s, noted that he had developed several of his fellow International Brigades veterans as Soviet espionage contacts, and referred briefly to his and Lona's postwar work with Rudolph Abel.[78]

Checking on the Smyth Report

In the fall of 1945 Gen. Leslie Groves, military director of the Manhattan Project, supervised the preparation and public release of a technical report on the development of the atomic bomb. Written by physicist Henry D. Smyth, it appeared under the title *General Account of the Development of Methods of Using Atomic Energy for Military Purposes*. The Smyth report was intended to satisfy the need for some sort of technical explanation for public consumption, but Groves also wanted to use the report to establish a maximum limit on what technical information the many scientists involved in the project could talk about without damaging American security and giving away the crucial secrets of the bomb.

Soviet scientists working on the atomic bomb read the Smyth report with great interest.[79] Soviet intelligence suspected that the report did not merely leave out certain highly sensitive information but also contained disinformation designed to lead the Soviets down technical blind alleys. Deciphered Venona messages show that the KGB sent an agent with the cover name Erie (later changed to Ernest) to check on this matter.[80] A November 1945 San Francisco KGB cable reported that Ernest had been sent to meet Morris Perelman, an engineer with the Los Alamos atomic bomb project, and a professor whose name was not recovered, both of whom had been in contact with Smyth regarding the report's authenticity. Ernest's mission was to find out what the two had to say about the report. There is no reason to suspect that either Perelman or the professor realized he was talking to a Soviet agent rather than to a fellow American scientist discussing something of mutual professional interest. Ernest also met with a third scientist, identified in the deciphered portions of the KGB's cable only by the initial D. Whoever he was, D. supplied Ernest with some of the information deliberately left out of the Smyth report. The portions of the KGB cable that can be read suggest that D. knew he was assisting Soviet espionage, as in a KGB reference to D.'s willingness to "turn [technical information] over to us at any time."[81]

The CPUSA and Attempted Recruitment for Atomic Espionage

The KGB used the American Communist party as its vehicle for an attempt to recruit Clarence Hiskey. A chemist, Hiskey had been doing research at Columbia University until September 1943, when he joined the Metallurgical Laboratory, a part of the atomic bomb project, at the University of Chicago. Hiskey had been active in the Communist party while in graduate school at the University of Wisconsin and was a natural target of KGB interest.[82] A May 1944 New York KGB message reported that Bernard Schuster, the CPUSA's liaison with the KGB, had been to Chicago at the KGB's direction. The cable passed on Schuster's description of those he had met: "Olsen is district leader of the Fraternal [Communist party] in Chicago. Olsen's wife, who has been meeting Ramsey [Hiskey], is also an active Fellowcountryman [Communist] and met Ramsey on the instructions of the organization. At our suggestion Echo [Schuster] can get a letter from Olsen with which one or other of our people will meet Ramsey and thereafter will be able to strike up an acquaintance."[83] Analysts at the NSA and the FBI did not identify Olsen, but it may have been the cover name or the party name of Morris Childs, at that time the head of the Communist party in Illinois. The message stated that Olsen's wife had been cultivating Hiskey, and the KGB wanted to use the relationship to put one of its agents in contact with him.

In July the New York KGB reported a follow-up to this May message.[84] It told Moscow that Schuster had passed along copies of two letters that had been sent to Hiskey by Victor (an unidentified cover name) and Rose Olsen. Rose, however, is probably not Morris Childs's wife but his sister-in-law, Roselyn. Roselyn's husband, Jack Childs, was a full-time CPUSA functionary whose work for the party was obscure and probably connected with its underground. The section of the cable describing the content of the letters was not deciphered. There was a garbled indication, however, that one of the KGB's veteran liaison agents, Joseph Katz, had been assigned to the Hiskey case. On September 18, 1944, the New York KGB office sent a cable responding to several inquiries from Moscow, one of which was about the status of the approach to Hiskey. The New York KGB deferred its report, on the grounds that its intermediaries in the matter, Bernard Schuster and Joseph Katz, were out of New York at the time and that Rose Olsen, at that point designated by the cover name Phlox, and her husband had traveled to "Ramsey's area."[85]

Finally, the New York KGB told Moscow in December 1944 that "Dick [Joseph Katz] is directly in touch with Phlox's husband and not with Phlox [Rose Olsen] herself. The intention of sending the husband to see Ramsey [Hiskey] is explained by the possibility of avoiding a superfluous stage for transmitting instructions."[86] Here the New York KGB is conveying its decision to Moscow that Jack Childs would make the approach to Hiskey. So far as is known, the approach, if carried out, was unsuccessful.[87]

The KGB's use of the CPUSA in its search for information on the

U.S. atomic program is reflected as well in a garbled November 1945 report from the San Francisco KGB station. The cable said that Jerome Callahan, a ship's clerk judged "trustworthy," had advised the KGB regarding something from (or about) Rudolph Lambert, head of the California Communist party's labor activities and chief of the party's security commission. The unrecovered sections of the message make it difficult to read, but it appears that Callahan and Lambert were the sources of information about uranium deposits. Neither Lambert nor Callahan would have been likely to take any interest in uranium ore had not the KGB put out feelers through the CPUSA.[88]

Other Facets of Soviet Atomic Espionage

Only a few GRU espionage cables were decrypted, yet it is clear from other sources that Soviet military intelligence also penetrated the Manhattan Project. Several attempted and probably partially successful penetrations were through an illegal GRU officer, Arthur Adams (chapter 6), who entered the United States in the late 1930s using a fraudulent Canadian passport.

By 1944 American counterintelligence had identified Adams as a Soviet agent and observed him meeting with Clarence Hiskey, the same Manhattan Project scientist the KGB had attempted to approach. Security officers suspected that his furtive meetings with an illegal GRU officer suggested espionage. They neutralized the situation by drafting Hiskey in mid-1944 and assigning him to routine Army duty in Alaska for the duration of the war. While Hiskey was en route to Alaska, American counterintelligence surreptitiously searched his belongings and found seven pages of classified notes on his work at the Metallurgical Laboratory. On a follow-up search, however, the notes were missing. Hiskey had either passed the information to a Soviet contact or, suspecting that he was under surveillance, destroyed them.[89]

Before Hiskey left for Army duty he made contact with John H. Chapin, a chemical engineer who also worked on the atomic bomb project, and arranged for him to meet with Adams. Security officials, however, observed the meeting. When questioned, Chapin admitted that Hiskey had told him that Adams was a Soviet agent, but he denied actually passing any secrets to him. Hiskey also put Edward Manning, a technician working on the bomb project, in touch with Adams. As with Hiskey, authorities had insufficient evidence for criminal charges and had to be content with simply neutralizing Manning and Chapin.[90]

Another Adams effort to penetrate the Manhattan Project took place in the winter of 1944. A counterintelligence officer caught one of Adams's contacts, Irving Lerner, an employee of the Motion Picture Division of the OWI, attempting to photograph the cyclotron at the University of California at Berkeley without authorization. (The cyclotron had been used in the creation of plutonium.) Again there was insufficient evidence for criminal action. Lerner resigned under pressure and went to work for Keynote Recordings, where Arthur Adams was employed.[91]

No Venona messages clearly refer to Adams, Chapin, Lerner, or Manning. One GRU message, however, may be related to Adams's attempts to obtain information at the Metallurgical Laboratory at the University of Chicago. In August 1943 Pavel Mikhailov, the GRU station chief in New York who met with Adams, sent a message to Moscow about William Malisoff, owner of Unified Laboratories in New York and a KGB spy. Mikhailov noted that Malisoff "knows people in Eskulap wife's special field and can recommend reliable people as candidates for her post in Chicago University." Eskulap was never identified. But, the frustrated Mikhailov reported, the GRU could not follow up on this possible lead because its agent Achilles—who may have been Arthur Adams—"was forbidden to meet Malisov [Malisoff] since the latter is connected with the Neighbors [KGB]."[92]

The GRU also attempted and achieved at least a limited penetration, and perhaps more, through the Radiation Laboratory at the University of California at Berkeley. Steve Nelson was both an open CPUSA official and a West Coast leader of its covert apparatus. The FBI placed listening devices in Nelson's residence and in October 1942 overhead Giovanni Lomanitz, a young scientist at the Radiation Laboratory, tell Nelson he was working on a highly secret weapon, a reference to the atomic bomb project. Nelson indicated prior knowledge of the project and advised Lomanitz, a Communist, to be discrete and to consider himself a undercover member of the party. In March 1943, another young Communist physicist, Joseph W. Weinberg, visited Nelson's home and talked about his confidential work at the Radiation Laboratory. Nelson took notes and several days later met with Peter Ivanov, nominally vice-consul at the Soviet consulate in San Francisco but in reality a GRU officer. Nelson gave Ivanov a package, believed by American security officers who watched the exchange to be his notes from Weinberg's briefing. When later asked by authorities about these events, Nelson took the Fifth, while Weinberg simply lied, denying that any meetings had occurred.[93]

Lomanitz and Weinberg were part of a group of a half-dozen Communist scientists working on the atomic bomb project at Berkeley's Radiation Laboratory. All were also active in attempts to establish a Radiation Laboratory local of the Federation of Architects, Engineers, Chemists, and Technicians (FAECT), a small white-collar CIO union, dominated by Communists, that shows up in several Soviet approaches to the atomic bomb project.

Although Nelson worked as a link between young Communist scientists at the Berkeley Radiation Laboratory and the Soviet intelligence officers, one chemist, Martin Kamen, met directly with Grigory Kheifets and Grigory Kasparov, KGB officers at the Soviet consulate in San Francisco. He was fired from the project in 1944 when security officers overheard him discussing the atomic bomb project with Kheifets. Unaware that they had been listening, he lied when questioned about the conversation.[94]

In August 1943 the New York KGB cabled to Moscow that it would approach a scientist, described as a "progressive professor" and one of the directors of a major radiation laboratory. The KGB said that the approach could be made through Paul Pinsky, a CPUSA member and organizer for FAECT in northern California. None of the subsequent deciphered Venona traffic, however, discusses the matter further.[95] Use of FAECT as a channel for Soviet espionage did not go unnoticed by American security officials. They made their concerns known to the White House, which got in touch with Philip Murray, national president of the CIO. He forced FAECT to cease organizing at the Radiation Laboratory for the duration of the war. Paul Pinsky attempted to delay the action, but he was overruled. The FBI later observed the GRU officer Ivanov visiting Pinsky's home in October 1943.[96]

It may be that FAECT also is the vaguely described organization in a September 1945 Venona message from the New York KGB to Moscow, which largely deals with the work of Julius Rosenberg but also mentions a source given the cover name Volok. Volok was a Communist working at an unidentified Manhattan Project facility. Unfortunately, the message noted, just a day earlier Volok had "learned that they had dismissed him from his work. His active work in progressive organizations in the past was the cause of his dismissal."[97] The passage immediately before the description of Volok was undeciphered, so it is not certain that Volok was a Rosenberg contact. Yet both the passage immediately before the undeciphered section and that immediately following the portion of the Volok passage that was decrypted deal with the Rosenberg ring. "Progressive" was standard Communist terminology for any Communist-aligned organization. Several engineers and scientists were dropped from the Manhattan Project when security officers discovered they were or had been FAECT militants, and FAECT would be a candidate for one of the "progressive organizations" referred to by this message.

The San Francisco office of the KGB also had a source, identified only by the cover name Brother-in-Law, who provided information on Lt. Col. Boris T. Pash, the U.S. Army counterintelligence officer who directed security for the atomic bomb program.[98] This assignment, too, reflects the intensity of the KGB interest in the Manhattan Project. In a poorly decrypted section of a 1944 message, the San Francisco KGB also appears to have discussed the possibility of approaching Frank Oppenheimer, brother of the scientific head of the Manhattan Project, J. Robert Oppenheimer. Frank, also a physicist, was a member of the Communist party. This cable, however, appeared to warn Moscow that Frank Oppenheimer was under close U.S. security surveillance.[99]

And what of J. Robert Oppenheimer himself? In the postwar period he came under suspicion when it was realized that the Manhattan Project had been penetrated by Soviet intelligence. The basis for the suspicion was Oppenheimer's background, ambiguous conduct, and reticence about his involvement with the CPUSA. He had been an ardent Popular Front liberal and an ally of the Communist party from the late 1930s until early 1942—an indication that his attachment to the Communist cause was strong enough to withstand the news of a Nazi-Soviet alliance in August 1939. Over that period Oppenheimer had given generous monetary contributions to the CPUSA, which he had often delivered to Isaac Folkoff, a senior leader of the California Communist party who also functioned as the party's West Coast liaison with the KGB. Further, until shortly before joining the Manhattan Project, Oppenheimer had socialized with Steve Nelson, another senior West Coast Communist, a leader of its secret apparatus, and, like Folkoff, a party contact with the KGB.

Oppenheimer's brother Frank and Frank's wife were concealed Communist party members. Frank vehemently denied Communist party membership until 1949. He then admitted he had joined the party in 1937 and remained a member until 1941. Robert's own wife, Katherine, had been a Communist and married to Joseph Dallet, a full-time functionary of the Communist party who had died while serving as a Communist political commissar with the International Brigades in the Spanish Civil War.

In addition to his background, Robert Oppenheimer's own conduct compounded counterintelligence concerns. Oppenheimer informed Manhattan Project security officers in August 1943 that he had indirect information that someone had approached several Manhattan Project scientists with requests that they provide sensitive information to the USSR. Pressed for details, Oppenheimer changed his story: the approach had been made directly to him. According to Oppenheimer's new version, Haakon Chevalier, a professor of Romance languages at the University of California, had asked him to divulge atomic bomb secrets in early 1943. Chevalier, a leading figure in Oppenheimer's Popular Front political circle of the late 1930s and early 1940s, said that he had been approached by George Eltenton, a chemical engineer who had worked in the Soviet Union. Eltenton asked Chevalier to act as an intermediary to feel out a number of Manhattan Project scientists about sharing information (a polite euphemism for spying) with the USSR. Oppenheimer said that he had rejected Chevalier's approach but had difficulty explaining why he had not reported the incident until months later and why his initial report had been a distortion. He than went on to supply information about several Manhattan Project scientists, including Giovanni Lomanitz, Joseph Weinberg, and David Bohm, whom he knew to be close to the Communist party and whose ideological loyalties raised questions about their trustworthiness.[100] (The three were among the young Communist scientists who had met with Steve Nelson.) To complicate matters more, Oppenheimer later made comments that repudiated parts of his revised statement about what happened.

Chevalier contested Oppenheimer's story. He denied Communist loyalties and said that he had only casually mentioned Eltenton's scheme to Oppenheimer and had rejected it at once. He also admitted meeting with Ivanov and Kheifets but insisted he had no idea that the two were Soviet intelligence officers. In looking back at the evidence, it is clear that Chevalier was a concealed Communist. Further, Eltenton was also a concealed Communist, whom U.S. security officers observed meeting on several occasions in 1942 with Peter Ivanov, the GRU officer operating out of the Soviet consulate in San Francisco.[101]

These circumstances contributed to Oppenheimer's losing his security clearance in 1954 and to suspicion that he had participated in espionage. What do the Venona cables have to say about J. Robert Oppenheimer? Directly, very little, but indirectly perhaps a bit more.

Oppenheimer's name appears in several messages in clear text where various Soviet sources reported on which scientists were supervising various aspects of the Manhattan Project. These are reports about him by Soviet spies, not reports from him. None suggests any compromising relationship with Soviet intelligence.[102] Two messages mention the cover name Veksel, whom FBI analysts identified as Robert Oppenheimer. These references also are benign. In one case Veksel is mentioned as directing a Manhattan Project facility to which the KGB had given the cover name Reservation, and the messages suggest that Reservation is Los Alamos, which Oppenheimer then directed.[103] In the other message, Moscow directed the New York KGB to send one of its agents, Huron, to Chicago to "renew acquaintance" and "reestablish contact" with two scientists working on the Manhattan Project, one of whom was Veksel. The other was Hyman H. Goldsmith, a physicist who worked at the Metallurgical Laboratory in Chicago. The most straightforward interpretation of this message is that the KGB hoped that Huron, who has never been identified but who was probably a scientist himself, was someone who had known the two in the past and would be able to learn something useful. Nothing in the message indicated that Goldsmith and Veksel had a compromising relationship with the KGB.[104]

In addition to what was said about Oppenheimer in Venona, what was not said is significant. Because only a portion of KGB cable traffic has been decrypted, silence on a particular person or subject often means nothing. The KGB traffic was not silent, however, on atomic espionage, on Los Alamos, or on J. Robert Oppenheimer. The messages on those subjects were written in a manner that suggests the absence of so knowledgeable a source as the director of Manhattan Project.

Another silence has to be taken into consideration. Although the archives of the Soviet intelligence agencies remain closed to research, the Russian government has released some documents dealing with the content of the intelligence delivered to the Soviet atomic bomb project. These documents do not provide much in the way of direct clues about who gave the information to the USSR but do show that the KGB and GRU sources provided the Soviets with rich and highly valuable information.[105] Oppenheimer, however, did not know just the secrets of some parts of the atomic bomb project. As scientific director at Los Alamos he knew all the secrets, and knew them nearly as soon as they came into being. Had Oppenheimer been an active Soviet source, the quality and quantity of what the Soviet Union learned would most likely have been greater than they actually were. Further, even in regard to what secrets the USSR did learn, if Oppenheimer had been a source, the Soviets would have learned them significantly sooner than they actually appear to have done.

The evidence suggests that Oppenheimer's ties to the Communist party up through 1941 were very strong. He was not simply a casual Popular Front liberal who ignorantly bumped up against the party in some of the arenas in which it operated. Until he went to security officials in 1943, Oppenheimer's attitude toward possible Communist espionage against the Manhattan Project came very close to complete indifference. It was as if in mid-1943 his views changed and he realized that there actually was a serious security issue involved. Even then, it appeared that he wanted only to give security officials enough information to bring about a neutralization of the problem but not enough to expose associates to retribution for what they might have already done. Throughout his life Oppenheimer declined to provide a detailed or accurate accounting of his relationship with the CPUSA in the late 1930s and early 1940s and of his knowledge of Communists who worked on the Manhattan Project. While the preponderance of the evidence argues against Oppenheimer's having been an active Soviet source, one matter cannot be ruled out. The possibility exists that up to the time he reported the Chevalier approach to security officials in mid-1943, he may have overlooked the conduct of others whom he had reasonable grounds to question, a passivity motivated by his personal and political ties to those persons.[106]

CHAPTER 11

SOVIET ESPIONAGE AND AMERICAN HISTORY

The deciphered cables of the Venona Project reveal that hundreds of Americans had formal ties to Soviet intelligence services in the 1930s and 1940s. Soviet intelligence achieved its greatest espionage success in hastily created wartime agencies that hired large numbers of people under procedures that bypassed normal Civil Service hiring practices. America's World War II intelligence agency, the Office of Strategic Services, was home to between fifteen and twenty Soviet spies. Four other wartime agencies—the War Production Board, the Board of Economic Warfare, the Office of the Coordinator of Inter-American Affairs, and the Office of War Information—included at least half a dozen Soviet sources each among their employees.

Although more established government agencies were less susceptible to penetration, they were not immune. At least six sources worked in the State Department. The two highest-ranking among these officials, Alger Hiss and Laurence Duggan, both aided Soviet intelligence for a decade. Thanks to the influence of Assistant Secretary Harry D. White, the Treasury Department was a congenial home for Soviet agents. Six of the eight known Soviet sources in the department were connected with the Division of Monetary Research, headed first by White and then by a second Soviet source, Frank Coe, after White moved farther up in the Treasury hierarchy.

The USSR's sources were impressive in their quality as well as their number. They included a presidential administrative assistant (Lauchlin Currie), scientists working at the heart of the atomic bomb project (Theodore Hall and Klaus Fuchs), a senior aide to the head of the Office of Strategic Services (Duncan Lee), an assistant secretary of the Treasury (Harry White), the secretary of state's assistant for special political affairs (Alger Hiss), the head of the State Department's Division of American Republics (Laurence Duggan), and dozens of well-placed mid-level officials scattered throughout the government.

Not all the Americans who cooperated with Soviet espionage were sources. For every Gregory Silvermaster or Maurice Halperin—frontline spies stealing secret documents—there were support and liaison agents, such as Amadeo Sabatini and Elizabeth Bentley, who made it possible for the actual sources to do their work. Every source must be supported by an elaborate apparatus: talent-spotters who suggest likely candidates for recruitment, vetters who check on the background of prospective sources, couriers who carry documents and instructions, and others to supply safe-houses, provide mail drops, help set up cover businesses, and assist in procuring fraudulent identifications. All are necessary parts of the espionage enterprise.

While the Venona cables document Soviet penetration of the American government, they are of less assistance in determining how much damage Soviet spies did to American security. Very little of the substantive information passed to Soviet intelligence agencies by their spies was transmitted to Moscow by the cables deciphered in the Venona Project. The bulk of the reports from sources and copies of stolen documents were sent by courier and resides in still-closed Russian archives. Only occasional items of exceptional interest or time-sensitive information were cabled. The Venona messages, the testimony of defectors, and the confessions of apprehended spies provide general descriptions of the type of information that was being transmitted but few details and, of course, little about what the Soviets did with the information.[1] The lack of specificity about the actual substance of the intelligence gathered by Soviet spies and the use to which the USSR put it renders an assessment of the extent of the damage to American interests tentative. That the damage was at the very least significant, however, is clear enough.[2]

The major exception to the lack of specific knowledge bears on atomic espionage. Since the collapse of the Soviet Union, Russian sources have made available a significant proportion of the intelligence "take" of the Soviet atomic spies. Given time and resources, the USSR's talented scientists and engineers would certainly have been able to construct an atomic bomb without assistance from spies. But because of the information gained from Klaus Fuchs, David Greenglass, Theodore Hall, and several as-yet-unidentified spies, the Soviet Union did not need to explore all the technical blind alleys that American and British scientists went down first; espionage revealed what worked and what did not. They did not have to expend enormous resources on the design and development of crucial technologies; espionage revealed the technical approaches that were practical and provided the data from expensive experiments free of charge. They did not have to depend on scientific insight for key conceptual breakthroughs; espionage revealed that implosion and plutonium offered tremendous savings in time and resources over the manufacture of a pure uranium bomb. Espionage saved the USSR great expense and industrial investment and thereby enabled the Soviets to build a successful atomic bomb years before they otherwise would have.

During World War II the CPUSA had more than fifty thousand members. Although, as we have noted, most American Communists were not spies, when the KGB and the GRU looked for sources and agents in the United States, they found the most eager and qualified candidates in the ranks of the American Communist party. Most of the Americans who betrayed their country and handed over its industrial, military, and governmental secrets to a foreign power did so not because they were blackmailed or needed money or were psychological misfits but out of ideological affinity for the Soviets. Throughout this book are examples of valuable Soviet sources, such as Theodore Hall, Klaus Fuchs, Julius Rosenberg, Gregory Silvermaster, Charles Kramer, and Victor Perlo, who were not recruited but who, prompted by ideological loyalty to communism, themselves sought out KGB or GRU contacts and volunteered to assist Soviet espionage. Others sources, of course, were approached and recruited. And though some American Communists who were asked to spy for the Soviet Union declined out of fear of being caught, there are no examples of Communists who indignantly rejected such overtures as unethical and reported the approaches to the U.S. authorities.[3]

The Soviet agents and sources came especially from three areas. First, there were the bright young idealists who had flocked to Washington in the heady days of the early New Deal. Several hundred of them had joined the Communist party and been assigned to secret party clubs. Many of these willingly turned government information over to the party in hopes of assisting Communist political goals or its labor cadre inside the CIO. And of this group a few score went further. When they found themselves in positions with access to secret government information helpful to the USSR, they did not hesitate to give it to Soviet intelligence officers. The Silvermaster and Perlo networks, among the largest Soviet spy rings, were both products of the Washington Communist underground. Second, several thousand young American Communists volunteered to fight in Spain in 1937–1938 in the ranks of the Comintern's International Brigades. The American volunteers sustained harrowing combat losses, but of those who survived, nearly a score enthusiastically continued their service to the cause by working in Soviet spy rings. One of them, Morris Cohen, became a career KGB officer who devoted his entire life to Soviet espionage. Third, several hundred committed CPUSA members worked for years in its "secret apparatus" which ensured internal security, prepared the CPUSA for the possibility of legal repression, and engaged in the infiltration and disruption of non-Communist organizations targeted by the party. The CPUSA functioned as an auxiliary to Soviet intelligence agencies, and its leading figures, such as Steve Nelson in California, performed a variety of tasks to assist Soviet espionage.

Why did American Communists spy for the USSR? The answer, at least in part, lies in the nature of American communism. We have read the remarks in which such spies as Theodore Hall, Gregory Silvermaster, David Greenglass, and Harry Gold professed their enthusiasm for Soviet communism and expressed their gratitude for the opportunity that espionage afforded to help strengthen the Soviet state. These attitudes were promulgated by the American Communist party. In 1935 a CPUSA spokesman wrote that Stalin "has directed the building of Socialism in a manner to create a rich, colorful, many-side cultural life among one hundred nationalities differing in economic development, language, history customs, tradition, but united in common work for a beautiful future. . . . [He is a] world leader whose every advice to every Party of the Comintern on every problem is correct, clear, balanced, and points the way to new, more decisive class battles."[4] In 1940 the American Young Communist League's journal, Clarity, proclaimed: "EVERY ONE OF COMRADE STALIN'S UTTERANCES IS A MIGHTY SEARCH-

LIGHT LIGHTING UP THE PATH OF THE REVOLUTIONARY YOUTH MOVE-
MENT. . . . The young workers and toilers of the capitalist countries who
are groaning under the yoke of capitalism look with great love and hope
to Comrade Stalin. . . . They see and know that the people of the Soviet
Union, whose happy life is for them a bright beacon, are indebted to
the Bolshevik Party and its great leader, Comrade Stalin, for the flour-
ishing of their youth and their happiness. Stalin rears the young generation like a careful, experienced gardener."[5]

In 1941 the party's theoretical journal, the *Communist,* declared
that Stalin was the "greatest man of our era. . . . With every passing
hour the titanic figure of this magnificent leader becomes more inextri-
cably bound up with the very destiny of world humanity."[6] In 1943
V. J. Jerome, the party's liaison with intellectuals, announced that "Stalin is the true forward-looking son of his epoch . . . the individually
gifted and socially endowed fighter for freedom."[7] And in 1949 Alexander Bittleman, one of the party's chief ideologists, asserted: "Stalin's
greatness and genius stand out so clearly and beautifully that progressive humanity has no difficulty in recognizing them. . . . To live with
Stalin in one age, to fight with him in one cause, to work under the
inspiring guidance of his teachings is something to be deeply proud of
and thankful for, to cherish."[8] Those who believed these statements had
no difficulty spying for Stalin's USSR if the opportunity presented itself.[9]

In some cases, the ideological attraction to the USSR was reinforced
by residual Russian patriotism, although of a nontraditional form. Some
of the Americans who spied for the Soviet Union were immigrants from
Russia or the children of immigrants. The parents of Saville Sax, a
young American Communist who worked for the KGB, were radical
Russian immigrants whom their grandson remembers as living in an
apartment building with similar families. The Sax family, he said, had
"barricaded themselves" in this "very closed community" that "identified American society with the people who were responsible for per-
secuting the Jews in czarist Russia."[10] Meanwhile, they believed that,
back in their native land, all that had been unjust had been made right
by the Bolshevik regime. The twin attraction of Communist and Russian
loyalties produced in these immigrants and their children a form of
Soviet patriotism that overwhelmed their weak ties to American national traditions.

By abetting Soviet espionage, these Communists and the CPUSA
itself laid the basis for the anti-Communist era that followed World

War II. The investigations and prosecutions of the American Communist movement undertaken by the federal government in the late 1940s and early 1950s were premised on an assumption that the CPUSA had assisted Soviet espionage. This view contributed to President Truman's executive order in 1947, reinforced in the early 1950s by President Eisenhower, that U.S. government employees be subjected to loyalty-security investigations. It also lay behind the 1948 decision by the Truman administration to prosecute Eugene Dennis and other CPUSA leaders under the sedition sections of the Smith Act. The government's loyalty-security program in the late 1940s had a rational basis—but that is not to say that the program was well designed or administered with skill and discretion, or that there were not serious abuses and injustices.[11]

With the advent of the Cold War, the decrypted Venona texts became a security nightmare. The identities of more than half the Americans who the deciphered Venona cables indicate cooperated with Soviet intelligence remained hidden behind cover names. How many of those nearly two hundred persons were still working in sensitive positions? Were they holding policy-making jobs? The hunt for these real but unidentified Soviet sources consumed the time and attention of hundreds of security officers for many years and subjected thousands of individuals to investigation. Particularly in the realm of diplomacy and defense policy-making, the knowledge that these unidentified Soviet agents existed diminished the mutual trust with which American officials could deal with each other. Further, the issue lent itself to partisan political exploitation. Republicans sought to discredit Democrats by painting the response of Democratic executive-branch officials as inadequate or even as constituting complicity in espionage. Democrats responded sometimes by covering up the problem, as in the *Amerasia* case, but more often, as with President Truman's personnel security order, by pre-empting the issue by taking a hard line against Communist subversion and spying.

By the mid-1950s American authorities understood that William Weisband and Kim Philby had betrayed to the Soviets the secret that Venona had succeeded in decrypting Soviet messages. American security officials calculated, however, that Soviet uncertainty about exactly what the Americans knew and what percentage of its wartime traffic had been penetrated was important, and Venona remained a closely held secret. But Venona's utility as a basis for gauging the accuracy or reliability of data from Soviet defectors diminished with time. The grounds for Venona's secrecy were much reduced by the 1970s, and its continued secrecy in the 1980s and until 1995 denied Americans a much-needed resource for understanding their own history.

Taken as a whole, the new evidence—from the deciphered Venona documents, the FBI files released in the past decades under the Freedom of Information Act, and the newly available documents from those Russian archives opened since the collapse of the USSR—along with the information produced earlier from defectors from Soviet espionage such as Whittaker Chambers and Elizabeth Bentley, testimony before various congressional committees, and the trials of major Soviet spies, shows that from 1942 to 1945 the Soviet Union launched an unrestrained espionage offensive against the United States. This offensive reached its zenith during the period when the United States, under President Franklin D. Roosevelt, adopted a policy of friendship and accommodation toward the USSR. The Soviet assault was of the type a nation directs at an enemy state that is temporarily an ally and with which it anticipates future hostility, rather than the much more restrained intelligence-gathering it would direct toward an ally that is expected to remain a friendly power. Stalin's espionage offensive was also a significant factor contributing to the Cold War. By the late 1940s the evidence provided by Venona and other sources of the massiveness and the intense hostility of the Soviet espionage attack caused American counterintelligence professionals and high-level American policy-making officials to conclude that Stalin was carrying out a covert assault on the United States. The Soviet espionage offensive, in their minds, indicated that the Cold War was not a state of affairs that had begun after World War II but a guerrilla action that Stalin had secretly started years earlier. They were right.

APPENDIX A

Source Venona: Americans and U.S. Residents Who Had Covert Relationships with Soviet Intelligence Agencies

This annotated list of 349 names includes U.S. citizens, noncitizen immigrants, and permanent residents of the United States who had a covert relationship with Soviet intelligence that is confirmed in the Venona traffic. It does not include Soviet intelligence officers operating legally under diplomatic cover but does show four Soviet intelligence officers operating illegally and posing as immigrants.

Of these 349 persons, 171 are identified by true names and 178 are known only by a cover name found in the Venona cables. A great many cover names were never identified. Many of these, however, are not listed here because the context indicates that the cover names refer to Soviet personnel operating under legal cover or because no judgment about the status of the person behind the cover name is possible. Only unidentified cover names that probably refer to Americans are included here.

Because cover names were changed from time to time, it is possible that a few of the unidentified cover names refer to persons known by another cover name or to persons named in the clear in another message. Some of the persons behind these unidentified cover names are very likely to be identified in appendix B as Americans who had a compromising relationship with Soviet intelligence but are not known to be documented in the Venona decryptions.

The persons identified in appendixes A and B represent only a partial listing of the total number of Americans and others who provided assistance to Soviet espionage in the Stalin era. The National Security Agency

followed Soviet intelligence cable traffic only for a few years in World War
II and decrypted only a small portion of that traffic.

Notes cite Venona messages regarding the person in question. Those
persons whose activities are discussed in the text are provided with brief
annotations, while those who are not are given fuller description. The Perlo
and Silvermaster groups, to which some of these persons belonged, were
founded as covert CPUSA networks but eventually were turned over to the
KGB. Cover names are given in italic type, and true names are given in
roman type.

A.: see Colloms, Anna.
Abram: see Soble, Jack.
Abt, John: labor lawyer and concealed Communist who turned the Perlo
   group over to the KGB in 1944.[1]
Achilles: unidentified asset of the New York GRU active 1941–1943 and
   involved in scientific-technical espionage at the University of Chicago.
   May be the illegal GRU officer Arthur Adams (see appendix B).[2]
Acorn: see Gold, Bela (William).
Ada: see Harris, Kitty.
Adam: see Getzoff, Rebecca.
Adler, Solomon. Treasury Department official and secret Communist.
   Source for the Golos-Bentley network. Cover name Sachs.[3]
Aida: see Rand, Esther Trebach.
Aileron: see Silverman, Abraham George.
Akhmed: unidentified asset reporting to the New York KGB office in 1944
   and 1945. Provided information on senior American journalists, reported
   on the activities of anti-Soviet émigrés, assisted in tracking the Soviet
   defector Victor Kravchenko, and served as the KGB liaison to a subset
   of other Soviet agents. Given the nature of his work, *Akhmed* may have
   been an immigrant from the USSR. Also carried under the cover name
   Thrush.[4]
Akhmerov, Iskhak Abdulovich: senior KGB illegal officer posing as an
   immigrant to America. Operated in the United States from the mid-
   1930s to the end of World War II. Credited by the KGB with the recruitment of scores of American sources. Known to have used the names
   William Grienke and Michael Green. Cover names in the Venona traffic
   are Mayor and Albert. On Akhmerov's full KGB career, see appendix
   E.[5]
Albert: see Akhmerov, Iskhak Abdulovich.
Aleksandr (Alexander): unidentified asset recruited by the New York KGB
   office in 1942 and mentioned in partially decrypted messages in 1943
   and 1944. The 1943 message suggests some connection with KGB activities in Mexico.[6]
Aleksandrov (Alexandrov): unidentified asset for the New York KGB office
   who reported on anti-Soviet émigrés in 1944 and 1945. Also accepted

payment. One message suggests that Aleksandrov was the father of Eugénie Olkhine (below).[7]

Ales: see Hiss, Alger.

Alma: see Levanas, Leo.

Altschuler, Lydia: functioned as a mail drop for the American end of the
KGB's anti-Trotsky operations in Mexico. Cover name Lidia.[8]

Antenna: see Rosenberg, Julius.

Arena: unidentified asset of the New York KGB holding a mid-level position in an unidentified government agency. Met directly with Vasily Zubilin. His residence was used as a safe-house.[9]

Armor: unidentified asset of the KGB who was employed at Bell Aircraft.
Also had the cover name Stamp.[10]

Arnold: see Fakir; Gold, Harry.

Arrow: unidentified asset of the KGB who carried out tasks among immigrants. Worked specifically among the Carpatho-Russians.[11]

Art: see Koral, Helen.

Arthur: see Bisson, Thomas Arthur.

Aster: unidentified asset of the KGB who may have worked on anti-
Trotskyist tasks.[12]

Ataman: see Gebert, Boleslaw K.

Attila: see Farish, Linn Markley.

Augur: unidentified Soviet contact who lived in Chicago and with whom
the KGB had no direct liaison. The New York KGB had difficulty approaching Augur and asked Moscow if it could use Soviet diplomats to
establish contact.[13]

Australian Woman: see Mitynen, Francia Yakilnilna.

Author: see Morkovin, Vladimir Borisovich.

B.: initial of an unidentified KGB source at Republic Aviation who provided
the New York KGB with information on American development of an
equivalent of the German V-1, an early cruise missile.[14]

Babin, Thomas: reported to the New York GRU office on ships leaving
the United States in 1943 and on his work with the OSS. Cover name
Brem.[15]

Baker, Rudy: head of the CPUSA's underground apparatus from 1938.
Baker shows up in the Venona traffic only under the cover name Son.
(Also see *Rudi.*) The identification comes from coded correspondence
between the Comintern and the CPUSA in Russia's RTsKhIDNI archive
(495-184), which contains dozens of messages from Brother in Moscow
to Father and Son in the United States. Annotations on these messages
identify Brother as Dimitrov and Father as Earl Browder. In these messages Son is the head of the CPUSA's covert arm, which Baker had taken
over in mid-1938. None of the Comintern messages to Son were sent
until after Baker had been to Moscow in January 1939 and had briefed
Comintern officials on his assumption of the leadership of the CPUSA
secret apparatus. Further, a May 1942 message from General Fitin, head

of the KGB's foreign intelligence directorate, to Dimitrov (in another Comintern collection) states, "We are forwarding a telegram we received from New York addressed to you from Rudy," and the telegram is signed "Son."[16]

Barash, Vladimir: Russian immigrant who approached a KGB asset and offered his services to the Soviet Union.[17]

Bark: unidentified asset who reported to the New York KGB office in 1943 and 1944. Checked out a Soviet sympathizer who worked for a major New York radio broadcaster as a candidate for KGB infiltration into the Office of War Information.[18]

Barr, Joel: concealed Communist, engineer, and part of the Rosenberg ring that reported to the New York KGB office. Cover names Scout and Meter (Metre).[19]

Barrows, Alice: employee of the Office of Education from 1919 to 1942, On the staff of the CPUSA's Abraham Lincoln School in Chicago in 1944. The KGB reported in 1945 that she gave Charles Kramer, one of its sources, some unspecified information.[20]

Bass: see Burd, Michael.

Bayer, Theodore: president of the Russky Golos Publishing Company, which published *Russky Golos,* the Russian-language newspaper allied to the CPUSA. Reported in 1943 to the New York GRU. Cover name Simon.[21]

Beam: unidentified asset of the New York KGB who appeared to work among immigrant groups, particularly Poles. In 1944 his work was of sufficient quality that the New York KGB proposed to Moscow that he receive a cash bonus.[22]

Beaver-Cloth: unidentified asset of the New York KGB who worked with the KGB illegal officer Iskhak Akhmerov in 1943.[23]

Beck: see Kurnakov, Sergey Nikolaevich.

Beer: see *El.*

Beiser, George: Bell Aircraft engineer who provided Andrey Shevchenko with information on machine tools. Described as a "left-winger" and an "idealist." Shevchenko was an inspector at Bell Aircraft, and Beiser may not have realized that he was also a KGB agent.[24]

Belenky, Aleksandr: Russian immigrant working at a General Electric plant. Provided material to the KGB through another immigrant.[25]

Belfrage, Cedric: journalist and concealed Communist, born in Britain, lived in the United States for many decades. Worked for British Security Co-ordination, a branch of British intelligence, in the United States during World War II. Reported both British and American information to the New York office of the KGB. Designated by Unbroken Cover Name No. 9.[26]

Ben: unidentified asset reporting to the New York KGB office in 1944. Worked with Joseph Katz, one of the KGB's most active American agents.[27]

Bentley, Elizabeth: joined the CPUSA in the mid-1930s and became part of its secret apparatus. Reported to the New York KGB office from 1943 to 1945 and managed several large rings (the Silvermaster group and the Perlo group) of secret CPUSA members who worked for the U.S. government. Cover names Clever Girl and Myrna.[28]

Berg: see Koral, Alexander.

Bernstein, Joseph Milton: journalist who reported to the GRU's New York office in 1943. Worked as GRU contact with Soviet agents employed in U.S. government agencies. Cover name Marquis.[29]

Bernstein, Walter Sol: journalist who the KGB said reestablished contact with the KGB in October 1944 and was preparing a report based on what he had learned during a trip abroad. Maintained in a memoir that he had met with representatives of the CPUSA at this time but denied any contact with Soviet intelligence.[30]

Bibi: unidentified asset who reported to the KGB New York office in 1943 and 1944. Worked for the economic mission of Charles de Gaulle's Free French movement in Washington, D.C., in 1944 and from that post sought to develop sources in the U.S. government's Lend-Lease Administration and Foreign Economic Administration. Also reported extensively on internal politics within the Free French movement. Appears to have been American but may have been French; gender unknown.[31]

Bisson, Thomas Arthur: Asia specialist, reported to the New York GRU office in 1943. Worked for the U.S. government's Board of Economic Warfare and for the private Institute for Pacific Relations. Cover name Arthur.[32]

Black: see Black, Thomas Lessing.

Black, Thomas Lessing: chemist engaged in industrial espionage on behalf of the Soviet Union starting in the mid-1930s. Cover names Black and Peter.[33]

Block: see *Osprey.*

Bob: see Menaker, Robert Owen.

Bolt: unidentified asset who provided the New York KGB office with documents on radio control technology in 1944.[34]

Borrow, Robinson: asset of the New York GRU in 1943. Cover name Richard.[35]

Bredan: unidentified asset of the New York KGB in 1942 who maintained contact with a target for Soviet recruitment.[36]

Brem: see Babin, Thomas.

Brook: unidentified asset for the Naval GRU office in Washington in 1943. Activities unknown.[37]

Brother: unidentified asset of the New York KGB office who appeared to have been involved in technical/scientific espionage, probably in the aviation industry. Also had the cover name Thomas.[38]

Brother-in-Law (Svoyak): unidentified asset of the San Francisco KGB in

1944 who provided information about U.S. atomic bomb project security.[39]

Brothman, Abraham: chemist and long-time KGB asset engaged in industrial espionage. Cover names Constructor, Chrome Yellow, and Expert.[40]

Browder, Earl: head of CPUSA from 1930 to 1945. Oversaw party's cooperation with Soviet espionage in the United States. Cover name Helmsman.[41]

Browder, Rose: courier between the CPUSA and the KGB. Wife of William Browder.[42]

Browder, William: Earl Browder's brother and longtime assistant. Met on several occasions with the head of the New York KGB office.[43]

Bugle: unidentified asset of the New York KGB office in 1944. Controlled by Andrey Shevchenko, a KGB officer who worked as an inspector at Bell Aircraft.[44]

Bumblebee: see Greenglass, David.

Burd, Michael: head of Midland Export Corporation. Played a key role in a complex KGB operation to arrange U.S. transit visas for Nicholas and Maria Fisher, two KGB agents. His firm also transmitted large amounts of money for the KGB. Cover names Tenor and Bass.[45]

Burns, Paul: member of the CPUSA secret apparatus and veteran of the International Brigades. Provided a safe-house for the KGB at the request of the CPUSA. Later became an employee of Soviet news agency TASS.[46]

Bursler, Norman: member of the Silvermaster group. Mid-level Justice Department official.[47]

Butcher: unidentified asset of the San Francisco KGB office in 1944. Identified possible recruits for Soviet espionage in the California oil and aviation industries. May be Steve Nelson (see appendix B).[48]

Caliber: see Greenglass, David.

Callahan, James: ship's clerk. Provided information in 1945 to the San Francisco KGB, which described him as "trustworthy."[49]

Callen, Sylvia: infiltrated the American Trotskyist movement on behalf of the CPUSA in the late 1930s and early 1940s. Later became part of the Soble espionage ring. Also used the surnames Franklin, Caldwell, and Doxsee. Cover name Satir (Satyr).[50]

Carmen: unidentified female courier who worked for the New York KGB office in 1942 and 1944. May have worked in the KGB's extensive Latin American operations in 1942 and 1943 but in 1944 was in New York, where the local KGB office planned to assign her to work with agents within the United States.[51]

Carter: see Coleman, Eugene Franklin.

Catalyst: unidentified asset of the New York KGB whom the Soviets were considering whether to continue to use in December 1942.[52]

Cautious: see Joseph, Julius J.

Cavalryman: see Kurnakov, Sergey Nikolaevich.

Cedar: see Perry, Burton.

Cerberus: unidentified employee of the U.S. Treasury Department. In a 1945 KGB message was identified as a GRU asset who in the view of the KGB had lost touch with the GRU and was attempting to reestablish contact through the CPUSA.[53]

Char . . . : partial decryption of the name of a member of one of Elizabeth Bentley's rings of former CPUSA covert sources taken over by the KGB in 1944. From description may be Charles Flato.[54]

Charlie: unidentified source of the New York KGB who provided sensitive official information on China and other subjects. May be Abraham Weinstein (see appendix B).[55]

Chef: unidentified asset of the New York KGB office in 1944. May have been a courier between KGB officers and their sources.[56]

Chen: (1) unidentified asset of the New York KGB in 1943 who reported information about the Czechoslovak government-in-exile and about the attitude of the U.S. State Department toward exile German groups.[57] (2) See Franklin, Zalmond David.

Chester: see Schuster, Bernard.

Chrome Yellow: see Brothman, Abraham.

Clemence: asset of the New York KGB who worked among German immigrants and exiles and ran a safe-house. Cover name later changed to Lee. May be Johanna Beker (see appendix B).[58]

Clever Girl: see Bentley, Elizabeth.

Coe, Virginius Frank: director of the Division of Monetary Research in the Treasury Department and after World War II a leading official of the International Monetary Fund. Member of the Silvermaster ring. Cover name Peak.[59]

Cohen, Lona: CPUSA activist, recruited into Soviet espionage by her husband, Morris. An active career agent in her own right, including as a courier on one mission to pick up reports from a Soviet spy working at the atomic bomb facility at Los Alamos. Cover name Lesley, also called Volunteer's Wife.[60]

Cohen, Morris: CPUSA activist and International Brigades veteran and career KGB spy. Cover name Volunteer.[61]

Coleman, Eugene Franklin: electrical engineer, secret CPUSA member recruited as a source by the Washington Naval GRU office in 1943. Cover name Carter.[62]

Colleague: see Joseph, Bella.

Colloms, Anna: New York City schoolteacher, worked as a courier linking the American and Mexican anti-Trotsky KGB operations. Called A. in a 1944 Venona cable reporting on her arrival in Mexico from the United States.[63]

Condenser: see Richardson, Kenneth.

Constructor: see Brothman, Abraham.

Coplon, Judith: concealed Communist and KGB asset in the Foreign Agents

Registration section of the Justice Department, where she had access to FBI counterintelligence information. Cover name Sima.[64]

Cora: member of CPUSA recruited by the New York KGB office in December 1944. Her husband and son-in-law were also party members. Iskhak Akhmerov was interested in using her and proposed drawing in her husband as well. Akhmerov planned to withdraw both of them gradually from CPUSA activities and move them to another city for KGB work. Subsequent activities unknown. Husband's cover name was Roy.[65]

Cork: see Pinsly, William.

Corporant: GRU cover name for member of the CPUSA or the CPUSA itself.

Costra, Louis: Puerto Rican Communist and International Brigades veteran whose address was proposed as a mail drop by a KGB asset.[66]

Crow: unidentified asset recruited by the New York KGB office in 1945. Nothing else known.[67]

Cupid: unidentified recruit of the New York KGB office in 1944. Considered for use as a "communications girl," possibly meaning a courier in the network supervised by Jack Soble. Also had the cover name Jeannette.[68]

Currie, Lauchlin B.: senior administrative assistant to President Roosevelt who served in a variety of positions, including that of the president's special representative to China and deputy administrator of the Foreign Economic Administration. Cooperated with Elizabeth Bentley's CPUSA-KGB Silvermaster network. Cover name Page.[69]

Czech: see Menaker, Robert Owen, and Soble, Jack.

D.: initial of a KGB source, probably a knowing one, who furnished information on the Manhattan Project.[70]

Danilov: see *Mok*.

Dasha: see Wicher, Maria.

Dauber, M.: of the Dauber and Pine Bookshop in New York City. Provided a mail drop for a KGB contact.[71]

Daughter: see Voge, Marietta.

Davis: (1) unidentified source of the New York KGB, possibly involved in industrial espionage.[72](2) See *Long* and *Spark*.

Davis, Marion: KGB source in the Office of the Coordinator of Inter-American Affairs Cover name Lou.[73]

Dennis, Eugene: senior member of the CPUSA leadership, in contact with a group of concealed Communists in the Office of Strategic Services and the Office of War Information.[74]

Dick: see Schuster, Bernard.

Dicky: see Steele, Johannes.

Dinah: see Kahn, Mrs. Ray (Gertrude).

Dir: see Price, Mary Wolfe.

Dodd, William E., Jr.: Popular Front activist. Father had been Roosevelt's ambassador to Nazi Germany. In 1944 the New York KGB asked Moscow if it was permissible, in light of Dodd's relationship to the KGB, for him to take a public job with TASS, the Soviet press agency. Cover name Sitsilla.[75]

Dodger: unidentified asset of the New York KGB who provided diplomatic information in 1943.[76]

Donald: unidentified U.S. Navy captain described by the Naval GRU in 1943 as "loyal to us." The description was part of a lengthy message about U.S. naval personnel in close contact with Soviet naval personnel in the United States. Unclear whether Donald is a real name or a cover name.[77]

Donald: (1) unidentified asset of the New York office of the GRU recruited in 1943 by the GRU agent Irving Velson.[78] (2) See Ullmann, William Ludwig.

Dora: see Silvermaster, Helen Witte.

Douglas: see Katz, Joseph.

Drugstore: unidentified asset recruited by the New York KGB office in 1945. Activities unknown.[79]

Duggan, Laurence: KGB asset beginning in the mid-1930s, headed the South American desk at the State Department until 1944. Served with the United Nations Relief and Rehabilitation Administration. Cover names Frank, Prince, and Sherwood.[80]

Duke: unidentified asset of the New York office of the KGB. The Russian name used in the messages is Gertsog, which means "duke" but may also transliterate the name Herzog. Appears to have been in or had some sort of contact with the French section of the OWI.[81]

Duya's son: unidentified son of Duya (also unidentified). In 1944 the New York KGB said that Duya's son was not now but had in the past been one of its assets. Duya is most likely a cover name.[82]

Dvoichenko-Markov, Demetrius: asset of the New York KGB 1943–1945, U.S. Army sergeant. Obtained, while assigned to military counterintelligence in Alaska, some sort of book or manual for the KGB. Cover name Hook. His mother, Eufrosina, also worked for the KGB.[83]

Dvoichenko-Markov, Eufrosina: asset of the New York KGB 1943–1945, provided information on exile groups in the United States, particularly Romanians and Carpatho-Russians, as well as on State Department personnel with whom she had contact. Cover name Masha.[84]

Dziedzik, Frank: employee of National Oil Products Company who supplied documentation on medical compounds to a KGB industrial espionage specialist.[85]

Eagle: unidentified asset of the New York KGB in 1944. In June 1944 placed by the KGB in cold storage for later use. Activities unknown.[86]

Echo: see Schuster, Bernard.

Economist: asset of the KGB likely involved in infiltration of the American Trotskyist movement.[87]

Egorn: see Einhorn, Nathan.

Einhorn, Nathan: journalist and executive secretary of the American Newspaper Guild in New York from 1938 to 1946. Helped to link CPUSA members to Soviet intelligence. Cover name Egorn.[88]

El: unidentified asset who worked with the Soviet illegal officer Iskhak Akhmerov in Washington, D.C., in connection with the Silvermaster group, as well as reporting to the New York KGB office in 1944 and 1945. Cover name changed to Beer in October 1944. Because of close relationship to Akhmerov, it is possible that El was merely a shortened form of Elsa, the cover name of Akhmerov's wife, Helen Lowry. El, which in Russian means "fir" or "spruce," is also used as a cover name for other unidentified persons and for Helen Keenan.[89]

Eleanor: asset of the Naval GRU in 1943 described as the daughter of Frank Gertsog, an immigrant from Russia in 1934 who became a naturalized U.S. citizen in 1935. Activities unknown.[90]

Ellis: unidentified female asset of the Naval GRU's Washington office in 1943. Passed on to the Naval GRU diplomatic information she had received from a luncheon with a "deputy minister of agriculture," presumably a deputy or assistant secretary of agriculture. Other activities unknown.[91]

Elsa: see Lowry, Helen.

Emilia: see *Stella.*

Emulsion: unidentified asset of the New York KGB in the military aircraft industry in 1944. Later had the cover name Signal.[92]

Engineer: unidentified asset of the KGB in 1944. The New York KGB feared that U.S. authorities had placed him under surveillance and observed him delivering documents to Amadeo Sabatini, one of its most active couriers. Sabatini was living on the West Coast at that time, so the document hand-over may have been there, suggesting that Engineer may also have been a West Coast resident. See York, Jones Orin.[93]

Epstein, Jacob: American Communist who had served with the International Brigades. Worked throughout 1943 and 1944 for the Mexico City KGB in its unsuccessful efforts to free Trotsky's assassin from a Mexican prison. Cover name Harry.[94]

Erie: see *Ernest* (KGB).

Ernest: unidentified asset of the New York KGB. Involved in scientific and technical espionage and may have been a scientist. Also had the cover name Erie.[95]

Ernest or *Ernst:* unidentified asset of the Naval GRU in 1943. Activities unknown.[96]

Expert: see Brothman, Abraham.

Express Messenger: see Setaro, Ricardo.

Fahy, Jack Bradley: asset of the Naval GRU. Worked for the Office of the Coordinator of Inter-American Affairs, the Board of Economic Warfare, and the Interior Department. Cover name Maxwell.[97]

Fakir: unidentified asset of the New York KGB office, 1943–1945. The KGB messages report that Fakir turned over State Department material to the KGB, discussed a contemplated trip to Moscow on behalf of an unnamed institution or agency, but also spoke of possibly taking a job with a CPUSA journal. Also had the cover name Arnold, and one KGB message makes a reference to information learned from an "officer" in "the statistical branch of Arnold's division," suggesting that Fakir/Arnold worked for a government agency.[98]

Fan: unidentified asset of the New York KGB in 1942 who provided vetting reports.[99]

Farish, Linn Markley: Communist, OSS officer, liaison with Tito's Partisan forces in Yugoslavia, and a KGB asset. Cover name Attila.[100]

Farley: unidentified asset of the New York office of the GRU, 1942–1943. Delivered information from the War Production Board and from the War Department.[101]

Farmhand: KGB contact of a KGB technical intelligence specialist. Described as having been on a long visit to a factory in New England in 1944.[102]

Fellowcountryman: generally a KGB term for any CPUSA member, but used in two 1944 messages as a cover name for a specific but unidentified asset of the New York KGB.[103]

Ferro: see Petroff, Aleksandr N.

Fighter: unidentified asset of the New York KGB who was recruited in 1942. Provided information on immigrant Ukrainians in the United States and Canada and investigated the attitudes of American journalists toward the Soviet Union. May be Albert Kahn (see appendix B).[104]

Fin: see Petroff, Aleksandr N.

Fir (or *Spruce*): see Keenan, Helen Grace Scott.

Fitzgerald, Edward J.: member of the Perlo group. Worked in the War Production Board. Cover name Ted.[105]

Flato, Charles: member of the Perlo group. Worked in the Board of Economic Warfare.[106]

Flora: New York KGB source who provided information on the United Nations Relief and Rehabilitation Administration.[107]

Fogel: unidentified asset of the New York KGB. Provided technical intelligence on the Manhattan Project and was most likely a scientist of some kind. Also had the cover name Pers or Persian.[108]

Folkoff, Isaac: senior member of the California Communist party and West Cost liaison between the KGB and the CPUSA. Worked as a courier passing information to and from Soviet sources, and as a talent-spotter and vetter of potential espionage recruits. Supervised several subagents. Cover name Uncle.[109]

Foster, Jane: a concealed Communist, worked for the Board of Economic Warfare in 1942 and then in the Indonesian section of the Office of Strategic Services from 1943 to 1947. After World War II became a member of the Soviet espionage ring managed by Jack Soble. Cover name Slang.[110]

Frank: see Duggan, Laurence, and Moosen, Arthur.

Franklin, Zalmond David: a CPUSA member and KGB asset, put into cold storage in 1944. Married at one time to Sylvia Callen. Cover name Chen.[111]

Fred: unidentified asset of the New York KGB who had a position in an unidentified U.S. government agency and dealt with Austria. May have been in the Office of War Information or had close contact with it.[112]

Friend: see Lange, Oskar.

Frost: see Morros, Boris Mikhailovich.

Gallardo, Isabel: Chilean, married to the American Lorren Hay, a Marine captain. Worked for the KGB on projects involving Chile.[113]

Gebert, Boleslaw K.: Communist union organizer and leader of pro-Communist activities among Polish-Americans. Reported to the KGB on the Polish-American community. Was a national officer of the Polonia Society of the International Workers Order. Cover name Ataman.[114]

Gel: unidentified asset of the New York KGB, 1942–1943. A journalist, worked for an unidentified magazine in 1943.[115]

George, Harrison: senior CPUSA figure, edited the party's West Coast newspaper, *People's World.* Assured the San Francisco KGB of the Communist loyalties of a target of KGB recruitment.[116]

Getzoff, Rebecca: KGB asset engaged in its anti-Trotskyist effort. Cover name Adam.[117]

Girl Friend: unidentified asset of the New York KGB, put into cold storage in 1944.[118]

Glasser, Harold: member of the Perlo group. An economist, worked in the Treasury Department. Cover name Ruble.[119]

Glory: see Wolston, Ilya Elliott.

Gnome: see Perl, William.

Godmother: asset of the New York KGB with access to diplomatic information.[120]

Gold, Bela (William): member of the Silvermaster group. Worked for the Senate Subcommittee on War Mobilization and Office of Economic Programs in the Foreign Economic Administration. Husband of Sonia Gold. Cover name Acorn.[121]

Gold, Harry: recruited in the mid-1930s for Soviet industrial espionage operations in the United States. Active courier for the New York KGB's scientific-technical espionage operations as well as liaison for several subagents. Cover names Goose and Arnold.[122]

Gold, Sonia Steinman: member of the Silvermaster group. Worked for the Division of Monetary Research of the Treasury Department. Wife of Bela Gold. Cover name Sonya (Sonia).[123]

Golos, Jacob: longtime senior official of the CPUSA and head of several groups of concealed party members within the U.S. government. Delivered information from his apparatus, spotted and vetted potential KGB recruits, and acted as a link between the KGB and the leadership of the CPUSA. Cover name Sound.[124]

Goose: see Gold, Harry.

Gorchoff, George: asset of the New York GRU in 1943. Cover name Gustav.[125]

Gordon, L.: asset of the New York GRU office described as female and a former CPUSA officer. Most likely Lottie Gordon, a former CPUSA official in Ohio. The GRU planned to establish Gordon as the head of a group of GRU sources in New York City and to provide her with a regular stipend.[126]

Green: provided information to the KGB about the Soviet defector Victor Kravchenko. May have been a cover name or possibly Abner Green, executive director of the American Committee for the Protection of the Foreign Born.[127]

Greenglass, David: member of the Young Communist League, recruited into Soviet espionage through the New York KGB office by his wife, Ruth, his sister, Ethel Rosenberg, and Ethel's husband, Julius. A soldier machinist working on the Manhattan Project at Los Alamos. Cover names Bumblebee and Caliber.[128]

Greenglass, Ruth: member of the Young Communist League, recruited into Soviet espionage through the New York KGB office by her sister-in-law, Ethel Rosenberg, and Ethel's husband, Julius. Assisted in drawing in her husband, David. Cover name Wasp.[129]

Growth: see *Odessan.*

Gustav: see Gorchoff, George.

Gymnast: KGB cover name for member of the Young Communist League.

Hall, Theodore Alvin: young physicist and Communist at Harvard, recruited to work on the Manhattan Project at Los Alamos. Volunteered to spy for the KGB and was an important Soviet atomic source. Cover name Youngster.[130]

Halperin, Maurice: secret Communist, became a KGB asset after obtaining the post of chief of the Latin American Division of the Research and Analysis section of the Office of Strategic Services, 1943–1945. After World War II, became a Latin American specialist for the State Department, 1945–1946. Cover names Hare and Stowaway.[131]

Hare: see Halperin, Maurice.

Harold: the New York KGB asked Moscow for permission to complete his recruitment in May 1944.[132]

Harris, Kitty: asset of the Mexico City KGB during World War II. Born in England, moved with her family to the United States via Canada, had close ties to the CPUSA. Joined the CPUSA in 1923, became a Comintern operative in the late 1920s, and at some point transferred to the KGB. Cover name Ada.[133]

Harry: see Epstein, Jacob.

Havre: cover name in the Venona cables for a person who worked for

British Security Coordination, a branch of British intelligence operating in the United States. The KGB reported that Havre delivered reports on the Czechoslovak government-in-exile and was a go-between with Cedric Belfrage, another officer of British Security Coordination who spied for the KGB. It is unclear whether Havre was American or British.[134]

Hedgehog: unidentified courier working for the New York KGB.[135]

Helmsman: see Browder, Earl.

Henry: see Malisoff (Malisov), William Marias.

Henwood, William: engineer for Standard Oil in California. Born in South Africa, became a naturalized U.S. citizen. Isaac Folkoff, the CPUSA West Coast liaison with Soviet intelligence, put Henwood in touch with the San Francisco KGB office in 1944.[136]

Hiss, Alger: senior American diplomat and important asset of the GRU. Cover name Ales.[137]

Hook: see Dvoichenko-Markov, Demetrius.

Horus: unidentified asset of the New York KGB, may have been in the Office of Strategic Services.[138]

Horvitz, Louis D.: member of the CPUSA secret apparatus and veteran of the International Brigades who provided a safe-house for the KGB at the request of the CPUSA.[139]

Hudson: unidentified asset of the New York KGB. Also had the cover name John. Activities included working in the KGB's "first line" (political intelligence), placing Soviet sources in Jewish and Zionist organizations, and maintaining liaison with various Soviet sources.[140]

Hughes: see Sarant, Alfred Epaminondas.

Huron: unidentified asset of the New York KGB, 1944–1945. Involved in scientific and technical espionage, may have been a scientist, perhaps Bruno Pontecorvo.[141]

I.: (1) unidentified asset of the New York KGB working in a scientific or technological field, possibly dealing with the oil industry. In 1944 the KGB said that I.'s coworkers made him useless for the moment, although he remained "loyal to the USSR."[142] (2) Unidentified asset of the Washington KGB who in 1945 delivered a secret Office of Strategic Services cable reporting on OSS operations in Yugoslavia.[143]

Iceberg: unidentified asset of the New York KGB. Provided information about the movement of American aircraft in Asia.[144]

Ide: see Krafsur, Samuel.

Informer: see Katz, Joseph.

Ipatov: unidentified contact in Chicago of the New York KGB.[145]

Isaak, Rosa: executive secretary of the American-Russian Institute. In 1945 advised the San Francisco KGB that she intended to resign from her job and would be breaking off contact with Soviet intelligence.[146]

Ivanov: see Scott, John.

Ivanova: female KGB asset who worked in the French section of the Office of War Information. Appears to have been an immigrant who applied for American citizenship in 1943.[147]

Ivy: see Joseph, Emma Harriet (appendix D).

Izra: see Wheeler, Donald Niven.

Jack: unidentified asset of the New York GRU in 1943 who provided information on the U.S. testing of guided bombs and shipping cargoes. Also vetted prospects for GRU recruitment. Was also an intermediary between the GRU and the CPUSA.[148]

Jacob: see Perl, William.

Jacobson, Herman R.: employee of Avery Manufacturing Company, worked with the New York KGB office. Cover name S-1.[149]

Jean: see Setaro, Ricardo.

Jeanne: see Krotkova, Christina.

Jeannette: (1) see *Cupid.* (2) Unidentified asset of the New York KGB in 1944.[150]

John: see *Hudson.*

Johnny: unidentified asset of the New York GRU office. In 1943 delivered a 150-page technical report.[151]

Joseph, Bella: secret Communist. Worked for the motion picture division of the Office of Strategic Services. Wife of Julius Joseph. Cover name Colleague.[152]

Joseph, Julius J.: secret Communist and member of the Golos-Bentley network who worked for the Far Eastern section (Japanese intelligence) of the Office of Strategic Services (1943–1945). Cover name Cautious. His wife also worked for the OSS.[153]

Julia: contact of Iskhak Akhmerov, a KGB illegal officer, described in a 1944 message as having been out of contact for several years and as living near Lake Geneva in New York on the resources of a wealthy father.[154]

Jupiter: unidentified asset of the New York KGB in 1944. Later had the cover name Original (or Odd Fellow).[155]

Jurist: see White, Harry Dexter.

Kahn, Mrs. Ray (Gertrude): suggested for foreign work by Moscow. The New York KGB told Moscow that this was unwise and advised that she was best used in a "passive" role. Cover name Dinah.[156]

Kant: see Magdoff, Harry Samuel, and Zborowski, Mark.

Karl: unidentified asset of the New York KGB in 1944. Appears to have been engaged in scientific-technical espionage. May have been a former member of a covert CPUSA apparatus inasmuch as in one message the New York KGB asks Moscow headquarters about the advisability of its picking up material Karl had delivered to Earl Browder. Also had the cover name Ray.[157]

Karr, David: journalist and asset of the New York KGB.[158]

Katz, Joseph: one of the KGB's most active American assets. Served as a courier to many Soviet sources, also vetted prospective recruits, photographed material, and carried messages to and from the CPUSA leadership. Cover names Informer, Douglas, and X.[159]

Keen: (1) see Wicher, Enos Regent. (2) See *Osprey*.

Keenan, Helen Grace Scott: asset first of the New York KGB office and then of the Washington KGB. Worked in 1945 for the Office of U.S. Chief of Counsel for Prosecution of Axis War Criminals, initially run by the OSS. Cover name Fir (or Spruce).[160]

Keeney, Mary Jane: secret Communist, recruited (along with her husband, Philip) by the GRU in 1940. Worked for the Board of Economic Warfare and, after World War II, for the United Nations. Taken over by the KGB in 1945.[161]

Keeney, Philip Olin: secret Communist, recruited (along with his wife, Mary Jane) by the GRU in 1940. Worked for the Office of the Coordinator of Information (later the Office of Strategic Services) in 1941. Taken over by the KGB in 1945.[162]

Khan: unidentified KGB asset who linked Soviet KGB officers with KGB sources, a number of whom were CPUSA activists (Albert Kahn, Boleslaw Gebert, Eufrosina Dvoichenko-Markov) involved in ethnic minority work. May be Avram Landy, a senior CPUSA official who supervised party work among ethnic groups. Also had the cover name Selim Khan.[163]

Khan's wife: wife of KGB asset Khan. Kept watch over a Finnish-American woman whom the KGB had recruited for intelligence work but had decided not to use, because she expressed doubts about the justice of Stalin's purges.[164]

Khazar: unidentified asset of the New York KGB. A naturalized American citizen, probably of Yugoslav origin. Provided information on Office of Strategic Services personnel being inserted into occupied Yugoslavia. Not clear whether he became an OSS operative.[165]

Khe . . . : see Miller, Floyd Cleveland.

Kinsman: see *Solid*.

Klara: see Stridsberg, Augustina.

Klo: see Rand, Esther Trebach.

Koch: see Lee, Duncan Chapin.

Koral, Alexander: CPUSA member who worked as a KGB courier along with his wife, Helen. Cover name Berg.[166]

Koral, Helen: asset of the New York KGB. Assisted the KGB illegal officer Iskhak Akhmerov and received a regular stipend. Cover names Miranda and Art.[167]

Krafsur, Samuel: CPUSA member and veteran of the International Brigades, an asset of the New York KGB working as a journalist for the Soviet news agency TASS. Used by the KGB to cultivate American journalists, with an eye to recruiting as KGB sources. Cover name Ide.[168]

Kramer, Charles: member of the Perlo group. An economist, worked for the Senate Subcommittee on War Mobilization and the Office of Price

Administration. Before the war, worked for the National Labor Relations Board. Cover names Plumb, Lot, and Mole.[169]

Krotkova, Christina: KGB asset who worked for the Office of War Information. Her chief target was the Soviet defector Victor Kravchenko. Cover names Jeanne and Ola.[170]

Kurnakov, Sergey Nikolaevich: former Czarist cavalry officer who had immigrated to the United States and become a Communist. Spied on Russian immigrants, served as a courier to various KGB sources, and acted as both a talent-spotter and a vetter of potential recruits. Cover names Cavalryman and Beck.[171]

Kurt: see *Plucky.*

Laird, Stephen: radio broadcaster, journalist, and filmmaker, KGB source in 1944 and 1945. Cover name Yun.[172]

Lambert, Rudolph Carl: California Communist party labor director and head of its security arm. Named in a garbled 1945 San Francisco KGB cable discussing information about uranium deposits in Western states.[173]

Lange, Oskar: Polish immigrant who became a naturalized citizen, A leading advocate of American support for a pro-Soviet Polish government, functioned as an agent of influence. Cover name Friend.[174]

Laszl: unidentified source of the New York GRU in 1943. Described as a friend of the GRU agent Joseph Bernstein. Unclear whether Laszl was a cover name or a real name, and unclear whether Laszl was a witting or unwitting source for Bernstein.[175]

Lava: see Schultz, Marion Miloslavovich.

Lawyer: see White, Harry Dexter.

Lee: see *Clemence.*

Lee, Duncan Chapin: highly placed officer of the Office of Strategic Services, serving as an assistant to William Donovan, head of the OSS, and as an OSS field officer in China. Came under KGB control via a CPUSA covert network. Cover name Koch.[176]

Lens: see Sidorovich, Michael.

Leona: unidentified female asset of the New York KGB. Attempted to get a job with the Office of War Information. Her husband appears to have been an employee of a large New York radio station and to have been aware of his wife's connection with Soviet intelligence. Activities unknown.[177]

Leshing, Michael S.: superintendent of Twentieth Century Fox film laboratories. In 1943 provided the Soviets with documents and formula for developing color motion pictures and other film-processing technology.[178]

Lesley: see Cohen, Lona.

Levanas, Leo: chemist with Shell Oil. After a meeting with a KGB agent, asked to meet with the head of the San Francisco KGB office to "explore helping us." Cover name Alma.[179]

Levenson, L.: employee of Electro-Physical Laboratories of New York City, provided a mail drop for a KGB contact.[180]

Levi: unidentified asset of the Washington KGB office who in 1945 delivered political intelligence. Possibly a real name.[181]

Lewis (Luis or *Louis):* unidentified asset recruited by the New York KGB in 1942. In 1944 and 1945 Alfred Stern had the cover name Louis, but it is unclear that this is the same person. In the Venona messages a different Luis (or Lewis or Louis) is also involved in the KGB's Latin American operations.[182]

Libau, Morris: German immigrant, a "walk-in" who in 1944 offered the Soviets information on the eastern front. The KGB turned him over to the GRU.[183]

Liberal: see Rosenberg, Julius.

Lidia (or *Lydia*): see Altschuler, Lydia.

Lily: see Olkhine, Eugénie.

Link: unidentified asset of the KGB New York, 1943–1944. Held some position in the U.S. government, most likely in the military but possibly in the Office of Strategic Services. According to one 1943 KGB message, Link completed a course in Italian, was on leave, and was expected to be sent to Britain shortly. (The KGB arranged a password allowing a KGB officer to approach Link in Britain.) In 1944 passed information to the New York KGB via his brother to Lona Cohen, a KGB asset. May be William Weisband (see appendix B).[184]

Lira: see Strong, Anna Louise.

Liza: unidentified asset of the New York KGB, a secretary in the War Department to Vladimir Pozner, and the link between him and the KGB.[185]

Liza: see Stern, Martha Dodd.

Loesh: unidentified asset of the GRU. In 1943 given $12,083 by the GRU. Activities unknown. It is not clear whether Loesh is a cover name or a real name.[186]

Long: unidentified asset of the New York KGB office, at least as early as 1941 and perhaps earlier. In 1941 changed residences and lost contact with the KGB when his Soviet controller, Gaik Ovakimian, was arrested by the FBI for espionage. In 1944 the New York KGB renewed contact through the KGB officer Aleksandr Raev, who reported that Long was apprehensive but had accepted five hundred dollars in payment and wanted more. Also had the cover name Davis.[187]

Lot: see Kramer, Charles.

Lou: see Davis, Marion.

Louis: see Stern, Alfred Kaufman.

Lowry, Helen: wife of Iskhak Akhmerov, the leading KGB illegal officer operating in the United States. Served as a courier between her husband and the KGB. Cover name Elsa. See also El.[188]

Lynch: provided to a KGB officer, according to a 1943 GRU message, information he had learned from a meeting with the vice-chairman of the War Production Board. Unclear whether informant acted wittingly or unwittingly. Unclear whether Lynch was a cover name or a real name.[189]

Lyuba: unidentified female asset of the New York KGB in 1944, connected in some way to the CPUSA. In New York City in 1944 but was planning to return to her permanent residence unless the KGB had an assignment in the near future.[190]

Mabel: unidentified asset of the Naval GRU in 1943.[191]

Mackey, William: resident of Portland, Oregon, who was doing some unspecified work for Isaac Folkoff, a senior Communist and liaison with the KGB. The San Francisco KGB appeared to be considering taking Mackey under its direct control.[192]

Magda: unidentified female asset of the New York KGB, 1944–1945, with links to journalists and *Time* magazine.[193]

Magdoff, Harry Samuel: member of the Perlo group, worked for the War Production Board and the Office of Emergency Management. Cover names Kant and Tan.[194]

Malisoff (Malisov), William Marias: KGB asset and owner of United Laboratories in New York City. Cover names Talent and Henry.[195]

Map: unidentified female asset of the San Francisco KGB, 1943–1945. Acted as a liaison between KGB officers and several intelligence sources. May be Louise Bransten (chapter 8).[196]

Margarita: KGB asset. Identified by NSA/FBI analysts, who redacted her real name in its release of the messages. Born in the United States to Finnish immigrant parents and emigrated with them in 1933 to settle in Soviet Karelia. Later worked for the *Moscow Daily News,* a Soviet-controlled English-language newspaper. After returning to the United States, she worked for the wartime U.S. government mail and press censorship office and for the United Nations Relief and Rehabilitation Administration. The KGB established a relationship with her through one of its agents, Joseph Katz. Although pro-Soviet, Margarita expressed anger about the treatment of the Finnish-Americans who had settled in Karelia and deep resentment about the conduct of the KGB during the purges. (Many Finnish-American immigrants had been executed or imprisoned during Stalin's Terror.) Under the circumstances, the KGB decided not to continue using her as an agent. Because its contacts with her might have made her a security risk, the New York KGB raised with Moscow the option of luring her back to the USSR through a letter from her brother, who had been wounded while fighting in the Red Army. The New York KGB noted that "this solution of the problems would be the most radical"—an understatement, because her return would certainly have resulted in imprisonment, given that the KGB had her on record as voicing anti-Soviet sentiments. In the end, however, the New York KGB decided that she was still sufficiently pro-Soviet that this plan was not necessary. Instead, she was put in cold storage and her activities were observed for signs that she might go to American authorities.[197]

Mark: asset of the New York KGB. Reported on Jewish and Zionist groups and on exiled European Social Democrats and Socialists. One message suggests that Mark was Menashe Unger, chairman of the American Committee of Jewish Writers, Artists, and Scientists. In 1944, put in cold storage by the KGB.[198]

Marquis: see Bernstein, Joseph Milton.

Masha: see Dvoichenko-Markov, Eufrosina.

Master (or *Master Craftsman*): see Sheppard, Charles Bradford.

Mateo: unidentified KGB asset who worked on obtaining false documents and arranging U.S.-Mexico border crossings. An asset of the Mexico City KGB. Unclear whether he was Mexican or American.[199]

Matvey: see Schwartz, Milton.

Max: unidentified asset of the New York GRU in 1943.[200]

Maxwell: see Fahy, Jack Bradley.

Mayor: see Akhmerov, Iskhak Abdulovich.

Menaker, Robert Owen: KGB asset involved in U.S. and Latin American operations. Cover names Bob and Czech.[201]

Meri: unidentified asset of the New York KGB in 1944. Activities unclear, but the messages suggest a close connection with the CPUSA.[202]

Meter: see Barr, Joel.

Miller, Floyd Cleveland: major KGB asset within the American Trotskyist movement. Also known as Mike Cort. Cover name in KGB messages, only partially deciphered, was Khe . . . [203]

Miller, James Walter: asset of the San Francisco KGB, 1943–1945. Recruited for Soviet intelligence by Isaac Folkoff of the CPUSA. Worked for the U.S. government wartime mail censorship office. Cover name Vague.[204]

Mins, Leonard Emil: concealed Communist and GRU agent. Held a position in the Russian section of the research and analysis division of the Office of Strategic Services. Cover name Smith.[205]

Mirage: unidentified asset of the New York office of the KGB in 1943. Was an employee either of the State Department or of an agency that received State Department documents. Provided the KGB with information about U.S. diplomatic activities in Latin America. May be Charles Page (chapter 7).[206]

Mirage's wife: provided information to the KGB on the pending trip to Sweden of an American journalist of interest to the KGB. May be Mary Page, wife of Charles Page and an employee of the postal censorship office.[207]

Miranda: see Koral, Helen.

Mitron: unidentified asset of the New York GRU in 1943.[208]

Mitynen, Francia Yakilnilna: illegal officer of the Naval GRU who was smuggled into the United States in 1943. Used the name Edna Margaret Patterson until she left in 1956. Cover names Sally and Australian Woman.[209]

Mok: GRU illegal operating under a false identify. Extracted from the United States in 1943 and returned to the USSR. Activities unknown.

May have been the GRU officer Vladimir V. Gavrilyuk. The KGB noted his removal under the cover name Danilov.[210]

Mole: see Kramer, Charles.

Moosen, Arthur: asset of the New York GRU in 1943. Cover name Frank.[211]

Morkovin, Vladimir Borisovich: aeronautical engineer at Bell Aircraft who provided technical information to Andrey Shevchenko, a KGB agent operating as an inspector at Bell. Shevchenko described Morkovin as cautious and as friendly to the Soviet Union but unaware that Shevchenko was a Soviet intelligence officer. Cover name Author.[212]

Morros, Boris Mikhailovich: Russian immigrant and Hollywood producer, was an asset of the New York KGB and later became an FBI double agent. Cover names Frost (the Russian word for frost is *moroz*) and a name with the initial V.[213]

Muse: see Tenney, Helen.

Musician: unidentified asset of the San Francisco KGB, 1943–1944.[214]

Myrna: see Bentley, Elizabeth.

Napoli, Nicola: president of Artkino, distributor of Russian films. Passed on information from the CPUSA to a KGB asset about people seeking contact with the KGB.[215]

Nat: unidentified asset of the San Francisco KGB, 1945–1946. Identified as a leading official of the Communist party in the San Francisco Bay Area. May be Nat Yanish.[216]

Needle: see York, Jones Orin.

Nelly: unidentified asset of the New York KGB in 1944 who appeared to be employed by the U.S. Lend-Lease Administration.[217]

Nemo: see Pinsly, William.

Neumann, Franz: KGB source working for the Office of Strategic Services. Cover name Ruff.[218]

Nick: see Sabatini, Amadeo, and Velson, Irving Charles.

Nile (or *Neil* or *Neale*): unidentified asset of the New York KGB. Originally passed material to the KGB through the CPUSA. Later appeared to have become part of the Rosenberg apparatus. Also had another cover name that was only partially deciphered: Tu . . . [219]

Nina: unidentified asset of the New York KGB in mid-1944.[220]

NN-32: unidentified asset of the New York KGB, 1943–1944. Put in cold storage in 1944. Allowed by the KGB to set up a mail drop for correspondence from Spain, and messages also suggest some connection with the International Brigades.[221]

Noah: unidentified asset of the New York KGB office, 1943–1945. The New York KGB regarded his reports about American data on internal German political conditions as "valuable."[222]

Noise: see *Splint*.

Nona: see Wilson, Ruth Beverly.

Octane: unidentified cover name of an asset in contact with Semyon Semenov, a KGB officer who specialized in scientific-technical intelligence. Active from 1943 to 1945 and perhaps as early as 1939.[223]

Odessan: unidentified asset of the New York KGB office, 1944–1945. Appeared to be engaged in scientific-technical espionage, maintained some sort of enterprise that was subsidized by the KGB. Also had the cover name Growth.[224]

Okho (possibly *Ojo*, Spanish "eye"): unidentified cover name for an asset of the New York KGB who furnished information on the OSS in 1944.[225]

Ola: see Krotkova, Christina.

Old (or *Oldster*): see Sax, Saville.

Olkhine, Eugénie: KGB asset. The KGB reestablished liaison with her in 1945 after a prolonged absence. American born of a Russian father, perhaps Aleksandrov. The KGB considered attempting to plant her in the FBI. Provided information on immigrant Russians and was promised Soviet citizenship by the KGB. Cover name Lily.[226]

Olsen: provided a letter of introduction for a KGB agent seeking in 1944 to contact a scientist working on the Manhattan Project. The scientist had been cultivated by members of the CPUSA, and Olsen was described as head of the Illinois Communist party. May be Morris Childs, head of the CPUSA in Illinois in 1944. Olsen may be a party name rather than a cover name.[227]

Olsen, Rose: See *Phlox.*

Oppen: unidentified asset of the New York office of the GRU in 1943. Provided information on U.S. military technology and assisted in recruiting new GRU agents.[228]

Original (or *Odd Fellow*): see *Jupiter.*

Orloff, Nicholas W.: asset of the New York KGB. Russian immigrant, member of the tsarist aristocracy. Received a regular KGB stipend, provided information on immigrant groups, and acted as a talent-spotter for new sources. In 1944 the KGB reported that he was applying for U.S. citizenship and hoped to get a job with the Office of Strategic Services or the State Department, and that he had told his wife, a native-born American, that he was breaking off all connections with Soviet intelligence in order to reduce the chance that she might turn him in to American authorities. According to OSS records, he obtained American citizenship in mid-1944 and, shortly thereafter, applied for a position with the OSS, citing his fluency in several European languages and his many years of residence in Europe. It appears, however, that his application was rejected. Cover name Osipov.[229]

Osipov: see Orloff, Nicholas W.

Osipovich, Nadia Morris: Asset of the San Francisco KGB. Naturalized American citizen living in Portland, Oregon. Cover name Watchdog.[230]

Osprey: unidentified asset of the New York KGB office who in 1944 was rewarded with a monthly stipend. Also had the cover names Block and Keen.[231]

Padva's wife (or *Padua*'s wife): in late 1944 Padva (otherwise unidentified) approached a KGB officer at the Soviet consulate about his wife, who, he explained, had once been in touch with another KGB officer and had material to give the Soviets.[232]

Page: see Currie, Lauchlin B.

Painter: unidentified asset of the New York KGB in 1944. Delivered documents and headed a group of sources in New York.[233]

Pal: see Silvermaster, Nathan Gregory.

Patriarch: unidentified asset of the New York KGB in 1944. Duties included providing background information on people of interest to the KGB, particularly American merchant seamen.[234]

Peak: see Coe, Virginius Frank.

Perch: see Tkach, Mikhail.

Perl, William: aeronautical scientist working on advanced-technology military projects, particularly jet aircraft. Member of the Rosenberg network of the KGB. Cover names Gnome and Jacob.[235]

Perlo, Victor: head of the Perlo group. An economist, during World War II worked for the Advisory Council of National Defense of the Office of Price Administration and the War Production Board. After the war, worked for the Division of Monetary Research of the Treasury Department. Cover name Raider.[236]

Perry, Burton: asset of the San Francisco office of the KGB. In 1944 Perry gave the KGB the technical particulars of a radar-guided glide bomb whose testing he was part of. Cover name Cedar.[237]

Pers (or *Persian*): see *Fogel*.

Peter: see Black, Thomas Lessing.

Petroff, Aleksandr N.: employee of Curtiss-Wright Aircraft, provided the KGB with information on aircraft production methods. Cover names Fin and Ferro.[238]

Phil: unidentified GRU liaison agent who linked sources within the U.S. military to Soviet military intelligence in 1943.[239]

Philip: unidentified contact of the San Francisco KGB in 1946 who met with a KGB officer and senior West Coast CPUSA officers.[240]

Philosopher: unidentified asset of the New York KGB, 1943–1944. Worked in the French section of the Office of War Information.[241]

Phlox: CPUSA contact in Chicago of the New York KGB used in an attempt to approach a senior Manhattan Project scientist targeted for recruitment. Also referred to in the Venona cables as Rose Olsen, likely a CPUSA party name. May be the wife of Jack Childs or Morris Childs.[242]

Phlox's husband: In 1944 the New York KGB told Moscow that it intended to use him to approach a senior Manhattan Project scientist targeted for recruitment. May be either Jack Childs, a full-time CPUSA functionary working in its underground apparatus, or his brother, Morris Childs, head of the Illinois Communist party.[243]

Pillar: unidentified asset of the New York KGB. Activities unknown. After

the return to the USSR of Pavel P. Klarin, a senior KGB officer who had
had been Pillar's liaison, the New York KGB had difficulty developing a
replacement.[244]

Pilot: see Ullmann, William Ludwig.

Pinsky, Paul: California Communist trade union official whom the KGB
planned to use to approach a scientist working on the Manhattan Project.[245]

Pinsly, William: employee of Curtiss-Wright Aircraft in Williamsville, New
York, an asset of the New York KGB office in 1944. Cover names Cork
and Nemo.[246]

Plato: see Pozner, Vladimir Aleksandrovich.

Plourde, William Alfred: engineer with Bell Aircraft in Buffalo, New York,
who was in contact with the KGB in 1944.[247]

Plucky: unidentified asset for the New York KGB office, 1941–1944.
Worked for the KGB for four years, but the only clear report about his
work refers to information he provided on exiled Bessarabians. Also had
the cover name Kurt.[248]

Plumb: see Kramer, Charles.

Pozner, Vladimir Aleksandrovich: asset of the New York KGB. Russian
immigrant who headed the Russian division of a photographic section
of the U.S. War Department. Cover name Plato.[249]

Pratt, Gertrude: active with the Student Antifascist Committee. In 1943 the
KGB proposed to use Pratt to "process" (gather background information
about) Eleanor Roosevelt.[250]

Price, Mary Wolfe: part of a CPUSA covert apparatus run by Jacob Golos
that was taken over by the KGB. A secretary of the journalist Walter
Lippmann, she acted as a courier to several Soviet sources. Cover name
Dir.[251]

Prince: see Duggan, Laurence.

Purser: KGB asset with whom the KGB lost contact when he entered the
Navy.[252]

Quantum: unidentified asset of the New York KGB. Provided highly technical information on the Manhattan Project at an early date, June 1943,
and appears to have been a scientist.[253]

R.: see Witczak, Ignacy.

Raider: see Perlo, Victor.

Rand, Esther Trebach: asset of the New York KGB who spied on Zionists,
part of the Soble espionage ring. Cover names Aida and Klo.[254]

Randolph: unidentified asset of the New York office of the GRU, 1943.
Appears to have been based in New York but made regular trips to
Washington, D.C. May have been a journalist, inasmuch as he reported
on what he had learned from prominent political and governmental figures as well as from major journalists.[255]

Ray: see *Karl.*

Redhead: Unidentified contact, mentioned in 1944 Venona cable, whom the illegal KGB officer Iskhak Akhmerov had known as early as 1940 and perhaps earlier. Possibly Hede Massing (appendix B), who is known to have had this cover name in 1936 when she supervised a KGB network in the United States.[256]

Reed: unidentified asset of the New York KGB. May have been a resident of Washington, D.C., where his KGB contact was assigned for a time.[257]

Relay: unidentified asset of the New York KGB in 1944, courier to several Soviet sources. Described as living in Philadelphia and having an artificial leg or foot. Cover name later changed to Serb.[258]

Rhodes, Peter: journalist and employee of the Foreign Broadcasting Monitoring Service, the psychological warfare section of Allied Military Headquarters in London, and the Office of War Information. In 1944 the New York KGB informed its headquarters that Rhodes had been connected with the KGB in earlier years through a CPUSA network but that the connection had been broken. The CPUSA's liaison with the KGB recommended that the connection be reestablished.[259]

Rich, Stephan: asset of the New York GRU in 1943. Cover name Sandi.[260]

Richard: see Borrow, Robinson, and White, Harry Dexter.

Richardson, Kenneth: employee of World Wide Electronics. Involved in scientific-technical intelligence with the New York KGB, 1943–1945. Cover name Condenser.[261]

Rit: unidentified asset of the New York KGB who was being replaced in 1944.[262]

Robert: (1) unidentified asset of the GRU in 1945. Name occurs in a list of KGB targets, most of whom have some State Department connection. The Moscow KGB headquarters warned its New York office away from him with the comment that he already was a GRU asset.[263] (2) See Silvermaster, Nathan Gregory.

Rodman, Samuel Jacob: journalist who for a time worked for the United Nations Relief and Rehabilitation Administration. In 1944 the KGB's CPUSA contact reported that Rodman was on his way to Yugoslavia on a UNRRA mission and that he had arranged for Rodman to gather information and carry out some unspecified task.[264]

Roman: see Soblen, Robert.

Rosenberg, Allan: member of the Perlo group. Rosenberg worked in the Board of Economic Warfare/Foreign Economic Administration.[265]

Rosenberg, Ethel: Communist and the wife of Julius Rosenberg. KGB messages show that she was fully informed about her husband's espionage activities and assisted in recruiting her brother and sister-in-law, David and Ruth Greenglass. She and her husband were convicted of espionage and executed in 1953.[266]

Rosenberg, Julius: engineer and concealed Communist who recruited a ring of engineers, most of whom were also concealed Communists, who gathered military scientific-technical intelligence for the New York KGB. He and his wife were convicted of espionage and executed in 1953. Cover names Antenna and Liberal.[267]

Ruble: see Glasser, Harold.

Rudi: unidentified contact of the New York GRU in 1943. Appears to have had responsibility for liaison with other sources, including some in Canada, and direct links with the CPUSA. May be Rudy Baker.[268]

Ruff: see Neumann, Franz.

S-1: see Jacobson, Herman R.

S-2: unidentified asset of the New York KGB. Described by the KGB in 1944 as female and forty-five years old. Appears to have been associated with Herman Jacobson (S-1).[269]

S-8: unidentified asset of the New York KGB in 1945.[270]

Sabatini, Amadeo: CPUSA member and veteran of the International Brigades, was one of the KGB's most active couriers and liaison agents. The KGB reimbursed him for travel and living expenses and paid a monthly stipend to his wife. Lived in California, and many of his assignments were in the West. Cover name Nick.[271]

Sachs: see Adler, Solomon.

Sally: see Mitynen, Francia Yakilnilna.

Sam: asset of the San Francisco KGB. Described as the younger brother of Burton Perry and helped to convince him to turn over the plans of a radar-guided glide bomb to the Soviets.[272]

Sandi: see Rich, Stephan.

Sarant, Alfred Epaminondas: concealed Communist, engineer, and part of the Rosenberg ring that reported to the New York KGB. Worked on military radar at the U.S. Army Signal Corps laboratories at Fort Monmouth, New Jersey. Cover name Hughes.[273]

Satir (Satyr): see Callen, Sylvia.

Sax, Saville: member of the Young Communist League at Harvard, roommate of Theodore Hall. Worked as a courier between Hall and the KGB. Cover name Old (or Oldster).[274]

Schultz, Marion (Marian) Miloslavovich: immigrant from Russia, an asset of the New York KGB for work among immigrants. Was a mechanic in a Philadelphia shipyard and chair of the United Russian Committee for Aid to the Native Country. Cover name Lava.[275]

Schuster, Bernard: official of the New York Communist party's internal security apparatus, also liaison between the New York KGB and the CPUSA national leadership. Performed a variety of other tasks for the KGB, including vetting potential KGB recruits and arranging for the use of CPUSA members for KGB courier work. Cover names Chester (his CPUSA party name), Echo, Dick, and South.[276]

Schwartz, Milton: asset of the New York GRU in 1943. The nature of Schwartz's work for the GRU is unknown, but he believed it valuable enough to ask the GRU for $1,200 to help him get out of a personal difficulty. Cover name Matvey.[277]

Scott, John: former Communist trade union organizer and asset of the New York KGB after he began work in the Russian section of the Office of Strategic Services. Cover name Ivanov.[278]

Scout: see Barr, Joel.

Second-Hand Bookseller: unidentified asset of the New York KGB in 1944. Put in cold storage in mid-1944 but brought back in the fall to assist with what appeared to be establishing a front enterprise for scientific-technical espionage. Also had close ties to the CPUSA.[279]

Selim Khan: see *Khan.*

Serb: asset of the New York KGB in 1945, In contact with Leonid Kvasnikov, a KGB officer who specialized in scientific-technical intelligence.[280]

Serpa: unidentified Soviet source. In 1944 the KGB headquarters told the New York KGB office to evaluate the information he was turning in and decide whether it wished to run him directly or indirectly, through its CPUSA liaison.[281]

Setaro, Ricardo: deputy chief of the Latin American department of CBS, a concealed Communist, and an asset of the New York office of the KGB, 1943–1944. Cover names Express Messenger and Jean.[282]

Sheppard, Charles Bradford: radio engineer working on radar in the design office of Hazeltine Electronics. Asked the KGB to arrange Soviet citizenship for him and his family and their eventual emigration to the USSR. Cover name Master or Master Craftsman.[283]

Sherwood: see Duggan, Laurence.

Sidorovich, Anne: member of the Rosenberg ring and the wife of Michael Sidorovich. Assisted her husband and received a monthly KGB stipend. Cover name Squirrel.[284]

Sidorovich, Michael: member of the Rosenberg ring. Did a great deal of courier work to sources, photographing their material and delivering to the KGB. Cover name Lens.[285]

Silverman, Abraham George: member of the Silvermaster group. During the war Silverman was an economic adviser to an assistant chief of the Army Air Force. Cover name Aileron.[286]

Silvermaster, Helen Witte: Active assistant in the management of the large Silvermaster group, headed by her husband, Nathan Silvermaster. Cover name Dora.[287]

Silvermaster, Nathan Gregory: head of the large and productive Silvermaster group of Soviet spies. An economist, his positions in the U.S. government during the war included posts with the Board of Economic Warfare/ Foreign Economic Administration and the War Assets Administration. Cover names Pal and Robert.[288]

Sima: see Coplon, Judith.

Simon: see Bayer, Theodore.

Sitsilla: see Dodd, William E., Jr.

Skrib: unidentified KGB asset in Alaska in late 1944.[289]

Slang: see Foster, Jane.

Smart: asset of the New York KGB who worked on technical intelligence in 1944. Not clear whether Smart was an American or a Soviet. The KGB also arranged for Smart to make contact with the GRU.[290]

Smith: see Mins, Leonard Emil.

Sobell, Morton: engineer and member of the Rosenberg apparatus. Worked for General Electric and Reeves Electronics on military and government contracts. Convicted of espionage against the United States in 1951 and imprisoned. That Sobell was a Soviet spy is clear, but it is not certain that he appears in the Venona cables. A New York KGB cable dated July 11, 1944, about providing a camera to a member of the Rosenberg apparatus with the cover name Relay is, according to an NSA/FBI footnote, a reference to Sobell. However, the footnote mentions that a September cable changes the cover name Relay to Serb, and the later occurrence of Serb is in the view of NSA/FBI not a reference to Sobell. A July 4, 1944, cable also uses the cover name Relay, and this Relay was not linked to the Rosenberg apparatus and had personal characteristics that rule out Sobell.[291]

Soble, Jack: long-term KGB agent who infiltrated the Trotskyist movement in the 1930s and early 1940s. In mid-1945 the KGB shifted Soble's emphasis from spying on Trotskyists to monitoring other targets. Brother of Robert Soblen. Cover names Abram and Czech.[292]

Soblen, Robert: long-term KGB agent who infiltrated the Trotskyist movement in the 1930s and early 1940s. Convicted of espionage in 1961. Brother of Jack Soble. Cover name Roman.[293]

Solid: unidentified asset of the New York KGB. Also had the cover name Kinsman.[294]

Son: see Baker, Rudy.

Sonya (or *Sonia*): see Gold, Sonia Steinman.

Sound: see Golos, Jacob.

Sounding Board: unidentified asset of the New York KGB.[295]

Source No. 12: GRU asset in 1943 who, from the nature of his reports and the documents he turned over, was probably on the Board of Economic Warfare.[296]

Source No. 13: asset of the New York GRU who, after repeated prodding, provided information in 1943.[297]

Source No. 19: unidentified highly placed asset who at the time of the Trident conference in 1943 reported to the KGB on a conversation with Roosevelt and Churchill.[298]

South: see Schuster, Bernard.

Spark: unidentified asset of the New York KGB who operated in the United States and Canada from 1943 to 1945. Activities unclear but appears to have had some quasi-public role: the KGB asked the CPUSA to check the authenticity of reports that while Spark's public statements were pro-Soviet, privately he was the source of anti-Soviet rumors. Also had the cover name Davis.[299]

Spline: source of KGB officer Andrey Shevchenko in the aircraft industry in New York in 1944. Also had the cover name Noise.[300]

Spruce: see Keenan, Helen Grace Scott.

Squirrel: see Sidorovich, Anne.

Staff-Man: unidentified asset of the New York KGB. In the U.S. Army in 1944. Provided with a KGB cipher to use for communications. Nothing else known.[301]

Stamp: see *Armor.*

Steele, Johannes: immigrant German journalist who arranged a meeting between a KGB officer and an exiled Polish journalist who offered his services to the USSR. Cover name Dicky.[302]

Stella: unidentified asset of the Naval GRU. Received a regular stipend and among other tasks assisted in vetting potential Soviet sources and served as a contact between the Naval GRU and its sources. Also had the cover name Emilia.[303]

Stern, Alfred Kaufman: wealthy Popular Front activist in Illinois. With his wife, Martha, invested in Boris Morros's Hollywood music publishing company. Cover name Louis.[304]

Stern, Martha Dodd: daughter of William Dodd, U.S. ambassador to Germany in the 1930s, and a prominent writer and Popular Front activist. Wife of Alfred Stern. Cover name Liza.[305]

Stevens, Edmund: journalist, secret Communist, and KGB contact.[306]

Storm: unidentified person connected with the Perlo group. May be Josef Peters.[307]

Stowaway: see Halperin, Maurice.

Stridsberg, Augustina (formerly Augustina Jirku): asset of the KGB in 1943 and 1944. Cover name Klara. Her daughter, Marietta Voge, also worked for the KGB.[308]

Strong, Anna Louise: radical journalist who championed the Soviet and Chinese Communist revolutions. Denied accusations of being a Communist and of being involved in Soviet espionage. Planned in 1944 to travel to Moscow. Messages show that she had some kind of relationship with the KGB, and the San Francisco KGB arranged with her a password that would allow her to identify her Moscow KGB contact. Cover name Lira.[309]

Suk: unidentified asset of the New York KGB, 1944–1945. Provided information on senior American journalists and senior Republicans close to Sen. Tom Dewey. Was probably a journalist.[310]

Talent: see Malisoff (Malisov), William Marias.

Tan: see Magdoff, Harry Samuel.

Ted: see Fitzgerald, Edward J.

Tenney, Helen: secret Communist and analyst in the Spanish section of the OSS. Source for the Golos-Bentley network. Cover name Muse.[311]

Tenor: see Burd, Michael.

Thomas: unidentified asset of the New York KGB in 1944. Earlier given the cover name Brother and was controlled by a KGB officer who concentrated on aviation technology intelligence. Activities unknown[312]

Thrush: see *Akhmed.*

Tkach, Mikhail: editor of the *Ukrainian Daily News* and a Communist activist. Carried out KGB tasks among Ukrainian immigrants and ran a group of subagents. Cover name Perch.[313]

Trio: unidentified asset of the New York KGB in 1943 who was reported not to have had any contact with the CPUSA. May be Frederick Thompson (see appendix D).[314]

Tu . . . : see *Nile.*

Tulip: see Zborowski, Mark.

Tur: unidentified source who reported on U.S. plans for the invasion of France.[315]

Tuvin: unidentified asset of the KGB. Appears to have been a pro-Communist activist among Polish-Americans. A 1944 KGB message notes that he was in difficulty because he was no longer being subsidized.[316]

Ullmann, William Ludwig: member of the Silvermaster group. Worked for the Division of Monetary Research of the Treasury Department and for the Material and Service Division of the Army Air Corps headquarters at the Pentagon. Cover names Pilot and Donald.[317]

Unbroken Cover Name No. 6: unidentified New York KGB asset. In mid-1943 was in Algeria with an Office of Strategic Services unit.[318]

Unbroken Cover Name No. 9: see Belfrage, Cedric.

Unbroken Cover Name No. 13: unidentified asset personally controlled by the head of the New York KGB in 1943.[319]

Unbroken Cover Name No. 14: unidentified asset of the New York KGB who provided liaison between the KGB and the CPUSA, 1943–1945.[320]

Unbroken Cover Name No. 19: a KGB asset in either the Office of Strategic Services or the Office of War Information in 1943. May be Julia Older (see appendix B.)[321]

Unbroken Cover Name No. 22: a KGB asset in touch with the illegal KGB officer Akhmerov. Anticipated being sent to Stockholm in 1943 as a press correspondent. The NSA deciphered enough of the cover name to determine that the last syllable was "gel."[322]

Uncle: see Folkoff, Isaac.

Unidentified KGB asset connected with the Council for Public Relations and described by the New York KGB as a "friend and fellow-countryman [Communist]." Warned the KGB that the State Department was asking questions about the brother of one of the KGB's American agents.[323]

Unidentified major in the U.S. Army Special Services Division who provided information on American industrial conditions to the Washington office of the Naval GRU in 1943. Unclear whether this source was witting or unwitting.[324]

Unidentified officer in the press section of the office of the U.S. Army Chief of Staff who provided information on discussions between Gen. George Marshall, President Roosevelt, and Prime Minister Churchill on the issue of a second front in October of 1943. Unclear whether this source was witting or unwitting.[325]

Unidentified source in the FBI. An October 27, 1944, New York KGB message refers to a Soviet source in the FBI. Unclear whether this was a reference to Judith Coplon or to another Soviet source.[326]

Unidentified source of the New York GRU in the U.S. Bureau of Shipping in 1943.[327]

Unidentified source working as a clerk in the Strategic Directorate of the Allied Joint Staff. Provided the Naval GRU in 1943 with American diplomatic reports from the U.S. embassy in Finland.[328]

V.: see Morros, Boris Mikhailovich.

Vague: see Miller, James Walter.

Valentina: unidentified asset of the KGB probably involved in infiltration of the American Trotskyist movement.[329]

Velson, Irving Charles: asset of the New York GRU. Among his duties was to control subagents and recruit additional Soviet sources. Also reported on weapons technology. Cover name Nick.[330]

Vick: unidentified asset of the New York KGB in 1943. Had contact with State Department officials and may have been a State Department employee.[331]

Vita: unidentified asset of the New York KGB put into cold storage in 1944.[332]

Voge, Marietta: née Jirku (see Stridsberg, Augustina). An asset of the San Francisco KGB. Cover name Daughter.[333]

Volunteer: see Cohen, Morris.

Volunteer's wife: see Cohen, Lona.

Vuchinich, George Samuel: of Serb ethnicity and an officer in the Office of Strategic Services. Provided information to Thomas Babin, a GRU asset and fellow OSS agent also assigned to duties dealing with Yugoslavia. Not clear whether a witting or an unwitting source.[334]

Wasp: see Greenglass, Ruth.

Watchdog: see Osipovich, Nadia Morris.

Wedge: unidentified asset of the New York KGB put into cold storage in mid-1944.[335]

Wheeler, Donald Niven: member of the Perlo group. Worked for the Research and Analysis Division of the Office of Strategic Services. Cover name Izra.[336]

White, Harry Dexter: member of the Silvermaster group. Assistant secretary of the Treasury and, later, director of the International Monetary Fund. Arguably the KGB's most valuable asset and the subject of a number of KGB cables. Cover names Jurist, Lawyer, and Richard.[337]

Whitefish: unidentified asset of the New York KGB in 1944. First provided information to the KGB via the CPUSA before it took over direct contact.[338]

Wicher, Enos Regent: onetime CPUSA organizer in Wisconsin, in 1945 was a KGB asset and worked for the Wave Propagation Group, Division of War Research, Columbia University. Wife (Maria Wicher) and stepdaughter (Flora Wovschin) were also KGB assets. Cover name Keen.[339]

Wicher, Maria: a Communist and a KGB asset, as were her husband (Enos Regent Wicher) and daughter (Flora Wovschin). In 1944 was in contact with KGB agent Sergey Kurnakov. Cover name Dasha.[340]

Wilson, Ruth Beverly: assisted her husband, the KGB asset Jacob Epstein, and had her own direct connections with the KGB. Cover name Nona.[341]

Witczak, Ignacy: illegal GRU officer who posed as a Canadian immigrant and lived quietly in Los Angeles from 1938 until identified by the FBI in 1945. Subsequently disappeared. Cover name identifed only by the initial R.[342]

Wolston, Ilya Elliott: KGB asset who was a U.S. Army military intelligence officer. He provided the KGB with details on the Army's military intelligence school and on soldiers being trained for intelligence work in areas of interest to the Soviets. Cover name Glory.[343]

Wovschin, Flora Don: asset of the KGB, 1943–1945, first in New York and then in Washington, where she worked for the Office of War Information. Mother (Maria Wicher) and stepfather (Enos Regent Wicher) were also KGB assets. Cover name Zora.[344]

X: see Katz, Joseph.

York, Jones Orin: aviation engineer and asset of the San Francisco KGB, first recruited in the mid-1930s. Gave the KGB microfilm of plans for experimental aircraft and was heavily subsidized. Cover name Needle. May also be Engineer.[345]

Youngster: see Hall, Theodore Alvin.

Yun: see Laird, Stephen.

Yur: asset of the New York KGB, 1943–1944, who worked on ethnic and émigré intelligence.[346]

Zaret, Daniel Abraham: safety inspector for the U.S. Army's Explosives Division. Turned over documents on explosives technology to the GRU. Was a Communist and a former officer in the International Brigades.[347]

Zborowski, Mark: long-term KGB infiltrator of the Trotskyist movement assigned by the KGB to get close to Victor Kravchenko, a Soviet defector. Cover names Tulip and Kant.[348]

Zone: unidentified cover name of a female asset of the New York KGB in 1944. The KGB lost contact with her and planned to reestablish contact through Earl Browder, who knew her. Browder, however, judged her untrustworthy and recommended that the KGB not reestablish contact.[349]

Zora: see Wovschin, Flora.

Americans and U.S. Residents Who Had Covert Relationships with Soviet Intelligence Agencies but Were Not Identified in the Venona Cables

The evidence for the covert relationship of these 139 persons with Soviet intelligence comes from sources other than the Venona decryptions. For those discussed in the text, documentation is cited there; otherwise, it is cited here. This list does not include Soviet intelligence officers operating under legal diplomatic cover. It is likely that some of the persons listed here are behind the unidentified cover names in appendix A. The list includes five Soviet illegal officers who posed as immigrants. Of the 139 persons, five are identified only by cover names (in italics).

Adamic, Louis: writer and spokesman for Yugoslav immigrants. During World War II, advised the OSS on Balkan questions. Minor source for Golos-Bentley network via Louis Budenz.[1]

Adams, Arthur: illegal GRU officer posing as an immigrant in the United States from 1938 to 1945. May be Achilles (see appendix A).[2]

Aden: unidentified KGB source recruited by Theodore Hall. Nuclear scientist, possibly working at the Hartford, Washington, facility that produced bomb-grade plutonium.[3]

Albam, Jacob: chief assistant to Jack Soble in the Soble espionage apparatus of the KGB in the postwar period. Pled guilty to espionage in 1957.[4]

Alleman, Otto: chemist who worked for Du Pont. Before 1945, was a contact of the KGB officer Gaik Ovakimian and was probably involved in industrial espionage. Employed in 1945 by an import company and suspected by the FBI of assisting in the covert transfer of Soviet intelligence funds.[5]

Anta: unidentified KGB source recruited by Theodore Hall. Nuclear scientist, or possibly the wife of a nuclear scientist (see *Aden*), working perhaps at the Hartford, Washington, facility that produced bomb-grade plutonium.[6]

Arenal (neé Biegel), Rose: American wife of Luís Arenal of Mexico. Lived in New York and was a communications link and mail drop between Jacob Golos and Mexican Communists working on the operation to murder Leon Trotsky.[7]

Aronberg, Philip: mid-level CPUSA activist in the 1920s. Undertook courier and other assignments for the Comintern, the GRU, and the KGB in the 1930s and early 1940s.[8]

Asimow, Morris: industrial spy for the Soviets at U.S. Steel in 1936.[9]

Baskind, Pauline: part-time New York schoolteacher who provided a mail drop for the American end of the KGB's anti-Trotsky operations in Mexico.[10]

Bedacht, Max: founding member of the CPUSA and part of its top leadership in the 1920s. In the early 1930s, oversaw the transfer of several party members from open party work to the underground and provided support for various Soviet intelligence missions.[11]

Beker, Johanna Koenen: daughter of the German Communist leader Wilhelm Koenen. Immigrated to the United States in 1938. Member of the Soble spy ring. May be Clemence and Lee (see appendix A).[12]

Bernay, Eric: Communist, headed Keynote Recording Company. Assisted in providing the illegal GRU officer Arthur Adams with a business cover and helped him to escape FBI surveillance in 1945.[13]

Bloch, Louis: New York film projectionist who provided a mail drop for the American end of the KGB's anti-Trotsky operations in Mexico.[14]

Booker, Lucy: worked for Soviet intelligence in the 1930s on missions to Germany, studied at the University of Berlin. Jacob Golos told Elizabeth Bentley that the KGB had temporarily lost touch with Booker and that he was assigned to reestablish contact. In 1951 Floyd Miller, a KGB agent, identified her as one of the intermediaries between him and Jack Soble, a KGB officer who supervised anti-Trotskyist work.[15]

Bransten, Louise: wealthy San Francisco–area Communist who linked Soviet intelligence officers working at the Soviet consulate to CPUSA members and sympathizers who were of intelligence value. May be Map (see appendix A).[16]

Browder, Margaret: sister of CPUSA leader Earl Browder, worked for the KGB in Europe in the 1930s.[17]

Budenz, Louis: editor of the *Daily Worker,* passed information from CPUSA members and sympathizers to the Golos-Bentley network.[18]

Buerger, Ruth Marie: active in the Communist-led Unemployment Councils in the early 1930s. American wife of Arnold Ikal, a GRU officer operating illegally in the United States in the 1930s.[19]

Burdett, Winston: journalist, recruited by Golos in 1940, worked for Soviet intelligence in Europe. Broke with the Communists in 1944 and later cooperated with U.S. authorities.[20]

Burtan, Valentine (William G.): born in Russia in 1900, came to the United States in 1907, and became a naturalized citizen in 1921. A CPUSA member in the 1920s, he was expelled in 1929 as a Lovestone supporter. Assisted Nicholas Dozenberg in establishing a cover business for Dozenberg's GRU work and attempted to launder $100,000 in counterfeit U.S. currency furnished by Dozenberg, for which he went to prison.[21]

Chambers, Whittaker: CPUSA activist in the late 1920s. Dropped out of open party work in the early 1930s and joined its underground apparatus, later supervised a network of sources that reported to the GRU. Defected in 1937 but did not approach U.S. authorities until 1939 and did not reveal the full extent of his role in Soviet espionage until 1948.[22]

Chapin, John Hitchcock: scientist at the Chicago Metallurgical Laboratory, part of the Manhattan Project. Met covertly with the illegal GRU officer Arthur Adams.[23]

Chapman, Abraham: journalist and official of the New York Communist party. In 1950 he and his family left the United States in panic for Mexico, where they lived in hiding. Soviet intelligence then covertly moved them to Czechoslovakia, where they received false identities and began a new life. Appears to have been withdrawn because of his knowledge of or participation in espionage operations in the United States. Activities unknown.[24]

Chevalier, Haakon: secret Communist and French professor at the University of California, Berkeley. Attempted to recruit J. Robert Oppenheimer as a Soviet source.[25]

Cohen, Leonard: attorney working for the Interior Department. Was a contact and exchanged material with the GRU illegal officer Ignacy Witczak.[26]

Collins, Henry: member of the CPUSA Washington underground and talent-spotter for Soviet intelligence.[27]

Crane, William: joined the CPUSA in 1932 and entered its underground almost immediately. Worked as a courier and as a photographer for the GRU-linked network that Whittaker Chambers supervised. Confessed after he was identified to authorities by Chambers in 1949.[28]

De Sveshnikov, Vladimir V.: ballistics expert who worked for the U.S. government. Supplied Soviet intelligence with American military information from the mid-1920s through the 1930s.[29]

Devyatkin, Boris: born in Russia in 1888, arrived in the United States in 1923, and became a naturalized citizen in 1929. Under the name Dick Murzin he assisted Moishe Stern, an illegal GRU officer in the United States in the late 1920s and early 1930s.[30]

Dozenberg, Nicholas: Latvian immigrant, founding member of the CPUSA, and mid-level party official in the 1920s. Became a GRU agent in 1928. Arrested in 1939, he confessed and on a plea bargain went to prison on a false passport charge.[31]

Eltenton, George Charles: chemist at Shell Oil in California, British subject who had worked for some years in the Soviet Union. Activist in the United States in the Federation of Architects, Engineers, Chemists and Technicians, a small Communist-led union. In 1942 met with Peter Ivanov, a Soviet diplomat and GRU officer, then approached, directly or through intermediaries such as Haakon Chevalier, several scientists working on the Manhattan Project regarding furnishing information to the Soviet Union.[32]

Feierabend, Albert: naturalized American citizen from Latvia, member of the CPUSA, Comintern courier. Worked with Nicholas Dozenberg's GRU apparatus. Arrested on smuggling charges in 1930 when returning from abroad. At that time claimed his name was Jacob Kreitz and carried a small, easily concealed white cloth ribbon signed by Max Bedacht, then a member of the CPUSA's executive secretariat, which stated that "the bearer of this credential is thoroughly trustworthy and should be given all possible support so that he may effectively accomplish the mission he is engages in." Arrested again in 1933 when arriving from abroad carrying a false American passport and $28,000 in cash, Soviet subsidies either for the CPUSA or for Soviet espionage operations. Skipped bail and was never apprehended.[33]

Field, Frederick Vanderbilt: secret Communist and a prominent Popular Front liberal. Acted as a recruiter for the CPUSA-GRU underground of which Whittaker Chambers was a part in the mid-1930s. Also provided his residence as a safe-house for a 1945 meeting between Elizabeth Bentley, then supervising of a CPUSA-KGB espionage network, and Earl Browder.[34]

Field, Noel: secret Communist, recruited by Hede Massing for a KGB network in the mid-1930s when he held a mid-level post in the State Department's West European division.[35]

Frankfurter, Gerta: part of Hede Massing's KGB network in the 1930s.[36]

Gayn, Mark: left-wing journalist, assisted Philip Jaffe in the *Amerasia* case.[37]

Glassman, Vivian: carried a warning and money from Soviet intelligence to William Perl urging him to flee to Mexico when the FBI began to roll up the Rosenberg network.[38]

Goldberg, Ben-Zion: journalist, identified in Soviet documents as a Soviet agent. Activities unknown.[39]

Granich, Grace: veteran CPUSA leader, acted as a talent-spotter for Jacob Golos.[40]

Greenberg, Michael: mid-level official specializing in Chinese matters for the Board of Economic Warfare and the Foreign Economic Administration and source for Golos-Bentley network.[41]

Gregg, Joseph: veteran of the International Brigades, source for Golos-Bentley network. Worked for the Office of the Coordinator of Inter-American Affairs and for the State Department.[42]

Hammer, Armand: son of a founding member of the American Communist movement. Laundered Soviet subsidies for the CPUSA in the 1920s and later used his position as a wealthy businessman with ties to the USSR to assist Soviet intelligence.[43]

Heiman, Julius: immigrant from Russia and a naturalized citizen, in the early 1920s worked in the jewelry business and was a secret Communist. Converted Soviet subsidies that came in the form of jewelry into cash. In the 1930s and early 1940s, undertook a variety of support tasks for GRU operations in the United States, most notably as an associate of the GRU illegal officer Arthur Adams.[44]

Heller, Ferdinand: son of a wealthy American Communist. Admitted to the FBI that he was recruited into Soviet industrial espionage in 1935 by Gaik Ovakimian.[45]

Hiskey, Clarence: scientist at the Chicago Metallurgical Laboratory, part of the Manhattan Project. Met covertly with the GRU illegal officer Arthur Adams. Hiskey was also a target of KGB recruitment and appears in KGB cables under the cover name Ramsey.[46]

Huettig, Lester M.: industrial spy at Remington Arms who supplied Soviet intelligence with blueprints for automatic shell loaders in the 1930s.[47]

Hutchins, Grace: socially prominent writer and secret Communist, assisted the CPUSA-GRU apparatus of which Whittaker Chambers was a part. After Chambers defected and was in hiding, she delivered an indirect warning to his brother-in-law that if he revealed Chambers's location to her, she would guarantee the safety of Chambers's wife and children.[48]

Ikal, Arnold: illegal GRU officer in the United States from the early 1930s to 1937. Married to an American Communist.[49]

Inslerman, Felix: part of the GRU-CPUSA network supervised by Whittaker Chambers. Later, in cooperating with U.S. authorities, stated that he had left Soviet service in 1939.[50]

Jacobson, Arvid: Finnish-American Communist, recruited for Soviet espionage in Finland by the CPUSA-GRU network of which Whittaker Chambers was a part. Arrested in Finland in 1933.[51]

Jaffe, Philip: longtime friend of Earl Browder and the CPUSA. As editor and publisher of *Amerasia,* illegally procured thousands of pages of classified government documents and attempted to make them available to Soviet intelligence. Convicted of unauthorized possession of government documents.[52]

Jerome, V. J.: veteran CPUSA leader chiefly involved in party work among intellectuals. Acted as a talent-spotter for Golos.[53]

Josephson, Leon: veteran Communist attorney and part of the CPUSA-Soviet false-passport operation in the 1930s.[54]

Kahn, Albert: journalist and secret member of the CPUSA, suggested for recruitment by the San Francisco KGB in 1946. However, Elizabeth Bentley told the FBI that in 1942 she and Jacob Golos had met with Kahn, who furnished information on immigrant Ukrainians hostile to the Soviets. May be Fighter (see appendix A).[55]

Kahn, M. G.: assisted in providing business cover for the illegal GRU officer Arthur Adams. Involved in smuggling jewels from the Soviet Union in 1919.[56]

Kamen, Martin: chemist working at the Radiation Laboratory at the University of California, Berkeley. Met with Grigory Kheifets and Grigory Kasparov, KGB officers at the Soviet San Francisco consulate. Fired from the Manhattan Project in 1944 when security officers overheard him discussing atomic research with Kheifets.[57]

Kaplan, Irving: secret Communist working at the War Production Board, source for Golos-Bentley network.[58]

Kazakevich, Vladimir: instructor at a wartime U.S. Army school, contact of Golos-Bentley network.[59]

Kent, Tyler: code clerk at the U.S. embassies in Moscow (1934–1939) and London (1939–1940). Arrested by British security officials in 1940 for theft of Roosevelt-Churchill correspondence. Convicted and imprisoned until 1945. American security officials later concluded that while serving in Moscow he had been compromised by the KGB and had provided the Soviets with American diplomatic communications. Kent's recruitment resulted not from ideological conviction but from a "honey trap," wherein a female KGB agent used sex to induce cooperation. His activities in London were not on behalf of the Soviets but stemmed from his opposition to possible American entry into that war and his involvement with antisemitic and pro-Nazi circles in Britain.[60]

Kowan, Maurice: Chicago doctor and Communist, acted as a mail drop for William Crane and John Loomis Sherman.[61]

Kruse, William: mid-level Communist activist in the 1920s. A Lovestoneite, he left the party in 1929 but in the 1930s assisted Nicholas Dozenberg in establishing a cover business for his GRU activities in the Philippines.[62]

Landy, Avram: senior CPUSA official chiefly involved in work with ethnic minorities. Acted as a talent-spotter for Golos. May be Khan (see appendix A).[63]

Larsen, Emmanuel: State Department researcher, one of Philip Jaffe's sources for stolen government documents in the *Amerasia* case. Convicted of illegal procurement of government documents, he lost his job with the State Department.[64]

Lerner, Irving: associate of the illegal GRU officer Arthur Adams and an employee of the Motion Picture Division of the Office of War Information. Attempted to photograph the cyclotron at the University of California without authorization.[65]

Leshinsky, Sol: official of the United Nations Relief and Rehabilitation Administration, member of the Perlo group, part of the Golos-Bentley network.[66]

Levin, Bernice: clerical employee of the Office of Emergency Management and the Office of Production Management. Minor source for Golos-Bentley network.[67]

Levy, Philip: secret Communist, close associate of Leon Josephson. His residence was used to store documents stolen by the CPUSA underground from the party's critics.[68]

Lieber, Maxim: literary agent, born in 1897 in Russian Poland, naturalized U.S. citizen. Active member of the CPUSA-GRU network of which Whittaker Chambers and John Loomis Sherman were members.[69]

Lomanitz, Giovanni Rossi: scientist working at the Berkeley Radiation Laboratory, met in 1942 with Steve Nelson of the CPUSA to discuss his work on the Manhattan Project.[70]

Lovestone, Jay: head of the CPUSA in the late 1920s, expelled in 1929. For a few years he and some of his followers assisted Soviet intelligence in hopes that this would win them readmission to the Communist movement.[71]

Marcus, James Lewis: headed Aldon Rug Mills, a firm that provided business cover for Soviet agents.[72]

Marzani, Carl: joined the Office of Strategic Services in 1942 and by 1945 had become deputy chief of the presentation branch, which prepared charts, graphs, and other pictorial displays of OSS information. Transferred to the State Department when the OSS dissolved. Convicted in 1947 of fraud for concealing his Communist party membership on various State Department employment documents.[73]

Massing, Hede: supervised a KGB network in the 1930s that included two State Department officials, Noel Field and Laurence Duggan. She and her husband dropped out of intelligence work for the Soviets and later broke entirely with communism. Went to the FBI in 1947. May be Redhead (see appendix A).[74]

Massing, Paul: KGB agent working in partnership with his wife, Hede.[75]

McPeek, Fanny: clerk at a New York City school, provided a mail drop for the American end of the KGB's anti-Trotsky operations in Mexico.[76]

Miller, Jenny Levy: wife of Robert T. Miller and a contact of Elizabeth Bentley. Worked for the Chinese Government Purchasing Commission in Washington during World War II.[77]

Miller, Robert T.: official of the Office of the Coordinator of Inter-American Affairs, source for Golos-Bentley network.[78]

Mink, George: American Communist union organizer in the 1920s. Worked on maritime unionism for the Comintern in the 1930s and assisted in its establishment of a covert courier system using Communist seamen. Arrested and imprisoned in Denmark for espionage.[79]

Minton, Bruce: editor of the CPUSA's literary-intellectual journal, *New*

Masses. Worked as a talent-spotter and put Jacob Golos in touch with Maurice Halperin, an OSS official who was one of the most productive spies the Soviets developed during World War II.[80]

Mitchell, Kate: co-editor of *Amerasia,* assisted Philip Jaffe.[81]

Miyagi, Yotoku: immigrated to the United States from Japan in 1919 as a teenager, joined the CPUSA in 1931 and was recruited for Soviet intelligence work through a Japanese Comintern agent assisting the CPUSA's work among Japanese-Americans. Returned to Japan in 1933 as part of a Soviet spy network headed by the KGB officer Richard Sorge. Arrested by Japanese police in 1941 and died in prison in 1943.[82]

Morgan, Will: seaman courier for the CPUSA secret apparatus carrying material via Iran for the Comintern in 1943.[83]

Morris: KGB contact originally made in Great Britain in the mid-1930s who moved to the United States. The KGB sought to reestablish contact in 1942 by sending its illegal officer Arnold Deutsch (who had known Morris) to the United States. Deutsch, however, died en route when his ship was sunk by a German U-boat.[84]

Moskowitz, Miriam: associate of Abraham Brothman. Convicted of obstruction of justice for her role in attempting to conceal Brothman's industrial espionage.[85]

Nelson, Steve: CPUSA official and figure in its secret apparatus. Assisted KGB and GRU officers. May be *Butcher* (see appendix A).[86]

North, Joe: senior CPUSA official and editor of the journal *New Masses.* Worked as a talent-spotter for Soviet intelligence, recruiting (among others) Winston Burdett and William Remington.[87]

Novick, Sam: Communist and head of Electronics Corporation of America. Provided business cover for the illegal GRU officer Arthur Adams and helped him to enter the United States using false documents in 1938.[88]

Older, Julia: Office of Strategic Services employee, dismissed for attempting to gain access to a file on Ukrainian nationalists on behalf of Albert Kahn. Reinstated on appeal but transferred to the Office of War Information. Lived in Moscow in the 1930s and worked for numerous CPUSA-linked bodies. Her brother, Andrew Older, was a secret party member and journalist. May be Unbroken Cover Name No. 19 (see appendix A).[89]

Osman, Robert: U.S. Army corporal assigned to the Panama Canal Zone, provided military documents to a GRU network.[90]

Park, Willard: employee of the Office of the Coordinator of Inter-American Affairs and later of the United Nations Relief and Rehabilitation Administration. Minor source for Golos-Bentley network.[91]

Perazich, George: official of the Yugoslav section of the United Nations Relief and Rehabilitation Administration. Minor source for Golos-Bentley network.[92]

Peters, Josef: head of the CPUSA secret apparatus from the early 1930s to mid-1938 and liaison with the GRU and the KGB. May be Storm (appendix A).[93]

Pigman, William Ward: secret Communist source at the National Bureau of Standards in the mid-1930s for Whittaker Chambers's CPUSA-GRU network.[94]

Poyntz, Juliet Stuart: founding member of the CPUSA, directed its women's department and the New York Workers School in the 1920s. On the staff of the Friends of the Soviet Union and International Labor Defense. In 1934 she dropped out of open party activities and into Soviet intelligence work. She disappeared from her New York City residence in 1937, and a police investigation turned up no clues to her fate. In early 1938 Carlo Tresca, a leading Italian-American radical, publicly accused the Soviets of kidnapping Poyntz in order to prevent her defection. He said that before she disappeared, she had come to him to talk over her disgust at what she had seen in Moscow in 1936 in the early stages of Stalin's Great Terror. Elizabeth Bentley, who had known her as Juliet Glazer, stated that in the late 1930s Jacob Golos and in 1945 the KGB officer Anatoly Gromov had told her that Poyntz had been a traitor and was dead. Whittaker Chambers related that he had heard that Poyntz had been killed for attempted desertion, and that this rumor had contributed to his caution when he defected in 1938.[95]

Price, Mildred: sister of Mary Price and leader of the China Aid Council. Talent-spotter for Golos-Bentley network.[96]

Rabinowitz, Gregory: KGB agent in the late 1930s who assisted in its anti-Trotsky campaign, including the American end of the KGB's murder of Leon Trotsky.[97]

Redmont, Bernard: journalist and official of the Office of the Coordinator of Inter-American Affairs. Minor source for Golos-Bentley network.[98]

Remington, William: official of the War Production Board, minor source for Golos-Bentley network. Convicted of perjury and murdered in prison in 1954.[99]

Reno, Vincent: employee at the U.S. Army proving grounds at Aberdeen, Maryland. Provided military information to the CPUSA-GRU network that Whittaker Chambers supervised. Later cooperated with U.S. authorities.[100]

Rivkin, Ruth: employee of a predecessor to the United Nations Relief and Rehabilitation Administration. Minor source for Golos-Bentley network.[101]

Rosenberg, Simon: naturalized American from Poland, engineer employed by Amtorg in the early 1930s and engaged in industrial espionage under the direction of the illegal KGB officer Gaik Ovakimian.[102]

Rosenblit, Philip: Communist dentist in New York, part of the courier system for delivering Soviet money to Soviet intelligence networks in the United States as well as funds to subsidize the CPUSA.[103]

Roth, Andrew: Office of Naval Intelligence liaison officer with the State Department, cooperated with Philip Jaffe in the *Amerasia* case.[104]

Salich, Hafis: naturalized American citizen from Russia who worked for the Office of Naval Intelligence. Recruited by Soviet intelligence in 1938. In 1939 he and his Soviet controller, Mikhail Gorin, head of the Los Angeles Intourist office, were arrested and convicted of espionage. Salich went to prison. Gorin, a Soviet national, was given probation; he paid a $10,000 fine and returned to the Soviet Union.[105]

Schuman, Irving George: used by the KGB agent Joseph Katz in surveillance of the Soviet defector Walter Krivitsky.[106]

Shepard, Barnett: provided a mail drop for the American end of the KGB's anti-Trotsky operations in Mexico.[107]

Sherman, John Loomis: CPUSA activist in the late 1920s, expelled from the party as a Lovestoneite in 1929 but almost immediately recruited to underground party work. Worked chiefly for the GRU in association with Whittaker Chambers and William Crane. Abandoned Soviet intelligence work in the late 1930s but remained a Communist.[108]

Silverman, Frances: CPUSA militant in the New York City teachers union, provided a mail drop for the American end of the KGB's anti-Trotsky operations in Mexico.[109]

Simon, Helen Levi: columnist for the CPUSA's *Daily Worker,* acted as a conduit for funds to assist Ramón Mercader, Trotsky's murderer.[110]

Slack, Alfred D.: chemist, in the early 1940s supplied information to the industrial espionage apparatus of which Harry Gold was a part. After Gold identified him, he confessed and received a fifteen-year prison sentence.[111]

Soble, Myra, wife of the KGB agent Jack Soble. Pled guilty to charges of espionage in 1957.[112]

Source No. 19: cover name of a KGB contact originally made in Great Britain in the mid-1930s who moved to the United States. The KGB sought to reestablish contact in 1942 by sending its illegal officer Arnold Deutsch (who had known this source) to the United States. Deutsch, however, died en route when his ship was sunk by a German U-boat in 1942. Unlikely to be the same as Source No. 19 in appendix A.[113]

Spiegel, William: Communist who made his apartment available for photographic work to the GRU-CPUSA network supervised by Whittaker Chambers.[114]

Spitz, Beatrice: physician and naturalized citizen. See Spitz, Henry.[115]

Spitz, Henry: physician and naturalized citizen, he and his wife, Beatrice, moved to Albuquerque, New Mexico, in 1950 and took photographs of atomic weapons research facilities that they passed to Robert Soblen of the KGB.[116]

Stahl, Lydia: American assistant to Alfred Tilton, an illegal GRU officer in the United States in the late 1920s.[117]

Steinberg, Arthur Gerald: Canadian, Columbia Ph.D. (1940) in zoology, worked for the U.S. Office of Scientific Research and Development in 1945. Source for a Canadian GRU network.[118]

Stenbuck, Joseph: acted as a mail drop and receiver of stolen blueprints for Robert Osman in 1933.[119]

Stern, Moishe (also known as Mark Zilbert): illegal GRU officer in the United States in the late 1920s and early 1930s.[120]

Stone, Victoria Singer: Communist who undertook a variety of support tasks for GRU operations in the United States, most notably as an associate of the GRU illegal officer Arthur Adams.[121]

Straight, Michael: American, became a secret Communist while at Cambridge University in the mid-1930s. Protégé of the Soviet spy Anthony Blunt, encouraged to return to the United States in a covert role. Became a speech writer for President Roosevelt, met on several occasions with Iskhak Akhmerov, an illegal KGB officer, but broke off the relationship in 1942.[122]

Switz, Robert Gordon: worked in the early 1930s as a clandestine photographer and courier for the GRU in the United States. Intermediary between Robert Osman and the GRU.[123]

Tamer, Joshua: member of the CPUSA-GRU network of which Whittaker Chambers was a part in the early 1930s.[124]

Taylor, William: Treasury Department official, source for Golos-Bentley network. Sued the publisher of Elizabeth Bentley's autobiography, who, over Bentley's objection, settled out of court. Presented a lengthy attack on Bentley's credibility. The FBI supported Bentley and prepared a detailed rebuttal to his attack.[125]

Tilton, Alfred: illegal GRU officer in the United States in the late 1920s. Posed as a Canadian immigrant with the name Joseph Paquett.[126]

Ulanovsky, Aleksandr Petrovich: illegal GRU officer operating in the United States in the early 1930s. Used, among others, the identity of Nicholas Sherman, an American.[127]

Ulanovsky, Nadezhda: illegal GRU officer and the wife of Aleksandr Ulanovsky.[128]

Unidentified Radar Source: recruited by the KGB agent Morris Cohen in the spring of 1942. The KGB officer Aleksandr Feklisov stated of this unidentified source that "every year he transmitted to us two or three thousand pages of photographs of secret materials [on radar development], the majority of which were appraised as either 'valuable' or 'extremely valuable.' "[129]

Vogel, Ethel: provided a mail drop for the American end of the KGB's anti-Trotsky operations in Mexico.[130]

Volkov, Anatole: son of Helen Silvermaster and stepson of Gregory Silvermaster, acted for a short time as a courier between the Silvermasters and the Golos-Bentley network.[131]

Wadleigh, Julian: mid-level State Department official, part of the CPUSA-GRU network that Whittaker Chambers supervised. Later cooperated with U.S. authorities.[132]

Weil, Ruby: secret Communist who infiltrated the American Trotskyist movement. Part of the KGB operation that murdered Leon Trotsky.[133]

Weinberg, Joseph W.: physicist and secret Communist at the Radiation Laboratory at the University of California, Berkeley. Met secretly with Steve Nelson, a CPUSA West Coast official, and gave him documents regarding the Manhattan Project. Nelson then met with Peter Ivanov, a Soviet intelligence officer under diplomatic cover at the Soviet consulate in San Francisco.[134]

Weinstein, Abraham: New York dentist who provided dental services for many CPUSA officials involved in its clandestine work as well as for many government employees who spied for the Soviets. The FBI concluded that Weinstein acted as a communications intermediary, that many of the dental visits were a cover for the passing of information to Weinstein, who then passed the information on to another party. Elizabeth Bentley identified a contact of Jacob Golos's who was a dentist and whom she knew only as Charlie. From her description, the FBI concluded that Weinstein was Charlie. May be Charlie in Venona (see appendix A).[135]

Weisband, William: linguist working for the U.S. Army Signals Security Agency during World War II, later joined the Venona Project. Fired in 1950 when another Soviet agent, Jones York, identified him as his Soviet contact in the early 1940s. Imprisoned for a year when he refused to answer a U.S. grand jury summons. May be Link (see appendix A).[136]

Yano, Tsutomu: Japanese-American CPUSA official who in 1931 recruited Yotoku Miyagi, a young Japanese-American, for Soviet intelligence work in Japan.[137]

Zilbert, Mark: See Stern, Moishe.

Zimmerman, David: mid-level official of the CPUSA in Maryland. Using the name David Carpenter, he was part of the GRU-CPUSA network supervised by Whittaker Chambers.[138]

Zlatowski, George: veteran of the International Brigades and secret Communist, became a U.S. Army intelligence officer. Married to Jane Foster (see appendix A), a Soviet agent in the Office of Strategic Services. Indicted on charges of espionage when the Soble spy ring was broken up after World War II. Abroad at the time and refused to return to the United States.[139]

Foreigners Temporarily in the United States Who Had Covert Relationships with Soviet Intelligence Agencies

These thirty-three foreigners and persons of unknown nationality temporarily resident in the United States had covert relationships with Soviet intelligence. Not included are nearly a hundred Soviet citizens, chiefly professional intelligence officers, who carried out espionage against the United States while on American soil under diplomatic cover. Cover names appear in italics.

Great Britain

Burgess, Guy: British diplomat and long-term Soviet spy who served in the British embassy in Washington, 1950–1951. Fled to Moscow in 1951.[1]

Eduard: KGB asset described in the Venona traffic as having served in Washington from 1939 until February 1945 and having contacts with prominent political figures. Likely but not certain to have been a British national.[2]

Fuchs, Emil Julius Klaus: part of the British contingent sent to assist the Manhattan Project. Confessed to espionage in 1950 and was imprisoned in Britain. Cover names Rest and Charles.[3]

Maclean, Donald: British diplomat and longtime Soviet spy who served in a senior position at the British embassy in Washington from 1944 to 1948. When British security began to close in on him in 1951, he fled to Moscow. Cover name Homer.[4]

Philby, H. R. (Kim): a senior British intelligence officer and also a longtime

Soviet agent who served as liaison with American intelligence in the late 1940s and early 1950s. Fled to Moscow in 1963.[5]

Canada

Losey, Mary [Mrs. Spencer Mapes]: employee of the Canadian National Film Board's office in Washington, D.C. Recruiter for a Canadian GRU network.[6]

May, Allan Nunn: part of the British contingent sent to assist the Manhattan Project. Worked chiefly in Canada but visited several American atomic research facilities. His role as a Soviet spy was revealed when Igor Gouzenko, a GRU code clerk at the Soviet embassy, defected in 1945 and identified several Soviet espionage sources. Confessed to espionage and was imprisoned.[7]

Pontecorvo, Bruno: refugee Italian physicist who was part of the British contingent inside the Manhattan Project. Worked largely in Canada and reported to the KGB through its Ottawa station. Moved in the late 1940s to England to work on the British atomic weapons program. Fled to the USSR after Fuchs was arrested in 1950. May be Huron (appendix A).[8]

Size, Hazen: secret Canadian Communist and veteran of the Spanish Civil War (medical unit), in Washington during World War II as a representative of the Canadian National Film Board. Minor source of Canadian and British embassy information for the Golos-Bentley network.[9]

France

Cot, Pierre: French political figure and KGB contact. Cover name Daedalus.[10]

Eliacheff, Boris: French diplomat born in Russia, longtime Soviet spy. Cover name Palm.[11]

Central and South America

Arthur: unidentified asset of the KGB. Central figure in the KGB's Latin American operations who came to New York frequently and reported to the New York KGB office. Link between the KGB and Soviet sources spread all over Central South America, with contacts in Spain as well. Probably held a position in government or industry that allowed extensive travel. May have been an illegal KGB officer.[12]

Muzquiz, Elena Huerta: resident of New York City, used for KGB Latin American operations. Cover name Southerner.[13]

Subercaseaux, Christian Casanova: Chilean diplomat and KGB asset involved in Latin American operations who traveled between New York, Portugal, and South America. Cover name Carlos.[14]

Romania

Davila, Carol A.: Romanian diplomat recruited as a KGB agent in 1944. Cover name Docker.[15]

Czechoslovakia

Fierlinger, Jan: information officer of the New York consulate of the Czechoslovak government-in-exile. Source for the KGB in 1943. Most of his reports dealt with diplomatic contacts between the United States and Britain and the Czechoslovak government-in-exile. Cover name Officer.[16]

Sukhomlin, Vasily: Russian Socialist Revolutionary exile, employed by the Czechoslovak Information Service (an arm of the Czechoslovak government-in-exile) in the United States, 1941–1945. KGB asset who reported to the New York KGB about the activities of the Czechoslovak government-in-exile and about other exiled European political figures in the United States, particularly exiled Social Democrats. Received a KGB stipend and was promised Soviet citizenship. Cover name Mars.[17]

Germany

Baerensprung, Horst: German refugee and former German police official, consultant to the Office of Strategic Services on German matters.[18]

Hirschfeld, Dr. Hans E.: German refugee, consultant to the Office of Strategic Services on German matters.[19]

Lund: unidentified illegal KGB officer inserted into the United States in 1943. Described as a German. Mission unknown.[20]

Mann, Heinrich Ludwig: reported to the San Francisco KGB about talks between the U.S. government and exiled German government officials.[21]

Poet: identified by the FBI as either Bertolt Brecht or Berthold Viertel. Brecht, the renowned German playwright, had entered the United States in mid-1941 and declared his intention (never carried out) to become an American citizen. He later became a leading intellectual figure under the East German Communist regime. Viertel, a writer who was a close friend and associate of Brecht, was also a German refugee. He entered the United States in 1942. In 1943 Poet supplied the San Francisco KGB with information about exiled German political figures.[22]

Poland

Moszulski, Roman: official of the Polish Telegraph Agency, a de facto arm of the Polish government-in-exile. Became a KGB asset in 1944. Cover name Canuck.[23]

Yugoslavia

Ivancic, Anton S.: KGB asset who arrived in the United States in 1940 and became active in Yugoslave exile politics. Early in 1944 he became head of the Yugoslav Seamen's Union in New York City. Cover name Crucian.[24]

Kosanovio, Sava N.: Yugoslav journalist and a politician in the Yugoslav government when Germany invaded. KGB asset, active figure in Yugoslav exile politics in the United States. After World War II he became an official in the Tito government. Cover name Kolo.[25]

Subasic, Ivan: exiled Yugoslav politician who became a KGB asset. Carried out KGB tasks among exiled Yugoslavs, reported on the initiatives of the U.S. government toward the exiles, and took part in the maneuvering for control of Yugoslavia after the defeat of the Nazis. Cover name Seres.[26]

The Netherlands

Dutch Naval Attaché in Washington (unidentified). In 1943 the Naval GRU office in Washington, which received information from him, referred to him as "loyal to us."[27]

Unknown Nationality

Contact: unidentified asset of the New York KGB who was part of a group of émigré agents.[28]

Dan: Agent with a U.S. connection to be greeted in London with the pass phrase "Didn't I meet you at Vick's restaurant on Connecticut Avenue?"[29]

Guard: unidentified asset of the New York KGB. Reported from Britain with information on British shipping and forwarded microfilm with encrypted letters to New York through Switzerland. One KGB cable also refers to "Guard's people" in Antwerp.[30]

Saffian, Alexander: appeared to represent either a foreign government or a foreign business firm in the United States. Reported to the New York KGB about negotiations regarding Middle Eastern oil concessions involving American companies. Cover name Contractor.[31]

Señor: unidentified cover name for someone who arrived in the United States from Denmark in September 1944 (but may have been in the United States earlier) and who was an active asset of the New York KGB during late 1944 and 1945. Received a monthly subsidy. Cover name changed to Berg in the fall of 1944.[32]

Yur: unidentified asset of the New York KGB who was part of a group of emigre agents.[33]

Americans and U.S. Residents
Targeted as Potential Sources by Soviet
Intelligence Agencies

The Venona decryptions and documents from Russian archives show that twenty-four persons were targeted by Soviet intelligence as candidates for some sort of relationship. There is no corroborative evidence, however, that their recruitment was accomplished. In several cases there is evidence that recruitment was not carried out, and in others it is likely that recruitment was aborted at an early stage when KGB approaches showed the target to be loyal to the United States. Cover names appear in italics.

Bachrach, Marion: sister of John Abt (see appendix A). Secretly joined the CPUSA in the early 1930s. Personal secretary and congressional office manager to Rep. John Bernard (Farmer-Labor, Minnesota) in 1937–1938 and correspondent for the newspaper *PM*. In 1942 the foreign intelligence arm of the KGB requested a background report on her from the Comintern and received a positive report.[1]

Barnes, Joseph: prominent journalist, former official of the Office of War Information, and manager of the foreign news department of the *New York Herald Tribune*. The KGB considered attempting to recruit Barnes because he had a number of friends in or close to the CPUSA, but it concluded that "the signing up of Barnes is not only inadvisable but unrealizable."[2]

Berger, Joseph Isadore: former assistant of the chairman of the Democratic National Committee and DNC speechwriter (1941–1946), U.S. delegate to the Allied Reparations Commission (1945). Cultivated by KGB agents for several years.[3]

Bloomfield, Samuel: staff member of the Eastern European division of the Research and Analysis section of the Office of Strategic Services in 1942, Also a secret Communist. The KGB, in reporting on him to Moscow, noted that he was also the manager of the Washington Progressive Book Store, a CPUSA-aligned firm. The U.S. government, however, noticed his Communist undertakings and opened an investigation into his activities. Left the OSS in 1943 for a job with the British Information Service in San Francisco.[4]

Bowen, Ralph: State Department economist. He and his wife were former members of the Young Communist League (YCL) and friends of the KGB agent Flora Wovschin, also a State Department employee and former YCL colleague. Cover name Alan.[5]

Breit, Gregory: émigré from Russia and a scientist working on the Manhattan Project. Mentioned in a 1945 cable in which the Moscow KGB headquarters lists possible targets for the New York KGB to consider. Unbeknownst to the Moscow KGB, Breit was a strong supporter of Manhattan Project secrecy and had left the project to protest what he regarded as loose security.[6]

Clarke: prospective GRU recruit who appears to have held a responsible position in a government agency, perhaps the Office of Strategic Services, inasmuch as one of the GRU agents who was engaged in feeling out his attitudes was Leonard Mins. All that is known about Clarke is that although pro-Soviet, he was not a CPUSA member. It is not known whether Clarke is a real name or a cover name.[7]

DuBois, Josiah Ellis: assistant to the secretary of the Treasury and a member of the U.S. delegation to the Allied War Reparations Commission meeting in Moscow in 1945. Harold Glasser, a senior Treasury Department official and a KGB spy, recommended DuBois to the KGB for consideration.[8]

Elitcher, Max: engineer with the Naval Ordnance Section of the National Bureau of Standards. Concealed member of the CPUSA. In 1944 Julius Rosenberg reported to the KGB that he had met with Elitcher and felt that Elitcher's response was sufficiently positive that recruitment should be pursued.[9]

Joseph, Emma Harriet: Communist and contact of the New York KGB via Elizabeth Bentley's apparatus. Worked for the OSS and in late 1944 received an assignment to go to Ceylon. Sister of the KGB agent Julius Joseph. Cover name Ivy.[10]

Larin: unidentified scientist or engineer considered for recruitment but rejected. Described as a CPUSA member, but a check by the KGB's CPUSA liaison showed that in the Federation of Architects, Engineers, Chemists and Technicians, a Communist-led union, Larin was "self-willed" and did not always carry out orders. On the basis of that report the New York KGB dropped its interest in recruiting him. It is not clear whether Larin is a cover name or a real name.[11]

Lauterbach, Richard T.: journalist and concealed Communist who worked for *Time* magazine. A leading KGB agent, Jack Soble, had a discussion with Lauterbach that led Soble and the New York KGB to ask the Moscow KGB headquarters to sanction his formal recruitment. Moscow's reply, however, was not among the Venona messages that were deciphered. Cover name Pa.[12]

Magidov, Nila: writer whom the *American Magazine* planned to send to the USSR as its correspondent for a year. In 1944 the New York KGB suggested that Moscow consider "eventually signing [her] on."[13]

Oppenheimer, Frank: physicist, secret Communist, brother of J. Robert Oppenheimer.[14]

Oppenheimer, J. Robert: physicist, supporter of the CPUSA until 1941, scientific head of the Manhattan Project.[15]

Rappoport, Joseph: veteran Communist party member. He and his wife, who had the cover name Lanya, appear to have been considered for recruitment in 1945.[16]

Roy: husband of Cora (see appendix A), whom Iskhak Akhmerov, the KGB's illegal agent, planned to use for KGB work.[17]

Steinberg, Isadore N.: artist-illustrator working for the Publications Division of the War Department. Concealed member of the CPUSA. Leonard Mins, a GRU agent working in the Office of Strategic Services, recommended his recruitment.[18]

Stone, Isidor Feinstein ("I. F."): journalist and commentator whom the KGB repeatedly attempted to approach. Cover name Pancake.[19]

Tanz, Alfred: lawyer and CPUSA member who, when serving with the Comintern's International Brigades in Spain, was identified in 1937 by Russian authorities as a "reliable" comrade and a candidate for "organizational-technical work." In 1943 the KGB's foreign intelligence arm sent a message to the Comintern inquiring about Tanz's background and received back a positive report.[20]

Thompson, Frederick: scion of a wealthy San Francisco area family, secret Communist. In May 1943 the KGB asked the Comintern for information on his activities during the Spanish Civil War, when he had worked with the Comintern. The message is typical of KGB messages of that period in which a candidate is being vetted for recruitment. May be Trio (see appendix A).[21]

Traugott, Lillian: official in the labor section of the Office of Strategic Services with assignments to OSS missions in England, Sweden, Norway, and France. Received in 1945 an assignment to watch for signs of Communist infiltration of the labor movement of liberated Norway. In 1944 the foreign intelligence arm of the KGB asked for a Comintern background report on Traugott. The Comintern reported that her brother was an "active member" of the CPUSA and that she was believed to have been a CPUSA member since 1937. The OSS appears to have been unaware of her links to the CPUSA. After World War II, she joined the national headquarters staff of the National Citizens Political Action Committee, a prominent Popular Front political group, and in 1948 became an assistant to and later married C. B. Baldwin, national presidential campaign manager for Henry Wallace.[22]

Tuzov: candidate for recruitment developed by the KGB agent Nicholas Orloff. In the final stages of recruitment Tuzov expressed fear of the consequences and indicated that he was reluctant to work for the KGB. The New York KGB decided that given that Tuzov was also elderly, it was inexpedient to pursue recruitment further.[23]

Volok: unidentified engineer or scientist who was fired from the Manhattan Project, reportedly for working for a "progressive organization." Reported by the KGB to be a concealed CPUSA member. The discussion of Volok occurs in a KGB message reporting on the activities of Julius Rosenberg's apparatus and his plans to recruit Communist engineers.[24]

Biographical Sketches of Leading KGB Officers Involved in Soviet Espionage in the United States

Career information is taken largely from *Veterany Vneshnei Razvedki Rossii* (Moscow: Russian Foreign Intelligence Service, 1995).

Akhmerov, Iskhak Abdulovich (1901–1975): of Tartar background, joined the Bolshevik party in 1919, attended the Communist University of Toilers of the East and the First State University [Moscow State University] and graduated from the latter's School of International Relations in 1930. Joined the KGB in 1930 and participated in the suppression of anti-Soviet movements in the USSR's Bukhara Republic (1930–1931). Transferred to the KGB foreign intelligence arm in 1932 and served as a legal intelligence officer under diplomatic cover in Turkey. Became an illegal field officer in China in 1934, entered the United States with false identify papers in 1935, and acted as head of the KGB illegal station in the United States from 1942 to 1945. In late 1945 or early 1946 he returned to the USSR and became deputy chief of the KGB's illegal intelligence section. Attained the rank of colonel and was awarded the Order of the Red Banner (twice), the Order of the Badge of Honor, and the badge of Honored Chekist.

Fitin, Pavel Mikhailovich (1907–1971): graduated from an engineering program at the Timiryazev Agricultural Academy in 1932, served in the Red Army, and worked as an editor for the State Publishing House for Agricultural Literature. In 1938 the CPSU selected him for a special course in foreign intelligence at the KGB's training institute. Made deputy chief of the KGB's foreign intelligence arm in 1938 and became its chief in

1939, at the age of thirty-one. The Russian Foreign Intelligence Service credits Fitin with rebuilding the purge-depleted foreign intelligence department and providing ample warning of the German attack in June 1941. Only the actual invasion saved Fitin from execution for providing Beria, head of the KGB, with information that Stalin did not want to hear and would not believe. Beria retained Fitin as chief of foreign intelligence until the war ended but then demoted him. In 1951 Beria discharged Fitin from the KGB and denied him a pension. Fitin was unable to find other employment until Beria himself was executed in 1953. Attained the rank of lieutenant-general and was awarded the orders of the Red Banner (twice), the Red Star, and the Red Banner of Tuva.

Gromov, Anatoly, pseudonym in the United States of Anatoly Veniaminovich Gorsky (dates unknown): joined the KGB in 1928 and worked in its internal political police section until transferring to foreign intelligence in 1936. Became deputy chief of the KGB station in London in 1936 and chief in 1940. Managed the "Cambridge Five" and the initial KGB penetration of the British atomic bomb project. Was recalled to the USSR in 1944 for work at the central KGB headquarters but was then hastily sent to Washington to become chief of the KGB station in the United States after the sudden recall of Vasily Zubilin. Returned to Moscow in 1947 to take a supervisory position in foreign intelligence and in 1953 shifted to internal security work. Attained the rank of colonel and was awarded the orders of the Red Banner, the Red Banner of Labor, the Badge of Honor, and the Red Star.

Kvasnikov, Leonid Romanovich (1905–1993): graduated with honors from the Moscow Institute of Chemical Machine-Building in 1934 and worked as an engineer for several years. Returned for postgraduate engineering studies and in 1938 entered the KGB as a specialist in scientific-technical intelligence, undertaking short-term assignments in Germany and Poland and rising swiftly to become deputy chief and then chief of the KGB scientific intelligence section. The Russian Foreign Intelligence Service credits Kvasnikov with sparking the KGB's interest in atomic research in 1940 when he noticed that British, American, and German scientists who had regularly published their findings on uranium and related atomic research had ceased to publish. Supervised from Moscow the initial KGB penetration of the British and American atomic bomb projects and in 1943 went to New York under diplomatic cover to supervise scientific-technical espionage with special attention to the atomic bomb project. Returned to the USSR in 1945 and in 1948 again became chief of KGB scientific intelligence, a position he held until 1963. Attained the rank of colonel and was awarded the orders of Lenin, the Red Banner of Labor (twice), and the Red Star (twice).

Ovakimian, Gaik Badalovich (b. 1898): of Armenian background, he joined the KGB in 1931 while a graduate student at Moscow's Bauman Higher Technical School and went immediately into foreign intelligence.

Undertook an assignment in Germany emphasizing scientific-technical espionage. Returned to the USSR in 1932 for advanced technical training at the Workers' and Peasants' Red Army Military-Chemical Academy. Went to the United States in 1933 as deputy head of the KGB's scientific-technical intelligence section, operating under the cover of being an engineer for Amtorg. Became chief of scientific intelligence in the United States in 1939 and also undertook study for a doctorate in chemistry at a New York university. Arrested in 1941 during a meeting with an agent who had been turned by the FBI. After the Nazi invasion of the USSR, the United States agreed to forgo prosecution and allowed him to return to Moscow. Became deputy chief of the KGB's foreign intelligence arm in 1943 and attained the rank of major-general. Left the KGB in 1947 for full-time scientific work.

Semenov, Semyon Markovich (1911–1986): graduated from the Moscow Textile Institute in 1936 with a specialty in power engineering. Joined the KGB in 1937 and was immediately sent to the United States as an intelligence officer. Enrolled at the Massachusetts Institute of Technology, from which he graduated in 1940. Worked under the cover of an Amtorg engineer while specializing in scientific and technical espionage. A Russian Foreign Intelligence Service history quotes his KGB personnel files as stating, "While working from 1938 through 1944 in the United States, Major Semenov showed himself to be one of the most active workers in the *rezidentura* [station]. He practically created the line followed by scientific-technical intelligence during the prewar years. He obtained valuable materials from dozens of agents dealing with explosives, radar technology, and aviation." Later undertook assignments in France and in Moscow and rose to the rank of lieutenant-colonel. Fired from the KGB in 1953 during an antisemitic purge. Rehabilitated in the 1970s.

Yatskov, Anatoly Antonovich (d. 1993): graduated from the Moscow Printing Institute in 1937 and, after joining the KGB in 1939, attended the KGB's training institute. Sent to the United States in 1940 or 1941 as a junior intelligence officer working under diplomatic cover. Specialized in scientific-technical intelligence. After the war he undertook numerous intelligence assignments and headed one of the schools of the KGB's Andropov Red Banner Institute for training of KGB personnel. Attained the rank of colonel and was awarded the orders of the October Revolution, the Red Banner of Labor, the Patriotic War, and the Red Star.

Zubilin, Elizabeth, pseudonym in the United States of Elizaveta Yulyevna Zarubina, and also known as Lisa Gorskaya (1900–1987): born in Russia of Romanian background, she attended universities in Russia, France, and Austria. Joined the Austrian Communist party in 1923 and became an agent of the KGB in 1925, working for its Vienna station until 1928. Undertook several short-term foreign assignments, including one to Turkey. There she alerted Moscow that Jacob Blumkin, a senior KGB officer with whom she was romantically involved, was in communication with Leon Trotsky. Blumkin was recalled and executed. Shortly thereafter she married Vasily Zubilin and, continuing to serve as a KGB officer, accompanied and assisted him in his many intelligence assignments, although occasionally undertaking independent missions. Credited by the Russian Foreign Intelligence Service with recruiting twenty sources for Soviet intelligence during her tour of duty in the United States in the early 1940s.

Zubilin, Vasily, pseudonym in the United States for Vasily Mikhailovich Zarubin (1894–1972): served with the Russian Imperial Army from 1914 to 1917 (wounded) and with the Red Army from 1918 to 1920. Joined the KGB in 1920 and served in its internal security section until 1925, when he transferred to foreign intelligence. Served as a legal officer in China (1925), a legal officer in Finland (1926), an illegal officer in Denmark and Germany (1927–1929), an illegal officer in France (1929–1933), and an illegal officer in Germany (1933–1937). Returned to the USSR in 1937 for work with the KGB's central apparatus. In 1940 he survived an accusation of working for Germany and had some unclear association with the KGB's murder at Katyn of more than fifteen thousand Polish prisoners of war (see chapter 2). Undertook an assignment in China in 1941 and is credited with obtaining information from a high-ranking German adviser to Chiang Kai-shek about Hitler's plans to attack the USSR in mid-1941. Became the chief of the KGB station in the United States in the fall of 1941. Recalled in 1944 to face a second accusation of working for the Germans, which he survived. Became deputy chief of foreign intelligence, attained the rank of major general, and was awarded the orders of Lenin (twice), the Red Banner (twice), and the Red Star.

Notes

Introduction: The Road to Venona

1. Robert Lamphere and Tom Shachtman, *The FBI-KGB War: A Special Agent's Story* (New York: Random House, 1986), 78–98; Ronald Radosh and Joyce Milton, *The Rosenberg File: A Search for the Truth* (New York: Holt, Rinehart and Winston, 1983; New Haven: Yale University Press, 1997), 130; David Martin, *Wilderness of Mirrors* (New York: Ballantine Books, 1981), 39–45. Martin also reported that deciphered messages had pointed to the British diplomat Donald Maclean as a spy. Christopher Andrew and Oleg Gordievsky, *KGB: The Inside Story* (New York: Harper-Collins, 1990), 373–376, 446–447.

2. Peter Wright, *Spy Catcher: The Candid Autobiography of a Senior Intelligence Officer* (New York: Viking, 1987), 239–241.

3. Harvey Klehr and John Earl Haynes, *The American Communist Movement: Storming Heaven Itself*. (New York: Twayne, 1992), 108.

Chapter 1: Venona and the Cold War

1. The basis for the rumors regarding a new Nazi-Soviet Pact is discussed in Vojtech Mastny, *Russia's Road to the Cold War: Diplomacy, Warfare, and the Politics of Communism, 1941–1945* (New York: Columbia University Press, 1979), 77–78, 83–84, 162.

2. Robert Louis Benson and Michael Warner, eds., *Venona: Soviet Espionage and the American Response, 1939–1957* (Washington, D.C.: National Security Agency, Central Intelligence Agency, 1996), xiii.

3. For a summary of Fitin's KGB career, see appendix E.

4. The KGB (Komitet Gosudarstvennoi Bezopasnosti or Committee for State Security) and its foreign intelligence arm have a complex organizational history. The pred-

ecessors to the KGB, which came into existence in 1954, include the Cheka (All-Russian Extraordinary Commission to Combat Counterrevolution and Sabotage), GPU (State Political Directorate), OGPU (United State Political Directorate), NKVD (People's Commissariat of Internal Affairs), GUGB (Main Administration of State Security), NKGB (People's Commissariat of State Security), MGB (Ministry of State Security), KI (Committee of Information), and MVD (Ministry of Internal Affairs). For simplicity, throughout this volume the term KGB will be used to designate these various predecessor organizations.

5. Muse and Mole were eventually identified, but not until many decades later—in Muse's case, not until 1998. After the dissolution of the OSS, Muse (Helen Tenney) had succeeded in transferring to the State Department, where she became a Soviet analyst, a perfect position for a Soviet spy. Mole (Charles Kramer) had become a senior staff member on a Senate committee. Although their Venona cover names were not broken at the time, both were identified as Soviet agents by Elizabeth Bentley, a defector from Soviet espionage, and they were quietly forced to resign. But security officers continued to hunt for Muse and Mole, not realizing that they had already been found.

6. Daniel Patrick Moynihan, *Secrecy: The American Experience* (New Haven: Yale University Press, 1998), 70–71; Benson and Warner, *Venona,* xxiv, xxx.

7. On White House consideration of these actions, see George Elsey to Clark Clifford, 16 August 1948, Clark M. Clifford papers, Harry S. Truman Library, "Loyalty Investigations," box 11, reproduced in Benson and Warner, *Venona,* 117.

8. See chapter 10.

9. It is likely that had the Venona messages been available to the public, both Rosenbergs would have escaped the death penalty, but it should also be kept in mind that both would have been spared execution had they confessed.

10. Joseph McCarthy speech, U.S. Senate, 14 June 1951, *Congressional Record,* vol. 97, part 5, p. 6602.

11. The authors have several times been asked if Senator McCarthy had knowledge of the Venona decryptions, perhaps leaked to him by a security official frustrated by the decision to keep the information secret. There is no evidence that McCarthy had any such information. The targets he picked for his accusations do not suggest Venona as a source. Further, McCarthy was not one to keep politically explosive information secret.

12. Richard M. Fried, *Nightmare in Red: The McCarthy Era in Perspective* (New York: Oxford University Press, 1990); David Caute, *The Great Fear: The Anti-Communist Purge under Truman and Eisenhower* (New York: Simon and Schuster, 1978), 11.

13. Caute, *The Great Fear,* 54. In italics in the original.

14. Ibid., 11.

15. To be exact, the USSR was only half an ally until the final weeks of the war. The Soviet Union stayed neutral in the Pacific theater until after the dropping of the atomic bomb on Japan. Britain and the United States, however, fought two-front wars in both Europe and Asia.

16. The GRU (Glavnoye Razvedyvatelnoye Upravleniye or Chief Intelligence Directorate of the Soviet General Staff) and Naval GRU were military agencies separate from the intelligence arm of the KGB, the Soviet secret political police. These two military intelligence agencies also went through complex organizational and title changes. For a brief period, in 1937 and 1938, the Soviet military intelligence agency even reported to the chief of the NKVD (a predecessor to the KGB), as did the NKVD's own foreign intelligence branch. It was, however, put back in the military chain of command. To avoid confusion, throughout this book the various predecessors to the two military intelligence agencies will be referred to as the GRU and the Naval GRU.

Chapter 2: Breaking the Code

1. This section follows the history of Venona in Robert Louis Benson and Michael Warner, eds., *Venona: Soviet Espionage and the American Response, 1939–1957* (Washington, D.C.: National Security Agency, Central Intelligence Agency, 1996), and in the NSA historical monographs prepared by Robert Louis Benson: "Introductory History of VENONA and Guide to the Translations" (1995), "The 1942–43 New York–Moscow KGB Messages" (1995), "The 1944–45 New York and Washington–Moscow KGB Messages," (1996), "The KGB in San Francisco and Mexico, The GRU in New York and Washington" (1996), "The KGB and GRU in Europe, South America, and Australia" (1996), and "VENONA: New Releases, Special Reports, and Project Shutdown" (1997).

2. A number of the Comintern radio messages and Mikhelson-Manuilov's background are discussed in Harvey Klehr, John Earl Haynes, and Kyrill M. Anderson, *The Soviet World of American Communism* (New Haven: Yale University Press, 1998). On Reid, see "Datos Biográficos de Arnold Reisky (nombre del Partido Arnold Reid)," circa 1937–1938, Archive of the International Brigades, RTsKhIDNI 545-3-453. The International Brigades were a Comintern-controlled military formation that fought with the Spanish Republican government in the Spanish Civil War. Reid was killed during that war.

3. Among other points, Mask messages destroy the view that foreign Communist parties were independent of the Comintern. Sets of the Mask messages are maintained in the United Kingdom by the Public Record Office and in the United States by the National Cryptologic Museum, Fort Meade, Md.

4. For an explanation by one of the Venona program's leading cryptanalysts, see Cecil James Phillips, "What Made Venona Possible?" in Benson and Warner, *Venona*, xv. The Soviet defectors are Igor Gouzenko, a GRU code clerk who defected in Canada in 1945, and Vladimir and Evdokia Petrov, the former a mid-level KGB officer and the latter a KGB code clerk who defected in Australia in 1954. Vladimir Petrov had also been a code clerk earlier in his KGB career. The Petrovs' defection is summarized in David McKnight, *Australia's Spies and Their Secrets* (St. Leonards, Australia: Allen & Unwin, 1994), 59–76. Gouzenko is discussed later in this book. Also see Igor Gouzenko, *Iron Curtain* (New York: Dutton, 1948).

5. The KGB procedure used a two-digit spell table for such names. The GRU used a spell table of mixed one- and two-digit entries for Latin-alphabet names, with a separate but similar table for Cyrillic words or names.

6. The pages of a one-time pad are always used in order, but since messages may be transmitted out of order it is important to have a way of identifying the correct page. Most of the Soviet diplomatic systems provided a page number running from 01 to 35 or from 01 to 50. However, on May 1, 1944, the KGB shifted to the procedure described here of using the first numerical key group on the page rather than a page number to tell the deciphering clerk what key page to use.

7. At one time it was less expensive to transmit letters than numbers. This practice probably originated when messages were transmitted by Morse code rather than teletype machine.

8. This is the "external" number from which is derived the NSA message number used in citing Venona messages.

9. The steps described above are intended to show each of the discrete processes that must be performed. According to Gouzenko, the encoding, encipherment, and typing of the cipher text into the ten-letter substitution was performed as a single operation because the code clerk was not allowed to write down either plain code or the enci-

pherment key, to prevent transmitting anything but fully completed cipher. For anyone working with such a system regularly, performing the encoding, encipherment, and conversion to letters as a single step would not have been difficult. The hardest part would have been keeping track of one's place in the one-time pad. This would have been aided by marking off the groups in the pad as they were used.

10. Phillips, "What Made Venona Possible?" The Army had recruited Phillips, an eighteen-year-old college sophomore, for work in its cryptographic operation at Arlington Hall in 1943 and assigned him to what became the Venona Project in May 1944. His talent was such that he became one of the National Security Agency's long-serving senior cryptanalysts.

11. The Soviet international diplomatic cable traffic during World War II was between 200,000 and 300,000 coded and enciphered messages.

12. Phillips, "What Made Venona Possible?" The NSA identified the use of thirty-five thousand duplicate key pages, but the total number was estimated at perhaps twice that.

13. One of the deciphered Japanese cables based on what had been learned from the Finns is Japanese Army General Staff to Berlin and Helsinki, Tokyo circular 906, 6 October 1942, reproduced in Benson and Warner, Venona, 43–45. See also U.S. Army Signals Security Agency, "Memorandum on Russian Codes in the Japanese Military Attaché System," 9 February 1943, excerpt reproduced in ibid., 47–48.

14. Phillips, "What Made Venona Possible?" Hallock, a Signal Corps reserve officer, had been an archeologist at the University of Chicago.

15. Among the leading cryptanalysts who contributed to breaking the overlying one-time pad cipher were Richard Hallock, Cecil Phillips, Genevieve Feinstein, Frank Lewis, Frank Wanat, and Lucille Campbell.

16. In these cases, to reduce the rapid depletion of one-time pad pages, when the KGB cipher clerks had used only part of a page they did not destroy it but used the rest of the page to encipher a second message. Phillips showed how these could be identified and a search for messages relying on the same page could be made.

17. The USSR had attacked and defeated Finland in the "Winter War" of 1939–1940, forcing the Finns to cede considerable territory. When Nazi Germany invaded the USSR in 1941, the Finns joined the attack in the hope of regaining their lost land.

18. Lt. Oliver Kirby recovered related cryptographic material on a similar mission in Schleswig, Germany. Neff and Kirby later became senior NSA officials.

19. Edward Stettinius, Jr., memorandum for the President, "Soviet Codes," 27 December 1944, President's Secretary's Files, "Russia—1944," box 49, Franklin D. Roosevelt Library. Before the NSA released Venona in 1995 and provided accurate information about the history of the project, one rumor (reported in several books, including one by these authors) erroneously conflated the 1944 OSS Finnish material with that obtained by Army intelligence in 1945.

20. Venona 1657 KGB New York to Moscow, 27 November 1944.

21. Meredith Gardner memorandum, "Covernames in Diplomatic Traffic," 30 August 1947, reprinted in Benson and Warner, Venona, 93–104.

22. Stephen Schwartz, "La Venona Mexicana," Vuelta (Mexico) (August 1997), 19–25.

23. McKnight, Australia's Spies and Their Secrets, 6–25; David McKnight, "The Moscow-Canberra Cables: How Soviet Intelligence Obtained British Secrets through the Back Door," Intelligence and National Security 13, no. 2 (Summer 1998), 159–170; Desmond Ball and David Horner, Breaking the Codes: Australia's KGB Network (St. Leonard's, Australia: Allen & Unwin, 1998).

24. Benson and Warner, *Venona*, xxxi.

25. Victor Navasky, publisher of *The Nation,* derided the decryptions as part of a sinister government covert project "to enlarge post–cold war intelligence gathering capability at the expense of civil liberty." The lawyer-activist William Kuntsler wrote that the messages should be treated as frauds because of their derivation from U.S. government agencies. Victor Navasky, "Tales from Decrypts," *The Nation* (28 October 1996), 5–6; William Kuntsler, letter to the editor, *The Nation* (16 October 1995).

26. Allen Weinstein and Alexander Vassiliev, *The Haunted Wood: Soviet Espionage in America—The Stalin Era* (New York: Random House, 1999). These comments are based on uncorrected proof made available to us by Allen Weinstein.

27. They are Solomon Adler, Iskhak Akhmerov, Joel Barr, Elizabeth Bentley, Abraham Brothman, Earl Browder, William Browder, Frank Coe, Lona Cohen, Morris Cohen, Judith Coplon, Lauchlin Currie, William Dodd, Edward Fitzgerald, Klaus Fuchs, Rebecca Getzoff, Harold Glasser, Bella Gold, Harry Gold, Sonia Gold, Jacob Golos, David Greenglass, Ruth Greenglass, Theodore Hall, Maurice Halperin, Alger Hiss, Julius Joseph, Irving Kaplan, Joseph Katz, Alexander Koral, Charles Kramer, Sergey Kurnakov, Duncan Lee, Donald Maclean, Harry Magdoff, Boris Morros, Victor Perlo, Mary Price, Allan Rosenberg, Ethel Rosenberg, Julius Rosenberg, Saville Sax, Bernard Schuster, George Silverman, Gregory Silvermaster, Helen Silvermaster, Jack Soble, Myra Soble, Alfred Stern, Martha Dodd Stern, Michael Straight, Helen Tenney, William Ullmann, William Weisband, Donald Wheeler, Harry White, Jones York, and Mark Zborowsky.

28. Almost all the KGB messages found in the Comintern records are signed by Lt. Gen. Pavel Mikhailovich Fitin, head of the KGB's First Chief Directorate, the KGB's foreign intelligence arm, from 1940 to 1946. These RTsKhIDNI documents will be described and cited along with the matching deciphered Venona messages in later chapters when we discuss KGB or GRU links with Josephine Adams, Rudy Baker, Earl Browder, Paul Burns, Norman Bursler, Eugene Coleman, Judith Coplon, Pierre Cot, Marion Davis, Edward Fitzgerald, Charles Flato, Harold Glasser, Louis Horvitz, Samuel Krafsur, Charles Kramer, Harry Magdoff, Victor Perlo, Peter Rhodes, and Donald Wheeler. A detailed examination of corroboration of Comintern documents and deciphered Venona cables is in John Haynes and Harvey Klehr, "Venona and the Russian Archives: What Has Already Been Found," a paper presented to the Seventh Symposium on Cryptologic History, 30 October 1997, Fort Meade, Maryland.

29. Venona 1253 KGB New York to Moscow, 30 July 1943.

30. Sharia to Dimitrov, 27 January 1943, Archive of the Dimitrov Secretariat of the Comintern, RTsKhIDNI 495-73-188.

31. Anonymous Russian letter to Hoover, 7 August 1943, reproduced in Benson and Warner, *Venona*, 51–54.

32. Zubilin headed the New York KGB station in 1942 and 1943, operating out of the Soviet consulate, and his move to Washington to work from the Soviet embassy in the second half of 1943 signaled the transfer of the headquarters of KGB operations in America. The New York station, however, remained a major KGB office. Zubilin's immediate replacement in New York was Pavel Klarin, followed in 1944 by Stepan Apresyan, both of whom officially held the title of Soviet vice-consul. Elizabeth Zubilin eventually attained the KGB rank of colonel. For summaries of the KGB careers of the Zubilins, see appendix E.

33. Kheifets, officially Soviet vice-consul, headed the KGB station in San Francisco from 1941 to 1944, when he was replaced by Grigory Kasparov. In 1945 Stepan Apresyan took over as head of the KGB's San Francisco office.

34. Secretary of the Central Committee, All-Union Communist Party [CPSU] to

Beria-NKVD, 5 March 1940, reproduced in Diane Koenker and Ronald D. Bachman, eds., *Revelations from the Russian Archives: Documents in English Translation* (Washington, D.C.: Library of Congress, 1997), 167–168. The Nazis announced the discovery in hopes of stirring up conflict between the anti-Nazi allies. It did. When the Polish government-in-exile refused to accept the Soviet declaration of innocence, the Soviets broke off diplomatic relations.

35. Venona 1033 KGB New York to Moscow, 1 July 1943.

36. Pavel A. Sudoplatov and Anatoli Sudoplatov, with Jerrold L. Schecter and Leona P. Schecter, *Special Tasks: The Memoirs of an Unwanted Witness* (New York: Little, Brown, 1994), 196–197. It is possible that Mironov's real name was Markov. See Ben Fischer, " 'Mr. Guver': Anonymous Soviet Letter to the FBI," *Newsletter of the Center for the Study of Intelligence,* no. 7 (Winter–Spring 1997), 10–11. Sudoplatov also confirmed that Zubilin had been involved in the Katyn operation, but said that Zubilin's role was to select a few of the condemned Polish officers as recruits for the KGB, and that he did not directly take part in the murder operation (pp. 277–278). See also a brief mention of Zubilin in Allen Paul, *Katyn: Stalin's Massacre and the Seeds of Polish Insurrection* (Annapolis, Md.: Naval Institute Press, 1996), 77–78.

37. FBI Comintern Apparatus file (FBI file 100-203581), serial 3378, 1 November 1944; FBI Comintern Apparatus file, serial 3702, "Comintern Apparatus Summary Report," 15 December 1944. This and other FBI files cited herein were obtained through Freedom of Information Act requests or are available at the FBI reading room at the FBI headquarters in Washington, D.C.

38. Frustration with the Justice Department's reluctance to prosecute may have contributed to the willingness of some FBI and other security officials to leak information on Soviet espionage to sympathetic journalists and members of Congress.

39. Benson and Warner, *Venona,* xiv, state that a reference (in Venona 441 KGB San Francisco to Moscow, 31 October 1943) to a new code book to replace the "Pobjeda" code was almost certainly to the replacement of the code book found by the Finns at Petsamo. Elizabeth Bentley FBI deposition, 30 November 1945, FBI file 65-14603, obtained under the Freedom of Information Act. The text of this deposition is also present in the Silvermaster file (FBI file 65-56402).

40. Moscow circular, 25 April 1944, reprinted in Benson and Warner, *Venona,* 259.

41. Clarke's discussion with Rowlett and Hays was reported to Robert Louis Benson in a 1992 interview with Rowlett and Oliver Kirby; see Michael Warner and Robert Louis Benson, "Venona and Beyond: Thoughts on Work Undone," *Intelligence and National Security* 12, no. 3 (July 1997), 1–13. The warning off of the OSS was reported in Timothy J. Naftali, "X-2 and the Counterintelligence Response to Soviet Espionage," a paper presented at the "Venona Conference," 4 October 1996, Washington, D.C.

42. Currie's intervention on behalf of Silvermaster was verbal, and a record exists only because two of the recipients of his efforts made written records of the contacts.

43. Michael Dobbs, "The Man Who Picked the Lock," *Washington Post* (19 October 1996); Benson and Warner, *Venona,* xxviii.

44. Venona messages regarding Link are cited in appendix A.

45. Benson and Warner, *Venona,* xxviii.

46. Larry Kerley testimony, 15 September 1949, "Communist Activities Among Aliens and National Groups," U.S. Congress, Senate, Committee on the Judiciary, Subcommittee on Immigration and Naturalization, 81st Cong., 1st sess., part 2, 811. Venona messages regarding Sabatini are cited in appendix A.

47. Mask 1959/H, Comintern Moscow to Amsterdam 13, 5 January 1935, and

Mask 3760/H, Comintern Moscow to Amsterdam 326, 3 September 1935, Mask collection, National Cryptologic Museum, Fort Meade, Md.; Roster and assignment list of American Communists with the International Brigades, Archive of the International Brigades, RTsKhIDNI 545-6-846; FBI memorandum, "Existing Corroboration of Bentley's Overall Testimony," 6 May 1955, FBI Silvermaster file (FBI file 65-56402), serial 4201.

48. Venona messages regarding York are cited in appendix A.

49. Jones York statement of 6 October 1953, in William Wolf Weisband background memo, 27 November 1953, in Office of Security, National Security Agency, reproduced in Benson and Warner, *Venona*, 167–169.

50. Weisband background memo in Benson and Warner, *Venona*, 170; also see xxviii. Weisband's wife, also an NSA employee, lost her job as well.

51. From a KGB document released in 1998, quoted in Nigel West and Oleg Tsarev, *The Crown Jewels: The British Secrets at the Heart of the KGB Archives* (London: HarperCollins, 1998; New Haven: Yale University Press, 1999), 182. Venona Project cryptanalysts comment that Philby's explanation, although adequate for warning Moscow that its cable traffic had been broken into, reflected a layman's muddled understanding of cryptanalysis in that it exaggerated the assistance provided by early computers in sorting messages for duplications, overplayed how the burnt code book (which was in American, not British, hands) had been used up to that time (only as a model of Soviet code-making), and misunderstood the way Trade messages assisted solutions.

52. There are many detailed books on the five; summaries of their espionage careers appear in Christopher Andrew and Oleg Gordievsky, *KGB: The Inside Story* (New York: HarperCollins, 1990), and West and Tsarev, *The Crown Jewels*. Burgess, the student, actually first recruited Blunt, the don.

53. Venona 1271–1274 KGB New York to Moscow, 7 September 1944. Venona messages regarding Maclean are cited in appendix C.

54. Venona 1105–1110 KGB New York to Moscow, 2–3 August 1944.

55. On the damage done to American security by the three, see Vern W. Newton, *The Cambridge Spies: The Untold Story of Maclean, Philby, and Burgess in America* (Lanham, Md.: Madison Books, 1991).

56. Based on KGB documents released in 1998, Nigel West concluded that Philby's warning about Fuchs, passed on to Guy Burgess in September 1949, did not reach Moscow until February 1950, by which time MI5 already had Fuchs under surveillance. The delay was due to poor microfilming and carelessness on Burgess's part, brought about by his alcoholism and increasingly erratic mental state. West and Tsarev, *The Crown Jewels*, 180–181.

Chapter 3: The American Communist Party Underground

1. "Communist Party Manifesto," reprinted in Joint Legislative Committee Investigating Seditious Activities, *Revolutionary Radicalism, Its History, Purpose and Tactics, with an Exposition and Discussion of the Steps Being Taken and Required to Curb It* (Albany: J. B. Lyon, 1920), 782. Emphasis in the original.

2. On the early history of the American Communist movement, see Harvey Klehr and John Earl Haynes, *The American Communist Movement: Storming Heaven Itself* (New York: Twayne, 1992); Theodore Draper, *The Roots of American Communism* (New York: Viking, 1957); Theodore Draper, *American Communism and Soviet Russia, The Formative Period* (New York: Viking, 1960).

3. On the relationship of the American Communist party to the Comintern in light

of documents from Russian archives, see Harvey Klehr, John Earl Haynes, and Kyrill M. Anderson, *The Soviet World of American Communism* (New Haven: Yale University Press, 1998).

4. Quoted in Theodore Draper, *American Communism and Soviet Russia,* 298.

5. William Z. Foster, *Toward Soviet America* (New York: International Publishers, 1932), 67, 212–213, 275, 317.

6. Protocol II, Session of the Illegal Commission, 4 May 1923, Archive of the Illegal Commission of the Comintern, RTsKhIDNI 495-27-1.

7. *Daily Worker* (17 October 1929); "Resolutions of the Political Secretariat of the ECCI on the Situation and Tasks of the CPUSA," folder 1, box 1, and B. Vasiliev, "How the Communist International Formulates at Present the Problem of Organization," folder 21, box 1, Theodore Draper papers, Emory University Library, Atlanta, Ga.; Lozovsky, "The Trade Unions and the Coming War," and Vasiliev, "The Communist Parties on the Anti-Militarist Front," both in *Communist International* 8, no. 14 (15 August 1931).

8. A detailed account of the CPUSA's underground, based on documents from Russian archives, can be found in Harvey Klehr, John Earl Haynes, and Fridrikh Igorevich Firsov, *The Secret World of American Communism* (New Haven: Yale University Press, 1995).

9. "Autobiography of J. Peter of C.P.U.S.A.," 25 January 1932, and "Report Peters, Joseph . . . ," 15 October 1947, both in Archive of Personnel Files of the Comintern, RTsKhIDNI 495-261-5584.

10. "Brief on the Work of the CPUSA Secret Apparatus," 26 January 1939, Archive of the Dimitrov Secretariat of the Comintern, RTsKhIDNI 495-74-472. Rudy Baker, Peters's successor as head of the secret apparatus, prepared this memo for the Comintern.

11. Paul Crouch testimony, "Communist Underground Printing Facilities and Illegal Propaganda," U.S. Congress, Senate, Committee on the Judiciary, Subcommittee to Investigate the Administration of the Internal Security Act and Other Internal Security Laws, 83d Cong., 1st sess., 4–9, 24–63.

12. On the Ware group, see Earl Latham, *The Communist Controversy in Washington: From the New Deal to McCarthy* (Cambridge: Harvard University Press, 1966), 101–123; Joseph Lash, *Dealers and Dreamers* (New York: Doubleday, 1988), 218. After leaving the AAA, Weyl directed the CPUSA's "School on Wheels," a mobile classroom that toured agricultural areas tutoring farmers in communism. He left the CPUSA in 1939 in reaction to the Nazi-Soviet Pact and broke his silence after the Korean War began. He wrote two books: *Treason: The Story of Disloyalty and Betrayal in American History* (Washington, D.C.: Public Affairs Press, 1950) and *The Battle Against Disloyalty* (New York: Crowell, 1951).

13. John Abt with Michael Myerson, *Advocate and Activist: Memoirs of an American Communist Lawyer* (Urbana: University of Illinois Press, 1993), 39–46.

14. Elinor Langer, "The Secret Drawer," *The Nation* (30 May 1994), 756.

15. The Nazi-Soviet Pact initiated a rethinking on Davis's part that led her out of the party. Earlier her husband had developed mental problems and killed himself. Hope Hale Davis, *Great Day Coming: A Memoir of the 1930s* (South Royalton, Vt.: Steerforth Press, 1994), 30–40, 66–69, 81, 98, 222, 331–332; Testimony of Herbert Fuchs, 13 December 1955, "Investigation of Communist Infiltration of Government," U.S. Congress, House of Representatives, Committee on Un-American Activities, 84th Cong., 1st sess., part 1, 2955–3033.

16. For documentation on the manipulation of government agencies see Klehr,

Haynes, and Firsov, *The Secret World of American Communism,* 96–106; Earl Latham, *The Communist Controversy in Washington,* 124–150.

17. Unsigned [William Dodd] to Mr. President, 19 October 1936, Archive of the Communist Party of the USA, RTsKhIDNI 515-1-4077. Dodd's copy of this letter is in box 49, William E. Dodd papers, Manuscript Division, Library of Congress, Washington, D.C. "Excerpt of a Letter Enclosed to Judge Moore," date-stamped 5 January 1937, archive of the CPUSA, RTsKhIDNI 515-1-4077. The description of Bullitt as "not undangerous" referred to his anti-Soviet attitudes. Bullitt was the first U.S. ambassador to Moscow following Roosevelt's diplomatic recognition of the Soviet Union in 1933. He began his service in Moscow as an enthusiastic supporter of American-Soviet friendship but ended it highly suspicious of Stalin's foreign policy. Among FDR's close advisers Bullitt was one of the strongest anti-Soviet voices.

18. Chambers's CPUSA-GRU network is described in great detail in Whittaker Chambers, *Witness* (New York: Random House, 1952), Sam Tanenhaus, *Whittaker Chambers: A Biography* (New York: Random House, 1997), and Allen Weinstein, *Perjury: The Hiss-Chambers Case* (New York: Random House, 1997), see particularly 115, 137, 204–211.

19. "Brief on the Work of the CPUSA Secret Apparatus."

20. New York FBI memo, 10 February 1947, Comintern Apparatus file (FBI file 100-203581), serial 5392.

21. Baker biographical report, January 1939, Archive of the Dimitrov Secretariat of the Comintern, RTsKhIDNI 495-74-472; "Brief on the Work of the CPUSA Secret Apparatus." On Baker's role in the Pan-Pacific Trade Union Secretariat, see Klehr, Haynes, and Firsov, *The Secret World of American Communism,* 59–60.

22. Venona 1043 KGB New York to Moscow, 25 July 1944; 1286 KGB New York to Moscow, 8 September 1944. Baker occurs in the Venona traffic only under his cover name, Son. NSA/FBI analysts never identified Son as Baker because the two messages about Son provided few clues to his identity. For the identification of Son as Baker see appendix A.

23. Father and Son to Brother, "We discussed . . . ," 13 February 1940, and "Propose you again . . . ," undated, both in Archive of the Secretariat of the Executive Committee of the Communist International: coded correspondence with Communist parties (1933–1943), RTsKhIDNI 495-184-4 (1939–1940 file); Son to Brother, 2 April 1942, RTsKhIDNI 495-184-19 (1942 files); Son to Brother with attached "Son Financial Statement for 1942," Archive of the Dimitrov Secretariat of the Comintern, RTsKhIDNI 495-74-480.

24. Son to Brother with attached "Son Financial Statement for 1942."

25. Brother to Son and Earl, 2 September 1939, and Brother to Earl for Son, 15 September 1939, both in Archive of the Secretariat of the Executive Committee of the Communist International: coded correspondence with Communist Parties (1933–1943), RTsKhIDNI 495-184-8 (1939 file).

26. Son to Brother with attached "Son Financial Statement for 1942."

27. Father and Son to Brother, "We discussed . . . ," 13 February 1940, and Son to Comintern, 22 February 1940, both in Archive of the Secretariat of the Executive Committee of the Communist International: coded correspondence with Communist Parties (1933–1943), RTsKhIDNI 495-184-4, 1939–1940 file. Microdots were extremely tiny bits of microfilm, generally holding the image of a single sheet of paper. They could be glued under a stamp or envelope flap or otherwise hidden in a letter so as to escape all but the most rigorous examination by a government inspector checking international mail.

28. Brother to Earl, 15 September 1939, Archive of the Secretariat of the Executive Committee of the Communist International: coded correspondence with Communist Parties (1933–1943), RTsKhIDNI 495-184-8 (1939 file).

29. Brother to Son, July 1942, Archive of the Secretariat of the Executive Committee of the Communist International: coded correspondence with Communist Parties (1933–1943), RTsKhIDNI 495-184-5 (1942 file).

30. Son to Dimitrov, 19 April 1943, Archive of the Secretariat of the Executive Committee of the Communist International: coded correspondence with Communist Parties (1933–1943), RTsKhIDNI 495-184-7 (1943 file).

31. George Mink autobiographical statement, 29 April 1932, Archive of Personnel Files of the Comintern, RTsKhIDNI 495-261-1667.

32. "Comintern Apparatus Summary Report," 15 December 1944, FBI Comintern Apparatus file, serial 3702.

33. Brother to Son, 2 October 1941, Archive of the Secretariat of the Executive Committee of the Communist International: coded correspondence with Communist Parties (1933–1943), RTsKhIDNI 495-184-3 (1941 file).

34. Son to Brother with attached "Son Financial Statement for 1942."

35. The FBI summary of the recorded conversation is found in "Interlocking Subversion in Government Departments," U.S. Congress, Senate, Committee on the Judiciary, Subcommittee to Investigate the Administration of the Internal Security Act and Other Internal Security Laws, 83d Cong., 1st sess., part 15, 1050–1051. See also Federal Bureau of Investigation, *Soviet Activities in the United States*, 25 July 1946, Clark M. Clifford papers, Harry S. Truman Library, Independence, Mo.; FBI memo on Nelson-Zubilin meeting, 22 October 1944, Comintern Apparatus file, serial 3515; J. Edgar Hoover to Harry Hopkins, 7 May 1943, and CIA memorandum "COMRAP—Vassili M. Zubilin," 6 February 1948, both reproduced in Robert Louis Benson and Michael Warner, eds., *Venona: Soviet Espionage and the American Response, 1939–1957* (Washington, D.C.: National Security Agency, Central Intelligence Agency, 1996), 49–50, 105–115.

36. A transcript of Miyagi's statement to Japanese security police about his recruitment by Yano is reprinted in "Hearings on American Aspects of the Richard Sorge Spy Case," U.S. Congress, House of Representatives, Committee on Un-American Activities, 82d Cong., 1st sess., 1190–1193. Also see discussions of Miyagi's role in the Sorge network in Gordon W. Prange with Donald M. Goldstein and Katherine V. Dillon, *Target Tokyo: The Story of the Sorge Spy Ring* (New York: McGraw-Hill, 1984); "The Case of Richard Sorge," in *Covert Warfare*, vol. 7, John Mendelsohn, ed. (New York: Garland, 1989); and Chalmers Johnson, *An Instance of Treason: Ozaki Hotsumi and the Sorge Spy Ring* (Stanford: Stanford University Press, 1990).

37. Dimitrov to Browder, 21 September 1940, Archive of the Secretariat of the Executive Committee of the Communist International: coded correspondence with Communist Parties (1933–1943), RTsKhIDNI 495-184-15 (1940 file).

38. Hede Massing, *This Deception* (New York: Duell, Sloan and Pearce, 1951), 164–178. KGB documents confirming Massing's account are cited in Weinstein, *Perjury*, 182–184.

39. Flora Lewis, *Red Pawn: The Story of Noel Field* (New York: Doubleday, 1965).

40. Fitin to Dimitrov, 2 November 1942, Archive of the Secretariat of the Executive Committee of the Communist International: coded correspondence with Communist Parties (1933–1943), RTsKhIDNI 495-74-485.

41. Brother to Earl, 13 September 1939, Archive of the Secretariat of the Executive

Committee of the Communist International: coded correspondence with Communist Parties (1933–1943), RTsKhIDNI 495-184-8 (1939 file).

42. FBI memorandum, "Existing Corroboration of Bentley's Overall Testimony"; Elizabeth Bentley, *Out of Bondage: The Story of Elizabeth Bentley* (New York: Ivy Books, 1988), 254–255, 327; Winston Burdett testimony, 29 June 1955, Hearings, Strategy and Tactics of World Communism, Recruiting for Espionage, U.S. Congress, Senate, Committee on the Judiciary, Subcommittee to Investigate the Administration of the Internal Security Act and Other Internal Security Laws, 84th Cong., 1st sess., part 14, pp. 1324–1363.

43. Son [Rudy Baker] to Comintern, 22 February 1940, Archive of the Secretariat of the Executive Committee of the Communist International: coded correspondence with Communist Parties (1933–1943), RTsKhIDNI 495-184-4 (1939–1940 file); New York FBI office memorandum, 3 December 1945, serial 292; Washington FBI office memo, 1 November 1946, serial 464; Scheidt to Hoover, 31 January 1947, serial 1976, all in FBI Silvermaster file (FBI file 65-56402).

44. Venona 1221 KGB New York to Moscow, 26 August 1944.

45. Rhodes background report, 16 November 1945, FBI Silvermaster file, serial 108.

46. Elizabeth Bentley FBI deposition, 30 November 1945, FBI file 65-14603.

47. Scheidt to Hoover, 3 June 1947, serial 2504; Rhodes interview report, 7 June 1947, serial 2583, both in FBI Silvermaster file.

48. Karl [Whittaker Chambers], "The Faking of Americans," Herbert Solow papers, Hoover Institution on War, Revolution and Peace, Stanford University, Stanford, Calif.

49. Karl, "The Faking of Americans."

50. Chambers, *Witness,* 355–356; Karl, "The Faking of Americans."

51. U.S. Department of State Passport Division brief on a conspiracy charge against World Tourists and the CPUSA, prepared in 1939–1940 by Anthony J. Nicholas, reprinted in "Scope of Soviet Activity in the United States," U.S. Congress, Senate, Committee on the Judiciary, Subcommittee to Investigate the Administration of the Internal Security Act, 85th Cong., 1st sess., appendix I, part 23-A, A8, A84, A85, A87, A94, A102, A116, A117, A121, A124.

52. Several Americans who served in the International Brigades in Spain reported seeing Mink there as an officer of the military security police, a body supervised by Aleksandr Orlov, a senior KGB officer. Some sources have it that Mink was later executed or imprisoned in the USSR in Stalin's purge of the International Brigades veterans who had sought exile in the Soviet Union in 1939. On Mink's later fate see Dorothy Gallagher, *All the Right Enemies: The Life and Murder of Carlo Tresca* (New Brunswick, N.J.: Rutgers University Press, 1988), 158–161; Testimony of William C. McCuiston, 12 April 1940, "Investigation of Un-American Propaganda Activities in the United States," U.S. Congress, House of Representatives, Special Committee on Un-American Activities, part 13, 7826–7828; Herbert Romerstein and Stanislav Levchenko, *The KGB Against the "Main Enemy"* (Lexington, Mass.: Lexington Books, 1989), 140.

53. State Department passport brief, A115–A116. Josephson's role in procuring Eisler's fraudulent passport is elaborated in "Investigation of Un-American Propaganda Activities in the United States," hearings of 6 February 1947, U.S. Congress, House of Representatives, Committee on Un-American Activities, 80th Cong., 1st sess., 14–19.

54. "Investigations of Un-American Propaganda Activities in the United States (Regarding Leon Josephson and Samuel Liptzen)," U.S. Congress, House of Representatives, Committee on Un-American Activities, 80th Cong., 1st sess., 5 and 21 March 1947.

55. FBI memorandum, "John Loomis Sherman Background and Personal History," FBI file 65-14920, serial 3221; Chambers, *Witness,* 52–54, 290–310; Weinstein, *Perjury,* 99, 105–110, 171, 204, 281; Allen Weinstein, "Nadya: A Spy Story," *Encounter* (June 1977); Tanenhaus, *Whittaker Chambers,* 85–86, 89–90; William Crane FBI file 74-1333, serial 2706.

56. Passport Division brief, A80, A89–90; David Hornstein, *Arthur Ewert: A Life for the Comintern* (Lanham, Md.: University Press of America, 1993), 153–154, 244–258.

57. Herbert Solow, "Stalin's American Passport Mill," *American Mercury* (July 1939).

58. Alan Cullison, "How Stalin Repaid the Support of Americans," Associated Press story, *Washington Times* (9 November 1997); Chambers, *Witness,* 355–357, 399–400; Weinstein, *Perjury,* 544n; Arnold Ikal suppression file, interrogation by NKVD [KGB], 8 January 1939. The authors thank the Associated Press reporter Alan Cullison for access to his copy of Ikal's NKVD suppression file.

59. Passport Division brief, A5–A32.

60. Two case studies of the mixture of success and excess of this system are Carl H. Chrislock's *Watchdog of Loyalty: The Minnesota Commission of Public Safety During World War I* (St. Paul: Minnesota Historical Society Press, 1991) and, on the American Protective League, Joan M. Jensen, *The Price of Vigilance* (Chicago: Rand McNally, 1968).

61. The titles of the FBI predecessors were the Bureau of Investigation, from 1908 to 1933, and the Division of Investigation, from June 1933 to July 1935.

62. Roosevelt to the Secretary of State et al., 26 June 1939, President's Secretary's Files (Confidential File), "State 1939–40," box 9, Franklin D. Roosevelt Library, Hyde Park, New York, reproduced in Benson and Warner, *Venona,* 13.

63. This description refers to security or counterintelligence. In regard to the gathering of foreign intelligence, FDR assigned chief responsibility to the Army for Europe, to the Navy for the Pacific, and to the FBI for the Western Hemisphere. The later creation of the Office of Strategic Services, however, would confuse this division of responsibility.

64. Hoover memo, "Present Status of Espionage and Counter Espionage Operations of the Federal Bureau of Investigation," 24 October 1940, attached to Hoover to Maj. Gen. Edwin Watson (secretary to the president), 25 October 1940, White House Official Files, "Justice Department—FBI Reports," box 12, FDR Library, reproduced in Benson and Warner, *Venona,* 15–26. On American counterintelligence against German and Japanese espionage, see Frank J. Rafalko, ed., *A Counterintelligence Reader,* vol. 2, *Counterintelligence in World War II* (n.p.: U.S. National Counterintelligence Center, 1998).

65. The Venona cables that deal with each of these persons are cited in appendix A.

66. For citations to the espionage activities of these persons see appendix B.

67. Berle diary entry of 2 September 1939, quoted in Weinstein, *Perjury,* 58. Berle's notes of his meeting with Chambers are reproduced in "Interlocking Subversion in Government Departments," 6 May 1953, part 6, 329–330. Levine's notes of the meeting are in the Chambers file of the Isaac Don Levine Papers, Emory University Library, Atlanta, Ga.

68. Joseph Lash, *Dealers and Dreamers,* 442.

69. For a chronology of the contact between Berle, Chambers, and the FBI, see Ladd to Hoover, 29 December 1948, reproduced in Benson and Warner, *Venona,* 121–128.

Chapter 4: The Golos-Bentley Network

1. Jacob Golos autobiographical questionnaire prepared by Golos, undated but information indicates post-1927, Archive of Personnel Files of the Comintern, RTs-KhIDNI 495-261-466; Elizabeth Bentley, *Out of Bondage: The Story of Elizabeth Bentley* (New York: Ivy Books, 1988), 143–144; Anthony Cave Brown and Charles B. MacDonald, *On a Field of Red: The Communist International and the Coming of World War II* (New York: Putnam, 1981), 340–342, 345. Golos's birth name is sometimes rendered Rasin. One 1946 FBI background memo on Golos puts his Siberian experience and escape via Japan in 1916–1918, but this dating seems erroneous; it was probably earlier. New York Field Office report, 7 January 1946, FBI Silvermaster file (FBI file 65-56402), serial 420.

2. One indirect (and inconclusive) piece of evidence supporting his having been in the Soviet Union in 1919–1923 is a 1928 letter from the Kuzbas Autonomous Industrial Colony to the Comintern. This colony had been founded in the early 1920s in the Kuzbas region of Siberia and consisted of coal mining and associated industrial projects staffed by American radicals who sought to bring American technology to the aid of the new socialist state. The letter announced that the project needed a new administrator and suggested that the Comintern consider Golos because he understood both American and Russian conditions. Possibly this is a reference to his having been in the Soviet Union in the early 1920s and even having been at the Kuzbas project itself; the story he told Bentley included his having been in Siberia and at a coal mine. L. J. Rutgers to Comintern, 8 October 1928, Archive of the Communist Party of the USA, RTsKhIDNI 515-1-507.

3. Jacob Golos later told Bentley that Bayer was part of a Soviet military intelligence (GRU) network. This is confirmed by Venona, in which three GRU messages refer to Bayer as a GRU source under the cover name Simon. Venona messages regarding Bayer are cited in appendix A.

4. FBI interview with John Reynolds, 7 June 1947, FBI Silvermaster file, serial 2503.

5. Venona 1673 KGB New York to Moscow, 30 November 1944; 1802 KGB New York to Moscow, 21 December 1944.

6. Elizabeth Bentley deposition, 30 November 1945, FBI file 65-14603; Bentley, *Out of Bondage*, 108, 176–177.

7. Rose Arenal later confirmed Bentley's story. FBI memorandum, "Existing Corroboration of Bentley's Overall Testimony," 6 May 1955, FBI Silvermaster file, serial 4201.

8. Venona messages regarding Price are cited in appendix A.

9. For a summary of Akhmerov's KGB career see appendix E. Venona messages about him are cited in appendix A.

10. Venona 1065 KGB New York to Moscow, 28 July 1944.

11. Don S. Kirschner, *Cold War Exile: The Unclosed Case of Maurice Halperin* (Columbia: University of Missouri Press, 1995), 130–131, 314–316.

12. Venona 887 KGB New York to Moscow, 9 June 1943; 921–922, 924 KGB New York to Moscow, 16 June 1943; 931 KGB New York to Moscow, 17 June 1943; 1019, 1021, 1024, 1034 KGB New York to Moscow, 29 June 1943; 1106 KGB New York to Moscow, 8 July 1943; 1162 KGB New York to Moscow, 17 July 1943; 1189 KGB New York to Moscow, 21 July 1943. See also Hayden B. Peake, "OSS and the Venona Decrypts," *Intelligence and National Security* 12, no. 3 (July 1997).

13. Venona messages regarding Halperin are cited in appendix A.

14. Kirschner, *Cold War Exile*, 76–77, 86–94, 98–104.

15. FBI report, 29 May 1947, FBI Silvermaster file, serial 2540; FBI report, 7 June 1947, FBI Silvermaster file, serial 2583; Kirschner, *Cold War Exile*, 282–288.

16. Kirschner, *Cold War Exile*, 272, 324.

17. Washington Field Office report, "Re: Lt. Col. Duncan C. Lee," 28 January 1946, FBI Silvermaster file.

18. Bentley deposition.

19. Bentley deposition.

20. Hitler got wind that his Hungarian allies were considering surrender, and in October 1944 German forces occupied Hungary, took direct control of its government, and imprisoned the OSS agents in Hungary who were negotiating the deal. The authors are grateful to Robert Goldberg, son of Arthur Goldberg (future Cabinet member and Supreme Court justice), one of the OSS authors of the Sparrow mission, for sharing his research into his father's suspicion that the Soviets, alerted to the Sparrow mission by Lee, deliberately leaked it to the Nazis to ensure that Hungary and the Balkans would come under Soviet domination.

21. Duncan Lee interview report, 4 June 1947, FBI Silvermaster file, serial 2530. Robert Goldberg brought the Lees' Moscow honeymoon to our attention.

22. Venona messages regarding Lee are cited in appendix A.

23. Venona 782 KGB New York to Moscow, 26 May 1943.

24. Bentley, *Out of Bondage*, 182.

25. Venona 1325–1326 KGB New York to Moscow, 15 September 1944.

26. Venona 1354 KGB New York to Moscow, 22 September 1944. In an act that is a serious barrier to historical accuracy, the NSA redacted—that is, blacked out—the names of Communists and Soviet sources contained in this message, with the single exception of the name of Donald Wheeler.

27. Venona 954 KGB Moscow to New York, 20 September 1944.

28. Testimony of Julius J. Joseph, 26 April 1953, "Interlocking Subversion in Government Departments," U.S. Congress, Senate, Committee on the Judiciary, Subcommittee to Investigate the Administration of the Internal Security Act and Other Internal Security Laws, 83d Cong., 1st sess., part 10, 605–621; FBI memo, "Underground Soviet Espionage Organization (NKVD) in Agencies of the United States Government," enclosed with D. M. Ladd to Director, 21 February 1946, serial 573, Hottel to Director, 13 January 1947, serial 2034, and Hottel to Hoover, 17 November 1947, serial 3009, all in FBI Silvermaster file.

29. Bentley deposition; Venona messages regarding Julius and Bella Joseph are cited in appendix A.

30. Julius Joseph testimony, 26 May 1953, "Interlocking Subversion in Government Departments," part 10, 615.

31. Venona 1464 KGB New York to Moscow, 14 October 1944. It is not known whether the KGB made contact with her in Ceylon.

32. Bentley deposition; Bentley, *Out of Bondage*, 139–140.

33. Cedric Belfrage interview, 8 June 1947, FBI Silvermaster file, serial 2522; Cedric Belfrage statement, 3 June 1947, FBI Silvermaster file, serial 2583.

34. Venona messages regarding Belfrage are cited in appendix A.

35. Cedric Belfrage, *The Frightened Giant: My Unfinished Affair with America* (London: Secker and Warburg, 1957) and *The American Inquisition, 1945–1960* (Indianapolis: Bobbs-Merrill, 1973).

36. Bentley deposition.

37. Bentley, *Out of Bondage,* 138–139; Bentley deposition; OSS report, secret, "Spain, Communist Party of Catalonia," 8 July 1943, archives of the Dimitrov Secretariat of the Comintern, RTsKhIDNI 495-74-481; Ladd memo on Mary Price interview, 18 April 1947, FBI Silvermaster file, serial 2340. Venona messages regarding Tenney are cited in appendix A.

38. Strickland memo on Tenney, 6 June 1946, FBI Silvermaster file, serial 1195; Ladd to Director 15 January 1947, FBI Silvermaster file, serial 2081.

39. Scheidt to Hoover, 12 February 1947, FBI Silvermaster file, serial 2407; Ladd to Hoover, 6 June 1947, FBI Silvermaster file, serial 2547; Bentley, *Out of Bondage,* 209–210.

40. Bentley deposition; Earl Latham, *The Communist Controversy in Washington: From the New Deal to McCarthy* (Cambridge: Harvard University Press, 1966), 306–307.

41. Michael Greenberg interview, 7 June 1947, FBI Silvermaster file, serial 2583.

42. Nor did either know that one of Miller's subordinates at the Office of the Coordinator of Inter-American Affairs, Charles Flato, was also a Soviet agent.

43. FBI report on Joseph Gregg, 11 March 1946, FBI Silvermaster file, serial 674.

44. FBI memo on Robert Talbott Miller III, 24 January 1948, FBI Silvermaster file, serial 3085; Robert T. Miller interview, 21 April 1947, FBI Silvermaster file, serial 2349.

Chapter 5: Friends in High Places

1. Venona messages regarding Perlo are cited in appendix A.

2. Bentley could not clearly remember the date, except that it was a rainy Sunday in March. She had also remembered that one participant, Harry Magdoff, had been on sick leave recovering from an operation and was about to return to work at the War Production Board. The FBI checked and found that Magdoff had been on sick leave from January 10 to March 7 for a gall bladder operation, and that it had rained in New York on both Sunday, February 27, and March 5. The bureau was inclined to regard the latter date as the most likely. Elizabeth Bentley FBI deposition, 30 November 1945, FBI file 65-14603; Elizabeth Bentley, *Out of Bondage: The Story of Elizabeth Bentley* (New York: Ivy Books, 1988), 163–165; New York FBI memo, 16 January 1947, FBI Silvermaster file (FBI file 65-56402), serial 1936.

3. Venona 588 KGB New York to Moscow, 29 April 1944; 687 KGB New York to Moscow, 13 May 1944; 769 and 771 KGB New York to Moscow, 30 May 1944.

4. Venona messages regarding each person are cited in appendix A.

5. Testimony of Herbert Fuchs, "Investigation of Communist Infiltration of Government"; Testimony of Allan Rosenberg, 21 February 1956, "Investigation of Communist Infiltration of Government," U.S. Congress, House of Representatives, Committee on Un-American Activities, 84th Cong., 2nd sess., part 4, 3300–3307; Earl Latham, *The Communist Controversy in Washington: From the New Deal to McCarthy* (Cambridge: Harvard University Press, 1966), 121–131.

6. Jane Foster, *An Un-American Lady* (London: Sidgwick and Jackson, 1980), 105.

7. Akhmerov's Storm/Peters cable is quoted in Allen Weinstein, *Perjury: The Hiss-Chambers Case* (New York: Random House, 1997), 184.

8. "Report Peters, Joseph . . . ," 15 October 1947, Archive of Personnel Files of the Comintern, RTsKhIDNI 495-261-5584.

9. The quoted material is from Bolshakov to Dimitrov, 5 May 1943, Archive of the Dimitrov Secretariat of the Comintern, RTsKhIDNI 495-74-486.

10. Ilichev to Dimitrov, 5 March 1943, Archive of the Dimitrov Secretariat of the Comintern, RTsKhIDNI 495-74-486. General Ilichev headed the GRU.

11. Venona 588 KGB New York to Moscow, 29 April 1944.

12. Also strengthening the possibility that Storm is Peters is the relationship with John Abt. In late 1943 the FBI opened an investigation of Abt, the intermediary with this group before it was handed over to Bentley and her CPUSA/KGB network. Its surveillance showed frequent meetings in the early months of 1944 between Abt and a man then known as Alexander Stevens, one of the several pseudonyms used by Josef Peters. New York FBI report, 9 April 1944, John Jacob Abt FBI file 100-236194, serial 6.

13. Venona 588 KGB New York to Moscow, 29 April 1944.

14. Fitin to Dimitrov, 28–29 September 1944, Archive of the Dimitrov Secretariat of the Comintern, RTsKhIDNI 495-74-485.

15. Bentley, *Out of Bondage,* 184. Given that Bentley reconstructed the conversation from memory, this should not be treated as if it were a transcript of Gromov's remarks.

16. Venona 1388–1389 KGB New York to Moscow, 1 October 1944.

17. On Bernard's secret relationship with the CPUSA and his later emergence as an open party member decades later, see John Earl Haynes, *Dubious Alliance: The Making of Minnesota's DFL Party* (Minneapolis: University of Minnesota Press, 1984), 29, 37, 55, 59, 224n.

18. Charles Kramer testimony, 6 May 1953, "Interlocking Subversion in Government Departments," Subcommittee to Investigate the Administration of the Internal Security Act and Other Internal Security Laws, U.S. Senate Committee on the Judiciary, 83d Cong., 1st sess., part 6, 327–381. Patterson had been discreetly allied with the CPUSA since the late 1930s. Harvey Klehr, *The Heyday of American Communism: The Depression Decade* (New York: Basic Books, 1984), 271–272, 403.

19. John Snyder to H. L. Lurie, 26 December 1947, reproduced in "Interlocking Subversion in Government Departments," part 2, 100.

20. Venona 769 and 771 KGB New York to Moscow, 30 May 1944.

21. Ladd to Director, 1 May 1947, serial 2380, memo on Glasser interview, 13 May 1947, serial 2429, both in FBI Silvermaster file; Glasser testimony, 14 April and 2 June 1953, "Interlocking Subversion in Government Departments," part 2, 53–100.

22. Whittaker Chambers, *Witness* (New York: Random House, 1952), 430.

23. Weinstein, *Perjury,* 326–327. The identification of Ales as Hiss is discussed in chapter 6.

24. Venona messages regarding Glasser are cited in appendix A.

25. Bentley deposition.

26. Venona 1759 KGB Washington to KGB Moscow, 28 March 1945.

27. Transcripts of Glasser's promotions and job rating forms signed by Coe, Ullmann, and White are in "Interlocking Subversion in Government Departments," part 2, 81–82, 98–99.

28. Hottel to Hoover, 14 January 1947, FBI Silvermaster file, serial 2028.

29. Edward Fitzgerald testimony, Harry Magdoff testimony, 1 May 1953, "Interlocking Subversion in Government Departments," part 5, 241–326; Perlo testimony, "Hearings Regarding Communist Espionage in the United States Government," U.S. Congress, House of Representatives, Committee on Un-American Activities, 80th Cong., 2d sess., 699–700; Victor Perlo, "Imperialism—New Features," *Political Affairs* (May 1981), 3; Vic Perlo, "Reply to Herbert Aptheker," *Political Affairs* (June 1992), 26.

30. Venona messages regarding these persons are cited in appendix A.

31. Venona 2011 KGB New York to Moscow, 11 December 1943.

32. Venona 1469 KGB New York to Moscow, 17 October 1944.

33. Real estate ad for 5515 30th Street, N.W., Washington, D.C., *Washington Star* (3 May 1947).

34. Kenneth Rexroth, *An Autobiographical Novel* (Santa Barbara, Calif.: Ross-Erikson, 1978), 278–279. The FBI's Seattle office identified Silvermaster as a Communist in 1922. See Silvermaster background memo, 16 November 1945, FBI Silvermaster file, Serial 26x1.

35. Patterson later became secretary of war under President Truman.

36. File card of Patterson contacts in regard Silvermaster, box 203, Robert P. Patterson papers, Library of Congress; General Bissell to General Strong, 3 June 1942, Silvermaster reply to Bissell memo, 9 June 1942, Robert P. Patterson to Milo Perkins of Board of Economic Warfare, 3 July 1942, all reprinted in "Interlocking Subversion in Government Departments," 30 August 1955, 84th Cong., 1st sess., part 30, 2562–2567; Lauchlin Currie testimony, 13 August 1948, U.S. Congress, House of Representatives, Committee on Un-American Activities, 80th Cong., 2d sess., 851–877. On Baldwin's secret Communist allegiances, see John Gates to Joseph Starobin, undated, box 10, folder 2, Philip Jaffe papers, Emory University Library, Atlanta, Ga.

37. Ladd to Hoover, 12 December 1945, FBI Silvermaster file, serial 235.

38. Paul Appleby to L. C. Martin and J. Weldon Jones, 23 March 1944, reprinted in "Interlocking Subversion in Government Departments," part 30, xii.

39. Venona 1388–1389 KGB New York to Moscow, 1 October 1944.

40. Venona 12, 13, 15, 16 KGB New York to Moscow, 4 January 1945.

41. Venona messages regarding Helen Silvermaster are cited in appendix A. Helen Silvermaster interview report, 21 April 1947, FBI Silvermaster file, serial 2349.

42. Venona 1635 KGB New York to Moscow, 21 November 1944. The reference to Silvermaster's wanting to "see the reward and the book" is to seeing the actual Soviet decoration and the official certificate ("book") in which the decoration is awarded to an individual. This was not the only KGB recognition Silvermaster received. He was at one time the only American citizen featured in the KGB's secret Hall of Fame in Moscow.

43. Venona messages regarding Gregory Silvermaster are cited in appendix A.

44. Venona messages regarding Ullmann are cited in appendix A.

45. Ladd to Hoover on White interview, 5 September 1947, FBI Silvermaster file, serial 2787; Ullmann interview report, 21 April 1947, FBI Silvermaster file, serial 2349.

46. Hope Hale Davis, "Looking Back at My Years in the Party," *New Leader* (11 February 1980).

47. Chambers, *Witness*; Weinstein, *Perjury*, 190–191.

48. Venona messages regarding Silverman are cited in appendix A.

49. Malcolm Hobbs, "Confident Wallace Aides Come Up with Startling Cabinet Notions," Overseas News Service dispatch, 22 April 1948, reprinted in "Interlocking Subversion in Government Departments," part 30, 2529–2530.

50. Bentley, *Out of Bondage,* 113.

51. Harvey Klehr and Ronald Radosh, *The Amerasia Spy Case: Prelude to McCarthyism* (Chapel Hill: University of North Carolina Press, 1996), 21–22, 37, 197, 159, 171–172. Mao Tse-tung and Chou En-lai to Dimitrov, 19 August 1940, Archive of the Secretariat of the Executive Committee of the Communist International: coded correspondence with Communist Parties (1933–1943), RTsKhIDNI 495-184-15, 1940 file.

52. Venona messages regarding White are cited in appendix A.

53. Venona 235–236 KGB San Francisco to Moscow, 5 May 1945.

54. Venona 1634 KGB New York to Moscow, 20 November 1944.

55. In the Venona cables White's cover name was first Jurist, then Lawyer, and finally Richard.

56. Venona 1119–1121 KGB New York to Moscow, 4–5 August 1944. The "new course" referred to a policy of American accommodation of Soviet foreign policy goals. Kolstov does not appear to have been a regular officer of the KGB stations in New York or Washington, but one visiting the United States from Moscow, probably posing as a diplomat in a high-level Soviet delegation, who could meet with a man of White's standing without attracting security attention.

57. Insert of 9 May 1945, *Morgenthau Diary (China)*, vol. 2, hearing of 5 February 1965, U.S. Congress, Senate, Subcommittee to Investigate the Administration of the Internal Security Act and Other Internal Security Laws, 89th Cong., 1st sess., 1043.

58. In regard to White as an agent of influence, Vladimir Pavlov, a retired KGB officer, published a description of a clandestine meeting with White in 1941. Pavlov stated that he had met with White on KGB orders to urge him to promote a stern American policy toward Japan in order to relieve Japanese pressure on the USSR. While denying that White was a spy, Pavlov said that White had been in contact with the KGB through Iskhak Akhmerov and that the meeting itself was arranged by a Soviet spy who worked at the U.S. Treasury. V. Pavlov, "The Time Has Come to Talk about Operation 'Snow,' " *Novosti razvedki i kontrrazvedki* (News of intelligence and counterintelligence, Moscow, in Russian), nos. 9–10 and 11–12, 1995. Pavlov, under the cover of being the second secretary of the Soviet embassy in Ottawa, was the chief of the KGB Canadian station from 1942 to 1946. Pavlov is vague—purposefully misleading, it appears—on dates and other matters regarding the operation. The article was one of a number sanctioned by the Russian Foreign Intelligence Service which praised historic Soviet intelligence successes. Pavlov's essay portrayed the KGB as having saved Russia from a two-front war by promoting via White a tough American policy that provoked Japan into attacking south against the United States rather than north against the USSR. This is certainly an exaggeration of White's influence, although White did provide memorandums supporting a firm stand to Secretary of the Treasury Hull to assist him in his discussion with other Roosevelt administration officials on what stance to take against Japan in the latter half of 1941. Like the similar Chikov article discussed in chapter 10, the mixture of truth, half-truth, and deliberate distortion in the essay makes Pavlov's reliability on any particular point uncertain.

59. Venona messages regarding Coe are cited in appendix A. His full name was Virginius Frank Coe.

60. Frank Coe testimony, 13 August 1948, "Hearings Regarding Communist Espionage in the United States Government," U.S. Congress, House of Representatives, Committee on Un-American Activities, 80th Cong., 2nd sess., 914–928; Frank Coe interview, 4 June 1947, FBI Silvermaster file, serial 2530; Benjamin Mandell report on Frank Coe, 12 November 1953, "Interlocking Subversion in Government Departments," part 16, 1073; Robert Alden, "Frank Coe Lauds Red China's Work," *New York Times* (21 February 1959), 4.

61. Solomon Adler interview, 19 December 1947, FBI Silvermaster file, serial 3030; Robert Morris statement, 18 November 1953, "Interlocking Subversion in Government Departments," part 16, 1163–1165.

62. Sidney Rittenberg and Amanda Bennett, *The Man Who Stayed Behind* (New York: Simon and Schuster, 1993), 251; *Selected Shanghai Culture and History Materials* (in Chinese), issue 43, April 1983, Shanghai People's Press; Henshen Chen, *Sige shidai de wo* (My life during four ages, in Chinese) (Beijing: Chinese Culture and History Press,

1988). The authors thank Professor Maochun Yu for calling our attention to the latter two Chinese sources. When the United States established diplomatic relations with the People's Republic of China, Adler petitioned for and received restoration of his American citizenship.

63. Anthony Kubek in *How the Far East Was Lost: American Policy and the Creation of Communist China, 1941–1949* (Chicago: Regnery, 1963) presents a scholarly version of this theme.

64. Chambers, *Witness,* 468; Berle's notes, reproduced in "Interlocking Subversion in Government Departments," 6 May 1953, part 6, 329–330.

65. Venona messages regarding Currie are cited in appendix A.

66. Venona 143 KGB Moscow to New York, 15 February 1945.

67. Venona 253 KGB Moscow to New York, 20 March 1945.

68. "Underground Soviet Espionage Organization (NKVD) in Agencies of the United States Government," 21 February 1946, FBI Silvermaster file, serial 573; Report on Currie interview, 31 July 1947, FBI Silvermaster file, serial 2794; Michael Warner and Robert Louis Benson, "Venona and Beyond: Thoughts on Work Undone," *Intelligence and National Security* 12, no. 3 (July 1997), 10–11; Anonymous Russian letter to Hoover, 7 August 1943, reproduced in Robert Louis Benson and Michael Warner, eds., *Venona: Soviet Espionage and the American Response, 1939–1957* (Washington, D.C.: National Security Agency, Central Intelligence Agency, 1996), 51–54.

69. Although an open ally of the CPUSA and an ardent Stalinist, Robeson refused to acknowledge his membership in the CPUSA during his lifetime. In 1998, however, the CPUSA announced that he had been a secret member. "World to Honor Robeson May 3," *People's Weekly World* (21 March 1998).

70. In the late 1930s the National Negro Congress grew rapidly and had prospects of becoming a major influence among African Americans. The CPUSA's insistence, however, that it follow the policy requirement of the Nazi-Soviet Pact caused many black activists who had joined it to leave in disgust, including the organization's most prominent figure, A. Philip Randolph.

71. Zola Clear, a member of the executive committee of the Washington Committee for Aid to China, resigned to protest the group's treatment of Pinchot and Roosevelt and testified to the Dies Committee with material supplied by Cornelia Pinchot. Clear to Pinchot, 6 October 1941, and Pinchot to Clear, 17 October 1941, both in the Washington Committee for Aid to China folders, box 398, Cornelia Pinchot Papers, Manuscript Division, Library of Congress; Zola Clear testimony and insert of 13 April 1941 statement of Cornelia Bryce Pinchot, 7 August 1941, "Investigation of Un-American Propaganda Activities in the United States," U.S. Congress, House of Representatives, Special Committee on Un-American Activities, 78th Cong., 2d sess., 2361–13881.

72. Currie testimony, U.S. Congress, House of Representatives, Committee on Un-American Activities, 13 August 1948, 80th Cong., 2d sess., 851–877.

73. Bentley and Rankin exchange, 31 July 1948, "Hearings Regarding Communist Espionage in the United States Government," 557–558.

74. The year 1950 was a high point in Soviet intelligence contacts' fleeing the United States. In addition to Currie, also emigrating that year (some publicly and some secretly) were Solomon Adler, Morris and Lona Cohen, Joseph Barr, Alfred Sarant, Henry and Beatrice Spitz, and Abraham Chapman. Also in 1950 the physicist Bruno Pontecorvo, a Soviet source who had worked on the American atomic bomb project, fled to the Soviet Union from Britain, where he then lived.

75. When the Bentley and Chambers cases became public, the FBI considered using

Katherine Perlo as a witness. Her mental condition, though, was poor: she had been admitted for a time to a mental institution, and she was likely to be an easy target for an aggressive defense lawyer. She was never called to testify. FBI background memo, 16 November 1945, FBI Silvermaster file, serial 26x1; Washington FBI Field Office to Hoover, 3 April 1947, FBI Silvermaster file, serial 2448.

76. New York FBI memo, 7 December 1945, FBI Silvermaster file, serial 248.

77. Ladd to Hoover, 12 December 1945, FBI Silvermaster file, serial 235.

78. Koral statement, 11 June 1947, FBI Silvermaster file, serial 2608; Alexander Koral interview summary, 9 June 1947, FBI Silvermaster file, serial 2571; FBI memorandum, "Existing Corroboration of Bentley's Overall Testimony," 6 May 1955, FBI Silvermaster file, serial 4201.

79. Venona messages regarding Alexander and Helen Koral are cited in appendix A.

80. Nigel West and Oleg Tsarev, *The Crown Jewels: The British Secrets at the Heart of the KGB Archives* (London: HarperCollins, 1998), 112, 116, 130, 133–134. Blunt's report is quoted on p. 130.

81. Michael Straight, *After Long Silence* (New York: Norton, 1983), 102.

82. Straight, *After Long Silence,* 104.

83. Straight, *After Long Silence,* 121.

84. Veterany Vneshney Razvedki Rossii (Veterans of Russian Foreign Intelligence Service), Russian Foreign Intelligence Service, Moscow, 1995. This biography states that while resident in the United States Akhmerov also undertook short-term missions to Europe and China.

85. On Akhmerov, see Robert Louis Benson, "The 1942–43 New York–Moscow KGB Messages" (NSA, 1995), and "The 1944–45 New York and Washington–Moscow KGB Messages" (NSA, 1996).

86. On Lowry as Browder's niece, see Christopher Andrew and Oleg Gordievsky, *KGB: The Inside Story* (New York: HarperCollins, 1990), 286; Pavel A. Sudoplatov, Anatoli P. Sudoplatov, with Jerrold L. Schecter and Leona P. Schecter, *Special Tasks: The Memoirs of an Unwanted Witness* (New York: Little, Brown, 1994), 83; Robert Louis Benson, "The 1944–45 New York and Washington–Moscow KGB Messages." A "J. C. Lowry" is one of the identifying witnesses for a passport obtained by Bill Browder, Earl's brother. Whether this person was related to Helen Lowry is unknown. U.S. Department of State Passport Division brief on a conspiracy charge against World Tourists and the CPUSA, reprinted in "Scope of Soviet Activity in the United States," U.S. Congress, Senate, Committee on the Judiciary, Subcommittee to Investigate the Administration of the Internal Security Act, appendix I, part 23-A (1957), A9.

87. Weinstein, *Perjury,* 183–184. Also see Vern W. Newton, *The Cambridge Spies: The Untold Story of Maclean, Philby, and Burgess in America* (Lanham, Md.: Madison Books, 1991), 218–221.

88. West and Tsarev, *The Crown Jewels,* 112–113. This account tends to support Straight's claims that he never became the spy that the KGB had hoped, because it appears that Deutsch was dispatched with a view to getting more out of him than Akhmerov had (p. 134).

89. West and Tsarev, *The Crown Jewels,* 174.

90. Straight had also known Guy Burgess as a fellow Cambridge Communist and likely an espionage recruit of Blunt's. He later wrote that in 1947 and 1949 he suspected that Burgess, then a British diplomat, might have been assisting Soviet intelligence and extracted promises from Burgess to leave the British Foreign Office. Burgess did not do so, and Straight did nothing.

91. David Caute, *The Great Fear: The Anti-Communist Purge under Truman and Eisenhower* (New York: Simon and Schuster, 1978), 156. Koral is named as "Koval" in Caute's book. The Akhmerovs and Alexander Koral were not the only members of the Bentley story for whom Straight gave corroboration. He also told the FBI that in 1938, during a period when he was out of touch with Akhmerov, Solomon Adler had approached him with the advice that he should "lay low" but that contact would be resumed. This was just after Chambers had dropped out of Soviet espionage, and his former contacts, of whom Akhmerov was one, feared he might go to government authorities. Straight also told the FBI that at his final meeting with Akhmerov in 1942, just before he entered the armed forces and severed contact with the KGB, he was asked about other possible contacts and mentioned another name that shows up in Bentley's story, Michael Greenberg. John Costello, *Mask of Treachery* (New York: Morrow, 1988), 380–381, 480–481. Straight initially remembered the name of the person who approached him as Solomon Leshinsky but identified a photograph of Solomon Adler as the man who had made contact with him. Bentley had named both Solomon Leshinsky and Solomon Adler as members of her network, and Straight had confused his Solomons.

92. Hoover to George Allen, 31 May 1946, FBI Silvermaster file, serial 1160.

93. On the FBI's conclusion that the Soviets warned Bentley's former contacts, see Hayden B. Peake, "Afterword," in Bentley, *Out of Bondage,* 290.

94. Venona messages regarding Coplon are cited in appendix A.

95. Fitin to Dimitrov, 19 October 1944, Archive of the Dimitrov Secretariat of the Comintern, RTsKhIDNI 495-74-485.

96. Venona 27 KGB New York to Moscow, 8 January 1945.

97. The FBI investigation of Coplon and the subsequent trial are discussed in Robert J. Lamphere and Tom Shachtman, *The FBI-KGB War: A Special Agent's Story* (New York: Random House, 1986), 97–125, and Sanche de Gramont [Ted Morgan], *The Secret War* (New York: Putnam, 1962).

98. Lovestone had publicly accused Leon Josephson of stealing his records, and in September 1938 Pat Toohey, the CPUSA's representative in Moscow, bragged to the Comintern that the party had carried out the theft. Toohey to Dimitrov, 19 September 1938, Archive of the Dimitrov Secretariat of the Comintern, RTsKhIDNI 495-74-466. The FBI report on the Levy entry was exhibit 119 in *United States* v. *Judith Coplon* (criminal case 381–49), United States District Court for the District of Columbia, 10 June 1949.

99. E. Morgan to H. H. Clegg, 14 January 1947, serial 2077. Other FBI expressions of the likelihood that prosecution would not be successful include Tamm to Director, 23 January 1947, serial 2007, and Nichols to Tamm, 14 February 1947, serial 2166. All three are in FBI Silvermaster file (65-56402).

100. Morgan to Clegg, 14 January 1947, FBI Silvermaster file, serial 2077.

101. Bentley deposition, 48; Bentley, *Out of Bondage,* 123–124.

102. FBI letter to John Steelman, 19 December 1946, FBI Silvermaster file, serial 2097x; regarding FBI interview with William Remington, 21 April 1947, FBI Silvermaster file, serial 2349; regarding FBI interview with William Remington, 28 April 1947, FBI Silvermaster file, serial 2381.

103. Gary May, *Un-American Activities: The Trials of William Remington* (New York: Oxford University Press, 1994). Remington was later killed in a prison fight.

104. Latham, *The Communist Controversy in Washington,* 160. Latham noted that he did not share the general view.

Chapter 6: Military Espionage

1. This shift is reflected in coded Soviet cable traffic. In 1940 the GRU transmitted nearly three times as many messages from New York to Moscow as did the KGB (992 versus 335). By 1942, however, the KGB had taken over many GRU agents, and its message traffic easily surpassed that of its brother agency. During most of World War II the GRU was clearly the lesser Soviet intelligence agency. The KGB had many more agents, developed a much more sophisticated support system of handlers and espionage controllers in the United States, and gathered more and better raw intelligence. Still, the relative inattention to GRU intelligence activity is partly due to the paucity of counterintelligence information about GRU operations. There were no defectors from the GRU comparable in importance to the KGB defector Elizabeth Bentley, and the agents that Whittaker Chambers exposed were (with the exception of Alger Hiss) from the KGB. Also, far fewer GRU messages were successfully decrypted by the Venona Project.

2. Robert Louis Benson, "The 1942–43 New York–KGB Messages" (NSA, 1996), 2.

3. Inserted statement of Nicholas Dozenberg, hearings of 8 November 1949, U.S. Congress, House of Representatives, Committee on Un-American Activities, 81st Cong., 1st and 2d sess.

4. "Comintern Apparatus Summary Report," 15 December 1944, FBI Comintern Apparatus file (FBI file 100-203581), serial 3702.

5. Lovestone later became a leading anti-Communist. On his links to Soviet intelligence in the 1930s, see Harvey Klehr, John Earl Haynes, and Fridrikh Igorevich Firsov, *The Secret World of American Communism* (New Haven: Yale University Press, 1995), 128–131.

6. On Rosenblit and Aronberg, see Klehr, Haynes, and Firsov, *The Secret World of American Communism,* 25–26, 46–49; Whittaker Chambers, "Statements to the Federal Bureau of Investigation," January–April 1949, 58–59; Adolf Berle memo of 1939 interview with Whittaker Chambers, "Interlocking Subversion in Government Departments," Subcommittee to Investigate the Administration of the Internal Security Act, Senate Committee on the Judiciary, part 6 (Washington, D.C.: GPO, 1953), 328–330; Allen Weinstein, *Perjury: The Hiss-Chambers Case* (New York: Random House, 1997), 106–107.

7. Testimony of William G. Burtan, 8 November 1949, U.S. Congress, House of Representatives, Committee on Un-American Activities, 81st Cong., 1st and 2d sess.

8. "Comintern Apparatus Summary Report." On Heiman's role in converting jewelry, see Benjamin Gitlow testimony, 11 September 1939, "Investigations of Un-American Propaganda Activities in the US," U.S. Congress, House of Representatives, Special Committee on Un-American Activities, 76th Cong., 1st sess., vol. 7, 4687–4688; William Crane memorandum, 14 February 1949, William Crane FBI File 74-1333, serial 213; Herbert Romerstein and Stanislav Levchenko, *The KGB Against the "Main Enemy"* (Lexington, Mass.: Lexington Books, 1989), 12–13.

9. For information on early Soviet military espionage, see David Dallin, *Soviet Espionage* (New Haven: Yale University Press, 1955). On the Osman case, see Louis Waldman, *Labor Lawyer* (Dutton: New York, 1944), 221–257. Waldman, Osman's lawyer, takes the view that his client was used by Communists, particularly Robert Switz, as an unwitting tool for espionage.

10. On the Gouzenko case, see Igor Gouzenko, *Iron Curtain* (New York: Dutton, 1948); Robert Bothwell and J. L. Granatstein, eds. *The Gouzenko Transcripts* (Ottawa: Deneau, 1982); and Royal Commission (Canada), *The Report of the Royal Commission,*

Appointed Under Order in Council P.C. 411 of 5 February 1946, to Investigate the Facts Relating to and the Circumstances Surrounding the Communications, by Public Officials and Other Persons in Positions of Trust, of Secret and Confidential Information to Agents of a Foreign Power, 27 June 1946 (Ottawa: Edmond Cloutier . . . Controller of Stationery, 1946).

11. The two most complete accounts of the Hiss-Chambers case are Allen Weinstein, *Perjury,* and Sam Tanenhaus, *Whittaker Chambers: A Biography* (New York: Random House, 1997). The 1997 edition of Weinstein's *Perjury* includes new evidence from Russian archives confirming Hiss's guilt.

12. Christopher Andrew and Oleg Gordievsky, *K.G.B.: The Inside Story* (New York: HarperCollins, 1990), 285–286.

13. Venona 1579 GRU New York to Moscow, 28 September 1943.

14. Richard Rhodes, *Dark Sun: The Making of the Hydrogen Bomb* (New York: Simon & Schuster, 1995), 54–47, 103–104.

15. Weinstein, *Perjury,* 326. Weinstein does not identify Ruble as Glasser. This identification is from Venona. Weinstein also quotes from KGB messages from 1936 that identify Hiss as a GRU agent (pp. 182–184).

16. Venona 1822 KGB Washington to KGB Moscow, 30 March 1945.

17. Tanenhaus, *Whittaker Chambers,* 519; Weinstein, *Perjury,* 321–322.

18. The April 1945 cable from Fitin to Merkulov (Weinstein, *Perjury,* 326–327), discussed in chapter 5, further corroborates that Ales is Alger Hiss.

19. Bentley deposition (FBI file 65-14603).

20. On Adams, see New York FBI report, 28 April 1945, serial 4378, and "Comintern Apparatus Summary Report," 15 December 1944, serial 3702, both in FBI Comintern Apparatus file, no. 100-203581, and Larry Kerley testimony, 15 September 1949, "Communist Activities Among Aliens and National Groups," Subcommittee on Immigration and Naturalization of the Committee on the Judiciary, 81st Cong., 1st sess., part 2, 803–805, 822.

21. Klehr, Haynes, and Firsov, *The Secret World of American Communism,* 129–132; Philip Levy testimony, 28 October 1953, "Interlocking Subversion in Government Departments," part 15, 1039–1045.

22. Benjamin Gitlow, *The Whole of Their Lives: Communism in America — A Personal History and Intimate Portrayal of Its Leaders* (New York: Scribners, 1948), 45; "Comintern Apparatus Summary Report."

23. On the surveillance of Adams and entries into his apartment see the FBI Comintern Apparatus file, serials 3428, 3434, and 3460.

24. "Comintern Apparatus Summary Report"; Kerley testimony, "Communist Activities Among Aliens and National Groups," 805.

25. Attention: Inspector M. E. Gurnea, 17 May 1945, FBI file 100-267360, serial 221, box 117, folder 4, and Washington FBI memo, 26 May 1945, FBI file 100-267360, serial 237, box 117, folder 6, Philip Jaffe papers, Emory University Library, Atlanta, Ga.

26. Ibid.

27. For a detailed examination of the *Amerasia* case, see Harvey Klehr and Ronald Radosh, *The Amerasia Spy Case: Prelude to McCarthyism* (Chapel Hill: University of North Carolina Press, 1996).

28. Venona messages regarding Bernstein are cited in appendix A.

29. Venona 927–928 GRU New York to Moscow, 16 June 1943. Mikhailov was officially a Soviet vice-consul. His true name is believed to have been Menshikov or Meleshnikov.

30. Emphasis in the original. T. A. Bisson, "China's Part in a Coalition War," *Far Eastern Survey* (July 1943), 139.

31. Bisson testimony, 9 April 1943, "Investigation of Un-American Propaganda Activities in the United States," U.S. Congress, House of Representatives, Special Committee on Un-American Activities, 78th Cong., 1st sess., vol. 7, 3467–3480; Venona 938 GRU New York to Moscow, 17 June 1943. Bisson is also mentioned in plain text in one KGB Venona message, but the deciphered portion is fragmentary and not revealing. Venona 1064 KGB New York to Moscow, 3 July 1943.

32. Venona 1103 GRU New York to Moscow, 8 July 1943; 1348 GRU New York to Moscow, 16 August 1943.

33. Background memorandums of Philip and Mary Jane Keeney, FBI Silvermaster file (FBI file 65-56402), serial 2127. Mary Jane Keeney's diary for June 17, 1939, notes: "Get to Mill Valley at 2:00. C.P. Marin County branch membership meeting from 2:00 to 6:00 P.M."

34. Venona messages regarding the Keeneys are cited in appendix A.

35. Venona 726–729 KGB New York to Moscow, 22 May 1942. The reply is very fragmentary, and the translator's note indicates that the material is not very firm. In both messages Keeney's name is in plain text.

36. Venona 1234 KGB New York to Moscow, 29 August 1944.

37. Excerpts from Mary Jane Keeney's diary and from the Keeneys' correspondence are in FBI Silvermaster file, serial 938 and 2661.

38. Ibid.

39. Ibid. Greg is Gregory Silvermaster.

40. Ibid.

41. Venona 1325 GRU New York to Moscow, 11 August 1943.

42. "Comintern Apparatus Summary Report"; Investigation of Un-American Propaganda Activities in the United States (Hearings Regarding Toma Babin), 27 May and 6 July 1949, U.S. Congress, House of Representatives, Committee on Un-American Activities, 81st Cong., 1st sess.

43. Venona messages regarding Babin are cited in appendix A.

44. Venona 1249 GRU New York to Moscow, 29 July 1943. In fact, Babin's group seems to have had its orders changed and been sent to England. In Venona 1350 GRU New York to Moscow, 17 August 1943, Mikhailov noted that consequently "the question of their being developed by us falls to the ground."

45. Testimony of Leonard Mins, 8 April 1943, "Investigations of Un-American Propaganda Activities in the U.S.," vol. 7, 3415–3437.

46. CPUSA Comintern Representative to CPUSA, 26 January 1935, Archive of the Communist Party of the USA, RTsKhIDNI 515-1-3750. In the document he is identified as L. Minz.

47. Markus Wolf, *Man Without a Face* (New York: Times Books, 1997), 304.

48. Elizabeth Bentley, *Out of Bondage: The Story of Elizabeth Bentley* (New York: Ivy Books, 1988), 111.

49. Venona messages regarding Mins are cited in appendix A.

50. Venona 1350 GRU New York to Moscow, 17 August 1943.

51. Venona 1373 GRU New York to Moscow, 23 August 1943.

52. New York FBI report, 5 April 1946, Comintern Apparatus file, serial 5236; FBI report, "Soviet Espionage Activities," 19 October 1945," attached to Hoover to Vaughan, 19 October 1945, President's Secretary's Files, Harry S. Truman Library, Independence, Mo.; FBI report, "Soviet Activities in the United States," 25 July 1946, Clark M. Clifford papers, Truman Library; Dallin, *Soviet Espionage,* 286; Robert J. Lam-

phere and Tom Shachtman, *The FBI-KGB War: A Special Agent's Story* (New York: Random House, 1995), 34–36. Venona 3, 4, 5 KGB San Francisco to Moscow, 2 January 1946; 25 KGB San Francisco to Moscow, 26 January 1946. The authors thank retired FBI agent John Walsh, who in 1946 tried to spot Bunia Witczak and her son on the deck of the *Sakhalin* when it docked in a South American port, for noting the likelihood that R. was Witczak.

53. Elizabeth Bentley FBI deposition, 30 November 1945, FBI file 65-14603; also see James Barros, *No Sense of Evil: Espionage, The Case of Herbert Norman* (Toronto: Deneau, 1986).

54. Venona 1328 GRU New York to Moscow, 12 August 1943.

55. Testimony of Charles I. Velson, 26 September 1951, "Unauthorized Travel of Subversives Behind the Iron Curtain on United States Passports," U.S. Congress, Subcommittee to Investigate the Administration of the Internal Security Act, Senate Judiciary Committee, 207–217; Robert Gladnick, "I Was a Fifth Columnist," Gladnick folder, Isaac Don Levine papers, Emory University Library, Atlanta, Ga.

56. Venona messages regarding Velson are cited in appendix A.

57. Martin Dies statement, *Congressional Record* (1 February 1943), 504–516; FBI memo, 17 June 1946, FBI Silvermaster file, serial 1364.

58. *Daily Worker* (17 October 1938): Hottel to Director, 28 February 1947, FBI Silvermaster file, serial 2437; Memo on Fahy, 17 April 1946, FBI Silvermaster file, serial 1364. Miller and Gregg became KGB sources.

59. Jack Fahy testimony, 8 April 1943, "Investigation of Un-American Propaganda Activities in the United States," vol. 7, 3453–3465; Kerr Commission report, 14 May 1943, box 856, Clinton Anderson papers, Library of Congress. The commission consisted of Representatives John H. Kerr (Democrat, North Carolina), Albert Gore (Democrat, Tennessee), Clinton P. Anderson (Democrat, New Mexico), D. Lane Powers (Republican, New Jersey), and Frank B. Keefe (Republican, Wisconsin).

60. Venona messages regarding Fahy are cited in appendix A.

61. Venona 115 Naval GRU Moscow to Washington, 20 January 1943; 360 Naval GRU Moscow to Washington, 26 February 1943; 366 Naval GRU Moscow to Washington, 28 February 1943.

62. Investigative administration, Main Naval Staff, USSR Navy to Dimitrov, 15 August 1942, Archive of the Dimitrov Secretariat of the Comintern, RTsKhIDNI, 495-74-478.

63. Venona messages regarding Coleman are cited in appendix A.

64. Venona 2505–2512 Naval GRU Washington to Moscow, 31 December 1942. Venona messages regarding are Mitynen cited in appendix A.

65. 1006 Naval GRU Moscow to Washington, 10 June 1943; Robert Louis Benson, "The KGB in San Francisco and Mexico, the GRU in New York and Washington" (NSA Historical Monograph, 1996), 9.

66. Venona messages regarding Bayer and Gordon are cited in appendix A. *People's Weekly World,* 1 May 1993.

67. Venona 82 New York to Moscow, 18 January 1945; 927–928 GRU New York to Moscow, 16 June 1943.

Chapter 7: Spies in the U.S. Government

1. William Donovan testimony, 13 March 1945, unpublished report of proceedings of hearing held before the Special Committee of the Committee on Military Affairs,

vol. 3, 189–190, Record Group 233, Center for Legislative Archives, National Archives, Washington, D.C.

2. The backgrounds of the four are discussed in Harvey Klehr, John Earl Haynes, and Fridrikh Igorevich Firsov, *The Secret World of American Communism* (New Haven: Yale University Press, 1995), 259–286. Fajans joined the Young Communist League in 1932, Lossowski in 1935, and Wolff in 1936. Goff was already a member of the CPUSA when he arrived in Spain in 1937 and after World War II became a full-time official of the CPUSA. Wolff joined the Spanish Communist party when in Spain and was commended by the Communist political committee in the International Brigades for his work in "executing a correct Party line." List of American Communists serving with the International Brigades, undated but probably 1938, Archive of the International Brigades, RTsKhIDNI 545-6-846; Milton Wolff biographical questionnaire for the Comisariado de Guerra de las Brigadas Internacionales, 1 November 1938, RTsKhIDNI 545-6-1015; Brigade party committee to Communist Party of Spain Central Committee, Milton Wolff evaluation, partly illegible date 1938, RTsKhIDNI 545-6-1015.

3. Donovan testimony, 179, 182.

4. After leaving the OSS, Dedijer joined the U.S. Army, became a paratrooper, and, to the amusement of his fellow troopers, when jumping insisted on shouting "Long Live Stalin!" After World War II, Dedijer directed atomic energy research for the Yugoslav government but later broke with Tito and left the country. R. Harris Smith, *OSS: The Secret History of America's First Central Intelligence Agency* (Berkeley and Los Angeles: University of California Press, 1972), 135.

5. Robert Hayden Alcorn, *No Bugles for Spies* (New York: David McKay, 1962), 134.

6. OSS Communists are identified or their role is discussed in Smith, *OSS;* Barry M. Katz, *Foreign Intelligence: Research and Analysis in the Office of Strategic Services, 1942–1945* (Cambridge: Harvard University Press, 1989); Earl Latham, *The Communist Controversy in Washington: From the New Deal to McCarthy* (Cambridge: Harvard University Press, 1966); Christopher Andrew and Oleg Gordievsky, *KGB: The Inside Story* (New York: HarperCollins, 1990); Robin W. Winks, *Cloak and Gown: Scholars in the Secret War, 1939–1961* (New York: Quill, 1988); Anthony Cave Brown, *The Last Hero: Wild Bill Donovan* (New York: Times Books, 1982).

7. Interdepartmental Committee on Investigations Pursuant to Public No. 135, "membership in the Communist Party or German American Bund as ground for dismissal from Federal employment," 18 May 1942, and "Disposition of Subversive and Disaffected Military Personnel," 5 February 1944, both in Record Group 226, OSS Washington Director's Office records, microfilm series M1642, reel 56, National Archives and Records Administration, Archives II, College Park, Md.

8. These included KGB assets Horst Baerensprung (OSS consultant on Germany), Jane Foster (OSS Far Eastern and Indonesian section), Maurice Halperin (chief of the Latin American Division of OSS Research and Analysis), Hans Hirschfeld (OSS consultant on Germany), Bella Joseph (motion picture section of OSS), Julius Joseph (OSS Far Eastern section), Duncan Lee (counsel to General Donovan and the OSS's Japanese intelligence section), Helen Tenney (OSS Spanish section), Donald Wheeler (OSS Research and Analysis), as well as GRU assets Thomas Babin (OSS section working with Yugoslav resistance), Philip Keeney (OSS librarian), and Leonard Mins (Russian section of OSS Research and Analysis).

9. Venona messages regarding all of the persons discussed here are cited in appendix A.

10. Venona 726–729 KGB New York to Moscow, 22 May 1942. Venona 387 KGB New York to Moscow, 12 June 1942 deals with Scott but is badly garbled.

11. John Scott, *Behind the Urals: An American Worker in Russia's City of Steel* (Boston: Houghton Mifflin, 1942), 248.

12. Venona messages regarding all these cover names are cited in appendix A.

13. The KGB assigned the task of preparing a report on the structure of the OSS in late 1944 to Bernard Schuster, its CPUSA liaison, a decision that probably reflects the Communist party's multiple sources inside the OSS. Venona 1668 KGB New York to Moscow, 29 November 1944.

14. Remarks of Representative Lesinski, *Congressional Record* (17 June 1943), 5999–6003; Elmer Davis testimony, 11 November 1952, "Hearings Before the Select Committee to Conduct an Investigation of the Facts, Evidence, and Circumstances of the Katyn Forest Massacre," U.S. House of Representatives, Select Committee, part 7, 1987–1994. Salman was also known as Stefan Arski. Irene Belinska, a member of the Polish section of the Office of War Information, was the daughter of Ludwig Rajchman, who became a high-ranking official of the Polish Communist regime. After World War II Belinska worked for a Polish-language newspaper aligned with the CPUSA. After the war, the husband of another staff member of the Polish OWI section, Mira Zlotowski, became a mid-level official in the Polish Communist government.

15. Ronald L. Filippelli, "Luigi Antonini, the Italian-American Labor Council, and Cold-War Politics in Italy, 1943–1949," *Labor History* 33, no. 1 (Winter 1992), 102–125.

16. Venona messages regarding these cover names are cited in appendix A. Several Soviet intelligence contacts—Peter Rhodes (chief of OWI's Atlantic news section), Christina Krotkova (it is unclear which OWI section employed her), and Irving Lerner (OWI's motion picture division)—were discussed in earlier chapters. As noted above, Unbroken Cover Name No. 19 denoted an unidentified Soviet agent in either the OWI or the OSS.

17. Venona messages regarding Wovschin are cited in appendix A.

18. Venona messages regarding the Wichers are cited in appendix A.

19. Fitin to Dimitrov, 24 September 1944, Archive of the Dimitrov Secretariat of the Comintern, RTsKhIDNI 495-74-485. Emphasis in original.

20. Venona messages regarding Davis are cited in appendix A.

21. Venona 1714 KGB New York to Moscow, 5 December 1944.

22. Venona 55 KGB New York to Moscow, 15 January 1945.

23. Venona 1714 KGB New York to Moscow, 5 December 1944.

24. Venona 1587 KGB New York to Moscow, 12 November 1944. Initially, in August, the New York KGB reported sending some UNRRA material from Wovschin, but in a September message it made the correction that the material was from the OWI.

25. Venona 1714 KGB New York to Moscow, 5 December 1944.

26. Venona 284–286, KGB Moscow to New York, 28 March 1945.

27. Lamphere to Gardner, memorandum on Flora Don Wovschin, 9 May 1949, reproduced in Robert Louis Benson and Michael Warner, eds., *Venona: Soviet Espionage and The American Response, 1939–1957* (Washington, D.C.: National Security Agency, Central Intelligence Agency, 1996), 131.

28. These sources include Thomas Bisson (BEW), Lauchlin Currie (FEA), Noel Field (State), Jack Fahy (Inter-American Affairs and BEW), Bela Gold (FEA), Michael Greenberg (BEW), Joseph Gregg (Inter-American Affairs and State), Maurice Halperin (OSS

and State), Alger Hiss (State), Mary Jane Keeney (BEW and the United Nations), Sol Leshinsky (UNRRA), Robert Miller (Inter-American Affairs), Willard Park (Inter-American Affairs and UNRRA), George Perazich (UNRRA), Allan Rosenberg (BEW/FEA), Gregory Silvermaster (BEW/FEA), Helen Tenney (OSS and State), and Julian Wadleigh (State). To this group one can add Ruth Rivkin (UNRRA) and Bernard Redmont (Inter-American Affairs), both minor sources of the CPUSA/KGB network supervised by Golos and Bentley.

29. Allen Weinstein, *Perjury: The Hiss-Chambers Case* (New York: Random House, 1997), 22, 175.

30. Weinstein, *Perjury,* 269.

31. Whittaker Chambers, *Witness* (New York: Random House, 1952), 30, 334, 339, 341, 381–382, 467, 469; Massing discussed her recruitment of Duggan in her 1951 memoir: Hede Massing, *This Deception* (New York: Duell, Sloan and Pearce, 1951), 206–211. Weinstein, *Perjury,* 181–183.

32. Venona messages regarding Duggan are cited in appendix A.

33. Venona messages regarding Keenan are cited in appendix A. See also Keenan section of "Underground Soviet Espionage Organization (NKVD) in Agencies of the United States Government," 21 February 1946, FBI Silvermaster file (FBI file 65-56402), serial 573.

34. Venona 3614, 3615 KGB Washington to KGB Moscow, 22 June 1945.

35. Venona 1553 KGB New York to Moscow, 4 November 1944. See also Rodman section of Robert Miller background memo, 26 December 1945, FBI Silvermaster file, serial 356.

36. Venona messages regarding these cover names are cited in appendix A.

37. A candidate for Mirage is Charles Albert Page, a mid-level cultural affairs officer for the State Department and the OWI in World War II who worked chiefly on South American matters. In 1945 he was assigned to the U.S. embassy in France. In 1944 the FBI identified Page as part of a shadowy Communist network but was unable to clearly distinguish between espionage activities and clandestine Communist political activities. He had access to the sort of information Mirage provided to the KGB. "Comintern Apparatus Summary Report," 15 December 1944, FBI Comintern Apparatus file (FBI file 100-203581), serial 3702; Larry Kerley testimony, 15 September 1949, "Communist Activities Among Aliens and National Groups," U.S. Congress, Senate, Committee on the Judiciary, Subcommittee on Immigration and Naturalization, 81st Cong., 1st sess., part 2, 810, 182.

38. Venona messages regarding Robert and Source No. 12 are cited in appendix A.

39. Venona 812 KGB New York to Moscow, 29 May 1943.

40. In one other message Wallace is designated by "Botsman" (Russian for Boatswain) but this may be simply an error by the cipher officer for "Lotsman." Venona 1625 KGB New York to Moscow, 3 October 1943. The messages in which Lotsman designates Wallace are Venona 1025, 1035–1936, KGB New York to Moscow, 30 June 1943; 590 KGB New York to Moscow, 29 April 1944; 744 and 746 KGB New York to Moscow, 24 May 1944; 759–760 KGB New York to Moscow, 27 May 1944; 1613 KGB New York to Moscow, 18 November 1944.

41. Venona 1350 KGB New York to Moscow, 23 September 1944; 1838 KGB New York to Moscow, 29 December 1944; 781–787 KGB New York to Moscow, 25–26 May 1945.

42. The historian Eduard Mark argues, on the basis on a close reading of the attendance records of the Trident conference and other archival evidence that most likely Deputy (Zamestitel) was Wallace and Source No. 19 was Hopkins. He concludes, fur-

ther, that the readable portions of the message do not allow a a clear determination of whether Hopkins/19 was a Soviet covert source or a benign "back-channel" diplomatic contact between Roosevelt and the Soviets. We agree that the partial decryption and ambiguity of the message does not allow a confident judgment on Source No. 19's relationship with the Soviets; while impressed by Mark's analysis, we view the evidence as too slim to enable us to reach a judgment about Source No. 19's identity. Edward Mark, "Venona's Source 19 and the Trident Conference of May 1943: Diplomacy or Espionage?" *Intelligence and National Security* 13, no. 2 (April 1998), 1–31.

43. Other chapters discuss the KGB sources Joel Barr (Army Signal Corps laboratories), Demetrius Dvoichenko-Markov (Army intelligence), Edward Fitzgerald (War Production Board), Klaus Fuchs (Manhattan Project), David Greenglass (Army/Manhattan Project), Theodore Hall (Army/Manhattan Project), Irving Kaplan (War Production Board), Charles Kramer (Office of Price Administration), Harry Magdoff (War Production Board and the Office of Emergency Management), William Perl (National Advisory Committee for Aeronautics), Victor Perlo (War Production Board), Vladimir Pozner (War Department), William Remington (War Production Board), Julius Rosenberg (Army Signal Corps), Alfred Sarant (Army Signal Corps laboratories at Fort Monmouth), George Silverman (Army Air Force), Ludwig Ullmann (Army Air Force), William Weisband (Army Signal Intelligence), Ilya Wolston (Army intelligence), and George Zlatovski (Army intelligence). Six GRU sources are also discussed elsewhere: John H. Chapin, (Manhattan Project), Clarence Hiskey (Manhattan Project), Edward Manning, (Manhattan Project), Robert Osman (Army, Panama Canal Zone), Vincent Reno (Aberdeen Army Proving Grounds), and Daniel Abraham Zaret (Army's Explosives Division).

44. Elizabeth Bentley FBI deposition, 30 November 1945, FBI file 65-14603; Elizabeth Bentley testimony, 13 May 1949, "Communist Activities Among Aliens and National Groups," Subcommittee on Immigration and Naturalization of the Committee on the Judiciary, U.S. Senate, 81st Cong., 1st sess., part 1, 106–123; FBI Washington Field Office memo, 26 August 1948, FBI Silvermaster file, serial 3430.

45. Venona messages regarding these cover names are cited in appendix A.

46. They include Solomon Adler (Treasury representative in China), Frank Coe (Division of Monetary Research), Sonia Gold (Division of Monetary Research), Victor Perlo (Division of Monetary Research), Gregory Silvermaster (War Assets Division), William Taylor (Division of Monetary Research, Treasury representative to China), Ludwig Ullmann (Division of Monetary Research), and Harry White (assistant secretary of the Treasury).

47. Venona 82 KGB New York to Moscow, 18 January 1945.

48. Venona 1522 KGB New York to Moscow, 27 October 1944.

49. Venona 1204 GRU New York to Moscow, 22 July 1943.

Chapter 8: Fellowcountrymen

1. Browder to Dimitrov, 19 January 1938, and reproduced in Harvey Klehr, John Earl Haynes, and Fridrikh Igorevich Firsov, *The Secret World of American Communism* (New Haven: Yale University Press, 1995), 241. At different times Margaret Browder adopted different spellings of her name.

2. Dimitrov to Yezhov, 24 January 1938, Archive of the Dimitrov Secretariat of the Comintern, RTsKhIDNI 495-74-465.

3. Walter G. Krivitsky, *Inside Stalin's Secret Service* (New York: Harper, 1939), 258–259.

4. Earl Browder testimony, 5 September 1939, William Browder testimony, 12 September 1939, "Investigations of Un-American Propaganda Activities in the United States," U.S. Congress, House of Representatives, Special Committee on Un-American Activities, 76th Cong., 1st sess., vol. 7, 4439, 4830.

5. U.S. Department of State Passport Division brief on a conspiracy charge against World Tourists and the CPUSA, prepared in 1939–1940 under the direction of Ashley J. Nicholas, reprinted in "Scope of Soviet Activity in the United States," U.S. Congress, Senate, Committee on the Judiciary, Subcommittee to Investigate the Administration of the Internal Security Act, 85th Cong., 1st sess., appendix I, part 23-A, A8, A93–A94, A107.

6. Report on New York FBI Interview with Margaret Browder dated 10 July 1951, SAC New York to FBI Director with report on Margaret Browder interview, and SAC New York to FBI Director dated 15 December 1952 with a Report on Margaret Browder Grand Jury Testimony, all in FBI file 100-59645; New York FBI synopsis of interview with Margaret Browder, 29 October 1957, FBI file 100-287645, serial 143. In the 1930s Zubilin used the cover of a Hollywood talent scout, a status provided by Boris Morros's film company. After the initial admissions to the FBI Margaret Browder refused to elaborate and in subsequent interviews refused to admit knowing the Zubilins. When she appeared before a grand jury she invoked the Fifth Amendment to refuse to testify. Booker had met the Zubilins and Margaret Browder in Berlin in the 1930s. On William Browder's meetings with Zubilin, see Venona 196 KGB New York to Moscow, 9 February 1944.

7. Venona messages regarding Browder are cited in appendix A.

8. Venona 14 KGB New York to Moscow 4 January 1945.

9. John Abt with Michael Myerson, *Advocate and Activist: Memoirs of An American Communist Lawyer* (Urbana: University of Illinois Press, 1993), 42.

10. Elizabeth Bentley FBI deposition, 30 November 1945, FBI file 65-14603.

11. Bentley deposition; Venona 2013 KGB New York to Moscow, 11 December 1943; 2011 KGB New York to Moscow, 11 December 1943; 2101 KGB New York to Moscow, 29 December 1943.

12. Jean Lacouture, *De Gaulle* (New York: New American Library, 1966), 79, 90.

13. Beria to Dimitrov, 29/30 November 1940, with attached Fitin memorandum, "The Secretary of the CC of the American Comparty . . . ," Archive of the Dimitrov Secretariat of the Comintern, RTsKhIDNI 495-74-478.

14. Venona 424 KGB Moscow to New York, 1 July 1942.

15. Venona messages regarding Cot are cited in appendix C.

16. Peter Wright, *Spy Catcher: The Candid Autobiography of a Senior Intelligence Officer* (New York: Viking, 1987), 239–241. Other KGB documents regarding Cot are cited and quoted in Thierry Wolton, *Le grand recrutement* (Paris: Grasset, 1993).

17. Venona 1163 KGB New York to Moscow, 18 July 1943. The latter point refers to the decision of the CPUSA to oppose an effort by New Jersey reformers and labor activists to split away from the Democratic party (dominated by Frank Hague's corrupt political machine) and form a new party modeled on the American Labor party of New York.

18. Venona 1164 KGB New York to Moscow, 18 July 1943.

19. Fitin to Dimitrov, 23 July 1943, and attached NKVD report "On 14 June of the Year, Com. Browder . . . ," Archive of the Dimitrov Secretariat of the Comintern, RTsKhIDNI 495-74-484.

20. Venona 1169 GRU New York to Moscow, 19 July 1943; 1258, 1259 GRU

New York to Moscow, 31 July 1943; 1350 GRU New York to Moscow, 17 August 1943.

21. Bolshakov to Dimitrov, 21 August 1944, Archive of the Dimitrov Secretariat of the Comintern, RTsKhIDNI 495-74-485. No reply was located in the Comintern's records. One should note that officially the Comintern had dissolved a year earlier. Dimitrov and sections of the Comintern headquarters lived on, however, as "institute 205" and were eventually absorbed into the international department of the Communist Party of the Soviet Union.

22. For a full discussion of Josephine Truslow Adams, see Harvey Klehr, "The Strange Case of Roosevelt's 'Secret Agent': Frauds, Fools, and Fantasies," *Encounter* [Great Britain] 59, no. 6 (1982), 84–91. See also Joseph P. Lash, *Eleanor and Franklin: The Story of Their Relationship, Based on Eleanor Roosevelt's Private Papers* (New York: Norton, 1971), 702–704.

23. Adams to Eleanor Roosevelt, January 1944, Eleanor Roosevelt to Adams, 13 July 1944, Eleanor Roosevelt papers, Franklin D. Roosevelt Library, Hyde Park, N.Y. One of Adams's letters to Mrs. Roosevelt contains a link, almost certainly an accidental one, to atomic espionage. Adams told Mrs. Roosevelt that there was a Nazi agitator at a tank factory run by Baldwin Locomotive Works near Philadelphia. The White House forwarded the letter to the FBI, which investigated the matter. It turned out that one of Adams's sources for the identify of the alleged Nazi was Robert Heineman, the husband of Klaus Fuchs's sister.

24. Even in the 1950s, when Adams's mental instability was apparent, Browder had difficulty believing that he had been hoodwinked. He insisted that Adams was not sufficiently politically sophisticated to make up the messages she delivered to him.

25. John Earl Haynes, *Dubious Alliance: The Making of Minnesota's DFL Party* (Minneapolis: University of Minnesota Press, 1984); Harvey Klehr and John Earl Haynes, *The American Communist Movement: Storming Heaven Itself* (New York: Twayne, 1992), 96–100. Hugh De Lacy, head of the Washington Commonwealth Federation (WCF), was elected to Congress as a Democrat in 1944. Howard Costigan, who had preceded De Lacy as head of the WCF, had been a secret member of the CPUSA in the 1930s. Costigan later became an anti-Communist and stated that Representative De Lacy was a secret Communist, a charge De Lacy denied. However, John Abt, a friend of De Lacy, confirmed De Lacy's Communist status in his autobiography. Abt and Myerson, *Advocate and Activist,* 117.

26. Browder's 1944 reforms and the Moscow origins of the Duclos article are discussed in Harvey Klehr, John Earl Haynes, and Kyrill M. Anderson, *The Soviet World of American Communism* (New Haven: Yale University Press, 1998). See also Maurice Isserman, *Which Side Were You On? The American Communist Party During the Second World War* (Middletown, Conn.: Wesleyan University Press, 1982).

27. John Lautner and Frank Meyer, two prominent defectors from the CPUSA, reported that they had heard of a secret Browder communications link to President Roosevelt.

28. Excerpts of Adams's testimony appear in the transcripts of the hearings of 25 and 26 February 1957, "Scope of Soviet Activity in the United States," part 54, 3590–3600.

29. Louis Budenz, *Men Without Faces: The Communist Conspiracy in the USA* (New York: Harper, 1948), 252.

30. His first book was *This Is My Story* (New York: McGraw-Hill, 1947), an autobiographical work, followed by *Men Without Faces* (1948), a book that presented primarily a fifth-column interpretation of the CPUSA. Budenz's early testimony and writ-

ings were largely accurate, and some points that were questioned at that time have been confirmed by documents appearing from Moscow's archives in recent years. Budenz, however, sometimes exaggerated his direct knowledge (conflating what he had personally observed with information he had gained at second hand) and sometimes gave his accounts a melodramatic aura.

31. Wolff gave false testimony about his Communist ties to a congressional investigating committee. See Klehr, Haynes, and Firsov, *The Secret World of American Communism,* 260–280.

32. To Foster, Minor from Dimitrov, 3 April 1942, Archive of the Secretariat of the Executive Committee of the Communist International: coded correspondence with Communist Parties (1933–1943), RTsKhIDNI 495-184-5 (1942 file). Browder was serving a jail sentence for traveling on false passports, so the cable was addressed to Robert Minor and William Foster, the ranking party officers.

33. Ryan [Dennis] to Dimitrov, 10 April 1942, Archive of the Secretariat of the Executive Committee of the Communist International: coded correspondence with Communist Parties (1933–1943), RTsKhIDNI 495-184-19 (1942 files).

34. Fitin to Dimitrov, 13 May 1942, Archive of the Dimitrov Secretariat of the Comintern, RTsKhIDNI 495-74-484.

35. Ibid.

36. The KGB had equally misplaced fears about British penetration. In 1942–1943 the KGB suspected that three of its most valuable spies inside the British government, Kim Philby, Anthony Blunt, and Guy Burgess, were double agents because it had difficulty believing their reports that after the development of the British-Soviet alliance the British had drastically reduced their intelligence actions directed at the USSR. The KGB's response to the same events had been the opposite: to see the British-Soviet alliance as an opportunity to increase its espionage assault on Great Britain. Nigel West and Oleg Tsarev, *The Crown Jewels: The British Secrets at the Heart of the KGB Archives* (London: HarperCollins, 1998), 147–153, 159–168.

37. Dimitrov to Fitin, 13 May 1942, Archive of the Dimitrov Secretariat of the Comintern, RTsKhIDNI 495-73-188; Fitin to Dimitrov, 13 May 1942.

38. Ryan to Dimitrov, enclosed in Fitin to Dimitrov, 1 June 1942, Archive of the Dimitrov Secretariat of the Comintern, RTsKhIDNI 495-74-484.

39. Ibid.

40. Venona 880 KGB New York to Moscow, 8 June 1943; Carl Marzani, *The Education of a Reluctant Radical,* book 4 (New York: Topical Books, 1995), 87.

41. Marzani, *The Education of a Reluctant Radical,* book 4, 3–7, 30; Oleg Kalugin, with Fen Montaigne, *The First Directorate: My 32 Years in Intelligence and Espionage Against the West* (New York: St. Martin's Press, 1994), 48–50.

42. Venona 1195 KGB New York to Moscow, 21 July 1943; 1206 KGB New York to Moscow, 22 July 1943.

43. Venona 846 KGB New York to Moscow, 3 June 1943.

44. Venona 142(a) KGB Moscow to Canberra, 12 September 1943.

45. Ladd memo to Director, 7 December 1945, FBI Silvermaster file (FBI file 65-56402), serial 118; see also background description of Schuster in serial 248.

46. Budenz, *Men Without Faces,* 127; Elizabeth Bentley, *Out of Bondage: The Story of Elizabeth Bentley* (New York: Ivy Books, 1988), 187; Bella Dodd, *School of Darkness* (New York: Kenedy, 1954), 96, 122, 207–209.

47. Venona messages regarding Schuster are cited in appendix A.

48. Venona KGB 283 KGB New York to Moscow, 24 February 1944; 598–599

KGB New York to Moscow, 2 May 1944; 605 KGB New York to Moscow, 2 May 1944. In 849 KGB New York to Moscow, 15 June 1944, New York reported that Browder's material was going to Moscow through Zubilin. Presumably this meant that Zubilin himself was meeting with Schuster.

49. Venona 579 KGB New York to Moscow, 28 April 1944.

50. Venona 1029 KGB New York to Moscow, 22 July 1944. The problem was complicated because Grohl was pregnant and the KGB agent, a Spanish Communist exile named José Sancha Padros, had a wife in Europe. The Mexico KGB, however, thought that marriage to an American might assist their agent in getting legal travel documents; see Venona 495–496 KGB Mexico City to Moscow, 12 June 1944; 506 KGB Mexico City to Moscow, 15 June 1944; 375 KGB Moscow to Mexico City, 18 June 1944.

51. Venona 1553 KGB New York to Moscow, 4 November 1944.

52. Venona 916 KGB New York to Moscow, 12 June 1945. Rappoport, who remained a Communist until his death, is the subject of Kenneth Kann's *Joe Rappoport: The Life of a Jewish Radical* (Philadelphia: Temple University Press, 1981). From the biographical facts he is clearly the same person as Rappoport in the Venona cable. According to Kann, Rappoport was vague about his activities during World War II.

53. Venona 1400 KGB New York to Moscow, 5 October 1944.

54. Venona 1328 KGB New York to Moscow, 15 September 1944; 295 KGB Moscow to New York, 30 March 1945.

55. Venona 1340 KGB New York to Moscow, 21 September 1944.

56. Venona 94 KGB New York to Moscow, 23 January 1945.

57. Venona 1166 KGB New York to Moscow, 16 August 1944; Fitin to Dimitrov, 19 August 1944, Archive of the Dimitrov Secretariat of the Comintern, RTsKhIDNI 495-74-485. When Burns was serving with the Comintern's International Brigades in Spain, Russian authorities identified him as "a reliable and honest member of the party" who was "suitable for organizational work." "Report on Americans," 27 September 1937, Archive of the International Brigades, RTsKhIDNI 545-3-453.

58. Venona 1769 KGB New York to Moscow, 15 December 1944.

59. Venona 1410 KGB New York to Moscow, 6 October 1944.

60. Venona 1457 KGB New York to Moscow, 14 October 1944.

61. Venona 1512 KGB New York to Moscow, 24 October 1944.

62. Ladd memo to Director, 7 December 1945, FBI Silvermaster file, serial 118; Venona 1668 KGB New York to Moscow, 29 November 1944.

63. Venona 1433–1435 KGB New York to Moscow, 10 October 1944; Pravdin's reply, making no mention of the CPUSA issue, is Venona 1442, 1447 KGB New York to Moscow, 11 October 1944.

64. Venona 12, 13, 15, 16 KGB New York to Moscow, 4 January 1945.

65. Venona 1818 KGB New York to Moscow, 16 December 1944.

66. "Comintern Apparatus Summary Report," 15 December 1944, FBI Comintern Apparatus file (FBI file 100-203581), serial 3702; Folkoff's CPUSA "Application for Permission to Leave the United States" under his party name of McLee, Archive of the Communist Party of the USA, RTsKhIDNI 515-1-3875.

67. William Crane memorandum, 14 February 1949, William Crane FBI File 74-1333, serial 213. Also see FBI file 65-59549, serial 1927.

68. FBI memorandum, "Information Regarding the Subject Furnished by William Edward Crane," 15 January 1951, FBI file 65-59549, serial 3; FBI memo, Re: William Edward Crane, 18 April 1949, FBI file 74-1333, serial 3570, and FBI teletype, 10 April 1949, FBI file 74-1333, serial 3042.

69. Allen Weinstein, *Perjury: The Hiss-Chambers Case* (New York: Random House, 1997), 111n, 138, 204, 208–209, 211, 274, 281n, 361–362, 363n, 374, 466.

70. Venona 172 KGB San Francisco to Moscow, 18 April 1945; 69 KGB San Francisco to Moscow, 20 February 1946. On behalf of his second-in-command in the underground, Leo Baroway, a.k.a. Gordon Stevens, Folkoff also inquired about the fate of Baroway's brother, Pavel, a Russian citizen who had worked in the Soviet consulate in New York in 1936–1937. Venona 266 KGB San Francisco to Moscow, 18 May 1945.

71. Venona 55 KGB San Francisco to Moscow, 8 February 1944; 101 KGB San Francisco to Moscow, 5 March 1944; 117 KGB San Francisco to Moscow, 11 March 1944, where it appears the KGB is "processing" William Mackie, a longshoreman who was working under Uncle.

72. Venona messages regarding Miller are cited in appendix A.

73. Venona 450 KGB San Francisco to Moscow, 1 November 1943; 472 KGB San Francisco to Moscow, 9 November 1943.

74. San Francisco FBI report of 1 July 1945 through 15 March 1947, Comintern Apparatus file, serial 5421 and "Comintern Apparatus Summary Report."

75. On Nelson's life and career in the party, see Steve Nelson, James Barrett, and Rob Ruck, *Steve Nelson, American Radical* (Pittsburgh: University of Pittsburgh Press, 1981).

76. Nelson, Barrett, and Ruck, *Steve Nelson,* 242–243. Nelson attributed the actual theft to an Associated Farmers office worker who had a change of heart. For RTsKhIDNI documents suggesting that the theft may have been carried out by secret Communist staff members of the La Follette subcommittee, see Klehr, Haynes, and Firsov, *The Secret World of American Communism,* 96–106, 132.

77. Son to Brother with attached "Son Financial Statement for 1942," Archive of the Dimitrov Secretariat of the Comintern, RTsKhIDNI 495-74-480; Venona 31 KGB San Francisco to Moscow, 17 January 1944; 133 KGB San Francisco to Moscow, 29 March 1944; CIA memorandum, "COMRAP—Vassili M. Zubilin," 6 February 1948, reprinted in Robert Louis Benson and Michael Warner, eds., *Venona: Soviet Espionage and the American Response, 1939–1957* (Washington, D.C.: National Security Agency, Central Intelligence Agency, 1996), 105–115. Nelson's family name in Croatia, then part of the Austro-Hungarian empire, was Mesarosh. In Croatian *mesaros* (pronounced "mesarosh") means meat-eater, while in Hungarian *meszaros* means butcher. Given what the Venona messages say about Butcher and the KGB's occasional habit of making cover names a play on the subject's name, it suggests Nelson as a candidate. The authors thank Stephen Schwartz for pointing out the translation from Hungarian and Richard Miller for elaborating on the linguistic variations of Croatian and Hungarian. Schwartz devotes one chapter, entitled "Charon's Shore," of his *From West to East: California and the Making of the American Mind* (New York: Free Press, 1998) to the intermeshing of Soviet espionage and the California Communist party in the 1940s.

78. FBI summary of Nelson/Cooper [Zubilin] conversation, 22 October 1944, FBI Comintern Apparatus file, serial 3515; Nelson also mentioned Doris Silver Amatniek, a student at City College of New York, as a courier. The FBI summary of the recorded conversation is found in "Interlocking Subversion in Government Departments," U.S. Congress, Senate, Committee on the Judiciary, Subcommittee to Investigate the Administration of the Internal Security Act and Other Internal Security Laws, 83rd Cong., 1st sess., part 15, 1050–1051. See also "COMRAP—Vassili M. Zubilin" and J. Edgar Hoover to Harry Hopkins, 7 May 1943, reproduced in Benson and Warner, *Venona,* 49–50.

79. "Comintern Apparatus Summary Report." Given the swift reaction to Nelson's

complaints, Zubilin must have endorsed them and passed them on to Earl Browder or Rudy Baker.

80. "Comintern Apparatus Summary Report"; *Daily World* (25 November 1982).

81. "Interlocking Subversion in Government Departments," part 15, 1050; FBI report, "Soviet Espionage Activities," 19 October 1945, attached to Hoover to Vaughan, 19 October 1945, President's Secretary's Files, Harry S. Truman Library, Independence, Mo.

82. "Comintern Apparatus Summary Report."

83. "Comintern Apparatus Summary Report" and memo on Bransten, 31 May 1944, serial 2753, 25 October 1944, serial 3341, all in FBI Comintern Apparatus file; Venona 294 KGB San Francisco to Moscow, 31 May 1945.

84. His son, also named Vladimir, became a spokesman for the Soviet Institute on the United States and Canada, a KGB-linked think tank, and was often on American television in the 1980s as an eloquent defender of the Soviet Union.

85. Pozner memo, 23 May 1944, Comintern Apparatus file, serial 2378; Venona 1132, 1133 KGB New York to Moscow, 13 July 1943. The same message referred to Pozner's sister, Ellen Kagan, who worked for the Office of Price Administration, but there is no indication that she was also being considered for recruitment. Another message discussed a second sister of Pozner's, Victoria Pozner-Spiri or Toto, but the context suggests only that someone she knew was being considered for recruitment. Venona 1148 KGB New York to Moscow, 14 July 1943.

86. Venona messages on Map are in appendix A.

87. Lower-level CPUSA functionaries and rank-and-file members involved with Soviet espionage are listed in appendixes A and B.

88. Harvey Klehr, *The Heyday of American Communism: The Depression Decade* (New York: Basic Books, 1984), 231–232; Budenz, *Men Without Faces,* 55–58, 60–61, 252. Gebert's wife was Jewish, and in one of the ironies of history his son became a well-known religious Jewish activist in Communist and post-Communist Poland.

89. Venona messages regarding Gebert are cited in appendix A.

90. Charles Sadler, "Pro-Soviet Polish-Americans: Oskar Lange and Russia's Friends in the Polonia, 1941–1945," *Polish Review,* 22, no. 4 (1977), 25–39.

91. Venona 700 KGB New York to Moscow, 17 May 1944; 759, 760 KGB New York to Moscow, 27 May 1944.

92. Venona 1135 KGB New York to Moscow, 8 August 1944.

93. Dimitrov to Molotov, 26 August 1942, Archive of the Dimitrov Secretariat of the Comintern, RTsKhIDNI 495-73-173. All of the Ross memorandums to Dimitrov and his cover notes conveying translated copies to Molotov are found in RTsKhIDNI 495-73-173. Ross's reports may also have led to the KGB's 1944 interest in Joseph Barnes, discussed below. Ross met Barnes in Moscow in 1942 when she accompanied prominent Republican Wendell Willkie to the USSR. She reported to the Comintern that she "had a personal conversation with Barnes. He and I have an acquaintance in common—one of the officers of our party in New York, a close friend of Barnes." Janet Ross to Dimitrov, "Wendell Willkie's Discussions with Correspondents," 23 September 1942, RTsKhIDNI 495-73-173.

94. Whittaker Chambers, *Witness* (New York: Regnery, 1997), 498; Sam Tanenhaus, *Whittaker Chambers* (New York: Random House, 1997), 182.

95. Venona 1754 KGB New York to Moscow, 14 December 1944; 20 KGB New York to Moscow, 4 January 1945.

96. Venona 1681 KGB New York to Moscow, 13 October 1943; 207 Moscow to New York, 8 March 1945.

97. Venona messages regarding Laird are cited in appendix A.

98. Venona 1154 KGB New York to Moscow, 12 August 1944. This message's reference to Elizabeth Zubilin corroborates reports that she worked on the West Coast, specifically in Hollywood.

99. Stephen Laird, "Report from Warsaw," *New Republic* (3 February 1947).

100. Venona 483–484 KGB San Francisco to Moscow, 13 September 1945.

101. Walter Bernstein, *Inside Out: A Memoir of the Blacklist* (New York: Knopf, 1996), 124, 228.

102. Venona 1509 KGB New York to Moscow, 23 October 1944.

103. Bentley, *Out of Bondage,* 108. Venona messages regarding Khan are cited in appendix A.

104. Venona messages regarding Steele are cited in appendix A.

105. Venona 1039–1041 KGB New York to Moscow, 24–25 July 1944.

106. Ibid.; Venona 1097, 1098 KGB New York to Moscow, 1 August 1944.

107. Venona messages regarding Setaro are cited in appendix A.

108. Venona 1234 KGB New York to Moscow, 29 August 1944. Setaro's cover name, Gonets, translates as Express Messenger or Courier.

109. Venona 1433–1435 KGB New York to Moscow, 10 October 1944.

110. Quoted in Harvey Klehr and Ronald Radosh, *The Amerasia Spy Case: Prelude to McCarthyism* (Chapel Hill: University of North Carolina Press, 1996), 67–68.

111. Venona messages regarding Krafsur are cited in appendix A.

112. Venona 705 KGB New York to Moscow, 17 May 1944.

113. Fitin to Dimitrov, 12 September 1944, Archive of the Dimitrov Secretariat of the Comintern, RTsKhIDNI 495-74-485.

114. Jerre Mangione, *The Dream and the Deal: The Federal Writers' Project 1935–1943* (Boston: Little, Brown, 1972), 211–215.

115. *New York Times* (12 November 1971).

116. Venona 777–779 KGB New York to Moscow, 25 May 1945.

117. Oliver Pilat, *Drew Pearson: An Unauthorized Biography* (New York: Harper's Magazine Press, 1973), 45, 170, 195, 297; Tyler Abell, ed., *Drew Pearson: Diaries, 1949–1959* (New York: Holt, Rinehart and Winston, 1974), 166–168, 172–173.

118. Venona 998 KGB New York to Moscow, 15 July 1944.

119. Statement of Rep. Fred E. Busbey, *Congressional Record* (18 February 1944), A876; Statement of Rep. Martin Dies, *Congressional Record* (1 February 1943), 504–516.

120. The story of Karr's journalistic coup is in the Henry Wallace Papers: see Harold Young from Oskar Lange, 3 July 1944; *Washington Post,* 3 July 1944; *Washington Post,* 4 July 1944; Arthur Schlesinger, Jr., to Klehr, 18 April 1990.

121. On Hammer's role in laundering Soviet subsidies to the CPUSA and cooperation with Soviet intelligence, see Klehr, Haynes, and Firsov, *The Secret World of American Communism,* 26–30; Harvey Klehr, John Earl Haynes, and Kyrill M. Anderson, *The Soviet World of American Communism* (New Haven: Yale University Press, 1998), 132–135; Edward Epstein, *Dossier: The Secret History of Armand Hammer* (New York: Random House, 1996).

122. Evgeniia Albats, "Senator Edward Kennedy Requested KGB Assistance with a profitable contract for his businessman-friend," *Izvestia* (24 June 1992), 5.

123. I. F. Stone, *The Hidden History of the Korean War* (New York: Monthly Review Press, 1952). Admiring biographies include Andrew Partner, *I. F. Stone: A Portrait* (New York: Pantheon Books, 1988), and Robert C. Cottrell, *Izzy: A Biography of I. F. Stone* (New Brunswick, N.J.: Rutgers University Press, 1992). For a discussion of

how Stone's views paralleled those of the Soviet Union until the mid-1950s, see Ronald Radosh, "A 'Jewish Dissident'?" *Forward* (23 October 1992).

124. Herbert Romerstein, "The KGB Penetration of the Media," *Human Events* (6 June 6 1992), 5–6; Andrew Brown, "The Attack on I. F. Stone," *New York Review of Books* (8 October 1992), 21; Oleg Kalugin, with Fen Montaigne, *The First Directorate: My 32 Years in Intelligence and Espionage Against the West* (New York: St. Martin's Press, 1994), 74.

125. Venona 1313 KGB New York to Moscow, 13 September 1944. All Venona messages regarding Stone are cited in appendix D.

126. Venona 1506 KGB New York to Moscow, 23 October 1944.

Chapter 9: Hunting Stalin's Enemies on American Soil

1. Albert Glotzer, *Trotsky: Memoir and Critique* (Buffalo: Prometheus Books, 1989), 76–80, 186; *How the GPU Murdered Trotsky* (London: New Park Publications, 1981), 21–25, 130–136. The latter book, compiled by American and British Trotskyists, consists largely of excerpts of testimony and exhibits from the trials of Jack Soble, Robert Soblen, and Mark Zborowski, as well as excerpts from FBI and Justice Department documents obtained under the Freedom of Information Act and by court action.

2. The international association of Socialist and syndicalist organizations that was founded in 1864 and collapsed in 1876 became known as the First International. European Socialist parties formed a new association, informally known as the Second International, in 1889. When Communists split from the socialist movement in the wake of the Bolshevik Revolution, Lenin formed the third international, the Comintern, in 1919.

3. Mark Zborowski testimony, 29 February 1956, part 4, 77–101, and 2 March 1956, part 5, 103–136, "Scope of Soviet Activities in the United States," Subcommittee to Investigate the Administration of the Internal Security Act, U.S. Senate, Committee on the Judiciary, 84th Cong., 2d sess.; Herbert Romerstein and Stanislav Levchenko, *The KGB Against the "Main Enemy"* (Lexington, Mass.: Lexington Books, 1989); Dimitri Volkogonov, *Trotsky: The Eternal Revolutionary* (New York: Free Press, 1996), 334–340, 347, 356–380, 388, 399–400, 426, 441–447, 456, 462, 467; KGB documents regarding his activities prior to his coming to the United States are in "Investigation File, Zborowski, Mark Grigorievich," box 4, Dimitri Volkogonov Papers, Library of Congress, Washington, D.C.

4. Venona messages regarding Zborowski are cited in appendix A.

5. Victor Kravchenko, *I Chose Freedom: The Personal and Political Life of a Soviet Official* (New York: Scribners, 1946), 4.

6. The trial is recounted in Victor Kravchenko, *I Chose Justice* (New York: Scribners, 1950).

7. Venona messages regarding Fighter are cited in appendix A.

8. Lilia Dallin testimony, 2 March 1956, "Scope of Soviet Activities in the United States," part 5, 136–150; *How the GPU Murdered Trotsky*, 178–189.

9. Venona 594 KGB New York to Moscow, 1 May 1944.

10. Venona 600 KGB New York to Moscow, 2 May 1944. NSA and FBI analysts were never sure whether Green was a cover name or referred to Abner Green, the Communist who headed the American Committee for the Protection of the Foreign-Born and who had many sources among immigrant Russians.

11. Venona 613–614 KGB New York to Moscow, 3 May 1944.

12. Venona 726 KGB New York to Moscow, 20 May 1944.

13. Venona 740 KGB New York to Moscow, 24 May 1944; 799 KGB New York to Moscow, 3 June 1944

14. Elizabeth Poretsky [Else Bernaut], *Our Own People* (Ann Arbor: University of Michigan Press, 1969), 262–274.

15. Kravchenko, *I Chose Freedom,* 309–311.

16. Venona 1143–1144 KGB New York to Moscow, 10 August 1944.

17. Venona 1457 KGB New York to Moscow, 14 October 1944; 1803 KGB New York to Moscow, 22 December 1944.

18. Alexander Orlov, *The Secret History of Stalin's Crimes* (New York: Random House, 1953). A more accurate account is John Costello and Oleg Tsarov, *Deadly Illusions: The KGB Orlov Dossier* (New York: Crown, 1993).

19. Mark Zborowski testimony, part 5, 107.

20. Some prominent anthropologists defended Zborowski as the victim of McCarthyite witch hunts. Isaac Don Levine, on the other hand, noted that he had "left behind a trail of duplicity and blood worthy of a Shakespearean villain." Isaac Don Levine, *The Mind of an Assassin* (New York: Farrar, Straus and Cudahy, 1959), 27.

21. Venona 217 KGB Moscow to New York, 10 March 1945.

22. Venona messages regarding these persons are cited in appendix A.

23. Venona messages regarding Kurnakov are cited in appendix A.

24. Venona messages regarding Tkach and the Sidoroviches are cited in appendix A.

25. Gennadi Kostyrchenko, *Out of the Red Shadows: Anti-Semitism in Stalin's Russia* (Amherst, N.Y.: Prometheus Books, 1995).

26. Kostyrchenko, *Out of the Red Shadows,* 78.

27. Venona messages regarding Mark and Hudson are cited in appendix A.

28. Venona 640 KGB New York to Moscow, 6 May 1944; 1251 KGB New York to Moscow, 5 September 1944.

29. In the late 1950s Rand founded the Metropolitan Council on Housing, a tenant's group in New York City. She remained a Communist activist until her death, in the Soviet Union, in 1981. *Daily World* (24 June 1981), 1.

30. Louis Budenz affidavit, 11 November 1950, "American Aspects of the Assassination of Leon Trotsky," U.S. Congress, House of Representatives, Committee on Un-American Activities, 81st Cong., 2d sess., part 1, v–ix; Louis Budenz, *Men Without Faces: The Communist Conspiracy in the USA* (New York: Harper and Brothers, 1948), 123–126.

31. Venona 749 KGB New York to Moscow, 26 May 1944.

32. New York FBI memo, serial 1980, FBI Silvermaster file (FBI file 65-56402). On Straight, see chapter 5.

33. *Sylvia Franklin Dossier* (New York: Labor Publication, 1977) contains excerpts from Callen's grand jury testimony.

34. Venona 851 KGB New York to Moscow, 15 June 1944. Venona messages regarding Callen are cited in appendix A.

35. Callen's grand jury testimony is in *The Gelfand Case: A Legal History of the Exposure of U.S. Government Agents in the Leadership of the Socialist Workers Party,* vol. 2 (Detroit: Labor Publication, 1985), 526–564.

36. FBI memorandum, "Existing Corroboration of Bentley's Overall Testimony," FBI Silvermaster file, serial 4201; Margaret Browder FBI file, 100-287645, serial 153; Booker interview in *Sylvia Franklin Dossier*. Booker is not identified in the cables deciphered in the Venona Project.

37. Venona messages regarding Miller are cited in appendix A.

38. Excerpts from Miller's trial testimony are published in *How the GPU Murdered Trotsky*, 146–153.

39. Venona messages regarding Getzoff are cited in appendix A.

40. Venona 846 KGB New York to Moscow, 14 June 1944.

41. Venona 556 KGB Mexico City to Moscow, 29 June 1944.

42. *How the GPU Murdered Trotsky*, 146–153.

43. Venona 1143–1144 KGB New York to Moscow, 10 August 1944.

44. Venona 776 KGB New York to Moscow, 25 May 1945. In this message Jack Soble is code-named Czech. Analysts mistakenly attributed this code name here to Robert Menaker, who was called Czech in earlier messages. *How the GPU Murdered Trotsky*, 146–153.

45. Venona 1143–1144 KGB New York to Moscow, 10 August 1944.

46. Franklin Folsom, *Days of Anger, Days of Hope: A Memoir of the League of American Writers* (Boulder: University Press of Colorado, 1994), 46–47; Daniel Menaker, *The Old Left* (New York: Knopf, 1987). Leopolo and Luís Arenal took part in the KGB's unsuccessful armed assault on Trotsky's residence in 1940. To add to these family ties, one of Robert Menaker's nieces was married to Victor Perlo, the Soviet spy discussed in chapter 5.

47. Menaker, *The Old Left*, 22, 42.

48. Venona messages regarding Menaker and Burd are cited in appendix A, those on Subercaseux in appendix C.

49. Venona 1313 KGB New York to Moscow, 13 September 1944.

50. Venona 1470 KGB New York to Moscow, 17 October 1944

51. Daniel Menaker telephone interview with Harvey Klehr, 23 June 1997.

52. Venona messages regarding Katz are cited in appendix A. On his background, see FBI memo, 27 October 1944, serial 3392, in FBI Comintern Apparatus file; FBI memo, "Existing Corroboration of Bentley's Overall Testimony," 6 May 1955, serial 4201, in FBI Silvermaster file.

53. Stalin's institution of an antisemitic purge of his intelligence services in this period may have played some role in Katz's severing links to the KGB.

54. Boris Morros, *My Ten Years as a Counterspy* (New York: Viking, 1959).

55. FBI memo, 8 September 1944, Comintern Apparatus file (FBI file 100-203581), serial 3318.

56. Romerstein and Levchenko, *The KGB Against the "Main Enemy,"* 187–188; Katrina vanden Heuvel, "Grand Illusions," *Vanity Fair* (September 1991), 219–225, 248–256. Vanden Heuvel takes the view that the Sterns did not cooperate with Soviet espionage.

57. Martin Dies statement, *Congressional Record* (1 February 1943), 504–516; Kerr Commission analysis of evidence in regard to William Dodd, analysis of evidence on Watson and Dodd, 21 April 1943, Report of the Kerr Commission, 14 May 1943, both in box 856, Clinton Anderson papers, Library of Congress; William Dodd, Jr., testimony, 5 April 1943, "Investigations of Un-American Propaganda activities in the United States," U.S. Congress, House of Representatives, Special Committee on Un-American Activities, 78th Cong., 1st sess., vol. 7, 3366–3382.

58. Venona 748 KGB New York to Moscow, 26 May 1944.

59. Venona 1824 KGB New York to Moscow, 27 December 1944; 4–5 KGB New York to Moscow, 3 January 1945; 11 KGB New York to Moscow, 4 January 1945; 18–19 KGB New York to Moscow, 4 January 1945. The KGB sent reports on the business to Moscow. By this time the Zubilins were there.

60. Vanden Heuvel, "Grand Illusions," 248.

61. Given that the anonymous Russian letter (see chapter 2) specifically named Morros as a KGB contact and its authenticity was accepted by the FBI, it may be that Morros in his autobiography exaggerated the extent to which he volunteered his services. The FBI most likely would by that time have gathered information about his espionage activities that would have provided leverage to encourage his cooperation.

62. Annotated list of CPUSA and Young Communist League members in the International Brigades, Archive of the International Brigades, RTsKhIDNI 545-6-846.

63. Jane Foster, *An Un-American Lady* (London: Sidgwick and Jackson, 1980), 99.

64. Venona 854 KGB New York to Moscow, 16 June 1942.

65. Venona 958 KGB New York to Moscow, 21 June 1943; 1025, 1035–1036 KGB New York to Moscow, 30 June 1943; 765, 771 KGB New York to Moscow, 30 May 1944.

66. *New York Times* (7 July 1961), 9.

67. *New York Times* (14 October 1961), 10; (7 July 1961), 9; (4 November 1961), 11; Romerstein and Levchenko, *The KGB Against the "Main Enemy,"* 195–196. Brandt, a Social Democrat, became one of West Germany's leading political figures.

68. Venona messages presumably regarding Beker are cited in appendix A.

69. Venona 48 KGB New York to Moscow, 11 January 1945.

70. *New York Times* (30 November 1960), 1.

71. Venona 777–781 KGB New York to Moscow, 26 May 1943. Other Venona messages regarding Wolston are cited in appendix A.

72. Venona 1824 KGB New York to Moscow, 27 December 1944. There is a Slava in a 1945 message (Venona 325 KGB Moscow to New York, 5 April 1945); it clearly is not Wolston but someone connected to the Rosenberg spy ring. This also suggests that by that time Wolston had a different cover name.

73. Venona 193–194 KGB Mexico City to Moscow, 14 March 1944; 474 KGB Mexico City to Moscow, 6 June 1944; 555 KGB Mexico City to Moscow, 29 June 1944; 812 KGB Mexico City to Moscow, 7 November 1944; 109 KGB Moscow to Mexico City, 20 February 1944; 355 KGB Moscow to Mexico City, 9 June 1944.

74. Pavel A. Sudoplatov, Antoli P. Sudoplatov, Jerrold Schecter, and Leona Schecter, *Special Tasks: The Memoirs of an Unwanted Witness* (New York: Little, Brown, 1994), 65–86.

75. Thomas Black testimony, 17 May 1956, "Scope of Soviet Activity in the United States," part 21, 1113–1124.

76. Levine, *The Mind of an Assassin*, 190.

77. In a 1944 Venona message Moscow informed the Mexico City KGB that Neruda, then Chilean consul-general, "is being developed" as an agent. Venona 287 KGB Moscow to Mexico City, 11 May 1944. Siqueiros later became a leader of the Mexican Communist party. His cover name in Venona was Chess Knight.

78. FBI memorandum, "Existing Corroboration of Bentley's Overall Testimony," 6 May 1955, FBI Silvermaster file, serial 4201.

79. Venona 1160 KGB New York KGB to Moscow, 17 July 1943. Other Venona messages regarding Rose Arenal are cited in appendix A.

80. Louis Budenz affidavit, 11 November 1950, "American Aspects of the Assassination of Leon Trotsky"; Don Levine, *The Mind of an Assassin,* is the fullest account of the assassination.

81. When a congressional committee asked Altschuler about her activities, she made a statement denying any criminal actions but then refused to answer any questions. Lydia

Altschuler testimony, 18 October 1950, "American Aspects of Assassination of Leon Trotsky," 3354–3360.

82. "Comintern Apparatus Summary Report," 15 December 1944, FBI Comintern Apparatus file, serial 3702.

83. Venona 177–179 KGB Mexico City to Moscow, 30 December 1943; 6 KGB Mexico City to Moscow, 3 January 1944, analyst footnote vi. In his memoir of growing up in a Communist family in New York, David Horowitz remembered Anna Colloms as a family friend who served as a courier to Mexico and later was distressed that she had been involved in Trotsky's assassination. David Horowitz, *Radical Son: A Generational Odyssey* (New York: Free Press, 1997), 76.

84. Anna Colloms testimony, 19 October 1950, "American Aspects of Assassination of Leon Trotsky," 3371–3377.

85. Letter no. 4 Buenos Aires to New York, 5 July 1942; Letter no. 5 Buenos Aires to New York, 1 August 1942; Letter no. 9 Buenos Aires to New York, 1 November 1942; Letter no. 11 Buenos Aires to New York, 6 December 1942. All of these "secret writing letters" were intercepted by American authorities and made public as part of the Venona Project.

86. Venona secret writing letters: Letter no. 12 KGB New York to Buenos Aires, 1 February 1943; Letter no. 14 KGB New York to Buenos Aires, 29 September 1943. Alexander was an unidentified KGB agent who had some connection with Mexico. In the Mexico City KGB traffic there is another cable, Venona 584 KGB Moscow to Mexico City, 6 October 1944, indicating that Altschuler was still serving as a mail drop as late as 1944.

87. Venona 193, 194 KGB Mexico City to Moscow, 14 March 1944. NSA analysts did not identify "A" as Colloms, but the context clearly refers to her.

88. Jacob Epstein testimony, 18 October 1950, "American Aspects of Assassination of Leon Trotsky," 3345–3354; "Comintern Apparatus Summary Report."

89. New York FBI memo, 1 April 1948, FBI Silvermaster file, serial 3187. Mercader had the cover name Rita until December 1943, when the designation was changed to Gnome.

90. Venona 193, 194 KGB Mexico City to Moscow, 14 March 1944.

91. Venona 800 KGB New York to Moscow, 28 May 1943; 816–817 KGB New York to Moscow, 30 May 1943; 899 KGB New York to Moscow, 11 June 1943. Another message, 1142 KGB New York to Moscow, 10 August 1944, contains identification routines for contacts with Epstein and two co-workers.

92. Venona 158 KGB Mexico City to Moscow, 23 December 1943. Klarin arrived in Mexico to take up duties as second secretary of the Soviet embassy on November 23; he left on May 24, 1944.

93. Venona 174–176 KGB Mexico City to Moscow, 29 December 1943; 177–179 KGB Mexico City to Moscow, 30 December 1943, 6 KGB Mexico City to Moscow, 3 January 1944; 193, 194 KGB Mexico City to Moscow, 14 March 1944.

94. Venona 193, 194 KGB Mexico City to Moscow, 14 March 1944; 212 KGB Mexico City to Moscow, 25 March 1944; 261–262 KGB Mexico City to Moscow, 16 April 1944; 281 KGB Mexico City to Moscow, 21 April 1944; 248 KGB Moscow to Mexico City, 27 April 1944; 288 KGB Moscow to Mexico City, 11 May 1944; 256 KGB Moscow to New York, March 21, 1945. Jacob Epstein, Anna Colloms, and several other people involved in the operation to free Mercader were later subpoenaed by the House Committee on Un-American Activities. They were all uncooperative witnesses. Jacob Epstein testimony, "American Aspects of Assassination of Leon Trotsky," 3349.

See also foreword to "American Aspects of Assassination of Leon Trotsky," part 2, ix–xv.

95. Venona 193, 194 KGB Mexico City to Moscow, 14 March 1944; 218 KGB Mexico City to Moscow, 29 March 1944.

96. Venona 474 KGB Mexico City to Moscow, 6 June 1944.

97. Venona 172–174 KGB Moscow to Mexico City, 9–10 March 1945; Sudoplatov and Schecter, *Special Tasks,* 80–81. Contributing to the KGB's failure to free Mercader was the intense security provided by Mexican counterintelligence. The Mexican political leadership, which had granted Trotsky exile, was deeply embarrassed by his murder on Mexican territory and determined that his assassin would serve out his term.

98. Harvey Klehr interview with Dr. Robert Harris, 19 August 1996. The details about Harris's sisters' employment is provided in Venona 347 KGB Moscow to Mexico City, 27 May 1945.

99. James Ryan, *Earl Browder: The Failure of American Communism* (Tuscaloosa: University of Alabama Press, 1997), 32–33, 283; Klehr, Haynes, and Firsov, *The Secret World of American Communism,* 45–46; Benjamin Gitlow, *I Confess* (Dutton: New York, 1940), 329–330; Klehr interview with Robert Harris. The complaint about Harris's lack of discipline is in J. Crosby and Marion to Alexander, 30 January 1929, Archive of the Red International of Labor Unions (Profintern), RTsKhIDNI 534-4-283.

100. It is not certain, but Harris may have used the name Adelina Zenejdas Gomez while in Mexico.

101. Venona 256 KGB Moscow to Mexico City, 29 April 1944.

102. Venona 492 KGB Mexico City to Moscow, 9 June 1944.

103. Venona 63–66 KGB New York to Moscow, 15 January 1945.

104. Venona 232 KGB Mexico City to Moscow, 3 April 1944; 208 KGB Moscow to Mexico City, 10 April 1944.

105. Venona 220 KGB Moscow to Mexico City, 16 April 1944.

106. Venona 327 KGB Mexico City to Moscow, 3 May 1944.

107. Venona 283 KGB Moscow to Mexico City, 10 May 1944. There is no decrypted message indicating the outcome.

108. Venona 129 KGB Mexico City to Moscow, 6 December 1943; 200 KGB Moscow to Mexico City, 8 April 1944; 243, 244 KGB Mexico City to Moscow, 10 April 1944; 283 KGB Moscow to Mexico City, 10 May 1944; 303 KGB Moscow to Mexico City, 17 May 1944; 347 KGB Moscow to Mexico City, 27 May 1945. Harris's nephew was astounded to learn that his aunt had communicated with her sisters in the 1940s; no one in the family ever mentioned that she was still alive at that late date. One of Harris's sisters was still alive in 1997; she refused to discuss Kitty Harris at all. Klehr interview with Robert Harris.

109. Venona 553, 554 KGB Mexico City to Moscow, 29 June 1944; 476 KGB Moscow to Mexico City, 29 July 1944.

110. Venona 312 KGB Moscow to Mexico City, 11 May 1945; 659 KGB Moscow to Mexico City, 7 September 1945; 238 KGB Moscow to Mexico City, 28 April 1946.

Chapter 10: Industrial and Atomic Espionage

1. Quoted in Ronald Radosh and Joyce Milton, *The Rosenberg File: A Search for the Truth* (New Haven: Yale University Press, 1997), 29. For the story of Gold and Black as industrial spies, see pp. 20–47.

2. Quoted in Radosh and Milton, *The Rosenberg File,* 30. Smith, Ruga, Fred, and

Semenov were Soviet intelligence officers. Brothman was a source, and Smilg was a target for recruitment.

3. For a summary of Semenov's KGB career, see appendix E.

4. Venona messages regarding Gold are cited in appendix A.

5. Venona 1390 KGB New York to Moscow, 1 October 1944; 1403 KGB New York to Moscow, 5 October 1944.

6. Radosh and Milton, *The Rosenberg File*, 152–153.

7. In recent decades Congress has enacted statutes that clearly define many types of industrial espionage as criminal acts. In the 1930s, however, few criminal statutes clearly applied to the stealing of scientific information or industrial techniques from private firms. There were remedies under civil law (patent and copyright infringement and the like), but such remedies were practical only when one firm could present evidence that another was marketing a product based on stolen proprietary information. Such remedies were rarely applicable when the thief was a Soviet intelligence agency stealing the information for use within the USSR's closed internal economy.

8. For a summary of Ovakimian's KGB career, see appendix E.

9. Thomas Black testimony, 17 May 1956, part 21, 1113–1124, and Harry Gold testimony, 26 April 1956, part 20, 1020, both in "Scope of Soviet Activity in the United States," U.S. Congress, Senate, Committee on the Judiciary, Subcommittee to Investigate the Administration of the Internal Security Act, 84th Cong., 2d sess.

10. Venona messages regarding Black are cited in appendix A.

11. In part due to the success of his field work in the United States, Kvasnikov later became overall head of KGB scientific intelligence. For a summary of Kvasnikov's KGB career, see appendix E. Venona messages regarding Malisoff are cited in appendix A.

12. Venona 622 KGB New York to Moscow, 4 May 1944.

13. Venona messages regarding Odessan and Second Hand Bookseller are cited in appendix A.

14. Venona messages regarding these individuals are cited in appendix A.

15. Alleman and Steinberg are discussed in appendix B.

16. Venona messages regarding all of these names are cited in appendix A.

17. Memo on Leona and Joseph Franey, 5 August 1944, FBI Comintern Apparatus file (FBI file 100-203581), serial 2919; memo on Leona and Joseph Franey, 21 August 1944, FBI Comintern Apparatus file, serial 2989; FBI memo on Shevchenko, 30 October 1944, FBI Comintern Apparatus file, serial Serial 3379; FBI memo on Shevchenko, 9 December 1944, FBI Comintern Apparatus file, serial 3612; Leona Franey testimony and Joseph Franey testimony, 6 June 1949, "Soviet Espionage Activities in Connection with Jet Propulsion and Aircraft," U.S. Congress, House of Representatives, Un-American Activities Committee, 81st Cong., 1st sess.

18. Venona 941 KGB New York to Moscow, 4 July 1944; Venona 1048 KGB New York to Moscow, 25 July 1944; Venona 1403 KGB New York to Moscow, 5 October 1944; Venona 1559 KGB New York to Moscow, 6 November 1944; Venona 305 KGB Moscow to New York, 1 April 1945.

19. Venona 1607–1608 KGB New York to Moscow, 16 November 1944; Loren Haas testimony, 6 June 1949, "Soviet Espionage Activities in Connection with Jet Propulsion and Aircraft."

20. Larry Kerley testimony, 15 September 1949, "Communist Activities Among Aliens and National Groups," U.S. Congress, Senate, Committee on the Judiciary, Subcommittee on Immigration and Naturalization, 81st Cong., 1st sess., part 2, 806.

21. Venona messages regarding all of these persons are cited in appendix A.

22. Radosh and Milton, *The Rosenberg File,* concentrates on the atomic espionage aspects of the Rosenberg apparatus, but it also has the most comprehensive examination of the Rosenberg network's scientific-technical espionage, including the activities of Morton Sobell, Max Elitcher, Joel Barr, and Alfred Sarant.

23. Elizabeth Bentley deposition, 30 November 1945 (FBI file 65-14603); Radosh and Milton, *The Rosenberg File,* 176.

24. Venona 628 KGB New York to Moscow, 5 May 1944. All Venona messages regarding Julius Rosenberg are cited in appendix A.

25. Venona 736 KGB New York to Moscow, 22 May 1944.

26. Venona 1053 KGB New York to Moscow, 26 July 1944.

27. Feklisov appears in numerous Venona messages under the cover name of Kalistratus. While in the United States as a KGB officer, he used the name Alexander Fomin. Michael Dobbs, "Julius Rosenberg Spied, Russian Says," *Washington Post* (16 March 1997); Joseph Albright and Marcia Kunstel, "Retired KGB Spymaster Lifts Veil on Rosenberg Espionage," *Washington Times* (16 March 1997). A Discovery Channel television documentary, "The Rosenberg File: Case Closed" (23 March 1997), featured lengthy interviews with Feklisov. See also Alexander Feklisov, *Za okeanom i na ostrove. Zapiski razvedchika* (Overseas and on the island: Notes of an intelligence officer, in Russian) (Moscow: DEE, 1994).

28. Venona messages regarding Sarant and Barr are cited in appendix A.

29. Venona 1600 KGB New York to Moscow, 14 November 1944.

30. Venona 1749–1750 KGB New York to Moscow, 13 December 1944.

31. Philip Morrison testimony, 7 and 8 May 1953, "Subversive Influence in the Educational Process," U.S. Congress, Senate, Committee on the Judiciary, 83rd Cong., 1st sess., part 9, 899–919.

32. Radosh and Milton, *The Rosenberg File,* xi–xiii; Michelle Locke, "Flight to Mexico with Lover Turns into 40 Years Behind Iron Curtain," *Los Angeles Times* (23 August 1992); Elizabeth Shogren, "Scientist for the Enemy," *Los Angeles Times* (14 October 1992); Irvin Molotsky, "Joel Barr, Defector Linked to Rosenberg, Dies," *New York Times* (16 August 1998); Alexei Kuznetsov and Carla Rivera, "Joel Barr: U.S. Defector, Electronics Whiz Helped Propel Soviets into Computer Age," *Los Angeles Times* (17 August 1998); John Corry, "Replaying the Best of Nightline's History," *Washington Times* (29 June 1996). Although Barr died in 1998 in St. Petersburg, Russia, he had established residency in California and collected both a federal Social Security pension and a California state supplemental old age benefit. His collecting U.S. government pensions inspired a group of congressmen to urge that the Justice Department open an inquiry into the possibility of prosecuting him. Nothing, however, came of the effort. Robert W. Stewart, "Inquiry Urged on Associate of Atom Spies," *Los Angeles Times* (24 June 1992).

33. Venona messages regarding Perl are cited in appendix A.

34. Venona 154 KGB Moscow to New York, 16 February 1945.

35. Venona 305 KGB Moscow to New York, 1 April 1945.

36. Radosh and Milton, *The Rosenberg File,* 299.

37. Venona 1491 KGB New York to Moscow, 22 October 1944. Five other Venona messages regarding the Sidorovichs are cited in appendix A. Julius Rosenberg's cover name in KGB cables initially was Antenna and was changed to Liberal in September 1944.

38. Radosh and Milton, *The Rosenberg File,* 299–300.

39. Venona messages regarding Nile are cited in appendix A.

40. American engineers succeeded in placing inside an artillery shell a tiny and very

rugged radar unit connected to the shell's fuse. The device set off the shell when it came close to (even if it did not hit) a target, a feature that greatly increased the efficiency of anti-aircraft shells. The device was called a proximity fuse because it set off the shell in the proximity of the target aircraft. Radosh and Milton, *The Rosenberg File*, 72. See also testimony of Col. Walter Edward Lotz, Jr., statement of O. John Rogge, and statement of David Greenglass, 24 November 1953, "Army Signal Corps—Subversion and Espionage," U.S. Senate, Committee on Government Operations, Permanent Subcommittee on Investigations of the Senate, 83rd Cong., 1st sess., part 1.

41. Venona messages regarding Julius Rosenberg are cited in appendix A.

42. David Martin, *Wilderness of Mirrors* (New York: Ballantine Books, 1981); Ronald Radosh and Joyce Milton in their 1983 edition of *The Rosenberg File: A Search for the Truth* (New York: Holt, Rinehart and Winston, 1983); Robert Lamphere and Tom Shachtman, *The FBI-KGB War: A Special Agent's Story* (New York: Random House, 1986).

43. There is one deciphered London GRU message regarding the initial establishment of Fuchs's relationship with Soviet intelligence: Venona 2227 GRU London to Moscow, 10 August 1941. This message is from a period antedating the Soviet duplication of one-time pads. Its decryption was made possible because the London GRU station in 1941 ran out of one-time pads and used its emergency back-up cipher system based on a standard statistical table to generate the additive key. British cryptanalysts working with the Venona Project recognized it as a nonstandard and vulnerable cipher and solved it, but not until well after Fuchs's arrest.

44. Venona messages regarding Fuchs are cited in appendix A.

45. Venona 345 KGB New York to Moscow, 22 September 1944; 1397 KGB New York to Moscow, 4 October 1944; 1403 KGB New York to Moscow, 5 October 1944; 1606 KGB New York to Moscow, 16 November 1944.

46. Quoted in Radosh and Milton, *The Rosenberg File*, 44.

47. [Lamphere to Gardner], "Study of Code Names in MGB Communications," 27 June 1950, National Security Agency, Venona Collection 50-025, box D045, reproduced in Robert Louis Benson and Michael Warner, eds., *Venona: Soviet Espionage and the American Response, 1939–1957* (Washington, D.C.: National Security Agency, Central Intelligence Agency, 1996), 153. Venona messages regarding the Greenglasses and the Rosenbergs are cited in appendix A.

48. Quoted in Radosh and Milton, *The Rosenberg File* (1997), 58–65.

49. There is no evidence that Greenglass's assignment to Los Alamos was anything but the chance working of the Army's personnel system.

50. Venona 1340 KGB New York to Moscow, 21 September 1944.

51. Quoted in Radosh and Milton, *The Rosenberg File*, 66.

52. Venona 1600 KGB New York to Moscow, 14 November 1944.

53. Venona 1657 KGB New York to Moscow, 27 November 1944.

54. Venona messages regarding Quantum are cited in appendix A.

55. Venona 972, 979, 983 KGB New York to Moscow, 22–23 June 1943.

56. Richard Rhodes, *Dark Sun: The Making of the Hydrogen Bomb* (New York: Simon and Schuster, 1995), 39.

57. Venona messages regarding Fogel/Pers are cited in appendix A.

58. On the intelligence information the KGB turned over to Soviet scientists in 1944, see Joseph Albright and Marcia Kunstel, " 'Did the United States Have *Any* Secrets?' " *The Bulletin of the Atomic Scientists* (January/February 1988), 53–54, and V. Merkulov to Lavrenti P. Beria, 28 February 1945, reprinted in *Voprosy Istorii Estestvoznaniia i Tekhniki*, Russian Academy of Science, no. 3 (1992).

59. Hall's name is given in clear text (no cover name) in the earliest message regarding him.

60. Michael Dobbs, "Code Name 'Mlad,' Atomic Bomb Spy," *Washington Post* (25 February 1996), and "Unlocking the Crypts: Most Spies Code Revealed Escaped Prosecution," *Washington Post* (25 December 1996); Joseph Albright and Marcia Kunstel, *Bombshell: The Secret Story of America's Unknown Atomic Spy Conspiracy* (New York: Times Books, 1997). *Bombshell* also contains extensive coverage of the espionage activities of Morris and Lona Cohen.

61. Venona messages regarding Hall are cited in appendix A.

62. Kurnakov's KGB career is discussed in chapter 6. Hall told Albright and Kunstel that he attempted to reach the Soviets by talking to staff members of Amtorg and was also directed to Kurnakov. The deciphered Venona cables refer only to Sax's approach. The decrypted parts of the Venona cable suggest that it may have been Nicola Napoli, head of Artkino, the distributor of Soviet films in the United States, who directed Sax to Kurnakov. Venona 1699 KGB New York to Moscow, 2 December 1944.

63. Venona 1585 KGB New York to Moscow, 12 November 1944.

64. Allen Weinstein, "Bombshell," *Los Angeles Times* (28 September 1997), 6.

65. Venona 298 KGB Moscow to New York, 31 March 1945.

66. Albright and Kunstel compare what is known of Hall's access to the secrets of Los Alamos with documents in papers of Igor Kurchatov and other Russian archives about espionage reports given to Soviet scientists. See *Bombshell,* chaps. 14–16.

67. Robert K. McQueen memo of 31 March 1951 on FBI interviews with Hall 16 and 19 March and with Sax 16 March, FBI file 65-3404 [65-3403], text available at *bombshell-1.com* website.

68. Vladimir Chikov, "How the Soviet Secret Service Split the American Atom," *Novoe Vremia* 16 (23 April 1991) and 17 (30 April 1991).

69. The Cohens' role in espionage against Great Britain is described in Rebecca West, *The New Meaning of Treason* (New York: Viking, 1964), 281–288, and in Albright and Kunstel, *Bombshell,* 244–253.

70. The FBI investigation of the Cohens can be followed in the FBI Morris and Lona Cohen file, 100-406659.

71. Russian Federal Foreign Intelligence Service, "Veterany vneshnei razvedki Rossii" (Veterans of Russian foreign intelligence service) (Moscow: Russian Federal Foreign Intelligence Service, 1995).

72. Chikov, "How the Soviet Secret Service Split the American Atom."

73. Michael Dobbs, "How Soviets Stole U.S. Atom Secrets," *Washington Post* (4 October 1992). Dobbs referred to the Perseus story when describing Yatskov's confirmation of the Cohens' role in atomic espionage, which has led some to think that Yatskov confirmed the Perseus cover name as well. Dobbs, however, says that Yatskov did not use the cover name Perseus. For a summary of Yatskov's KGB career, see appendix E.

74. In an earlier book the authors discussed Morris Cohen's background and his activities in Spain as well as a report written by Rudy Baker, head of the CPUSA's underground arm. Baker's report described the work during 1942 of a covert network, one that included a covert radio operator with the cover name Louis. Cohen was trained as a covert radio operator and, according to Chikov, had the cover name Louis in 1942. This led the authors to conclude that the Louis in Baker's report was Morris Cohen. Since that time the authors have found a document in the archive of the Communist International that disproves this identification. Specifically, in 1943 Earl Browder, head of the CPUSA, sent a coded message to the Comintern stating that he was sending Louis

to Mexico to establish a new clandestine radio station. This Louis was clearly the same one as in Baker's report, but it cannot have been Cohen, who by that point had been drafted into the U.S. Army. Harvey Klehr, John Earl Haynes, and Fridrikh Igorevich Firsov, *The Secret World of American Communism* (New Haven: Yale University Press, 1995), 205–226; Browder to Comintern, 15 January 1943, Archive of the Secretariat of the Executive Committee of the Communist International: coded correspondence with Communist Parties (1933–1943), RTsKhIDNI 495-184-7 1943 file.

75. Pavel A. Sudoplatov, Anatoli Sudoplatov, Jerrold Schecter, and Leona Schecter, *Special Tasks: The Memoirs of an Unwanted Witness* (New York: Little, Brown, 1994); Rhodes, *Dark Sun,* 71; *Voprosy Istorii Estestvoznaniia i Tekhniki,* Russian Academy of Science, no. 3 (1992), document 4; Albright and Kunstel, *Bombshell,* 76–77, 317n–318n.

76. Venona 50 KGB New York to Moscow, 11 January 1945.

77. Venona 239 KGB New York to Moscow, 30 August 1944; 50 KGB New York to Moscow, 11 January 1945.

78. New York FBI to Director, 8 May 1957, FBI Morris and Lona Cohen file, 100-406659, serial 33; Transcript of videotaped interview of Morris Cohen by a historian of the KGB oral history project in Moscow, 19 July 1993, and shown by the Russian Foreign Intelligence Service to Joseph Albright and Marcia Kunstel on 15 July 1995, *bombshell-1.com* website.

79. On the Smyth report's impact on the Soviet bomb program, see Rhodes, *Dark Sun,* 182, 215–17, 221–22.

80. Venona messages regarding Erie and Ernest are cited in appendix A.

81. Venona 619–620 KGB San Francisco to Moscow, 27 November 1945.

82. Venona messages regarding Hiskey are cited in appendix B.

83. Venona 619 KGB New York to Moscow, 4 May 1944.

84. Venona 1020 KGB New York to Moscow, 20 July 1944.

85. Venona 1332 KGB New York to Moscow, 18 September 1944.

86. Venona 1715 KGB New York to Moscow, 5 December 1944.

87. While it is most likely that Rose Olsen/Phlox is Roselyn Childs and that Jack Childs was designated to approach Hiskey, an alternative would be that Rose was the cover name for Morris's wife and that it was Morris himself who was picked to approach Hiskey.

88. Venona 580–581 San Francisco to Moscow, 13 November 1945.

89. Testimony of James Sterling Murray and Edward Tiers Manning, 14 August and 5 October 1949, U.S. Congress, House of Representatives, Committee on Un-American Activities, 81st Cong., 1st sess., 877–899.

90. Excerpts From Hearings Regarding Investigation of Communist Activities in Connection with the Atom Bomb, U.S. Congress, House of Representatives, Committee on Un-American Activities, 80th Cong., 2d sess., 1948; Testimony of James Murray and Edward Manning.

91. FBI memo, "Soviet Activities in the United States," 25 July 1946, Papers of Clark Clifford, Harry S. Truman Library.

92. Venona 1276 GRU New York to Moscow, 2 August 1943.

93. "Report on Atomic Espionage (Nelson-Weinberg and Hiskey-Adams Cases)," 29 September 1949, U.S. Congress, House of Representatives, Committee on Un-American Activities, 89th Cong., 1st sess., 1–15; San Francisco FBI report of 1 July 1945 through 15 March 1947, Comintern Apparatus file, serial 5421.

94. Report of 11 January 1944, serial 3378, FBI Silvermaster file (FBI file 65-56402); "Comintern Apparatus Summary Report," 15 December 1944 "Comintern Apparatus Summary Report," 15 December 1944, serial 3702, FBI Comintern Apparatus

file; "The Shameful Years: Thirty Years of Soviet Espionage in the United States," 30 December 1951, U.S. Congress, House of Representatives, Committee on Un-American Activities, 39–40.

95. Venona 1328 KGB New York to Moscow, 12 August 1943. The Venona message gives the professor's name in clear text, but the NSA chose to black it out in its release. Internal and other evidence suggests that the name was that of Ernest Lawrence, in which case the New York KGB most likely soon learned that Lawrence was not recruitable. This cable erroneously located the radiation laboratory at Sacramento rather than at Berkeley.

96. San Francisco FBI report, 22 April 1947, serial 5421 and "Comintern Apparatus Summary Report," 15 December 1944, serial 3702, both in FBI Comintern Apparatus file. Pinsky also had a brother-in-law who was a physicist and who worked at Los Alamos on the bomb project. In 1944 Pinsky may have traveled to New Mexico to contact him. Pinsky himself later became research director for the California CIO while it was headed by Harry Bridges, a concealed Communist.

97. Venona 340 KGB New York to Moscow, 21 September 1944.

98. Venona 132 KGB San Francisco to Moscow, 18 March 1944.

99. Venona 580–581 KGB San Francisco to Moscow, 13 November 1945.

100. Oral transcription of interview between Lt. Col. John Landsdale, Jr., and Dr. J. Robert Oppenheimer, 12 September 1943, inserted in hearing of 3 May 1954, "In the Matter of J. Robert Oppenheimer," U.S. Atomic Energy Commission, 871–886. In 1949 Bohm refused to answer congressional committee inquiries about his relations with the CPUSA. He moved to Brazil in 1951 and became a Brazilian citizen in 1954. Having lost his belief in communism, in the early 1960s Bohm applied for and got an American passport, stating that he had not intended to repudiate his American citizenship. He also told American authorities that he had been a CPUSA member while at the radiation laboratory during World War II. F. David Peat, *Infinite Potential: The Life and Times of David Bohm* (Reading, Mass.: Helix Books, 1997).

101. San Francisco FBI report of 1 July 1945 through 15 March 1947, Comintern Apparatus file, serial 5421. Chevalier later wrote *Oppenheimer: The Story of a Friendship* (New York: Braziller, 1965).

102. Venona 1773 KGB New York to Moscow, 16 December 1944; 580–581 KGB San Francisco to Moscow, 13 November 1945.

103. Venona 799 KGB New York to Moscow, 26 May 1945. The identification of the Reservation as Los Alamos comes from matching up the information (from a deciphered message) that Klaus Fuchs was working at the Reservation and the fact that at the time, February 1945, Fuchs was at Los Alamos. Venona 183 KGB New York to Moscow, 27 February 1945.

104. Venona 259 Moscow to New York 21 March 1945. Arnold Kramish, a physicist who was at Los Alamos, has offered an alternative set of identifications. He suggests that the Reservation was not Los Alamos but rather the Manhattan Project's Argonne Laboratory at Chicago, and that Veksel was not Oppenheimer but Enrico Fermi. Fermi, one of the Manhattan Project's key scientists, headed much of the scientific work at its Chicago facilities until he moved to Los Alamos in September 1944, but he retained the his post at the Argonne Laboratory. Kramish adds to this the suggestion that Huron was the cover name for Bruno Pontecorvo, a refugee Italian physicist who was part of the British atomic program and spent most of the war at the British-Canadian nuclear research facility at Chalk River, Ontario. Pontecorvo was a Soviet spy, probably recruited in 1943. After the war he continued to work for the British atomic program and

fled to the USSR in 1950 when British and American security officials uncovered several Soviet atomic spies. Pontecorvo had been a friend of Fermi in Italy in the 1930s and indeed visited the Chicago Metallurgical Laboratory in May 1944. Arnold Kramish, "The Manhattan Project and Venona," 1997 Cryptologic History Symposium, 29–31 October 1997, Fort George Meade, Md.

105. On the Soviet atomic bomb project and the role of espionage in it, see Rhodes, *Dark Sun;* David Holloway, *Stalin and the Bomb* (New Haven: Yale University Press, 1994); German A. Goncharow, "Thermonuclear Milestones," *Physics Today* 49, no. 11 (November 1996), 44–61. Some of the Soviet documents on World War II atomic espionage are reproduced in appendixes 1–4 of the Sudoplatovs and the Schecters' *Special Tasks* and in *Voprosy Istorii Estestvoznaniia i Tekhniki*, Russian Academy of Science, no. 3 (1992), 107–134.

106. Sudoplatov in his memoir describes both Oppenheimer and Fermi as persons who turned a blind eye to Soviet espionage, but his discussion of the two is ambiguous and vague compared with his detailed discussion of other Soviet intelligence operations in which he was involved. In December 1943 FBI listening devices in Steve Nelson's residence picked up a conversation between Nelson and Bernadette Doyle, organizational secretary of the CPUSA's branch in Alameda County, which included Berkeley. Nelson and Doyle spoke of both Oppenheimer brothers as CPUSA members, but Nelson referred to Robert as having become inactive. J. Edgar Hoover to Maj. Gen. Harry Vaughn, 28 February 1947, President's Secretary's Files, Papers of Harry Truman, Harry S. Truman Library. A February 1944 KGB memo quoted in Allen Weinstein and Alexander Vassiliev, *The Haunted Wood: Soviet Espionage in America—The Stalin Era* (New York: Random House, 1999), identifies both Oppenheimer brothers as having been secret members of the CPUSA. This memo also indicates that Frank had been a more active Communist than Robert, that Robert was a target for recruitment by the KGB and the GRU, but that, in part because of the heavy security around him, nothing had been achieved.

Chapter 11: Soviet Espionage and American History

1. Stalin and his inner circle placed a high value on information gained by espionage. See Vladislav Zubok and Constantine Pleshakov, *Inside the Kremlin's Cold War: From Stalin to Khrushchev* (Cambridge: Harvard University Press, 1996), 14, 40, 101, 105–107.

2. The value of the stolen secrets does not affect the inherent nature of the acts of espionage themselves, any more than a burglar is less a burglar if he makes off only with the everyday tableware rather than the sterling silver.

3. See, however, the discussion of the murky matter of Robert Oppenheimer's cooperation with American security officials in chapter 10.

4. M. J. Olgin, *Trotskyism* (New York: Workers Library, 1935), 148–149.

5. N. Slutsker, "Lenin, Stalin and the Communist Youth Movement," *Clarity* 1 (April–May 1940), 70, 72. Capitalization in the original.

6. Donald MacKenzie Lester, "Stalin—Genius of Socialist Construction," *Communist* 20 (March 1941), 257–258.

7. V. J. Jerome, "The Individual in History," *New Masses* (18 May 1943), 19.

8. Alexander Bittleman, "Stalin: On His Seventieth Birthday," *Political Affairs* 28 (December 1949), 1–2.

9. These and a plethora of other citations regarding the CPUSA's Stalin worship

are found in Aileen S. Kraditor, *"Jimmy Higgins": The Mental World of the American Rank-and-File Communist, 1930-1958* (New York: Greenwood Press, 1988), particularly chapters 5 and 6.

10. Michael Dobbs, "Unlocking the Crypts: Most Spies Code Revealed Escaped Prosecution," *Washington Post* (25 December 1996).

11. America's bureaucratic regime of Cold War secrecy is described in Daniel Patrick Moynihan, *Secrecy: The American Experience* (New Haven: Yale University Press, 1998).

Appendix A

1. Venona 588 KGB New York to Moscow, 29 April 1944; 687 KGB New York to Moscow, 13 May 1944.

2. Venona 335 GRU New York to Moscow, 18 April 1941; 1276 GRU New York to Moscow, 2 August 1943.

3. Venona 14 KGB New York to Moscow, 4 January 1945. Sachs is identified as Adler in Allen Weinstein and Alexander Vassiliev, *The Haunted Wood: Soviet Espionage in America—The Stalin Era* (New York: Random House, 1999).

4. Venona 1202 KGB New York to Moscow, 23 August 1944; 1322 KGB New York to Moscow, 15 September 1944; 1515 KGB New York to Moscow, 25 October 1944; 1584 KGB New York to Moscow, 12 November 1944; 1766 KGB New York to Moscow, 15 December 1944; 18-19 KGB New York to Moscow, 4 January 1945; 49 KGB New York to Moscow, 11 January 1945; 239 KGB Moscow to New York, 17 March 1945.

5. Venona 812 KGB New York to Moscow, 29 May 1943; 846 KGB New York to Moscow, 3 June 1943; 871 KGB New York to Moscow, 8 June 1943; 925 KGB New York to Moscow, 16 June 1943; 958 KGB New York to Moscow, 21 June 1943; 991 KGB New York to Moscow, 24 June 1943; 1000 KGB New York to Moscow, 24 June 1943; 1025, 1035-1036, KGB New York to Moscow, 30 June 1943; 2013 KGB New York to Moscow, 11 December 1943; 278 KGB New York to Moscow, 23 February 1944; 283 KGB New York to Moscow, 24 February 1944; 380 KGB New York to Moscow, 20 March 1944; 588 KGB New York to Moscow, 29 April 1944; 687 KGB New York to Moscow, 13 May 1944; 769, 771 KGB New York to Moscow, 30 May 1944; 776 KGB New York to Moscow, 31 May 1944; 854 KGB New York to Moscow, 16 June 1944; 918 KGB New York to Moscow, 28 June 1944; 928 KGB New York to Moscow, 1 July 1944; 973 KGB New York to Moscow, 11 July 1944; 975 KGB New York to Moscow, 11 July 1944; 1009 KGB New York to Moscow, 19 July 1944; 1052 KGB New York to Moscow, 26 July 1944; 1065 KGB New York to Moscow, 28 July 1944; 1114 KGB New York to Moscow, 4 August 1944; 1155 KGB New York to Moscow, 12 August 1944; 1208 KGB New York to Moscow, 23 August 1944; 1215 KGB New York to Moscow, 25 August 1944; 1388, 1389 KGB New York to Moscow, 1 October 1944; 1393 KGB New York to Moscow, 3 October 1944; 1442, 1447 KGB New York to Moscow, 11 October 1944; 1463 KGB New York to Moscow, 14 October 1944; 1465 KGB New York to Moscow, 14 October 1944; 1481-1482 KGB New York to Moscow, 18 October 1944; 1613 KGB New York to Moscow, 18 November 1944; 1634 KGB New York to Moscow, 20 November 1944; 1635 KGB New York to Moscow, 21 November 1944; 1636 KGB New York to Moscow, 21 November 1944; 1691 KGB New York to Moscow, 1 December 1944; 1757 KGB New York to Moscow, 14 December 1944; 1791 KGB New York to Moscow, 20 December 1944; 1798 KGB

New York to Moscow, 20 December 1944; 1803 KGB New York to Moscow, 22 December 1944; 1818 KGB New York to Moscow, 26 December 1944; 1824 KGB New York to Moscow, 27 December 1944; 12, 13, 15, 16 KGB New York to Moscow, 4 January 1945; 14 KGB New York to Moscow, 4 January 1945; 18–19 KGB New York to Moscow, 4 January 1945; 21 KGB New York to Moscow, 8 January 1945; 26 KGB New York to Moscow, 8 January 1945; 50 KGB New York to Moscow, 11 January 1945; 71 KGB New York to Moscow, 17 January 1945; 79 KGB New York to Moscow, 18 January 1945; 82 KGB New York to Moscow, 18 January 1945; 143 KGB Moscow to New York, 15 February 1945; 179, 180 KGB Moscow to New York, 25 February 1945; 195 KGB Moscow to New York, 3 March 1945; 221 KGB Moscow to New York, 11 March 1945; 248 KGB Moscow to New York, 19 March 1945; 253 KGB Moscow to New York, 20 March 1945; 292 KGB Moscow to New York, 29 March 1945; 328 KGB Moscow to New York, 6 April 1945; 337 KGB Moscow to New York, 8 April 1945; 1822 KGB Washington to Moscow, 30 March 1945 ("A." in this message was judged to be the initial of Albert, then Akhmerov's cover name).

6. Venona 448 KGB Moscow to New York, 9 July 1942; 899 KGB New York to Moscow, 11 June 1943; 148 KGB New York to Moscow, 29 January 1944.

7. Venona 1322 KGB New York to Moscow, 15 September 1944; 1586 KGB New York to Moscow; 12 November 1944; 243 KGB New York to Moscow, 18 March 1945; 163 KGB Moscow to New York, 19 February 1945; 239 KGB Moscow to New York, 17 March 1945. In connection with the other messages about Eugénie Olkhine, 1322 KGB New York to Moscow suggests that *Aleksandrov* was her father.

8. Venona 584 KGB Moscow to Mexico City, 6 October 1944. Also see "Comintern Apparatus Summary Report," 15 December 1944, FBI Comintern Apparatus file (FBI file 100-203581), serial 3702.

9. Venona 984 KGB New York to Moscow, 23 June 1943; 588 KGB New York to Moscow, 29 April 1944; 769, 771 KGB New York to Moscow, 30 May 1944. NSA and FBI analysts indicated that Arena may have been a cover name for Mary Price, along with Director. Documents in Weinstein and Vassiliev, *The Haunted Wood*, confirm that Director is Mary Price but indicate that Arena was used for an unidentified source working for the Civil Service Commission.

10. Venona 1403 KGB New York to Moscow, 5 October 1944; 1559 KGB New York to Moscow, 6 November 1944; 793–794 New York to Moscow, 25 May 1945.

11. Venona 626 KGB New York to Moscow, 5 May 1944; 864 KGB New York to Moscow, 16 June 1944.

12. Venona 1146 KGB New York to Moscow, 10 August 1944.

13. Venona 652 KGB New York to Moscow, 9 May 1944.

14. Venona 1327 KGB New York to Moscow, 15 September 1944.

15. Venona 927–928 GRU New York to Moscow, 16 June 1943; 1026 GRU New York to Moscow, 30 June 1943; 1027 GRU New York to Moscow, 30 June 1943; 1030 GRU New York to Moscow, 1 July 1943; 1123 GRU New York to Moscow, 11 July 1943; 1171 GRU New York to Moscow, 19 July 1943; 1249 GRU New York to Moscow, 29 July 1943; 1250 GRU New York to Moscow, 29 July 1943; 1324 GRU New York to Moscow, 11 August 1943; 1329 GRU New York to Moscow, 12 August 1943; 1350 GRU New York to Moscow, 17 August 1943; 1365 GRU New York to Moscow, 19 August 1943; 1488 GRU New York to Moscow, 15 September 1943; 1385 KGB New York to Moscow, 1 October 1944.

16. Fitin to Dimitrov, 22 May 1942, RTsKhIDNI 495-74-484. The Venona messages with Son/Baker are Venona 1043 KGB New York to Moscow, 25 July 1944; 1286 KGB New York to Moscow, 8 September 1944.

17. Venona 865–866 KGB New York to Moscow, 8 June 1943.

18. Venona 975 KGB New York to Moscow, 11 July 1944.

19. Venona 914 KGB New York to Moscow, 27 June 1944; 1251 KGB New York to Moscow, 2 September 1944; 1429 KGB New York to Moscow, 9 October 1944; 1600 KGB New York to Moscow, 14 November 1944; 1657 KGB New York to Moscow, 27 November 1944; 1715 KGB New York to Moscow, 5 December 1944; 1749–1750 KGB New York to Moscow, 13 December 1944.

20. Venona 3706 KGB Washington to Moscow, 29 June 1945.

21. Venona 1169 GRU New York to Moscow, 19 July 1943; Venona 1258–1259 GRU New York to Moscow, 31 July 1943; 1350 GRU New York to Moscow, 17 August 1943.

22. Venona 1954 KGB New York to Moscow, 27 November 1943; 864 KGB New York to Moscow, 16 June 1944.

23. Venona 958 KGB New York to Moscow, 21 June 1943.

24. Venona 780, 792, KGB New York to Moscow, 25 and 26 May 1945.

25. Venona 1341 KGB New York to Moscow, 21 September 1944.

26. Venona 592 KGB New York to Moscow, 29 April 1943; 725 KGB New York to Moscow, 19 May 1943; 810 KGB New York to Moscow, 29 May 1943; 952 KGB New York to Moscow, 21 June 1943; 974 KGB New York to Moscow, 22 June 1943; 1430 KGB New York to Moscow, 2 September 1943; 1452 KGB New York to Moscow, 8 September 1943.

27. Venona 618 KGB New York to Moscow, 4 May 1944; 1050 KGB New York to Moscow, 26 July 1944; 1351 KGB New York to Moscow, 23 September 1944.

28. Venona 2011 KGB New York to Moscow, 11 December 1943; 2013 KGB New York to Moscow, 11 December 1943; 278 KGB New York to Moscow, 23 February 1944; 588 KGB New York to Moscow, 29 April 1944; 687 KGB New York to Moscow, 13 May 1944; 973 KGB New York to Moscow, 11 July 1944; 1065 KGB New York to Moscow, 28 July 1944; 1353 KGB New York to Moscow, 23 September 1944; 1464 KGB New York to Moscow, 14 October 1944; 1673 KGB New York to Moscow, 30 November 1944; 1802 KGB New York to Moscow, 21 December 1944; 954 KGB Moscow to New York, 20 September 1944; 275 KGB Moscow to New York, 25 March 1945.

29. Venona 927–928 GRU New York to Moscow, 16 June 1943; 938 GRU New York to Moscow, 17 June 1943; 948 GRU New York to Moscow, 19 June 1943; 1103 GRU New York to Moscow, 8 July 1943; 1325 GRU New York to Moscow, 11 August 1943; 1348 GRU New York to Moscow, 16 August 1943; 1448 GRU New York to Moscow, 6 September 1943.

30. Venona 1509 KGB New York to Moscow, 23 October 1944.

31. Venona 874–875 KGB New York to Moscow, 8 June 1943; 1197 KGB New York to Moscow, 22 July 1943; 1207 KGB New York to Moscow, 22 July 1943; 695 KGB New York to Moscow, 16 May 1944; 1508 KGB New York to Moscow, 23 October 1944. The NSA has redacted the identification of Bibi.

32. Venona 1064 KGB New York to Moscow, 3 July 1943; 927–928 GRU New York to Moscow, 16 June 1943; 938 GRU New York to Moscow, 17 June 1943; 948 GRU New York to Moscow, 19 June 1943; 989 GRU New York to Moscow, 24 June 1943; 1348 GRU New York to Moscow, 16 August 1943.

33. Venona 1370 KGB New York to Moscow, 27 September 1944; 1403 KGB New

York to Moscow, 5 October 1944; 1429 KGB New York to Moscow, 9 October 1944; 1430 KGB New York to Moscow, 10 October 1944; 1557 KGB New York to Moscow, 6 November 1944; 1055 KGB New York to Moscow, 5 July 1945; 83 KGB Moscow to New York, 28 January 1945; 259 Moscow to New York, 21 March 1945.

34. Venona 1804 KGB New York to Moscow, 22 December 1944; 86 KGB New York to Moscow, 19 January 1945.

35. Venona 1579 GRU New York to Moscow, 28 September 1943.

36. Venona 726–729 KGB New York to Moscow, 22 May 1942.

37. Venona 1934 Naval GRU Washington to Moscow, 11 August 1943.

38. Venona 705 KGB New York to Moscow, 18 May 1943; 943 KGB New York to Moscow, 4 July 1944; 1403 KGB New York to Moscow, 5 October 1944; 1559 KGB New York to Moscow, 6 November 1944.

39. Venona 132 KGB San Francisco to Moscow, 18 March 1944.

40. Venona 1390 KGB New York to Moscow, 1 October 1944; 1403 KGB New York to Moscow, 5 October 1944; 1797 KGB New York to Moscow, 20 December 1944; 18–19 KGB New York to Moscow, 4 January 1945. Brothman is identified as Chrome Yellow in Weinstein and Vassiliev, *The Haunted Wood.*

41. Venona 774 KGB New York to Moscow, 26 May 1943; 820 KGB New York to Moscow, 31 May 1943; 846 KGB New York to Moscow, 3 June 1943; 1047 KGB New York to Moscow, 2 July 1943; 1163 KGB New York to Moscow, 18 July 1943; 1164 KGB New York to Moscow, 18 July 1943; 1430 KGB New York to Moscow, 2 September 1943; 1999, 2000 KGB New York to Moscow, 10 December 1943; 2011 KGB New York to Moscow, 11 December 1943; 588 KGB New York to Moscow, 29 April 1944; 598–599 KGB New York to Moscow, 2 May 1944; 605 KGB New York to Moscow, 2 May 1944; 687 KGB New York to Moscow, 13 May 1944; 823 KGB New York to Moscow, 7 June 1944; 849 KGB New York to Moscow, 15 June 1944; 973 KGB New York to Moscow, 11 July 1944; 1065 KGB New York to Moscow, 28 July 1944; 1328 KGB New York to Moscow, 15 September 1944; 1410 KGB New York to Moscow, 6 October 1944; 1433, 1435 New York to Moscow, 10 October 1944; 1457 KGB New York to Moscow, 14 October 1944; 1512 KGB New York to Moscow, 24 October 1944; 1818 KGB New York to Moscow, 26 December 1944; 14 KGB New York to Moscow, 4 January 1945; 236 KGB Mexico City to Moscow, 1944 April; 1258–1259 GRU New York to Moscow, 31 July 1943.

42. Venona 11 KGB New York to Moscow, 4 January 1945.

43. Venona 196 KGB New York to Moscow, 9 February 1944; 11 KGB New York to Moscow, 4 January 1945.

44. Venona 1559 KGB New York to Moscow, 6 November 1944.

45. Venona 492 KGB Mexico City to Moscow, 9 June 1944; 526 KGB Moscow to Mexico City, 2 September 1944; 985 KGB New York to Moscow, 23 June 1943; 1000 KGB New York to Moscow, 24 June 1943; 1044 KGB New York to Moscow, 2 July 1943; 1088 KGB New York to Moscow, 7 July 1943; 786 KGB New York to Moscow, 1 June 1944; 889 KGB New York to Moscow, 23 June 1944; 943 KGB New York to Moscow, 4 July 1944; 1102–1103 KGB New York to Moscow, 2 August 1944; 1163 KGB New York to Moscow, 15 August 1944; 1239 KGB New York to Moscow, 30 August 1944; 1313 KGB New York to Moscow, 13 September 1944; 1336 KGB New York to Moscow, 18 September 1944; 1353 KGB New York to Moscow, 23 September 1944; 1470 KGB New York to Moscow, 17 October 1944; 1509 KGB New York to Moscow, 23 October 1944; 1741 KGB New York to Moscow, 12 December 1944; 1821 KGB New York to Moscow, 26 December 1944; 25 KGB New York to Moscow, 8 January 1945; 37 KGB New York to Moscow, 9 January 1945; 63–66 KGB New York

to Moscow, 15 January 1945; 77 KGB New York to Moscow, 17 January 1945; 95 KGB New York to Moscow, 23 January 1945; 329 KGB Moscow to New York, 7 April 1945.

46. Venona 1166 KGB New York to Moscow, 16 August 1944.

47. Venona 1619–1620 KGB New York to Moscow, 20 November 1944.

48. Venona 31 KGB San Francisco to Moscow, 17 January 1944; 133 KGB San Francisco to Moscow, 29 March 1944.

49. Venona 580–581 San Francisco to Moscow, 13 November 1945.

50. Venona 899 KGB New York to Moscow, 11 June 1943; 926 New York to Moscow, 16 June 1943; 670 KGB New York to Moscow, 11 May 1944; 751–752 KGB New York to Moscow, 26 May 1944; 851 KGB New York to Moscow, 15 June 1944.

51. Venona 722 KGB New York to Moscow, 21 May 1942; 854 KGB New York to Moscow, 16 June 1944.

52. Venona 865 KGB Moscow to New York, 26 December 1942.

53. Venona 82 KGB New York to Moscow, 18 January 1945.

54. Venona 769, 771 KGB New York to Moscow, 30 May 1944.

55. Venona 1905 KGB New York to Moscow, 17 November 1943; 776 KGB New York to Moscow, 31 May 1944.

56. Venona 1003 KGB New York to Moscow, 18 July 1944; 1328 KGB New York to Moscow, 15 September 1944; 1430 KGB New York to Moscow, 10 October 1944; 1523 KGB New York to Moscow, 27 October 1944. Chef is identified in Weinstein and Vassiliev, *The Haunted Wood,* as Franklin Zelman, which may be a garbled translation of Zalmond Franklin.

57. Venona 860 KGB New York to Moscow, 6 June 1943; 1398 KGB New York to Moscow, 26 August 1943. In 1944 Chen is the cover name used by the KGB for Zalmond Franklin, but this 1943 Chen appears to be a different person.

58. Venona 1207 KGB New York to Moscow, 22 July 1943; 682 KGB New York to Moscow, 12 May 1944; 1251 KGB New York to Moscow, 2 September 1944.

59. Venona 1243 KGB New York to Moscow, 31 August 1944; 1838 KGB New York to Moscow, 29 December 1944; 179–180 KGB Moscow to New York, 25 February 1945.

60. Venona 1239 KGB New York to Moscow, 30 August 1944; 50 KGB New York to Moscow, 11 January 1945.

61. Venona 50 KGB New York to Moscow, 11 January 1945.

62. Venona 704 Naval GRU Washington to Moscow, 1 April 1943; 1934 Naval GRU Washington to Moscow, 11 August 1943; 1969 Naval GRU Washington to Moscow, 13 August 1943; 2933 Naval GRU Washington to Moscow, 14 November 1943; 115 Naval GRU Moscow to Washington 20 January 1943; 1194 Naval GRU Moscow to Washington 10 July 1943.

63. Venona 193–194 Mexico City to Moscow, 14 March 1944. Also see "Comintern Apparatus Summary Report," 15 December 1944, FBI Comintern Apparatus file, serial 3702; Colloms testimony, "American Aspects of Assassination of Leon Trotsky," U.S. Congress, House of Representatives, Un-American Activities Committee, 82nd Cong., 1st sess., 1951.

64. Venona 1014 KGB New York to Moscow, 20 July 1944; 1050 KGB New York to Moscow, 26 July 1944; 1385 KGB New York to Moscow, 1 October 1944; 1587 KGB New York to Moscow, 12 November 1944; 1637 KGB New York to Moscow, 21 November 1944; 1714 KGB New York to Moscow, 5 December 1944; 1845 KGB New York to Moscow, 31 December 1944; 27 KGB New York to Moscow, 8 January 1945; 55 KGB New York to Moscow, 15 January 1945; 76 KGB New York to Moscow,

17 January 1945; 992 KGB New York to Moscow, 26 June 1945; 1053.KGB New York to Moscow, 5 July 1945; 268 KGB Moscow to New York, 24 March 1945; 284, 286 KGB Moscow to New York, 28 March 1945. Coplon may be the subject of Venona 1522 KGB New York to Moscow, 27 October 1944, in which the KGB agent Joseph Katz, who had liaison responsibilities for Coplon at one point, reports the arrival of "our source in the FBI."

65. Venona 1791 KGB New York to Moscow, 20 December 1944. The NSA redacted Cora's identity.

66. Venona 1053 KGB New York to Moscow, 2 July 1943.

67. Venona 257 KGB Moscow to New York, 21 March 1945.

68. Venona 823 New York to Moscow, 7 June 1944; 1275 KGB New York to Moscow, 7 September 1944; 1403 KGB New York to Moscow, 5 October 1944; 1754 KGB New York to Moscow, 14 December 1944.

69. Venona 928 KGB New York to Moscow, 30 June 1943; 1317 KGB New York to Moscow, 10 August 1943; 1431 KGB New York to Moscow, 2 September 1943; 900 KGB New York to Moscow, 24 June 1944; 1243 KGB New York to Moscow, 31 August 1944; 1463 KGB New York to Moscow, 14 October 1944; 1634 KGB New York to Moscow, 20 November 1944; 143 KGB Moscow to New York, 15 February 1945; 253 KGB Moscow to New York, 20 March 1945.

70. Venona 619, 620 KGB San Francisco to Moscow, 27 November 1945.

71. Venona 1031 KGB New York to Moscow, 1 July 1943; 1045 KGB New York to Moscow, 2 July 1943.

72. Venona 1557 New York KGB to Moscow, 6 November 1944.

73. Venona 708 KGB Moscow to Mexico City, 8 December 1944; 1714 KGB New York to Moscow, 5 December 1944; 55 KGB New York to Moscow, 15 January 1945.

74. Venona 1195 KGB New York to Moscow, 21 July 1943; 1206 New York to Moscow, 22 July 1943.

75. Venona 748 KGB New York to Moscow, 26 May 1944.

76. Venona 1776 KGB New York to Moscow, 26 October 1943.

77. Venona 834, 846–848, Naval GRU Washington to Moscow, 18 April 1943.

78. Venona 1456 GRU New York to Moscow, 8 September 1943.

79. Venona 871–872 KGB New York to Moscow, 6 June 1945.

80. Venona 1025, 1035–1936, KGB New York to Moscow, 30 June 1943; 380 KGB New York to Moscow, 20 March 1944; 744, 746 KGB New York to Moscow, 24 May 1944; 916 KGB New York to Moscow, 17 June 1944; 1015 KGB New York to Moscow, to Victor [Fitin], 22 July 1944; 1114 KGB New York to Moscow, 4 August 1944; 1251 KGB New York to Moscow, 2 September 1944; 1613 KGB New York to Moscow, 18 November 1944; 1636 KGB New York to Moscow, 21 November 1944.

81. Venona 726–729 KGB New York to Moscow, 22 May 1942; 865, 866 KGB New York to Moscow, 8 June 1943; 1132–1133 KGB New York to Moscow, 13 July 1943; 1148 KGB New York to Moscow, 14 July 1943; 1930 KGB New York to Moscow, 21 November 1943; 853 KGB New York to Moscow, 16 June 1944.

82. Venona 853 KGB New York to Moscow, 16 June 1944.

83. Venona 894 KGB New York to Moscow, 10 June 1943; 627 KGB New York to Moscow, 5 May 1944; 864 KGB New York to Moscow, 16 June 1944; 1053 KGB New York to Moscow, 5 July 1945.

84. Venona 894 KGB New York to Moscow, 10 June 1943; 627 KGB New York to Moscow, 5 May 1944; 864 KGB New York to Moscow, 16 June 1944; 1053 KGB New York to Moscow, 5 July 1945; 1182 KGB New York to Moscow, 19 August 1944; 1508 KGB New York to Moscow, 23 October 1944.

85. Venona 1055 KGB New York to Moscow, 5 July 1945.

86. Venona 823 KGB New York to Moscow, 7 June 1944; 881 KGB New York to Moscow, 20 June 1944.

87. Venona 1557 KGB New York to Moscow, 6 November 1944.

88. Venona 749 KGB New York to Moscow, 26 May 1944.

89. Venona 1388–1389 KGB New York to Moscow, 1 October 1944; 1403 KGB New York to Moscow, 5 October 1944; 1635 KGB New York to Moscow 21 November 1944.

90. Venona 104 Naval GRU Moscow to Washington 17 January 1943; 155 Naval GRU Moscow to Washington 26 January 1943.

91. Venona 1934 Naval GRU Washington to Moscow, 11 August 1943; 2278 Naval GRU Washington to Moscow, 10 September 1943; 2346 Naval GRU Washington to Moscow, 15 September 1943.

92. Venona 651 KGB New York to Moscow, 9 May 1944; 943 KGB New York to Moscow, 4 July 1944; 972 KGB New York to Moscow, 11 July 1944; 1403 KGB New York to Moscow, 5 October 1944.

93. Venona 1220 KGB New York to Moscow, 26 August 1944.

94. Venona 800 KGB New York to Moscow, 28 May 1943; 816–817 KGB New York to Moscow, 30 May 1943; 899 KGB New York to Moscow, 11 June 1943; 1142 KGB New York to Moscow, 10 August 1944; 174–176 KGB Mexico City to Moscow, 29 December 1943; 193–194 KGB Mexico City to Moscow, 14 March 1944; 212 KGB Mexico City to Moscow, 25 March 1944; 261–262 KGB Mexico City to Moscow, 16 April 1944; 281 KGB Mexico City to Moscow, 21 April 1944; 553–554 KGB Mexico City to Moscow, 29 June 1944; 893 KGB Mexico City to Moscow, 28 November 1944; 237 KGB Moscow to Mexico City, 20 April 1944; 248 KGB Moscow to Mexico City, 27 April 1944; 288 KGB Moscow to Mexico City, 11 May 1944; 511 KGB Moscow to Mexico City, 24 August 1944; 626 KGB Moscow to Mexico City, 29 October 1944; 634 KGB Moscow to Mexico City, 5 November 1944.

95. Venona 912 KGB New York to Moscow, 27 June 1944; 1403 KGB New York to Moscow, 5 October 1944; 989 KGB New York to Moscow, 26 June 1945; 164 Moscow to New York, 20 February 1945; 619–620 San Francisco to Moscow, 27 November 1945.

96. Venona 1192 Naval GRU Washington to Moscow, 4 June 1943.

97. Venona 115 Naval GRU Moscow to Washington, 20 January 1943; 360 Naval GRU Moscow to Washington, 26 February 1943; 366 Naval GRU Moscow to Washington, 28 February 1943; 849 Naval GRU Washington to Moscow, 20 April 1943; 901 Naval GRU Washington to Moscow, 27 April 1943; 393 Naval GRU Moscow to Washington, 5 March 1943; 427 Naval GRU Moscow to Washington, 11 March 1943.

98. Venona 656 KGB New York to Moscow, 9 May 1944; 939 KGB New York to Moscow, 18 June 1943; 823 KGB New York to Moscow, 7 June 1944; 881 KGB New York to Moscow, 20 June 1944; 905 KGB New York to Moscow, 26 June 1944; 1275 KGB New York to Moscow, 7 September 1944; 1403 KGB New York to Moscow, 5 October 1944; 275 KGB Moscow to New York, 25 March 1945.

99. Venona 854 KGB New York to Moscow, 16 June 1942.

100. Venona 1397 KGB New York to Moscow, 4 October 1944.

101. Venona 287 GRU Moscow to New York, 4 May 1942; 1348 GRU New York to Moscow, 16 August 1943; 1351 GRU New York to Moscow, 18 August 1943; 1448 GRU New York to Moscow, 6 September 1943; 1498–1499 GRU New York to Moscow, 17 September 1943.

102. Venona 1769 KGB New York to Moscow, 15 December 1944.

103. Venona 823 KGB New York to Moscow, 7 June 1944; 1275 KGB New York to Moscow, 7 September 1944.

104. Venona 865 KGB Moscow to New York, 26 December 1942; 939 KGB New York to Moscow, 18 June 1943; 165 KGB New York to Moscow, 2 February 1944; 823 KGB New York to Moscow, 7 June 1944; 881 KGB New York to Moscow, 20 June 1944; Elizabeth Bentley FBI deposition, 30 November 1945, FBI file 65-14603.

105. Venona 588 KGB New York to Moscow, 29 April 1944; 687 KGB New York to Moscow, 13 May 1944; 769, 771 KGB New York to Moscow, 30 May 1944; 179, 180 KGB Moscow to New York, 25 February 1945.

106. Venona 588 KGB New York to Moscow, 29 April 1944. Flato is a candidate for the partially decrypted Char. . . . in Venona 769, 771 KGB New York to Moscow, 30 May 1944.

107. Venona 1155 KGB New York to Moscow, 12 August 1944.

108. Venona 212 KGB New York to Moscow, 11 February 1944; 854 KGB New York to Moscow, 16 June 1944; 1251 KGB New York to Moscow, 2 September 1944; 1749, 1750 KGB New York to Moscow, 13 December 1944.

109. Venona 429 KGB San Francisco to Moscow, 23 October 1943; 450 KGB San Francisco to Moscow, 1 November 1943; 55 KGB San Francisco to Moscow, 8 February 1944; 101 KGB San Francisco to Moscow, 5 March 1944; 117 KGB San Francisco to Moscow, 11 March 1944; 136 KGB San Francisco to Moscow, 2 April 1945; 138 KGB San Francisco to Moscow, 3 April 1945; 143 KGB San Francisco to Moscow, 6 April 1945; 172 KGB San Francisco to Moscow, 18 April 1945; 238, 239 KGB San Francisco to Moscow, 7 May 1945; 266 KGB San Francisco to Moscow, 18 May 1945; 310 KGB San Francisco to Moscow, 9 June 1945; 320 KGB San Francisco to Moscow, 13 June 1945; 69 KGB San Francisco to Moscow, 20 February 1946.

110. Venona 854 KGB New York to Moscow, 16 June 1942; 958 KGB New York to Moscow, 21 June 1943; 1025, 1035–1036, KGB New York to Moscow, 30 June 1943; 769, 771 KGB New York to Moscow, 30 May 1944.

111. Venona 749 KGB New York to Moscow, 26 May 1944.

112. Venona 629 KGB New York to Moscow, 5 May 1944.

113. Venona 768 KGB New York to Moscow, 25 May 1943.

114. Venona 700 KGB New York to Moscow, 17 May 1944; 759–760 KGB New York to Moscow, 27 May 1944; 761 KGB New York to Moscow, 27 May 1944; 763 KGB New York to Moscow, 29 May 1944; 823 KGB New York to Moscow, 7 June 1944; 928 KGB New York to Moscow, 1 July 1944; 956, 957 KGB New York to Moscow, 6 July 1944; 1229 KGB New York to Moscow, 29 August 1944; 1410 KGB New York to Moscow, 6 October 1944.

115. Venona 865 KGB New York to Moscow, 18 June 1942; 925 KGB New York to Moscow, 16 June 1943.

116. Venona 472 KGB San Francisco to Moscow, 9 November 1943.

117. Venona 826 KGB New York to Moscow, 7 June 1944; 851 KGB New York to Moscow, 15 June 1944; 907 KGB New York to Moscow, 26 June 1944; 942 KGB New York to Moscow, 4 July 1944; 292 KGB Moscow to New York, 29 March 1945.

118. Venona 823 KGB New York to Moscow, 7 June 1944; 881 KGB New York to Moscow, 20 June 1944.

119. Venona 1195 KGB New York to Moscow, 21 July 1943; 1206 KGB New York to Moscow, 22 July 1943; 588 KGB New York to Moscow, 29 April 1944; 769, 771 KGB New York to Moscow, 30 May 1944; 79 KGB New York to Moscow, 18 January 1945; 179–180 KGB Moscow to New York, 25 February 1945; 1759 KGB

Washington to Moscow, 28 March 1945; 3598 KGB Washington to Moscow, 21 June 1945; 3600 KGB Washington to Moscow, 21 June 1945; 3645 KGB Washington to Moscow, 23 June 1945; 3688 KGB Washington to Moscow, 28 June 1945.

120. Venona 1398 KGB New York to Moscow, 26 August 1943; 144 KGB New York to Moscow, 27 January 1944.

121. Venona 12, 13, 15, 16 KGB New York to Moscow, 4 January 1945; 18–19 KGB New York to Moscow, 4 January 1945.

122. Venona 195 KGB New York to Moscow, 9 February 1944; 912 KGB New York to Moscow, 27 June 1944; 1233 KGB New York to Moscow, 29 August 1944; 1345 KGB New York to Moscow, 22 September 1944; 1390 KGB New York to Moscow, 1 October 1944; 1397 KGB New York to Moscow, 4 October 1944; 1403 KGB New York to Moscow, 5 October 1944; 1536 KGB New York to Moscow, 28 October 1944; 1606 KGB New York to Moscow, 16 November 1944; 1749, 1750 KGB New York to Moscow, 13 December 1944; 1797 KGB New York to Moscow, 20 December 1944; 183 KGB Moscow to New York, 27 February 1945; 257 KGB Moscow to New York, 21 March 1945; 275 KGB Moscow to New York, 25 March 1945.

123. Venona 918 KGB New York to Moscow, 28 June 1944; 12, 13, 15, 16 KGB New York to Moscow, 4 January 1945; 79 KGB New York to Moscow, 18 January 1945.

124. Venona 325 KGB Moscow to New York, 17 May 1942; 959 KGB New York to Moscow, 8 July 1942; 725 KGB New York to Moscow, 19 May 1943; 810 KGB New York to Moscow, 29 May 1943; 846 KGB New York to Moscow, 3 June 1943; 928 KGB New York to Moscow, 30 June 1943; 1052 KGB New York to Moscow, 2–4 July 1943; 1143 KGB New York to Moscow, 14 July 1943; 1163 KGB New York to Moscow, 18 July 1943; 1253 KGB New York to Moscow, 30 July 1943; 1430 KGB New York to Moscow, 2 September 1943; 1431 KGB New York to Moscow, 2 September 1943; 1586 KGB New York to Moscow, 29 September 1943; 2101 KGB New York to Moscow, 29 December 1943; 588 KGB New York to Moscow, 29 April 1944; 769, 771 KGB New York to Moscow, 30 May 1944; 1076 KGB New York to Moscow, 29 July 1944; 1221 KGB New York to Moscow, 26 August 1944; 1388, 1389 KGB New York to Moscow, 1 October 1944.

125. Venona 1579 New York GRU to Moscow, 28 September 1943.

126. Venona 927–928 GRU New York to Moscow, 16 June 1943.

127. Venona 600 KGB New York to Moscow, 2 May 1944; 601 KGB New York to Moscow, 2 May 1944; 694 KGB New York to Moscow, 16 May 1944.

128. Venona 1340 KGB New York to Moscow, 21 September 1944; 1549 KGB New York to Moscow, 3 November 1944; 1600 KGB New York to Moscow, 14 November 1944; 1749, 1750 KGB New York to Moscow, 13 December 1944; 1773 KGB New York to Moscow, 16 December 1944; 28 KGB New York to Moscow, 8 January 1945.

129. Venona 1340 KGB New York to Moscow, 21 September 1944; 1549 KGB New York to Moscow, 3 November 1944; 1600 KGB New York to Moscow, 14 November 1944; 1749–1750 KGB New York to Moscow, 13 December 1944; 1773 KGB New York to Moscow, 16 December 1944; 28 KGB New York to Moscow, 8 January 1945.

130. Venona 1585 KGB New York to Moscow, 12 November 1944; 1749–1750 KGB New York to Moscow, 13 December 1944; 1773 KGB New York to Moscow, 16 December 1944; 94 KGB New York to Moscow, 23 January 1945; 799 KGB New York to Moscow, 26 May 1945; 298 Moscow to New York, 31 March 1945; 709 Moscow

to New York, 3 July 1945. Venona 1699 KGB New York to Moscow, 2 December 1944, does not mention Hall, but its text very likely is a report delivered by Hall.

131. Venona 880 KGB New York to Moscow, 8 June 1943; 887 KGB New York to Moscow, 9 June 1943; 921, 922, 924 KGB New York to Moscow, 16 June 1943; 931 KGB New York to Moscow, 17 June 1943; 993 KGB New York to Moscow, 24 June 1943; 1019, 1021, 1024, 1034 KGB New York to Moscow, 29 June 1943; 1106 KGB New York to Moscow, 8 July 1943; 1162 KGB New York to Moscow, 17 July 1943; 1189 KGB New York to Moscow, 21 July 1943; 206 KGB New York to Moscow, 10 February 1944; 611 KGB New York to Moscow, 3 May 1944; 694 KGB New York to Moscow, 16 May 1944; 748 KGB New York to Moscow, 26 May 1944; 993 KGB New York to Moscow, 13 July 1944; 1214 KGB New York to Moscow, 25 August 1944; 1325, 1326 KGB New York to Moscow, 15 September 1944; 1333 KGB New York to Moscow, 18 September 1944; 1437 KGB New York to Moscow, 10 October 1944; 1438 KGB New York to Moscow, 10 October 1944; 1453 KGB New York to Moscow, 12 October 1944; 1484 KGB New York to Moscow, 19 October 1944; 954 KGB Moscow to New York, 20 September 1944.

132. Venona 627 KGB New York to Moscow, 5 May 1944.

133. Venona 1999–2000 KGB New York to Moscow, 10 December 1943; 129 KGB Mexico City to Moscow, 6 December 1943; 232 KGB Mexico City to Moscow, 3 April 1944; 243–244 KGB Mexico City to Moscow, 10 April 1944; 327 KGB Mexico City to Moscow, 3 May 1944; 343 KGB Mexico City to Moscow, 5 May 1944; 553–554 KGB Mexico City to Moscow, 29 June 1944; 893 KGB Mexico City to Moscow, 28 November 1944; 167 KGB Moscow to Mexico City, 17 March 1944; 200 KGB Moscow to Mexico City, 8 April 1944; 220 KGB Moscow to Mexico City, 16 April 1944; 256 KGB Moscow to Mexico City, 29 April 1944; 283 KGB Moscow to Mexico City, 10 May 1944; 303 KGB Moscow to Mexico City, 17 May 1944; 476 KGB Moscow to Mexico City, 29 July 1944; 533 KGB Moscow to Mexico City, 7 September 1944; 653 KGB Moscow to Mexico City, 15 November 1944; 312 KGB Moscow to Mexico City, 11 May 1945; 347 KGB Moscow to Mexico City, 27 May 1945; 472 KGB Moscow to Mexico City, 4 August 1945; 559 KGB Moscow to Mexico City, 7 September 1945; 238 KGB Moscow to Mexico City, 28 April 1946.

134. Venona 974 KGB New York to Moscow, 22 June 1943; 977 KGB New York to Moscow, 22 June 1943. NSA redacted the identify of Havre.

135. Venona 764, 765 KGB New York to Moscow, 24 May 1943; 1056 KGB New York to Moscow, 3 July 1943.

136. Venona 55 KGB San Francisco to Moscow, 8 February 1944; 101 KGB San Francisco to Moscow, 5 March 1944.

137. Venona 1822 KGB Washington to Moscow, 30 March 1945.

138. Venona 1019, 1021, 1024, 1034, KGB New York to Moscow, 29 June 1943; 1056 KGB New York to Moscow, 3 July 1943; 1428 KGB New York to Moscow, 9 October 1944.

139. Venona 1166 KGB New York to Moscow, 16 August 1944.

140. Venona 640 KGB New York to Moscow, 6 May 1944; 823 KGB New York to Moscow, 7 June 1944; 1275 KGB New York to Moscow, 7 September 1944; 1403 KGB New York to Moscow, 5 October 1944; 1754 KGB New York to Moscow, 14 December 1944.

141. Venona 912 KGB New York to Moscow, 27 June 1944; 1403 KGB New York to Moscow, 5 October 1944; 1429 KGB New York to Moscow, 9 October 1944; 164 Moscow to New York, 20 February 1945; 259 Moscow to New York, 21 March 1945.

142. Venona 193 KGB New York to Moscow, 8 February 1944.

143. Venona 3711 KGB Washington to Moscow, 29 June 1945.

144. Venona 210 KGB New York to Moscow, 10 February 1945.

145. Venona 847 KGB New York to Moscow, 14 June 1944.

146. Venona 294 KGB San Francisco to Moscow, 31 May 1945.

147. Venona 1148 KGB New York to Moscow, 14 July 1943; 1930 KGB New York to Moscow, 21 November 1943.

148. Venona 927–928 GRU New York to Moscow, 16 June 1943; 989 GRU New York to Moscow, 24 June 1943; 1116 GRU New York to Moscow, 9 July 1943; 1456 GRU New York to Moscow, 8 September 1943.

149. Venona 917 KGB New York to Moscow, 28 June 1944; 943 KGB New York to Moscow, 4 July 1944; 971 KGB New York to Moscow, 11 July 1944.

150. Venona 1275 KGB New York to Moscow, 7 September 1944.

151. Venona 1427 GRU New York to Moscow, 1 September 1943.

152. Venona 880 KGB New York to Moscow, 8 June 1943. Bella Joseph is identified as Colleague in Weinstein and Vassiliev, *The Haunted Wood*.

153. Venona 880 KGB New York to Moscow, 8 June 1943; 1454 KGB New York to Moscow, 13 October 1944; 1464 KGB New York to Moscow, 14 October 1944.

154. Venona 975 KGB New York to Moscow, 11 July 1944.

155. Venona 652 KGB New York to Moscow, 9 May 1944; 1403 KGB New York to Moscow, 5 October 1944; 1716 KGB New York to Moscow, 5 December 1944.

156. Venona 1000 KGB New York to Moscow, 24 June 1943; 1136 KGB New York to Moscow, 13 July 1943; 1205 KGB New York to Moscow, 22 July 1943.

157. Venona 1403 KGB New York to Moscow, 5 October 1944; 1429 KGB New York to Moscow, 9 October 1944; 1557 KGB New York to Moscow, 6 November 1944; 1818 KGB New York to Moscow, 26 December 1944. The NSA redacted Karl's identify. There is also a cover name Karl, also redacted, in the 1945 message traffic of the San Francisco KGB: Venona 433 KGB San Francisco to Moscow, 11 August 1945.

158. Venona 998 KGB New York to Moscow, 15 July 1944.

159. Venona 1694 KGB New York to Moscow, 16 October 1943; 221 KGB New York to Moscow, 12 February 1944; 486 KGB New York to Moscow, 11 April 1944; 546 KGB New York to Moscow, 20 April 1944; 605 KGB New York to Moscow, 2 May 1944; 618 KGB New York to Moscow, 4 May 1944; 638 KGB New York to Moscow, 6 May 1944; 676 KGB New York to Moscow, 12 May 1944; 749 KGB New York to Moscow, 26 May 1944; 942 KGB New York to Moscow, 4 July 1944; 976 KGB New York to Moscow, 11 July 1944; 1015 KGB New York to Moscow, 22 July 1944; 1020 KGB New York to Moscow, 20 July 1944; 1050 KGB New York to Moscow, 26 July 1944; 1087 KGB New York to Moscow, 30 July 1944; 1190 KGB New York to Moscow, 21 August 1944; 1196 KGB New York to Moscow, 22 August 1944; 1220 KGB New York to Moscow, 26 August 1944; 1251 KGB New York to Moscow, 2 September 1944; 1266 KGB New York to Moscow, 6 September 1944; 1313 KGB New York to Moscow, 13 September 1944; 1328 KGB New York to Moscow, 15 September 1944; 1332 KGB New York to Moscow, 18 September 1944; 1337 KGB New York to Moscow, 19 September 1944; 1351 KGB New York to Moscow, 23 September 1944; 1370 KGB New York to Moscow, 27 September 1944; 1410 KGB New York to Moscow, 6 October 1944; 1411 KGB New York to Moscow, 6 October 1944; 1457 KGB New York to Moscow, 14 October 1944; 1470 KGB New York to Moscow, 17 October 1944; 1512 KGB New York to Moscow, 24 October 1944; 1522 KGB New York to Moscow, 27 October 1944; 49 KGB Moscow to New York, 19 January 1944.

160. Venona 326 KGB Moscow to New York, 5 April 1945; 3614–3615 KGB Washington to Moscow, 22 June 1945.

161. Venona 1234 KGB New York to Moscow, 29 August 1944.

162. Venona 726–729 KGB New York to Moscow, 22 May 1942; 1234 KGB New York to Moscow, 29 August 1944; 325 KGB Moscow to New York, 17 May 1942.

163. Venona 823 KGB New York to Moscow, 7 June 1944; 864 KGB New York to Moscow, 16 June 1944; 928 KGB New York to Moscow, 1 July 1944; 956, 957 KGB New York to Moscow, 6 July 1944; 1146 KGB New York to Moscow, 10 August 1944; 1337 KGB New York to Moscow, 19 September 1944; 1509 KGB New York to Moscow, 23 October 1944.

164. Venona 1337 KGB New York to Moscow, 19 September 1944.

165. Venona 1462 KGB New York to Moscow, 9 September 1943; 913 KGB New York to Moscow, 27 June 1944; 1016 KGB New York to Moscow, 20 July 1944; 1039–1041 KGB New York to Moscow, 24–25 July 1944; 1397 KGB New York to Moscow, 4 October 1944.

166. Venona 1251 KGB New York to Moscow, 2 September 1944; 1332 KGB New York to Moscow, 18 September 1944; 1582 KGB New York to Moscow, 12 November 1944; 1636 KGB New York to Moscow, 21 November 1944; 1803 KGB New York to Moscow, 22 December 1944; 50 KGB New York to Moscow, 11 January 1945; 1052 KGB New York to Moscow, 5 July 1945; 275 KGB Moscow to New York, 25 March 1945; 337 KGB Moscow to New York, 8 April 1945. Koral is identified as Berg in Weinstein and Vassiliev, *The Haunted Wood.*

167. Venona 1251 KGB New York to Moscow, 2 September 1944; 1524 KGB New York to Moscow, 27 October 1944; 1582 KGB New York to Moscow, 12 November 1944; 1636 KGB New York to Moscow, 21 November 1944; 1791 KGB New York to Moscow, 20 December 1944; 1052 KGB New York to Moscow, 5 July 1945; 337 KGB Moscow to New York, 8 April 1945.

168. Venona 705 KGB New York to Moscow, 17 May 1944; 734 KGB New York to Moscow, 21 May 1944; 738 KGB New York to Moscow, 23 May 1944; 789 KGB New York to Moscow, 1 June 1944; 847B, 848 KGB New York to Moscow, 15 June 1944; 998 KGB New York to Moscow, 15 July 1944; 1178 KGB New York to Moscow, 17 August 1944; 1291 KGB New York to Moscow, 9 September 1944; 1312 KGB New York to Moscow, 14 September 1944; 1313 KGB New York to Moscow, 13 September 1944; 1433, 1435 New York to Moscow, 10 October 1944; 1506 KGB New York to Moscow, 23 October 1944; 1535, 1537, 1538 KGB New York to Moscow, 28 October 1944; 777–779 KGB New York to Moscow, 25 May 1945.

169. Venona 588 KGB New York to Moscow, 29 April 1944; 687 KGB New York to Moscow, 13 May 1944; 1015 KGB New York to Moscow, 22 July 1944; 1163 KGB New York to Moscow, 15 August 1944. NSA and FBI analysts list the cover name Mole as unidentified, but the fit between the information reported by Mole and Kramer's activities at the time is extremely tight. Mole also appears only after Plumb, Kramer's prior cover name, disappears. Venona 3612 KGB Washington to Moscow, 22 June 1945; 3640 KGB Washington to Moscow, 23 June 1945; 3655 KGB Washington to Moscow, 25 June 1945; 3706 KGB Washington to Moscow, 29 June 1945; 3709 KGB Washington to Moscow, 29 June 1945; 3710 KGB Washington to Moscow, 29 June 1945.

170. Venona 613–614 KGB New York to Moscow, 3 May 1944; 654 KGB New York to Moscow, 9 May 1944; 724 KGB New York to Moscow, 19 May 1944; 1145 KGB New York to Moscow, 10 August 1944; 1403 KGB New York to Moscow, 5 October 1944; 87 KGB New York to Moscow, 19 January 1945; 229 KGB Moscow to New York, 15 March 1945.

171. Venona 833 KGB New York to Moscow, 10 June 1942; 929–930 KGB New York to Moscow, 17 June 1943; 936 KGB New York to Moscow, 17 June 1943; 952 KGB New York to Moscow, 21 June 1943; 985–986 KGB New York to Moscow, 23 June 1943; 1120 KGB New York to Moscow, 10 July 1943; 1251 KGB New York to Moscow, 2 September 1944; 1322 KGB New York to Moscow, 15 September 1944; 1404 KGB New York to Moscow, 5 October 1944; 1438 KGB New York to Moscow, 10 October 1944; 1449 KGB New York to Moscow, 12 October 1944; 1584 KGB New York to Moscow, 12 November 1944; 1585 KGB New York to Moscow, 12 November 1944; 1586 KGB New York to Moscow, 12 November 1944; 1699 KGB New York to Moscow, 2 December 1944; 1714 KGB New York to Moscow, 5 December 1944; 18–19 KGB New York to Moscow, 4 January 1945; 94 KGB New York to Moscow, 23 January 1945; 243 KGB New York to Moscow, 18 March 1945.

172. Venona 851 KGB New York to Moscow, 15 June 1944; 928 KGB New York to Moscow, 1 July 1944; 1154 KGB New York to Moscow, 12 August 1944; 1198 KGB New York to Moscow, 23 August 1944; 433 KGB San Francisco to Moscow, 11 August 1945; 483–484 KGB San Francisco to Moscow, 13 September 1945. Venona 1136 KGB New York to Moscow, 8 August 1944, reports confidential information from Laird's office, and he is the obvious source, but the message does not clearly state that he is.

173. Venona 580–581 San Francisco to Moscow, 13 November 1945.

174. Venona 700 KGB New York to Moscow, 17 May 1944; 759–760 KGB New York to Moscow, 27 May 1944; 761 KGB New York to Moscow, 27 May 1944; 956, 957 KGB New York to Moscow, 6 July 1944; 1000 KGB New York to Moscow, 15 July 1944; 1135 KGB New York to Moscow, 8 August 1944; 1229 KGB New York to Moscow, 29 August 1944.

175. Venona 1103 GRU New York to Moscow, 8 July 1943.

176. Venona 782 KGB New York to Moscow, 26 May 1943; 880 KGB New York to Moscow, 8 June 1943; 887 KGB New York to Moscow, 9 June 1943; 830 KGB New York to Moscow, 9 June 1944; 1325–1326 KGB New York to Moscow, 15 September 1944; 1354 KGB New York to Moscow, 22 September 1944 (does not mention Lee by name but is a follow-up to Venona 1325–1326); 1353 KGB New York to Moscow, 23 September 1944; 1437 KGB New York to Moscow, 10 October 1944; 954 KGB Moscow to New York, 20 September 1944. In addition to these, in Venona 726–729 KGB New York to Moscow, 22 May 1942, the KGB reports on those sections of the OSS of chief interest to the Soviets and mentions in a partially deciphered but garbled section the name Lee. This may be a reference to Duncan Lee, who was about to join the OSS and was already in touch with Golos through Mary Price.

177. Venona 975 KGB New York to Moscow, 11 July 1944.

178. Venona 512 KGB San Francisco to Moscow, 7 December 1943.

179. Venona 31 KGB San Francisco to Moscow, 17 January 1944; 133 KGB San Francisco to Moscow, 29 March 1944.

180. Venona 1031 KGB New York to Moscow, 1 July 1943.

181. Venona 3616, 3617, 3619, 3620 KGB Washington to Moscow, 22 June 1945.

182. Venona 373 KGB Moscow to New York, 3 June 1942.

183. Venona 602 KGB New York to Moscow, 2 May 1944; 982 KGB New York to Moscow, 12 July 1944.

184. Venona 981 KGB New York to Moscow, 23 June 1943; 1239 KGB New York to Moscow, 30 August 1944; 154 KGB Moscow to New York, 16 February 1945.

185. Venona 1132, 1133 KGB New York to Moscow, 13 July 1943.

186. Venona 882 GRU New York to Moscow, 8 June 1943.

187. Venona 1050 KGB New York to Moscow, 26 July 1944; 1403 KGB New York to Moscow, 5 October 1944; 1557 KGB New York to Moscow, 6 November 1944; 1706 KGB New York to Moscow, 4 December 1944.

188. Venona 1582 KGB New York to Moscow, 12 November 1944; 1635 KGB New York to Moscow, 21 November 1944; 11 KGB New York to Moscow, 4 January 1945; 275 KGB Moscow to New York, 25 March 1945; 337 KGB Moscow to New York, 8 April 1945.

189. Venona 952 GRU Washington to Moscow, 4 May 1943.

190. Venona 939 KGB New York to Moscow, 3 July 1944.

191. Venona 1934 Naval GRU Washington to Moscow, 11 August 1943.

192. Venona 117 KGB San Francisco to Moscow, 11 March 1943.

193. Venona 1337 KGB New York to Moscow, 19 September 1944; 71 KGB New York to Moscow, 17 January 1945.

194. Venona 629 KGB New York to Moscow, 5 May 1944; 687 KGB New York to Moscow, 13 May 1944; 769, 771 KGB New York to Moscow, 30 May 1944; 179, 180 KGB Moscow to New York, 25 February 1945. Magdoff is identified as Tan in Weinstein and Vassiliev, *The Haunted Wood.*

195. Venona 1276 GRU New York to Moscow, 1943; 193 KGB New York to Moscow, 8 February 1944; 620 KGB New York to Moscow, 4 May 1944; 622 KGB New York to Moscow, 4 May 1944; 1077 KGB New York to Moscow, 29 July 1944; 1403 KGB New York to Moscow, 5 October 1944; 1680 KGB New York to Moscow, 30 November 1944; 1706 KGB New York to Moscow, 4 December 1944; 1755 KGB New York to Moscow, 14 December 1944.

196. Venona 450 KGB San Francisco to Moscow, 1 November 1943; 472 KGB San Francisco to Moscow, 9 November 1943; 161 KGB San Francisco to Moscow, 13 April 1944; 136 KGB San Francisco to Moscow, 2 April 1945; 138 KGB San Francisco to Moscow, 3 April 1945; 167 KGB San Francisco to Moscow, 16 April 1945.

197. Venona 676 KGB New York to Moscow, 12 May 1944; 1196 KGB New York to Moscow, 22 August 1944; 1337 KGB New York to Moscow, 19 September 1944; 1351 KGB New York to Moscow, 23 September 1944; 1370 KGB New York to Moscow, 27 September 1944; 1411 KGB New York to Moscow, 6 October 1944; 1429 KGB New York to Moscow, 9 October 1944; 1430 KGB New York to Moscow, 10 October 1944.

198. Venona 766 KGB New York to Moscow, 24 May 1943; 1055 KGB New York to Moscow, 2 July 1943; 823 KGB New York to Moscow, 7 June 1944; 881 KGB New York to Moscow, 20 June 1944; 958 KGB New York to Moscow, 7 July 1944.

199. Venona 221 KGB Mexico City to Moscow, 31 March 1944; 327 KGB Mexico City to Moscow, 3 May 1944; 283 KGB Moscow to Mexico City, 10 May 1944.

200. Venona 1116 GRU New York to Moscow, 9 July 1943; 1456 GRU New York to Moscow, 8 September 1943.

201. Venona 694 KGB New York to Moscow, 15 May 1943; 1044 KGB New York to Moscow, 2 July 1943; 1185 KGB New York to Moscow, 21 July 1943; 1031 KGB New York to Moscow, 24 July 1944; 1143–1144 KGB New York to Moscow, 10 August 1944; 1313 KGB New York to Moscow, 13 September 1944; 1337 KGB New York to Moscow, 19 September 1944; 1430 KGB New York to Moscow, 10 October 1944; 1470 KGB New York to Moscow, 17 October 1944; 1512 KGB New York to Moscow, 24 October 1944; 1522 KGB New York to Moscow, 27 October 1944; 1613 KGB New York to Moscow, 18 November 1944; 1637 KGB New York to Moscow, 21 November 1944; 1716 KGB New York to Moscow, 5 December 1944; 77 KGB New York to Moscow, 17 January 1945; 55 KGB Moscow to New York, 10 January 1943.

202. Venona 854 KGB New York to Moscow, 5 June 1943; 1100 KGB New York to Moscow, 7 July 1943.

203. Venona 727 KGB New York to Moscow, 20 May 1944; 751–752 KGB New York to Moscow, 26 May 1944; 826 KGB New York to Moscow, 7 June 1944; 846 KGB New York to Moscow, 14 June 1944; 851 KGB New York to Moscow, 15 June 1944; 1143–1144 KGB New York to Moscow, 10 August 1944.

204. Venona 450 KGB San Francisco to Moscow, 1 November 1943; 472 KGB San Francisco to Moscow, 9 November 1943; 511 KGB San Francisco to Moscow, 7 December 1943; 539 KGB San Francisco to Moscow, 31 December 1943; 147 KGB San Francisco to Moscow, 27 March 1944; 68 KGB San Francisco to Moscow, 27 February 1945.

205. Venona 1131 GRU New York to Moscow, 12 July 1943; 1348 GRU New York to Moscow, 16 August 1943; 1350 GRU New York to Moscow, 17 August 1943; 1373 GRU New York to Moscow, 23 August 1943; 1456 GRU New York to Moscow, 8 September 1943.

206. Venona 842 KGB New York to Moscow, 3 June 1943; 1179 KGB New York to Moscow, 20 July 1943; 1625 KGB New York to Moscow, 3 October 1943; 1681 KGB New York to Moscow, 13 October 1943.

207. Venona 1681 KGB New York to Moscow, 13 October 1943; "Comintern Apparatus Summary Report."

208. Venona 1325 GRU New York to Moscow, 11 August 1943.

209. Venona 2505–2512 Naval GRU Washington to Moscow, 31 December 1942; 1016 Naval GRU Washington to Moscow, 10 May 1943; 1040–1041 Naval GRU Washington to Moscow, 13 May 1943; 1080 Naval GRU Washington to Moscow, 19 May 1943; 1209 Naval GRU Washington to Moscow, 5 June 1943; 1252 Naval GRU Washington to Moscow, 10 June 1943; 1271 Naval GRU Washington to Moscow, 12 June 1943; 1348 Naval GRU Washington to Moscow, 19 June 1943; 1600 Naval GRU Washington to Moscow, 12 July 1943; 1902 Naval GRU Washington to Moscow, 8 August 1943; 1983 Naval GRU Washington to Moscow, 14 August 1943; 2124 Naval GRU Washington to Moscow, 27 August 1943; 126 Naval GRU Moscow to Washington, 22 January 1943; 394 Naval GRU Moscow to Washington, 5 March 1943; 452 Naval GRU Moscow to Washington, 16 March 1943; 484 Naval GRU Moscow to Washington, 20 March 1943; 611 Naval GRU Moscow to Washington, 8 April 1943; 835 Naval GRU Moscow to Washington, 12 May 1943; 846 Naval GRU Moscow to Washington, 14 May 1943; 863 Naval GRU Moscow to Washington, 17 May 1943; 1006 Naval GRU Moscow to Washington, 10 June 1943.

210. Venona 895 GRU New York to Moscow, 10 June 1943; 927–928 GRU New York to Moscow, 16 June 1943; 987 GRU New York to Moscow, 24 June 1943; 1014 GRU New York to Moscow, 28 June 1943; 1295 GRU New York to Moscow, 6 August 1943; 1456 GRU New York to Moscow, 8 September 1943; 1008 KGB New York to Moscow, 26 June 1943; 985–986 KGB New York to Moscow, 23 June 1943.

211. Venona 1579 New York GRU to Moscow, 28 September 1943.

212. Venona 943 KGB New York to Moscow, 4 July 1944; 1341 KGB New York to Moscow, 21 September 1944.

213. Venona 1824 KGB New York to Moscow, 27 December 1944; 4–5 KGB New York to Moscow, 3 January 1945; 18–19 KGB New York to Moscow, 4 January 1945.

214. Venona 513 KGB San Francisco to Moscow, 7 December 1943; 268 KGB San Francisco to Moscow, 21 June 1944.

215. Venona 1699 KGB New York to Moscow, 2 December 1944.

216. Venona 172 KGB San Francisco to Moscow, 18 April 1945; 69 KGB San Francisco to Moscow, 20 February 1946.

217. Venona 1009 KGB New York to Moscow, 19 July 1944; 1465 KGB New York to Moscow, 14 October 1944.

218. Venona 846 KGB New York to Moscow, 3 June 1943; 854 KGB New York to Moscow, 5 June 1943; 880 KGB New York to Moscow, 8 June 1943; 917 KGB New York to Moscow, 15 June 1943. There is also a Ruff in a 1945 KGB message, but that is clearly a different person from the Ruff of 1943. 876 KGB New York to Moscow, 6 June 1945. The identification of Neumann as Ruff is in Weinstein and Vassiliev, *The Haunted Wood*.

219. Venona 863 KGB New York to Moscow, 16 June 1944; 1251 KGB New York to Moscow, 2 September 1944; 1657 KGB New York to Moscow, 27 November 1944; 200 Moscow to New York, 6 March 1945; 325 Moscow to New York, 5 April 1945.

220. Venona 943 KGB New York to Moscow, 4 July 1944. Separately there was also a Nina in KGB traffic who was a clerical worker in the KGB office.

221. Venona 1031 KGB New York to Moscow, 1 July 1943; 1045 KGB New York to Moscow, 2 July 1943; 1053 KGB New York to Moscow, 2 July 1943; 1582 KGB New York to Moscow, 12 November 1944.

222. Venona 846 KGB New York to Moscow, 3 June 1943; 1644 KGB New York to Moscow, 9 October 1943; 336 KGB Moscow to New York, 8 April 1945.

223. Venona 801 KGB New York to Moscow, 28 May 1943; 1054 KGB New York to Moscow, 5 July 1945.

224. Venona 1002 KGB New York to Moscow, 17 July 1944; 1203 KGB New York to Moscow, 23 August 1944; 1251 KGB New York to Moscow, 2 September 1944; 1275 KGB New York to Moscow, 7 September 1944; 1336 KGB New York to Moscow, 18 September 1944; 1430 KGB New York to Moscow, 10 October 1944; 1829 KGB New York to Moscow, 28 December 1944; 14 KGB New York to Moscow, 4 January 1945.

225. Venona 993 KGB New York to Moscow, 13 July 1944.

226. Venona 1438 KGB New York to Moscow, 10 October 1944; 1586 KGB New York to Moscow, 12 November 1944; 20 KGB New York to Moscow, 4 January 1945; 239 KGB Moscow to New York, 17 March 1945. The link to Aleksandrov is suggested in Venona 1322 KGB New York to Moscow, 15 September 1944.

227. Venona 619 KGB New York to Moscow, 4 May 1944.

228. Venona 1324 GRU New York to Moscow, 11 August 1943; 1350 GRU New York to Moscow, 17 August 1943; 1362 GRU New York to Moscow, 19 August 1943. NSA redacted the identities of two candidates for Oppen.

229. Venona 854 KGB New York to Moscow, 5 June 1943; 934–935 KGB New York to Moscow, 17 June 1943; 952 KGB New York to Moscow, 21 June 1943; 613–614 KGB New York to Moscow, 3 May 1944; 725 KGB New York to Moscow, 19 May 1944; 750 KGB New York to Moscow, 26 May 1944; 163 KGB Moscow to New York, 19 February 1945; 239 KGB Moscow to New York, 17 March 1945; 767 KGB Moscow to New York, July 1945. On Orloff's attempt to gain OSS employment, see Nicholas W. Orloff autobiography and offer of service, attached to Horace W. Peters of OSS X-2 branch to Darwin Marron, 11 August 1944, Office of Strategic Services records, record group 226, entry 171, box 25, folder 370, National Archives and Records Administration, Archives II, College Park, Maryland.

230. Venona 151 KGB San Francisco to Moscow, 1944 March 30.

231. Venona 943 KGB New York to Moscow, 4 July 1944; 1052 KGB New York to Moscow, 26 July 1944; 1251 KGB New York to Moscow, 2 September 1944; 1403

KGB New York to Moscow, 5 October 1944; 1661–1662 KGB New York to Moscow, 28 November 1944.

232. Venona 1517 KGB New York to Moscow, 25 October 1944.

233. Venona 1465 KGB New York to Moscow, 14 October 1944; 1661–1662 KGB New York to Moscow, 28 November 1944.

234. Venona 864 KGB New York to Moscow, 16 June 1944; 1206 KGB New York to Moscow, KGB New York to Moscow, 23 August 1944; 1828 KGB New York to Moscow, 28 December 1944.

235. Venona 717 KGB New York to Moscow, 10 May 1944; 732 KGB New York to Moscow, 20 May 1944; 854 KGB New York to Moscow, 16 June 1944; 1048 KGB New York to Moscow, 25 July 1944; 1251 KGB New York to Moscow, 2 September 1944; 1314 KGB New York to Moscow, 14 September 1944; 1491 KGB New York to Moscow, 22 October 1944; 1536 KGB New York to Moscow, 28 October 1944; 1797 KGB New York to Moscow, 20 December 1944; 954 KGB Moscow to New York, 20 September 1944; 154 KGB Moscow to New York, 16 February 1945; 224 KGB Moscow to New York, 13 March 1945; 305 KGB Moscow to New York, 1 April 1945.

236. Venona 588 KGB New York to Moscow, 29 April 1944; 687 KGB New York to Moscow, 13 May 1944; 769, 771 KGB New York to Moscow, 30 May 1944; 1003 KGB New York to Moscow, 18 July 1944; 1015 KGB New York to Moscow, 22 July 1944; 1214 KGB New York to Moscow, 25 August 1944; 79 KGB New York to Moscow, 18 January 1945; 1823, 1824, 1825 KGB Washington to Moscow, 30 March 1945; 3707 KGB Washington to Moscow, 29 June 1945; 3708 KGB Washington to Moscow, 29 June 1945; 3713, 3715 KGB Washington to Moscow, 29 June 1945.

237. Venona 232 KGB San Francisco to Moscow, 1944 May 25.

238. Venona 995 KGB New York to Moscow, 24 June 1943; 1403 KGB New York to Moscow, 5 October 1944; 1559 KGB New York to Moscow, 6 November 1944; 154 KGB Moscow to New York, 16 February 1945; 305 KGB Moscow to New York, 1 April 1945.

239. Venona 882 GRU New York to Moscow, 8 June 1943; 1325 GRU New York to Moscow, 11 August 1943; 1393 GRU New York to Moscow, 25 August 1943; 1456 GRU New York to Moscow, 8 September 1943.

240. Venona 69 KGB San Francisco to Moscow, 20 February 1946. The cover name Philip also occurs in a number of Venona KGB San Francisco cables from the first half of 1945, but that Philip was clearly a KGB officer working at the Soviet consulate.

241. Venona 1930 KGB New York to Moscow, 21 November 1943; 853 KGB New York to Moscow, 16 June 1944.

242. Venona 619 KGB New York to Moscow, 4 May 1944; 1020 KGB New York to Moscow, 20 July 1944; 1332 KGB New York to Moscow, 18 September 1944; 1715 KGB New York to Moscow, 5 December 1944; 295 KGB Moscow to New York, 30 March 1945.

243. Venona 1715 KGB New York to Moscow, 5 December 1944.

244. Venona 621 KGB New York to Moscow, 4 May 1944; 853 KGB New York to Moscow, 16 June 1944.

245. Venona 1328 KGB New York to Moscow, 12 August 1943.

246. Venona 941 KGB New York to Moscow, 4 July 1944; 943 KGB New York to Moscow, 4 July 1944; 1403 KGB New York to Moscow, 5 October 1944; 1559 KGB New York to Moscow, 6 November 1944.

247. Venona 1151 KGB New York to Moscow, 12 August 1944.

248. Venona 864 KGB New York to Moscow, 16 June 1944; 1341 KGB New York to Moscow, 21 September 1944.

249. Venona 1132–1133 KGB New York to Moscow, 13 July 1943; 1930 KGB New York to Moscow, 21 November 1943.

250. Venona 786–787 KGB New York to Moscow, 26 May 1943.

251. Venona 868 KGB New York to Moscow, 8 June 1943; 1065 KGB New York to Moscow, 28 July 1944.

252. Venona 682 KGB New York to Moscow, 12 May 1944.

253. Venona 961 KGB New York to Moscow, 21 June 1943; 972, 979, 983 KGB New York to Moscow, 22–23 June 1943; 1405 KGB New York to Moscow, 27 August 1943.

254. Venona 640 KGB New York to Moscow, 6 May 1944; 1251 KGB New York to Moscow, 2 September 1944.

255. Venona 1074–1075 GRU New York to Moscow, 5 July 1943; 1172–1173 GRU New York to Moscow, 19 July 1943; 1243–1244 GRU New York to Moscow, 28 July 1943; 1312–1313 GRU New York to Moscow, 9 August 1943; 1456 GRU New York to Moscow, 8 September 1943; 1498–1499 GRU New York to Moscow, 17 September 1943; 1523 GRU New York to Moscow, 21 September 1943.

256. Venona 975 KGB New York to Moscow, 11 July 1944.

257. Venona 1557 KGB New York to Moscow, 6 November 1944.

258. Venona 943 KGB New York to Moscow, 4 July 1944.

259. Venona 1221 KGB New York to Moscow, 26 August 1944.

260. Venona 1579 New York GRU to Moscow, 28 September 1943.

261. Venona 1047 KGB New York to Moscow, 2 July 1943; 918 KGB New York to Moscow, 12 June 1945.

262. Venona 1410 KGB New York to Moscow, 6 October 1944.

263. Venona 227 KGB Moscow to New York, 13 March 1945.

264. Venona 1553 KGB New York to Moscow, 4 November 1944.

265. Venona 1810 KGB New York to Moscow, 23 December 1944.

266. Venona 1340 KGB New York to Moscow, 21 September 1944; 1657 KGB New York to Moscow, 27 November 1944.

267. Venona 628 KGB New York to Moscow, 5 May 1944; 736 KGB New York to Moscow, 22 May 1944; 845 KGB New York to Moscow, 14 June 1944; 911 KGB New York to Moscow, 27 June 1944; 976 KGB New York to Moscow, 11 July 1944; 1053 KGB New York to Moscow, 26 July 1944; 1251 KGB New York to Moscow, 2 September 1944; 1314 KGB New York to Moscow, 14 September 1944; 1327 KGB New York to Moscow, 15 September 1944; 1340 KGB New York to Moscow, 21 September 1944; 1491 KGB New York to Moscow, 22 October 1944; 1600 KGB New York to Moscow, 14 November 1944; 1609 KGB New York to Moscow, 17 November 1944; 1657 KGB New York to Moscow, 27 November 1944; 1715 KGB New York to Moscow, 5 December 1944; 1749–1750 KGB New York to Moscow, 13 December 1944; 1773 KGB New York to Moscow, 16 December 1944; 1797 KGB New York to Moscow, 20 December 1944; 28 KGB New York to Moscow, 8 January 1945; 200 KGB Moscow to New York, 6 March 1945; 325 Moscow to New York, 5 April 1945.

268. Venona 927–928 GRU New York to Moscow, 16 June 1943; 987 GRU New York to Moscow, 24 June 1943; 1116 GRU New York to Moscow, 9 July 1943; 1456 GRU New York to Moscow, 8 September 1943.

269. Venona 917 KGB New York to Moscow, 28 June 1944. NSA redacted the identify of S-2.

270. Venona 186 KGB Moscow to New York, 2 March 1945.

271. Venona 942 KGB New York to Moscow, 4 July 1944; 1015 KGB New York to Moscow, 22 July 1944; 1087 KGB New York to Moscow, 30 July 1944; 1220 KGB

New York to Moscow, 26 August 1944; 1266 KGB New York to Moscow, 6 September 1944; 1313 KGB New York to Moscow, 13 September 1944; 1370 KGB New York to Moscow, 27 September 1944; 1523 KGB New York to Moscow, 27 October 1944; 1649 KGB New York to Moscow, 25 November 1944; 29 KGB New York to Moscow, 8 January 1945; 130 KGB Moscow to New York, 11 February 1945; 446 KGB San Francisco to Moscow, 31 October 1943; 55 KGB San Francisco to Moscow, 8 February 1944; 298 KGB San Francisco to Moscow, 13 July 1944.

272. Venona 232 KGB San Francisco to Moscow, 25 May 1944.

273. Venona 628 KGB New York to Moscow, 5 May 1944; 1600 KGB New York to Moscow, 14 November 1944; 1715 KGB New York to Moscow, 5 December 1944; 1749–1750 KGB New York to Moscow, 13 December 1944.

274. Venona 1585 KGB New York to Moscow, 12 November 1944; 1699 KGB New York to Moscow, 2 December 1944; 94 KGB New York to Moscow, 23 January 1945.

275. Venona 579 KGB New York to Moscow, 28 April 1944; 1661–1662 KGB New York to Moscow, 28 November 1944.

276. Venona 283 KGB New York to Moscow, 24 February 1944; 598–599 KGB New York to Moscow, 2 May 1944; 605 KGB New York to Moscow, 2 May 1944; 619 KGB New York to Moscow, 4 May 1944; 749 KGB New York to Moscow, 26 May 1944; 911 KGB New York to Moscow, 27 June 1944; 939 KGB New York to Moscow, 3 July 1944; 1020 KGB New York to Moscow, 20 July 1944; 1029 KGB New York to Moscow, 22 July 1944; 1166 KGB New York to Moscow, 16 August 1944; 1221 KGB New York to Moscow, 26 August 1944; 1313 KGB New York to Moscow, 13 September 1944; 1328 KGB New York to Moscow, 15 September 1944; 1332 KGB New York to Moscow, 18 September 1944; 1337 KGB New York to Moscow, 19 September 1944; 1340 KGB New York to Moscow, 21 September 1944; 1400 KGB New York to Moscow, 5 October 1944; 1410 KGB New York to Moscow, 6 October 1944; 1430 KGB New York to Moscow, 10 October 1944; 1457 KGB New York to Moscow, 14 October 1944; 1512 KGB New York to Moscow, 24 October 1944; 1522 KGB New York to Moscow, 27 October 1944; 1553 KGB New York to Moscow, 4 November 1944; 1637 KGB New York to Moscow, 21 November 1944; 1668 KGB New York to Moscow, 29 November 1944; 1715 KGB New York to Moscow, 5 December 1944; 1803 KGB New York to Moscow, 22 December 1944; 1818 KGB New York to Moscow, 26 December 1944; 94 KGB New York to Moscow, 23 January 1945; 49 KGB Moscow to New York, 19 January 1944; 14 KGB New York to Moscow, 4 January 1945; 194 KGB Moscow to New York, 3 March 1945; 295 KGB Moscow to New York, 30 March 1945.

277. Venona 1456 GRU New York to Moscow, 8 September 1943; 1579 GRU New York to Moscow, 28 September 1943.

278. Venona 726–729 KGB New York to Moscow, 22 May 1942; 1681 KGB New York to Moscow, 13 October 1943; 207 KGB Moscow to New York, 8 March 1945.

279. Venona 823 KGB New York to Moscow, 7 June 1944; 881 KGB New York to Moscow, 20 June 1944; 1203 KGB New York to Moscow, 23 August 1944; 1275 KGB New York to Moscow, 7 September 1944.

280. Venona 50 KGB New York to Moscow, 11 January 1945.

281. Venona 49 KGB Moscow to New York, 19 January 1944.

282. Venona 764, 765 KGB New York to Moscow, 24 May 1943; 886 KGB New York to Moscow, 9 June 1943; 967–968 KGB New York to Moscow, 22 June 1943; 1234 KGB New York to Moscow, 29 August 1944; 1403 KGB New York to Moscow, 5 October 1944.

283. Venona 1589, 1590 KGB New York to Moscow, 30 September 1943; 886 KGB New York to Moscow, 22 June 1944; 943 KGB New York to Moscow, 4 July 1944.

284. Venona 210 KGB Moscow to New York, 9 March 1945.

285. Venona 1491 KGB New York to Moscow, 22 October 1944; 1536 KGB New York to Moscow, 28 October 1944; 1609 KGB New York to Moscow, 17 November 1944; 1797 KGB New York to Moscow, 20 December 1944; 210 KGB Moscow to New York, 9 March 1945; 224 KGB Moscow to New York, 13 March 1945.

286. Venona 928 KGB New York to Moscow, 30 June 1943; 1057 KGB New York to Moscow, 3 July 1943; 1081 KGB New York to Moscow, 6 July 1943; 1317 KGB New York to Moscow, 10 August 1943; 1243 KGB New York to Moscow, 31 August 1944; 1463 KGB New York to Moscow, 14 October 1944; 12, 13, 15, 16 KGB New York to Moscow, 4 January 1945.

287. Venona 1508 KGB New York to Moscow, 23 October 1944; 1635 KGB New York to Moscow, 21 November 1944; 12, 13, 15, 16 New York to Moscow, 4 January 1945; 337 KGB Moscow to New York, 8 April 1945.

288. Venona 678–682 KGB New York to Moscow, 14 May 1942; 746–748 KGB New York to Moscow, 25 May 1942; 763–765 KGB New York to Moscow, 27 May 1942; 833 KGB New York to Moscow, 10 June 1942; 732, 735 KGB New York to Moscow, 21 May 1943; 794–799 KGB New York to Moscow, 28 May 1943; 888 KGB New York to Moscow, 9 June 1943; 977 KGB New York to Moscow, 22 June 1943; 1017, 1022 KGB New York to Moscow, 29–30 June 1943; 1057 KGB New York to Moscow, 3 July 1943; 1176, 1177, 1178 KGB New York to Moscow, 20 July 1943; 1189 KGB New York to Moscow, 21 July 1943; 1431 KGB New York to Moscow, 2 September 1943; 278 KGB New York to Moscow, 23 February 1944; 588 KGB New York to Moscow, 29 April 1944; 655 KGB New York to Moscow, 9 May 1944; 687 KGB New York to Moscow, 13 May 1944; 827 KGB New York to Moscow, 7 June 1944; 918 KGB New York to Moscow, 28 June 1944; 927 KGB New York to Moscow, 1 July 1944; 973 KGB New York to Moscow, 11 July 1944; 1003 KGB New York to Moscow, 18 July 1944; 1155 KGB New York to Moscow, 12 August 1944; 1243 KGB New York to Moscow, 31 August 1944; 1388, 1389 KGB New York to Moscow, 1 October 1944; 1463 KGB New York to Moscow, 14 October 1944; 1469 KGB New York to Moscow, 17 October 1944; 1481–1482 KGB New York to Moscow, 18 October 1944; 1483 KGB New York to Moscow, 18 October 1944; 1508 KGB New York to Moscow, 23 October 1944; 1606 KGB New York to Moscow, 16 November 1944; 1619–1620 KGB New York to Moscow, 20 November 1944; 1634 KGB New York to Moscow, 20 November 1944; 1635 KGB New York to Moscow, 21 November 1944; 1691 KGB New York to Moscow, 1 December 1944; 1751–1753 KGB New York to Moscow, 13 December 1944; 1787, 1788 KGB New York to Moscow, 19 December 1944; 1789 KGB New York to Moscow, 19 December 1944; 1798 KGB New York to Moscow, 20 December 1944; 1821 KGB New York to Moscow, 26 December 1944; 12, 13, 15, 16 KGB New York to Moscow, 4 January 1945; 14 KGB New York to Moscow, 4 January 1945; 21 KGB New York to Moscow, 8 January 1945; 55 KGB New York to Moscow, 15 January 1945; 71 KGB New York to Moscow, 17 January 1945; 79 KGB New York to Moscow, 18 January 1945; 82 KGB New York to Moscow, 18 January 1945; 83 KGB New York to Moscow, 18 January 1945; 205 KGB New York to Moscow, 10 February 1945; 143 KGB Moscow to New York, 15 February 1945; 173 KGB Moscow to New

York, 22 February 1945; 179, 180 KGB Moscow to New York, 25 February 1945; 186 KGB Moscow to New York, 2 March 1945; 195 KGB Moscow to New York, 3 March 1945; 248 KGB Moscow to New York, 19 March 1945; 253 KGB Moscow to New York, 20 March 1945; 268 KGB Moscow to New York, 24 March 1945; 292 KGB Moscow to New York, 29 March 1945; 328 KGB Moscow to New York, 6 April 1945; 336 KGB Moscow to New York, 8 April 1945; 337 KGB Moscow to New York, 8 April 1945.

289. Venona 1824 KGB New York to Moscow, 27 December 1944.

290. Venona 912 KGB New York to Moscow, 27 June 1944; 1267 KGB New York to Moscow, 6 September 1944; 1332 KGB New York to Moscow, 18 September 1944; 1370 KGB New York to Moscow, 27 September 1944.

291. Venona 943 KGB New York to Moscow, 4 July 1944; 976 KGB New York to Moscow, 11 July 1944; 1251 KGB New York to Moscow, 2 September 1944; 50 KGB New York to Moscow, 11 January 1945.

292. Venona 992 KGB New York to Moscow, 24 June 1943; 1086 KGB New York to Moscow, 6 July 1943; 625 KGB New York to Moscow, 5 May 1944; 851 KGB New York to Moscow, 15 June 1944; 1146 KGB New York to Moscow, 10 August 1944; 1251 KGB New York to Moscow, 2 September 1944; 1353 KGB New York to Moscow, 23 September 1944; 1449 KGB New York to Moscow, 12 October 1944; 1754 KGB New York to Moscow, 14 December 1944; 48 KGB New York to Moscow, 11 January 1945; 776 KGB New York to Moscow, 25 May 1945.

293. Venona 791–792 KGB New York to Moscow, 27 May 1943; 1118 KGB New York to Moscow, 9 July 1943; 1146 KGB New York to Moscow, 10 August 1944; 1353 KGB New York to Moscow, 23 September 1944; 1517 KGB New York to Moscow, 25 October 1944; 1553 KGB New York to Moscow, 4 November 1944; 1789 KGB New York to Moscow, 19 December 1944; 48 KGB New York to Moscow, 11 January 1945; 776 KGB New York to Moscow, 25 May 1945.

294. Venona 1405 KGB New York to Moscow, 27 August 1943; 1403 KGB New York to Moscow, 5 October 1944; 1509 KGB New York to Moscow, 23 October 1944.

295. Venona 1016 KGB New York to Moscow, 20 July 1944; 1042 KGB New York to Moscow, 25 July 1944.

296. Venona 882 GRU New York to Moscow, 8 June 1943; 986 GRU New York to Moscow, 23 June 1943; 1084 GRU New York to Moscow, 6 July 1943; 1433 GRU New York to Moscow, 3 September 1943.

297. Venona 1456 GRU New York to Moscow, 8 September 1943.

298. Venona 812 KGB New York to Moscow, 29 May 1943.

299. Venona 583 KGB New York to Moscow, 28 April 1943; 867 KGB New York to Moscow, 8 June 1943; 194 KGB Moscow to New York, 3 March 1945.

300. Venona 998 KGB New York to Moscow, 24 June 1943; 943 KGB New York to Moscow, 4 July 1944; 1403 KGB New York to Moscow, 5 October 1944; 1559 KGB New York to Moscow, 6 November 1944; 780, 792 KGB New York to Moscow, 25 and 26 May 1945.

301. Venona 669 KGB New York to Moscow, 11 May 1944; 981 KGB New York to Moscow, 12 July 1944; 1142 KGB New York to Moscow, 10 August 1944.

302. Venona 734 KGB New York to Moscow, 21 May 1944; 1039–1041 KGB New York to Moscow, 24–25 July 1944; 1393 KGB New York to Moscow, 3 October 1944; 1814, 1815 KGB New York to Moscow, 23 December 1944.

303. Venona 704 Naval GRU Washington to Moscow, 1 April 1943; 1934 Naval GRU Washington to Moscow, 11 August 1943; 1969 Naval GRU Washington to Moscow, 13 August 1943; 115 Naval GRU Moscow to Washington, 20 January 1943; 155

Naval GRU Moscow to Washington, 26 January 1943; 1194 Naval GRU Moscow to Washington, 10 July 1943; 1251 KGB New York to Moscow, 2 September 1943.

304. Venona 1824 KGB New York to Moscow, 27 December 1944; 4–5 KGB New York to Moscow, 3 January 1945; 11 KGB New York to Moscow, 4 January 1945; 18–19 KGB New York to Moscow, 4 January 1945.

305. Venona 854 KGB New York to Moscow, 16 June 1942.

306. Venona 927, 928 KGB New York to Moscow, 3 July 1942. "Stevenson" in 1681 KGB New York to Moscow, 13 October 1943, is probably an error for "Stevens." See also Fitin to Dimitrov; 8 July 1942, and Vilkov memo on Stevens, 21 July 1942, both in RTsKhIDNI 495-74-485, and Harvey Klehr, John Earl Haynes, and Fridrikh Igorevich Firsov, *The Secret World of American Communism* (New Haven: Yale University Press, 1995), 299–303.

307. Venona 687 KGB New York to Moscow, 13 May 1944; 769, 771 KGB New York to Moscow, 30 May 1944.

308. Venona 500 KGB San Francisco to Moscow, 27 November 1943; 26 KGB San Francisco to Moscow, 17 January 1944; 39 KGB San Francisco to Moscow, 22 January 1944; 104 KGB San Francisco to Moscow, 5 March 1944; 725 KGB New York to Moscow, 1944 May 19.

309. Venona 132 KGB San Francisco to Moscow, 18 March 1944; 257 KGB San Francisco to Moscow, 7 June 1944; 270 KGB San Francisco to Moscow, 22 June 1944.

310. Venona 1048 KGB New York to Moscow, 25 July 1944; 71 KGB New York to Moscow, 17 January 1945.

311. Venona 756 KGB New York to Moscow, 27 May 1944; 769 and 771 KGB New York to Moscow, 30 May 1944; 940 KGB New York to Moscow, 4 July 1944; 1118 KGB New York to Moscow, 4 August 1944; 1352 KGB New York to Moscow, 23 September 1944. Tenney was not identified as Muse until the appearance in 1999 of Weinstein and Vassiliev, *The Haunted Wood.*

312. Venona 1403 KGB New York to Moscow, 5 October 1944; 1559 KGB New York to Moscow, 6 November 1944.

313. Venona 1056 KGB New York to Moscow, 3 July 1943; 823 KGB New York to Moscow, 7 June 1944; 881 KGB New York to Moscow, 20 June 1944; 1076 KGB New York to Moscow, 29 July 1944; 202 KGB New York to Moscow, 10 February 1945; 116 KGB Moscow to New York, 9 February 1945; 143 KGB Moscow to New York, 15 February 1945.

314. Venona 622 KGB New York to Moscow, 4 May 1943.

315. Venona 927 KGB New York to Moscow, 1 July 1944.

316. Venona 700 KGB New York to Moscow, 17 May 1944; 761 KGB New York to Moscow, 27 May 1944.

317. Venona 928 KGB New York to Moscow, 30 June 1943; 1081 KGB New York to Moscow, 6 July 1943; 278 KGB New York to Moscow, 23 February 1944; 590 KGB New York to Moscow, 29 April 1944; 656 KGB New York to Moscow, 9 May 1944; 927 KGB New York to Moscow, 1 July 1944; 1122 KGB New York to Moscow, 8 August 1944; 1214 KGB New York to Moscow, 25 August 1944; 1243 KGB New York to Moscow, 31 August 1944; 1251 KGB New York to Moscow, 2 September 1944; 1325, 1326 KGB New York to Moscow, 15 September 1944; 1388, 1389 KGB New York to Moscow, 1 October 1944; 1481–1482 KGB New York to Moscow, 18 October 1944; 1634 KGB New York to Moscow, 20 November 1944; 1721–1728 KGB New York to Moscow, 8 December 1944; 1822 KGB New York to Moscow, 27 December 1944; 1836 KGB New York to Moscow, and to 8th department, 29 December 1944; 12, 13, 15, 16 KGB New York to Moscow, 4 January 1945; 71 KGB New York to

Moscow, 17 January 1945; 210 KGB New York to Moscow, 10 February 1945; 211–212 KGB New York to Moscow, 10 February 1945; 289 KGB Moscow to New York, 28 March 1945; 328 KGB Moscow to New York, 6 April 1945. Although unnamed, Ullmann may be the source of stolen documents discussed in 1751–1753 KGB New York to Moscow, 13 December 1944. See Robert Louis Benson and Michael Warner, eds., *Venona: Soviet Espionage and the American Response, 1939–1957* (Washington, D.C.: National Security Agency, Central Intelligence Agency, 1996), xxi.

318. Venona 884 KGB New York to Moscow, 8 June 1943.

319. Venona 846 KGB New York to Moscow, 3 June 1943.

320. Venona 846 KGB New York to Moscow, 3 June 1943; 1248 KGB New York to Moscow, 29 July 1943.

321. Venona 880 KGB New York to Moscow, 8 June 1943.

322. Venona 1000 KGB New York to Moscow, 24 June 1943.

323. Venona 1351 KGB New York to Moscow, 23 September 1944.

324. Venona 2693 Naval GRU Washington to Moscow, 15 October 1943.

325. Venona 2693 Naval GRU Washington to Moscow, 15 October 1943.

326. Venona 1522, KGB New York to Moscow, 27 October 1944.

327. Venona 1204 GRU New York to Moscow, 22 July 1943.

328. Venona 1804 Naval GRU Washington to Moscow, 31 July 1943.

329. Venona 1557 KGB New York to Moscow, 6 November 1944.

330. Venona 1324 GRU New York to Moscow, 11 August 1943; 1456 GRU New York to Moscow, 8 September 1943.

331. Venona 959 KGB New York to Moscow, 21 June 1943.

332. Venona 853 KGB New York to Moscow, 16 June 1944.

333. Venona 500 KGB San Francisco to Moscow, 27 November 1943; 515 KGB San Francisco to Moscow, 7 December 1943; 26 KGB San Francisco to Moscow, 17 January 1944; 39 KGB San Francisco to Moscow, 22 January 1944; 104 KGB San Francisco to Moscow, 5 March 1944; 167 KGB San Francisco to Moscow, 15 April 1944.

334. Venona 1324 GRU New York to Moscow, 11 August 1943.

335. Venona 823 KGB New York to Moscow, 7 June 1944; 881 KGB New York to Moscow, 20 June 1944; 958 KGB New York to Moscow, 7 July 1944.

336. Venona 769, 771 KGB New York to Moscow, 30 May 1944; 1325, 1326 KGB New York to Moscow, 15 September 1944; 1354 KGB New York to Moscow, 22 September 1944; 1388, 1389 KGB New York to Moscow, 1 October 1944; 954 KGB Moscow to New York, 20 September 1944.

337. Venona 590 KGB New York to Moscow, 29 April 1944; 1119–1121 KGB New York to Moscow, 4–5 August 1944; 1251 KGB New York to Moscow, 2 September 1944; 1271–1274 KGB New York to Moscow, 7 September 1944; 1388–1389 KGB New York to Moscow, 1 October 1944; 1634 KGB New York to Moscow, 20 November 1944; 79 KGB New York to Moscow, 18 January 1945; 83 KGB New York to Moscow, 18 January 1945; 248 KGB Moscow to New York, 19 March 1945; 292 KGB Moscow to New York, 29 March 1945; 328 KGB Moscow to New York, 6 April 1945; 230 KGB San Francisco to Moscow, 4 May 1945; 235–236 KGB San Francisco to Moscow, 5 May 1945; 259 KGB San Francisco to Moscow, 13 May 1945; 312 KGB San Francisco to Moscow, 8 June 1945.

338. Venona 823 KGB New York to Moscow, 7 June 1944; 863 KGB New York to Moscow, 16 June 1944; 881 KGB New York to Moscow, 20 June 1944.

339. Venona 1714 KGB New York to Moscow, 5 December 1944; 76 KGB New York to Moscow, 17 January 1945; 1137 KGB New York to Moscow, 17 July 1945.

340. Venona 1146 KGB New York to Moscow, 10 August 1944; 1714 KGB New York to Moscow, 5 December 1944.

341. Venona 256 KGB New York to Moscow, 21 March 1945; 193–194 KGB Mexico City to Moscow, 14 March 1944.

342. Venona 3, 4, 5 KGB San Francisco to Moscow, 2 January 1946; 25 KGB San Francisco to Moscow, 26 January 1946; FBI report, "Soviet Espionage Activities, 19 October 1945," attached to Hoover to Vaughan, 19 October 1945, President's Secretary's Files, Harry S. Truman Library, Independence, Mo.; FBI report, "Soviet Activities in the United States," 25 July 1946, Clark M. Clifford papers, Truman Library.

343. Venona 777–781 KGB New York to Moscow, 26 May 1943; 893 KGB New York to Moscow, 10 June 1943; 325 Moscow to New York, 5 April 1945. It is not clear that the Glory in the 1945 message is Glory/Wolston as in 1943.

344. Venona 1589, 1590 KGB New York to Moscow, 30 September 1943; 144 KGB New York to Moscow, 27 January 1944; 1014 KGB New York to Moscow, 20 July 1944; 1050 KGB New York to Moscow, 26 July 1944; 1155 KGB New York to Moscow, 12 August 1944; 1321 KGB New York to Moscow, 15 September 1944; 1385 KGB New York to Moscow, 1 October 1944; 1397 KGB New York to Moscow, 4 October 1944; 1587 KGB New York to Moscow, 12 November 1944; 1637 KGB New York to Moscow, 21 November 1944; 1714 KGB New York to Moscow, 5 December 1944; 1716 KGB New York to Moscow, 5 December 1944; 1845 KGB New York to Moscow, 31 December 1944; 55 KGB New York to Moscow, 15 January 1945; 76 KGB New York to Moscow, 17 January 1945; 221 KGB Moscow to New York, 11 March 1945; 227 KGB Moscow to New York, 13 March 1945; 229 KGB Moscow to New York, 15 March 1945; 268 KGB Moscow to New York, 24 March 1945; 284, 286 KGB Moscow to New York, 28 March 1945.

345. Venona 446 KGB San Francisco to Moscow, 31 October 1943; 457 KGB San Francisco to Moscow, 2 November 1943; 1266 KGB New York to Moscow, 6 September 1944; 1523 KGB New York to Moscow, 27 October 1944.

346. Venona 1435 KGB New York to Moscow, 4 September 1943; 864 KGB New York to Moscow, 16 June 1944.

347. Venona 1325 GRU New York to Moscow, 11 August 1943.

348. Venona 790 KGB New York to Moscow, 27 May 1943; 1184 KGB New York to Moscow, 21 July 1943; 594 KGB New York to Moscow, 1 May 1944; 740 KGB New York to Moscow, 24 May 1944; 799 KGB New York to Moscow, 3 June 1944; 851 KGB New York to Moscow, 15 June 1944; 907 KGB New York to Moscow, 26 June 1944; 1143, 1144 KGB New York to Moscow, 10 August 1944; 1145 KGB New York to Moscow, 10 August 1944; 1251 KGB New York to Moscow, 2 September 1944; 1353 KGB New York to Moscow, 23 September 1944; 1449 KGB New York to Moscow, 12 October 1944; 1457 KGB New York to Moscow, 14 October 1944; 1500 KGB New York to Moscow, 20 October 1944; 1548 KGB New York to Moscow, 3 November 1944; 1803 KGB New York to Moscow, 22 December 1944; 87 KGB New York to Moscow, 19 January 1945; 954 KGB Moscow to New York, 20 September 1944; 323 KGB Moscow to New York, 5 April 1945.

349. Venona 1251 KGB New York to Moscow, 2 September 1944; 1328 KGB New York to Moscow, 15 September 1944.

Appendix B

1. Elizabeth Bentley FBI deposition, 30 November 1945, FBI file 65-14603.

2. See chapters 6 and 10.

3. Joseph Albright and Marcia Kunstel, *Bombshell: The Secret Story of America's Unknown Atomic Spy Conspiracy* (New York: Times Books, 1997), 193–195.

4. See chapter 9.

5. FBI report, "Soviet Espionage Activities, 19 October 1945," attached to Hoover to Vaughan, 19 October 1945, President's Secretary's Files, Harry S. Truman Library, Independence, Mo.

6. Albright and Kunstel, *Bombshell*, 193–195.

7. See chapter 9.

8. See chapter 6.

9. See chapter 8.

10. See chapter 9.

11. See chapter 8.

12. See chapter 9.

13. See chapter 6.

14. See chapter 9.

15. See chapter 9.

16. See chapter 8.

17. See chapter 8.

18. Bentley deposition.

19. See chapter 3.

20. See chapter 3.

21. See chapter 6.

22. See chapters 3 and 6.

23. See chapter 10.

24. Ann Kimmage, *An Un-American Childhood* (Athens: University of Georgia Press, 1997).

25. See chapter 10.

26. FBI report, "Soviet Espionage Activities, 19 October 1945"; New York FBI report, 5 April 1946, Comintern Apparatus file (FBI file 100-203581), serial 5236.

27. See chapters 3, 5, 7, and 9.

28. See chapter 8.

29. See chapter 8.

30. Inserted statement of Nicholas Dozenberg, hearings 8 November 1949, U.S. Congress, House of Representatives, Committee on Un-American Activities, 81st Cong., 1st and 2d sess.; Herbert Romerstein and Stanislav Levchenko, *The KGB Against the "Main Enemy": How the Soviet Intelligence Service Operates Against the United States* (Lexington Books, 1989), 16.

31. See chapter 6.

32. "Comintern Apparatus Summary Report," 15 December 1944, FBI Comintern Apparatus file, serial 3702; see also memo of 1 November 1944, serial 3378; see chapter 10.

33. U.S. Department of State Passport Division brief on a conspiracy charge against World Tourists and the CPUSA, reprinted in "Scope of Soviet Activity in the United States," appendix 1, part 23-A, U.S. Congress, Subcommittee to Investigate the Administration of the Internal Security Act, Senate Judiciary Committee (Washington, D.C.: GPO, 1957), A110–111; Harvey Klehr, John Earl Haynes, and Fridrikh Igorevich Firsov, *The Secret World of American Communism* (New Haven: Yale University Press, 1995), 296–297.

34. Whittaker Chambers, *Witness* (New York: Random House, 1952), 382; Scheidt to Director, 31 January 1947, FBI Silvermaster file (FBI file 65-56402), serial 1976.

35. See chapter 3.

36. Hede Massing, *This Deception* (New York: Duell, Sloan and Pearce, 1951), 139, 182–183, 195, 202–204, 218–19.

37. Harvey Klehr and Ronald Radosh, *The Amerasia Spy Case: Prelude to McCarthyism* (Chapel Hill: University of North Carolina Press, 1996).

38. See chapter 10.

39. Gennadi Kostyrchenko, *Out of the Red Shadows: Anti-Semitism in Stalin's Russia* (Amherst, N.Y.: Prometheus Books, 1995), 78–79.

40. Elizabeth Bentley, *Out of Bondage: The Story of Elizabeth Bentley* (New York: Ivy Books, 1988), 108.

41. See chapter 4.

42. Bentley deposition; Ladd memo to Director, 7 December 1945, serial 118, Ladd memo to Director 12 December 1945, serial 235; FBI Washington Field Office report, 11 March 1946, serial 674, both in FBI Silvermaster file.

43. See chapter 8.

44. See chapter 6.

45. Robert Lamphere and Tom Shachtman, *The FBI-KGB War: A Special Agent's Story* (New York: Random House, 1995), 143, 164–165, 171.

46. See chapter 10.

47. See chapter 8.

48. Allen Weinstein, *Perjury: The Hiss-Chambers Case* (New York: Random House, 1997), 96, 146, 280, 342.

49. See chapter 3.

50. Chambers, *Witness*, 41, 422–424; Weinstein, *Perjury*, 208, 210, 226–227, 444–445.

51. Weinstein, *Perjury*, 106.

52. Klehr and Radosh, *The Amerasia Spy Case*.

53. Bentley deposition.

54. See chapters 3, 5, and 6.

55. Bentley deposition. Also see Venona 247 KGB San Francisco to Moscow, 14 June 1946, for an ambiguous mention of Kahn in the clear.

56. See chapter 6.

57. Report of 11 January 1944, FBI Silvermaster file, serial 3378; "Comintern Apparatus Summary Report"; "The Shameful Years: Thirty Years of Soviet Espionage in the Untied States," 30 December 1951, U.S. Congress, House of Representatives, Committee on Un-American Activities, 39–40.

58. Bentley deposition.

59. Bentley deposition.

60. Ray Bearse and Anthony Read, *Conspirator: The Untold Story of Tyler Kent* (New York: Doubleday, 1991).

61. William Crane memorandum, 14 February 1949, William Crane FBI File 74-1333, serial 213.

62. See chapter 6.

63. Bentley deposition.

64. Klehr and Radosh, *The Amerasia Spy Case*.

65. See chapter 10.

66. Bentley deposition.

67. Elizabeth Bentley testimony, 13 May 1949, "Communist Activities Among Aliens and National Groups," Subcommittee on Immigration and Naturalization of the Committee on the Judiciary, U.S. Senate, 81st Cong., 1st sess., part 1, 106–

123; FBI Washington Field Office memo, 26 August 1948, FBI Silvermaster file, serial 3430.

68. Klehr, Haynes, and Firsov, *The Secret World of American Communism*, 131–132; "Comintern Apparatus Summary Report."

69. Testimony of Maxim Lieber, 13 June 1950, U.S. Congress, House of Representatives, Committee on Un-American Activities, 81st Cong., 1st and 2d sess.; Chambers, *Witness*, 280–291, 408–413; Sam Tanenhaus, *Whittaker Chambers: A Biography* (New York: Random House, 1997), 80–83, 100–102.

70. See chapter 10.

71. See chapter 6.

72. See chapter 9.

73. Oleg Kalugin, with Fen Montaigne, *The First Directorate: My 32 Years in Intelligence and Espionage Against the West* (New York: St. Martin's Press, 1994), 48–50.

74. Massing, *This Deception*.

75. Ibid.

76. See chapter 9.

77. Elizabeth Bentley testimony, "Communist Activities Among Aliens and National Groups."

78. Bentley, *Out of Bondage*, 107.

79. See chapter 4.

80. See chapter 4.

81. Klehr and Radosh, *The Amerasia Spy Case*.

82. See chapter 3.

83. Son to Dimitrov, 19 April 1943, Archive of the Secretariat of the Executive Committee of the Communist International: coded correspondence with Communist Parties (1933–1943). RTsKhIDNI 495-184-5 (1942 file).

84. Nigel West and Oleg Tsarev, *The Crown Jewels: The British Secrets at the Heart of the KGB Archives* (London: HarperCollins, 1998), 112–113.

85. Ronald Radosh and Joyce Milton, *The Rosenberg File: A Search for the Truth* (New Haven: Yale University Press, 1997), 153–156.

86. See chapters 3, 8, and 10.

87. See chapter 3 and 5.

88. See chapter 6.

89. FBI memo, 23 December 1946, Silvermaster file, serial 1938.

90. Romerstein and Levchenko, *The KGB Against the "Main Enemy,"* 17.

91. Bentley deposition; Ladd to Director, "Underground Soviet Espionage Organization (NKVD) in Agencies of the United States Government," 21 February 1946, serial 573, and Scheidt to Director, 31 January 1947, serial 1976, both in FBI Silvermaster file.

92. Ibid.

93. See chapter 3.

94. Weinstein, *Perjury* (1997), 206, 209, 211, 214–215.

95. Dorothy Gallagher, *All the Right Enemies: The Life and Murder of Carlo Tresca* (New Brunswick, N.J.: Rutgers University Press, 1988), 170–176; Bentley deposition; Bentley, *Out of Bondage*, 108, 176–177; Chambers, *Witness*, 36. The FBI conducted an extensive and fruitless investigation into Poyntz's disappearance: FBI Poyntz file 100-206603.

96. See chapter 4.

97. See chapter 9.

98. Bentley deposition; "Underground Soviet Espionage Organization (NKVD) in

Agencies of the United States Government," serial 573, and FBI Washington Field Office report, 21 April 1947, serial 2349, both in FBI Silvermaster file.

99. See chapter 5.

100. Weinstein, *Perjury,* 206, 209–11, 214, 279.

101. Bentley deposition.

102. "The Shameful Years," 15–16.

103. See chapter 3.

104. Klehr and Radosh, *The Amerasia Spy Case.*

105. Hoover to San Francisco FBI, 22 November 1944, FBI Comintern Apparatus file, serial 3474.

106. FBI memorandum, "Existing Corroboration of Bentley's Overall Testimony," FBI Silvermaster file, serial 4201.

107. See chapter 9.

108. Weinstein, *Perjury,* 98, 105, 109, 111–114, 208, 273–274, 288, 361.

109. See chapter 9.

110. See chapter 9.

111. Radosh and Milton, *The Rosenberg File* (1997), 152–153.

112. See chapter 9.

113. West and Tsarev, *The Crown Jewels,* 112–113.

114. Chambers, *Witness,* 421n.

115. See chapter 9.

116. See chapter 9.

117. Inserted statement of Nicholas Dozenberg.

118. FBI report, "Soviet Espionage Activities, 19 October 1945"; FBI report, "Soviet Activities in the United States," 25 July 1946, Clark M. Clifford papers, Harry S. Truman Library, Independence, Mo.

119. New York FBI report, 19 January 1945, Comintern Apparatus file, serial 3899.

120. Inserted statement of Nicholas Dozenberg; Romerstein and Levchenko, *The KGB Against the "Main Enemy,"* 16.

121. See chapter 6.

122. Michael Straight, *After Long Silence* (New York: Norton, 1983); John Earl Haynes, "Speak No Evil: Michael Straight and *After Long Silence,*" *Chronicles of Culture* 7, no. 11 (1983); Sidney Hook, "The Incredible Story of Michael Straight," *Encounter* (December 1983); Robert King, "Treason and Traitors," *Society* 26, no. 5 (July/August 1989); Weinstein, *Perjury,* 183–184; West and Tsarev, *The Crown Jewels,* 112–113, 116, 130, 133–134, 174.

123. See chapter 6.

124. Weinstein, *Perjury,* 107.

125. Bentley deposition; "Existing Corroboration of Bentley's Overall Testimony"; "Underground Soviet Espionage Organization (NKVD) in Agencies of the United States Government." Taylor's points are discussed in detail in Hayden Peake's Afterword to the 1988 reissue of Bentley's *Out of Bondage,* and the principal part of the FBI analysis of Taylor's attack on Bentley charges is reproduced in appendix B of the same book.

126. Inserted statement of Nicholas Dozenberg; "Comintern Apparatus Summary Report."

127. See chapter 3.

128. Weinstein, *Perjury,* 107–108, 110, 138n, 204, 281.

129. Albright and Kunstel, *Bombshell,* 49; Aleksandr Feklisov, *Za okeanom i na ostrove. Zapiski razvedchika* (Moscow: DEE, 1994), 76; Vladimir Chikov, "How the

Soviet Secret Service Split the American Atom," *Novoe vremia,* no. 16, 17 (23, 30 April 1991).

130. See chapter 9.

131. Bentley deposition; "Underground Soviet Espionage Organization (NKVD) in Agencies of the United States Government," serial 573, and New York FBI to Director, 13 February 1947, serial 2466, both in FBI Silvermaster file.

132. Weinstein, *Perjury,* 57, 102-103, 137, 172, 204-206, 225, 228, 247, 293, 346, 466, 515.

133. Klehr, Haynes, and Firsov, *The Secret World of American Communism,* 142; Louis Budenz, *Men Without Faces* (New York: Harper and Brothers, 1948), 126-129.

134. See chapter 10.

135. Bentley deposition; "Underground Soviet Espionage Organization (NKVD) in Agencies of the United States Government"; Ladd memo, 15 December 1945, serial 367; New York FBI to Hoover, 6 February 1946, serial 452; Ladd to Director, 21 February 1946, serial 573; last three in FBI Silvermaster file.

136. See chapter 2.

137. See chapter 3.

138. Weinstein, *Perjury,* 137, 192, 209-210, 214-215, 246, 342, 357, 386.

139. Romerstein and Levchenko, *The KGB Against the "Main Enemy,"* 193-194.

Appendix C

1. See chapter 2.

2. Venona 13 KGB Moscow to London, 16 September 1945.

3. Venona 2227 GRU London to Moscow, 10 August 1941; 195 KGB New York to Moscow, 9 February 1944; 645 KGB New York to Moscow, 8 May 1944; 850 New York to Moscow, 15 June 1944; 1049 KGB New York to Moscow, 25 July 1944; 1345 KGB New York to Moscow, 22 September 1944; 1397 KGB New York to Moscow, 4 October 1944; 1403 KGB New York to Moscow, 5 October 1944; 1606 KGB New York to Moscow, 16 November 1944; 183 KGB Moscow to New York, 27 February 1945; 298 KGB Moscow to New York, 31 March 1945; 349 KGB Moscow to New York, 10 April 1945.

4. Venona 915 KGB New York to Moscow, 28 June 1944; 1105, 1110 KGB New York to Moscow, 2-3 August 1944; 1114 KGB New York to Moscow, 4 August 1944; 1146 KGB New York to Moscow, 10 August 1944; 1263 KGB New York to Moscow, 5 September 1944; 1271-1274 KGB New York to Moscow, 7 September 1944; 1788 KGB Washington to KGB Moscow, 29 March 1945; 1791 KGB Washington to KGB Moscow, 29 March 1945; 1793 KGB Washington to KGB Moscow, 29 March 1945; 1808-1809 KGB Washington to KGB Moscow, 30 March 1945; 1826 KGB Washington to KGB Moscow 31 March 1945.

5. See chapter 2.

6. FBI report, "Soviet Espionage Activities, 19 October 1945," attached to Hoover to Vaughan, 19 October 1945, President's Secretary's Files, Harry S. Truman Library, Independence, Mo.

7. "The Report of the Royal Commission, Appointed Under Order in Council P.C. 411 of 5 February 1946, to Investigate the Facts Relating to and the Circumstances Surrounding the Communications, by Public Officials and Other Persons in Positions of Trust, of Secret and Confidential Information to Agents of a Foreign Power, 27 June 1946" (Ottawa: Edmound Cloutier . . . Controller of Stationery, 1946); Robert Bothwell and J. L. Granatstein, eds., *The Gouzenko Transcripts* (Ottawa: Deneau, 1982), 74, 97;

U.S. Joint Committee on Atomic Energy, 82d Cong., 1951, *Soviet Atomic Espionage*, 58.

8. Richard Rhodes, *Dark Sun: The Making of the Hydrogen Bomb* (New York: Simon & Schuster, 1995), 127–128.

9. Elizabeth Bentley FBI deposition, 30 November 1945, FBI file 65-14603.

10. Venona 424 KGB Moscow to New York, 1 July 1942; 894 KGB New York to Moscow, 26 June 1942; 846 KGB New York to Moscow, 3 June 1943; 1032 KGB New York to Moscow, 1 July 1943; 1107 KGB New York to Moscow, 8 July 1943; 1137 KGB New York to Moscow, 13 July 1943; 1197 KGB New York to Moscow, 22 July 1943; 1198 KGB New York to Moscow, 22 July 1943; 847B, 848 KGB New York to Moscow, 15 June 1944; 1453 KGB New York to Moscow, 12 October 1944; 1741 KGB New York to Moscow, 12 December 1944; 447 KGB San Francisco to Moscow, 31 October 1943.

11. Venona 448 KGB San Francisco to Moscow, 31 October 1943; 523 KGB San Francisco to Moscow, 14 December 1943; 538 KGB San Francisco to Moscow, 31 December 1943; 1 KGB San Francisco to Moscow, 2 January 1944; 212 KGB Moscow to Canberra, 29 August 1944.

12. Venona 317 KGB Moscow to New York, 15 May 1942; 722 KGB New York to Moscow, 21 May 1942; 719–720, 722 KGB New York to Moscow, 19 May 1943; 764–765 KGB New York to Moscow, 24 May 1943; 804, 805 KGB New York to Moscow, 29 May 1943; 821, 823, 825 KGB New York to Moscow, 31 May 1943; 899 KGB New York to Moscow, 11 June 1943; 904–907 KGB New York to Moscow, 12 June 1943; 908–910 KGB New York to Moscow, 12 June 1943; 916 KGB New York to Moscow, 15 June 1943; 965–966 KGB New York to Moscow, 21 June 1943; 967–968 KGB New York to Moscow, 22 June 1943; 1011 KGB New York to Moscow, 27 June 1943; 1979 KGB New York to Moscow, 4 December 1943; 722 KGB New York to Moscow, 19 May 1944; 747 KGB New York to Moscow, 25 May 1944; 851 KGB New York to Moscow, 15 June 1944; 1142 KGB New York to Moscow, 10 August 1944; 1234 KGB New York to Moscow, 29 August 1944; 1470 KGB New York to Moscow, 17 October 1944; 1821 KGB New York to Moscow, 26 December 1944.

13. Venona 327 KGB Moscow to Mexico City, 17 May 1945.

14. Venona 768 KGB New York to Moscow, 25 May 1943; 1088 KGB New York to Moscow, 7 July 1943; 747 KGB New York to Moscow, 25 May 1944; 1142 KGB New York to Moscow, 10 August 1944.

15. Venona 827 KGB New York to Moscow, 1 June 1943; 1182 KGB New York to Moscow, 19 August 1944; 1333 KGB New York to Moscow, 18 September 1944; 1431 KGB New York to Moscow, 10 October 1944.

16. Venona 860 KGB New York to Moscow, 6 June 1943; 974 KGB New York to Moscow, 22 June 1943; 1094, 1095 KGB New York to Moscow, 7 July 1943; 1207 KGB New York to Moscow, 22 July 1943; 1209 KGB New York to Moscow, 22 July 1943; 1435 KGB New York to Moscow, 4 September 1943; 1461 KGB New York to Moscow, 9 September 1943; 1039–1041 KGB New York to Moscow, 24–25 July 1944.

17. Venona 833 KGB New York to Moscow, 10 June 1942; 925 KGB New York to Moscow, 2 July 1942; 830 KGB New York to Moscow, 1 June 1943; 857, 863–864 KGB New York to Moscow, 5 June 1943; 860 KGB New York to Moscow, 6 June 1943; 952 KGB New York to Moscow, 21 June 1943; 1070 KGB New York to Moscow, 4 July 1943; 1209 KGB New York to Moscow, 22 July 1943; 1398 KGB New York to Moscow, 26 August 1943; 1776 KGB New York to Moscow, 26 October 1943; 725 KGB New York to Moscow, 19 May 1944; 726 KGB New York to Moscow, 20 May 1944; 1183 KGB New York to Moscow, 19 August 1944; 1370 KGB New York to Moscow, 27 September 1944.

18. See chapter 9.

19. See chapter 9.

20. Venona 55 KGB Moscow to New York, 10 January 1943.

21. Venona 445 KGB San Francisco to Moscow, 31 October 1943.

22. Venona 445 KGB San Francisco to Moscow, 31 October 1943.

23. Venona 1954 KGB New York to Moscow, 27 November 1943; 1039–1041 KGB New York to Moscow, 24–25 July 1944; 1097–1098 KGB New York to Moscow, 1 August 1944.

24. Venona 810 KGB New York to Moscow, 29 May 1943; 833 KGB New York to Moscow, 2 June 1943; 1207 KGB New York to Moscow, 22 July 1943; 699 KGB New York to Moscow, 17 May 1944; 817 KGB New York to Moscow, 6 June 1944; 847 KGB New York to Moscow, 14 June 1944; 1385 KGB New York to Moscow, 1 October 1944.

25. Venona 952 KGB New York to Moscow, 21 June 1943; 1207 KGB New York to Moscow, 22 July 1943; 1016 KGB New York to Moscow, 20 July 1944; 1042 KGB New York to Moscow, 25 July 1944; 1397 KGB New York to Moscow, 4 October 1944.

26. Venona 952 KGB New York to Moscow, 21 June 1943; 612 KGB New York to Moscow, 3 May 1944; 617 KGB New York to Moscow, 4 May 1944; 639 KGB New York to Moscow, 6 May 1944; 695 KGB New York to Moscow, 16 May 1944; 1042 KGB New York to Moscow, 25 July 1944.

27. Venona 1012 Naval GRU Washington to Moscow, 9 May 1943.

28. Venona 1207 KGB New York to Moscow, 22 July 1943.

29. Venona 6 KGB Moscow to London, 15 September 1945.

30. Venona 911 KGB New York to Moscow, 12 June 1943; 916 KGB New York to Moscow, 15 June 1943; 1207 KGB New York to Moscow, 22 July 1943; 1777 KGB New York to Moscow, 26 October 1943; 669 KGB New York to Moscow, 11 May 1944.

31. Venona 976 KGB New York to Moscow, 11 July 1944; 1286 KGB New York to Moscow, 8 September 1944; 17 KGB New York to Moscow, 4 January 1945.

32. Venona 1251 KGB New York to Moscow, 2 September 1944; 1267 KGB New York to Moscow, 6 September 1944; 1332 KGB New York to Moscow, 18 September 1944; 1582 KGB New York to Moscow, 12 November 1944; 1636 KGB New York to Moscow, 21 November 1944; 1803 KGB New York to Moscow, 22 December 1944; 50 KGB New York to Moscow, 11 January 1945; 1052 KGB New York to Moscow, 5 July 1945; 275 KGB Moscow to New York, 25 March 1945; 337 KGB Moscow to New York, 8 April 1945.

33. Venona 1207 KGB New York to Moscow, 22 July 1943; 1435 KGB New York to Moscow, 4 September 1943; 864 KGB New York to Moscow, 16 June 1944.

Appendix D

1. Dimitrov to Fitin, 20 November 1942, RTsKhIDNI 495-74-484. See also Harvey Klehr, John Earl Haynes, and Fridrikh Igorevich Firsov, *The Secret World of American Communism* (New Haven: Yale University Press, 1995), 318–319.

2. Venona 1433, 1435 KGB New York to Moscow, 10 October 1944.

3. Venona 705 KGB New York to Moscow, 17 May 1944; 738 KGB New York to Moscow, 23 May 1944; 777–779 KGB New York to Moscow, 25 May 1945.

4. Venona 726–729 KGB New York to Moscow, 22 May 1942; FBI report of 31 May 1944, FBI Comintern Apparatus file (FBI File 100-203581), serial 2753; Comintern Apparatus Summary Report, 15 December 1944, FBI Comintern Apparatus file, serial 3702.

5. Venona 227 KGB Moscow to New York, 13 March 1945.

6. Venona 259 Moscow to New York, 21 March 1945.

7. Venona 1116 GRU New York to Moscow, 9 July 1943; 1456 GRU New York to Moscow, 8 September 1943.

8. Venona 1759 KGB Washington to KGB Moscow, 28 March 1945.

9. Venona 1053 KGB New York to Moscow, 26 July 1944.

10. Venona 1464 KGB New York to Moscow, 14 October 1944.

11. Venona 1340 KGB New York to Moscow, 21 September 1944.

12. Venona 1754 KGB New York to Moscow, 14 December 1944; 20 KGB New York to Moscow, 4 January 1945.

13. Venona 1692 KGB New York to Moscow, 1 December 1944.

14. See chapter 10.

15. See chapter 10.

16. Venona 916 KGB New York to Moscow, 12 June 1945.

17. Venona 1791 KGB New York to Moscow, 20 December 1944. The NSA redacted Cora's identity.

18. Venona 1350 GRU New York to Moscow, 17 August 1943.

19. Venona 1313 KGB New York to Moscow, 13 September 1944; 1433, 1435 KGB New York to Moscow, 10 October 1944; 1506 KGB New York to Moscow, 23 October 1944.

20. "Report on Americans," 27 September 1937, RTsKhIDNI 545-3-453; Dimitrov to Fitin, 27 March 1943, RTsKhIDNI 495-74-485.

21. Fitin to Dimitrov, 6 May 1943, RTsKhIDNI 495-74-485. On Thompson's relationship with the CPUSA and the KGB vetting message see Klehr, Haynes, and Firsov, *The Secret World of American Communism,* 303-305.

22. On Traugott's OSS career, see Klehr, Haynes, and Firsov, *The Secret World of American Communism,* 307-308. On her postwar career see Traugott to National Citizens PAC State Coordinators, 19 April 1946, and Traugott to Steefel, 19 July 1948, box 1, Minnesota Progressive Party (Genevieve Steefel) Papers, Manuscript Division, Library of Congress, Washington, D.C.

23. Venona 767 KGB Moscow to New York, 17 July 1945.

24. Venona 1340 KGB New York to Moscow, 21 September 1944.

Index

This is an index to persons, organizations, and concepts in the text. There are names of persons in the alphabetical entries of the appendixes that are not listed in this index.

DISCARDED
from
New Hanover County Public Library

NEW HANOVER COUNTY PUBLIC LIB.

3 4200 00517 0283

NEW HANOVER COUNTY PUBLIC LIBRARY
201 Chestnut Street
Wilmington, N.C. 28401

GAYLORD S